RELIGION AND ANTHROPOLOGY

This important study provides a critical introduction to the social anthropology of religion, focusing on more recent classical ethnographies. Comprehensive, free of scholastic jargon, engaging, and comparative in approach, it covers all the major religious traditions that have been studied concretely by anthropologists – Shamanism, Buddhism, Islam, Hinduism, Christianity and its relation to African and Melanesian religions, and contemporary Neo-Paganism. Eschewing a thematic approach and treating religion as a social institution and not simply as an ideology or symbolic system, the book follows the dual heritage of social anthropology in combining an interpretative understanding and sociological analysis. The book will appeal to all students of anthropology, whether established scholars or initiates to the discipline, as well as to students of the social sciences and religious studies, and to all those interested in comparative religion.

Brian Morris is Emeritus Professor of Anthropology at Goldsmiths College, at the University of London. His many publications include *Chewa Medical Botany* (1996), *Animals and Ancestors* (2000), *Kropotkin: The Politics of Community* (2004), *Insects and Human Life* (2004), and *Anthropological Studies of Religion: An Introductory Text* (Cambridge, 1987).

Religion and Anthropology

A Critical Introduction

BRIAN MORRIS
University of London

CAMBRIDGE UNIVERSITY PRESS
Cambridge, New York, Melbourne, Madrid, Cape Town, Singapore, São Paulo

Cambridge University Press
40 West 20th Street, New York, NY 10011-4211, USA

www.cambridge.org
Information on this title: www.cambridge.org/9780521852418

First published 2006

Printed in the United States of America

A catalog record for this publication is available from the British Library.

Library of Congress Cataloging in Publication Data

Morris, Brian, 1936–
Religion and anthropology : a critical introduction / Brian Morris.
p. cm.
Includes bibliographical references (p.) and index.
ISBN 0-521-85241-2 (hardcover) – ISBN 0-521-61779-0 (pbk.)
1. Ethnology – Religious aspects. 2. Religions. I. Title.
BL256.M67 2006
218 – dc22 2005023290

ISBN-13 978-0-521-85241-8 hardback
ISBN-10 0-521-85241-2 hardback

ISBN-13 978-0-521-61779-6 paperback
ISBN-10 0-521-61779-0 paperback

To James Woodburn
Who guided my first
steps in Social Anthropology

Advance Praise:

"Brian Morris' *Religion and Anthropology* is at once remarkably comprehensive and situated. He manages to include most of the religious endeavors of the world and of world history while situating each in social context, elucidated by anthropological fieldwork. The resulting volume is an excellent resource for thinking and teaching about religion in a specifically anthropological perspective. I plan to assign the book for my own course on the topic."

– James L. Peacock, *University of North Carolina, Chapel Hill*

"As a sequel and complement to Morris's previous reader on theoretical approaches to religion, this book of impressive scholarship is an admirable success and a thoroughly enjoyable read. The book is characterized by a refreshing, commonsense approach to religion that is eminently accessible due to the consistent avoidance of unnecessary jargon, psychobabble or lyrical prose. The sympathetic and nonjudgmental ethnographic descriptions, the dynamism of the theoretical polemic, the clear use of English, and the elegance of the narrative structure made this book difficult to put down. A rare experience when reading much modern anthropological writing."

– Jerome Lewis, *London School of Economics and Political Science*

Contents

Preface

I have been teaching a course on the Anthropology of Religion at Goldsmiths' College, off and on, for almost thirty years. My writing of *Anthropological Studies of Religion* was in fact motivated by a felt need for an introductory text on the subject, even though I knew that some elitist Oxbridge scholars held such texts in general disdain. Indeed, one well-known anthropologist severely rebuked me for even teaching anthropology as a subsidiary subject at Goldsmiths, insisting that anthropology could be taught adequately only at a postgraduate level. Having failed my eleven-plus, I left school at the age of fifteen to work in an iron foundry, and, failing to get into a university because I lacked any 'A' levels, I have always found such elitist attitudes quite deplorable. When, along with Jane Hoy of the University of London Extra-Mural Department, I initiated a Certificate of Anthropology, supported by my colleagues at Goldsmiths' College, I found great difficulty in convincing my anthropological colleagues at other universities that the certificate had any value as an access course. Typically, more than a decade later, when academics had discovered that anthropology was being widely taught outside of universities, a resource guide was published, *Discovering Anthropology*, that completely ignored these earlier initiatives. It is worth noting also that, because of these elitist attitudes, anthropology is the only university discipline that is not a part of the school curriculum, even though Britain is a multicultural society! Unlike some pretentious academics, ensconced in some elite university, I have always found introductory texts extremely useful as teaching aids, in the same way as travel guides are useful in exploring the landscape, and true scholars, like Ernst Mayr (for example), do not feel that the writing and the use of introductory texts is in the least demeaning. In fact, some introductory texts offer more critical insights into the subject matter than many articles in academic journals where obscurantist, neo-Baroque jargon is often a cover for sociological platitudes. I thus make no apology for offering a sequel and an update of my earlier text, and it has the same purpose, namely, to be a helpful guide to anthropological studies of religion – comprehensive, stimulating I hope, critical, sympathetic, and above all, readable, that is, free of obscurantist jargon. It will, I trust, appeal to all students of anthropology, whether established scholars or initiates on access courses, as well as to the students of the social sciences generally, and to all those interested in comparative religion.

Over the years I have been very appreciative of many friends and colleagues in anthropology who have given me encouragement and intellectual support, and I would especially like to thank the following: Tony Atcherly, Barbara Bender, Alan Barnard, Maurice Bloch, Peter Baynes, Pat Caplan, Roy Ellen, Simeren and the late Alfred Gell, Victoria Goddard, Susan Greenwood, Olivia Harris, Signe Howell, Tim Ingold, Jean La Fontaine, Ioan Lewis, Murray Last, Josep Llobera, Nici Nelson, Stephen Nugent, Judith Okely, David Parkin, Johnny Parry, the late Madan Sarup, Laura Rival, Mary Searle-Chatterjee, Cris Shore, Shelagh Weir, Roy Willis, James Woodburn, and Justin Woodman.

In addition I should like to thank the many students who have sat in my seminars – around 2,000 too many to mention by name! – for all their insights, feedback, and often warm friendships.

Finally, I should like to thank my family and colleagues at Goldsmiths' College for their continuing support, and Sheila Robinson and Emma Svanberg for kindly typing my manuscript.

Brian Morris
August 7, 2004

Introduction

This book is in a real sense an update and a sequel to my text *Anthropological Studies of Religion* (1987). It thus offers a critical introduction or guide to the extensive anthropological literature on religion that has been produced over the past forty years or so – with a specific focus on the more well-known and substantive ethnographic studies. My earlier text gave a broad, historical but critical survey of the many different theoretical approaches to religion that had emerged since the end of the nineteenth century – a path that has since been well trod by several other scholars (e.g., Hamilton 1995, Pals 1996, Cunningham 1999, and D. Gellner 1999).

With regard to the present text, I adopt a very different strategy; I take a more geographical approach, for in an important sense the major religious systems – Islam, Buddhism, Hinduism, African, Melanesian – are regional phenomena, even though they may have universalizing tendencies. It must be emphasized at the outset, however, that not only is religion a complex and variable phenomenon, but also it is essentially a *social* phenomenon. Religion is a social institution, a socio-cultural system; and it is thus ill understood when viewed simply as an ideology, or as a system of beliefs, still less as merely a 'symbolic system' (Geertz), an 'awareness of the transcendent' (Tambiah), or a 'feeling of the numinous' (Otto).

There has, of course, been a plethora of books and articles that have attempted to define 'religion', which is (in case you haven't heard!) a 'Western' category. Thus – like economy, culture, realism, and reason – it has a historical trajectory and in different contexts diverse meanings. But, as a general working definition, we can follow Melford Spiro in defining religion as 'an *institution* consisting of culturally patterned interaction with culturally postulated superhuman beings' (1987, 197) – although one can easily suggest other terms that refer to a person's involvement with a meta-empirical realm – the sacred, spiritual beings, divinity, supernaturals, numinals, or occult powers.

A distinction is often made between substantive and functional definitions of religion, but the latter tend to be quite vague, as in J. Milton Yinger's well-known definition of religion as a 'system of beliefs and practices by means of which a group of people struggles with the ultimate problems of human life' – problems relating to human mortality, suffering, and injustice; to the need to infuse human life with meaning and intellectual coherence; and the crucial importance of upholding moral precepts and patterns of social life. (1970, 5–7; see also Nadel 1954, 259–73, on the "competences" of religion.) But, of course, such human problems can equally well be addressed by secular ideologies – historical materialism, dialectical or evolutionary naturalism, or secular humanism. Indeed, given such a wide definition, Dewey's empirical naturalism and secular humanism have, in the United States at least, both been declared a 'religion' (Kurtz 1983; Rosenbaum 2003; for useful discussions on the definition of religion, see Geertz 1975, 87–125; Asad 1993, 27–54; Horton 1993, 19–49; Saler 1993).

As a social institution, religion is thus neither a static nor a unitary phenomenon; but as a widespread institution, it is characterized by a number of 'dimensions', or what Southwold, in his polythetic approach to religion, describes as 'attributes'. These include the following: ritual practices; an ethical code; a body of doctrines, beliefs, scriptures, or oral traditions; patterns of social relations focussed around a ritual congregation, church, or moral community; a hierarchy of ritual specialists; a tendency to create a dichotomy between the sacred and profane; and, finally, an ethos that gives scope for emotional or mystical experience (Southwold 1978, 370–1; Smart 1996, 10–11).

Anthropology, despite its diversity, has a certain unity of purpose and vision. It is unique among the human sciences in both putting an emphasis and value on cultural difference, thus offering a cultural critique of western capitalism and its culture, and in emphasizing people's shared humanity, thus enlarging our sense of moral community and placing humans squarely 'within nature'. As a discipline, anthropology has therefore always placed itself – as a comparative social science – at the 'interface' between the natural sciences and the humanities. Sadly, in recent years, given the increasingly arrogant and intolerant rhetoric of postmodern anthropologists who seem to repudiate empirical science entirely, and the equally dismissive attitude some positivist anthropologists have towards hermeneutics (Tyler 1986; E. Gellner 1995), a 'wide chasm' seems to have emerged between these various traditions (Burofsky 1994, 3). I have elsewhere offered my own reflections on this sad state of affairs and have emphasized that an understanding of human social life should entail both hermeneutic understanding (humanism) as well as explanations in terms of causal mechanisms and historical understanding (naturalism) (Morris 1997). Anthropology has historically always tended to combine both approaches – hermeneutics and naturalism, interpretive understanding and scientific explanations – and has thus tended to avoid either a one-sided emphasis on hermeneutics, which in its extreme form, 'textualism', denies any empirical science, or the equally one-sided emphasis on naturalism, which in its extreme form, as crude positivism, oblates or downplays cultural meanings and human values (Morris 1997). As Jackson writes, 'people cannot be reduced to texts any more than they can be reduced to objects' (1989, 184). The notion that anthropology is simply a 'romantic rebellion against the enlightenment' (Shweder 1984) is thus completely misleading, for anthropology has always drawn equally on the insights of both the romantic (humanist) and the enlightenment (empirical science) traditions.

Emphasizing the 'dual heritage' of anthropology, Maurice Bloch has also bewailed the spirit of 'fundamentalism' that has entered anthropology in recent years. Thus one type of fundamentalism, associated with hermeneutic and postmodernist scholars, conceives of anthropology as purely a 'literary enterprise' and repudiates social science entirely, while the other type of fundamentalism, embraced by anthropologists who take their bearings from socio-biology and cognitive psychology, is aggressively naturalistic and wishes to 'purify' anthropology of the other orientation. Bloch himself affirms the 'hybrid character' of anthropology (1998, 39–41). In this study, I avoid both these forms of 'fundamentalism' and focus on those scholars – the majority – who have remained true to the dual heritage of anthropology.

My earlier text focussed specifically on exploring the many different theoretical approaches to the study of religion; and, although described as a *tour de force*, it was never designed to herald a 'Hegelian renaissance', as one reviewer bizarrely suggested. These approaches may be briefly summarized here under the following seven headings.

1. INTELLECTUALIST APPROACHES

This approach, derived from the classical studies of Edward Tylor and James Frazer, suggests that religion can best be understood as a way of explaining events in the world. As Robin Horton puts it, religious beliefs are 'theoretical systems intended for the explanation, prediction and control of space–time events' (1971, 94). Thus Horton considered African religious thought as akin to science. Evans-Pritchard's classic study of Azande witchcraft is seen as exemplifying this style of analysis. The problem with this approach to religion is that it is extremely partial, and religious explanations of events hardly seem plausible when contrasted with those of science (on this approach, see Morris 1987, 91–106, 304–9; Horton 1993).

2. EMOTIONALIST APPROACHES

Psychological theories of religion have a long history going back to Hume and Spinoza. This approach suggests that religion is a response to emotional stress and thus serves to alleviate fears and anxieties. Malinowski's biological functionalism and Freud's psychoanalytic theory are classical examples of this approach to religions and magic. Although Wittgenstein considered that any attempt to explain social life was 'mistaken', he also thought, as did other logical positivists, that religious rituals had primarily a cathartic function (Tambiah 1990, 56–7). In recent years psychoanalytic and emotionalist theories of religion have gone out of fashion, although they form an important dimension to the work of Melford Spiro and Gananath Obeyesekere, which is discussed in Chapter 2 (on religion and the emotions, see Morris 1987, 141–63; Cunningham 1999, 23–31).

3. STRUCTURALIST APPROACHES

Invariably identified with the important work of Claude Levi-Strauss, the structuralist approach emphasizes that culture is a form of communication, and, influenced by structural linguistics, especially the theories of Saussure, it seeks to elucidate the 'grammar' of culture. Systems of thought, especially mythology, magic, symbolism, and totemic classifications, are thus analysed in terms of binary oppositions in order to reveal their underlying, and often hidden, 'symbolic logic'. The approach was seen by Levi-Strauss as exemplifying the scientific method, and a focus was placed squarely on what he described as the 'thought-of-orders' – ideological structures. Levi-Strauss was little concerned with religion per se, but for a while structuralism was embraced with enthusiasm by many anthropologists and, in the work of Maurice Godelier, was combined with a Marxist approach. Levi-Strauss' structuralist theory gave rise to a plethora of critical studies and commentary, and the approach was seen as essentially synchronic and ahistorical, as downplaying human agency, and as divorced from social and political realities (Morris 1987, 264–91; Johnson 2003).

4. INTERPRETIVE APPROACHES

This approach, variously described as semantic, symbolic, semiotic, or hermeneutic, represents a development of as well as a reaction against earlier sociological approaches to religion, especially structural–functionalism. Interpretive anthropology puts an emphasis on religion as a cultural or symbolic system, as essentially a system of meanings that both express and shape social reality, as well as people's dispositions and sense of identity. This symbolic or interpretive approach has been closely identified with the work of Clifford Geertz (1975) but is also embraced by many other scholars; among the better known are Mary Douglas, Marshall Sahlins, John Beattie, Victor Turner, and Stanley Tambiah. Although the interpretive approach is an important and integral part of the 'dual heritage' of anthropology, adherents of the symbolic or hermeneutic approach have increasingly tended to repudiate social science and comparative analysis and to embrace a rather idealist metaphysic, one that is antirealist and implies an extreme epistemological relativism (on the interpretive approach to religion, see Geertz 1975; Morris 1987, 203–63; Hamilton 2001, 177–84).

5. COGNITIVE APPROACHES

In recent decades some anthropologists have enthusiastically embraced sociobiology and its offshoot, evolutionary psychology, as a strategy by which to advance a truly 'scientific' study of religion. The basic idea is that religious systems can be explained in terms of 'basic or pan-cultural human psychological characteristics'

(Hinde 1999, 14). The emphasis, however, is specifically on cognitive 'mechanisms' or propensities that have been adaptive in a biological sense, namely, in fostering the survival or reproductive success of humans in the past. Religious beliefs and rituals are described as 'counterintuitive', that is, contrary to commonsense assumptions and experience (hardly news!) but nevertheless as 'natural'; and an explanation for such beliefs and rituals is to be found 'in the way all human minds work' (Boyer 2001, 3). The 'mind', however, according to this approach, is not simply a 'blank slate' on which culture writes its script, but rather it consists of a 'whole variety' of cognitive mechanisms that collectively not only explain the very existence of religious concepts but also their persistence in human cultures, as well as explaining the way in which religion has 'appeared in human history' (Boyer 2001, 342). Even atheism is explained by reference to these same cognitive mechanisms and presumably Boyer's own theory too. Pascal Boyer tends to be dismissive of other approaches to religion – intellectualist, emotionalist, sociological – and makes some rather grandiose claims for the cognitive approach. Essentially this approach is 'atomistic', and there appear to be no mediating factors – such as human agency and human social life – between the units of culture or 'memes' (which seemingly have a life of their own!) and the determining psychological instincts – the various cognitive mechanisms (for critiques of socio-biology and evolutionary psychology, see Morris 1991, 132–42; Rose and Rose 2000).

A further cognitive approach is expressed by Stewart Guthrie (1993), who suggests that all religion is a kind of 'anthropomorphism' – anthropomorphism being the attribution of human characteristics to nonhuman things and events. He thus comes to view religion as essentially an 'illusion'. Although anthropomorphism was heralded as a new theory of religion, Max Muller – like Levi-Strauss – had much earlier defined religion in similar terms, as the 'personification' or anthropomorphism of natural phenomena (on the cognitive approach to religion, see also Boyer 1993; McCauley and Lawson 2002).

6. PHENOMENOLOGICAL APPROACHES

This is the classical approach of religious-studies scholars and essentially derives from the writings of the German philosopher Edmund Husserl. It is exemplified particularly in the work of Rudolf Otto, Carl Jung, Gerardus Van Der Leeuw, and Mircea Eliade. Phenomenology essentially implies a philosophical method that attempts to provide a neutral description of human experience. This essentially entails two steps: first, the notion of 'epoche' – the suspension of prior judgements and the 'bracketing' of the 'natural attitude' – commonsense understandings – so that a focus can be put purely on conscious experience, allowing the 'phenomena to speak for themselves'; and second, the notion of 'eidetic intuition', discovering through intuition the 'essence' – the essential meanings – of the phenomena. In recent decades many anthropologists have explicitly embraced phenomenology, although by this term they do not intend Husserl's 'rigorous science' but rather a repudiation of social science and comparative analysis and a narrow focus on the interpretation of cultural phenomena through either thick description or hermeneutics. In essence it implies making a fetish of culture and the reduction of social life to language or discourses – religious beliefs and ritual practices being reduced in the process to 'texts'.

Ironically, while many postmodern anthropologists have been embracing religious phenomenology and New Age theology, religious-studies scholars, in contrast, have been stressing the importance of developing a more secular and scientific approach to religion. In the process they have offered some cogent criticisms of the phenomenological approach to religion, namely, it treats religion as 'sui generis' and as an autonomous realm independent of social life and human psychology; it posits a divine realm (or spiritual entities) not as a social construct but as having ontological reality; it suggests that the 'origins' of religion are in the private experiences of awe or mystery; and finally, it relies entirely on 'intuitive understanding' and thus ignores the importance of *explaining* religion as a social phenomenon (Jensen and Rothstein 2000).

It is worth noting, of course, that there is a good deal of overlap and common ground among the structuralist, interpretive, and phenomenological approaches to religion, for they all treat religion as essentially a symbolic system, divorced from the wider social world of politics and economics. They differ in what they seek to uncover – a symbolic code or schema, cultural meanings, archetypes, or universal 'essences'. Examples of the latter are the 'sacred' (Eliade) or 'personal faith' (Cantwell Smith) – which is hardly enlightening! (Cox 1992, 38–9). What is significant about phenomenology is that it emphasizes the importance of an empathetic approach towards other cultures and the need to 'walk in the moccasins of the faithful', taking a neutral standpoint, and thus looking at religious phenomena from the viewpoint of the people themselves. Anthropologists like Boas and Malinowski had, of course, adopted this phenomenological approach long before Husserl's philosophical musings on the human everyday 'life-world' [*Lebenswelt*], and it is intrinsic to anthropological scholarship (on the phenomenological approach to religion, see Morris 1987, 174–81; Erricker 1999).

7. SOCIOLOGICAL APPROACHES

This is the approach adopted by the great majority of anthropologists and sociologists over the past half century, and it essentially derives from the seminal writings of Karl Marx, Max Weber, and Emile Durkheim. It thus includes classical structural functionalism, associated with A. R. Radcliffe-Brown, Raymond Firth, and John Middleton; the neo-Marxist approach advocated by such anthropologists as W. M. Van Binsbergen, Peter Worsley, and Maurice Godelier; and the historical sociology that was expressed by neo-Weberian scholars such as Gananath

Obeyesekere and Ernest Gellner. The work of many of these anthropologists is discussed later in the study. Central to all sociological approaches is the idea that religion is essentially a social phenomenon, a 'human construct', and thus can be understood only when it is placed within its socio-historical context. Religious beliefs and values, ritual practices, and organizational structures are thus seen as the products of social processes and wider social structures – patterns of social relations. Religion is not therefore an autonomous realm of social life but is intrinsically related to such issues as health, gender, social identity, and the wider political economy, and to such social processes as globalization and intergroup relations. It is recognized, of course, that religion, in turn, influences social life and cultural meanings in various degrees, whether as an ideology legitimating class oppression (Marx), or functioning to maintain enduring patterns of social life (Durkheim), or as an important factor in the rise of capitalism (Weber). Sociological approaches to religion have therefore always combined interpretive understanding with sociological analysis. As Weber famously put it, sociology is defined as 'a science which attempts the interpretive understanding of social action in order thereby to arrive at a causal explanation of its causes and effects' (1947, 88).

It thus implies the method of inquiry known as *Verstehen*, the emphathetic understanding of subjective meanings (i.e., phenomenology) as well as being centrally concerned with the explanation of social facts.

Raymond Firth has cogently expressed the aim of the social anthropology of religion as a field of inquiry, in that it not only consists of personal observations but also involves 'actually taking part in the religious practices of the people being studied and [the] systematic discussion of their religious beliefs with them'. But it also involves, he writes, studying religion 'in its social setting and noting the economic and political parameters to religious ideas and operations' (1996, 3). The most succinct statement of the sociological approach to religion was expressed by Beckford in suggesting that it 'studies the processes whereby religion, in all its variety and complexity, is interwoven with other social phenomena' (1986, ix).

The sociological approach to religion has been much criticized by hermeneutic scholars who suggest that such sociological analyses do not fully engage in the drama and intensity of religious ritual and symbolism and involve the imposition of western theories and categories upon the ethnographic data (Fernandez 1978). Although one can acknowledge the insights offered by deeply textured ethnographies of specific rituals within a narrow ethnic context, anthropologists like Van Binsbergen have defended a more synthetic, sociological approach. He points out that his own studies, like those of such scholars as Firth, Horton, and Middleton, arise out of fieldwork that was both experiential and participatory, and that one cannot pursue any kind of anthropology completely outside of the western intellectual tradition (Van Binsbergen 1981, 34–6). Indeed, treating religious ritual as an autonomous realm and focussing exclusively on symbolism, aesthetics, and personal idiosyncratic experiences also reflect the imposition of western values and intellectual preoccupations upon other cultures. We thus need to combine hermeneutics with sociological analysis.

At this juncture a brief discussion of what has been described as 'postmodernism' (or poststructuralism) may perhaps be of some value. Both of these concepts are, of course, somewhat vague, implying a rather simplistic and unilinear conception of intellectual history, such that until the likes of Baudrillard, Lyotard, and Derrida arrived on the intellectual scene, all social scientists were either modernists (advocates of Cartesian metaphysics) or structuralists. Around twenty years ago, postmodernism became all the rage in anthropology. It was interesting to see scholars who only a decade earlier were making a fetish out of science and Marxism suddenly repudiate them entirely and embrace postmodernism with an uncritical fervour. Difficult to define – as it includes scholars with very contrasting approaches to social life – postmodernism as an intellectual ethos has been described as having the following tenets.

First, as we have no knowledge of the world except through 'descriptions' (to use Rorty's term), the 'real' is conceived as an 'effect' of discourses. Ideas, linguistically encoded, are thus all that there is, or at least, all that one can ever hope to know. There is then, so we are told, no objective reality. Postmodernism thus propounds an idealist and subjectivist metaphysic that denies the reality of the material world. In Mary Douglas' memorable phrase, 'all reality is social reality' (1975, 5).

Second, as there is no immediate relationship between consciousness (or language) and the world – an idea that has been part of the common currency of the social sciences ever since Marx – postmodernists take this premise to extremes and posit no relationship between language and the world, and thus espouse an absolute epistemological (and moral) relativism. Truth is either repudiated entirely (Tyler) or seen simply as an 'effect' of local cultural discourses (Rorty, Geertz, Flax) or is seen as something that will be 'disclosed' or 'revealed' by elite scholars through poetic evocation (Heidegger). Cultural relativism is thus embraced, and all claims to truth are seen as masking power relations or, in fact, constituting that power.

Third, there is a rejection of all 'metanarratives' (Lyotard) (science, Marxism, liberalism, Christianity, Buddhism, for example) and a strident celebration of the postmodern condition. The so-called 'postmodern condition' – with its alienation, fragmentation, nihilism, cultural pastiche, relativistic theory, antirealism, and 'decentred' subjectivity – describes, however, not so much a new epoch but rather the cultural effects of global capitalism. But such a stance leads postmodernists to repudiate objective knowledge and empirical science.

Finally, there has been a growing tendency among postmodern academics – following Heidegger – to express themselves in the most obscure and impenetrable jargon, under the misguided impression that obscurity connotes profundity and that a scholastic, neo-Baroque prose style is the hallmark of radical politics. It isn't! (Morris 1997; Hay 2002, 322).

All these tenets of postmodernism have been severely critiqued by many scholars over the past two decades and from various theoretical persuasions (Gellner 1992, Bunge 1996; Callinicos 1997; Kuznar 1997; Searle 1999; Bricmont 2001). Not only has postmodernist theory been found wanting, but the political radicalism of the postmodernists has also been questioned. Indeed, in their rejection of history, in reducing social reality to discourses, in their epistemic relativism, and in their seeming obsession with consumer capitalism, many have remarked that there seems to be an 'unholy alliance' between postmodernism and the capitalist triumphalism of the neo-liberals.

Postmodernism is, of course, like structural Marxism, now 'history', as Alex Callinicos puts it (2003, 13), and we have entered a period, according to some scholars, of 'after postmodernism'. Nevertheless, postmodernism continues to be extremely fashionable among litterateurs and cultural idealists in many departments of anthropology. For many interpretative and literary anthropologists studying religion tend to follow in its wake and thus continue to disparage and ridicule, or even repudiate entirely, empirical social science. This has entailed a growing obsession with symbolism, rhetoric, ritual, aesthetics, metaphor, and language more generally, and anthropology among some scholars has been reduced to semiotics or hermeneutics, or even to autobiography. As one doyen of postmodern anthropology put it, ethnography should 'break' with the 'trope' of history and social structure and be simply a kind of autobiography (Marcus 1995). Social life, indeed the world, has therefore been seen as a 'text' to be interpreted rather than as something real to be described and explained. Viewing social life as a 'text', or as a collection of discourse, is an 'idealist extravagance' that undervalues the natural world and bypasses economic and political realities (Bunge 1996, 343–6).

Hermeneutics, of course, is a scholarly tradition that goes back to the nineteenth century and is particularly associated with Wilhelm Dilthey, and in recent times with the writings of Ricoeur (both of whom I have discussed at length elsewhere: Morris 1991, 143–52; 1997, 334–5). It has to be recognized, however, that hermeneutics, interpretive understanding, or Verstehen, has always been an intrinsic part of social anthropology, and scholars like Boas, Malinowski, and Evans-Pritchard were engaged in hermeneutics long before it became a fashionable term among postmodernists. As this present text is focussed around ethnographic studies, it is, in a sense, all about hermeneutics. For the sociological approach to religion, as earlier emphasized, has always combined hermeneutics – interpretive understanding – with sociological and historical analysis.

Although the sociological approach to religion does not entail a 'cold, detached, value-free orientation', which, as Marvin Harris suggests, represents a total distortion of an earlier generation of social scientists (1980, 12), it usually implies what has been described as 'methodological agnosticism'. Thus anthropologists adopting a sociological approach are not concerned with the truth status or morality of specific religious concepts or beliefs, nor with the authenticity of the personal experiences that are often attributed to religious devotees or prophets (Hamilton 1995, 5–12; Beckford 2003, 2–3). This is because, ever since Durkheim, anthropologists have made an implicit distinction between philosophical issues relating to existence (ontology), truth (epistemology), and morality (ethics) – which has not been their main concern – and the role of the anthropologist as a social scientist. In this role they employ what Wright Mills (1959) called the 'sociological imagination' to both understand religion as a system of meanings and to explain religion within its socio-historical context by means of comparative, functional, or causal analysis. Anthropologists as social scientists have thus, following their vocation, been neither for nor against religion, neither engaged in theology, apologetics, or advocacy, nor in explicitly attacking or dismissing religion as meaningless or irrational in the style of the logical positivists. As empirical naturalists, most anthropologists have thus been concerned with knowledge and the understanding of human cultures, not with eternal truths, ultimate meanings, self-enlightenment, or the morality or otherwise of people's religious concepts. Recent discussions of the 'rationality debate' have emphasized, like Firth and Foucault, the importance of a critical rationalism when approaching religion and the need to separate philosophical issues relating to truth and existence from the scientific approach to religion (see Firth 1996 and Jensen and Martin 1997; but cf. Lett 1997, who suggests that anthropologists as empirical scientists should, to maintain their own integrity, fervently and publicly declare that religious beliefs are 'nonsensical' and 'demonstrably untrue' and that religion is a 'thicket of superstition').

Many contemporary postmodern anthropologists, often advocating a kind of New Age theology, have followed religious phenomenologists like Eliade in adopting a very condescending or dismissive attitude towards social science. Sociological analysis is thus repudiated with such negative epithets as 'positivist' or 'detached' or 'reductionist', and social scientists are accused, often in the most oracular fashion, of 'reifying' social phenomena or as treating religion as 'epiphenomena'. Even more perverse is that New Age anthropologists derogate an earlier generation of social scientists for having a 'unitary' conception of the human subject, as if anthropologists were still stuck in the seventeenth century! Such New Age and postmodern anthropologists seem to be discovering for themselves what has been common knowledge among social scientists ever since Marx, namely, that humans in all cultures are intrinsically social beings and that self-identity – personhood – is complex, shifting, composite, relational, and involves multiple identities (see Morris 2000, 41–8). As I shall explore in this study, most of these adverse criticisms of the social scientific approach by postmodern and New Age anthropologists are unwarranted, prejudiced, and verge on caricature (on the sociological approach to religion, see Morris 1987, 23–90, 106–40; Hamilton 2001; Beckford 2003; specifically on the Marxist approach, see Siegel 1986).

There is a common tendency among many scholars of religion to exaggerate or overemphasize the importance of religion in human social life, such that religion is described as forming the basis for almost everything that humans do or think. Religion, one scholar tells us, 'is very much and always with us. It is with us at every moment of life' – and with regard to *all* the events of life (Idowu 1973, 1). This is about as valid and as enlightening as the suggestion that all human life has a material or biological dimension or that everything is political or economic. I thus tend to think, like Clifford Geertz, that nobody, not even religious mystics or saints or Catholic priests, live in the 'world' that religious symbols formulate all the time, and that the majority of humans live it only at moments, or not at all; 'the everyday world of common sense objects and practical acts is . . . the paramount reality in human experience' (Geertz 1975, 119). Even Husserl acknowledged this, in spite of his tendencies towards subjective idealism. Religion is thus only one perspective in terms of which humans construe the world, and it is certainly not the most basic.

As religion is a complex and multifaceted phenomenon, one can thus understand it fully only by adopting an integral approach, in which all approaches to religion must be taken into account. But in this present text I focus almost exclusively on the sociological approach to religion, not only because this has been by far the most dominant trend in social anthropology over the past fifty years or so, but also because in the recent decade this approach has tended to be marginalized or ignored in many introductory texts and anthologies. The emphasis in such texts is on such topics as the aesthetics of religion, body symbolism, the semiotics of magic and ritual, and a general focus on the more exotic aspects of religion – to the exclusion often of any discussion of Buddhism and Islam or on the political economy of religion.

It must be emphasized that this present text is focussed almost entirely on ethnographic studies; not because I see such ethnographies as case study material to illustrate the sociological approach, but rather because I see them as substantive studies in their own right – texts that, within their own pages, combine the interpretation of cultural phenomena (religious ideas and practices) with theory, in the form of sociological analysis. As my main concern in this book is expository, to offer a critical guide to the social anthropology of religion, I have quoted liberally from the writings of various scholars, both to give the flavour of their work and to avoid any misunderstandings. I have also, as in my earlier studies, attempted to approach the work of other scholars with an attitude of critical sympathy. At times, exasperated by the pretensions of some postmodernists, or by the rather arrogant and disparaging denunciations of social science by hermeneutic anthropologists, I may at times have been a little harsh in my criticisms. But please note: they are criticisms, and nowhere in these pages do I intend to belittle the work of the many scholars that I discuss.

This book has a regional and ethnographic focus and is in eight chapters, the contents of which are summarized thus:

Chapter 1 is on shamanism. After an initial discussion on the relationship of shamanism to spirit-possession and altered states of consciousness, I explore shamanic rituals and the role of the shaman in two ethnographic contexts – with respect to the Siberian peoples and the Inuit of North America. I conclude the chapter with a discussion of neo-shamanism and the various interpretations of shamanism as a social phenomenon.

Chapter 2 is devoted to an exploration of the complex relationship between Buddhism and spirit-cults, and its focus is on South-East Asia. After an initial discussion of Buddhism, in the classical sense as a religion of salvation, I explore the relationship between Buddhism and spirit-cults in four societies – Burma, Thailand, Sri Lanka, and Tibet – drawing on some important and comprehensive ethnographic studies. I conclude the chapter with a brief look at the relationship between Buddhism and state power.

Chapter 3 is focussed on Islamic societies and is particularly centred on anthropological studies that have explored the nature of Islam as a popular religious form, especially the relationship between Islam as a religion of salvation and the spirit-cults. After outlining the early history of Islam and its basic 'orthopraxy', I discuss the nature and function of Zar cults in two ethnographic contexts – Somalia and the Sudan. I then turn to the more political aspects of Islam and discuss Gellner's theory of 'two styles' of Islam: the Hamadsha sufi brotherhood in Morocco and the relationship between Islam and political rule in Morocco, focussing particularly on the political sociology of the reformist movement.

Chapter 4 is on popular Hinduism. After an initial section on what is usually described as 'Sanskritic' Hinduism, I give an account of popular Hinduism, its gods and rituals, and illustrate this popular Hinduism by exploring a number of ethnographic contexts – religion among the Coorgs of South India, the cult of the goddess in Orissa, and the Radha-Krishna Bhakti cult in Madras. I then give an account of a new religious movement that has emerged from the Hindu tradition and that has had an important cultural impact in both India and the West – the Hare Krishna movement. I conclude the chapter with a discussion of the role of religious gurus in the contemporary resurgence of a militant Hindu nationalism.

Chapter 5 is on Christianity and religion in Africa. After outlining the Christian tradition and the religious concepts and practices that constitute what is generally described as 'traditional' African religion, I discuss this religion in relation to specific ethnographic contexts. I focus on some key anthropological texts that have attempted to go beyond a narrow hermeneutical approach and to explore African religions, within their socio-historical context, particularly in regard to the impact of Christianity. I thus discuss the following subjects: religion among the Kongo of Zaire; religious change in Zambia; and the relation between the religious cosmology of the Tshidi of Mafeking and both the Christian missions and the expanding capitalist economy. The chapter concludes with a brief note on the pentecostalist movement in Africa.

Chapter 6 is focussed on African-based religions in the 'New World' – the Americas. After an initial discussion on the impact of the Atlantic slave trade on

African cultures, I discuss the emerging African religions in three specific contexts – Haiti, Jamaica, and Brazil. I thus focus on Vodou religion, Revivalism, and the Rastafari movement in Jamaica, and on Candomble in Brazil.

Chapter 7 is specifically concerned with the religions of Melanesia and is focussed on some key ethnographic studies, dealing respectively in the first part of the chapter with the religions of the Kwaio and Tsembago. I then turn to a discussion of millennial movements in Melanesia, the well-known cargo cults, examining the historical background of these movements, some specific ethnographic examples, and the various interpretations that have been suggested by anthropologists to explain them.

Chapter 8 examines the recent upsurge of Neopaganism and New Age religion in Western Europe and North America. After exploring the basic worldview and historical roots of this Neopagan revival, which is a diverse and eclectic movement, I discuss in turn its main forms, Wicca, feminist witchcraft, Druidry and the northern tradition, and ritual magic, and conclude the chapter with a discussion of the Western Mystery tradition and its most recent manifestation – New Age religion.

Although it has not been possible to cover every region and topic, overall the book provides a comprehensive introduction to the social anthropology of religion. It is thus focussed on the ethnographic studies of those scholars who have continued to embrace the 'dual heritage' of anthropology, combining the interpretive understanding of subjective meanings with a social scientific perspective that situates religion within its wider socio-historical context.

1

Shamanism

1.1. PROLOGUE

When I was a student-novitiate in anthropology in the 1970s, shamanism was something of an unknown and esoteric subject among the general public. Even among anthropologists the topic of shamanism was disparaged. That doyen of postmodern anthropologists, Clifford Geertz, famously declared that shamanism was one of those 'dessicated types' or 'insipid categories' by means of which ethnographers of religion 'devitalize their data' (1975, 122). A cultural transformation has taken place over the past two decades, and there has been a renaissance in studies of shamanism. For not only has shamanism – as a social phenomenon – become an important topic of research in the fields of anthropology and religious studies, but it is also now widely practised as a mode of spiritual or self-enlightenment among New Age adherents.

In recent years, however, postmodern anthropologists have been telling us that as shamanism is a 'made-up, modern, western category' (in case you didn't know!) and as it does not exist as a 'unitary and homogeneous' phenomenon, we should stop talking about 'shamanism' and instead write only of 'shamanisms' or 'shamanry' or 'shamanizing'. By these criteria they themselves should stop writing about 'anthropology', 'western', 'time', and the 'Evenki'! Such semantic quibbles and banal nominalism seem to be unnecessary and stultifying and cannot be sustained even by their advocates. Indeed, far from being an 'outmoded western category' as postmodern anthropologists suppose, shamanism has become an important research topic as well as showing a surprising capacity to adapt to new urban contexts (Saladin D'Anglure 1996, 507). Here I use the term *shamanism* simply as a concept to refer to a complex set of beliefs, ritual practices, and social relationships that have worldwide occurrence, which I subsequently define and explore.

Two other rather banal observations coming from postmodern students of religion are also worth noting. One is the suggestion that tribal people conceptualize the spirits and deities as 'persons' – 'dividual' is the current fashionable label – as if anthropologists had never before been aware of this obvious fact. The second is the rather oracular pronouncements against the use of the term *spirit*. The term *spirit* is unhelpful, Graham Harvey tells us, because it has diverse meanings and is 'nothing less than a mystification contrived by sceptical outsiders' (2003, 11). But in contradictory fashion he also tells us that the term *spirit* is 'empty of meaning', that it implies a dualistic metaphysic and suggests that spiritual beings are beyond sensual experience. The implication that anyone using the term *spirit* – scholars as diverse as Evans-Pritchard, Hultkrantz, Middleton, Lewis, Siikala, Harner, Fortes – is thereby engaged in mystification and embraces a Cartesian metaphysic is not only completely fallacious but also demeaning towards a generation of anthropologists, all of whom, unlike Harvey, had spent many years engaged in ethnographic fieldwork. Anthropologists have long recognized that *spirits* are conceptualized as 'persons' and addressed as such, that there are many different kinds of spiritual beings within a specific context, and that the spirits manifest themselves sensuously (how else!) as humans, in dreams, in the form of animals or birds, as masked dancers, or embodied in artefacts (amulets, figurines, sculptured images). Like some Victorian scholars, Harvey has the quaint idea that tribal people talk to the trees and propitiate bears and plovers, whereas these are only hierophanies (to use Eliade's term) of spirits or deities. For example, in Malawi, god [*mulungu*] and the ancestral spirits [*mizimu*] are conceptualized as persons and addressed as grandparent [*ambuye*]. People do not address prayers to clay pots or puff adders but to the spirits [*mizimu*], which are embodied in these (and other) natural features. The alternatives to the term *spirit* – superpersons, shades, numinals, personages, other than human persons, powers – that have been suggested are hardly more enlightening. Following Hallowell, Harvey opts for 'other than human persons' (the Ojibway seem to have addressed them as 'grandfathers'); it is a rather vague concept, for it not only covers spiritual beings (god, deities, spirit) but, in different contexts, a host of entities – motorbikes, animals, divining instruments, business corporations, and boats – but excludes malevolent spirits and witches, which, in Malawi at least, are not conceived as 'persons' (see Morris 2000, 41–68).

Personally, I prefer the term *spirit* (as a translation, for example, of *mzimu*) as it still retains the connotation of its original Latin meaning – despite the dualistic emphases of Christian Neoplatonism and Cartesian philosophy – namely, that of breath, life, wind, awe, mystery, and invisibility. Harvey still seems stuck in Christian theology, with its psychologistic emphasis, and ignores the fact that the term *spirit* not only predates Descartes (let alone anthropology!) but that the dualistic, spiritualist metaphysic he alludes to is not a characteristic of a mystifying secular humanism but of religious thinkers such as Plato, Augustine, and Descartes.

In this chapter I simply follow and employ the terms used for spiritual beings by the scholars and ethnographers themselves, even though in some contexts it might have been helpful to distinguish between gods, who have full moral personhood and rarely possess humans, and spirits who are only minimally persons, often capricious and amoral, and are the main focus of spirit-possession rituals (Mageo and Howard 1996). Harvey's contention that shamans are not primarily concerned with 'spirituality' but rather strive for basic subsistence needs, health, and prosperity (2003, 8) has, of course, been affirmed by generations of anthropologists, ever since the time of Durkheim and Weber.

This chapter is focussed on shamanism in its widest sense. In the first three sections I address the question 'What is shamanism?' and discuss the relationship of shamanism to altered states of consciousness and to spirit-possession. In Sections 1.5 and 1.6, I explore shamanic rituals and the role of the shaman in two ethnographic contexts – with respect to Siberian peoples and the Inuit, of Arctic Canada and Greenland. In Section 1.7, I describe a recent social movement, neo-shamanism, which has become a key part of the western New Age culture. In the final sections, I discuss two comparative studies and various interpretations of shamanism as a social phenomenon.

1.2. WHAT IS SHAMANISM?

The term *shaman* is taken from the language of the Evenki (Tungus), a hunting and reindeer-herding people of eastern Siberia, and was used to refer to their spirit-mediums [*saman*]. It has been suggested that the word is derived from the Indo-European verb root *sa*, meaning 'to know' (in Pali, *samana*; in French, *savoir*) and that the cultural–historical foundations of shamanism may be sought in Buddhism or in other scriptural traditions of Asia. The evidence indicates, however, that Siberian shamanism at least is probably endemic, having its origins or roots in early Palaeolithic hunting and gathering cultures, even though the word *saman* itself may be of foreign origin, as Shirokogoroff suggested. Indeed, the term *samana (or shamana)* is the Pali term for a Buddhist monk (Shirokogoroff 1935, 266–9; Ripinsky-Naxon 1993, 69; Siikala and Hoppal 1998, 2; Hutton 2001, 114).

Several writers have viewed shamanism, that is, communion with the 'spirit world' through trance states or out-of-body experiences, as the ancient or 'ur-religion' of humankind, as virtually co-terminous with humanity. It is seen as having its source in the pan-human 'existential quest for meaning' or in being functional in enabling early humans to cope with the serious problems of health and survival. An intrinsic link is therefore made between shamanism and altered states of consciousness (La Barre 1972; Harner 1980, 53; Ripinsky-Naxon 1993, 9).

The first description of a shamanic séance was recorded in the thirteenth century, when a Franciscan monk visited the Mongolian court. He described how the shaman, as oracle, beating a drum during a night ceremony invoked the (evil) spirits. Throughout the eighteenth and nineteenth centuries, eyewitness accounts of Siberian and Inner Asian shamanism continued to be recorded by travellers and missionaries, especially from Russian sources. Shamanism thus from an early period became the subject of the European cultural imagination, and the shaman was portrayed in diverse ways – as an expression of demonic forces, the source of art and esotericism, as an archaic magician, and as a wounded healer. Even Enlightenment figures such as Diderot, Herder, and Goethe were fascinated by Siberian shamanism (Flaherty 1992; Siikala and Hoppal 1998; Hutton 2001, 29–44).

It was, however, the phenomenologist and well-known scholar of comparative religion, Mircea Eliade (1907–1986), who offered perhaps the first comprehensive study of shamanism. Indeed, his book, *Shamanism: Archaic Techniques of Ecstasy* (1964), has become something of a classic, a pioneering study that has had a wide appeal and influence. For Eliade, shamanism was pre-eminently a religious phenomenon of Siberia and Central Asia, and he virtually equated shamanism with 'techniques of ecstasy' and the shaman's 'magical flight'. The shaman was thus interpreted as an inspired priest who 'specializes in a trance during which his soul is believed to leave his body and ascend to the sky or descend to the underworld' (1964, 5). Eliade distinguished the shaman as a mystic who engaged in such ecstatic journeys from other ritual specialists, such as magicians and 'medicine-men' (herbalists), and he emphasized that the shaman controlled his tutelary spirits. The shaman is thus a kind of spirit-medium who interacts with the 'spirit world' on behalf of his community and engages in such social practices as divination, particularly in relation to the presence of game animals, healing rites, and the protection of the kin group or community from malevolent spiritual influences. But Eliade made a clear distinction between shamanism – implying ecstasy (or trance), soul flight, and the mastery of the spirits – and spirit-possession. The latter, involving the 'embodiment' of the spirits by the shaman, Eliade recognized as almost a universal phenomenon; nevertheless, he was adamant that being 'possessed' by spirits was not a part of shamanism in the strict sense. Thus the shamanism of the Evenki (Tungus), as recorded by Shirokogoroff (1935), having been deeply influenced by Buddhism from the South, was regarded by Eliade as a syncretic, decadent form of an original authentic shamanism (1964, 500). Many scholars have questioned this formulation and have stressed that spirit-possession may often be a functional alternative to the 'soul flight' and is thus an intrinsic aspect of the shamanic complex (Lewis 1986, 84–6; Siikala and Hoppal 1998, 21).

Eliade's study was not restricted to Siberia and the Eurasian context. He ranged widely and noted, even if only implicitly, the presence of shamanism in North and South America, in South-East Asia, and in Oceania – although significantly he completely ignored the African context. Subsequent research has indicated that shamanism is a worldwide phenomena and is by no means restricted to Siberia and Central Asia (Lewis 1971; Harner 1980; Vitebsky 1995a).

The entire raison d'etre of shamanism, wrote Joan Townsend, 'is to interact with the spirit world for the benefit of those in the material world' (1997, 431). The shaman is thus essentially a spirit-medium who serves as a 'bridge' between the 'spirit world' and the world of the living. Ioan Lewis, following Shirokogoroff, has thus defined the shaman as

> an inspired prophet or leader, a charismatic religious figure with the power to control the spirits, usually by incarnating them. If spirits speak through him, he is also likely to have the capacity to engage in mystical flight and other 'out-of-body' experiences. (1986, 88)

As misfortunes in many societies are believed to be caused by spirits, and as such misfortunes can be countered only with the aid of 'helping spirits', the shaman essentially acts as the intermediary in order to alleviate many diverse problems. Essential to this endeavour is the mastery or control of spirits.

This question is often asked: Is shamanism a religion? Most scholars suggest that shamanism is not a 'religion' in the sense of an organized or institutionalized social phenomenon – but nevertheless they frequently aver to describing it as a 'world-view', or as an 'ideology', or as a 'hunter's religion' (Vitebsky 1995a, 11; Townsend 1997, 431–3). Ake Hultkrantz rightly suggests that shamanism is best described as a complex of various beliefs and practices *within* a religion and not a religion in itself. Although shamanism is often identified with the religious cosmology of the Siberian peoples, as explored by Eliade, with its multilayered universe (heaven, earth, underworld) connected by a cosmic pillar or tree, shamanism, of course, is to be found in many different societies, with widely differing religious concepts and cosmologies – even within the Siberian context. Hultkrantz specifically defines religion as a belief in gods and spirits and as involving 'faith in the existence of a supernatural world' – although he eschews the concept of transcendental. As religion is thus the 'intuitive certainty of another world', shamanism is viewed as being explicitly grounded in a two-world theory. Thus we have the ordinary world as experienced in everyday life and the 'supernatural' or 'hidden world' experienced only during trance states (Hultkrantz 1988, 36–9).

This notion of shamanism as being embedded within a dualistic worldview is expressed even more clearly by Michael Harner:

> A perception of two realities is typical of shamanism, even though some western armchair philosophers have long denied the legitimacy of claiming such a dual division between the ordinary world and a hidden world among primitive peoples. (1980, 60)

Thus the shaman is seen as existing in two worlds: in the ordinary world of daily life and in the hidden world of the spirits into which he or she enters during a trance state. Townsend described these 'two realities' as the 'material reality' in which we live and the 'spiritual reality', which is the abode of spirits, souls of the dead, deities, and other beings. Thus, by falling into a trance, the shaman is interpreted as entering the other reality, the unseen world (Townsend 1997, 437; Hultkrantz 1988, 38).

But, of course, people in their ordinary working life also communicate with the spirits, and thus spiritual beings are equally to be seen as existing within the world of commonsense experience. Ronald Hutton has thus affirmed, at least in relation to the Siberian cosmologies, that the spirits 'were fully integrated with the natural and human environments; indeed they were an aspect of them' (2001, 67). The important point is how the events and concrete things of ordinary experience and perception are interpreted and conceptualized within particular social contexts.

Following Shirokogoroff and Lewis, we can therefore define a shaman as a person who is able to control the spirits. What is crucial is not the 'ecstatic magical flight', as a visionary journey, but the ability to contact and possess spirits, so that a dialogue or relationship can be established between the spirit and the local community. He or she is therefore a specific kind of spirit-medium.

1.3. SHAMANISM AND ALTERED STATES OF CONSCIOUSNESS

Mircea Eliade, influenced by phenomenology, suggested that religion must be understood only in its own terms and so repudiated any attempt to relate religious phenomena to sociological and psychological factors. To try to grasp the essence (meaning) of religion by reference to sociology and psychology he thus considered false and reductive. Yet, in closely identifying shamanism with trance and defining the former specifically as 'techniques of ecstasy', Eliade himself has been much criticized by scholars for his own reductive, psychological approach to shamanism. In fact, in adopting a comparative approach, he was deviating substantially, as he admitted, from the kind of phenomenology advocated by Husserl (on Eliade's approach to religion, see Altizer 1963; Allen 1978; Morris 1987, 174–81; and the short but useful review essay by Pals 1996, 158–97).

As the shamanic séance involves what is described as a 'shift' in consciousness, trance (or ecstasy), as earlier noted, is invariably seen as a key feature of shamanism. The terms *trance* and *ecstasy* are often used by scholars as almost interchangeable, indeed as synonyms, with *trance* tending to be favoured by psychologists and anthropologists, *ecstasy* by students of comparative religion. Both terms have their problems. The word *ecstasy* derives from the Greek *ekstasis*, meaning to displace or drive out, and its usual connotations may be misleading, as they tend to imply frenzy, euphoria, rapture, or intense emotions, or, in a theistic context, union with the divine. *Trance*, on the other hand, often implies a hypnotic or unconscious state and may be used to cover a wide range of different mental states (Pattee 1988, 18–19; Townsend 1997, 441). Thus, over the recent decades, and given the interest in 'transpersonal psychology' and the emerging drug culture in Europe and North America, the rubric 'altered states of consciousness' has come into vogue. In fact, it has become something of a 'buzzword' in interdisciplinary studies of shamanism, to the neglect often of the social and cultural aspects of shamanism (Atkinson 1992, 310). Harner, however, refers specifically to a *shamanic* state of consciousness, which the shaman enters only when performing the shamanic tasks – that is, only during a ritual séance – and notes that this altered state of consciousness includes varying degrees of trance. But he affirms that 'what *is* definite is that *some* degree of alteration of consciousness is necessary to shamanic practice' (his emphasis, 1980, 59–62).

Altered states of consciousness have been particularly emphasized in the writings of Michael Winkelman. He suggests that such states – expressed in dreams, soul flights or out-of-body experiences, meditative and mystical states, possession rites, and visionary experiences – form a biological basis for many aspects of religious behaviour. As with la Barre (1972), Winkelman suggests that the altered states of consciousness evident in shamanic activities provide a basis for explicating the 'ontogenesis of religious experience' (1997, 393).

The induction of such altered states of consciousness has been explored by many scholars; and it may be accomplished in many different ways by use of a variety of agents and procedures. These include, in particular, the use of psychotropic plants and fungi to induce trance or visionary experiences. Among the more well known are the fly agaric (*Amanita muscaria*), tobacco (*Nicotiana spp*), ayahuasca or yagé (*Banisteriopsis spp*), and the peyote cactus (*Lophophora sp*). Although in Mexico, Siberia, and the Amazon region hallucinogenic plants or fungi are often used to ritually induce an altered state of consciousness, they are by no means essential, or even widely practised. More common is the use of the drum and rhythmic dancing. In his own system of neo-shamanic healing and counselling, Michael Harner advocates rhythmic drumming and chanting, not drugs, to induce the 'shamanic' state of consciousness (1980, 64–6; on hallucinogenic plants, see Furst 1972; Schultes and Hofmann 1979; Ripinsky-Naxon 1993, 131–50).

Besides drumming, chanting, and the use of psychotropic plants, many other activities can induce ecstasy, visionary experiences, or other altered states of consciousness – namely, sensory and social deprivation (isolation, fasting, and exposure to extreme temperatures), intensive physical movement (dancing, long-distance running, or the use of swings), sleep deprivation, mental concentration as in meditative states, or physical pain (including torture). But such changes in states of consciousness and how they are interpreted – whether, for example, simple inebriation or possession by the god Dionysus – are influenced and shaped by many factors: the expectations, dispositions, and motives of the individual person, cultural beliefs and schemas, and the social context. Thus, with altered states of consciousness, whether induced by drumming or psychotropic plants, '*what* will be perceived and *how* it will be experienced is related to the cultural context and the traditional meanings provided by the individual' (Bourguignon 1979, 242; for further discussions of altered states of consciousness, see Ludwig 1968; Bourguignon 1979, 233–69; Winkelman 1997; Siikala and Hoppal 1998, 26–31).

Although writers like Winkelman suggest there is a 'common mode of consciousness' utilized in shamanic rituals (as well as in visionary experiences and meditative states), they also emphasize that there are significant physiological and phenomenological differences within the altered state of consciousness (Winkelman 1997, 410). *What* is experienced – a soul flight or out-of-body experience, possession, a mystical state of pure being (what Eliade described as entasis), or a visionary experience; the *degree* of consciousness or amnesia; and whether the experience is interpreted in secular or religious terms – all these seem to be extremely variable. Harner suggests that the altered (shamanic) state of consciousness is a 'conscious waking state' while Winkelman emphasizes that, although possession usually entails amnesia, meditative states may bring a heightened sense of awareness (Harner 1980, xx; Winkelman 1997, 413–5).

The close identification of shamanism with altered states of consciousness (especially with psychotropic plants) has led many recent scholars to interpret the rock paintings of Siberia, Western Europe, and Southern Africa as products of shamanic rituals. Whether anthropomorphic figures, polychromatic paintings of animals, schematic (or entopic) images, or portraits of masked figures (such as the famous 'sorcerer' of the Les Trois Frères Cave in the Pyrenees), all have been associated with shamanism and trance states. They are thus seen as reflecting the religion of hunter–gatherers in the upper Palaeolithic (Pfeiffer 1982; Lewis-Williams and Dowson 1988; Clottes and Lewis-Williams 1998; Siikala and Hoppal 1998, 132–49; Pearson 2002).

Although often denying that their analyses are reductive, anthropologists have the tendency to identify shamanism with altered states of consciousness, which tends to put an emphasis on psychology and to downplay the social and cultural dimensions of shamanism. As Atkinson cogently puts it

> Certainly shifts in consciousness are a key part of shamanic practice. But to analyse shamanism primarily as a trance phenomenon is akin to analysing marriage solely as a function of reproductive biology. (1992, 311)

In relation to the Daur Mongols, Caroline Humphrey is critical of seeing trance–ecstasy as the defining characteristic of shamanism and emphasizes that shamanic practices deal with a range of different mental states. These include

> different kinds of dreaming, assumption of other identities, having visions, the exaltation of calling for blessings, various states of dissociation, achieved by shamans, and even fever-induced delirium or drunkenness. (1996, 31)

States of dissociation are what are ordinarily meant by the term *trance*, and most of these states seem to fall under Winkelman's rubric of 'altered states of consciousness'. But what was essential to someone's being called a shaman [*yadgan*], Humphrey writes, 'was the ability to become at one with a spirit, and consequently able to journey in the cosmos' (1996, 31).

This does not seem very different from Eliade's conception of the shaman.

There are serious limitations when discussing shamanism, of focussing exclusively on altered states of consciousness: but it is, I think, equally unhelpful to deny any connection between shamanism, and religion more generally, and ecstatic states.

1.4. SPIRIT-POSSESSION AND SHAMANISM

Ioan Lewis' important study, '*Ecstatic Religion*', is a sustained attempt, in the structural–functionalist tradition – which for Lewis did not imply the 'teleological mystique of status-quo maintenance' or a repudiation of history – to offer a sociological interpretation of shamanism and spirit-possession. His aim, as he puts it, is to try and isolate 'the particular social and other conditions which encourage the development of an ecstatic emphasis in religion' (1971, 28). He is critical of cognitive anthropology and Levi-Straussion structuralism for ignoring the social context. Such analyses, in treating religion as a thing in itself 'with a life of its own' are, Lewis feels, consonant with a theological perspective and the contemporary interest in the occult.

Lewis' interest in spirit-possession was derived from his own fieldwork experiences among the pastoral nomads of the Somali republic. Here, although an Islamic culture, spirit-possession plays an important role as a peripheral cult associated primarily with women who become possessed by Zar spirits. The nature of this ecstatic cult I explore more fully in Chapter 3. But here I must outline Lewis' general theory of spirit-possession and shamanism, which is clearly expressed in his essay on 'The Shaman's Career' (1986, 78-93).

The term *spirit-possession* generally denotes the incarnation or possession of an individual by some spiritual being and not by some vague 'external forces'. According to the culture, the spirit may 'possess' or control the individual person in a number of different ways – it may reside in the head, 'ride' the individual as a horse, or a spirit might fully incarnate the person, taking full control of his or her body – and the person is 'seized' by the divinity or spirit. He or she then becomes a 'vessel' or 'temple' or the embodiment of the spirit.

Long ago, Raymond Firth, writing about Tikopia religious beliefs and rituals, made a useful distinction among spirit-possession, spirit-mediumship, and shamanism. Spirit-possession entails abnormal personal behaviour being interpreted by other members of a society as evidence that a spirit is controlling the person's actions, probably inhabiting his or her body. Spirit-mediumship means simply communication with what are understood in a community to be entities in the spirit world. The person is conceived as serving as an intermediary between a human community and the spirits, as in many divinatory rites. Finally, shamanism is a social phenomenon in which a person, whether or not a spirit-medium, is regarded as controlling the spirits, exercising his or her mastery over them (1967, 296). Lewis suggests that all these three modes of communication with the spirit world are involved in shamanic rites.

The possessing spirit may be of various kinds – mythical culture-heroes, ancestral spirits or ghosts, legendary kings or historical personalities, nature spirits, and various types of deities. Significantly, where there is a belief in a high god, belief in possession by such a god is rare, and in the Christian tradition, possession is usually envisaged as by the 'holy ghost' or 'holy spirit'. In a wider context it tends to be spirits rather than gods that possess humans (Mageo and Howard 1996, 11–27). Such spirits may be conceived as malevolent, but most spirits are not regarded as wholly bad, even though their beneficent aspect may often consist simply of leaving people alone. Spirits may be communicated with and contacted in various ways – through sacrifice, prayer, dreams, or rituals – but the shamanic rituals involving possession entail a close and immediate relationships with the divinities or the spirits.

It might be worth mentioning that the most famous shaman or spirit-medium in history was, of course, Jesus of Nazareth, although many Christians and even some anthropologists seem to baulk at the idea. From the New Testament record, it is evident that Jesus had visionary experiences, believed himself to be possessed by god the father – 'The words that I speak unto you I speak not of myself, but the father that dwelleth in me' (John 14: 9–10) – and interpreted illness and misfortunes as being due to 'unclean spirits' and devils. Jesus is described as being 'full of the holy ghost' and being 'led by the spirit', and there are numerous instances of Jesus 'casting out' malevolent spirits. There is no mention at all of medical herbalism in the gospels, and Jesus seems to have been essentially a spirit-healer and exorcist. Even the early Christian church under Paul seems to have all the hallmarks of a spirit-possession cult (Morris 1975).

In his study of ecstatic religion, Ioan Lewis fully explores the relationship between spirit-possession and other related phenomena – such as trance states, soul loss, and shamanism. Although he suggests that spirit-possession is often closely associated with trance or ecstasy, there is, however, no intrinsic connexion. Altered states of consciousness occur in many different social contexts, both secular and religious, and are not necessarily associated with spirit-possession per se but may be interpreted in many other ways. Lewis mentions trance states among the Samburu of Kenya. Pastoral nomads, Samburu men of the warrior age group typically fall into a trance on particular occasions. Such trances are viewed as culturally conditioned responses to tension and danger, in which there is no mystical interpretation (Spencer 1965; Lewis 1971, 40). In the trance performances of the !Kung bushmen, there is also no incarnation of spirits (see Lee 1968; Katz 1976, 1982; Guenther 1999).

Conversely, in many social contexts, spirit-possession involves no dissociation or altered states of consciousness. For example, Harper (1957) records one South Indian shaman who incarnated a local deity, Siddheshavana, at will, and who, although alleged to go into a trance, seemed to be fully conscious during the séance, answering any questions put to him at what amounted to an open discussion forum. Lewis also stresses that there is a widespread belief in many societies that illness is a form of spirit-possession without this implying that the patient is in a trance state.

Soul loss too may or may not be linked with spirit-possession. Among members of the vodou cult in Haiti (discussed fully in Chapter 6), it is believed that the loa spirits incarnate a person only after first displacing the *gros bon ange* [the big good angel], one of the two souls a person is said to possess. Similarly, the Akawaio Indians of Guyana believe that during a trance séance, the shaman's soul or spirit leaves his body, and he is then able to incarnate various forest spirits (Butt 1966). But as Lewis indicates, this is not always the case, for among the Somali nomads a person may become possessed by a Zar spirit, without this implying the doctrine of soul loss. Conversely, soul loss is believed to occur in many African societies without this involving spirit-possession. Lewis therefore feels that it is best to take a phenomenological approach to the issue of possession and that if a person is considered in his or her own cultural milieu to be possessed by a spirit, then this can be taken as spirit-possession.

The question then arises as to the relationship between shamanism and spirit-possession. As already described, Eliade (1964) and several other scholars have seen shamanism and spirit-possession as antithetical phenomena. For these scholars, shamanism involves a 'soul flight', a disembodied mystical experience – an 'ascent of man towards the gods' – and entails the control or 'mastery' of the spirits. On the other hand, spirit-possession is postulated as having no intrinsic link with shamanism and is viewed in a negative sense as implying only an involuntary, unconscious passive state. The shaman is one who is 'inspired' rather than possessed and seeks to 'cure possession' (de Heusch 1981, 151–63; Pattee 1988, 22).

In an examination of the ethnographic record on the Evenki (Tungus) of Siberia, specifically the classic studies of the Russian scholar Shirokogoroff (1935), Lewis argues that the rigid demarcation between shamanism and spirit-possession is untenable. He suggests that trance states, soul loss, magical flight, and spirit-possession should not be seen as separate, self-sustaining forms of religiosity, as they coexist in many societies. They should therefore be seen as essentially 'constituent elements in the composite shamanic complex' (1986, 85).

In fact, he quotes Shirokogoroff's definition of the shaman to emphasize that spirit-possession is an intrinsic component of shamanism:

> In all the Tungus languages the term [shaman] refers to both sexes who have mastered the spirits, who at their will can introduce these spirits into themselves and use their power over their spirits in their own interests, particularly helping other people who suffer from the spirits: in such a capacity they may possess a complex of special methods for dealing with the spirits. (Shirokogoroff 1935, 269)

Thus shamans had a variety of different ways of engaging with the spirits, including possession, and sought the aid of specific tutelary or 'helping spirits'. A shaman therefore was a spirit-medium who often became possessed as well as having 'mastery' of the spirits. Lewis therefore suggests that shamanism among the Siberian peoples like the Evenki (Tungus) was in no sense a unique phenomenon, but that their séances had affinities to those recorded elsewhere in other spirit-possession cults. The important distinction therefore, for Lewis, was not between shamanism and spirit-possession but between two forms of possession, an initial 'uncontrolled' possession, at the assumption of the shamanic role, and 'controlled' possession. For after an initial traumatic experience, a person may become a shaman and, by developing a relationship with one or more tutelary spirits, come to achieve some degree of control over the spirits, particularly those malevolent spirits who may be the agent of some illness or misfortune. Significantly, any spirit may be malevolent, benevolent, or neutral, according to the local context and interpretation, and this depends particularly on whether or not it is controlled by a shaman on behalf of a local community (Shirokogoroff 1935, 21–2; Lewis 1986, 86). Some of these issues are explored further in the next section, which deals specifically with Siberian shamanism.

1.5. SIBERIAN AND INNER ASIAN SHAMANISM

There were considerable differences in the ecology, social life, and religious culture of the peoples of Siberia and Inner Asia (Mongolia). People like the Yukaghir and Evenki (Tungus) in central and north-eastern Siberia were largely hunters of deer and elk and nomadic reindeer herders who had a well-developed clan system. On the other hand, along the Pacific coast, the Chukchi and Koryak had a weakly developed clan system, and, while the Chukchi were essentially reindeer herders, the Koryak had an economy focussed around the hunting of sea mammals – whales, walruses, and seals. In southern Siberia and Inner Asia, such peoples as the Sakha (Yakuts) and Buryats had a more complex society, with a hierarchic social structure and a developed pastoral and farming economy. Influenced by Buddhism, they often had a more complex ritual and cosmological system. Throughout the region, there was a wide variety of different kinds of shamans and other religious specialists, and they varied in relation to their function, the kinds of spirits they invoked, and the degree of prestige and professionalism they indicated. This was the case even within a specific ethnic group (Vitebsky 1995a, 34–7; Siikala and Hoppal 1998, 2–4; Hutton 2001, 48–50).

Among the Evenki (Tungus), the shaman was often one of the leaders of the clan, who conducted calendrical rites to ensure the success of hunting and was concerned in helping clan members; curing illness, disease, and infertility; conducting divinatory rites; and preventing misfortunes threatened by the spirits. For among the Evenki, sickness and misfortune were believed to be due either to the neglect of the ancestral clan spirits or to the attacks of alien spirits. The shaman was thus centrally concerned with the well-being of the kin community, through either propitiating the clan spirits or by warding off or exorcising alien spirits. Lewis graphically remarks that the shaman was virtually involved in maintaining a 'mystical iron curtain' to protect his kinfolk from misfortune (1971, 156). Although the shaman conducted a number of religious rituals, the main religious rite performed by the shaman was the shamanic séance.

The Evenki, as with other peoples of Siberia, have a complex cosmological system that suggests a multilevel cosmos: the upper world inhabited by the supreme nature deities, the middle world containing humans and spirits of the earth, and the underworld. The worlds are connected by a stream or cosmic pillar or tree. Besides the ancestral spirits, the spirits that were important among these Siberian peoples were mainly nature spirits – the spirits of the wolf, raven, bear, eagle, and plover. Particularly important were the spirits of ancestral shamans, who often acted as the shaman's tutelary or guardian spirit. The relationship between the spirits and the shaman was usually close and intimate, and often erotic, the spirit being conceived as the wife (or husband) of the shaman. There was also a close relationship between the spirits and animals. Spirits and shamans were able to transform themselves into animals (metamorphosis) and, as Shirokogoroff records, the spirits had to be 'placed' in a physical body – a bird or animal – for the shaman to deal successfully with the spirit. Equally important, local beliefs suggest that the spirits – as 'keepers' or 'masters' of the animals (which also have spirits) – allow the animals to be killed as food for humans. Thus the marriage between the shaman and his spirit (in the role as wife) is important in the successful maintenance of a 'game supply contract'. Animals are not spirits, but spirits take animal form, and their propitiation is essential for hunting success (Ripinsky-Naxon 1993, 75–7; Lewis 1999, 109; Baldick 2000, 134–7; and the interesting article by Balzer 1996).

The initiation of the shaman was a long and complex process and has been the subject of many studies and reports. Three features seem to have been common in the Siberian context: an initial traumatic experience – what Siikala describes as the 'shaman's disease'; the shaman's initial encounter with the spirits and his or her acquisition of one or more tutelary spirits, the 'spirit-helpers', while in an ecstatic state; and, finally, the recognition of the new shaman by members of his or her own community.

Although social and personal reasons, such as striving for prestige and material success, may often have led a person to becoming a shaman, most of the shaman's own personal reports and ethnographic studies suggest that an illness or traumatic experience was the initial stimulus. Indeed, one early anthropologist, Maria Czaplicka (1914), in a general study of Siberian people, specifically explained shamanism by reference to the well-known 'arctic hysteria'. But what seems to have been generally the case is that a potential shaman could be recognized by abnormal behaviour – mental unbalance, periods of seclusion, a propensity for dreaming, fits of hysteria, unusual visions, or the hearing of voices. Particularly important was that a serious illness, interpreted as possession by spirits, was frequently seen as a prelude to the assumption of the shamanic role. The sickness, as Anna-Leena Siikala writes, was interpreted as the 'call of the spirits to become a shaman' (Siikala and Hoppal 1998, 6). Whether they do eventually become a 'master of spirits' depended on a number of factors – often the position of shaman was inherited within the family – but essentially it involved overcoming the illness with the aid of the spirit-helpers – with which a relationship had been established – and being able to induce a state of controlled possession. Thus a traumatic episode or illness interpreted as possession by a spirit; the identification of the offending spirit and its adoption as a tutelary spirit; the acquisition of the necessary ritual paraphernalia and support and tuition by an established shaman; and the eventual control of the possessing spirit and the trance state – these seem to have been the essential steps in becoming a shaman (see Halifax 1979 for interesting narrative accounts of shamanic initiations and visionary experiences in a wide range of societies).

Given the close association between the shaman's initial 'sickness' and hysteria, early scholars, especially those influenced by psychoanalysis, often contended that the shaman was mentally ill, neurotic, paranoid, or even psychotic (e.g., Devereux 1961; Silverman 1967; La Barre 1972, 107). This has been disputed by later scholars, who have argued that shamanism is not a function of mental illness and that shamans are usually among the more intelligent, socially aware, and capable members of a community; indeed, quintessentially normal. In fact, even performing the shamanic role, as an intermediary between the spirit world and the local community, demands that the shaman be a competent, balanced, and sober individul (Murphy 1964; Lewis 1971, 179–83; Noll 1983; Townsend 1997, 454–6).

The shamanic séance was a complex ritual in which humans are able to make direct contact with the spirits. Although Eliade was centrally concerned to highlight the ecstatic flight achieved by the shaman during the séance, it is of interest that his own account of a typical séance among the Evenki (Tungus) seems to confirm what Shirokogoroff and Lewis emphasize, namely, that it involved spirit-possession. Eliade writes that, after a series of misfortunes in a community,

> the shaman, bidden to determine the cause, incarnates a spirit and learns the reason why the spirits . . . are causing the disequilibrium: he also learns what sacrifice can placate them. The community then decides to undertake the sacrifice. (1964, 238)

The séance is usually held at night, as spirits are thought to be afraid of light. Darkness is thus a prerequisite for a shamanic ritual. After preparations for the séance have been made, the shaman dons his or her costume and invokes the ancestral spirits. The shaman's costume is made of cloth or leather and is adorned with bits of metal or bone that represent the spirits in human or animal form. A sacrifice is often made, usually a reindeer, and then the shaman begins drumming, singing, and dancing. These gradually become louder and more frenzied as the shaman, concentrating on the spirits, achieves an altered state of consciousness. The eating of Amanita mushrooms, or the consumption of alcohol or tobacco, or the use of aromatic herbs may serve to achieve an altered state of consciousness, but Siikala suggests that the use of hallucinogens is not 'essential to or even a vital factor in the shaman's trance technique' (Siikala and Hoppal 1998, 11; cf. Hutton 2001, 100–2).

During the ritual, the shaman's helping spirit enters the body of the shaman and speaks through him or her. As Eliade put it, 'The shaman's body is now inhabited by a spirit, and it is the spirit that answers in his stead' (1964, 239).

Thus the shaman fully identifies with the spirit: 'he in fact turns into the spirit and manifests this change in his gestures, movements and speech' (Siikala and Hoppal 1998, 11).

Another person, usually the shaman's assistant, then becomes the shaman. Importantly, besides the shaman and the assistant and the spirits that are invoked and possessed by the shaman, the audience are also active participants in the shamanic ritual. In her important studies of the Siberian shaman's technique of ecstasy, Siikala (1978) shows that the visionary journey of the shaman and spirit-possession are simply functional alternatives in the process of communicating with the spirit world and that the key feature of the séance is not only the 'mastery of the spirits' but also the 'role-taking' techniques of the shaman. Sometimes the shaman identifies completely with the spirit role; at other times, through ventriloquism, he sets up a dialogue between himself or herself and the spirit, while at other stages of the ritual, he or she may simply offer invocations or requests to the spirits. The depth and intensity of the altered state of consciousness – the trance – vary throughout the séance, but the shaman always attempts to keep in contact with the audience (Siikala and Hoppal 1998, 26–40).

Thus a typical séance usually involved spirit-possession and undoubtedly had a therapeutic value. The highly charged emotional atmosphere of the séance, when it was applied to healing the sick, was, as Lewis wrote, probably highly effective in the treatment of certain neurotic and psychosomatic illnesses. Moreover, as Shirokogoroff pointed out, even in the case of organic ailments, the shamanic séance was probably significant in strengthening the patient's will to recover (Lewis 1971, 53).

For many centuries, of course, the Siberian peoples have been influenced by outside forces. The intrusions of the Russian state, first under the tsar and then under the Soviet regime, the spread of capitalism – the fur trade and mining were especially important – as well as the spread of Christian evangelism, all had a profound impact on the social life and culture of Siberian peoples. Buddhism was also influential among the Buryats and peoples to the south. There is ample evidence to indicate that shamans were harassed and persecuted throughout this period, by both Buddhists and orthodox Christians, and it is suggested that by about 1900 most Siberian peoples were nominally Christian, their shamanic practices often being highly syncretic and conducted in secrecy. Among the Khanty during the 1930s, Marjorie Balzer (1983) writes, shamanism began to seriously decline when, with collectivization, Soviet officials took away the drums and other equipment of the shamans and began an active campaign against them. Shamans were denounced as 'deceivers' and as overcharging their patients, and there was a general discrediting of the shamanic (i.e., spiritualist) worldview. Hospitals and mobile medicine were introduced to Siberian peoples, although the focus was on biomedicine. As Balzer suggests, people often recognized that biomedicine was in many ways more effective than the shamanic rituals, but nevertheless still practiced spiritual healing, particularly in relation to such illnesses as depression, arthritis, and menstrual and reproductive disorders. This would suggest that shamanism in Siberia has become something of a peripheral cult.

In recent years, however, there seems to have been a renaissance and reaffirmation of shamanism and folklore among many Siberian people, which seems to be related to a reassertion of ethnic identity. (For important studies of shamanism in Siberia and central Asia, see Dioszegi and Hoppal 1978; Balzer 1983, 1997; Humphrey 1980, 1996; Hutton 2001).

1.6. INUIT SHAMANISM

The northern periphery of North America is inhabited by people popularly known as 'Eskimos'. They are almost entirely coastal people, with an economy based on hunting, particularly of whales, seals, and caribou, and fishing. Almost all of these people have now become Christians, but their earlier animistic religion and shamanic rituals have been recorded in great detail and have always been of interest to European scholars. The ethnographic studies of the Danish explorer and scholar Knud Rasmussen, who saw himself as an advocate of the Eskimo people and his writings as the 'voice of the people' are particularly noteworthy (Jakobsen 1999, xiii). Here I want to focus on two groups of Eskimo (Inuit) that have been the focus of ethnographic studies relating to shamanism – the Netselik or Seal Eskimos of Arctic Canada and the Inuit (Eskimo) people of Greenland.

In pre-contact times, the economic life of the Netselik had a migratory pattern. Spending the winter in a large encampment on the coast, with the men collectively hunting seals on the ice, they spent the summer months in small family parties, the hunting of caribou (reindeer) being important during the autumn. Women and children often helped men with seal hunting, and everyone engaged in fishing (Balikci 1970, 82–3). In 1920 traps and guns were introduced into the community, and their economy became adapted to fur trading. Their migratory pattern, based on ecological factors, was reflected in their cosmological ideas, and they had an 'intricate taboo system' that was essentially designed to keep summer and winter game animals apart (Lewis 1971, 164; see the classic study by Mauss 1979 on the seasonal variations of Eskimo life).

The Netselik lived in extended family-like kinship groupings, an individual's kin including about thirty to fifty people. Marriage tended to be endogenous within this group. The communities, however, were loosely structured, and there were no formal political leaders. Because of the harsh environmental conditions and the importance of hunting, female infanticide was practiced to a high degree, and this, Asen Balikci suggests in his lucid article on Inuit (Eskimo) shamanism (1963), created anxiety and tension in interpersonal relationships. There was also a high rate of suicide. Thus Netselik Inuit social life, unlike that of many other hunter–gatherers, was one based on suspicion, anxiety, and hostility towards others.

The Inuit universe was peopled by a vast number of spirits, mostly malevolent. These consisted of various nature spirits, mythical monsters, and ancestral ghosts. Certain spirits, called *tunraqs*, were, however, of particular importance for these were those spirits and ghosts that were deemed to have a protective relationship towards and under some degree of control by a specific shaman [*angatkok*]. Traumatic encounters or affliction often served as a prelude to the assumption of the shamanistic role, but essentially it was a vocation that required a long period of training under an elderly angatkok–teacher. During his initiation, the shaman observed certain taboos, learnt the secret formulas and shamanistic techniques, and through intermittent sleep began to have visions. Assisted by his teacher, the novice came, by degrees, to learn to 'control' one or more tunraq spirits.

Sickness and misfortune (or lack of game) among the Netselik were often interpreted as caused by some malevolent ghost or spirit, usually angered by a breach of taboo. The patient was believed to be possessed by a particular evil spirit, and the shaman was called in to treat the illness by means of a shamanistic séance. In a typical performance, writes Balikci,

> the shaman adorned in his paraphernalia, crouched in the corner of the igloo . . . covered with a caribou skin. The lamps were extinguished. A protective spirit called by the shaman entered his body and, through his mouth, started to speak very rapidly, using shaman's secret vocabulary. (1963, 196)

While the shaman was in a trance, the malevolent spirits left the patient's body and hid outside the igloo. Combat then ensued between the shaman's tunraq spirits, helped perhaps by the benevolent ghost of some deceased shaman, and the offending spirits, who were either killed or chased away. Other curing rituals were performed besides the séance, but as with the séance, the curing typically involved the questioning of the helping spirits with a view to discovering the broken taboo and the exorcising of the offending spirit.

The taboo system itself was complex, but it was focussed around two essential concerns. The first related to the ecological division, previously noted, and involved the transgression of what Lewis has graphically described as 'mystical game laws' (1971, 64). The second relates to the gender division of labour, particularly menstrual taboos. In addition, incest was believed to anger the spirits and thus to cause misfortunes. An important aspect of the shamanistic séance was therefore the confession, and it was the shaman's function to encourage people to admit any taboo transgressions. Such infractions invariably involved women, whose public confessions formed an important part of the therapeutic procedure – for any taboo infraction was believed to affect the whole community. With the Netselik, shamanism was inextricably linked with sorcery, for although the shamans were usually looked on as good persons and essential by their kinfolk and community, it was also felt that shamans often dealt in harmful magical practices [*ilisiniq*] and could 'send' their tunraq spirits against rivals or cause harm. As with the Evenki and other Siberian peoples, the Netselik recognized three worlds – one in the sky, one just under the surface of the earth, and the third as an underworld. Shamans could visit the ancestral spirits in these spirit worlds, and there was also a close interrelationship between the various 'souls' of humans (living and dead) and animals. Sickness could also be interpreted as 'soul loss' and some shamans even had their own souls temporarily taken by their helping tunraq spirits.

In an important essay on the psychotherapeutic aspects of the Inuit of St. Lawrence Island, Alaska, who have a similar pattern of shamanism to that of the Netselik, Jane Murphy (1964) described in some detail their etiologies of disease and misfortune. Essentially, as with other Inuit communities, five distinct categories were evident.

1. *Soul loss.* The Inuit believe that a person's soul wanders abroad at night while that person is asleep or may depart from the body if a person is suddenly frightened. Thus a person's soul may be captured by a malevolent spirit, and, until it returns to the patient's body, disease or illness hold sway.
2. *Breach of taboo.* As already noted, the belief that disease is caused by the transgression of a ritual prohibition (taboo), or by a moral violation, was common currency among the Inuit. Failure to show proper respect to animals or to maltreat them, not sharing meat equitably, incest, and sexual perversions were all believed to be disease-provoking transgressions. The essence of the shamanic séance was therefore to find what wrong had been committed and, through consultation with helping or familiar spirits, to ascertain what sacrifice or atonement was necessary to rectify the situation and return the patient to health.
3. *Sorcery.* The Inuit make a clear distinction between the healing magic of the shaman and that of the sorcerer or witch – a person (often thought to be a shaman from some other community) who uses magical formulas and secret rites to cause illness. The shaman's role was thus to discover the possible identity of the witch and to counter the witch's harmful influences.
4. *Object intrusion.* The belief that disease was caused by the intrusion of a foreign object into the patient's body was well developed among the Inuit. Thus the shamanic cure involved the extraction of this object if health was to be restored. It was important therefore for the shaman during the séance to produce one or more objects – usually a stone – that could be shown to the audience as evidence that the cause of the disease had been removed.
5. *Spirit-intrusion.* The belief that disease could also be caused by the intrusion of a foreign spirit was not well developed, Murphy suggests, among the

> Alaskan Inuit, although this was usually invoked for insanity or episodic hysteria. Spirit-intrusion involved diagnostic techniques to ascertain the spirit's identity and the therapeutic procedure of ritual exorcism. Murphy thus makes a distinction between spirit-intrusion and spirit-possession, which seems to be akin to the distinction suggested by Lewis between uncontrolled and controlled spirit-possession, as previously discussed (Murphy 1964, 62–83).

As with other peoples of the Arctic region, the Inuit of Greenland have long been Christians and have thus abandoned their 'old beliefs' and rituals relating to shamanism. In other parts of the Arctic, however, a strong undercurrent of animistic belief remains, and among the Caribou Inuit of the Hudson Bay region, people have recently been attracted to those Protestant denominations whose rituals involve visions and 'speaking in tongues'. These have affinities, in many ways, to traditional shamanic performances (Burch 1999, 59). But, in her important study of shamanism among the Greenland Inuit, using earlier Danish sources, Merete Jakobsen (1999) emphasizes that shamanism is now a lost tradition among these people and that, unlike in other societies, shamanism has not been revived in Greenland.

In the past the Greenland Inuit, Jakobsen writes, 'lived in an animated world surrounded by mostly hostile and dangerous spirits' (1999, 72). It was less a sense of perceiving the whole world as 'alive' or 'animate' but as envisioning a surrounding world where things and events were charged with *spiritual* agency and power. But although the spirits were often conceived as malevolent, there were also, as Rasmussen wrote, 'the mountain spirits, sea spirits, underground spirits, giants and goblins' that could be utilized as helping spirits [*torngak*]. These spirits were stronger and more powerful than humans, but by following their forebears, the shamans, through amulets, magical formula, and the shamanic séance, were able to counter the evil spirits and sorcery for the benefit of the community (Jakobsen 1999, 72). These helping spirits, which according to Jakobsen were visible only to the initiated – although in the séance, the community (audience) could come face to face with the spirit in human form – were either nature spirits or spirits of the dead. Thus the Greenland Inuit recognized the existence of a 'spiritual' realm, a separate dimension to human existence, and thus, as Jakobsen writes, 'the notion of dualism in every walk of life was prominent in the mind of the Greenlander' (1999, 115).

Although Jakobsen mentions the spirits of the ancestors and the spirits of certain animals (walrus, polar bear) who were often the helping spirits [*torngak*], three spirits seem to have particular significance for the Greenland Inuit in combatting illness and misfortune. These were the 'moon spirit', who was responsible for taboo transgressions and human fertility and was associated with adverse weather conditions; the 'mother of the sea', who was seen as controlling the animals of the sea, which were so crucial to Inuit livelihood; and the 'toornaarsuk spirit', which was described in a variety of ways but often seen as manifested in animal form – as a large seal or an 'immense white bear' (Jakobsen 1999, 65–72).

The initiation of the shaman among the Greenland Inuit followed a pattern similar to that described elsewhere. After an initial calling – a severe illness, a fearful encounter with a spirit when experiencing 'great solitude' (as Rasmussen [1927, 65] described it) – the potential shaman [*angakkoq*] learns to overcome his fear, transforms his relationship to the spirits so that they become 'helping spirits', and through a long apprenticeship learns the skills requisite to becoming a shaman. According to Rasmussen, it took several years to become a shaman. In Greenland, shamans were mostly men, but women could become shamans – although childbearing was often seen as antithetical to shamanic inspiration. As with the Netselik, although shamans have essentially a positive role, they may in certain circumstances be described as a witch [*ilisiitsoq*], an evil person, often a woman, who brought misfortune, illness, or even death on their fellow humans. To this end, witches often utilized malevolent spirits and magic – powerful ritual medicines [*tupilak*] (Jakobsen 1999, 75, 95–8). It is important to note, however, that the protective amulets, the ritual stones used by the shamans to invoke the spirits, and the *materia medica* employed for malevolent purposes [*tupilak*] were all made 'alive' by ritual invocations or by being conceived as having spiritual agency.

The attitude of the Greenland Inuit to their shamans was therefore essentially ambivalent; hence, the shaman was often held in awe and sometimes feared. They thus often exhibited considerable authority and had a political role as 'law-givers' and in resolving social conflicts and tensions. The male shaman also had the prerogative, it seems, of sleeping with the wives of other men (Jakobsen 1999, 133).

Illness among the Greenland Inuit, as with other Eskimos, was due to the transgression of ritual prohibitions (taboos), soul loss, object intrusion, or through the intervention of spirits, and the shamanic séance involved both spirit-possession and a visionary journey. In the so-called 'magical flight', the shaman in deep trance travelled 'to get in contact with the spirits and the souls of the dead' (Jakobsen 1999, 89). Healing thus involved identifying the offending spirit, restoring the soul to the patient, ritual blowing or sucking to remove an intrusive object, or exorcising or placating the malevolent spirit. This was sometimes done outside the shamanic séance. Significant, however, is the fact that there seems among the Greenland Inuit to have been no recourse to medical herbalism (Jakobsen 1999, 94).

One important aspect of Inuit shamanism was perhaps best expressed by a Caribou Inuit shaman who, in his discussion with Rasmussen about his life experiences, suggested that knowledge about hidden things and the spirits was to be sought away from people: 'solitude and suffering open the human mind, and therefore a shaman must seek his wisdom there' (Halifax 1979, 69; for other important studies of Inuit shamanism, see Rasmussen 1929; Merkur 1985; Riches 1994).

1.7. NEO-SHAMANISM

Over the past thirty years, there has been a resurgence of interest in shamanism, not only amongst academic scholars but also in the popular culture. With regard to the latter, there has been a blossoming of what has been variously described as 'urban' or 'neo-shamanism'. This has generally been seen as a strand of the New Age movement, or part of what Joan Townsend describes as a 'new mystical movement' (1988, 73). Spiritualism – a belief in a spiritual reality – has of course always been a part of western culture, but in recent decades a new shamanic movement has sprung up in North America and Europe. Various factors have been adduced for this resurgence of (neo-) shamanism: the drug cultures of the 1960s and 1970s; an increasing interest in non-western religions coupled with a general disenchantment with Christianity; a search for new forms of spirituality in an era of global capitalism, when nihilism, consumerism, and instrumental reason seem to be all-pervasive; the rise of the human potential movement, with its emphasis on counselling, self-help, and self-realization; and finally, the feminist and ecology movements that have critiqued the dominant tendencies of western capitalism and its culture. But crucial in the emergence of neo-shamanism have been the writings of three popular anthropologists: Carlos Castaneda, Michael Harner, and Joan Halifax. Indeed, the publication of Castaneda's book *The Teachings of Don Juan* (1968) has been described as the 'most significant event' in the rise of neo-shamanism (Townsend 1988, 75). Describing his (alleged) apprenticeship to a Yaqui shaman [*brujo*], this book was but a prelude to a stream of best-selling books by Castaneda on his visionary experiences, helped by the use of hallucinogenic plants, especially peyote. The authenticity of these books has been questioned by anthropologists familiar with Yaqui culture, and it is now widely recognized that Castaneda's work lacks ethnographic substance and is based largely on his own fertile imagination (De Mille 1976; Drury 1989, 81–7; Noel 1997, 42–62; compare the effusive review of Castaneda by Douglas 1975, 193–200, with that of Churchill 1992, 43–64).

Michael Harner's work is of a very different order; for his well-known study, *The Way of a Shaman* (1980), is largely based on his own ethnographic studies of shamanism among the Jivaro of Ecuador and the Conibo of the Peruvian Amazon. But the book also aimed to provide an introductory handbook to 'shamanic methodology for health and healing' (1980, xxi), and in this regard it has been especially influential. Harner established an institute in California devoted to shamanic studies and held 'shamanic training workshops' in order to promote what he described as 'core shamanism'. It is a form of shamanism particularly attuned to western people who had no direct experience of 'traditional' shamanism, and who, as Jakobsen puts it, felt the need to overcome a 'sense of a social and spiritual void' (1999, 151).

Daniel Noel has gone so far as to suggest that without Castaneda and his 'hoax', there would have been no neo-shamanism and that Harner's *The Way of the Shaman* was almost a 'devotional tract' for the new movement. He implies that shamanism is largely a product of the western imagination and that Harner is a kind of Merlin figure (1997, 37, 92–8). But Noel emphasizes that the anthropologist Joan Halifax also had an important influence on the emergence of neo-shamanism through her useful anthology of accounts of visionary experiences, *Shamanic Voices* (1979).

During the past twenty years, neo-shamanism has thus become established as a major part of the contemporary New Age movement, though its adherents tend to emphasize that it is an 'earth-based' form of spirituality.

There are a number of key elements in what is envisaged as 'core shamanism'. It is seen first and foremost as a revival or a continuation of an 'ancient' visionary or spiritual tradition, one involving the utilization of altered states of consciousness to make contact with a spiritual reality – the latter conceived as the domain of gods and spirit. It tends to conflate consciousness with reality – if you imagine something as real, it is real – and to propound a dualistic metaphysic. The 'core belief' of neo-shamanism is thus the existence of two 'realities': the ordinary reality associated with waking, everyday experience, and an 'alternate' spiritual reality, which is the 'abode of spirits'. At the same time, it is argued that shamanism constitutes a '*new* worldview', which suggests that humans are an intrinsic part of nature and that the 'interconnectedness of all things' is a fundamental tenet of shamanism (Townsend 1988, 79–83). That humans are a part of nature and that all things are interconnected in a web of life are, of course, integral to our commonsense understandings of the world, an empirical naturalism that has precious little to do with shamanic rites. The conflation of an ecological worldview with spiritualism is quite misleading. Some scholars (e.g., Kalweit 1992, 103) are quite unable to conceive of any perspective on the world other than spiritualism and mechanistic science – the latter misleadingly equated with western culture (see Morris 1996, 7–36, for a critique of such gnostic perspectives).

In neo-shamanism, contact with the spirit world is achieved through an altered state of consciousness, with the emphasis on drumming and chanting – Harner in his shamanic workshops does not advocate drugs – the shamanic ritual being envisaged as a 'journey', usually into the earth. Here a person makes contact with his or her personally imagined guardian spirits or 'power animals'. For Harner and his associates, the shamanic ritual is essentially concerned with healing and with restoring the well-being of the individual. This may involve extracting harmful intrusions from the patient by sucking – although this would seem to be largely symbolic – implying the removal of the 'spiritual essence' of the intrusive object – insect, snake, spider – rather than the removal of the thing itself (Harner 1980, 150–2).

In her studies of neo-shamanism, Merete Jakobsen highlights the contrasts between the shamanic rituals of the Greenland Inuit and that of neo-shamanism – as practised in shamanic workshops in Denmark. The first obvious contrast is that while it took many, many years to become a shaman among the Inuit and the Siberian people, and often involved a traumatic experience, becoming a contemporary shaman can be achieved during a weekend workshop – which can be quite expensive. Moreover, alluding to a democratic ethos, in contemporary shamanism the clients heal themselves through the shamanic experience. It is thus highly individualistic and instrumental, and the crucial emphasis is less on the curing of ailments than on self-help, self-actualization, and achieving rather rapid results – according to Harner, sometimes in only a 'few days' (1980, xix). The emphasis in neo-shamanism is essentially on personal empowerment. It is of interest also that the spirits involved in neo-shamanism, the 'spirit-helpers' or 'power animals', tend to be conceived as rather benevolent or benign spirits, and thus, unlike the Evenki and Inuit, there is little engagement with malevolent spirits (Jakobsen 1999, 186). Nor is any link made between the 'power animals' and hunting, which was so crucial among the Inuit and Evenki. Equally important, whereas the shaman in tribal societies acts on behalf of a local community, the 'urban' shamans reconfigure the shamanic tradition to accord with western conceptions of self-actualization and personal power. Indeed, it has been suggested that neo-shamanism simply reflects the culture of 'radical modernity' (i.e., global capitalism), with is obsession with the 'self', individual agency, subjectivity, and reflexivity (Johnson 1995).

One key motif expressed by the advocates of neo-shamanism is that, through the experience of shamanic consciousness and contact with the world of the *spirits*, people will be able to rediscover their 'connections with *nature*'. Indeed, Nevil Drury suggests that shamanism is, if nothing else, 'a religious perspective which venerates nature' (1989, 102). New Age enthusiasts have the strange idea that everybody but themselves, and tribal people, are Cartesian dualists alienated from the natural world!

Shamanism, as an ancient method of healing involving contact with spirits through altered states of consciousness, has certainly been transformed in the urban context. What is of interest, however, is the degree to which anthropologists themselves have been influential in the neo-romantic appropriation of shamanic traditions, combining this with a 'back-to-nature' ethic (Siikala and Hoppal 1998, 208–9). The tendency, however, to equate shamanism with Jung's psychology and the mystical traditions of all the major religions (Christianity, Buddhism, Islam, Judaism, Hinduism) to view shamanism as a branch of the 'perennial philosophy', involving a mystical belief in a vague 'numinous unity', seems to me unhelpful and misleading and tends to gloss over ontological distinctions, as well as their diverse social and cultural contexts (for interesting studies and advocacy of New Age shamanism, which often express this tendency, see Nicholson 1987; Doore 1988; Goodman 1990; Walsh 1990; Drury 1991).

It is of interest to note the transformation in the western imagination: Whereas in the past shamans were depicted in a wholly negative fashion, as devil-worshippers, charlatans, or neurotics, now they are seen wholly positively as religious mystics and visionary ecologists.

1.8. COMPARATIVE STUDIES

Shamanism, like all complex social phenomena, has many different aspects or dimensions and can therefore be approached in many different ways – social, economic, political, medical, psychological, aesthetic. This section is devoted to a discussion of two comparative studies of shamanism and spirit-possession, those of Erika Bourguignon and Ioan Lewis. In the final section I focus more generally on other interpretations of shamanism.

In a series of important essays, Bourguignon has sought to explore the relationship among trance, possession, and altered states of consciousness and to delineate their socio-cultural correlates. Undertaking ethnographic studies on Haitian vodou religion in the late 1940s, she has since directed and sponsored a number of important fieldwork studies and cross-cultural surveys (Bourguignon 1973, 1976; Goodman, Henney, and Pressel 1974). Her discussion of altered states of consciousness in her text *Psychological Anthropology* (1979; 233–69) is a useful resumé of her ideas, though it is largely focussed on trance states and does not discuss shamanism per se.

Bourguignon initially outlines (1979, 237–9) three contrasting examples of typical trance states – taken from the ethnographic record. The first is an account of a possession rite among the peasants of Haiti in which the cult members are 'mounted' by the Loa spirits. The whole ritual has a theatrical air about it, and the trance state is induced by dancing and drumming. The dancer may be possessed by any number of spirits, and each Loa has its own specific symbolism and personal characteristics. I discuss the nature of these vodou cult rituals in Chapter 6.

Bourguignon's second example is a shamanic séance typical of many South American Indians, in which the male shamans achieve spirit visions by taking hallucinogens. With the Amahuaca Indians described, an infusion of the narcotic plant *Banisteriopsis caapi* is used. After the drug is taken, the hallucinations that appear are interpreted as Yoshi spirits communicating with the individual. Importantly, the vision, though experienced during a collective rite, is essentially of a private nature (Carneiro 1964, 8–9). (For further studies of shamanism among South American societies, see Wilbert 1972; Reichel-Dolmatoff 1975, 1997; Siskind 1975, 130–68; Luna 1986; Taussig 1987.)

The final example is the familiar 'vision quest' of the Native American. Bourguignon quotes from the autobiography of John Lame Deer, an Oglala Sioux, who, when a youth, went to search for a personal guardian spirit. He thus went alone (for the first time in his life) and spent four days fasting on an isolated hilltop. The experience led him to hear voices, including the voice of his great-grandfather, and to have visions. This gave him a feeling of power, and he thus became a shaman (medicine man) (Lame Deer and Erdoes 1972, 157–8).

All three examples of an altered state of consciousness involve contact with the spirits and are thus religious experiences. Although they are induced in different ways – through drums and dancing, drugs, or sensory deprivation, respectively – Bourguignon stresses that such experiences are neither spontaneous nor idiosyncratic. Nor are they necessarily similar cross-culturally. For although sensory deprivations, drugs, or rhythmic drumming set up the conditions favourable to an altered state of consciousness, *what* will be experienced – its actual content – and *how* it will be experienced are largely functions of the intentions, expectations, and beliefs of the individual and the social and cultural context (Bourguignon 1979, 242; Weil 1986).

Bourguignon goes on to make a distinction between trance (as a religious phenomena) and possession-trance, and notes that the former is closely associated with hunting, gathering, and fishing economies. In such societies, she suggests, there is a strong emphasis that men be independent and self-reliant and that this has psychological consequences in the way of increased anxiety. She thus concludes that

> Visionary trance, whether part of the guardian spirit complex or drug-induced in other settings, is far more frequently reported as practised by men than by women. (1979, 254)

Possession-trance, on the other hand, Bourguignon notes, is much more widely distributed cross-culturally and, being associated with agricultural production, implies a very different value orientation – that of nurturance, reliability, and obedience. These values are commonly associated with women and are more emphasized in their socialization patterns. Evidence from a variety of spirit-possession cults seems to suggest that possession-trance is a 'typically female phenomenon' and that women use these cults, as Lewis (1971) suggests, as an indirect way of airing grievances and of asserting their autonomy and independence of men. In Chapter 3, I discuss these cults more fully, particularly in relation to Zar cults in the Sudan.

There is therefore, Bourguignon stresses, an interesting contrast between visionary trance and possession-trance. The former, whether induced by mortification, isolation, or drugs, is more likely to be found in small-scale foraging societies and is experienced primarily by men. Possession-trance, on the other hand, is associated with complex, stratified societies, where agriculture is predominant. In these situations, it is women who mainly go into trance, the authoritative spirits acting in their place by means of incarnation. Trance, she suggests 'is an experience; possession trance is a performance' (1979, 261).

Trance is more likely to be induced by sensory deprivation and drugs (as are mystic states), while possession-trance is induced by drumming, singing, dancing, and crowd contagion, but only rarely by drugs. The imagery of both kinds of trance, she suggests, involves two kinds of motifs: mastery (power) and sexuality. But whereas the physically passive trance involves an *active* imagery – the spirit journey or struggle with the spirits to gain power or knowledge – the active possession-trance involves a *passive* imagery. The woman in a trance is possessed, mounted, and ridden by the spirit. The trancer remains himself and gains power by intercourse with the spirit; the possessed women ceases to be herself, becoming merely the vehicle or vessel of the spirit. The spirit-possession rite is 'basically one of submission' and replete with sexual imagery (Bourguignon 1979, 262–3).

Although this comparative analysis is suggestive, it tends to downplay the fact that in many ethnographic contexts – such as among the Evenki and Inuit – visionary trances and spirit-possession actually coexist, and both may be expressed by the shaman even within a single shamanic ritual. Equally in both hunter–gathering and agricultural contexts, sexual imagery and an emphasis on controlling the spirits and thus achieving self-empowerment are both important motifs (cf. Lewis 1986, 82–3).

Bourguignon's interpretation of shamanism, or more specifically trance states, is similar to that of many other anthropologists, who see altered states of consciousness as the normal individual's response to stressful conditions. Such mental states therefore, whether manifested in crisis or millenial cults, visionary experiences, or possession rites, are seen as essentially adaptive mechanisms. Some scholars have gone even further in adopting a psychoanalytic interpretation that suggests that visionary experiences (or dreams) are the source or, as Laing put it, 'the original well spring of all religion' (1967, 112; La Barre 1972, 1975; for other studies that have linked altered states of consciousness [and religion] to stress and deprivation, see Aberle 1966; Lewis 1971, discussed in the following paragraph). Bourguignon's approach is thus both functional and psychological and therefore tends to ignore, as noted earlier, the specific social, cultural, and historical context of shamanism.

The comprative approach to Ioan Lewis (1971) is also functional and puts an important emphasis on stress and deprivation, but, unlike Bourguignon, he advocates a more sociological approach to shamanism and spirit-possession. He is thus interested in exploring the social conditions that give rise to ecstatic phenomena. He suggests that spirit-possession cults can be divided into two basic types. On the one hand, there are what Lewis terms *peripheral possession cults*. These are spirit-possession cults that coexist with more dominant moralistic religions, such as Christianity, Islam, and Buddhism, which are non-ecstatic and supportive of the status quo. The spirit cult is peripheral in three senses: first, its membership comprises categories that are peripheral to the authority structures of the society, for members of such groups largely consist of women, men from low-status groups, or other deprived categories; second, the cult is peripheral to the moral order, being largely unconcerned with upholding social mores; and, finally, the possessing spirits tend to be peripheral, often being foreign, alien, or amoral spirits. In subsequent chapters with specific reference to Afro-American cults and the spirit cults associated with Islam and Buddhism, I discuss this mode of religious expression and organization in more detail.

The second type Lewis terms *central possession cults*, and this refers to a social context in which the main form of religion is focussed around spirit-possession rites. The societies described in this chapter – Evenki, Inuit – typically represent this type of cult, and the possession rites essentially serve to uphold the social and moral order.

Lewis' study has been subjected to much criticism; his approach has been described as 'ahistoric' and his distinction between central and peripheral cults considered a 'static categorization' that has little explanatory value (Hultkrantz 1989, 46; Linden 1979, 199). These criticisms seem somewhat misplaced, for Lewis' study *Ecstatic Religion* (1971) takes a historical and comparative approach and is replete with examples illustrating the historical transformations of possession cults. Boddy's suggestion (1994) that Lewis' typology is not explanatory (did he ever suggest it was?) and that because membership of Candomble cults in Brazil is largely middle class and supportive of Brazilian nationalism, it is not therefore a 'peripheral' cult are also completely misplaced criticisms, as Lewis did not see the peripheral – central distinction as implying static categories. In fact, his whole book not only attempts to put possession cults in their cultural and socio-historical context – Boddy's approach therefore is hardly new or original – but, as said, also explores historical transformations of ecstatic cults.

Lewis' general approach is essentially to see shamanism and spirit-possession cults as 'religions of the oppressed'. The peripheral possession cults are, in his view, 'protest cults' that enable individuals who lack political influence – especially women – to 'advance their interest and improve their lot, even if only temporarily, from the confining bonds of their allotted stations in society' (1971, 127).

In his discussion of central possession cults, Lewis offers a similar interpretation, relating the ecstatic tendency to external pressure. Factors that explain why people like the Akawaio and Evenki have possession cults, Lewis suggests, include 'the existence of overwhelming physical and social pressures, where social groups are small and fluctuating, and general instability prevails'. Thus both central and peripheral ecstatic cults 'are forms of religious expression which imply the existence of acute pressures' (1971, 175–6).

I have discussed elsewhere the limitations of this thesis, as well as those of Douglas' (1970) contrasting symbolic approach, which tends to interpret religious symbolism as simply a reflection of social structure, and thus sees trance states and spirit-possession as essentially expressing a society in which relationships are loosely structured and fluid. Both theories have their limitations but are salutary in attempting to place ecstatic religious forms in their wider social context (see Morris 1987, 229–33).

1.9. THE INTERPRETATION OF SHAMANISM

Anthropologists have long emphasized that the key role of the shaman, in many different contexts, is that of a healer or, more precisely, that of a spiritual healer. A question that has long intrigued anthropologists is therefore this: Whence the power of the shaman? What are the reasons behind the alleged efficacy of shamanic rites, when, to the western observer, many of the therapeutic procedures were based on sleight of hand or on spiritual concepts? In his now-classic articles on shamanism, Claude Levi-Strauss (1963, 167–205) addressed this issue with regard to a Kwakuitl Indian shaman named Quesalid (whose biography had been recorded by Boas) and to shamanic or ritual healing among the Cuna Indians, and the effectiveness of symbols in assisting a difficult childbirth. Although Levi-Strauss accepted that part of the success of the shaman may be due to empirical knowledge, his main emphasis is that shamanism is a form of symbolic healing. As he put it,

> Quesalid did not become a great shaman because he cured his patients; he cured his patients because he had become a great shaman. (1963, 180)

Levi-Strauss goes on to compare the role of the shaman with that of the psychoanalyst. But whereas the psychoanalyst interprets a personal trauma, the shaman provides the individual patient with a social myth that integrates and gives meaning to his or her disordered state or misfortune. The shamanic cure, Levi-Strauss suggests, lies therefore on the borderline between contemporary biomedicine and such psychological therapies as psychoanalysis (1963, 198).

Although written some fifty years ago, these tentative thoughts by Levi-Strauss, though subjected to much critique on various grounds, have nonetheless been essentially confirmed by recent researches. For ample studies have indicated that in all systems of medicine – including biomedicine – psychological and emotional states are important factors in the therapy. Just as negative emotions such as depression, anxiety, and fear can impede health, or even lead to serious illness, so can a patient's state of mind effect the healing process itself. There have been numerous studies exploring the therapeutic functions of shamanism and on what has been described as 'symbolic healing' (Kleinman 1979; Moerman 1979; Peters 1981; Dow 1986; Atkinson 1987, 1992, 313–4).

But, of course, shamanism is not exclusively focussed on healing, and an important aspect of shamanic or trance rituals among many hunter–gathering societies relates to the hunting of game animals and therefore has an essentially economic function. The emphasis on the spirit guardians of the animals among the Inuit and Evenki and the divinatory rites to ascertain the whereabouts of game animals exist primarily because animals play such a vital role in their subsistence economy. It has indeed been argued that the shaman functions primarily as an 'intermediary' between the human community and the natural world, and only secondarily as a healer. His primary allegiance, we are told, is not to the human community per se, but to the 'earthly web of relations' in which the community is embedded. By focussing on the shaman as healer, countless anthropologists, David Abram suggests, have thus overlooked 'the ecological dimension of the shaman's craft' (1996, 8). To interpret, as Abram does, 'European civilization' in simplistic, monadic fashion as having a 'disdain' for nature and to look at the shaman as a kind of 'ecomanager' both seem somewhat exaggerated, but nevertheless the shaman can be interpreted as having an economic or ecological function. For the shaman mediates between the human community and the natural world and is concerned with people's basic subsistence and livelihood as well as with their health. But it is worth distinguishing between empirical and shamanic knowledge. Through their subsistence activities, tribal people like the Evenki and Akawaio are closely engaged with the natural world. Thus many people in such communities have an intimate and extensive knowledge of the biology, life-history, and ecology of plants, fungi, and animals. But this empirical knowledge should not be equated with shamanism, for hunters, women who regularly gather mushrooms and food plants, and herbalists are, as I know from my own experiences, often much more knowledgeable than shamans – whose knowledge is largely esoteric and spiritual, and who often do not in fact hunt.

But shamans, as noted earlier, also have a political side. In pre-contact situations, they often wielded considerable informal power within a community, as with the Inuit and Akawaio. But it is important to stress, as Piers Vitebsky (1995b, 116) suggests, that shamanism is not a timeless and unchanging social phenomenon, which expresses some archetypal essence (or meaning) – which is how Eliade tends to describe it – for it has continually changed in response to external pressures and influences. Throughout the world, the incorporation of tribal people into state structures, the spread of capitalism, and the cultural influences of such hegemonic religious traditions like Islam, Buddhism, and Christianity, all have had an enormous impact on tribal peoples – on both their religious forms and shamanic practices. This impact has been extremely variable. Recent social change among the Sora, a tribal people of Orissa, India, as Vitebsky (1995b) records, has led younger members of the community to abandon shamanism and the 'cult of the ancestors' and to become Christians, specifically Baptists. Among the Sakha (Yakut) of Siberia, on the other hand, there has been a revival of shamanism, particularly among the urban intelligentsia. The emphasis here is on shamanism as an ancient religion; it is part of a 'spiritual revival', in many ways a backlash, a reaction against the rigid, stultifying ethos of the Soviet rule. It is thus closely bound up with the emergence of an ethnic identity and ethnic nationalism – the autonomy of the Sakha republic having been declared in 1990 with the break-up of the Soviet Union. Shamanism has also played a crucial role in the ethnic identity of Hungarian peoples. A revival of 'old religiosity' or 'ethnic wisdom' (shamanism) thus continues to play a role in contemporary world politics (Vitebsky 1995b; Balzer 1995; Siikala and Hoppal 1998, 169–75). In recent years, therefore, there have been a number of important studies that have attempted to explore the history and political economy of shamanism in many different contexts (Taussig 1987; Balzer 1997; Sergei 1991; Humphrey and Thomas 1994).

A shamanic ritual is, of course, a performance and self-evidently a mode of communication, although this obvious fact is now heralded as offering new insights into shamanism by hermeneutic scholars! Dancing, music, songs, chants, dialogue are all intrinsic to the shamanic séance, as they are to many initiation and spirit rituals throughout the world. During the rites, the shaman, as already discussed, embodies the spirits and thus may initiate or voice their various forms – as animals or birds, as historical personages, or as ancestors. Thus 'role-taking' – acting – is a crucial aspect of the shamanic ritual, as Siikala stressed. The shaman's relationship with the spirits is therefore not only spiritual but also corporeal – he or she 'embodies' the spirit. Rhythmic drumbeats, which may of course induce a trance state, also relate to specific kinds of spirits, and it has long been recognized that the shaman is the 'poet' or 'singer' of oral traditions. Eliade, in fact, described the Buryat shamans as 'principal guardians' of their rich oral literature and continually alludes to the fact that, besides being involved in curing and divination, the shaman was a singer, poet, and musician. The shamanic trance is thus one of the universal sources of lyrical poetry, which, like religion itself, is deemed by Eliade to reveal the 'essence of things' (1964; 30, 510). Likewise, Marjorie Balzer (1995) has noted that during an altered state of consciousness, people are often receptive to creativity and that there is an aesthetic power in the shamanic chants of the Sakha (Yakut) of north-eastern Siberia. The chants, which she suggests are 'intensely functional', represent several sacred genres of poetry – sacred epics, improvised songs, musical lyrics.

All this means, of course, that the shamanic séance can be interpreted as an 'art form', for it clearly has an aesthetic dimension, as a performance or musical experience. But the tendency to overemphasize the aesthetics of shamanism, and, like Eliade, to dismiss sociological approaches to shamanism as 'reductionist' seems to me to simply reflect the religious prejudices of many 'religious studies' scholars (cf. Harvey 2003, 443; Wiebe 1981).

2

Buddhism and Spirit-Cults

2.1. PROLOGUE

"Buddhism is a very ancient religion: it has behind it two thousand five hundred years of history" – so wrote the founder of the Western Buddhist Order, Sangharakshita (1990, 26). Yet contemporary scholars continually tell us, usually those of postmodernist persuasion, that Buddhism as a religion is purely a western invention; or that it does not exist as a 'single entity'. It is not a monolithic institution, Damien Keown writes, 'which was everywhere the same' (1996, 2). We should therefore speak of Buddhisms (plural) only as if this statement does not imply the existence of something called 'Buddhism', which is then the subject of a book! And one may well ask this question: What scholar or anthropologist has ever failed to recognize the diverse manifestations of Buddhism as it has adapted to local cultural and social conditions in its spread across Asia? People, of course, in many parts of Asia have always recognized themselves as Buddhists (long before European scholars arrived on the scene), usually expressed in terms of following the *dharma*, the teachings of the Buddha.

In essence, Buddhism is a way of salvation: It is not concerned with god or the world, but with human life, or rather with sentient beings, and with the elimination of suffering. The attainment of salvation depends neither on ritual sacraments, nor faith, nor on divine grace, but only on a deep understanding of the way 'things really are' (Gombrich 1984, 9–11).

The first question we might well ask regarding the essential tenets of Buddhism – and many have posed such a question – is whether or not Buddhism is a religion? Some have suggested, following Tylor's well-known definition of religion as a 'belief in spiritual beings' (1871, 1/424), that Buddhism is not really a religion even though such an idea seems to contradict our everyday usage. The argument is that Buddhism is an atheistic system of thought. Several different issues are involved, as Edward Conze (1951) long ago suggested. The first relates to whether Buddhism entails the notion of a creator-spirit, the belief in a deity that transcends or stands outside the world. The Buddhist tradition denies the existence of a creator-god and thus, in terms of western categories, it is atheistic. Indeed, it suggests that preoccupation with such a being is a waste of time, for it is not conducive to salvation. In Buddhist scriptures the way of the Buddha is always considered superior to Brahma, who, in Hindu theology, is thought of as the creator. If indifference to a creator-god is atheism, then, as Conze writes (1951, 39), Buddhism is indeed atheistic. Walpola Rahula, himself a Buddhist monk, stresses this atheism even more strongly, suggesting that Buddhism stands unique in the history of human thought in denying the existence of both the soul [*atman*] and a god. These concepts he suggests are connected with two ideas that are psychologically deep-rooted in human beings – self-preservation and self-protection. In denying these, Buddhism offers no such consolation. According to Buddhism, he writes, 'our ideas of God and Soul are false and empty' (1959, 52). Buddhism is thus viewed by many western interpreters as an essentially ethical religion, akin to secular humanism (Spiro 1970, 8).

But it has to be recognized, of course, that in Buddhist cosmology several realms of beings are recognized, besides humans and animals – deities [*deva*], malevolent spirits [*yaksha*], ghosts [*pretas*], and tormented beings. Incorporated into the Buddhist scriptures, the existence of these beings has always been believed in by Buddhists, and early texts give instructions to the laity regarding the performance of rituals to propitiate these gods and spirits (Lehman 1971; Sangharakshita 1990, 81–5; Lewis 1997, 343). Spirits are thus, as we shall observe, a constituent part of folk Buddhism, although animistic beliefs are not, in essence, a part of Buddhism as a religion of salvation – for salvation [*nirvana*] cannot be achieved through the aid of spirits.

Finally, there is the issue as to whether Buddhism implies the mystical notion of an ultimate or divine reality that is substantial to the material world. Is the conception of god, especially as expressed by Christian and Islamic mystics, akin to the Buddhist concept of nirvana – as many writers have suggested? Indeed, Aldous Huxley's famous study of mysticism, *The Perennial Philosophy* (1946), includes many references to the Buddha; and Conze, too, opens his discussion with the statement that Buddhism is a form of spirituality that is 'identical' with other mystical teaching. But it is extremely misleading to view the Buddhist concept of nirvana in religious terms and to equate the 'ultimate' realities of different systems of thought. The 'intuition of oneness with the cosmic absolute' or with an 'all-embracing spiritual essence' – to cite two definitions of the mystical experience (Bharati 1976, 25; De Marquette 1965, 24) – has a religious and theistic bias. The nirvana of Buddhism, often glossed as the 'mysterious void; the Sufi, Christian, and Vedanta concept of the deity or brahman; the notion of Tao expressed by Lao Tzu; and the nature mysticism of Richard Jefferies can in no meaningful sense be equated – other than the fact that there is a perception of a reality (or psychological experience) that is distinct from phenomenal reality (for other accounts of mysticism, cf. Suzuki 1957; Zaehner 1957; Happold 1963; Katz 1983).

Such issues take us beyond our present discussion, but clearly it would be appropriate to concede that Buddhism is a religion but that it fits uneasily into a theistic definition. This was precisely Durkheim's position, for he argued that the 'Buddhist was not interested in knowing whence came the world in which he lives and suffers, he takes it as a given fact, and his whole concern is to escape it' (1915, 37). Thus there is no necessary recourse to divinity. In a useful discussion on Buddhism and the definition of religion, Martin Southwold (1978) argues that Sinhalese concepts very largely conform with Durkheim's thoughts on religion. For the Sinhalese classify everything as either of the world [*laukika*] or not of the world [*lokottara*] – and the latter would seem to be close to what Durkheim meant by the term *sacred* (cf. Ames 1964, 23). Southwold gives a rough translation of *lokottara* as 'supra-wordly', and of course Buddhism is essentially concerned with such other-worldly ends. But Southwold finds the Durkheimian definition equally limiting and proposes a polythetic definition of religion that incorporates a number of attributes or elements that are normally associated with 'religion' as a cultural system.

In his study *Ecstatic Religion*, Ioan Lewis briefly mentions the Nat cults of Burma as an example of a peripheral cult. And he notes how these cults, associated primarily with women, coexist with the official Buddhist religion 'dominated by men' (1971, 85). It is the purpose of this present chapter to explore the relationship between these two religious systems, spirit religion and Buddhism, focussed as they are on the worldly and other-worldly (transcendent) concerns of humankind. The literature on Buddhism is of course vast, even in relation to its social aspects, and I therefore focus my discussion on some key anthropological texts. It is, however, worth noting that Buddhism is completely bypassed in many recent texts on the anthropology of religion (Klass and Weisgrau 1999; Bowie 2000; Lambek 2002).

During the past half century, there has been a renaissance of Buddhism in the 'West', both as a subject of study and as a new religious movement(s). Associated with such scholars as Dharmapala, Daisetz Suzuki, Christmas Humphreys, and Sangharakshita, this movement tends to advocate what has been described as modern Buddhism. In this modern form, there is an emphasis on meditation and on the rationality of Buddhism, a stress on its compatibility with modern science and western philosophy (especially existentialism), a tendency to disparage or reject spirit religion or the ritual aspects of earlier forms of religion, and finally, it emphasizes that Buddhism is an egalitarian, universal, radical, and socially committed form of spirituality (Bechert 1984; Sangharakshita 1992; Batchelor 1994; Baumann 1995; Lopez 2002).

This 'western' form of Buddhism is similar to the Protestant Buddhism that has developed in Sri Lanka, which I describe in Section 2.5.

Let me now outline the content of this chapter.

After an initial discussion in the next section of the essential doctrines of Buddhism, in its classical sense as a religion of salvation, I explore the relationship between Buddhism and spirit-cults in three Theravadin societies – Burma, Thailand, and Sri Lanka. I focus the discussion on three seminal anthropological texts by, respectively, Spiro (1970), Tambiah (1970), and Gombrich and Obeyesekere (1988). This forms the substance of Sections 2.3–2.5. I then, in Section 2.6, explore the relationship of Buddhism to folk religion in Tibet, concentrating on Samuel's (1993) comprehensive study, and the distinction he makes between shamanic and clerical Buddhism. I conclude the chapter with a brief look at the relationship between Buddhism and the state.

2.2. THE BUDDHIST DHARMA

Buddhism essentially is that religious tradition that is associated with the teaching of Siddhartha Gautama, the Buddha, who was born around 483 B.C.E. at Kapilavastu, a small city–state in the basin of the River Ganges. His father was a Kshatriya chieftain, and thus the Buddha was of aristocratic lineage, specifically a member of the Sakya clan. The sixth century B.C.E. was a significant period in human history, and it has been described by Karl Jaspers (1953) as the Axial Age, for the era produced some important figures in terms of religious innovation – Confucius, Pythagoras, Zarathustra, Lao Tzu, Mahavira, and the prophet Isaiah, all living around this time. It was a period, too, when many Asian communities were undergoing radical transformations, with the break-up of tribal society and the emergence of large-scale state empires. Bellah's discussion of religious evolution (1964) described the important changes he believed to have occurred in the first millenium B.C.E., which saw the emergence of the phenomenon of 'world rejection'. This implied a negative evaluation of the world and society and the exaltation of a spiritual realm. As Arnold Toynbee put it in discussing this issue and the five 'seers' of the period,

> The most momentous common feature is the attainment, by an individual human being, of a direct personal relation with the ultimate spiritual reality in and behind the Universe in which man finds himself. (1976, 178)

After the achievement of 'civilization' – equated with the rise of agrarian states and literacy – 'man had shifted his approach to ultimate reality' (1976, 178). It was indeed a turning point in human history and, if one is to judge from the earliest Chinese literature, a time of violence and disorder, quite different from the earlier tribal period. It was into such a situation that Gautama was born.

Given his aristocratic background, Gautama was probably to some extent shielded from the malaise and suffering that then existed but, one day, according to Buddhist legend, he was suddenly confronted with the stark reality of life. He met an old man in the last stages of senility; then he was drawn by the cries of a man afflicted with a terrible disease; and finally, passing by the riverbank, he saw a procession of mourners, carrying a dead person and weeping bitterly. These sights made him think deeply about the meaning and purpose of human existence, and as he went his way pondering such issues, he met – and on the same day – an ascetic monk walking calmly and confidently along the road. This convinced him of the value of the ascetic life. He therefore renounced his inheritance to his father's kingdom, and left his wife and children, in order to devote himself to a search for the means of escape from this world of suffering. For about six years he practised an extreme ascetic life until he was all but wasted away but then realized that such austerities did not lead to any understanding. He therefore left the five ascetics with whom he had associated. He was then about thirty-five years old. But he was also convinced that the 'truth' about suffering would not be attained by engaging in sensuous pleasures – so he followed a 'middle way' between the extremes of asceticism and pleasure-seeking. He eventually gained enlightenment whilst sitting under a Bo tree (*Ficus religiosus*) on the banks of a river near Gaya (in modern Bihar), meditating on the nature of human existence.

According to tradition, Gautama spent a further four weeks in meditation beneath the Bo tree and then set out to preach his understanding to the world. The first preaching of the dharma, or four Noble Truths, is said to have taken place in the deer park near Benares. Like many other religious leaders, he gathered around him a group of disciples and converts, and for the next forty or so years travelled around north-east India preaching his doctrine of salvation. He died at about the age of eighty, having just eaten some pork at the house of a blacksmith. For most of his life, Gautama was an itinerant teacher, and, though concerned with establishing an order of monks, he did not actively seek the patronage of political authorities (for useful studies of the life of the Buddha, see Saddhatissa 1976; Pye 1979; Carrithers 1983a; Armstrong 2000).

It is important to realize that the achievement of Buddha-hood (enlightenment) was not unique to the historical Gautama, but rather that he was considered to be the latest in a long line of Buddhas and the fourth in the present cosmic cycle. Moreover, there is a general belief, expressed in the scriptures and in folk culture, of an apocalypse, of the end of the present world and the coming of a future Buddha, Maitreya, to begin the next. Towards the end of the present era, associated with Gautama, Buddhism will decline, and people will die at an earlier age. Thus no one will be able to attain salvation until the appearance of Maitreya, who will rediscover the Truth and expound it all. There is a messianic theme here, although no one knows exactly when the next Buddha will appear.

Importantly, Buddhism was not established as a major religious system until more than 200 years after the death of Gautama, when Emperor Ashoka was converted to Buddhism. Experiencing remorse after the slaughter and devastation he had caused in building up his empire, Ashoka made Buddhism the state religion. It was during or near his reign that a council of monks agreed on the contents of the Pali canon. Known as the *Tripitaka* [three baskets], this canon consists of three sections: the Vinaya Pitaka, which is the corpus of rules governing the life of the monks; the Sutra-Pitaka, which consists of sermons and discourses (sutras) of the Buddha; and the Abhidharma, books of scholastic philosophy of relatively later origin. Thus Buddhist doctrines as expressed in these scriptures have been handed down relatively unchanged for many centuries. It is this Pali canon that is important for Theravada Buddhists.

Buddhist cosmology is both complex and variable. In Burma it is believed that there are three different worlds of existence, each of these worlds (or *lokas*) having their characteristic forms of life. The upper loka or heavens has twenty levels of byama or devas and six levels of Nat spirits. (In Thailand, the latter category is replaced with the phii spirits, in Sri Lanka with the yakas.) Below these levels is the world in which villagers physically exist, while in the lower world are the ghosts of dead humans [*pretas*], suffering animals, monsters, and a place of intense misery and pain. What is important about this Buddhist conception is that although six basic forms of existence are recognized – god, spirit, humans, animal, ghost, and soul in hell – these distinctions are only of a temporary nature, for a person is subject to the wheel of rebirth [*samsara*] that constitutes the world. According to one's *karma* [the sum of one's acts], a person may be 'reborn' as a god or as an animal; it all depends on one's past deeds and the moral balance of good and evil that goes on from existence to existence. Sometimes known as reincarnation, this theory of rebirth has the status of an ineluctable natural law like gravity. It was a system of thought that Gautama derived from Hinduism, and the essence of both Buddhism and Hinduism is that they offer a means of salvation or escape from this world of rebirth. But, important in the Buddhist tradition, one can achieve this liberation only whilst in the human condition: The gods merely enjoy the fruits of previous karma and must be reborn human to achieve salvation. What is also important in Buddhism – and this has been noted earlier – is that laukika [this world] incorporates all forms of existence, so that even the gods and spirits are considered profane. The realm of lokottara thus means not simply the sacred, or 'other-worldly', but complete liberation from sentient existence. This can be achieved only through salvation, as expressed in the basic doctrines advocated by Gautama the Buddha.

The essential doctrine of Buddhism, embodied in the four Holy Truths taught by Gautama at Benares, constitutes the dharma. This term is difficult to translate into English, but it essentially means something that exists in its own right, without dependence on any prior reality. The dharma consists of four essential truths.

The first is that everything in the world is bound up with suffering [*dukkha*]. It is not a matter of original sin – life is suffering. Human life, Buddha considered, was like a chain:

> The first link in the chain is contact with matter, and this produces sensation. Out of sensation comes desire, out of desire attachment to the illusions of life, out of attachment karma, out of karma comes birth, and out of birth – age, sickness and death – the springs of suffering. (Vaswani 1960, 55)

There is no way out – human life implies suffering, even though to think about it runs counter to our usual inclinations. For, as Conze suggests, most people cannot live happily without adopting some kind of ostrich attitude to this existential fact. To understand this first truth, Buddha held, demanded penetration and awareness: 'Birth is suffering, decay is suffering, sickness is suffering, death is suffering,' said the Buddha. He put his cardinal thoughts succinctly when he said 'one thing I teach is suffering, and the ending of suffering' (Humphreys 1951, 81).

This awareness implies neither a pessimistic or optimistic attitude towards life but, as Rahula suggests, a realistic one. It is to look at the world objectively. The Buddha did not deny the enjoyment and happiness, both material and spiritual, that there are in life, but stressed that these are transient and impermanent. Nor did this emphasis on the reality of suffering suggest a rejection of the world – a repugnant attitude to the world. Suffering for the Buddha is a fact, not an evil, and there is nothing to be gained by expressing anger, gloom, or impatience about it (Rahula 1959, 16–28).

The second truth postulates the cause of suffering: 'It is that craving which leads to rebirth, accompanied by delight and greed . . . i.e. craving for sensuous experience, craving to perpetuate oneself' (Conze 1951, 43). Desire then is the cause of suffering. It therefore follows – and this is the third Noble Truth – that the elimination of desire will abolish suffering. The third Noble Truth suggests that there is emancipation and liberation from suffering and that to eliminate dukkha completely, one has to eliminate the main root of dukkha, which is thirst, desire, craving (Rahula 1959, 29–35). How then do we go about eliminating desire and craving? By accepting the fourth Noble Truth and following the Noble eightfold path that leads to the ultimate ideal and value of Buddhism – nirvana, salvation through the extinction of desire. As said, this path involves the avoidance of two extremes, namely the search for freedom and happiness through the pleasures of the senses on the one hand and self-mortification and various forms of asceticism on the other, which is deemed to be equally 'painful, unworthy and unprofitable'. The eightfold path essentially involves three aspects. First, there is ethical conduct [*sila*], which involves compassion and love for the world, attitudes, and actions that promote harmony and happiness – Buddhism is strongly opposed to any kind of war or the involvement in any work or activities that involve suffering or harm to others – and the abstention from slanderous, idle, or dishonest speech. The second aspect is mental discipline or meditation [*samadhi*], which stresses the cultivation of mental effort and concentration and an awareness of all forms of bodily feelings and sensation. The third aspect of the path is wisdom [*panna*], which demands a radically new way of looking at the world, the cultivation of a sense of detachment, and an understanding of the true nature of reality, as embodied in the four Noble Truths. Buddhism thus combines compassion and wisdom, love, and knowledge. To what extent this path involves the assumption of a monastic life or at least a life of mendicancy is none too clear, for Rahula suggests that the attainment of nirvana can be realized by men and women living ordinary normal lives (Rahula 1959, 45–50, 77; Carrithers 1983a, 71–3). There is, however, an important sense in which, as Carrithers has put it, Buddhism is a 'psychological pragmatism', involving a 'practical path to overcoming suffering' (1983, 47–8). Liberation did not imply an end to physical pain but rather to mental suffering.

The whole worldview of Buddhism, Nash suggests (1965, 112) is summed up in this constantly heard refrain: *dukkha, anicca, anatta* – the 'three signs of being'. These three premises constitute and embody the major characteristics of all existence and form the basis of the dharma. Dukkha, as already noted, implies that all existence involves suffering. Anicca means change and impermanence and holds that all earthly experiences are transient and that there is an unrelenting law of change and decay observable in all things. And, finally, anatta is the doctrine of 'non-self' and is an extreme empiricist doctrine that holds that the notion of an unchanging permanent self is a 'fiction' and has no reality. According to Buddhist doctrine, the individual person consists of five *skandhas* or heaps – the body, feelings, perceptions, impulses, and consciousness. The belief in a 'self' or 'soul', over these five skandhas, is illusory and the cause of suffering. Thus the essence of salvation is 'de-individualization', the eradication of all notions of the ego, for when the individual ceases to exist, the result is nirvana, the goal of Buddhism. This doctrine of 'no soul' is intimately associated with the notion of anicca or impermanence, for in Buddhist terms the universe itself is in a state of perpetual flux. But, as Spiro notes, Buddhism makes an even more radical claim, for it does not suggest that there is any permanent or eternal reality. As he puts it, 'Rather than aspiring to an eternal existence, the Buddhist (in theory) aspires to the extinction of existence' (1970, 8). Thus Buddhism is a radical form of salvation or mysticism, the experience of 'emptiness' or 'void' being associated with the state of nirvana. There has been some dispute as to the exact meaning of nirvana, but clearly the Buddhist theory of no soul seems to imply quite a different perspective from that of Vedantist philosophy, in which the individual soul or self [*atman*] is seen as identical with the world soul or Brahman [god] (on the doctrine of anatta [no soul], see Rhys Davids 1912, 48–77; Murti 1955; Collins 1982; Morris 1994, 49–69).

There has been some dispute among Buddhists regarding the exact nature of nirvana. The well-known Buddhist scholar Christmas Humphreys tended to give the Buddhist conception of enlightenment a religious or idealist gloss, writing of what is essentially a human experience as the 'absolute all-mind'. In this 'ultimate spiritual experience', the self, he writes, becomes emerged in the 'all self' and consciousness becomes coeval with the universe, the latter being 'mind-only' (1987, 15–19). Similarly, Sangharakshita suggests that through insight mediation, one recognizes that the world is conditioned, impermanent, unsatisfactory, and unreal, and thus gains a spiritual vision, the direct experience of the 'ultimate reality'. This reality is 'beyond the world' and is unconditioned, transcendent, permanent, real, and blissful (1966b, 22). This vision is reminiscent of both Vedanta and Platonic idealism.

But other scholars have stressed that the principles of impermanence [*anicca*] and dependent origination [*Paticca Samuppada*] are the fundamental 'bedrock' of Buddhism. The latter notion emphasizes the interdependence and conditioned nature of *all* phenomena – physical, biological, psychological. It is therefore quite misleading to equate nirvana with some unconditioned 'metaphysical absolute'. Such scholars stress that there is no underlying entity of a divine, transcendental, eternal, or metaphysical nature that lies beyond the manifest phenomena of this world and that is experienced as nirvana (Macy 1991, 58–61; Brazier 2001, 146). To these scholars, Buddhism is a form of secular humanism and to be enlightened is to be

> compassionate, tolerant, reasonable, moral, and engaged in a life that benefits humankind – that contributes to the emancipation of all sentient beings from avoidable suffering and exploitation. (Brazier 2001, 1)

The implication of the anatta doctrine seems to be that Buddhism is both nihilistic and pessimistic, and in a radical way, for it repudiates everything that constitutes or attracts the empirical self and regards all sensory experience, all life, as something to be totally rejected. Since as long as there is life there is suffering, then according to Spiro the 'only reasonable goal to aspire to, according to Buddhism, is the extinction of life as we ordinarily understand it' (Spiro 1970, 9), or more accurately the extinction of ego. Nirvana is essentially the transcending of individuality. But as Conze writes in discussing this 'radical pessimism', if this world is indeed a vale of tears, as Buddhists hold, 'there is joy in shedding its burden' (1951, 21). A further implication of these doctrines is that nothing but one's own efforts will bring salvation. In a sense, Buddhism is an extreme form of individualism, for there is no recourse to a deity or saviour, no prayer or sacrament, no religious grace, and not even an enduring soul. Whereas other religions see death, though inevitable, as the ultimate tragedy, they offer hope by offering eternal life; for Buddhism, death is but the continuation of life through endless rebirths – and equally tragic. Only salvation, self-extinction, offers a release. Importantly, given this concept of anatta, Theravada Buddhism offers only one way to salvation – and this is through systematic meditation. There is no salvation through ritual or devotion [*bhakti*] as in Hinduism.

Because renunciation, or rejection of the world, is implied by the Buddhist dharma – for attachment to the world is seen as the cause of suffering – Buddhism is a religion, par excellence, of what Weber called 'world-rejecting asceticism' (1966, 169). Thus the core of the Buddhist movement has always consisted of followers of the monastic life, who have embraced poverty, celibacy, and non-violence as a way of life.

Although the Buddhist path to salvation is open to all regardless of caste or sex, those who have attained, or at least have approached, the state of nirvana are few indeed, and consist of three kinds of people. The Buddha; those who are on the threshold of Buddha-hood [*bodhisattva*]; and the ascetic monk [*arahat*], who by practising meditation [*dhyana*] has entered the path of salvation and attained mystic power. At his death he will reach the state of nirvana. In Mahayana Buddhism, found in Tibet, China, and Japan, the bodhisattva doctrine is more developed, a bodhisattva being someone who, out of love for humanity, renounces his own Buddha nature in order to help the salvation of others. This ideal has a place, however, in the Jataka tales of Sri Lanka (Carrithers 1983a, 90–103).

The paradox, of course, is how a religion that seemingly advocates a complete renunciation of the world comes to terms with social realities. Two points may be made: one relating to Buddhist politics, for there has always been a symbiotic relationship between Buddhism and state power; the other relating to the village context.

Although Buddhism has often been defined as an other-worldly religion from its inception, it was essentially a social movement, and the community of monks [*sangha*], as we shall explore, has always been closely involved, indeed intertwined, with everyday social life and politics. Early Buddhism has been interpreted in many ways as a revolutionary movement, which emphasized an egalitarian ethos, and thus challenged the caste hierarchy of Hindu society. And throughout its long history there has been a close and intricate relationship between Buddhism and state politics, ever since Emperor Ashoka made Buddhism the official religion of the Magadhan Empire (circa 250 B.C.E.). The expansion as well as the decline of Buddhism was closely related to the fortunes of various Asian empires (Ling 1968, 232–54). Cynthia Mahmood has indeed suggested that Max Weber's approach to the Buddhist religion was virtually devoid of sociology (1997, 309).

With regard to the immediate everyday life, there is this question:

If nirvana is seemingly such a remote possibility, and the monastic ideal an unenviable way of life for most people, how does Buddhism manifest itself in 'practical' terms in the village context?

In subsequent sections we shall explore this issue more fully, but here it is worth noting what many anthropologists have stressed, namely, that the preceding doctrines do not constitute an esoteric body of knowledge available and of interest only to religious specialists. On the contrary, the basic principles of what Spiro (1970) calls 'Nibbanic [salvation] Buddhism' are known to everyone, including the humblest villager (cf. Ames 1964; Carrithers 1983b, 90–4). And though much of the Pali canon may be unknown to villagers, nonetheless throughout most of Thailand, Burma, and among the Sinhalese, Buddhism is a living tradition. The five basic precepts of Buddhism – not to kill, steal, engage in sexual misconduct, lie, or drink intoxicants – are upheld, and along with the famous 'triple Jewel' – 'I take my refuge in the Buddha, I take my refuge in the Dharma, I take my refuge in the Sangha' – are recited every day by almost every villager. Importantly, though such devotions are said before an image of the Buddha, the Buddha is not considered a god, though such images, as well as the famous relics, are often conceived as having spiritual power.

2.3. BUDDHISM AND NAT CULTS IN BURMA

The relationship between Theravada Buddhism and the spirit-cults, or what is often described as animism, has given rise to some controversy and to varying types of interpretation. Some have seen the two religious systems as hopelessly intertwined, forming a syncretic religion, whose components can be distinguished only at an analytical level (Brohm 1963). Nash stresses that to a Burmese villager these systems form a 'coherent whole' (1965, 166), while Tambiah in his study of Thai Buddhism goes even further and offers, as subsequently discussed, an analysis of a 'total' ritual field. Others have stressed the pre-eminence of the spirit-cults and have suggested that the ordinary villager of South-East Asia is essentially an animist, following the rites and practices of a pre-Buddhist religion, and that Buddhism is simply a 'thin veneer of philosophy' (Temple 1906). Melford Spiro considers both these interpretations misleading. As Buddhism is deeply embedded in the thought and culture of the people – it was a 'pervading force' in Burmese society, wrote Nash (1965, 104) – the second approach is clearly untenable. Thus Spiro argued in his pioneering studies (1967, 1970) that there existed in Burma two distinct systems of thought, Buddhism and supernaturalism, each offering its own interpretation and rituals in the alleviation of suffering. Between these 'two religions', with conflicting and incompatible orientations, there existed a state of tension.

Following Spiro's own approach, we can perhaps describe these two religious systems, the spirit-cults and Buddhism, separately. I also follow Spiro in utilizing the term 'supernatural', although many scholars are now reluctant to use this concept, as it seems to imply a dualistic metaphysic, even though they themselves often define Buddhism or shamanic religion in terms of a two-world theory. In Burma, two religous 'systems' are seen to coexist, for Buddhism 'requires', as Nash suggests (1965, 166), some set of complementary activities for handling immediate, day-to-day emergencies and misfortunes. These are provided for by what Spiro calls 'supernaturalism'. His studies of Burmese religion (1967, 1970) deal respectively with the two religious 'systems', Buddhism and spirit-cults, his earlier study dealing specifically with the latter cults. Spiro's approach to religion combines psychoanalytic theory with structural–functionalism; in fact, he describes himself as an 'unregenerate functionalist' and, like Lewis, expresses misgivings about all forms of cognitive anthropology. Responding to Levi-Strauss' work on totemism, he expresses the view that religious ideas are not so much used to think about or classify with as to *live* by (1970, 6).

Burmese religion recognizes five main categories of supernaturals, and these are briefly outlined.

First, there are the various deities [*devas*] who reside in the Buddhist heavens. They are looked on as beneficent supernaturals and considered to be the guardians of Buddhism. They are prayed to and given offerings, particularly fruit. As they are considered vegetarians, they are never offered meat. It is recognized that the intercession of the devas is inconsistent with the Buddhist doctrine of karma, but nevertheless they are believed to protect people from harm.

Second, there is a belief in various demons [*baw*] and mythical, ogre-like beings. Despite the fact that they feature prominently in sculptures, they have little significance in Burmese life.

Third, there are witches: individuals who possess mystical power and who cause harm to others. Two types are distinguished: the *aulan* [lower-path] *hysaya*, invariably a male who causes sickness and death by sending malevolent spitis, and the *sonma*, who are chiefly women. According to Spiro, there is much anxiety expressed about witchcraft, though no one is ever openly accused of being a witch.

Fourth, there are ghosts [*pretas*], disembodied spirits that have their origin in the death of a person through unnatural causes or through some evil committed in their past lives. They are looked on as especially malevolent.

And, finally, and most importantly, there are the Nat spirits, whose culture comprises an organized and elaborate system of beliefs and rituals.

With the exception of the devas, most of these supernaturals are considered to be potentially malevolent and are frequently cited as the causal agents of illness and misfortunes. The Nat spirits themselves, as said, are the object of an elaborate cult, which, Spiro suggests, can be viewed as an organized religious system that rivals Buddhism in its cognitive and ritual systemization. The Nats, thirty-seven in number, are conceived to be fundamentally the spirits of deceased human beings who, because of their violent deaths, became Nats. Few people are acquainted with all the Nats, even though many have an associated mythology, and some have the status of royal ancestral spirits. The Nats can be grouped into three categories, according to their ritual congregations. There are first the territorial Nats that are known throughout a region. Of special importance in this context is the house Nat *min mahagiri*, who is represented in each household by a coconut and propitiated with flowers and cooked rice. Second, each village has a special shrine or Nat house, usually near the village gate, dedicated to the village guardian Nat [*ywadawyin*]. This Nat is propitiated once a year. And third, there are inherited Nats associated with a specific family and kinship group. Although men express a good deal of scepticism about the reality and importance of the Nat spirits, women are deeply involved in Nat propitiation. As Spiro records, it is women who most fear the Nats and who regularly tend the village shrines. The Nats are propitiated at various life-cycle rituals and at various stages of the agricultural cycle – and many of these ceremonials are attended almost exclusively by women. But most important is the regional Nat festival at the village of Taungbyon, about twenty miles from Mandalay, which is attended by cult followers from all over Burma. This festival lasts five days and is similar to a Catholic fiesta; indeed, Spiro stresses that it has a Bacchanalian character, with dancing and drinking. Female spirit-mediums, *nat-kadaw* [Nat wife], wearing red turbans (a colour especially liked by the Nats), play a prominent part in the rituals, propitiating the Nat spirits (known as Taungbyon brothers) and, helped by country spirits, going into trance states.

In the Burmese context, the treatment of illness involving spirit-possession takes one of two forms. In the first instance, the services of the magician or exorcist *ahtelan* [upper-path] *hsaya* is sought; and he is able, with the assistance of the 'devas', to induce the offending spirit to incarnate the patient. The patient acts as a medium for the spirit, which is then questioned with respect to its requirements. The exorcist attempts to induce the spirit to leave the patient alone. It is often literally a struggle between good and evil, the exorcist endeavouring to enlist the support of Buddhism. In the second form, the shaman enters a trance state and becomes the medium for the spirit. What is of interest is the contrasting roles of exorcist and shaman. Whereas the former is always a man and a strict Buddhist, the shaman is invariably a woman, the wife of the Nat spirit, and is both a diviner and a cult officiant. This distinction therefore reflects the cosmological division between Buddhism and Nat cults that Spiro sees as central to Burmese religion, Buddhism being concerned with other-worldly salvation, the spirit-cult with the attainment of worldly ends. In his concluding chapter, Spiro links these two religious systems to the well-known Appollian–Dionysian dichotomy, as noted by Ruth Benedict (1934); this can be roughly tabulated as follows:

	Buddhism	**Nat Cults**
Morality	Moral	Amoral
Sensuality	Ascetic	Libertarian
Reason	Rational	Non-rational
Personality	Serenity	Turbulence
Society	Other-worldly	Worldly

Spiro considers these two religious systems to be absolutely distinct – at least at a conceptual level. 'If Buddhism', he writes, stresses the rational, the Nat cult stresses the non-rational. If reason is the foundation stone of the former, emotion is the basis of the latter.... Unlike the Buddhist monk, who seeks truth through study and meditation, in consciousness and self-awareness, the shaman achieves her revelation by means of Nat possession, in states of unconsciousness and trance'. Spiro stresses that both Buddhism and the spirit-cults are concerned with suffering and the need to avoid suffering, but rather than rejecting the world, the Nat cult embraces it. Thus the Nat spirits themselves exemplify craving and desire – for power, sexuality, and material pleasure. And Spiro stresses too that Buddhism is the dominant cult and that its values permeate all levels of Burmese culture. But because it sets an ideal of other-worldly salvation, animism has a significant role to play in the attainment of worldly goals, thus rendering the persistence of Buddhism possible.

Yet although Spiro presents a radical dichotomy between Buddhism and the Nat spirit-cults, he does not view Buddhism, as a cultural system, in monolithic terms. For he suggests that Buddhism in Burma consists of three distinct systems, although not implying that living Buddhism itself can be neatly packaged into distinct bundles of belief and practices.

The first of these is Nibbanic Buddhism, focussed around the monks [*bhikkhu*] and the monastic life. This largely accords with the Buddhist dharma described in the previous section, with its emphasis on nihilism, asceticism, renunciation, and detachment from worldly concerns. The monk, Spiro writes, is the 'true Buddhist' (1970, 279). Although in the past an order of female monks was recognized, at the present time in Burma only males are eligible to join the order of monks – the Sangha. Monks are essentially concerned with their own salvation and their own spiritual welfare, and essentially devote their lives to morality – the sentiment of loving kindness [*metta*] is particularly emphasized – spiritual discipline, the study of the scriptures, and meditation. Few people in Burma engage in meditation apart from the monks, but two forms are practised by the bhikkhu, one emphasizing serenity and tranquillity [*bhavana*], the other insight [*vipassana*]. Through meditation, the monk becomes intuitively aware that there is no self and thus attains wisdom [*panna*] and possible release from the wheel of rebirth – enlightenment or nirvana [*nibbana*]. As the monk does not engage in production, he is thus dependent on the villagers for support, but he relates to the wider society in teaching Buddhism to lay people and in being centrally involved in funeral rituals. Spiro, indeed, remarks that

> If birth and childhood ceremonies are primarily concerned with the Nat [spirits], death ceremonies are the concern primarily of Buddhism. (1970, 248)

Nibbanic Buddhism is thus a religion of 'radical salvation' and primarily the concern of monks. Spiro argues that the bhikku are not priests as they are in no sense an intermediary between humans and the spirit world.

The second form of Buddhism, Kammatic Buddhism, is that practised by the majority of the populace who are essentially concerned not with rejecting the world but with improving their position within the wheel of rebirth [*samsara*] by enhancing their own karma [*kamma*]. This is achieved by the acquisition of merit [*ku thou*], which, in turn is attained in three ways: by giving [*dana*], morality [*sila*], or meditation [*bhavana*] (Spiro 1970, 94). But whereas meditation is important in Nibbanic Buddhism, giving – particularly to the monks – is the means par excellence for acquiring merit in Kammatic Buddhism. Indeed, Spiro suggests that it is through Kammatic Buddhism that the Burmese people are able to affirm their loyalty to orthodox Buddhism while at the same time rejecting the orthodox emphasis on 'other-worldly' salvation. The Buddhism of the great majority of contemporary people in Burma, Spiro writes, 'is best characterized as a religion of proximate salvation' (1970, 67). In Kammatic Buddhism, a pleasurable rebirth is therefore considered preferable to extinction – nirvana.

The third system of Buddhism Spiro refers to as Apotropaic Buddhism, which is essentially concerned, like the Nat cults, in protecting the individual from existential problems – illness, drought, snake-bites, and other misfortunes. Even Kammatic Buddhism does not deal adequately with the problems and sufferings of everyday life. Thus the recitation of specific spells or chants [*paritta*] derived from the Buddhist canon, the enactment of special rituals before images of the Buddha, the invocation of certain Buddhist gods or deva, all these serve to protect the individual from harm and bring about a variety of worldly benefits. They thus constitute a 'powerful magical technology' that deals with the mundane concerns and problems of everyday experience – not with salvation. This is the system of Apotropaic Buddhism.

Although Melford Spiro makes a rather stark dichotomy between spirit cults and Buddhism, his studies of Burmese religion are detailed and substantive and indicate that it is both complex and multifaceted. He eschews homiletic interpretations of religious doctrine and rituals – currently fashionable – and, though acknowledging the importance of hermeneutics, Spiro's primary concern is to explore the functions of Buddhism and spirit cults in Burma at both a social and psychological level. But two important themes are worth noting in conclusion. One is the importance of the monk in Burmese society; for the bhikkhu is not only a symbol of worldly renunciation but also venerated to an extraordinary degree as the epitome of the devout Buddhist. Indeed, Spiro writes that the feeding of the monks and the maintenance of the monastery is almost the raison d'etre of the Burmese village, serving to integrate the village as a social unit (1970, 472). The second is the fact that the Burmese tend to maintain a clear distinction between the ultimate values and perspective of Nibbanic Buddhism [*lokuttara*] and the practical and empirical perspective of worldly existence [*loki*]. (For an important collection of Spiro's theoretical writings, see Spiro 1987; for a general account of Buddhism in Burma, see Bechert 1984.)

2.4. BUDDHISM AND SPIRIT-CULTS IN THAILAND

In this section we focus on Stanley Tambiah's important study of Thai religion. Tambiah, influenced by Levi-Strauss and Leach, attempts to provide a synchronic, structuralist approach to Buddhism and spirit-cults and, as such, attempts to conceptualize the religious system as a 'total field'. This means that he does not stress, like Spiro, the duality and contrast between Buddhism and animism but rather discusses separately four ritual complexes and attempts, by means of formal concepts – hierarchy, opposition, complementarity – to analyse these cult activities and the relationship among them. The first of these ritual complexes relate to the Buddhist monks, and there are, I think, three interrelated aspects of what has been described as "practical Buddhism" that Tambiah's study highlights.

First, the monastic life is not seen as something entirely separate from the world for, as noted earlier in relation to Burma, there is a symbiotic relationship between the Buddhist laity and the monks, the latter offering spiritual gifts in return for material support. The Buddhist monk is therefore very different from the two religious specialists of Hinduism. Although like the Sannyasin, the monk renounces the world and devotes himself to the religious life, the Sangha has a structured relationship with the laity. Unlike the Sannyasin, the Buddhist monk is not outside the social structure. Moreover, whereas the status of homeless wanderer (Sannyasin) was seen as the final stage in the theory of *asrama* (the Hindu stages of life), monkhood for the many male Buddhists in South-East Asia is a role they adopt when young adults – though they may intensify their religious piety towards the end of their life. Unlike the brahmans, monks do not form a caste and, in fact, given the rule of celibacy, they could never be one. In fact, in the Indian context, the Brahman priest and the Buddhist bhikku were in many ways opposed and antagonistic.

In Thailand, the Buddhist temple [*wat*] is ecologically separated from the village settlement and reflects the separation of the monk from the ordinary villager or householder. Within the temple, the monks constitute a monastic community, which in essence is a self-governing community under the loose governance of a senior monk or abbot. They form what Tambiah calls a 'confraternity' (1970, 73) devoted to the religious life; the internal organization of the community is thus rather loose, and the community to a large degree has political autonomy. Within the community there is no stress on central authority, and seniority is based on the number of years since full ordination as a monk. Importantly, the Sangha or monastic community is an open institution; any man can become a monk, and though there is a ceremony of ordination, the monk takes no vows of obedience and is free to leave the order at any time. There is no equivalent status for women, though in Buddhism, *bhikkhunis* [nuns] are in fact recognized. As Tambiah writes, 'The salvation quest is very much a male pursuit. The inferiority of women in respect of the Buddhist quest is doctrinally well established' (1970, 98).

But though the political structure of the Sangha is antihierarchical in many respects, there is nonetheless a rigid enforcement of disciplinary rules. The more important of these relate to sexual misconduct and the impropriety of even associating with women; to the drinking of wines and spirits; and to injunctions against trade, luxurious living, the taking of life, and the eating of food after midday. Poverty, celibacy, and non-violence form therefore the three essentials of monastic life, but significantly, unlike with most Christian monks, there is no stress on manual labour or on obedience. The monk, whose life is oriented towards his own salvation, is supported by the contributions and gifts of the Buddhist laity. An ordinary villager, by observing the Buddhist precepts in a strict fashion, may gain piety, and it is common for men and women in later life to retreat from worldly concerns; but these people are not monks. Although some individuals devote their life to the Sangha and become full-time monks, the usual pattern in Thailand (but not in

Sri Lanka) is for every male to spend some time in the monastery as a novice monk. He is initiated as a monk, usually through an ordination ceremony sponsored by his family, and for a time lives in the monastery, observing the rules of discipline, wearing the ochre robe, and having his head shaven. He performs many of the functions of a monk and, besides undertaking some of the more menial tasks in the monastery, devotes his time to studying and learning the Buddhist scriptures – memorizing in particular the various sermons and chants. Traditionally, before the advent of public schooling, the period a man spent as a monk was important in acquiring literacy. Thus typically the Sangha is composed primarily of celibates in the prime of adult life, and, as Tambiah writes, the ordination as a monk in Thailand is 'distinctly a rite of passage for young men before they marry and set up their own households' (1970, 101). Many in later life, and as village elders, continue to support the Sangha, either materially through alms and gifts or in the administration of the temple, through the Wat committee.

Second, the monks play an important role in conducting many of the village rites. The most important of these are the cycle of collective calendrical rites connected with agriculture (Tambiah 1970, 152–75, for a detailed account of those undertaken in a Thai village) and the funerary rites. The latter rituals – unlike the rites associated with marriage and birth – are presided over by monks and are conceived of as essentially Buddhist rites. The monks act as mediators between death and rebirth, and the whole focus of the ritual is to secure for the dead person a good status in afterlife by the transfer of merit. An important distinction is made between those who have died a violent death through unnatural events – accident, injury, or suicide – and those who have died of natural causes at the end of the normal life span. A violent death is looked on as highly inauspicious, for it is believed that a person's spirit [*winjan*] will become a malevolent *phii*. The person is therefore given a hurried burial; there is no cremation and the monks do not participate in the funeral ceremony. In contrast, the monks officiate at the mortuary rites associated with normal death, the purpose of the rite, as said, being to lead the dead man's spirit to heaven and make possible a better rebirth (Tambiah 1970, 179–90).

It is in relation to the latter concept that the third aspect of practical Buddhism pertains, namely, the notion that merit-making leads to better rebirth. It is in fact the ideology of merit that links together Nibbanic Buddhism, exemplified by the monks, and the everyday world of the villager. For the chief activity involved in being an ordinary Buddhist is concerned with gift-giving. Almsgiving, as Ames writes (1964, 30) is the first and foremost duty of all Buddhists. By giving food, gifts, and support to the Buddhist monks and the Buddhist Sangha, a person obtains merit [*bun*], and, by increasing his fund of merit in this life, he or she thereby ensures a rebirth blessed with happiness and prosperity and, more important, with the possibility of obtaining salvation in a future life.

Thus most Buddhists in Thailand, as in Burma, are not concerned with renunciation and with obtaining salvation but only with 'a happy rebirth'. It is merit-making rather than meditating that has practical significance, and, as Tambiah writes (1970, 54), merit-making need not be an individual activity, for the family household or kin group may engage in merit-making activities. But significantly, the act of voluntary giving, without a thought of immediate advantage, though giving merit to the individual, can also be seen as a form of sacrificial act, for by giving, a person registers less attachment to the things associated with the self (Nash 1965, 115). There are therefore two distinct paths to salvation: what Spiro refers to as *Nibbanic* and *Kammatic* Buddhism. The one is associated with monks and world-renunciation, and seeks salvation through meditation; the other, undertaken by ordinary Buddhists, is concerned with accumulating merit by gift-giving and thereby gaining a better rebirth to facilitate one's future salvation.

Given the difficult and world-negating path that the nirvana ideal implies, the latter path represents the religious orientation of most Theravada Buddhists, and it is functional to the support of the monastic order. Essentially, the requirements of the monks and the local Wat, including daily food, are supplied entirely by the laity. In return, the monks perform their sermons, officiate in village rituals, and, by their example and studies, uphold the Buddhist ideal.

The three other ritual complexes that Tambiah describes as important in Thailand are also worth outlining.

Buddhists in Thailand conceptually distinguish two spiritual essences associated with the person. *Winjan*, or spirit, leaves the person only at death and may then become either a malevolent phii spirit in the event of an unnatural death or continue the cycle of rebirths, hopefully in heaven. The *khwan*, or life soul, on the other hand, is associated with a person only during his or her earthly life, and its presence in the body is essential for a person's well-being. 'Soul loss' leads to suffering, illness, and misfortune. There is therefore a class of rituals, the Sukhwan rites, whose essential purpose is to ensure that the khwan is either restored to or bound to the body. The rites therefore have both a therapeutic and a prophylactic function. The essence of the rite, which is performed by the village elders, is the calling of the khwan soul and the binding of the person's wrist with a cord – symbolically signifying the attachment of the khwan to the person. Such rites are undertaken at times of crisis or misfortune and as part of important transition rites – marriage, ordination to monkhood, and pregnancy. The elder who officiates at the Sukhwan rituals is termed *Paahm*, which derives from the word *Brahman*; and Tambiah suggests that the elder performs auspicious rites in some ways reminiscent of the Brahman priest in the Hindu context. Importantly, such elders are always ex-monks who are literate and versed in the Pali scripture, so that the roles of 'priest' and 'monk' in the Thai context, Tambiah suggests, are not antagonistic but complementary (1970, 255).

The third class of rites in Thailand is focussed around the cult of the guardian spirits. These are phii spirits who, though seen as distinct from the *thewada* [*devas*] – the heavenly gods – are nonetheless, like these deities, seen as essentially benevolent supernaturals. In Thai villages, two phii spirits have particular importance in this respect, the *tapubaan* [grandfather or village ancestor], who is the guardian of the land and settlement, and the *chao phau phraa khao* [holy father–monk], who is associated with the temple. The first spirit is of the laity, and his shrine is placed at the edge of the village; the second spirit is that of a pious man, and his shrine, in the form of a wooden statue, is next to that of the Buddha, in the village temple. Offerings made to these spirits reflect, as among the Sinhalese, the pure–impure distinction. Both spirits are believed to cause misfortunes, but they are not capricious, and their inflictions reflect transgressions of certain norms – the breaking of taboos relating to the Buddhist sabbath, for instance (Tambiah 1970, 263–9).

The general procedure when a person becomes ill is to consult the *mau song*, or diviner, who diagnoses whether or not the illness has been caused by a spirit. If this is indeed the case, and the offending spirit is one of the guardian spirits, recourse has to be made to the services of a spirit medium [*tiam*], whose mediumship is publicly ratified by the village community. Such mediums are often women but, unlike the paahm, they are neither literate nor involved or generally interested in Buddhist doctrine and rites. They differ from other ritual specialists – specifically the monk [*bikkhu*] and paahm – in being recruited through possession and, as Tambiah writes, 'the distinctive features of their rituals are ecstatic possession and dance, and oracular statements – which characteristics are altogether different from those exhibited by monks and the paahm who conduct Sukhwan rituals' (1970, 283).

The final ritual complex in Thailand is associated with those phii spirits that are deemed to be malevolent. These are invariably the spirits of people who have died under abnormal circumstances, though they may also be nature spirits associated with the hills and rivers. One particular spirit *phii paub* has a permanent human host, and affliction can be remedied only by exorcism. It is women who are believed to be the most likely victims of this spirit. Significantly, the ritual offerings undertaken with respect to those afflictions caused by the malevolent phii are made not by the tiam but by other spirit mediums, *mau phii*. This leads Tambiah to suggest that the phii spirits are of two types, the guardian and the malevolent phii, each with its own complex of rites and specialists.

Although Tambiah's central concern is to offer a synchronic approach and to suggest that the relationship between Buddhism and spirit-cults is complex and cannot be seen simply as a dichotomy, he was also interested in the relationship between the 'grand Buddhist tradition', as expressed in the classical literature, and the folk religion, the religious beliefs as observed in the context of village life. This relates to the well-known paradigm of the great and little traditions (Marriott 1955) as well as to Dumont's and Pocock's distinction between Sanskritic civilization and popular Hinduism – both of which Tambiah discusses. His main criticism is that these writers assume that the classical literary tradition (whether Sanskrit Hinduism or Pali Buddhism) is a homogeneous body of literature, whereas in fact it is a miscellaneous collection of writings spread over many centuries. Thus the notion of a 'great tradition' is largely the 'fabrication of anthropologists' (Tambiah 1970, 371) and reflects a profoundly ahistorical viewpoint. Tambiah suggests that this 'two-level' approach is misleading. In fact, at the village level, the ordinary monk combines these two levels, for he chants verses and preaches sermons that are taken from the classical Pali texts while at the same time being an active member – through these rites – of a local community. Tambiah therefore suggests that we should take a historical approach and look at two kinds of links between the Buddhist past and the contemporary context, at the continuities that are evident, and at the transformations that have taken place. Looking at the relationship between Buddhism and the spirit-cults in structural terms may, he felt, give us insights into the historical processes by which Buddhism, as it spread from India, came to terms with the indigenous religions (for other interesting studies of Thai Buddhism, particularly on the role of the Sangha, see Terwiel 1975; Tambiah 1976; Bunnag 1973).

2.5. RELIGIOUS CHANGE IN SRI LANKA

Early studies of Buddhism in Sri Lanka tended to suggest that among Sinhalese Buddhists, two forms of religion coexisted: a spirit religion, often referred to as animism and that dealt with worldly concerns; and Buddhism in the strict sense, which was concerned mainly with other-worldly salvation. The latter was focussed specifically around the sangha, the order of monks. In his study of Sinhalese Buddhism, Michael Ames (1964), for example, suggests that Buddhism and animism form two distinct systems, even though they are inextricably linked in practice. Although Buddhism is not an esoteric doctrine and was open to all, those wishing to become true Buddhists had to join the sangha and, as a monk, renounce all sexual and economic activity.

As in Burma and Thailand, in Sri Lanka there was a clear distinction between the religious statuses of the layperson and the monk, the latter being supported by the laity. With regard to the spirit-cults, Ames suggests that they have a tripartite structure, for there are three main categories of spirits, each with its associated ritual system and specialist. The first system is concerned with the higher spirits [*deviyas*], who are propitiated through ritual offering [*puja*] by a priest. Only the shrines of these spirits are found in conjuction with Buddhist temples and shrines. The second is associated with astrology and planetary deities who represent astral powers and to whom offerings are made. And, finally, there are the spirits [*yakas*] and ghosts, who are warded off or exorcised from the patient by means of offerings or a spirit dance. The offerings made to the various spirits reflect a purity–pollution hierarchy, and Ames notes that all these rites begin and end with the magician or priest expressing his veneration of the Buddha. But though fused in practice, Buddhism and the spirit-cults are held to be distinct by the Sinhalese, and the latter are considered inferior to Buddhism and wholly profane. Typically, a person will first visit the Buddhist temple to venerate the Buddha and his symbols (monks, relics, Bo tree), and then go to the spirit shrine to propitiate the deities. Importantly, the spirit-cults are seen by the Sinhalese as distinct from magic (trickery) and as a form of science [*vidyava*] that is concerned with the provision of consolation and 'worldly relief' from temporary misfortunes. Between Buddhism and the spirit-cults, there is therefore a division of labour, Buddhism being concerned with karma and individual destiny, the 'science of spirits' being concerned with events brought about by other 'natural laws'. Ames succinctly indicates the relationship between these two religious systems:

> Although the two realms of Buddhism and magical-animism are completely separate and distinct in Sinhalese theory, they are complementary in function. This is why the Sinhalese fuse them in practice. (1964, 39)

This is why Ames considers the theory that Buddhism is the religion of the literati and spirit-cults the folk religion to be misleading, and for two reasons. First, as in Burma, in Sri Lanka Buddhism itself has a sophisticated and popular level of participation, the one focussed on the ascetic ideal of salvation, the other on merit-making. Second, all Buddhists, whatever their status within the Buddhist hierarchy, tend to participate in spirit propitiation. The following extract neatly summarizes what Ames is proposing:

> The primary division in Sinhalese religion is therefore not between big and little traditions at all, but between lokottara and laukika value orientations. . . . Two important religious sub-systems have combined to solve this dual problem of human life – happiness in it and salvation from it. Spirit cults, oriented to worldly (laukika) concerns, deal with the misfortunes of daily life; Buddhism is concerned with personal destiny, with what is beyond (lokottara) the ordinary. . . . The Sinhalese, both literate and non-literate . . . participate in both sub-systems. (1964, 41)

The important studies of Ames on Sinhalese Buddhism and spirit-cults (1964, 1968) relate to the 1960s, when Theravada Buddhism was still largely the 'religion of a rice-growing peasant society' (Gombrich and Obeyesekere 1988, 5). Its main institutional feature was the distinction between the laity and the sangha, it being the duty of the laity to give material support to the order of monks. The sangha, in turn, embodied and preserved the ideals of Buddhism. Equally important, as Ames emphasized, there was a clear distinction made between Theravada Buddhism and the spirit-cults, each with distinct social functions. Indeed, these two forms of religiosity had probably coexisted in Sri Lanka since time immemorial. Over the past forty years, however, Buddhism has been transformed in Sri Lanka, along with the spirit-cults, and these religious changes have been explored in a detailed and interesting study by Richard Gombrich and Gananath Obeyesekere (1988).

In the past, Sinhala Buddhist society was primarily based on peasant agriculture, and daily life focussed around kin groups and the village community. The sangha was a key institution and, as said, the distinction between the laity and the monks was an important fulcrum around which social life was organized. Over the past forty years or so, this pattern of life has been fundamentally transformed by socio-economic changes. The population of Sri Lanka has more than doubled since independence and now stands at around 15 million. This has led to impoverishment in rural areas and to increased urbanization, and many of the villages around the capital, Colombo, are now little more than suburbs (or slums) of the city. Political and economic power has become more and more centralized in Colombo, and this has led to the emergence of both a new middle class and an impoverished urban proletariat. These profound social changes have created a 'disoriented society' and have entailed dramatic religious changes – a 'new religious culture' that Gombrich and Obeysekere explore in great depth. Fundamentally, there have been two basic changes – the development within the bourgeois culture of a 'Protestant Buddhism' and the transformation of the spirit-cults into a Hindu-style bhakti religious tradition. These developments in Buddhism and spirit religion are briefly described separately – for this distinction is acknowledged by the Sinhalese themselves and the anthropologists in their own exposition.

Protestant Buddhism had its origins in the latter part of the nineteenth century, and the key figure in its emergence was Anagarika Dharmapala (1864–1933), who is also seen as an important figure in the creation of 'modern' Buddhism (Lopez 2002, 54). This is the assumed name of David Hewavitarne and literally means the 'homeless defender of the doctrine [Buddhism]'. Born in Colombo and an early member of the Theosophical Society, Dharmapala visited India in 1891 and was shocked to see the decay of the great pilgrimage sites, especially Bodh Gaya, where Buddha first experienced enlightenment. In 1891, he therefore founded the Maha Bodhi society, whose primary aim was to restore Bodh Gaya to Buddhist control. Through his writings and activities, Dharampala played an important role in promoting Buddhism as a world religion (Rahula 1978, 123–5; Gombrich 1988, 188–91).

There are a number of key features that define modern or Protestant Buddhism.

First, it emphasizes a spiritual egalitarianism and stresses equality over hierarchy. Thus it denies that only through the sangha can a person find salvation. Religion therefore becomes personal, reflecting an 'inner-worldly asceticism', and Dharmapala in particular strongly emphasized thrift and hard work. The hallmark of Protestant Buddhism is then 'its view that the layman should permeate his life with his religion; that he should strive to make Buddhism permeate his whole society; and that he should try to reach nirvana' (Gombrich and Obeyesekere 1988, 216). The quest for salvation was therefore no longer confined to the monk.

Second, it emphasizes a fundamentalist approach to religion and advocates a return to origins, to the Buddhism of the Buddha himself, stressing that contemporary

Buddhism, especially Mahayana Buddhism, has become degenerate, corrupt, and moribund.

Third, Protestant Buddhism presents itself as less of a religion than as a philosophy, almost a spiritual form of atheism. Not only compatible with modern science, it was considered more ancient and the equal of if not superior to Christianity as a mode of enlightened ethics. Early Protestant Buddhists often made use of the anti-Christian writings of western rationalists, and thus Buddhism came to be viewed as a rational mysticism (Gombrich 1988, 172–97; Gombrich and Obeyesekere 1988, 202–36).

Besides taking a polemical stance and engaging in public debate, Protestant Buddhists like Dharmapala also make great use of English-language writings and concepts.

In an interesting essay, Martin Southwold (1982) refers to this Protestant Buddhism as 'true Buddhism', which tends to be practised by English-speaking middle-class Sinhalese, who disparage what they describe as 'village Buddhism'. The small group of forest-dwelling monks in Sri Lanka, perceptively described by Michael Carrithers (1983b), are seen as part of modern or Protestant Buddhism – and as largely the outcome of European inspiration (Gombrich 1971, 283–4).

Although Protestant Buddhists do not renounce family life or economic activities, they nevertheless dedicate their spare time to religious concerns and assume an ascetic lifestyle – becoming vegetarian, refusing to drink alcohol, wearing white clothes, and sometimes leading a celibate life. Meditation centres have been established, and the widespread practice of meditation by the laity has been, Gombrich and Obeysekere suggest, "the greatest single change to have come over Buddhism in Sri Lanka . . . since the Second World War" (1988, 237).

Whereas in the past monks officiated only at funerary rites, now the marriage ceremony has become infused with Buddhist values or rather has adopted Victorian sexual mores – with its emphasis on strict monogamy and puritanical attitudes towards sexuality. The contemporary Sinhala middle class now see these as quintessential Buddhist values (Gombrich and Obeysekere 1988, 255–6). Also significant in recent years has been the resurgence of nuns. Although not belonging to a clearly defined order, such women put on yellow robes, shave their heads, follow the essential Buddhist precepts, and often live together in retreats, and, like monks, they devote their lives to the attainment of salvation.

A final important feature of Protestant Buddhism has been the emergence of the Sarvodaya movement – Sarvodaya being a Sanskrit term meaning *the welfare of all.* Founded by A. T. Ariyaratne in 1958 and influenced by Gandhi's philosophy, Sarvodaya aims to foster a model of balanced development, based on basic human needs, that is consonant with Buddhist doctrine and ethics. Its philosophy stresses the basic values of equality, loving kindness, sharing, compassionate action, equanimity, and unselfish joy. But Gombrich and Obeyesekere suggest that Sarvodaya's vision of a 'village society' and the past Sri Lankan civilization is idealized and romantic and is essentially 'a projection of the bourgeoisie, a fantasy that has no social reality' (1988, 250).

In all this, Protestant Buddhism undercuts the prestige and importance of the monk, for it holds that 'it is the responsibility of every Buddhist both to care for the welfare of Buddhism and to strive himself for salvation' (Gombrich and Obeyesekere 1988, 7).

For Dharmapala himself, the 'model Protestant Buddhist', the spirit-cults were viewed as a 'mass of superstition' that no self-respecting Buddhist could believe in or practise. But what has also occurred over the past half century has been a transformation of spirit religion in Sri Lanka, which, under the influence of Hinduism, has developed into Bhakti – like devotional cults. Whereas in the past, possession tended to be viewed negatively, as possession by malevolent spirits [*yaka*] or ghosts [*preta*], it now has a more positive evaluation. As Gombrich and Obeyesekere write, 'the most striking recent change in the Sinhala religious scene has been the widespread acceptance of possession as something positive' (1988, 37).

For what has emerged are female priests who are devotees of some of the more powerful Hindu deities – such as Pattini, Kali, Kataragama (Skanda), and Huniyam. These deities possess a woman, and so she becomes the accredited vehicle of the deity – and as a female priest (maniyo) she sets up her own shrine, and the god becomes her own guardian deity and the relationship often has an erotic quality. Counterpart to that of the traditional priests [*kapurala*], who usually came from the dominant caste and acted as intermediaries for the deities [*devata*], this new religious role is mainly associated with women. And, as in other spirit-possession cults, after an initial personal crisis, a woman may be converted from a patient into an ecstatic priestess. Thus

> the theory of divine possession enhances the self respect of the possessed person and becomes a source of 'liberation' (increased dignity, social independence, earning power) for women and indeed many other people who see no hope of other success or fulfilment. (Gombrich and Obeyesekere 1988, 41)

The *maniyo* come from the poorer sections of the community and, as diviners and curers, largely serve an impoverished urban proletariat. Whereas the nun has a vocation of salvation, the ecstatic priestess has a vocation of healing. This distinction reflects the Sinhalese saying, 'The Buddha for refuge: the gods for help'. Also important has been the emergence of the *sami*, a kind of urbanized, self-recruited priest who, influenced by Hinduism, also engages in benign possession. Gombrich and Obeyesekere give a detailed account of the various spirit-cults and rituals associated with such deities as Huniyam, Kali, and Kataragama (Skanda), all of whom have become popular deities in recent decades (1988, 96–199; see also Obeyesekere 1981, for interesting life-histories of individual women devotees and for an account of how cultural symbols have personal significance and meaning for individuals).

Of especial interest is the Kataragama shrine in the south-east corner of Sri Lanka, which has become an important pilgrim centre. Since the 1950s, most pilgrims to the shrine of Kataragama, who is associated with the Hindu god Skanda, have been Buddhists, and they visit the shrine in the thousands – the annual pilgrim traffic has indeed been estimated as exceeding a half million. It has become a 'great melting pot' of Sri Lankan society and is renowned for its more exuberant forms of religiosity – fire-walking, various forms of self-mortification, and the Kavadi ecstatic dance – a combination of eroticism and devotionalism, in which the devotees of the god, men, women, and children, dance together in ecstatic trance. It appears that the deity Skanda has almost universal appeal – and he is the god even of local politicians, businessmen, and 'big-time crooks' in the city of Colombo. Kataragana represents, Gombrich and Obeyesekere conclude, a kind a Hindu–Buddhism syncretism – the invasion of Sinhalese region by Tamil Bhakti religiosity (1988, 163–99; Obeyesekere 1981).

Gombrich and Obeyesekere affirm that the important function of Buddhism in Sri Lanka is to provide life with meaning and a sense of purpose and that the spirit cults have a largly communal function (1988, 22). But eschewing neither functional or causal analysis, they go beyond hermeneutics and semiology – with its narrow emphasis on 'meaning' – and give a rich and fascinating account of Buddhism and spirit religion in Sri Lanka, situating it, in Weberian fashion, in its socio-historical context. It is thus refreshingly free of any reference to fashionable postmodern icons! (For further studies of Buddhism and spirit-cults in Sri Lanka, see Gombrich 1971; Evers 1972; Yalman 1964; Southwold 1983. For an important study of Theravada Buddhism, see Gombrich 1988; and for an account of the aesthetics and cultural logic of exorcism as a form of ritual healing in Sri Lanka, see Kapferer 1983.)

2.6. BUDDHISM AND FOLK RELIGION IN TIBET

In the preceding sections we have focussed specifically on Theravada Buddhism – 'the school of the elders,' reputed to be the most ancient of all the schools of Buddhism – as it was practised in three social contexts: Burma, Thailand, and Sri Lanka. We turn now to Tibetan Buddhism, which in many ways represents a synthesis of the three major forms or paths of Buddhism – Hinayana (Theravada), Mahayana (the great vehicle), and Vajrayana, or Tantric Buddhism. Indeed, it has been suggested that these represent three different stages in the development of Buddhism, each with its own value orientation: early Theravada Buddhism emphasized psychology, ethical discipline, and monastic rule; Mahayana Buddhism added an emphasis on metaphysics and devotional rituals, together with the development of the Bodhisattva doctrine; and finally, after about 500 C.E., came the emergence of Vijrayana, with its emphasis on yoga and esoteric meditation (Sangharakshita 1990, 27; 1996, 29–30).

An aura of mystery surrounds Tibet, and, as Stephen Batchelor writes, the very thought of Tibetan Buddhism evokes a colourful and exotic imagery (1987, 14). Indeed, the well-known spiritualist Helena Blavatsky, a founder of the Theosophical Society (in 1875) is reputed to have had telepathic communications from spiritual beings in Tibet, whom she described as *Mahatmas* [great souls]. But whether or not she can be considered one of the founders of modern Buddhism is debatable (Lopez 2002, 1–5). In this section, however, I steer clear of the many esoteric books on Tibetan Buddhism and focus instead on Geoffrey Samuel's comprehensive anthropological and historical study, *Civilized Shamans* (1993).

In a decade when postmodernism was all the rage in academia, and anthropology was being systematically reduced to hermeneutics or to egocentric scholastic reverie, it was refreshing indeed to encounter a scholar – Geoffrey Samuel (1990) – who was advocating a reconstruction of anthropology as a 'natural science of society' (1990, 4), with an emphasis, like that of Radcliffe-Brown, on situating human life not in 'culture' but within social life as a historical process. Although many of Samuel's suggestions for a new social scientific paradigm – which he terms a 'multimodal framework' – were not quite as novel as he envisaged, it nevertheless represented a worthy attempt to advance scholarship beyond the narrow confines of interpretive or symbolic anthropology, which is still in vogue (advocated, of course, by Clifford Geertz). Most of the essential tenets of Samuel's supposedly new paradigm – a move beyond positivistic science, a synthesis of the two dominant social epistemologies – methodological individualism (Popper) and holism (Durkheim), and the repudiation of Cartesian metaphysics with its inherent dualism (individual–society, body–mind, subject–object) – are, of course, hardly new; such tenets have long been a part of the social sciences (Morris 1991, 1997; Bunge 1996).

But what was important about Samuel's text is his insistence that there are 'multiple ways of knowing', that within any human society (or individual) one always finds the coexistence of several conceptual frameworks or cultural patterns. This too is hardly news, for in my earlier text, *Anthropological Studies of Religion* (1987), I emphasized that within the social sciences there are many different ways of interpreting or explaining religious phenomena – indeed, I suggested that even with writings of a single scholar many diverse theoretical (cultural) perspectives may be expressed. But Samuel's emphasis on a 'multimodal framework' is important, given the tendency of many anthropologists to conceive of 'culture' either as a 'totalising ritual schema' or, in equal monadic fashion, as a 'symbolic order' (Douglas 1966), or, alternatively, as with the postmodernists, to emphasize, almost to the point of *Reductio ad Absurdum*, the incoherence and fragmentary nature of cultural discourses, as a 'montage of polyphony', even questioning whether the very concept of 'culture' has any meaningful place in anthropological theory (Morris 2000, 99). Samuel steers his analysis between these two extremes, emphasizing the diversity of different cultural schemas or conceptual frameworks within any historical or social context (1990, 59–61).

In premodern Tibet the main forms of subsistence focussed around agriculture and pastoralism, although long-distance trade was important and was largely under the control of the monks within the religious establishments. The society was diverse and complex. In remote areas, relatively autonomous agricultural communities and pastoralists were found; several independent petty states also existed, but in the agricultural heartland of central Tibet around Lhasa there developed a highly stratified society, with large estates owned by aristocratic families or monasteries, and with a highly centralized and powerful theocracy under the Dalai Lama, who was both a religious leader and head of the government administration, thus combining spiritual and temporal power. Peasants were tied to the land as 'serfs' and under the control of the landed aristocracy, and although one may debate whether this system can be described as 'feudal', nevertheless prior to the Second World War there were large monastic centres near Lhasa (of the Gelugpa tradition), highly exploitative reltations between the rulers and peasants, and a political regime that wielded great power, bolstered by shamanic Buddhism. Between ten and fifteen per cent of the male population were monks, which constituted a large section of the population to be supported by the labour of others. Some of the larger monasteries housed several thousand monks. But Samuel emphasizes that the Dalai Lama's regime at Lhasa, though a powerful state, did not cover the whole of Tibet, and, compared with the states that developed in Sri Lanka and South-East Asia, it was a relatively weak (i.e., a feudal-like) state. He suggests that the Tibetan state and estate system was not 'oppressive' (a highly debatable issue), and the fact that it was not effectively 'centralized' allowed tantric or shamanic Buddhism to develop and become dominant in Tibetan society (1993, 39–142).

Following an earlier generation of Buddhism scholars, Samuel suggests that within Tibet there are three basic religious orientations or spheres of activity. These are as follows:

1. **Pragmatic.** This orientation is concerned with this-worldly goals, such as health, prosperity, and social well-being. In religious terms – Samuel tends to completely bypass secular modes of thought – this involves interactions with and often protection against local gods and spirits. This is carried out by a variety of ritual practitioners within the folk religion, but whereas in Theravada societies this tends *not* to be the concern of the Buddhist monks, in Tibet the Buddhist lamas also employ tantric rituals to deal with these this-worldly problems and issues.
2. **Karma.** This orientation – Spiro's Kammatic Buddhism – is focussed around the doctrine of rebirth and the 'ideology of merit', as mediated by both the Buddhist monks and lamas. Samuel suggests that this is the primary realm of clerical Buddhism.

3. **Bodhi.** This is the salvation tradition of Buddhism, which Spiro describes as Nibbanic Buddhism, and which in Theravadin societies is almost exclusively the concern of monks. But in Tibet, the Bodhi sphere of religious activity is associated not only with celibate monks, clerical Buddhism, but also with the lamas, and what Samuel describes as shamanic Buddhism, and is thus carried out largely through tantric practices (Samuel 1993, 5–32).

Thus in Tibet we find, according to Samuel, two radically different forms of Buddhism, clerical and shamanic, which are seen to coexist with the folk religion, the latter being interpreted by Samuel as a separate religious tradition involving spirits and deities. There are thus essentially three religious traditions in Tibet, and we discuss each of these in turn, although in practice they are closely interwoven and cannot be identified with any specific person or social institution.

The pre-Buddhist religion of Tibet was probably some form of animism or spirit religion, and has often been described as Bon religion. Focussed around deities and spirits, it has been described as the 'indigenous shamanistic religion' of Tibet (Sangharakshita 1996a, 21). Early scholars all described Bon as a form of shamanism and suggest that it entailed a belief in the spirits of the earth and sky and in various deities, and that the principal rites involved propitiation, exorcism, and divination (Waddell 1972, 19; Bell 1992, 8–10; Hoffmann 1979). Although recognizing that there may be grounds for describing the early religion of Tibet as Bon, Samuel prefers to describe the contemporary cults of gods and spirits as 'folk religion' (1993, 12). He agrees with the earlier scholars that the folk religion is shamanic, and, like Michael Harner (1980), he defines shamanism as involving altered states of consciousness and as constituting a dualistic worldview. As he writes, shamanic ritual practitioners are held 'to communicate with a mode of reality alternative to, and more fundamental than, the world of everyday experience' (1993, 8).

In these terms, it is akin to the ultra-rationalism of Plato and Descartes, implying a dualistic and idealist metaphysic and a devaluation of empirical experience. Yet Samuel also tells us that the universe the Tibetans 'perceive' includes gods, demons, and enlightened beings (1993, 157). Granting that life in Tibet has an element of risk and unpredictability, Samuel finds it understandable that the activities of the deities associated with natural phenomenon are a major focus of concern (1993, 161).

In general terms, there are four categories of spiritual beings [*lha*]: the tantric gods [*yidam*], who form a group of 'powerful symbolic entities', who act as protectors, and who are contacted through rituals or experienced through visionary states; the Buddhist deities who are generally well disposed towards humans; the local deities that are associated with lakes, mountains, and other natural phenomena; and, finally, the malevolent spirits and ghosts that are opposed to humans and the dharma (Samuel 1993, 161–6). Throughout Tibet there are what one writer calls 'power places' (Dowman 1988), sites that have specific meanings or associations with particular deities or people; mountains and lakes identified with specific deities, caves where in the past holy lamas have meditated, particularly those associated with Padmasambhava, otherwise known as Guru Rimpoché. Padmasambhava is one of the most remarkable figures in the entire history of Buddhism in Tibet. A native of Swat (in north-east Pakistan), Padmasambhava was a tantric teacher and adept at magical rites and was mainly responsible, during a short visit, for establishing Buddhism in Tibet towards the end of the eighth century. Through his occult powers he was able, as an enlightened Buddhist, to 'conquer' or 'tame' the deities and spirits associated with the Tibetan landscape – and such spiritual agencies were obliged to submit to the Buddhist dharma (Snelling 1987, 196). The Guru Rimpoché – the term *Rimpoché* means 'great jewel' and is used to address high-ranking monks and incarnate lamas – is now regarded as a major tantric deity. Padmasambhava is also considered the founder of the *nyingma*, or 'old school', of Tibetan Buddhism and as the ideal exemplar of Buddhahood, or the enlightened being. Samuel notes that the tantric deities are considered more powerful than the 'worldly gods' and thus 'enable a competent lama to keep the worldly gods in order' (1993, 167–8).

Throughout Tibet there are shrines and temples dedicated to various spirits and deities, and offerings are made to them through specific rituals [*sang*]. Spirit-mediums [*lhapa* – literally, a spirit-person], who may include both men and women and who become shamans through the classical form of initiation, often overcoming a serious illness, play an important role as mediators between the deities and spirits and humans. This is mainly achieved through possession, and the spirit-mediums have essentially a 'pragmatic' orientation and are primarily involved in curing rituals and divination. Samuel's study, however, has little detail on their medical functions or on whether or not the spirit-mediums may be a focus of peripheral cults in rural areas. Many of the spirit-mediums are, in fact, attached to the monasteries and serve as 'oracle priests', acting on behalf of the dharma in controlling 'disorderly' spirits and deities. But in 'premodern' Tibetan society, there were many other 'unorthodox' ritual practitioners – including 'crazy siddhas' [*drubnyon*], finders of hidden treasure [*terton*], and visionary bards [*babdrung*] (Samuel 1993, 290–308).

Shamanic rituals, however, are only *one* aspect of the folk religion, and most rituals do not involve altered states of consciousness. One scholar, in fact, has suggested that to refer to the pre-Buddhist religion in Tibet as 'shamanism' is entirely misleading, as it essentially involved non-shamanic rituals (Kvaerne 1984, 269).

What is of particular interst to Samuel is the similarity between spirit-possession and the system of incarnate lamas [*trulku*], for such lamas are seen as incarnations or 'emanations' of specific Buddhist personages – bodhisattva (enlightened beings) or Buddhist tantric deities (Samuel 1993, 195).

For Samuel, clerical Buddhism is equivalent to what Spiro refers to as Nibbanic Buddhism – an activity focussed almost exclusively around celibate monks [*gelong*], who are concerned primarily with salvation and thus express most clearly the Bodhi orientation. Their primary mode of activity, Samuel suggests, is scholarship, philosophical analysis, and monastic discipline, and its typical figure is the scholar– monk studying texts or involved in philosophical debates. Clerical Buddhism is focussed on Hinayana and Mahayana texts [*sutras*], and Indian Buddhist philosophy, with its emphasis on insight meditation [*prajna*] and the understanding and experience of the void or emptiness [*sunyata*]. Buddhist monks within the gelugpa school, founded by Tsongkhapa in the fourteenth century and otherwise known as the 'yellow hats', are seen by Samuel to emphasize the clerical approach. The gelugpa school rose to political dominance from the sixteenth century onwards, the state ruler, the Dalai Lama, belonging to this tradition, combining spiritual and temporal power, and some of its larger monasteries near Lhasa housed around 5,000 monks. But Samuel also emphasizes that the gelugpa expressed a 'synthesis' of clerical and shamanic Buddhism (1993, 499). Samuel suggests that clerical Buddhism *both* dismisses activity within the cycle of 'rebirth' as 'irrelevant' and that the karma orientation is the 'primary realm' of clerical Buddhism (1993, 10–31). But essentially, the karma orientation and the importance of merit or virtuous action [*sodnam*] is primarily the concern of neither shamanic nor clerical monks but of the Buddhist laity. For the celibate Buddhist monks who observe the ethical precepts and follow moralistic discipline, the bodhi orientation is their paramount concern, while Samuel suggests that the tantric practices of shamanic Buddhism tends to weaken the significance of both karma and monaticism (1993, 207).

The final religious tradition in Tibet that Samuel describes is that of shamanic Buddhism. This is the well-known tantric Buddhism (Vajrayana) that is focussed around the lama, who is usually a kind of monk proficient in both the theory and practice of the tantras. The term *lama* is roughly equivalent to the Indian *guru*, and essentially means a religious teacher, but in Tibet it can have diverse meanings, including that of a tantric practitioner. A lama does not necessarily have to be a celibate monk. Certain lamas are seen as reincarnations of their predecessors, or past Bodhisattva, and are thus described as *tulkus* – incarnate lamas (Sangharakshita 1996a, 61–3). The Dalai Lama, the head of the Tibetan state, is regarded as a manifestation of Avalokiteshvara, a tantric deity–bodhisattva who personifies compassion. Shamanic or tantric Buddhism involves rituals of prostration, the chanting of mantras, and, most important, an altered state of consciousness involving visualizations. Indeed, as Sangharakshita emphasizes, visualization plays an extremely important part in tantric meditation (1996a, 112). The visualization may be of tantric deities or personages such as Avalokitesvara, Tara, or Amitabha; of a mandala, which is a symbolic representation of the cosmos, incorporating several deities; or of Sambiyogakaya, which is conceived as a subtle manifestation of a Buddha's presence. But as Sangharakshita and Samuel stress, these visions or images are seen less as some kind of spirit entity, but rather as the emanation of specific qualities or consciousness of a Bodhisattva. As Samuel puts it, the tantric deities [*yidam*] 'are less autonomous spirit entities than symbolic devices to activate particular modes of being or particular ways of living' (1993, 247–8; Sangharakshita 1996a, 109–13). Indeed, visionary experiences of tantric deities–bodhisattva are seen as more 'real' than the experiences of everyday life.

What is important about shamanic (tantric) Buddhism in Tibet is that it is not only focussed on salvation for its practitioners – the Bodhi orientation–but that the tantric lama is also engaged in using his occult powers to help the lay population. Thus the lama also has a pragmatic or this-worldly orientation, conducting rituals to empower the individual and to counteract the influence of malevolent spirits (Samuel 1993, 259–67).

Samuel is concerned to emphasize the aesthetic and psychological aspects of shamanic Buddhism, tends to downplay its political significance, and is clearly unhappy with the suggestion that it may have an ideological function in bolstering the power of the Tibetan theocratic state. As he clearly put it,

> 'I am more inclined to view Tibetan Buddhism as one of the great spiritual and psychological achievements of humanity than as an ideological justification for the oppression of Tibetan serfs by their overlords.' (1993, 5)

Like many contemporary anthropologists, Samuel seems to have the mistaken impression that any emphasis on the political and economic aspects of religious phenomena implies either a reductive form of materialism or a Cartesian dualistic metaphysic that rigidly separates the 'material' and the 'mental'. Marxists, emergent materialists, and critical realists repudiate *both* these theoretical strategies, as well as the spiritualist metaphysic that Samuel seems implicitly to uphold and endorse (cf. Collier 1994; Bunge 1996; Callinicos 1999; Reyna 2002). (For further studies of Tibetan Buddhism, see Dargyay 1978; Tucci 1980; Paul 1982.)

2.7. BUDDHISM AND THE STATE

It is beyond the scope of this present study to explore in detail the complex and intrinsic relationship between religion and politics, but I conclude this chapter with a brief discussion of the relationship between the Buddhist dharma and the state. As noted earlier, Buddhism has often been characterized as an other-worldly religion, especially by Max Weber (1958), as essentially apolitical, the monks divorcing themselves from worldly concerns and, following Buddha's message, being focussed entirely on their own salvation and that of other sentient beings. This is indeed how many Buddhist monks and lay people interpret their religion and may be deeply opposed to the involvement of the sangha or Buddhists generally, in political activities. They base this opposition on the classical Buddhist distinction between the empirical world [*laukika*] and the sacred or supraworldly domain [*lokotarra*] (Spiro 1970, 392; Sangharakshita 1986, 84–91).

But this interpretation of Buddhism in somewhat misleading, for throughout its history there has been something of a 'symbiotic relationship', as Spiro describes it (1970, 379), between the monastic order of Buddhism [*sangha*] and state power – or at least the government as the embodiment of the state. Studies of early Indian political philosophy suggest that the Buddhist attitude to the state (kingship) was one of 'antagonistic symbiosis' (Gunawardana 1979, 344), the state using its coercive power to protect, support, and maintain the sangha, and if need be purify the Order; while the order of monks, though theoretically independent of the state and aloof from politics, nevertheless gave the state ideological support and moral justification. The order became the 'conscience of the government' while at the same time serving to legitimate state power. As in Islamic societies, the existence of coercive state power and centralized government was taken for granted in Buddhist writings. Throughout the history of Buddhism in South-East Asia, the king and the sangha have always therefore tended to support to each other. This was equally true in Tibet, with its theocratic state based at Lhasa in the agricultural 'heartland' of central Tibet. This state was less an expression of a symbiosis between state power and Buddhism than a melding together of political (coercive), economic (trade being especially important), and ideological (shamanic) forms of power. The traditional formula for the Tibetan state under the Dalai Lama was 'religion and politics' combined – even if the powers of the state did not extend to all Tibetan-inhabited regions (Schwartz 1999, 230). However, it is worth noting that almost all early states and empires were based on shamanic power, or ritual suzerainty, including that of Genghis Khan as well as that of the Dalai Lama. Samuel tends, rather misleadingly, to associate shamanism with equality, mutual aid, and insurgency against state power, while reason is almost identified with bureaucratic rationality, clerical Buddhism, state power, and the ethic of domination over nature (1990, 122–7). But shamanism itself implies a spiritual hierarchy, a devaluation of the empirical world, and evinces not equality and reciprocity but charismatic (shamanic) power. This form of power is intrinsically related to the rise of the early states, even if these tributary or feudal-like states, like those of Tibet, Mongolia, or early-modern Europe, may have had limited coercive power (Mann 1986).

Many studies have explored the complex and intrinsic 'symbiotic' relationship between state power and the Buddhist sangha. They have shown how the order of monks received material privileges from the government, how often monks played important roles in the bureaucratic administration, and how they often served as essential 'middle men' between the people and the government. Equally important, the monastic foundations, supported by the state, were primary seats of literacy and learning. In return, the sangha has generally supported state power, although given their different historical trajectories, the relationship between politics and Buddhism in Asian societies has been complex and somewhat variable (Smith 1965; Spiro 1970, 378–95; Tambiah 1976; Harris 1999).

But Buddhism, specifically the monks, has also played an important role in both anticolonial struggles and independence movements throughout Asia, but particularly in Burma and Sri Lanka. In both countries, Buddhist monks were active in resistance movements against colonial rule and, particularly in the years prior to the Second World War, played a leading role in the independence movement. Buddhism thus became, as Spiro put it, 'the rallying cry of the early nationalists' in Burma, as well as in Sri Lanka (1970, 384). Equally important, in both countries, Buddhism was transformed from a universal religion into an 'ethnic religion' and came to be identified with Burmese and Sri Lankan nationalism. After independence, in both countries, Buddhism came to be interpreted in fundamentalist terms; Burmese and Sri Lankan identity was thus identified with Buddhism. In Burma (Myanmar), for example, under U Nu, who was prime minister in the years after independence (in 1948) and a devout Buddhist, Buddhism became the state religion. Ecclesiastical courts and a Buddhist Council were established, with Buddhism and the sangha restored to their pre-colonial status and pre-eminence, and Buddhism, through a constitutional amendment, was established as the state religion. There was thus a fusion of Buddhism and national identity. Some Buddhist monks, filled with more nationalist fervour than U Nu, pillaged Indian shops, burned mosques, and generally harassed non-Buddhists and insisted that Buddhists be given preferential treatment in all social matters (Spiro 1970, 385–91; Matthews 1999, 33–5).

A similar state of affairs emerged in Sri Lanka, where Buddhism was intrinsically identified with Sinhalese nationalism. This was particularly well expressed in the treatise, *The Betrayal of Buddhism* (1956), which stressed the historical links among Buddhism, the state, and the Sinhalese people. It was also well expressed by the radical scholar–monk Walpola Rahula (1974), who closely identified Buddhism with Sinhalese nationalism (see the critique of Sangharakshita 1986, 69–91). This intrinsic linkage between Sinhalese nationalism and Buddhism is related to the current ethnic conflict and collective violence in Sri Lanka, which has been critically explored by several anthropologists (Kapferer 1988; Spencer, 1990; Tambiah 1992; Bartholomeusz 1999).

We can but conclude therefore that Buddhism was not only a powerful factor in anti-colonial struggles but has also played an important role in the formation of the modern state in many Asian countries.

3

Islam and Popular Religion

3.1. PROLOGUE

Contemporary anthropologists continually inform us – as if this had not been recognized by an earlier generation of scholars – that Islam, like shamanism, is not some monolithic entity with a unitary 'essence', but rather a cultural tradition that takes diverse forms, according to various social and historical contexts. As Dale Eickelman wrote, the main challenge for the study of Islam in its local contexts 'is to describe and analyse how the universalistic principles of Islam have been realised in various social and historical contexts without representing Islam as a seamless essence on the one hand, or as a plastic congeries of beliefs and practices on the other' (1982, 1–2). This is not, of course, how many Muslims view Islam. The well-known Islamic scholar, Seyyid Hossein Nasr, for example, suggests that Islam 'is at once a religion, and a civilisation and social order based upon the revealed principles of the religion. It is an archetypal reality, residing eternally in the Divine Intellect'. And he goes on to emphasize the integrity and unity of the Islamic tradition (1981, 1–2). The view that Islam is to be defined essentially as a religious 'tradition' is also confirmed by Talal Asad, who writes, 'Islam is neither a distinctive social structure nor a heterogeneous collection of beliefs, artefacts, customs and morals. It is a tradition' (1986, 14). Yet though a tradition, this does not imply an unchanging or unitary set of principles that exist independently of social life and historical circumstances. Moreover, within any particular socio-historical context there may coexist, within the Islamic tradition, several alternative and often competing ideologies and practices, each with their own adherents and advocates. Often particular individuals or groups, especially Islamic reformists, will declare that their own brand of Islam is the only 'true' Islam and come to dismiss, or disparage, many local cultural practices as non-Islamic. Thus what is important is not only the diversity of different beliefs and practices within Islam but also the structures of authority and power that determine which ideas and institutions are given priority. Asad goes so far as to suggest that a practice is Islamic 'because it is authorised by the discursive traditions of Islam' (1986, 15). Although emphasizing the link between belief and authority, it leaves open the question as to exactly which cultural traditions are considered Islamic. As Gregory Starrett writes, 'the definition of what is or is not "Islamic" is likely not to be about how closely society mirrors a known textual blueprint as about how and by whom specific texts are used to underwrite specific practices and general notions of authority' (1997, 288). Islamic orthodoxy therefore is an expression of a relationship of power.

Another misleading tendency is to identify Islam with the Middle East, whereas in fact the majority of Muslims do not speak Arabic and are not from this region. Some forty per cent of the total Muslim population is to be found in South Asia, and nearly half of the world's 1 billion Muslims live in South-East Asia. Indonesia alone contains almost as many Muslims as in all of the Arab states of the Middle East (Ahmed 1988, 5; Eickelman 2002, 13. For useful studies of the Indonesian context, see Peacock 1978; Woodward 1989; Hefner 2000).

One final point before the contents of the present chapter are outlined relates to the tendency of many scholars to overemphasize the importance of religion and to suggest that all cultural practices are 'basically religious' and that religion permeates all aspects of everyday life in Muslim countries. Culture is thus almost equated with religion, and Islam is seen as a motivational system that determines the social activities of all Muslims (Patai 1952). Although religion undoubtedly has an important influence on people's lives and their sense of identity, many other beliefs, concepts, motivations, and activities influence their social life, besides those of religion (Starrett 1997, 282). Indeed, Mary Douglas suggested that the Basseri nomads of Persia, though Muslims, have a secular orientation and take their religion about as seriously as do members of a typical London suburb. She therefore suggested that anthropologists should 'ditch the myth of the pious primitive' that she had earlier espoused (1975, 81).

Let me now outline the content of this chapter on Islam. In the next section I give, in broad outline, an account of the Islamic tradition as a religion of revelation – which contrasts of course with Buddhism as a religion of discovery (Sangharakshita 1987, 146–55). After outlining the early history of Islam, I discuss some of its essential tenets – its lack of a priesthood and the Five Pillars that constitute its orthopraxy, or core rituals of the faith. In the following two sections (Sections 3.3 and 3.4), I outline the nature and function of Zar cults in two ethnographic contexts – Somalia and the Sudan. Focussed largely around women, these spirit-cults represent an alternative form of religiosity to that of the dominant Islam, even though they form an intrinsic part of folk Islam. I then turn to the more political aspects of Islam and in Section 3.5 discuss Gellner's theory of 'two styles' of Islam and the role of the religious cleric [*ulama*] and the saint in Islam. In the following section, I discuss the Hamadsha Sufi brotherhood in Morocco, and in the last section of the chapter I outline the relationship between Islam and politics in Morocco, focussing on the political sociology of the reformist movement. The chapter as a whole is thus essentially focussed around the role of scholars, saints, and spirit-cults in contemporary Islamic societies.

3.2. THE ISLAMIC TRADITION

As a religion, Islam, as is well known, derives from the visionary revelations of one Muhammad Ibn Abdullah, who was born in Mecca around 570 C.E. Orphaned as a boy, he grew up under the care of his maternal uncle and other relatives, members of the Quraysh tribe, who were important locally as merchant traders. Mecca at that period was an important commercial centre situated on the trade route between the Byzantium and Persian empires and the South Arabian kingdoms. A mercantile economy, as Rodinson writes, was 'growing up in the chinks of the nomadic world', market transactions were becoming commonplace, and the 'disintegration of tribal society had begun' (1971, 36). Mecca was also an important pilgrim centre, for one of its shrines held the Ka'ba, a black stone of meteoric origin, which was held in special veneration by the surrounding tribes.

As a young man, Muhammad became an employee of a rich widow named Khadija, whom he later married at the age of twenty-five, she being somewhat older. Under her employ he travelled widely as a merchant. Well-respected and trusted, comfortably placed, and seemingly happily married and the father of four daughters (two sons died in infancy), Muhammad nevertheless appears to have spent long periods alone, meditating on a nearby hillside. Around the age of forty, he began to have visions, the Angel Gabriel appearing to him and ordering him to 'recite'. Troubled by these visions initially, Muhammad, supported by his wife and his cousin Ali, eventually came to see himself as a prophet or messenger of God, and the Arabic verses [*suras*] that were disclosed to him came to form the Quran. Although Jewish communities and various Christian groups had long been settled among the Bedouin tribes of western Arabia, and so monotheistic ideas were familiar, coexisting with the animistic beliefs of the tribal peoples, the essential message of the Quran was an uncompromising monotheism.

Muhammad clearly believed himself to be the last – the 'seal' – of a long line of prophets (which included Abraham, Moses, and Jesus) and to have been commissioned with the sole duty of conveying God's message of salvation to humankind. He claimed no miraculous powers, nor did he see himself as incarnating the spirit of God; Jesus too in the Quran is held to be simply a messenger, a prophet, not God incarnate (Gibb 1969, 40–1). Islam is therefore very much the religion of the 'book', for the words of the Quran, as revealed to Muhammad, are believed to be those of God. Also prominent in the message is the notion of a coming day of judgement, a cataclysmic event, the timing of which is known only to God. On this last day, both humans and jinns (who, unlike humans, are created of fire, not of earth) will be called to account.

Conscious of being a prophet for the Arabs – who had not as yet been sent a prophet – Muhammad nonetheless preached a universal message. But besides a few close kin and friends, who accepted his prophetic vision, Muhammad's claims and message were ill-received among the Quraysh tribes of Mecca. His message was treated with scepticism and mockery and some hostility, no doubt because he proclaimed against the pagan rites and the unscrupulous pursuit of profit and wealth, and this, it was sensed, would adversely affect the trade associated with Mecca as a pilgrim centre. Thus it was that the prophet and his supporters were eventually forced to leave Mecca, and the year of this migration (hijrah or flight), 622 C.E., marks the beginning of the Muslim chronology. Muhammad was fifty-two years old. But his departure from Mecca was not under conditions of panic and desperation for, impressed by his political sagacity, the people of the neighbouring town of Yathrib (Medina) invited Muhammad to take refuge there and to mediate between the various contending factions that threatened the stability of the town. Lying some 200 miles north-west of Mecca, Muhammad already had connections with Medina; it was the home of his grandmother, and his father Abdullah had died and was buried there.

At Medina, his visions continued, and it was there that he organized a religious community as a theocratic city–state. In setting up such a community [*umma*], Muhammad seemed to combine both religious charisma and a high degree of moral rectitude and courage, with remarkable political acumen, especially in suggesting ways of compromise and conciliation. Eventually, after several years of shifting fortunes, he led an army that defeated the Quraysh tribes of Mecca and returned in triumph to the town in 630 C.E., two years before his death (for important studies of Muhammad's life, see Watt 1961; Rodinson 1971; Lings 1983; Combs-Schilling 1989, 49–76).

Having united the Bedouin tribes of western Arabia into a political unit, Muhammad laid the foundation for its further expansion, and in less than a century Islam had spread through the entire Near East, and Arab supremacy ranged from Persia, Iraq, and Syria, west to Morocco and Spain. It thus became one of the world's great religions, and it has exerted an enormous influence not only on the cultural and political life of these regions but also on the development of western culture itself (for useful discussions on the history and culture of Islam, see Rahman 1967; Gibb 1969; Hitti 1971; Hodgson 1974; Ahmed 1988; Esposito 1988; and on western views of Islam, see Said 1978; Rodinson 1987).

An Islamic anthropologist suggests that perhaps one of the appeals of Islam was its essential simplicity (in spite of its underlying profundity): one god, one book, one prophet. And it was a tidy, rather uncomplicated form of religion with a clearly defined set of core rituals (Ahmed 1988, 17). Much earlier, Cantwell Smith had noted that Islam tended not to have a clearly defined set of orthodox beliefs but rather an orthopraxy, a common core of ritual practices (1957, 28). These are embodied in the 'Five Pillars' of Islam.

Islam, unlike orthodox Christianity, has no hierarchy of priests, no clergy, no body of dogma laid down by a religious elite. And although it has religious scholars [*ulama*], these are in no sense mediators between the individual and God. In an important sense, as Gellner (1981) observes, the divine message of Islam is complete and final and is set fourth in the holy book, the Quran, and in the body of traditions [*hadith*] relating to what the prophet said and did in various circumstances. The term *sunna* refers to the customs and codes of behaviour indicated in these oral traditions. Given these guidelines, it is not surprising that Islam is a legalistic and ritualistic religion that places a great stress on the observance of the law [*shari'a*] as denoted in the Quran. The term *Islam*, in fact, connotes 'submission' or 'surrender' to the will of God. There can therefore be no rigid demarcation between the secular and sacred dimensions of social life, and the ulama are both lawyers and theologians. Moreover, there is a pronounced egalitarian emphasis in Islam, for the individual believer has a direct, unmediated relationship with God, and his or her religious duties are clearly laid down in the well-known 'Five Pillars' of Islam:

First, the explicit profession of faith, *shahadah*, embodied in this simple formula: '*la ilaha illa allah, Muhammadum rasula allah*' [there is no god but god, and Muhammad is the messenger (*rasul*) of god].

Second, prayer, *salah*. There is an obligation on every Muslim to pray five times a day, after performing the necessary ablutions for ritual cleanliness. All Muslims should therefore ritually cleanse themselves, face Mecca, and pray at dawn, noon, mid-afternoon, sunset, and dusk. Only one congregational prayer is enjoined – on Friday at noon. It is suggested by many Muslims that the prayers symbolize humanity's equality before god and their submission or surrender (*islam*) to god's will – although there is always a strict separation of men and women.

Almsgiving (*zakah*) is the Third Pillar of the Islamic faith, canon law suggesting that a person should give up a portion of his or her wealth, beyond that needed for sustenance, to 'purify' what is retained. This portion is put aside for the welfare of the poor and needy and is in effect a tax on one's possessions.

The Fourth Pillar of Islam is fasting [*sawn*], to be undertaken from dawn until dusk during the month of Ramadan, the ninth month of the calendar year and the one in which the Quran was revealed. It is said to be the month of repentance and purification.

The pilgrimage [*haj*] to Mecca is the last and final pillar, and all Muslims are expected, if economically and physically able to do so, to visit Mecca at least once during their lifetime. Mecca is the centre of Islam's sacred geography, and the pilgrimage has important social and symbolic significance, reflecting an ethos of what Victor Turner (1969) called *communitas* (on the Five Pillars, see Mawdudi 1980, 93–100; Glassé 1989; Eickelman 2002, 250–6).

Although Islam as a religious tradition is complex and multifaceted, it is, as Ioan Lewis writes, first and foremost a creed enjoining specific, public, and observable ritual practices, which are embodied in the Five Pillars (1999, 98).

The philosopher and sociologist Ernest Gellner suggested that there was a close, indeed intrinsic, relationship between Islam as a religious system and normative social life. As he wrote,

Islam is the blueprint of a social order. It holds that a set of rules exists, eternal, divinely ordained, and independent of the will of man, which defines the proper ordering of society. This model is available in writing; it is equally and symmetrically available to all literate men, and to all those willing to heed literate men. These rules are to be implemented throughout social life. (1981, 1)

This perspective, which reflects that of many educated Muslims, tends to imply that Islam, as a normative system, exists independently of any social context. Yet although the blueprint can be located with some precision, its implementation and manifestation in specific historical contexts are extremely variable. There is thus no simple relationship between what is expressed in the textual tradition – what Gellner and Starrett refer to as the 'high culture' and the local social manifestations of the Islamic tradition (Starrett 1997, 282).

3.3. ZAR CULTS IN NORTHERN SOMALIA

Ioan Lewis has written extensively both on the modern history of Somalia and on the social dynamics of spirit-possession cults in north-east Africa. His comparative studies of shamanism and spirit-possession have been seminal, though the subject of much controversial debate. But before discussing his more general theories, I outline the role of spirit-possession among the Somali pastoralists, as described by Lewis (1969, 1971).

The northern Somali are essentially pastoral nomads living in what is generally an arid and uncertain environment. Their principal wealth consists of sheep, goats, and camels. Strongly patrilineal, their social organization is focussed around small lineage groups, which are mobilized in disputes and feuds. In contrast with many Muslim communities, marriage within these groups is forbidden. Sexual relationships among the northern Somali are decidedly unequal, and women are subject to direct jural control by their menfolk. Although men can divorce their wives very easily, it is much more difficult for the latter to instigate divorce, and a woman's right to inherit property, accepted under Islamic law, is very rarely honoured. Throughout most of their lives, Lewis suggests, women are treated very much as 'second-class citizens' (1969, 195). A woman is traditionally conceived as being weak and submissive, in contrast to men, who are culturally expected to show initiative, courage, and aggressiveness. It is considered 'unmanly' for men to show open affection for their wives or to reveal that they are emotionally dependent on them. Indeed, as Lewis notes (1971, 73), while the open display of affection and love between men and women is suppressed, the expression of love towards God is highly approved and is reflected in Somali mystical poetry. While woman's activities are generally confined to the domestic sphere and to the herding of sheep and goats, the men, as heads of household, have overall responsibility for the management of the herds and spend much of their time in political activities. They are thus often away from their wives and tents.

This pattern of activities is reflected in their religious activities, for Islam, as a public cult, is almost exclusively dominated by men, who hold all the major positions of religious authority and prestige. Although women are frequent visitors to the shrines of saints, they are not admitted to the mosques where men regularly pray. Nor do they participate in the activities of the mystical religious orders or 'brotherhoods', which play such a vital role in men's religious life (Lewis 1955). And finally, while a considerable number of men succeed in making the pilgrimage to Mecca [*haj*] – one of the Five Pillars of Islam – only a few women accomplish this act of devotion.

Islam, Lewis suggests, has none of the immediacy that is characteristic of tribal religion, for its orthodox doctrine stresses that man's conduct is judged in the hereafter. And this implies a separation between the social order and divine retribution, even though Muhammad's message is essentially this-worldly. Through prayer and sacrifice and the mediation of the prophet, God is approached to intervene in human affairs. But because the Somali consider that man is inherently sinful, and far removed from God's grace, they believe, Lewis writes, that powerful intermediaries are needed to plead with God, through the prophet. In this task, the Somali seek the help of holy men [*wadaad*] or saints [*weli*], who are believed to be endowed with mystical power, manifested in their blessing [*baraka*] and through their ability to administer sorcery or a curse to uphold their authority. Interestingly, as Lewis explores in another article (1963), there is a clear division amongst the Somali between secular and religious authority. Mystical power, however, extends over a wide spectrum, ranging from the power of the saints – whose power emanates directly from God – to that of the low-status Yibir soothsayers whose mystical power is associated with the devil [*shaydaan*]. Among the Somali, witchcraft, as this phenomenon is known elsewhere, does not figure prominently in the interpretation of misfortunes but spirit-possession does. Thus although Islam, at the level of orthodoxy, would appear to be strictly monotheistic, and the Somali have an extensive knowledge of herbal lore, nonetheless afflictions are often interpreted as the result of possession by certain spirits.

Known as *jinn* or *saar* (Zar) spirits they have spiritual warrant, being mentioned in the Quran. These spirits, which are anthropomorphic in character, are looked on as essentially malevolent. The fact that they are ultimately seen as under the control of God leads Lewis to suggest that they indicate the essential 'ambiguous character of the divinity' (1969, 192). There is no connection between the Zar spirits and either the lineage ancestors or the souls of the dead, and as the 'spirits cause disease [but] do not cure it', spirit-possession in the Somali context is distinct from shamanism. The spirits are found everywhere but are particularly associated with wild animals and with dark empty places. Incense is thought of as giving protection against the spirits and is therefore employed in exorcising them.

Although spirit-possession is associated with a wide range of illness and misfortune, ranging from bodily aches and pains and depression to epilepsy, it figures in only a limited and fairly clearly defined range of contexts. The general term for possession in Somali is *gelid*, meaning literally 'entering', and it is believed that the person is 'caught' and thus controlled by the spirit. Although the most common form of possession in Somali is that affecting women, young men in particular often become possessed by spirits. One form occurs in a situation of unrequited love, where a boy may have jilted a girl. In these circumstances, if the young man falls ill, it is often suspected that the girl who desires him, and whom he has abandoned, has possessed him. It is the 'girl' who is said to have 'entered' the boy, but this is seen metaphorically, for when pressed, the Somali explanation suggests that the girl has sent a jinn to trouble the man. Treatment of this illness consists in the exorcism of the offending 'spirit'. This is done by a holy man [*wadaad*] who recites passages from the Quran and burns incense – both of which have mystical power. During the treatment, the invading 'spirit' reveals herself and is alternately cajoled and threatened by the power of God to leave the man. In this context, the attack by the 'spirit' is direct and reflects private misunderstandings and disputes that cannot be vented in public, given the puritanical nature of Somali society.

Before marriage, young Somali men live a Spartan existence as camel herders. In the dry season especially, when water is scarce, they have to endure the rigours of hunger, thirst, and social isolation. In these circumstances, young herders often become 'hysterical', and this is interpreted as possession by a saar spirit. His companions arrange a ritual dance, known as 'beating the spirit', during which the man goes into a trance state and eventually collapses exhausted. It is explicitly cathartic, and when he recovers he speaks the Muslim creed 'There is no God but Allah and Muhammad is his prophet' – and this signifies his return to normal health.

In contrast to these two contexts, the spirit-possession associated with women is more complex, though it does not take on the form of an organized cult as in Ethiopia and elsewhere. The emphasis in Somali is on exorcism rather than on shamanism. A number of named saar spirits are believed to be responsible for the afflictions that affect women, especially married women. The term *saar* describes not only the spirit but the illness attributed to them. The stock epidemiological situation, writes Lewis, is,

> that of the hard-pressed wife, struggling to survive and feed her children in the harsh nomadic environment, and liable to some degree of neglect, real or imagined, on the part of her husband. Subject to frequent, sudden and often prolonged absences by her husband . . . to the jealousies and tensions of polygamy which are not ventilated in accusations of sorcery and witchcraft, and always menaced by the precariousness of marriage in a society where divorce is frequent and easily obtained by men, the Somali women's lot offers little stability or security. (1971, 75)

Lewis disclaims that this is an ethnocentric portrait but rather reflects the reality of the woman's position in Somali. It is in such circumstances that women's ailments, whether or not accompanied by physical symptoms, are interpreted as possession by the saar spirits. In their treatment, however, two interesting features emerge.

First, the treatment is always undertaken not by a holy man or saint but by a woman specialist or shaman [*alaaqad*] who is regarded as having authority over the spirits. Such ritual experts are invariably widows, childless women, or divorcees. Indeed, Lewis makes the significant point that women involved in the spirit-possession cults are usually those who do *not* conform to the Somali ideal of 'womanhood'.

Second, the treatment, which if serious may involve an elaborate costly séance, consists essentially of the appeasement of the possessing spirit by the presentation of luxurious gifts to the patients. The requests are articulated by the spirits, speaking through the afflicted women – and consumed with envy and greed, they demand such things as perfume, fine clothes, and expensive foods. The more elaborate rituals involve sacrificial offerings and a communal feast, all paid for by the husband of the patient. The standard male reaction to this situation, Lewis writes, is one of scepticism and to regard them as feigned, or as trivial complaints assumed by their wives to extort unnecessary luxuries and attentions from their menfolk. But as the reality of the spirits is not questioned – for they are mentioned in the Quran – men's attitudes towards these cult activities are ambivalent. Much depends on the marital circumstances as to whether the husband gives in to his wife's demands, articulated through the possession séance. Thus Lewis suggests that amongst the Somali, the spirit-possession cults focussed around women constitute a 'counterpart' to the 'official' cult of Islam, and operate as a

> limited deterrent against the abuses of neglect or injury in a conjugal relationship which is heavily biased in favour of men. Where they are given little domestic security and otherwise ill-protected from the pressures and exactions of men, women may thus resort to spirit-possession as a means both of airing their grievances obliquely, and of gaining some satisfaction. (1971, 77)

Lewis denies that this is an androcentric or ethnocentric portrayal of the predicament of Somali women and suggests that such women are far from being naïve, nor do they passively accept or endorse the subordinate position accorded to them by men (1971, 75).

Thus, as with many earlier scholars, Lewis concludes that the prominent role of women in spirit-possession cults can be interpreted as a 'compensation for their exclusion and lack of authority in other spheres' (1986, 27).

As we noted in Chapter 1, Lewis essentially interprets shamanism and spirit-possession cults as 'religions of the oppressed'.

With peripheral possession cults, these are considered 'protest cults' that enable individuals who lack political influence – especially women – to 'advance their interests and improve their lot, even if only temporarily, from the confining bonds of their allotted stations in society' (Lewis 1971, 127). Such cults often occur in societies where possession plays no part in the central religion, and, unlike the shamanistic cults described in Chapter 1, peripheral cults do not function to uphold a society's moral code. It is the central religion – Hinduism, Islam, Buddhism, Christianity, or in the African context, ancestral cults – that is moralistic and whose spirits support the status quo, afflictions being related to moral transgressions. There is a sense in which cults like that of the Zar are amoral and unconcerned with the social order. Thus Lewis suggests that these cults are 'peripheral' in three senses.

First, its membership comprises categories that are peripheral to the authority structure of the society, for members of such groups largely consist of women, men from low-status groups, and other deprived categories.

Second, the cult is peripheral to the moral order, being largely unconcerned, Lewis suggests, in upholding social mores. For instance, cult leaders or shamans often lead 'immoral' lives without this necessarily affecting their role as a 'medium' for the spirit.

And third, the spirits themselves are peripheral, invariably originating from or being associated with a domain outside the social order – they are, perhaps, nature or foreign spirits.

An interesting question arises regarding the relationship of spirit-possession to witchcraft, social phenomena that are related and that coexist in many communities. In such situations, Lewis suggests, spirit-possession can be seen as an oblique form of 'mystical attack', a form of redress that ventilates frustration and grievances without disturbing the established order of things. In the Zar cults, a woman's needs and aspirations are given expression without this necessarily leading to a rupture in the conjugal relationship. Indeed, the cults, as Constantinides suggests, are a subtle way in which an individual can adjust her position (given the support of the group) in 'relation to the instruments of social pressure' (1977, 84). Although Lewis sometimes overstresses the 'sex war' viewpoint, this too reflects his own standpoint. In contrast, Lewis suggests, witchcraft accusations represent a more drastic strategy, a direct form of 'attack' that seeks to break the relationship.

It is important to note that Lewis does not view the distinction between 'central' and 'peripheral' cults as ideal types but as functional categories reflecting the spirit-possession cults' relationship to power. Whether or not a particular cult is peripheral depends on a particular historical context, and Lewis is interested in exploring the historical transformations of such cults in relation to the power structures of a society.

An interesting aspect of Lewis' study is therefore his discussion of the relationship between the ecstatic and the ritual forms of religious expression and the 'cyclical' nature of religious movements. Following Weber, he writes that the 'extinction of enthusiasm is a built-in tendency' in the development of religious movements, and that many world religions – Christianity and Islam are cited as examples – had their origins as ecstatic cults. He therefore links spirit-possession cults with millenarian-type movements and other 'religions of the oppressed'

(Lanternari 1963), and suggests that such cults have either been discredited or have, in time, simply fizzled out. Some have retained a marginal and 'unofficial' existence as popular 'superstitions' or as separatist sects. But significantly, where peripheral cults have managed to establish themselves and become a dominant cult, then possession invariably tends 'to become relegated to the background and to be treated as a sign of dangerous potential subversion'. And Lewis continues,

So if it is the nature of new religions to herald their advent with a flourish of ecstatic effervescence, it is equally the fate of those which become successfully ensconced at the centre of public morality to lose their inspirational savour. (1971, 132)

But Lewis notes that complex economic and political factors influence the development of religious movements and that there is therefore no simple pattern. In given circumstances central shamanistic cults focussed on ancestral spirits may have a resurgence, and play a dynamic role in the reassertion of ethnic identity, and in countering political oppression through cultural forms. With the Kaffa of south-west Ethiopia, for example, their traditional ancestral cults have a political significance and coexist alongside Amhara Christianity, even though the Kaffa political system has been destroyed (1971, 147).

In subsequent essays, Lewis tended to reaffirm the essential premises of his study, *Ecstatic Religion* (1971). He is thus critical of the excessive concentration by anthropologists on the aesthetic, dramatic, and 'expressive' aspects of possession – the hermeneutic focus on 'meaning' and on the cognitive function of culture – to the exclusion of a sustained enquiry into the social and psychological functions of spirit-possession rites. He thus stresses that possession should be treated as a 'social institution', not simply as a cultural text, as with scholars like Boddy (discussed in the next section). Lewis also affirms the distinction between main morality cults that tend to relate misfortunes to moral transgressions and peripheral cults, in which the spirits (usually of foreign origin) bring disease and afflictions on a person, without any reference to moral infringements. Peripheral cults are thus non-moral in this specific sense. And, finally, Lewis argues that the prevalence of women in spirit-cults is essentially a reflection of the frustrations associated with their subordinate position in a male-dominated society. They thus enable women, for a limited time, to transcend the subordinate status normally accorded to them, putting pressure on their husbands and male kin, and thus achieving a degree of 'status enhancement' – without seriously challenging the established order of society (Lewis 1986, 96–103; 1999, 80–94).

The spirit-cults are thus essentially healing cults, a form of 'women's medicine', in which the responsibility for providing treatment for the spirit-afflicted wife falls largely on the husband. Hence, Lewis writes, in a context of domestic conflict 'the sick role has its compensations and strategic value, and can even be materially productive, not least when, through the demands of the spirit, the patient seeks relief in the regular performance of costly, placatory rituals' (1991, 2). But while stressing the essential dynamic aspects of the spirit-cults, and the fact that the spirit beliefs constitute a kind of 'spiritual reservoir' on which the afflicted women can draw, Lewis nevertheless affirms that the Zar therapy is essentially conservative, 'enabling women to adjust to and accept pressures in ways which do not radically challenge the existing, male-dominated order' (1991, 7). (For a further study of spirit-possession cults in southern Somalia, see Luling 1991.)

3.4. ZAR CULTS IN THE SUDAN

The 'Zar–Bori complex', as it was described by the French scholar Maxime Rodinson, is a widespread healing cult found throughout much of northern and north-eastern Africa, as well as in parts of the Middle East. It takes various forms in the Sudan, the Zar–Bori cults being particularly associated with women, while Zar–Tumbura is associated more particularly with men, especially those belonging to low-status groups, such as the descendants of ex-slaves (Constantinides 1991). The Zar–Bori cults have been the subject of numerous studies, but in this section I focus on the Sudan and draw on the important writings of two anthropologists in particular – Pamela Constantinides (1977, 1978) and Janice Boddy (1989).

Although widespread in the Islamic world, spirit-cults have periodically been condemned by the educated elite as unorthodox and as a type of superstition that inhibits progress. Nevertheless, as Constantinides points out, with respect to the Sudan, the Zar spirit-cults are by no means 'traditional' cults but were introduced into the Sudan in the early decades of the last century and seem to be indubitably associated with increasing urbanization and the pressures of modern life. They are essentially a means, she writes, of adapting to urban society. In the northern Sudan, such Zar cults are extremely popular among women. They constitute an ego-based group focussed around healing rites that in an important sense make the group.

Prior to the Turko-Egyptian conquest in 1821, much of the Sudan was characterized by a tribal pattern of social organization, each tribe having recognized tribal base. With the establishment of the colonial capital at Khartoum, this pattern began to break down, and subsequent decades saw much expansion in trade and in the development of administration and transport. The process of urbanization also increased, and there was an expansion of labour migration from the rural areas into the towns. However, large areas of rural Sudan still have a tribal orientation and there is a close association between tribe and territorial area. Within the tribal community, the villages are based on patrilineages, and marriage patterns on the whole are characterized by lineage and village endogamy. Thus, within the village community, an individual can trace some form of relationship with almost all other members of the village. This has important implications for the status of women, for it means that the system of sexual segregation and the seclusion of women, characteristic of town life, is much less marked in the rural areas. Coupled with the fact that a great reliance is placed on the labour of women in the rural economy – both domestic and agricultural – women in the villages have a certain degree of personal autonomy, and can, through their kinship ties, assert moral pressure on the men (Constantinides 1978, 192).

When a family moves into the urban situation, however, the range of a woman's social activity becomes severely restricted. She becomes isolated from her kin group, while at the same time the urban Islamic culture demands that she should seclude herself from unrelated males. In addition, the cash economy removes certain subsistence tasks from her, and allows her father and husband to support her in seclusion. It is in this social (and urban) context that the Zar cults assume a fundamental importance for women, and because they do not generally attend the formal group rituals of Islam, their participation in the Zar cults, as Constantinides writes, 'parallels men's participation in the religious brotherhoods' (1977, 64). In fact, as she notes, there are many similarities between the Zar cults and the brotherhoods.

The primary basis for recruitment into a Zar cult group is illness. The concept of illness in the Sudanese context is a wide one, for it not only includes a range of organic ailments but also a variety of social distresses such as anxieties about conflicts or problems in the home. Severe behavioural disorders, however, are classified as possession by jinn spirits that have to be exorcised by a male Islamic healer. But milder emotional disorders, which some might term neurotic, tend to be ascribed to possession by the Zar spirits. Such spirits are merely placated and remain bound to their hosts for life. The majority of cult leaders are women, and they are addressed as Shaikha. They normally become cult leaders by first suffering a spirit-caused illness, usually of a severe kind. Generally speaking, cult leaders attempt to seek a following that cuts across kinship and ethnic lines, though Constantinides suggests that their role is more that of a "fellow sufferer" than a shaman. When a new patient consults a cult leader, the diagnosis takes one of two forms. Either the cult leader will have what are thought to be spirit-inspired dreams and convey to the patient the nature of the demands made by the Zar spirit, or the patient will be invited to a cult ritual and there encouraged to enter into a trance and thus become a medium for a particular Zar spirit. Drumming and the administering of incense – specific to each spirit – are important elements in the ritual. When in a trance, the patient will speak in a spirit voice and through gestures indicate the spirit possessing her. Through the cult leader, the gestures will be interpreted and the requirements of the spirit ascertained. Often the demands of the spirit will include the mounting of a ritual, with spirit costumes and a sacrifice in its honour.

Although cult dogma has it that there are seven categories of spirits – seven having a mystical significance in Islam – Constantinides found that there were many types of spirit groups: Muslim saints, early administrators (including General Gordon), and a diverse number of spirits associated with ethnic categories. Each spirit has its associated drumbeat and incense.

The main possession ritual is an elaborate affair, lasting several days and involving considerable expense – which is met by the woman's husband. It is attended each day by, on average, thirty to a hundred women, those attending being either cult members or friends and kin of the patient. The symbolism of the rite is reminiscent of marriage, for the patient is called a 'bride of the Zar', and she is dressed as a bride with a red henna dye applied to her hands and feet. During the rite, although the focus of attention is on the patient, anyone initiated into the cult may dance and become possessed. As Constantinides writes,

> During the course of the dancing several women may achieve, or assume, a state of dissociation, the drumming, incense, rhythmic bodily jerking, and overbreathing, all being employed as techniques. Trance allows for considerable bodily and emotional abandon. The same women whose culture normally demands of them sedate, restrained behaviour may weep, tremble, rage, shriek, yelp, beat themselves violently against the ground, smoke and drink openly, or strut about arrogantly. (1977, 74)

However, this abandon occurs in a controlled manner, for different states of bodily abandon are associated with different spirit categories. The drumming and dancing continues for several days, the climax of the rite involving the sacrifice of two animals – a black male goat and a white or reddish male sheep. The sacrifice is considered a form of thanksgiving [*karaama*], as in the other principal Muslim festivals. During the sacrificial rite, the patient rides the animal, and, after the killing, she is anointed with the blood of the animal. She is also given a red handkerchief and the blood-stained knife of the sacrifice to hold in her right hand. The finale of the rite involves a symbolic purification with water, the cult leader and the patient washing in the river, where the remnants of the sacrifice are also disposed of.

Constantinides notes the colour symbolism involved in the possession rite, and the similarity in the meanings of the basic colour categories, white, black, and red, in Sudanese ritual to those postulated by Turner (1967). In Islam, white indicates divine blessing and purity and is the colour of mourning because it signifies spiritual rebirth. Holy men wear white. Black, in contrast, is an undesirable colour associated with sorcery and the evil eye, with severe illness leading to death, and with madness. The pervasive colour of the possession rite, however, is red. The Zar spirits themselves are said to be 'red winds', and the colour red is associated with heat, fertility, and earthly rebirth. It therefore mediates between black and white and reflects the fact that the possession rite is essentially a transition ritual.

Besides being a healing rite and offering an explanation for illnesses and misfortunes (however defined), the Zar cults also serve important social functions. They provide an opportunity for drama and entertainment, for those possessed enter a trance state and are able to express, through behaviour appropriate to specific spirits, a wide range of experience. The Zar cult, as Constantinides suggests, is also 'a key which opens out the social life of women in the towns', and membership of the cult counteracts the shrinkage of the woman's sphere of social activity in the urban setting. It provides for the social solidarity of women and represents not an attack on men in general, nor a repudiation of the women's traditional role, but rather 'backing' and support for women against individual men – the husband or father on whose interest and support a woman's status ultimately rests. A woman's aspirations centre on financial security and on her own and her husband's health and fertility. Anything that threatens these, be it her own ill health, infertility, or inadequate support by her spouse, needs to be counteracted – and this is often done through the Zar cult. A husband's willingness to accept a spirit-possession diagnosis and to bear the costs of a Zar ritual is a public affirmation of his concern for his spouse – supported as she is by the cult members (1978, 203).

Constantinides emphasizes that Sudanese women, whose lives are 'so immensely constricted by social forces outside their control', explain their misfortunes not as a result of their own moral transgressions but as due to external powers – the Zar spirits. After an initial 'personal crisis' they thus attempt to forge with these spirits an ongoing relationship. Those who adopt what she calls the 'sick role' tend to be women who for some reason or other fail to live up to their expected gender role – being unable to find a suitable, supportive husband; having an unsatisfactory marriage; failing to reproduce (she notes the high frequency of reproductive problems that are due to the practice of infibulation); or, more generally, failing to find any satisfaction in her life circumstances. Thus, through the Zar rituals, a woman can indirectly and symbolically regain some control over the conditions of her own existence. Thus, spirit-possession is centrally concerned with crises relating to marriage, fertility, and childbirth (Constantinides 1985, 688–9).

But Constantinides also emphasizes that women who are cult leaders, the Shaikha, generally do not conform to the norms and ideals of Sudanese womanhood – they are either divorced or widowed, and several are childless. They often engineered their own divorce, refused to be submissive to men, affirmed their own freedom of movement and action, and, as a medium for the spirits, suggested they had no real need for men (1985, 690).

In her studies of Zar cults in the market town of Sennar in central Sudan, Susan Kenyon (1995) likewise suggests that the Zar rituals are largely in the hands of women and provide a forum for women to voice their 'indirect opposition to developments that do not bode well for them'. As a form of embodied knowledge, Zar thus represents a set of strategies that enable women to make sense of their changing life circumstances and is therefore a form of 'modernization' (i.e., they relate to contemporary changing conditions). Kenyon notes that Zar rituals have been officially banned in the Sudan since 1992, but that the 'drums' still beat in the town.

Although Zar cults are particularly associated with urban contexts in the Sudan, for in places like Khartoum they are greatly elaborated and form organized cults – and sometimes media events – they are by no means restricted to the urban context. Janice Boddy's substantive ethnographic study, *Wombs and Alien Spirits* (1989), is thus specifically focussed on Zar cults in a small village in northern Sudan. Rich in ethnographic detail, the study largely confirms and illustrates the sociological theories of Lewis and Constantinides. The book, however, is mainly an exercise in cultural hermeneutics, and although she describes Lewis' work as 'illuminating' and engages herself in historical and sociological analysis, Boddy never loses an opportunity in the book, and in her review article (1994), to criticize, disparage, and denigrate any anthropologist who takes a social-scientific approach to spirit-possession or attempts in any way to go beyond the narrow contextual hermeneutics that she espouses. In her review article, for example, Boddy writes,

> spirit-possession rests on epistemic premises quite different from the infinitely differentiating, rationalising, and reifying thrust of global materialism and its attendant scholarly traditions. (1994, 407)

Besides stating the obvious, this invidious statement and her subsequent discussion tend to suggest that rationalism, philosophical materialism, and social science (all lumped together by Boddy) imply 'mystifying', 'dehumanising', and 'reductive' models that ignore cultural logics and the imagination; that they involve the 'reification' and 'decontextualizing' of social phenomena; and she even has the gall to equate such epistemologies with global capitalism. She also seems quite unable to distinguish social science from positivism. She herself advocates taking an interpretative approach to spirit-possession and thus to examine this phenomena within its social context, as if this constitutes a new approach to anthropology. Anthropologists, of course, have long attempted to combine both the interpretation of cultural and social phenomena and the explanation of such phenomena by placing them within a causal, or socio-historical, context. They have thus tried to avoid the fundamentalist approaches of both the positivists and postmodern textualists like Boddy (Fuller 1992, 8; Morris 1997; Bloch 1998, 39–42).

The book, *Wombs and Alien Spirits*, consists essentially of three parts, dealing respectively with the cultural logics of gender in the village of Hofriyati, the social aspects of the Zar rituals, and the cultural aesthetics of the Zar spirit beliefs. We discuss each of these in turn.

Zar cults in the Sudan, as Constantinides earlier suggested (1991), developed in the Sudan during the nineteenth century, virtually in 'tandem', Boddy writes, with the spread of radical Islam and the incorporation of Sudan into the global political economy (i.e., capitalism) largely through invasions. The Hofriyati village, some 200 kilometres north of Khartoum, has long been incorporated into this economy, and local people are wary of outsiders. The cultivation of sorghum, maize, legumes, and fodder crops are important for the local economy, but women generally do not cultivate, and their main duty, besides domestic work, is to care for the family's goats and sheep. But in recent decades migrant labour has become important in sustaining the village economy, and many men work outside the village, often in Saudi Arabia or the Gulf States. Many women have therefore become de facto heads of household. Thus, some women have a relative autonomy, but marriages are fragile, and husbands, Boddy writes, are 'an increasing source of worry and frustration' (1989, 27–41).

Hofriyati women and men, Boddy suggests, 'regard each other as different kinds of human beings' and live in segregated worlds. Although putting a great emphasis on the 'complementarity' of the gender roles, Boddy largely seems to agree with Lewis in describing the women's subordination to men and their peripheral status in regard to both Islam and the dominant political structures. Women are subject to overt control by men, they are rarely free to articulate their own interests, they have no independent legal status and come under the authority of their husbands or male kin, and they are relatively powerless in relation to the political domains of the state. Men are entitled to be polygamous and can easily divorce their spouses; women describe their own position in society as being like that of domestic livestock – 'we are cattle' [*nihna bahaim*], they say (Boddy 1989, 113). This hardly suggests that women meekly acquiesce to their gender subordination.

But Boddy outlines an underlying 'cultural logic' that indicates that women symbolically represent the essence of the village society and that suggests a complementary opposition between spiritual power associated with Islam and men and generative power associated with women. Female circumcision is thus of crucial significance in culturally defining a woman as 'enclosed', as ritually pure, and the embodiment of the moral order (identified with kinship). Female identity is thus centrally focussed on her reproductive role, to the virtual repudiation of a woman's sexuality (Boddy 1989, 57). Thus women symbolize, in this cultural logic, the 'earthly stability of the village culture', and come to perceive themselves, Boddy writes, as 'the inner core of the village life: fertile, enclosed, domesticated; bound by custom, husbands and kin' (1989, 114–5). Thus Boddy postulates a 'cultural logic' that consists of a symbolic complementary dichotomy focussed around gender.

Men	**Women**
Outside	Inside
Outside world	Village domain
Politics	Morality
Spiritual power	Generative power
Motion	Stasis
Openness	Enclosure
Production	Reproduction
Substance	Fluid

Although reducing the complexity of Hofriyati culture to a single symbolic schema based on gender, this cultural analysis, in the style of Douglas, allows Boddy to affirm that, in many important respects, women are not peripheral to Sudanese society. For they are centrally concerned with reproduction, with the domestic sphere, and are the fulcrum around which village identity and moral rectitude are organized. The emphasis that Boddy puts on 'balance' in this cultural logic runs completely counter, of course, to the realities of Hofriyati social life, which emphasizes the subordination of women in many different contexts.

In the second part of the book, Boddy focusses on the Zar cults and on the relationship of the spirits to social life. She emphasizes that spirit-possession is a 'holistic social reality' and thus can be approached in many different ways – psychological, aesthetic, religious, social, and medical. But she suggests that its 'province is meaning' and that it 'defies simple explanation' – what anthropologists would disagree with this? – but then proceeds to repudiate or downplay any approach other than her own rather narrow hermeneutics that puts a focal emphasis on cultural forms and aesthetics, and she views spirit beliefs as 'texts' and women as 'metaphors' (1989, 136–7). Such an approach seems to me far more 'reifying' and 'reductive' than the sociological approaches she continually berates. And viewing spirit-possession as an 'idiom of communication' is hardly news to anthropologists.

Like Constantinides, Boddy emphasizes that the Zar cults are closely linked with fertility and marital problems, and though 'counter-hegemonic' – and thus peripheral to Islam and the dominant political structures – they largely serve as a 'conservative force'. Although her ethnography largely confirms Lewis' own theory, she continually distances herself from his account, suggesting that Lewis presents an 'androcentric portrayal' of women, seeing them as 'reacting to men rather than acting for themselves within a specific cultural context' (1989, 40). Lewis, of course, continually emphasizes the subjective agency of women, but conflating individuality and subjective agency with the possessive individualism of bourgeois ideology, Boddy also berates Lewis for his 'instrumentality'. It's a case of heads I win, tails you lose!

Boddy's whole analysis is based on a somewhat dubious psychological theory, derived from Geertz, that makes a radical and rather exotic dichotomy between the individual (equated with the abstract, asocial, monadic subject of bourgeois ideology) and the relational identity of Hofriyati women – a dichotomy that is misleading and obfuscating. For as social scientists and social psychologists have long been telling us – long before postmodern scholars arrived on the intellectual scene – that humans in all cultures, including Europeans, are both individuals, with unique personalities and subjective agency, and intrinsically social beings, such that self-identity – personhood – in all cultures is complex, embodied, shifting, composite, relational, and involves multiple identities. Hofriyati women are therefore hardly unique in having a selfhood that 'inheres in relationships' (1989, 119). But then, following the culture and personality theorists, Boddy suggests an extreme cultural determinism, such that the selfhood of Hofriyati women is culturally 'overdetermined'. They thus, Boddy informs us, are not individuals, have no subjective agency or self-awareness, and their personality is completely absorbed or identified with their social role – the 'cultural image of womanhood' (1989, 252–3).

This questionable portrait of Hofriyati women not only fails to distinguish between the self and the cultural conceptions of the person but also allows Boddy to imply – as against Lewis – that outside the ritual context, Hofriyati women have no subjective agency, nor do they make a determined effort to further their own material interests (instrumentally). Marriage is thus portrayed by Boddy as devoid of 'conflict', and women are seen as in no sense 'deprived' but as passively accepting their subordinate role – wholly determined by the cultural logic.

In arguing against Lewis, Boddy offers a thesis that is largely in contradiction to her own ethnographic data, which indicate that in everyday life women *do* challenge their subordinate status, that they *do* assert their own individual identity, and through the idiom of the Zar illness that they *do* mobilize in an oblique way support in order to obtain material satisfactions and redress from difficult circumstances.

But then, surprise, surprise! In the ritual context, through the Zar cults and possession, women are able, Boddy argues, to achieve 'self-transcendence' and full personhood and are able to achieve an integrated self – they become an individual?! She is able to 'transcend the categories which have constrained her, recognise them for what they are; cultural constructs' (1989, 257). Boddy offers little evidence for this theory, which suggests that Zar possession is a 'journey to self-awareness' (1989, 301). Although berating social scientists for being unaware of the cultural assumptions underlying their own theories, she herself seems oblivious to the fact that this emphasis on self-transcendence and on achieving full personhood or individuality only through religious rituals largely reflects the preoccupations of the western advocates of 'New Age' spiritualism and Jungian psychology. As the majority of women do not become possessed, one wonders if they even recognize themselves as individuals or simply remain cultural clones?

In the final part of the book, Boddy largely engages in what Gellner describes as 'hermeneutic intoxication' (1995, 22), for she gives a very detailed account of the Zar spirits as a 'system of meanings'. It is largely an exercise in Zar theology, though informative and interesting. Her main suggestion is that the Zar spirits provide a 'parallel universe' to that of humans and offer a 'cultural resource' or 'text' from which women can idiosyncratically draw on in their possession rituals (1989, 148). But, as other scholars have suggested, the Zar is also an important ritual drama, which encapsulates historical events and personages, and is essentially 'counter-hegemonic'. But Boddy seems to get lost in extravagant lyricism in suggesting that spirit-possession enables its adherents

> to explore multiple refractions of order and morality; to distil the lessons of history; to sift, evaluate and situate external influences and to respond. (1994, 414)

Such grandiose functionalism trumps that of any positivist. Boddy even suggests, and this is the acme of vacuity dressed up as postmodern profundity, that 'mimesis is dependent on alterity, the existence of an Other' (1994, 425). True!

Although the spirit world of the Hofriyati is complex, consisting of diverse spiritual agencies, the villagers essentially recognize three kinds of jinn, which are coded by colour. The white jinn are benign and principally Muslim, and possession by them is not considered serious. The black jinn are malevolent, usually of African or pagan origin, and are associated with intractable mental illness. Possession by these spirits is extremely serious and can be cured only through exorcism. And, finally, there are the red jinn, or 'red winds', the ambivalent and capricious Zar spirits, which are the central concern of women and the Zar cults and, as already discussed, usually involve milder forms of illness or other forms of distress (Boddy 1989, 187).

Although, for many Muslim clerics, Zar cults are not officially part of Islam, for the women themselves the Zar rituals are intrinsic to their Islamic faith. Boddy affirms that the Zar and orthodox Islam are not competing religious ideologies, but are different aspects of a single conceptual system, the Zar dealing with earthly existence, Islam with ultimate causes and the afterlife (1989, 279). The suggestion that Islam is other-worldly is, however, quite misleading, for as we shall observe in the rest of this chapter, Islam is very much involved in worldly politics.

(For further studies of Zar and other related cults, see Messing 1958; Lambek 1981; Lewis 1991; Kramer 1993; Rasmussen 1995).

3.5. THE SAINTS AND SCHOLARS OF ISLAM

Ernest Gellner was one of the major intellectual figures of the twentieth century. A polymath, a passionate liberal, and hence a staunch defender of modernity (embracing capitalism, science, and the modern nation – state), he was a brilliant cosmopolitan scholar – profound, witty, irreverent, incisive, and iconoclastic. He wrote in an engaging and lucid style, so different from the 'portentous obscurity' that tends to be highly esteemed in academia (Lessnoff 2002, 3). His trenchant critiques of the antirealism and self-indulgent subjectivism of many hermeneutic and postmodern scholars were particularly refreshing, even if somewhat overstated, in that 'hermeneutics' is conceived by Gellner almost as if it were some kind of ailment or delusion (Gellner 1992, 22–71; 1995, 236–40).

But throughout his life, Gellner was a serious, if controversial, student of Islam; and his *Muslim Society* (1981) has become something of a classic text. A decade earlier, however, Gellner had published his ethnographic study on the saints of the Atlas Mountains, Morocco (1969), and in his last years he wrote a highly polemical and acerbic text, *Postmodernism, Reason and Religion* (1992), in which Islam is interpreted as the veritable prototype of religious fundamentalism. Gellner's exuberant and insightful writings on Islam are worthy of a study in itself, but here I briefly focus not on his polemics but rather on two themes – his discussion on the 'two styles' of Islam and on the role of the saint in the High Atlas region of Morocco, as described in his ethnographic studies (1969, 1972, 1984).

Earlier scholars often made a contrast between two religious emphases that are evident within the Islamic tradition. Gibb, for example, spoke of 'two channels of

Muslim religious life' – the orthodox and the mystical (1969, 12). But the scholar who has most fervently stressed that there are two styles of religious life within Islam is, of course, Gellner, in his theory of the 'pendulum swing' of Islam. As he puts it

> Within Muslim societies, there is a permanent, if sometimes latent, tension and opposition between two styles of religious life. On the one hand, there is a puritanical, unitarian, individualist, scripturalist ideal of a single deity, which has disclosed its final message in a definitive revelation available to all who care to read. This version spurns mediation and neither requires nor formally allows clergy; it presupposes only a literate class of scribes who act as guardians and exegetes of the revelation. (1981, 159)

This is the 'orthodox' style of Islam represented by the ulama scholars. In contrast to this vision, Gellner continues, 'there is the "associationist" ideal . . . which allows mediation, propitiation, ritual and devotional excess, and religious hierarchy'. This 'pole' is represented by the Sufi brotherhoods, the popular ecstatic cults associated with holy men or saints, and the spirit-cults. Drawing on the early ideas of Hume and the Islamic sociologist Ibn Khaldun, Gellner suggests that each of these 'styles' serves different social needs, and though there are specific circumstances in which the two styles coexist peacefully and even interpenetrate each other, at other times, the 'pendulum' swings to one extreme. In particular, the puritanical, scripturalist stress is thought not only to be associated with urban Islamic civilization but to be related to the many reform movements within Islam. As Gellner notes, within Islam, and unlike Christianity, it is the central, orthodox tradition that has the 'protestant' characteristics – a tradition without clergy, based on trading towns, stressing literacy and learning, and generally hostile to the popular cults focussed around the saints. Geertz (1968) has written perceptively of the Islamic reform movements in Indonesia and Morocco and how the 'radical fundamentalism' and 'scripturalism' associated with the ulama formed both a prologue to the nationalist movement and was instrumental in encouraging certain 'modernizing' trends. Many have noted the 'selective affinity' between a stress on Islamic orthodoxy, often of a puritanical kind, and a reformist social programme, although in different contexts the political role of the ulama has varied enormously (Keddie 1972; Eickelman 1976; Gilsenan 1983, 27–54).

The other end, as it were, of the spectrum – the ecstatic, mystical, devotional end of the pendulum swing – is, however, by no means unitary; and, in fact, as Ahmed (1976, 151) suggests but does not develop, there is a certain 'frailty' about Gellner's typological approach, useful though it is as a heuristic aid. Studies of popular religious cults and the Sufi brotherhoods within Islam have indicated that these vary enormously with regard to their social functions and their political role in different contexts. Several studies have indicated that in a 'tribal' milieux, certain holy men or saints, known for their piety and belonging to lineages claiming descent from the prophet, have functioned as political mediators, arbitrating in disputes (Barth 1959; for some interesting studies of Islam in 'tribal' societies, see

Ahmed and Hart 1984). In specific circumstances, particularly in the context of colonial oppression, such saints, who were invariably associated with Sufi orders, have often been instrumental in politically uniting through their charismatic appeal diverse elements of the population. Often with a millennial aspect, the movements they have led have sometimes resulted in the establishment of centralized states (for illustrative material on such movements, see Evans-Pritchard 1949; Holt 1958; Brown 1971; Ahmed 1976). In other contexts, however, the Sufi brotherhoods are associated with the working classes and the lumpenproletariat of urban areas, particularly the shanty towns [*bidonvilles*] of North Africa and the Middle East. In the cults associated with such brotherhoods, spirit-possession and ecstatic states are prominent.

In later writings, Gellner referred to these 'two variants of the faith' as the 'high' and 'low' cultures of Islam. The high or scripturalist tradition is linked to the urban context and to the ulama. As he wrote

> Scholars, often of urban background and rooted in the trading bourgeoisie of the towns, project a corresponding vision of the faith – scripturalist, rule-oriented, puritanical, literal, sober, egalitarian, anti-ecstatic. (1994, 18)

In contrast, rural or folk Islam, focussed around what he described as the 'rustic tribal', took the form of an ecstatic Islam, a tradition that was associated with Sufi saints and emphasized mystical and ecstatic experiences – through dance, music, and spirit-possession rituals. In contrast to Christianity, in which Protestantism as the scriptural tradition emerged as a dissident form of religion, in Islam, Gellner continually stressed, it is the central tradition, the high culture – that is, egalitarian, scripturalist, devoid of hierarchy, and puritanical.

But importantly for Gellner, this scripturalist tradition in Islam – which in its extreme form is fundamentalist – had an 'elective affinity' with the 'virtues' required by a 'disciplined, modern, industrial society' (i.e., capitalism). For it possesses such features as sobriety, puritanism, an aversion to 'disorderly' folk practices and 'mystical indulgence', individualism, and rule-observance, as well as an emphasis on literacy. Islam is thus seen by Gellner as playing a similar role to that of nationalism, and that nationalism and scripturalist (fundamentalist) Islam are often conflated (1994, 22). But the reality of contemporary Islamic politics he describes as *clientism,* government-by-network, combined with a religious moralism (1994, 25–57).

These two styles of Islam may be summarized as follows:

Scripturalist	**Ecstatic**
Ulama	Saint
Urban	Rural
Puritanical	Ritualistic
Literate	Oral
Egalitarian	Hierarchical
Orthodox	Marginal

Gellner's theory of two styles of religious life within Islam, which has generally been equated with the distinction between the great and little traditions formulated by Redfield (1956), has been the subject of a wealth, indeed a barrage, of criticism. Gellner's dichotomy has thus been described as vague, inadequate, simplistic, and unenlightening. The central problem is that the dichotomy between scriptural orthodoxy and Sufi mysticism – 'magical macraboutism' – does not have any matching social correlates and cannot be unambiguously identified with the dichotomies of town and tribe, literate and non-literate. The Sufis can hardly be described as simply tribal 'rustics' and identified with the popular tradition, for they were mostly associated with urban contexts and put an emphasis on learning and scriptures – particularly the study of the Quran. Lewis quotes the distinguished scholar Arberry to emphasize the link between Sufis and scripturalism. As Arberry wrote, 'the esoteric exposition of the Quran became the central point of the hard training of the Sufi' (1950, 23; Lewis 1986, 96). Although conceding that the distinction between popular and orthodox Islam has some validity in Morocco, Henry Munson emphasizes that the Muslim clerics [*ulama*] whom Gellner sees as embodying orthodoxy were often themselves Sufi mystics, and that both the ulamas and Sufis were part of the same urban elite. Equally important, as Gellner himself admits, popular religion involving spirit-cults and ecstatic rites was not only a tribal or rural phenomenon but, as we shall see with the Hamadsha, also existed among the urban poor. Gellner indeed speaks of Sufism and the ecstatic cults as offering 'consolation' for the urban poor and as being the 'opium of the people' (1981, 54; Munson 1993, 81–4). Thus Sufism – and the religion of the Shi'ites – seems to uncomfortably 'straddle' the two forms of religious life that Gellner stridently separates (Holy 1991, 2–3; for a further critique of Gellner's theory, see Asad 1986).

Let me now turn to Gellner's account of the role of the saints in the political life of the people of the High Atlas, Morocco.

Throughout much of its history, Morocco has been a monarchy, its inhabitants recognizing the sultan as their spiritual leader. But his political power was largely confined to the cities and coastal plain, and this region was known as Blad L-Makhzan, or 'government land'. The Atlas Mountains, largely inhabited by Berber-speaking people, was known as Blad S-Siba, 'land of dissidence'. Berber society had a segmentary political system, consisting of tribal communities that were associated with a common territory and that claimed to be descendants of a common patrilineal ancestor. Such tribes were known as the people [*ait*] of a particular ancestor (Hart 1984, 67–8). The boundaries of the land of 'dissidence' or anarchy tended to be unstable as well as ill-defined, and the Berber tribes often resisted paying taxes to the central government. The Berbers of the Central High Atlas – the Ait'Atta – were a transhuman segmentary society with a strong tendency to endogamy and with preferred marriage to fathers' brothers' daughters (sons).

Chieftainship among the tribal groupings is elective and the election is undertaken annually at local Sufi lodge [*zawiya*], under the auspices of the saints, and by men of the various clans that constitute the tribe. Eligibility to the chieftainship is through rotation, each of the clans providing a chief for one year. The powers of the chieftainship are weak, and Gellner describes all the chiefs as 'lame ducks' (1984, 26), for they have no coercive sanctions, and the power they have is through the influence of public opinion. Order among the Berber tribes is not maintained, Gellner argues, by central government – to the contrary, 'the tribes ensure that the central government does not interfere in their affairs' (1984, 27). How then is order maintained? Gellner suggests that it is through two essential mechanisms:

1. through the segmentary political system, as described by Evans-Pritchard for the Nuer, which involves the resolution of conflict through the balancing of clan or tribal segments, and
2. through the influence of the saints (Berber, Igurramen, sing Agurram), 'holy men' belonging to saintly lineage who claim descent from the prophet.

In the area where Gellner undertook his research, this descent was through the lineage of Sidi Said Ahansal. The settlement around his shrine was quite large, with about 300 inhabitants. Not all descendants of the founding saint have effective political influence; only a few have a political role as mediators, as these men are thought to possess *baraka* [blessing or grace].

The role of the saints contrasts with those of the chief. Whereas the lay chiefs are chosen by the people and hold power for only one year, the saints are chosen by god and have in principle a permanent role. Thus the political system of the Berber tribes, the 'maraboutic state' as Gellner rather misleadingly describes it, consists of 'two systems' or two kinds of politics. Among the tribes in general, everything is organized so as to prevent the emergence of power and to limit its duration and effectiveness. With regard to the saints, however, there is a concentration of power, though this power is not absolute. Between the tribes, there is much litigation and feuding – Gellner suggests they are 'addicted' to it – but the saints have a reputation for piety and pacifism: they do not dance like ordinary Berbers, they keep their wives in seclusion, they possess baraka, and they do not fight or litigate.

The saints, according to Gellner, have a number of important political functions in Berber society: They supervise the election of chiefs each year; they act as mediators or arbitrators in disputes, providing the "cornerstone" of the legal system, in which decisions are made through arbitration and by collective oaths; and they 'anchor' local Berber society in the wider system of Islam. As most Berbers are non-literate and are seen by more urban Muslims to be somewhat heretical, they affirm and display through the saints their Muslim status and identity (1984, 30). Although the saints are linked in terms of terminology and organization to the mystical Sufi brotherhoods in urban centres, Gellner suggests that these two phenomena are quite distinct in nature and function (1984, 37). With the advent of French colonial rule, saints often became allies of the French and incorporated into the system of indirect rule. But with independence and the setting up of the

Moroccan state, deprived of sources of revenue, they have now lost most of their power and influence.

Gellner describes, in summary fashion, the political system of the Berber tribes as one 'in which permanent and pacific saints divide the political role with elective, secular, and feud-addicted tribal chieftains', and that it is one that is structurally sufficient unto itself – though conceptually linked to wider Islamic society (1984, 31).

Gellner thus, in the Moroccan context, makes a clear distinction between the 'genuine mystics', the urban Sufis – who are seen as an alternative to the ulama – and the 'tribal holy men', whose connection with mysticism is limited and who function not as religious scholars but as political mediators. But with regard to Islamic politics generally, Gellner describes three major types of legitimation: the book – and by extension the Islamic traditions [*hadith*]; the consensus of the community [*umma*]; and the line of succession from the prophet. In practice, he writes

> the Book required scholars to read it and consensus to interpret it, and hence, concretely speaking, the authority of the ulama as religious scholars, and that of the community as the interpreters of the words, were in harmony. (1984, 23)

The third principle of legitimation, that of succession, is particularly associated with Shi'a Islam and is not always in harmony with the other two. But within Moroccan tribal society, this mode of legitimation becomes evident in the role of the saints – the 'tribal holy men', as Gellner describes them – through whom the 'word becomes flesh'. They thus provide an alternative to the ulama as a source of political authority (1984, 23–4).

With regard to Gellner's account of the segmentary political system of the Ait'Atta, there is little evidence to suggest that this is a clearly articulated ideology among them or that feuding or conflict ever conformed to the 'segmentary model' of a balanced and complementary opposition between groups (Munson 1993; Eickelman 2002, 125–6; cf. Kuper 1988). (For an excellent study of Islam in a tribal society – the Berti of Western Sudan – see Holy 1991, which explores the relationship between gender and two forms of the religious life, one focussed on local Islamic orthodoxy, predominantly the concern of men, the other on the customary rituals largely focussed around women.)

As already noted, Gellner suggests that there is almost an 'elective affinity' between orthodox scriptural Islam and 'modernity' (i.e., capitalism), and he continually emphasizes the similarities between this style of Islam and protestantism. Thus what makes Islam so acceptable to the modern world, he writes, is its 'puritanical, egalitarian, scripturalist face' (1992, 17). Gellner even suggests that the Iranian revolution was an expression of this form of Islam. For although the Shi'ite Islam of Iran, with its highly emotional martyr cult, seems to differ from orthodox Sunni scripturalism, Gellner contends that the Ayatollah Khomeini essentially advocated a puritanical version of High Islam, focussed around the rule of the clerics [*ulama*].

These theses will no doubt be the subject of continuing debate (Gellner 1992, 16–22; Lessnoff 2002, 77–89. On the Iranian revolution, see Keddie 1981; Bashiriyeh 1984; Mottahedeh 1985; Salehi 1988; Abrahamian 1993; Beyer 1994).

3.6. THE HAMADSHA: A SUFI BROTHERHOOD IN MOROCCO

In this section, I focus the discussion specifically on Vincent Crapanzano's lucid study of the Hamadsha, a loosely organized religious brotherhood found in Morocco. A study in ethnopsychiatry, Crapanzano is primarily concerned with exploring the therapeutic aspects of this co-fraternity, but his ethnography has a much wider interest.

Islamic mysticism is known universally as Sufism, a term originally derived from the Arabic word for wool [*suf*] and alludes to the coarse woollen garment said to have been worn by the prophet. Sufism, however, is distinct from the Shi'ite tradition within Islam, which, with its cult of the martyred personality, also has a stress on divine mediation. Unlike the Sunni tradition, embraced by ninety per cent of Muslims, the Shi'ite tradition looks to a descendant of Ali, the prophet's son-in-law, and the fourth caliph of Islam, as the only legitimate ruler of the Muslim community. Until the expected revelation and return of this 'hidden Imam', guidance of the community is meanwhile in the hands of religious scholars [*ulama*] (Gilsenan 1983, 55–74). Sufism is an unorthodox religious movement of a very different kind, and it arose quite early in the history of Islam. By the end of the ninth century, a number of ascetic or devotional cults had emerged that stressed a path [*tariqa*] towards a specific goal, namely, union with the ultimate reality or godhead. This often involved an immanent or pantheistic conception of the deity, and it is not surprising that these Sufi orders were strongly condemned by orthodox Muslims. The mystic Mansur Al Hallaj, for example, was executed at Baghdad in 922 C.E. for blasphemy and for refusing to recant the utterance 'I am the truth' [*Ana'L-Haqq*]. By the twelfth century, a number of Sufi orders had been established, each associated with a particular saint or *wali*, who was held in veneration as the founder of a particular path. Such orders were often referred to as the Dervish brotherhoods and as an 'ascetic protest'. Sufism seems to have been focussed on Iraq, where in Baghdad much of the early devotional literature originated. The Qadiriyyah, owing their original inspiration to the Persian saint Abd Al-Qadir, and the order known as the Maulawiya, founded by the mystical poet Jalal Al-Din Rumi who was also a Persian, are two well-known examples of early Sufi orders (for a general account of these early Sufi orders and the religious aspects of Sufism, see the classics of Nicholson 1914 and Arberry 1950; for more recent accounts, see Evans-Pritchard 1949; Abun-Nasr 1965; Gilsenan 1973; Martin 1976).

The Hamadsha of Morocco is a religious brotherhood associated with the veneration of two Moroccan saints, Sidi-Ali, an eighteenth-century scholar and mystic, and his servant, Sidi Ahmed. Both saints are buried some 16 miles north-west of the city of Meknes. The Hamadsha are almost exclusively Arabs and look on themselves as orthodox [*sunni*] Muslims, recognizing the fundamental importance of the Five Pillars of Islam. Although not as well known as the other Sufi orders, the Isawiyya and Tijaniyya, and often frowned on as a degenerate form of Sufism, the Hamadsha are nonetheless part of the cult of saints, often known as *Maraboutism*, a term derived from the Arabic *Murabit*, which describes a man attached to God. The social and economic organization of the Hamadsha brotherhood is divided into three distinct complexes.

First, there are the two saintly villages, Beni Rachid and Beni Ourad. Here the tombs and various shrines associated with the saints are to be found, and these are tended by the patrilineal descendants of the saints, known as *Wulad Siyyid*, the children of the saint. Comprising about half of the village population, the 'children of the saint' are believed to be endowed with *baraka*, usually translated as grace or blessing. It is a kind of mystical beneficent power, which in special circumstances has a contagious quality. The descendants of the saint, Crapanzano suggests, are endowed with institutional baraka, and it is particularly evident in the person of the Mizwar, the leader of the saintly lineages, who has complete control over the affairs of the saint's complex, particularly the care and maintenance of the saint's tomb. But baraka may also be of a personal kind, reflected in an individual's character and piety and in his therapeutic gifts and ability to perform 'miracles' (for further discussions on the concept of baraka, cf. Geertz 1968, 44–5; Gilsenan 1983, 79–80). The saintly lineages in this part of Morocco have almost no institutional political role, partly because of the wider influence of another local saint, Moulay Idriss, and partly because the villages have long been subjected to a central authority. Central to the village complex is the annual pilgrimage to the saint's shrine, undertaken by the followers and devotees of the Hamadsha order. Money and gifts – wealth – are given to the adepts of the order and to the saint and by extension to his children, the incoming wealth being controlled, of course, by the lineage head, the Mizwar, who is responsible for the proceeds coming to the shrine. In return for their gifts, the donors obtain baraka, which, as Crapanzano writes, is a 'potentialising force'. The saint is indeed, through his descendants, a 'continual and inexhaustible source of baraka' (1973, 121). Thus material wealth is exchanged for baraka, and the pilgrim, in asking the saint to intercede with God, receives some beneficence – a child, a spouse, business success, or the cure of an illness. The principal aim of the pilgrimage seems to be therapeutic.

The second aspect of the Hamadsha brotherhood is the cult lodges [*zawiyas*], associated with the old quarter of Meknes. Under the leadership of a local Muqaddim (who is formally approved by the Mizwar even though selected by members of the lodges themselves), these lodges consist of some fifteen adepts, all men who regularly attend and organize the cult ceremonies. They usually belong to the lowest economic strata and are petty traders, artisans, or manual workers. Also associated with the lodge are the devotees [*muhibbin*], men, women, and children who are also attracted to the ceremonies and take part in the trance dances.

Finally, there are the various unstructured groups of Hamadsha to be found in the shanty towns. Mostly consisting of recent migrants, they are also focussed around a cult leader or Muqaddim. The vast majority of the Bidonville Hamadsha are devotees, mostly women and unskilled workers. As Crapanzano writes,

> There are many more female Muhibbin in the bidonvilles than there are among the Zawiya – affiliated devotees; and the women, who are not as restricted as women in the old town, play a more active part in the ceremonies. (1973, 112)

The most important of these ceremonies for both the lodges and the shanty town groups is the *hadra*, or trance dance. Involving the chanting of litanies, rhythmic music and drumming, and the making of a sacrifice, these ceremonies are designed to lead devotees, including the patient, into a trance or ecstatic state [*hal* or *wajo*]. Women, who fall into trances much easier than men do, remain in the audience until they 'are driven by the music' into a trance. Various-named jnun [singular *jinn*], who are spiritual agencies associated with rivers and springs, are often invoked during these ceremonies. Being sensitive to insult or injury, the jnun often retaliate by striking or possessing those who commit wrongs against them, and many illnesses, both physical and mental, are said to be caused by these spirits. Women are particularly prone to an attack by the jnun. To bring about a cure, the offending spirit must be appeased, or exorcised. The exorcism is done by a Quaranic teacher. But to appease the spirit, a 'symbiotic relationship' may be established between the jinn and the patient, and the latter, as Crapanzano writes, 'in the case of a symbiotic cure, is incorporated into a cult, and as a member of that cult he (or she) must go through "curing" periodically'. The hadra ceremony is thus essentially a curing rite, a therapeutic procedure that is pleasing not only to the saints but to the jnun as well. Like the pilgrimages, the trance dance is a form of therapy, a 'sharing of illness' as well as having a cathartic function for the individual devotees. Crapanzano gives a vivid account of these ceremonies, which often involve head slashing and other forms of self-mutilation by the men, and frenetic and convulsive dancing by the women (1973, 185–211). It is of interest to note that these Sufi brotherhoods, as Keddie (1972, 10) has indicated, are not concerned with the achievement of a mystical union between humans and God, the alleged aim of Sufi mystics. (For further studies of Sufi brotherhoods, see Lewis 1955; Gilsenan 1973; Eickelman 1976; Cornell 1998.)

3.7. RELIGION AND POLITICS IN MOROCCO

There have been a number of excellent anthropological studies on the relationship between Islam and politics in Morocco. One of the most seminal and well known was Clifford Geertz's comparative and historical study, *Islam Observed*

(1968). Geertz explicitly describes the study as an exercise in macrosociology, in the style of Weber, thus avoiding the 'pallid mindlessness' of cultural relativism – which his own advocacy of interpretive anthropology tends to entail! – and the 'shabby tyranny' of historical determinism (by which he evidently means the kind of analysis suggested by Marx, Engels – and Weber?). The study describes the 'classical style' of Moroccan religious expression as 'maraboutism', the importance of scripturalism as a powerful force in renovating and reaffirming the classical tradition, and suggests that with Muhammid V, who ruled Morocco until 1961, 'maraboutic kingship returned to Morocco' (1968, 74). Geertz in the study emphasizes that religion is concerned with meaning, functioning to give unity to experience and to overcome the felt inadequacies of commonsense ideas. He thus tends to ignore or underplay what he terms the comparative or 'scientific' approach to religion, which is concerned with the 'uncovering of the forces' (political and economic) through which cultural forms come into existence (1968, 96). Geertz's whole outlook remains close to the German idealist tradition and thus puts an emphasis on hermeneutics and the interpretation of meaning – rather than following the historical sociology of Marx and Weber.

Elaine Combs-Schilling's excellent study of the Moroccan monarchy, *Sacred Performances* (1989), though also seen as an exercise in historical anthropology, tends to follow Geertz in viewing the Islamic monarchy as largely a cultural phenomenon. She thus focusses on the contribution of various Islamic rituals to the stability of the Moroccan monarchy – the oldest ruling dynasty in the world we're told – and tends to downplay the importance of King Hasan II's control of economic, administrative, and coercive power. But in this section, I want to focus on a study that is also in the tradition of historical anthropology but that offers a comprehensive and instructive counter to the cultural emphases of Geertz and Combs-Schilling – Henry Munson's *Religion and Power in Morocco* (1993).

Politics and religion are intrinsically connected in Islam, and it is worth beginning by quoting the words of Muhammad Al-'Alawi (1880–1964), a Moroccan Sufi who played an important role in the Moroccan nationalist movement. When told by a French colonial officer to avoid political issues in his lectures on Islam, he is reported to have said

Anyone who claims to give lectures on the religion of Islam without discussing politics is either a liar, a hypocrite, or an ignoramus. For Islam demands the liberation of the human being and calls for both justice and freedom and the quest for knowledge. (Munson 1993, 80)

Al-'Alawi is seen by Henry Munson as a classic example of a Sufi and reformist scholar who embodies that myth of the 'righteous man of god', one who dares to defy the unjust ruler – Al'-Alawi in his latter years defying both French colonial rule and later in the 1960s the government of King Hassan II. But although religious scholars [*ulama*] throughout the history of Morocco have tended to support or remain passive in relation to the various political rulers, there has been a long series of mystical saints who have defied political authority and have embodied the classical theme of the Moroccan moral imagination, 'the myth of the righteous man of God who dares to defy an unjust sultan' (Munson 1993, 27). One of the most famous of these saints is Al-Yusi (1631–1691), who is the subject of many popular folk tales. Al-Yusi was a Berber, a largely pastoral community, as we have noted, living in the Atlas Mountains of Morocco. For almost twenty years he lived in a Sufi lodge [*zawiya*] in the western foothills of the Middle Atlas Mountains, but when this lodge was destroyed in 1668, Al-Yusi began a wandering existence that was to last for the rest of his life. This is not because 'restlessness' is an essential attribute of the Moroccan ethos or 'mode of being' – as Geertz suggests (1968, 31–2) – but because the sultans of Morocco feared his popularity and often ordered him to move from place to place to stop him becoming a political threat. The folk tales particularly concern the tensions and conflicts between the Sufi saint [*wali, sayyidi – sidi* in colloquial Arabic] and the Moroccan sultan Mulay Isma'il, who reigned from 1672 to 1727.

Al-Yusi was a Sufi *Shaykh*, which essentially means an elderly man or mystical religious teacher, and was believed to possess baraka mystical power or blessedness. Geertz tends to treat baraka as an endowment, a talent or capacity of certain individuals – such as extraordinary physical courage or ecstatic intensity (1968, 33), whereas Munson argues that baraka, as a concept, has a much wider semantic and social significance. It means essentially 'blessedness', and the conventional way of saying 'thank you' in Moroccan Arabic is *baraka allahu fik*, meaning *God bless you.* But the Quran is believed to be full of baraka, and all amulets worn to ward off and protect a person from the jnun [jinn, spirits] are imbued with baraka derived from the verses of the Quran that they contain. But baraka is also associated with the notion of purity [*tahara*] and the descendants of the prophet. Throughout Morocco, in almost every village and in all the popular quarters of every city, there are tombs of saints, and the veneration of saints is an important aspect of both Sufism and popular religion. All popular saints in Morocco, including Al-Yusi, who is buried near Sefrou in the Atlas Mountains (Rabinow 1975), are thought to be descendants, through the patrilineal line, of the prophet Muhammad. As the sons of the prophet died in infancy, the descendants of the prophet – referred to as 'people of the house' – trace their descent to his daughter Fatima and her husband Ali, who was also Muhammad's cousin, son of his father's brother. Such descendants are known throughout North Africa as *Shurafa honoured ones* [sing. *Sharif(a)*]. From the earliest years of Islam, there has thus always been a tension between the veneration of the descendants of the prophet – who are often thought to have a special right to be the imams, or spiritual leaders of the community [*umma*] – and the belief in the essential equality of all Muslims. For honour [*sharaf*] is also to be derived from righteous conduct independent of birth.

Equally important, the *baraka* [blessedness] of the descendants of the prophet [*shurafa*] is also intrinsically linked to their ritual purity [*tahara*]. Ritual purity is an important aspect of Islamic religious life, and a person must not pray, or touch the Quran, or enter a mosque, without being in a ritually pure condition, which is achieved by ablutions with water. Baraka and purity are intrinsically linked in Moroccan thought, and a boy who has recently been circumcised and a person who has recently returned from a pilgrimage to Mecca are both believed to be imbued with baraka, as well as being ritually pure (Munson 1993, 11–12).

Sufism as a mystical doctrine implies the effacement or 'extinction' [*fana*] of the individual self and desires and the experience of a spiritual unity that transcends the multiplicity of things and is interpreted as the knowledge or the experience of the presence of God. But because in the Moroccan context, the Sufi Shaykh was seen as a spiritual heir of the prophet Muhammad as an intercessor on the day of judgement, 'it became common for Sufis to think of this inheritance in genealogical terms' (Munson 1993, 16). It thus followed that the prominent Sufi Shaykh were invariably seen as Shurafa – as descendants of the prophet. Equally important, most of the Muslim dynasties that have ruled Morocco have claimed sharifian ancestry at one point or another (Munson 1993, 16–19).

Thus throughout most of Moroccan history, and the figure of Al-Yusi exemplifies this, the categories of Sufi Shaykh, saint (*Wali Allah* [one who is close to god]) and sharif (a descendant of the prophet) often tended to coalesce (Munson 1993, 18) – and all are associated with the possession of baraka. But although Al-Yusif's life exemplifies the righteous man of God who dares to defy an unjust ruler, this Sufi mystic never questioned the sultan's right to rule. He was thus rooted in the classical tradition of Islamic political thought that emphasized that the sultan had three basic political obligations: the collection of taxes according to what is right and not oppressive, to conduct holy war [*jihad*] to spread the word of God, and to provide justice for the oppressed (Munson 1993, 29–30). If the sultan did not fulfil these obligations, he could rightly be rebuked, challenged, or deposed. Al-Yusi therefore followed what Munson describes as the *contractual* form of government, which suggests that being a just ruler means implementing Islamic law as it is interpreted by the ulama, the religious scholars.

Munson argues that political life in Morocco over the centuries, and the authority of the various sultans in particular, has been based on two distinct conceptions of monarchy. On the one hand, with the contractual form of government, as expressed by Al-Yusi, rulers are considered legitimate only by virtue of the fact that they have been selected by representatives of the Islamic community [*umma*], in particular the religious scholars [*ulama*] and only so long as they implement Islamic law and rule justly. Orthodox Sunni Muslims in Morocco have tended to follow this contractual form of government, recognizing that Muslims through the ulama have the right to depose any ruler who failed to uphold the laws of Islam or who ruled unjustly. On the other hand, the other form of legitimacy is hierocratic, which suggests that monarchs are sacred kings, representatives of God and the prophet who must be obeyed unconditionally. This position is associated with the Shi'ite sects – the term being derived from *Shi'at'ali* [the faction of Ali]. For this sect the imam or leader of the Islamic community should be a descendant of Ali, for they alone had inherited the purity of the prophet. What is of interest is that, although Moroccan Muslims are Sunnis, the conception of authority that has been favoured by the Moroccan rulers has been of the hierocratic form, and closer to that of the Shi-ites (Munson 1993, 37).

Islam has always acknowledged the importance of political authority, for the famous Quranic verse reads 'O you who believe, obey God, obey the messenger and those in authority' (4.59). The term *sultan* originally meant 'authority' or 'government' and came into use after the demise of the Abbasid caliphate (750–1258). But the sultans of many early Islamic states also claimed the title *Khalifa* – which means 'successor' or 'deputy' (of the prophet) – although in principle there is supposed to be only one caliph for the entire Islamic world. Now although the ulama saw themselves as the guardians of God's law, and in principle considered that the caliph was to be selected by them as the representatives of the Islamic community [*umma*] – and a caliph or sultan was legally recognized only when he had received the *bay*'a or oath of allegiance of the ulama and other notables – in practice, from the time of the Umayyad dynasty (661–750) up until the twentieth century, Sunni rulers considered themselves as God's deputy and established dynastic rule. So there was, in essence, a built-in tension between the hierocratic rule of the sultans – who pressed for dynastic succession and saw themselves as God's deputy (a sacred kingship) – and the contractual form of authority advocated by the ulama. The word *ulama* is derived from the verb '*alima* [to know] (sing. '*alim*), and essentially refers to religious scholars who have knowledge of Islamic law. They are not priests, for any virtuous man in Islam can lead prayers – and traditionally the ulama functioned as scholars, teachers, and judges. Ideally, they were supposed to live simply without wealth and to avoid government positions. According to Al-Yusi, the ideal scholar should 'sit in his house, surrounded by books of knowledge' (Munson 1993, 44). He was also fond of quoting the *hadith*:

> The best kings are those who visit the ulama and the worst ulama are those who visit kings.

But in practice, of course, the ulama relied on the ruler for their livelihood and for a regular income derived from positions such as teachers, judges, or administrators. Thus a symbiotic relationship tended to emerge between the sultans and the ulama and, as Munson writes, 'the attitude of scholars to sultans in precolonial Morocco was usually one of servile submission' (1993, 54), and only a few scholars ever conformed to the ideal of the righteous man of God and overtly criticized and defied the sultan. Equally, few sultans conformed to the ideal of the just Islamic ruler;

they just found it useful not to overtly defy the ulama. Munson notes that in the early years of the last century when Morocco was being colonized by the French, the guardians of the law, the ulama, played a rather passive role, offering little resistance (1993, 66). And throughout the colonial period they generally supported the French administration. One important religious scholar, Muhammad Al-Kattani (1873–1909), who did actively defy the sultan and resist the French occupation, was flogged to death and buried in the middle of the night (Munson 1993, 74). Al-Kattani's rebellion against both the sultan and the French was short-lived, and most of his supporters were Berbers and poor artisans rather than the ulama.

At the end of the nineteenth century, the Salafiyya reformist movement emerged in Morocco, having spread from Egypt where it had originated. Its members sought to purify Islam of what they considered heretical innovations – in particular, Sufism and the veneration of saints. The reformists thus advocated a return to the pristine Islam of the 'virtuous forefathers' [*Al-Salaf Al-Salih*] as a means of overcoming European domination. As a form of scripturalism, they were also opposed to the idea of divine kingship or the idea that the sultan was in any way a representative of God. They thus advocated the contractual conception of political authority. Munson notes that throughout Islamic history, reformists or revivalists – such as the Wahhabis in early nineteenth-century Arabia – have urged Muslims to return to the pristine Islam of the Quran and the Sunna (the customary practices of the prophet as recorded in the hadith), and that rebellions against political rulers were almost always legitimated in these terms. But Munson is critical of Gellner's (1981) famous thesis on the 'pendulum' swing of Islam. Gellner, as described in an earlier section, interpreted Moroccan Islam as historically oscillating between two polar conceptions – a puritanical, scripturalist religion (orthodox) of the urban bourgeoisie and the ritualistic religion of the rural peasants. Gellner thus argued that the tribes of the Atlas Mountains would periodically revolt against the reigning but corrupt dynasty, in the name of the puritanical Islam normally associated with the urban areas (1969, 4). Munson concedes that puritanical reformist movements did periodically emerge in Morocco, advocating a return to the pristine Islam of the Quran, often drawing on the support of the Berber tribes. But he also emphasizes the point that not since the twelfth century have any of these reformist movements ever managed to seize or retain control of the Moroccan state. Moreover, Munson notes that Sufism is not simply a rural phenomenon and a component of popular religion but from the fifteenth century has pervaded both orthodox and popular forms of Islam. Both Al-Yusi and Al-Kattani were ulama as well as Sufis, and religious scholarship relating to law and mystical experience were considered by them as complementary rather than as antithetical. There was, indeed, a long-standing tension between orthodoxy and Sufism, but the Sufis who were persecuted by the sultan and orthodox ulama were often themselves urban ulama (Munson 1993, 83). Munson is equally critical of Geertz's view that Moroccan scripturalism sought to separate religion from secular life (1968, 105–6). To the contrary, Munson suggests,

'The Salafis actually tended to stress that Islam should govern *all* aspects of life – precisely the opposite of the argument Geertz attributes to them' (1993, 80). While Gellner's theory, he suggests, is 'anachronistic', that of Geertz is simply 'inaccurate'. Munson notes, however, that in the early years of the present century, Salafi scripturalist reformism did not necessarily coincide with the anti-colonial resistance movement. Al-Dukkali (1878–1937), for example, though hostile to popular Sufism and to many rural customs – such as the hanging of amulets on sacred trees – came from a family of ulama, was himself a Sufi as well as a Salafi reformist, and throughout his life supported the French protectorate government. On the other hand, Al-Alawi (1880–1964) combined Salafi reformism with Moroccan nationalism and was staunchly anti-colonial in his politics. He embodied the myth of the righteous man of god, for he shunned both wealth and power and lived in a little house on the outskirts of Fez, selling the produce of his three cows and flock of chickens. At the age of seventy-nine, he became an active member of the newly formed socialist party – the Union Nationale des Forces Populaires (UNFP) and became a hostile critic of King Hassan II. He considered royal succession by primogeniture and the right that rulers like Hassan had given themselves to formulate a national constitution both to be contrary to the principles of Islam and the national interest.

Earlier anthropologists – such as Geertz (1968) and Combs-Schilling (1989) – tended to see the Moroccan monarchy as the pivotal institution both of the religion and of the politics of Moroccan social life. For Geertz, the monarchy was not only the primary political institution but also the 'key institution in Moroccan religious life'. He argues that the power of King Hassan II – who took the title of king [*malik*] rather than that of sultan and who ruled Morocco from 1961 – rests 'almost entirely on the legitimacy of the sultanate in the eyes of the masses' (1968, 75–88; Munson 1993, 115). Likewise, Combs-Schilling affirms that the monarchy is of fundamental religious significance in Morocco, and that 'the King is the centre of the most important rituals of the faith' (1989, 21). Munson stridently argues that these accounts present a very distorted picture of Moroccan political life, as well as being apologetic towards Hassan's authoritarian rule. Their accounts ignore the fact that the basic rituals of Islam – such as daily prayers, the Friday prayers, and sermon – have a specifically religious significance for ordinary people, and have little or nothing to do with the monarchy, while politics in Morocco is not just an exercise in ideology but also involves fear, force, and repression. Combs-Schilling argues that one of the public holidays, the feast of sacrifice, is 'the most important ritual support for the Moroccan monarchy' (1989, 223) because the king's own sacrifice is repeatedly shown on television. But she fails to mention, Munson writes, that *everything* the king does publicly is endlessly covered in the government-controlled media (1993, 122) or to recognize that the king is almost never mentioned in the basic Muslim rituals. Munson thus affirms the need to distinguish between religion as a conceptual system in terms of which people interpret and relate to the world and political institutions that are legitimated through religion.

What was important about Hassan II was that he reaffirmed the hierocratic conception of monarchy, seeing himself as both a caliph and as a sharif, the 'commander of the faithful', who demands absolute obedience and devotion from his subjects – symbolized as 'slaves' [*adiduhu*] of the monarch. He himself is king [*malik*], which is derived from the verb *malaka*, meaning 'to possess, control, rule'. But Munson argues that the majority of Moroccans see government as a rather alien phenomenon, that affects them but over which they have little control and that the sycophantic displays of devotion to the monarch that one sees displayed on television 'reflect fear rather than reverence, servile submission rather than real loyalty' (1993, 147). He details the repression, the periodic Berber revolts – much of the Rif remained under military rule for three and a half years after the revolt of 1958–9, the suppression of public dissent or opposition – several hundred people being killed by government troops in 1959 in attempting to quell the strikes and demonstrations, the assassination of all political opponents by the secret police, and the use of arbitrary imprisonment and torture – in what amounted to a reign of terror – none of this is ever mentioned, Munson writes, in anthropological studies of Morocco's sacred kinship:

> Anthropologists, like many other Western observers, have tended to exaggerate both the religious and political significance of Hasan II's sanctity while completely overlooking his use of force and fear. (1993, 147)

People may believe in the monarch's baraka, especially rural peasants, but this is not the central feature of Moroccan religious life, nor does it imply any strong political commitment to the regime – which rules largely by fear and terror. There are some who echo the classical themes of Islamic political theory, that even an unjust ruler is better than no ruler at all – but most politically aware Moroccans saw Hassan's sacred kingship as a medieval anachronism that was kept alive by French colonialism. (For further studies of religion and politics in Morocco, see Waterbury 1970; Zartman 1987; for a discussion of the relationship between Islam and democracy by a Moroccan scholar, who stresses the importance of the 'rebel tradition' in Islam and the 'fragility' of the power of the caliph, see Mernissi 1993).

4

Hinduism and New Religious Movements

4.1. PROLOGUE

> Oh east is east and west is west and never the twain shall meet. So sang a Western bard – Rudyard Kipling – in the arrogant heyday of British imperialism

These are the opening words of a book on ayurvedic medicine. The author, however, does not challenge this dichotomy; on the contrary, he emphasizes it. Western and Indian culture, he tells us, are 'poles apart'. Western culture is aggressive, extroverted, selfish, analytic, and a 'real curse to the cosmos', while Indian culture – ancient Indian culture – is co-operative, synthetic, introverted, hospitable, and generous (Garde 1975, 1).

No one will dispute that there are not crucial differences between western and Indian cultures. The hegemony of positivistic science in western culture, with its dualistic metaphysics, its reductive materialism, and its individualism, inevitably leads to such a contrast: markedly with that of Indian culture, in which Hindu religion is seen as an 'encompassing' phenomenon. Indeed, Agehananda Bharati has written of the way in which he feels metaphysical conceptions, drawn from ancient Brahmanic doctrines, have permeated all aspects of Indian social life (1985, 189). But such contrasts, based on monolithic conceptions of particular cultural traditions, seem to me, whilst having some validity, to be extremely misleading, if not obfuscating. There is thus a tendency to equate Indian culture with Hinduism, and the suggestion that Hinduism is not a religion like Islam and Christianity but rather a civilization that expresses a universal 'spirituality'. With Hindu nationalists such as Vinayak D. Savarkar, there is even the suggestion of a primordial sense of being a Hindu – Hindutva – that is essentially spiritual (Bhatt 2001, 94–7). There is, in fact, a widely propagated 'fiction' that holds that the basis of Indian thought and culture is fundamentally 'spiritual', and moreover this spirituality is in essence that of Advaita Vedanta. The clearest proponent of this view is the Indian philosopher Sarvepalli Radhakrishnan (1888–1975), himself a high-caste Brahman, who at the end of his life became the Indian president. His voluminous writings on Indian religion, philosophy, and culture are well known. A typical quotation from his writings will cogently express this standpoint:

> Philosophy in India is essentially spiritual. It is the intense spirituality of India, and not any great political structure or social organization that it has developed, that has enabled it to resist the ravages of time and the accidents of history.... The spiritual motive dominates life in India.

He continues:

> The dominant character of the Indian mind which has coloured all its culture and moulded all its thought is the spiritual tendency. Spiritual experience is the foundation of India's rich cultural history.

He even suggests that such spirituality is in essence a 'mysticism' that leads to the realization of the spiritual (1933, 1/24–5, 41). These extracts are from his treatise on Indian philosophy. In his *An Idealist View of Life* (1932), a study that expresses very well his conservatism, he writes in a similar fashion contrasting the rationalistic logic of the West with the 'mystic contemplation' inherent in the Hindu system of philosophy (on Radhakrishnan's conception of Hinduism, see Minor 1981).

This 'myth of Indian spirituality' has been questioned by such scholars as M. N. Roy and Debiprasad Chattopadhyaya. The propagation of the 'myth' was certainly influenced by the German romantic movement of the early nineteenth century, which in a necessary critique of the mechanistic tendencies of the Enlightenment took an especial interest not only in the European folk tradition but also in Indian culture and religion. Max Müller, the famous Sanskrit scholar, inherited this perspective. What the myth does in essence is to equate one school of Indian philosophy, Advaita Vedanta, with Indian thought generally. The Vedanta tradition, systemized by the idealist philosopher Shankara in the eighth century, and popularized and propagated not only by Müller but by such luminaries as Vivekananda and Aurobindo, is in fact less of a philosophy than a theology.

What Roy and Chattopadhyanya conclusively demonstrated was that the religious and idealist perspective in early Indian philosophy, rather than being the dominant tendency, was in fact a minority one. They showed that the major schools of Indian philosophy – Samkhya, Nyaya, and Vaisesika – were all essentially materialist philosophies as well as expressing, like early Buddhism, an atheistic viewpoint. They thus stressed that these philosophical writings, together with those associated with Lokayata – the 'philosophy of the people' – were in their critique of religious conceptions and ritual, and in their defence of the reality of the material world, essentially characterized by secularism, a rationalistic logic and science (Roy 1940, 76–112; Chattopadhyaya 1959, 1969; Morris 1990, 71–2; for a useful study of Müller emphasizing the important influence of the German romantic movement, see Chaudhuri 1974).

In this chapter, I focus specifically on popular Hinduism, as studied by anthropologists, and therefore I steer clear of the rather philosophical accounts of

Hinduism, as described in many introductory texts. Such texts tend to give a rather scriptural and philosophical account of Hinduism and equate the latter with the worldview of Advaita Vedanta, with its emphasis on a 'universal soul'. Popular theism tends therefore to be bypassed, and from such texts you would hardly be aware of the importance of ritual worship [*puja*] and pilgrimages in the life of ordinary Hindus (see, for example, Radhakrishnan 1927; Nirvedananda 1944; Sen 1961).

There is another misleading tendency in popular philosophical accounts of Hinduism, and that is the suggestion that, because Hinduism is an 'encompassing' religion, historically incorporating many diverse beliefs and practices, it is essentially a religion of tolerance. This again is well expressed by Radhakrishnan: 'Hinduism absorbs everything that enters into it, magic or animism, and raises it to a higher level'. Different religious conceptions, and many different deities within Hinduism, are therefore simply manifestations of the 'absolute reality' – Brahman (1927, 34). Thus Hinduism is essentially a tolerant religion and lacks any proselytizing spirit. Even an atheist can become a Hindu – if he or she follows the Hindu code of conduct (Sen 1961, 38). Unlike other religions, Hinduism developed what Radhakrishnan describes as an 'attitude of comprehensive charity' (1927, 28). He therefore considers Buddhism to be simply a Hindu reformist movement and thus a constituent part of the Indian religious tradition, which in turn is conflated with Hinduism. The Buddha, of course, is considered by many Hindus to be simply an avatar [reincarnation] of the god Vishnu (Diwakar 1980).

But as Cynthia Mahmood (1997) has argued, there has been a long history of extensive persecution by the Brahmanic establishment of Buddhism, and even the famous scholar Saint Shankara called the Buddha an 'enemy of the people' and is reputed to have destroyed Buddhists throughout India. Mahmood emphasizes the dangers of 'overmysticizing' the religions of Asia (particularly Hinduism) and failing to recognize the religious pluralism of India, by privileging the perspective of idealist philosophers like Radhakrishnan.

In the following section, I give a brief account of what is usually described as Sanskritic Hinduism, although, as Van Der Veer suggests, there is no 'great Sanskritic tradition' in Hindu India, only a great many interacting traditions – local, regional, and national (1988, 61). But there are a number of key notions or principles intrinsic to Hinduism, and these I discuss: the doctrine of karma [reincarnation]; the caste system, and the principle of 'hierarchical inequality' that it implies; the concept of a world soul (or spirit) (Brahman); and the four main Hindu paths to salvation [*moksha*] – knowledge, action, devotion, and yoga. In Section 4.3, I then turn to popular Hinduism, drawing on the important work of Chris Fuller. Here I outline the various deities – gods, goddesses, and spirits – encountered in the Hindu tradition and, as a way of illustration, discuss Srinivas' classic study of the Coorgs of South India. I conclude the section with an account of Hindu rituals and the contrast that is often found within popular Hinduism between the high gods – Shiva and Vishnu – who are the focus of Sanskritic rituals, and the village deities and spirits, whose associated rituals are often conducted by a non-Brahmin priest and are particularly related to misfortunes.

In the next section, I discuss the cult of the goddess in Orissa and the importance of pilgrimages in the Hindu tradition (Section 4.4). I then turn to a discussion of new religious movements in Section 4.5, which is devoted to Bhakti cults and focuses on two religious movements, the Rhadha-Krishna Bhajanas of Madras and the Hare Krishna movement. The final section is devoted to a discussion of the role of religious gurus in the contemporary resurgence of a militant Hindu nationalism.

4.2. SANSKRITIC HINDUISM

In discussing Buddhism and Islam in the previous chapters, there was a brief mention of the theoretical distinction made by Robert Redfield and his associates between the great tradition of what he came to describe as an 'indigenous civilization' (such as India) and the little tradition of the folk communities. During the early 1950s, when this distinction was being formulated, Redfield was conscious that there was something of a division of labour between the writings of humanistic scholars and orientalists, who focussed their studies on the literate tradition embodied in sacred religious writings – the text – and the writings of anthropologists who tended to focus their ethnographic studies on tribal or village communities as if these were social isolates. The anthropologists' focus was on the folk community – in the context of a culture. Redfield wanted to bring these two kinds of study together in order to examine the relationship between the literate tradition and the culture of the peasant communities. With this kind of perspective, as Milton Singer put it, 'the anthropologist becomes interested in how the great tradition emerges from the culture of the folk and in how the two kinds of cultural traditions and two kinds of community, little and great, inter-relate' (1972, 55). Redfield appears not to have seen these two traditions as distinct cultural types, but rather the great tradition emphasized and abstracted certain 'aspects of the cultural heritage of the folk'. This systematization of the folk tradition was often esoteric and was done by a specialist literati associated with urban centres. The great tradition, for Redfield, was essentially a literate tradition, indigenous in its formation, and was embedded in a specific social context. Such a distinction was consonant with the 'folk–urban continuum', which Redfield had developed in his anthropological studies of Yucatan, Mexico (Redfield 1956; Singer 1972, 250–71). A number of early anthropologists working in India used this perspective in describing the religious culture of the village communities they studied, and in one well-known study, McKim Marriott concluded this:

Seen through its festivals and deities, the religion of the village of Kishan Garhi [in Uttar Pradesh] may be conceived as resulting from continuous processes of communication between a little, local tradition and greater traditions which have their places partly inside and partly outside the village. Only residual fragments of the religion of such a little community can be conceived as distinctive or separable. (1955, 218)

Such a perspective suggested that the earlier, holistic studies of anthropologists, which conceived of the folk culture or village as isolated from or a microcosm of the wider culture, were inadequate. There is thus a complex interrelationship between local religious traditions and the religious culture or what can be termed classical or Sanskritic Hinduism.

Anthropological studies over the past forty years have questioned whether Hinduism can usefully be understood by radically distinguishing two separate traditions, each with its own distinctive beliefs and ritual practices. But as Chris Fuller suggests in his excellent study of popular Hinduism, it is equally unhelpful to overstate the unity of Hinduism and fail to recognize that there are often institutional separations between different bodies of religious beliefs and practices. Thus, throughout India, as we shall subsequently discuss, temples devoted to the major deities such as Shiva and Vishnu (in his various manifestations) tend to be served by Brahman priests who use Sanskrit as a ritual language and make only vegetarian offerings. Such temples tend to attract mainly high-caste devotees. In contrast, the temples of other deities tend to be patronized by the low castes and have non-Brahman priests, who utilize vernacular languages in rituals and sometimes make animal sacrifices (Fuller 1992, 26–8; Morris 1981).

Unlike Islam, Hinduism has no founder, and all attempts, as M. N. Srinivas remarked, 'to define an enormously complex and amorphous phenomenon like Hinduism have usually ended in failure' (1952, 213). As a religious system, it is one of 'vast syncretism', a veritable melting pot of the myths, beliefs, rites, and spiritual entities of many cultures and communities – the Aryans, the so-called Dravidians, and innumerable 'tribal' communities. The term *Hindu* is derived from the Persian word for the country beyond the River Sindhu (Indus), and thus Hinduism would appear to mean the religion of the Indian people (Sen 1961, 17). The earliest codification of this religion is contained in the Vedic scriptures. Consisting of four collections of texts, of which the most important are the Rigveda [knowledge of hymns], these were written in Sanskrit between 1500 and 800 B.C.E. The religion depicted in these scriptures, like that of the early Greeks, is polytheistic, many of the deities being personified natural phenomena – Agni [fire], Indra [thunder], Surya [sun]. Many of these deities were masculine, and the central rite of the cults associated with them was sacrifice, performed by priests. One god, Soma, was associated with special rites involving the induction of a hallucinogenic herb (from which the deity took its name) and ecstatic dances. There has been much controversy over the identification of the herb, but modern research suggests that it is the fungi *Amanita muscaria*, which is widely used in religious rites among Eurasian peoples (Wasson 1972; Emboden 1979, 58–65). Basham, in his invaluable account of the early history and culture of India, suggests that the religion of the

Rigveda is an 'imperfect syncretism of many tribal beliefs and cults' (1967, 240). Later Vedic scriptures, the Brahmanas, the doctrinal texts dealing with priestly sacrifices and rites, and the Upanishads, philosophical discourses that are often referred to as the Vedanta (the conclusion of the Vedas), express a more abstract, esoteric, and mystical conception of religion. In fact, the Upanishads, which have had such a profound influence on Indian philosophy, were written at a period when fundamental social changes were taking place, with the break-up of tribal communities, and the rise of Asiatic city–states. Basham suggests that the emergence of mysticism and asceticism was directly related to these social changes and the psychological anxiety that they caused (Basham 1967, 248–9; Toynbee 1976, 176–83). Robert Bellah in his important essay on religious evolution (1964) writes that the social transformations involving the development of a class structure, literacy, and a market economy was directly related to the emergence of 'historic religion' with its notion of a transcendent realm beyond the natural cosmos, and a devaluation of the empirical world. Classical Hinduism is an example of this kind of religion.

These later Vedic scriptures express two interrelated conceptions.

The first is embodied in the notion of karma. The doctrine of karma (which means literally action or deed) is fundamental to most Indian thought and implied a belief in a cosmic or moral order, in which one's actions in this – and previous lives – determine the fate of one's reincarnation. All living things, including spirits and deities, are part of this cycle of rebirth [*samsara*]. This conception suggests that the life process itself is without beginning and without end and that every event is determined by its antecedents (Hiriyanna 1949, 46–50). Such beliefs are not merely part of the literary tradition, but as Ursula Sharma (1973) indicated, are also a part of the folk culture, providing an ultimate explanation for suffering, even though coexisting with more immediate explanations of misfortunes – such as witchcraft or spirit illness. Karma is thus a theory of moral causation and implies that every human action has consequences for good or ill. According to Hindu doctrine, therefore, a person is not born a *tabula rasa* but is endowed with certain fundamental characteristics that were largely determined by actions in a previous life. As the Chandogya Upanishad puts it

> Those whose conduct here has been good will quickly attain a good birth, the birth of a Brahman, the birth of a Kshatriya, or the birth of a Vaishya. But those whose conduct has been evil, will quickly attain an evil birth, the birth of a dog, the birth of a hog, the birth of a [low-caste] Chandala. (4.10.7)

The notion of karma is therefore intimately related to the caste system, which as Srinivas (1952) noted, forms the structural basis of Hinduism. In the Indian context, dharma essentially refers to the caste system, which is a hierarchical social system that proclaims the fundamental inequality of humans. In the classical literature, four castes (*varna*, meaning colour) are outlined and given divine sanction – the

Brahmans [priests], Kshatriyas [rulers and soldiers], Vaishyas [merchants and traders], and Shudras [the service castes]. There is also a group of 'outcastes' mentioned, which refers to marginal tribal people in the process of being incorporated into the caste system. The varna was essentially an *ideal* model of Hindu society, and the caste hierarchy essentially formed a part of a cosmic order, which had important symbolic correlates, viz.:

Caste	**Brahman**	**Kshatriya**	**Vaishya**	**Shudra**
Social Function	Priest	King Warrior	Merchant	Service
Colour	White	Red	Yellow	Black
Direction	East	North	South	West
Body Part	Head	Heart	Loins	Feet
Path of Salvation	Jnana	Karma	Bhakti	Yoga
	Knowledge	Action	Devotion	Meditation

This is purely an ideological construct, and there is little evidence to suggest that the castes of medieval and modern India emerged from this ideal classification. In fact, in reality the caste system is complex and variable, numerous castes [*jati*] being evident within the Indian context. Each village had a number of hereditary castes linked together by ritual obligations and economic ties, which were usually focussed around members of the dominant land-owning caste. Pollution rules enforced a high degree of cultural segregation, and the low castes, who perform the essential agricultural work, were subject to much harassment and exploitation. In an important study, Louis Dumont (1970*a*) emphasized that the opposition between ritual purity and pollution was the fundamental ideological principle of the caste system. There has been a vast amount of literature on the caste system, and some scholars seem to suggest that it is largely the product of the western imagination, but as Fuller suggests, caste is not some abstract concept but is a 'visible dimension of everyday life in rural India, which is part of everyone's social and personal identity in a very real sense' (1992, 13). But scholars such as Declan Quigley (1993) have emphasized the limitations of interpreting 'caste' as simply a religious or cultural phenomenon, thus ignoring the political dimension, particularly the importance of kingship and the dominant land-owning castes. Thus, though the caste-system may not be the 'essence' of Indian society, only extreme cultural idealists will question its social reality and its cultural and political significance (for useful studies of the caste system, see Beteille 1971; Kolenda 1978; Parry 1979; Raheja 1988; Fuller 1996; Sharma 1999).

The principle of 'hierarchical inequality' is then an essential element of Hinduism – both Sanskritic and popular – but as Fuller emphasizes, there is no radical dichotomy between humans and various forms of divinity (1992, 4). Indeed, the Indian psychoanalyst Sudhir Kakar suggests that the 'Hindu world image' implies a 'unitary vision' with no radical dichotomy between the self and the world (1981, 33).

This leads us to the second important conception evident in the Upanishads and the later Vedic writings: that of Brahman, an impersonal, all-pervading world spirit, sustaining but beyond the phenomenal world. The individual soul, or *atman*, is considered to be an aspect or manifestation of this 'eternal substrata of the universe', as Zaehner (1962, 5) describes it. The eternal dharma or moral law has its origin in this 'world spirit'. 'Oriental' religion is often seen as quite distinct from the Christian tradition and 'Occidental' thought, but this conception has close affinities to gnosticism, even though the latter is often described as dualistic, in its rigid separation of spirit and matter. But in its stress on salvation through knowledge (Greek *gnosis*), in its devaluation of the mundane world as a realm of 'unreality' and illusion [*maya*], and in its advocacy of a mystical union [*unio mystica*] between the individual (soul) and this transcendental realm (Brahman), Upanishadic doctrine resembles, it seems to me, that of gnostic religion (Jonas 1958; Pagels 1982). In the writings of the famous South Indian philosopher Shankara, this doctrine was developed as the Vedanta system of philosophy (salvation). Shankara (788–820) advocated a non-dualistic [*advaita*] thesis, suggesting that at a higher level of truth the phenomenal universe, including the gods themselves, was unreal – *maya* – and that the ultimate reality was Brahman, the impersonal world soul of the Upanishads, with which the individual soul was identical (Hirayanna 1949, 152–69; Basham 1967, 330–1; Menon 1976).

Taken together, a belief in the transmigration of souls and the cycle of rebirths [*samsara*] and the devaluation of this phenomenal 'cosmic' order in relation to a higher primordial 'spiritual' reality – such a notion having ascetic and pessimistic overtones – implied that a way out of the world of samsara was both possible and necessary. Thus, in common with Buddhism, Hinduism developed the concept of liberation [*moksha*] from the transient empirical world of samsara. The Upanishads in fact reflect a shift of emphasis from a religion of sacrifice to a religion of salvation. But whereas in Buddhism, there is only one way of liberation – the Middle Way – Hinduism recognized several paths to salvation; the most important of these are *jnana* [knowledge], *yoga* [meditation], *karma* [action], and *bhakti* [devotion]. We shall briefly discuss each of these paths in turn, drawing on my earlier study (Morris 1994, 82–6).

1. *Jnana Marga.* The way of knowledge. In Hindu culture, it has been said that a knowledge of reality is the key to self-realization. Knowledge and learning have always been given high priority, and both Samkhya and Vedanta scholars see *jnana* [knowledge] as the way to liberation. As the Bhagavad-Gita put it, 'Even if you be the most sinful of all sinners, yet shall you cross over all sin by the raft of knowledge' (4: 36). But such knowledge was centred on the human subject and subordinated to the desire for liberation. Shankara put an important emphasis on liberation through knowledge, although he accepted religious worship and devotion.

One of the most well-known advocates of Jnana Yoga is Ramana Maharshi, who follows the Advaita–Vedanta teachings of Shankara. And the teachings of this modern mystic echo those of Shankara in making it clear that the self is in no way related to the body but is identified with an impersonal deity (Mahadevan 1977).

It has to be stressed, however, that knowledge in this context is not empirical knowledge of the world and of human existence but religious knowledge or gnosis. As Jonathan Parry has written of the Brahmanical tradition, 'real knowledge is knowledge of a metaphysical truth which liberates the soul from the endless cycle of existence – a knowledge which is revealed in the texts but which is generally thought to be obtained only by years of submission to a rigorous ascetic discipline' (1985, 206). The 'self' therefore in the Hindu tradition is essentially a metaphysical self.

2. *Karma Marga.* The way of action. This path of liberation stresses the importance of social duty and the performance of selfless actions. It is given its classic expression in the Bhagavad-Gita and is a path clearly associated with the Kshatriya caste. The epic Bhagavad-Gita [the Song of the Lord] records the moral dilemma of one of the Panava brothers, Arjuna, who on the battlefield of Kurushetra faces many of his own kinsmen in battle. He is moved and disturbed at the thought of killing his own kindred and turns to his charioteer, Krishna, for advice. The charioteer reveals himself as an incarnation of the god Vishnu, and what ensues in the dialogue is that Krishna convinces Arjuna that it is his duty to fight and thus to kill his own kith and kin. It symbolizes the dominance of the state or territorial principle over the kinship ethics of tribal society (Sardesai and Bose 1982, 23). The message of the Gita is that one should follow the dharma and so through selfless action [karma] achieve salvation.

   It is somewhat ironic that the Gita had such a strong appeal to Mahatma Gandhi, when the text is fundamentally a defence of militarism and the caste hierarchy. Yet although the Karma Marga stresses the importance of activity in the world and action, its aim is to transcend dharma. 'The notion of agency must be given up. The act is to be disinterested' (Organ 1970, 247). The notion of an empirical self is thus transcended.

3. *Bhakti Marga.* The way of devotion. The Bhagavad-Gita discusses not only Jnana and Karma Yoga but also introduces a third path, that of Bhakti. The term comes from the root *bhaj*, meaning to be attached to, to be devoted to, and essentially means the unconditional surrender to the deity, with profound feelings of love and devotion. It represents the theistic tendency in Hinduism, and was given its fullest expression in the hymns of the early Tamil devotees of South India. Bhakti cults flourished during the medieval period, and were particularly associated with those religious scholars who

accepted a qualified form of Vedanta – like Madhava and Ramanuja. These cults focussed around two deities – Krishna (an incarnation of the god Vishnu and hence called Vaishnavism) and Shiva (the Saiva cults). The Bhakti path implied no lengthy meditation, no penance, no intellectual insights into the mysteries of Brahman–Atman – simply loving devotion directed towards the deity. Its advocates stressed its superiority to the other paths: The Bhagavad-Gita clearly implies that this path is the one most suited to those of 'inferior birth' – the Vaisyas, Shudras, and women (9.32).

Bhakti, as with the other paths, is a form of salvation that involves then a detachment from the empirical world. This is particularly evident in a contemporary devotional cult, the Hare Krsna movement (International Society for Krsna Consciousness), which is discussed more fully in Section 4.5.

4. *Yoga Marga.* Besides being one of the six systems of philosophy, Yoga also constitutes a system of discipline that leads to salvation and thus represents one of the four paths [Marga]. The term *Yoga* is derived from the Sanskrit root *yuj*, which means to join, to bind, to yoke together. It thus implies the union of the individual soul with the universal spirit. This is possible, as Mircea Eliade suggests, only if the 'bonds' that unite the spirit to the world are detached. This implies a preliminary detachment from matter (1958, 7). The term Yoga is therefore often applied to the three Hindu paths to salvation, Karma Yoga, Bhakti Yoga, and Jnana Yoga. But the classical system of Yoga, known as Raja Yoga, was that described by Patanjali in his Yoga Sutras.

In his Yoga Sutras, Patanjali defined Yoga as the control of thought processes in the mind and following Samkhya doctrine, the mind [*chitta*] is made up of several functions, *manas* [mind as a sensing organ], *buddhi* [intelligence or intellect], and *ahamkara* [ego or self-consciousness] (Chennakesavan 1960, 17–34). Such thought processes take into account perception, knowledge, delusions, dreams, sleep, memory. Through non-attachment, one achieves freedom, freedom from desire for what is seen or heard. The aim of Yoga, as with the other three paths, is to achieve salvation, defined as non-attachment to the empirical world.

'When, through knowledge of the Atman, one ceases to desire any manifestation of nature, then that is the highest kind of non-attachment' (1.16). Patanjali also notes that concentration may be attained also through devotion to god (Isvara). But Patanjali's scheme of salvation is less concerned with knowledge and devotion than with outlining a course of graded mental concentration or spiritual discipline in order to obtain 'union' [*yoga*] (Prabhavananda 1953, 10–12; for classic texts on yoga, see also Eliade 1975; Wood 1959). The Bhagwan Shree Rajneesh incorporated the tantric version of the yoga path into his own 'dynamic meditation' (Myers 1985; Thompson and Heelas 1986; Gordon 1987; Mann 1991).

Although in the caste hierarchy the Brahman priest is often seen as of the highest rank, in fact within the Hindu context, there are at least three 'hierarchical models', suggesting varying relationships among the Brahman priest, the king, and the ascetic renouncer. According to Richard Burghart (1978), who based his theory on research studies from the Hindu kingdom of Nepal, each of these persons claimed supreme rank according to his own hierarchical model of social relations. Thus while according to the varna model and in terms of ritual purity and function, the Brahman priest considered himself superior and as ideally constituting a caste that has the power of sacred knowledge, in other contexts it was the king [*raj*] who claimed priority. As upholders of the dharma [the moral order of society], the king did not necessarily subordinate himself ritually to the Brahman and was usually considered a divine ruler, an incarnation of the god Vishnu. The ascetic renouncer [*sannyasin*], on the other hand, practising complete non-attachment and focussed completely on liberation [*moksha*] from the eternal cycle of rebirths [*samsara*] was seen as the 'exemplar' of the supreme religious ideal (Fuller 1992, 17). He was thus, as a wandering ascetics and in his own terms, superior to both the Brahman and king. As Fuller suggests, the sannyasin, whether ascetics in ochre robes or half-clad figures with matted hair living in seclusion or as itinerant mendicants, are familiar figures in India. Often seen near the major temples or gathering at pilgrimage sites, they enjoy a significance out of all proportion to their actual numbers, and many ascetic renouncers are men of very high status. Even Brahmans and kings, Fuller writes, 'will bow down to acknowledge his superiority' (1992, 18), for most renouncers are men. Burghart suggests that throughout the history of Nepal (and India) there has been a complex relationship among these three ritual figures, and often 'mutual antagonism' was expressed between the Brahmans and the ascetic renouncers (1978, 533; for further studies on this topic, see Das 1977, 18–56; Burghart 1983).

Although India is now a democratic republic with no 'kingdoms' – the 'princely states' remain as viable political entities – nevertheless the rituals of kingship still play an important part in popular Hinduism (Fuller 1992, 106–27). It is to popular Hinduism that we may now turn.

4.3. POPULAR HINDUISM

In this section, I want to outline, in contrast to 'Sanskritic' Hinduism, the popular Hinduism that is to be found in the cities, towns, and villages throughout India, drawing on the work of Fuller (1992) and focussing specifically on the classical study of the Coorgs by M. N. Srinivas (1952).

Although Hinduism, as Srinivas writes, has a 'bias towards pantheism' (1962, 148) of an acosmic variety, for ordinary Hindus it may best be described as a form of polytheism. Thus popular Hinduism is theistic, and within both the village and the urban context, people believe in the existence of a variety of deities, both male and female, and of many kinds of spirits. Following Fuller, and using the term *deity* to cover gods, goddesses, and spirits, there is within the Hindu pantheon a superabundance of different deities or spiritual agencies. But as Fuller emphasizes, Hindu polytheism is extremely complex, amorphous, and flexible. Thus the majority of the important deities have numerous forms and manifestations, and most have a multitude of names. One deity can become many, and many deities can become one, and within the Sanskritic tradition stressed by Radhakrishnan, all deities are simply manifestations of one spiritual absolute – Brahman. Equally important, there is no radical dichotomy between deities and humans, and in many contexts, as we shall explore, human persons may become gods, either through possession or by being seen as manifestations of a deity. Both the Brahman priest and the devotees may take the form of a god during worship, if only temporarily, and the identification with the deity, as Fuller writes, 'is a fundamental objective in Hindu worship [*puja*]' (1992, 31). What essentially distinguishes humans from deities is that the deities are immortal and have mystical power.

Given this complexity, we can nevertheless broadly discuss the Hindu deities under three headings: what are usually described as Sanskritic or 'great gods'; the goddess and her many forms; and the village deities – the numerous gods and spirits that are important for local communities.

The two most important deities of popular Hinduism are the great gods [*deva*], Vishnu and Shiva, which have temples and shrines dedicated to them throughout India. Many of these temples are famous pilgrimage centres. In the literature, Vishnu is often described as the 'preserver' and Shiva as the 'destroyer' while Brahma, which also has prominence in the classical literature, is denoted as the 'creator'. But it is of interest that while Brahman as a universal spirit is important for philosophers, Brahma is rarely worshipped by ordinary Hindus. The god Vishnu, whose consort is Lakshmi, the goddess of wealth and good fortune, is essentially a celestial deity that takes many different forms and is invariably looked on as a beneficial deity. Of especial importance is that Vishnu has many distinct incarnations [*avataras*], the most important being that of Rama, the king of Ayodhya and the hero of the epic Ramayana, and Krishna, whose life and heroics is recorded in the Bhagavad-Gita. Many temples are dedicated to the incarnations Rama and Krishna throughout India, and Krishna, as we subsequently discuss, is the focus of many Bhakti devotional movements. Vishnu is especially associated with particular kingdoms; for example, as Padmanabha at Trivandrum (the Travancore state) and as Jagannatha at Puri (the kingdom of Orissa). On the other hand, unlike Vishnu, Shiva is rarely represented in the form of incarnations [*avataras*], but nevertheless takes many different forms – as lord of the dance [*Nataraja*], as the malevolent Bhairava, which is often a tutelary village deity, or most commonly in the form of a *linga*, a short cylindrical pillar that represents his phallus. This usually stands on a base representing the female sexual organ [*yoni*], identified as the goddess Shakti. But Shiva also takes the form of an ascetic, the great yogi, such as at Mount Kailasa in the

Himalayas, and is generally thought to be the patron deity of ascetics. At the famous Madurai temple in South India, Shiva, in the form of Sundareshwara, is married to Minakshi, the daughter of the Pandyan king, both deities being the focus of elaborate rituals (Fuller 1984). The usual consort of Shiva, however, is Parvati, and they are depicted as having two sons, Ganesha and Skanda, both important deities in their own right. Ganesha (or Ganapathi), the famous elephant-headed god, is popular throughout India, while Skanda is particularly associated with South India (and also, as we have seen, with Sri Lanka) and in Tamilnadu is known as Subrahmanya or Murugan. He is the presiding deity of many large temples and is usually depicted holding a spear and mounted on a peacock.

Although an important form of the mother goddess depicts her as the wife of Shiva, called in her benevolent form Parvati or Mahadevi [great goddess], the goddess [*devi*] takes many diverse forms. These can be seen either as distinct deities or as simply manifestations of the one goddess. In vernacular terms, she is usually known as the mother [*mata* or *ammai*]. But the goddess may often take a malevolent, ferocious, or destructive form – as Durga who slays the buffalo-demon, or as Kali, the black one. The goddess is also known as Shakti, expressing female power, energy, and independence. The powers of the goddess, like those of Shiva, are thus essentially ambivalent. Forms of the goddess are often associated or identified with particular kingdoms (such as Mysore) and throughout India may be the tutelary deity of a local community. Indeed, almost every village or local settlement has its own tutelary goddess [Gramadevata], even if only in the form of a shrine set up under a sacred tree. In South India, such goddesses as Sitala and Mariyammai are often associated with smallpox.

The final category of deities is that of the village gods and spirits that are associated with specific local regions or communities. These range from malevolent ghosts and spirits that lack any associated cult [*preta, bhuta*] to prominent local deities that may or may not be manifestations or forms of more 'Sanskritic' or 'great' gods. But given what Fuller describes as a 'polytheistic logic of fluid continuity', there is usually no clear-cut separation between the great deities and the more local deities and spirits within the village context (1992, 55–6). This can be illustrated if we turn now to Srinivas' classic study of the Coorgs (1952) (for discussions of Hindu deities, see Basham 1967, 302–22; Fuller 1992, 29–56).

What is of interest about Srinivas' study, *Religion and Society Among the Coorgs of South India*, is that although it is considered a classic statement of functionalist anthropology, and clearly shows the influence of Radcliffe-Brown, the main thrust of the work analyzes the manner in which the domestic and village cults of the region are linked to the wider culture and suggests a process by which communities are drawn into the Hindu fold.

The Coorgs are a dominant land-owning caste of south-west Mysore (now southern Karnataka). With a strong martial tradition, they have looked on themselves as Kshatriyas and, under the Lingayat Rajas of the eighteenth century and during the colonial period, they constituted like the Nayars of Malabar (Fuller 1976), an aristocratic warrior caste, holding important positions in the administration and nearly monopolizing the army. The village economy was focussed around members of this land-owning caste and included such castes as the Kaniya [astrologers]; Brahmin [priests]; Meda [basketmakers]; such low castes as Banna, Panika, and Poleya, who perform important ritual functions for the Coorgs; and several artisan castes. For the Coorg community, the most important social group was the *okka*, the patrilineal joint family of twenty to thirty members: Srinivas indeed describes it as the 'basic unit of society' (1952, 55). Under the leadership of a senior male, the okka was a corporate group with an ancestral estate, rights in which were mainly restricted to male members. The group was exogamous, and on marriage there were elaborate ceremonies transferring rights between the respective kin groups. Indeed, the marriage rite involved essentially the granting of rights to the bride in the groom's okka and the severance of her own natal ties. Cross-cousin marriage was preferred and common, and there were close affinal links between different okka. There was a clear sexual division of labour: the men cultivating or supervising the cultivation of the land by low-caste labourers, many Poleyas being in the past attached by hereditary ties to a Coorg family; the women were mainly involved in domestic work and seem formerly to have enjoyed greater freedom. As indicated, Coorg men also served in the army, and when Srinivas was undertaking his researches in the early 1940s, many had professional occupations.

Many religious rites are focussed around the patrilineal joint family, and in a sense each okka has its own religious cult. Each estate has an ancestral shrine, for at any given time an okka consists of a group of agnatically related males descended from a common ancestor [*karanava*]. During the harvest festival and on important ritual occasions, particularly during the marriage and funerary ceremonies, elaborate propitiations are made to the ancestors. These consist of offerings of meat curry and rice offered to the ancestors on a plantain leaf; in the funerary rite, this is the dominant motif. The departed ancestors are also saluted and prayed to every day. Two ritual specialists are important to the cult of the okka. The first is the astrologer, who belongs to the Kaniya caste, whose function it is not only to see, by the examination of horoscopes, whether the marriage of two people is compatible but also whether a particular time is appropriate for the holding of a ceremony. Srinivas suggests that astrology is a Sanskritizing agent and that the more a tribe or local community 'resorts to astrology the more do its beliefs become Sanskritized' (1952, 75). We shall return to this process in a moment. The second important specialist is the spirit oracle, usually a man belonging to the Banna caste, who incarnates the ancestral spirit of the Coorg family. The spirit-possession rite has the quality of a drama and usually takes place after sundown at the ancestral shrine. In a possessed state, the oracle often asks to be conducted around the – his – ancestral estate and may sharply rebuke his – for the oracle is simply a spirit medium – descendants for neglecting the estate. Sacrifices of a fowl or pig are often made during these ceremonies, and in an important sense, as Srinivas writes, the Banna oracle and his family almost become the repository of the traditions and history of the Coorg okkas. Many villagers, particularly those expressing preference for the Vedanta doctrine, often express opposition to the ancestor cult. At these ceremonies, no Brahmin priests are present and no Sanskrit mantras are chanted.

Although the harvest festival is strictly that of the Coorg landowners, every caste in the village co-operates in the festivals, and gifts are exchanged between different castes. Srinivas suggests that the festival stresses 'the unity of the village' (1952, 44). Hunting rituals and communal dancing by the Coorg men are important on these ceremonial occasions. It is worth noting that low-caste people, such as Medas and Poleyas, were not allowed to enter the Coorg ancestral house, and that cobra deities, associated with the god Subramanya, the son of Shiva, often had shrines within the compound of the Coorg house. Brahmin priests often made propitiations at these shrines by using Sanskrit mantras on behalf of the Coorg family.

Besides the cults associated with the kin groups [*okkas*] of the land-owning caste, there are important rituals focussed on the village deities. Each village in the region has one or more temple or shrine. A particular temple derives its name from a specific deity, who is often the 'village deity' – although several villages may combine to celebrate the festival of the deity. Besides the shrine of this chief deity, which is represented in the temple by an icon or image, the shrines of several other deities may be present. The Bhadrakali temple at Kuklur, Srinivas notes, contained the shrines of Ganesha, Sartavu (Ayyappa), and the Shiva linga, while in the compound were the shrines of several other deities and spirits. These other deities were considered subordinate to Bhadrakali. Village deities are found throughout peninsular India and include such deities as Ayyappa (Shasta), Bhagavati, Ketrappa (Kshetrapala), Chamundi, and Ayyanar.

The deities protect and watch over the village community. They are often females like the mother goddesses Kali, Ellamma, and Mariamma, the latter being particularly associated with smallpox and cholera (for a useful account on the village gods of South India, see Whitehead 1921).

The temples dedicated to Bhagavati, Mahadeva (Shiva), and Ayyappa have Brahmin priests who propitiate and worship the deities by using Sanskrit mantras. Only vegetarian offerings are made. In the past, such temples, which often have a regional significance and are important pilgrim centres, were not open to untouchable castes like the Poleya. There are also temples where the Brahmins are normally priests and the mode of worship Sanskritic, but on certain occasions the Brahmin priests withdraw to allow the temple to be used by non-Brahmins.

In the festival of Bhadrakali described by Srinivas (1952, 187–200), which lasts a week or more, a Coorg man acts as an oracle medium for the goddess, giving instructions for the organization of the festival while in a possessed state. Standing near the shrine, the Bhadrakali oracle also receives offerings and answers questions put to him on matters of welfare by the villagers. During the festival, many members of the Poleya caste become possessed outside the temple, incarnating the various spirits associated with their caste. In their ecstatic state, the Poleya oracles may be called on to exorcise evil spirits from people, and in a manner reminiscent of devotees of Hamadsha brotherhood, the Poleya oracles may gash themselves while possessed. The festival usually ends, like the harvest festival, with a communal meal. During the festival of the village deity, Srinivas stresses, Sanskritic and non-Sanskritic rites are combined in varying proportions. The propitiation of these deities during the annual festival is a village purification and serves to keep epidemics such as smallpox, plague, and cholera away from the village and to grant the community good crops, children, and longevity (1952, 184).

There is thus an interesting correlation between the caste system and the religious structure. The Sanskrit deities like Bhagavati and Mahadeva are served by Brahmin priests, using Sanskritic mantras. No possession is usually involved, and propitiations are vegetarian. These deities often have an all-India significance. Village deities like Bhadrakali and Ketrappa, on the other hand, usually involve spirit mediums or priests who are non-Brahmins, and propitiations may include non-vegetarian food. Coorgs we may note were, as the dominant caste, involved in hunting and were meat-eaters. And, finally, castes like the Poleyas propitiate more local spirits, which often have locus outside the temple. Possession rites are mainly connected with these spirits. Given his focus on the Coorg caste, Srinivas does not explore the cult activities of those 'untouchable' communities (for an interesting study of the religion of a Harijan community, see Moffatt 1979, 219–89). Also important is the fact that whereas the high gods – Shiva, Vishnu – are considered beneficent and protective at a village level, the non-vegetarian deities have a more malevolent aspect. Local deities or spirits may not be directly associated with the Sanskritic literature, their significance local or caste-specific, and they may have a free-floating or uncontrolled nature. Such deities are mainly associated with 'untouchable' castes and may be seen as primarily malevolent. This situation where 'the order of gods is . . . parallel to the order of men' has been reported in many communities (Harper 1959; Beals 1962, 47–9; Morris 1981).

In noting the coexistence of Sanskritic and non-Sanskritic elements in the rituals and beliefs of the Coorgs and other castes of Mysore, and conscious that Hinduism is a dynamic and not a static phenomena, Srinivas, in his conclusions to the study, examines the 'spread' of classical Hinduism in two ways. The first is spatial. Noting that the deities and rituals evident in a Coorg village have a differential spread – local, regional, and all-India – he writes that the 'Hinduism with an all-India spread . . . is chiefly Sanskritic in character' (1952, 214). Brahmins everywhere, he suggests, have much Sanskritic ritual in common. He notes too how the epics Ramayana and Mahabharata have played an important part in the spread of Hinduism, and how deities, events, and places mentioned in the myths have been identified with specific localities. As he writes, 'The presence, within Sanskritic Hinduism, of a vast and ever-growing mythology, the worship of trees, rivers and mountains, and the association of deities and epic heroes with local spots everywhere in India, makes easy the absorption of non-Sanskritic cults and deities' (1952, 227).

The second way he describes is temporal – the process of Sanskritization whereby tribal communities and low castes are absorbed into Hinduism or attempt to raise their social status by adopting the customs and rites of the higher castes. The classic statement of this process is Aiyappan's perceptive study of the Iravas of Kerala. Focussing on a single village, Aiyappan (1965) explores how this caste community, traditionally toddy-tappers and considered untouchables, acquired a knowledge of Sanskrit and Ayurvedic medicine, adopted puranic deities like Vishnu, Shiva, and Shasta (Ayyappa), and under the leadership of Sri Narayana Guru formed an association to build temples and propagate philosophic Hinduism. But this process of Sanskritization, it is worth noting, was an accompaniment of a change in the economic circumstances of the Iravas, as feudal reciprocities were gradually eroded in the village context. As Parry writes, in discussing the Kolis, a scheduled caste of Kangra in north-west India, Sanskritization was usually necessary, but it was seldom a sufficient condition for the upward social mobility of a caste community (1970, 99).

The concept of Sanskritization introduced by Srinivas stimulated a good deal of research, comment, and criticism. Milton Singer (1972, 45) questioned if it was possible to equate all-India Hinduism with 'Sanskritic' Hinduism, for many beliefs and practices that are widespread throughout India have no sanction in scripture. These include witchcraft beliefs and much 'popular Hinduism'. Others have noted that the Brahmin is not the only model for Sanskritization, and that other processes, glossed under such terms as 'modernization' and 'secularization', have been taking place within the Indian context. Indeed, Bernard Cohn, in his study (1955) of the changing status of the Chamars of Uttar Pradesh, noted that while members of this 'untouchable' caste have been fighting for their social and economic rights, and in the process adopting elements of the religious culture of the higher castes, the dominant castes themselves are becoming secularized as they are increasingly drawn into the urban economy and culture.

To conclude this section on popular Hinduism, we may briefly explore the two main forms of Hindu ritual – worship [*puja*] and sacrifice [*bali*], and discuss Louis Dumont's classic article on the Tamil village deity Aiyanar (1970*b*, 20–32).

Puja [worship], as Fuller affirms, is the core ritual of popular theistic Hinduism. It consists of making offerings – of food, flowers, water, incense – and conducting services for the deity, who is represented usually by a sculptured image [*murti*]. Cast in bronze or carved in stone, the image may take many different forms, but is usually an anthropomorphic representation of the deity. The deity is installed in the image through a consecration ritual, and thus a distinction is made between the image and the deity, and, as Fuller writes, 'the object of worship is not the image, but the deity whose power is inside it' (1992, 60). But during the ritual act, the image and deity tend to be identified. The puja is an act of 'respectful honouring', of expressing devotion towards the deity and involves the ritual exchange of 'vision' [*darshana*] between the deity and the worshipper. The crucial importance of visual contact, which implies an extremely intimate form of communion between the god (or guru) and the devotee, needs to be stressed in the Hindu context (Eck 1981; Babb 1986, 214–6). This leads one to seriously question the suggestions of postmodernist scholars who interpret 'vision' as predominantly a western emphasis, with connotations of distance, objectivity, and dominance (cf. Fabian 1983 and Everden 1985 on the 'despotism' of the eye).

The importance of light and fragrance, however, expressed by the camphor flame, suggests that the essence of the puja ritual is the identification of the deity with the human devotee, and thus the worshipper can potentially 'transcend' the human condition. Importantly, of course, people seek divine support for earthly problems, and at the conclusion of the puja ritual, they usually receive *prasada*, 'grace' or blessing in the form of ashes or red powder that is rubbed on the forehead by the priest. These represent the ritual transmutation of the substances offered to the deity and embody the power and grace of the divinity (Fuller 1992, 74).

Although recognizing that the puja ritual expresses a hierarchical relationship between the deities and humans – and Fuller suggests that hierarchical values are intrinsic to Hinduism – and thus that rituals may reflect or legitimate social inequalities, Fuller nevertheless questions whether the ritual has only a political function. The theory of Nicholas Dirks (1987), who contends that puja is simply a 'root metaphor' for political relations that centred on the king, who is viewed a superior to the Brahman, Fuller thus suggests is a rather limited perspective (1992, 81; for a useful booklet on temple rituals, see Ramachandra Rao 1985).

Although animal sacrifice [*bali*] was an important ritual in Vedic religion, with the decline of Buddhism in the early centuries of the Christian era and the emergence of what Fuller describes as the 'Brahmanical synthesis' – that is, Sanskritic Hinduism – there has developed a general antipathy towards this form of ritual. For the Brahmanic tradition puts a focal emphasis on non-violence, vegetarianism, and puja, or devotional rituals. Since the nineteenth century, reformist movements within Hinduism have also been opposed to animal sacrifice, and Srinivas noted that the Indian National Congress had been more or less successful in 'opposing the propitiation of village-deities with blood sacrifices' (1952, 182). Yet, as already discussed, the Coorgs themselves were meat-eaters and animal sacrifices were still practised in the village. But despite the opposition to this type of ritual, animal sacrifice is still widely practised in India and is an important aspect of popular Hinduism. It is particularly prominent among the Shaivas, the devotees of Shiva, and reaches its most striking form in the cult rituals associated with the mother goddess, Durga, in Orissa and Bengal. We shall discuss the cult of the goddess in Section 4.4.

What is of interest with regard to Dumont's well-known essay on the folk deity Aiyanar in Tamilnadu (1970b, 20–32) is the suggestion that the gods themselves in their relationships reflect the structure of the caste system – particularly the opposition between purity and impurity that Dumont sees as the fundamental principle of the caste system – and the distinction between puja (vegetarianism) and sacrifice (meat-eating). Thus although Mariyamma is the main village goddess concerned with the protection and prosperity of the village, the god Aiyanar also has prominence, and he has a temple devoted to him in almost every village of the region. According to Dumont, Aiyanar is associated with Shiva and is a 'pure vegetarian god' while his servant Karuppan, the black god, is meat-eating and is propitiated by blood sacrifices as well as being associated with malevolent spirits [*pey*]. Dumont, as a structuralist, emphasizes the relational aspect of the deities, and that the relationship between Aiyanar and Karuppan mirrors that of the caste system and the complementary opposition between purity and impurity. The cultural context is no doubt more complex – for puja is also offered to Karuppan, and the priest of the Aiyanar temple is generally a meat-eating potter, and the god himself is usually represented as a warrior and associated with the hunt. Thus, as with the Coorgs, Kshatriya status is associated with meat-eating.

It has to be noted, of course, that while the 'great gods' of the Sanskritic traditions, such as Shiva and Vishnu, are associated with cosmic events and are normally seen as distancing themselves from the mundane problems of ordinary people, most misfortunes and everyday problems are associated with the minor deities and malevolent spirits. Particularly troublesome are unsettled spirits or the 'ghosts' [*pretas*] of people who have met with an untimely death – through suicide, accident, snake-bite, murder, or while young. Many of these spirits afflict women and are associated with fertility – and treatment consists of exorcism or possession rituals that determine the identity of the offending spirits and offer means of placating the spirits. As with the Zar cults, Fuller suggests that women's possession episodes are 'culturally tolerated opportunities to complain about female inferiority and subordination within Indian society' (1992, 233). But what is crucial in the Hindu context – in contrast to both Islam and Buddhism – is that an important means of coming to terms with the possessing spirit is to settle or enshrine the spirit. Its malevolent power can then be controlled and it can be worshipped as a deity. In essence, this involves the 'deification of spirits', or as Dumont puts it, 'often a spirit is malevolent only as long as it lacks a cult: once a cult is provided, it becomes tutelary' (1986, 449, cited in Fuller 1992, 49). Illness and misfortune are therefore very much within the domain of the village deities (on spirit healing in the Indian context, see Freed and Freed 1964; Kakar 1982, 53–88).

4.4. CULT OF THE GODDESS

The mother goddess, in her many forms, is worshipped throughout India, and, as we have seen, is often the tutelary deity of a village or settlement, protecting and upholding the prosperity of the community. Some feminist scholars have suggested, following the theory of Bachofen, that mother-goddess religion or goddess 'spirituality' is associated with an early Eden-like phase of human history, one of universal egalitarian matriarchy that existed prior to the rise of patriarchy, the formation of the state, and patriarchal monotheism (Eisler 1987). I have elsewhere offered some critical reflections on this theory of the 'ancient religion' of the goddess, emphasizing that bipolar conceptions of human history are limited and theoretically suspect, that there is no intrinsic relationship between matrilineal kinship and mother-goddess cults, and that the latter are certainly not a universal feature of pre-state or tribal societies. Indeed, mother-goddess religion seems to happily coexist with both theocratic states and patriarchy (Biehl 1991; Morris 1998). But here I want to focus on mother-goddess cults in India. Such cults have undoubtedly ancient roots in South Asian prehistory, for terra cotta figurines of the goddess have been dated back to 3000 B.C.E. But devotion to the goddess probably emerged as a distinct cult around the seventh century with the rise of Sanskritic Hinduism as a coherent religious tradition or synthesis. Importantly, however, goddess worship is almost always only a part of the larger and more comprehensive Hindu tradition of beliefs and practices (Preston 1980, 10–16).

But, as we have earlier noted, the goddess takes many different forms or manifestations, both benign and malevolent, and is often localized. The goddesses Parvati, Sita, Saraswati, and Lakshmi are all considered to be manifestations of the goddess [*devi*] but as consorts of the 'high gods' – Shiva, Rama, Brahma, and Vishnu, respectively – they take a passive role and are always subordinate to their divine husbands. On the other hand, in the form of Kali, the goddess is autonomous, aggressive, powerful, malign, and is sometimes depicted as standing on the corpse of her consort Shiva. As Durga, the 'inaccessible' and the destroyer of the buffalo-demon, the goddess is identified with the earth and fertility. And, as noted earlier, as Sitala or Mariyamma, the goddess is not only a tutelary deity but is also associated with smallpox and other epidemic diseases – both causing the disease and being its cure. Complex rituals may therefore be performed to ritually 'cool' the wrath of the goddess (Fuller 1992, 45). What is important in regard to the goddesses Kali and Durga is that they not only possess people, particularly women, but that they are appeased by blood sacrifices. Fuller emphasizes a structural but complementary opposition between the high gods Shiva and Vishnu, who represent celestial space and transcendence, and the goddess, who is linked to the earth, both as soil and territory and to worldly concerns (1992, 44). This has affinities to Mandelbaum's (1966) well-known distinction between two basic functions of religion, the transcendental (concerned with long-term welfare and ultimate goals in salvation) and the pragmatic (focussed on earthly concerns and personal or local problems).

In his ethnographic study of the cult of the goddess in Orissa, based on researches undertaken in the early 1970s, James Preston (1980) noted that temples devoted to the goddess varied along a spectrum. Those on the eastern coast were characterized by the dominance of the Brahman caste, the absence of animal sacrifices, vegetarian deities, and generally had close ties to the well-known Jagannath (Shiva) temple at

Puri, which is an important pilgrimage centre. In contrast, temples to the goddess located near the inland mountains, as 'strong tribal roots', are distinguished by having non-Brahman priests, non-vegetarian deities, animal sacrifices, and tend to be independent of the Jayannath cult. Preston's study was focussed on the Chandi temple, in the commercial city of Cuttack near the coast, which has a population of nearly 200,000 people. The deity Chandi is a form of the goddess Durga, and her devotees are known as *shakta.* The priests of the Chandi temple are Brahmans, all members of a single family, and within the temple there is not only the main sanctuary dedicated to the goddess but also the shrines of other deities – Shiva, Lakshmi, Narayan (Vishnu), and Hanuman, the monkey-god and the devoted servant of Rama.

The temple is supported and patronized by the merchants and middle classes of the city, and over the past thirty years it has been transformed from a small neighbourhood shrine to that of a major temple – and has become one of the more commercial centres of Cuttack (Preston 1980, 46).

The temple is the main place of devotion for the devotees of the goddess, and they regularly conduct the sacred rites [*puja*] – making offerings of sweetmeats and plantains to the deity, through the mediation of the Brahman priests. The most important of these rituals is held at night when hundreds of ghee lamps are lit and are placed by the devotees before the image of the goddess in the central shrine. This is an act of *darshana* – the vision of the deity. But, as Preston writes,

> All the senses are stimulated in the act of darshan. There is a profusion of colours, sweet incense, garlands of tropical flowers, the smell of sweetmeats in preparation, and the odour of livestock that have been tethered in the courtyard. (1980, 49)

Although caste distinctions and the norms of purity–impurity are observed within the temple, nevertheless the ultimate goal of goddess worship, Preston writes, is 'to reach emancipation through total identity with the deity' (1980, 50). Equally important, through the mediation of the priests, the transmuted offerings are returned to the devotees in the form of *shakti,* sacred power or blessing, thus enabling them to cope with their worldly sufferings (1980, 50–6).

But the most important ritual at the Chandi temple is the Durga Puja, a festival that takes place in October and that celebrates the destruction of evil by the goddess. The Durga Puja is celebrated in many parts of India, but the festival at Cuttack is one of the largest and most popular in Orissa. The festival lasts several days, and in 1972 around 70,000 people from all over the state attended the Chandi temple. There is much festivity and gift-giving, people spending hundreds of rupees buying ornaments or exchanging gifts. Two rituals performed during the festival are particularly noteworthy. One is a large procession in which over a hundred life-size statues of various deities, which have been skilfully made out of clay by various artisans, are taken to the river, where they are submerged. The procession is followed by dancing and singing in the streets. The second ritual is the animal sacrifice, and in 1972 over 500 goats and 30 chickens were offered to the goddess. The Brahman priests first perform special rites of purification and worship the goat by offering it flowers, incense, food, and water. But the goat is actually sacrificed by a non-Brahman, who kills the animal with the single stroke of a sword – and its head is then placed before the goddess. Most of the people who sacrificed animals at the Chandi temple were from the lower castes, who sought material help from the goddess – jobs, money to send children to school, or a cure for illness or infertility. Because of the widespread opposition to animal sacrifices among high-caste and professional people, it was mainly those from the lower castes who sacrificed the goats and chickens (1980, 62–70). Recourse to the goddess in relation to problems and illness is, Preston suggests, usually a 'last resort', when other strategies have failed (1980, 78).

Affirming that there is no validity in the notion of a 'spiritual east and material west', for in the Hindu context material needs and spiritual aspirations are inextricably linked, Preston suggests that the rise in the popularity of mother-goddess worship in the recent decades is closely linked to the problems of urban living. With the decline of royal patronage after independence, a new urban middle class has emerged to patronize and administer the temple – giving rise to a good deal of conflict among the merchants, educated elite, and government bureaucrats. Indeed, Preston writes that temples are 'notorious places of scandal, fraud and deceit' (1980, 32). But this increasing 'commercialism' has gone hand-in-hand with the growing popularity of mother-goddess worship. Equally important, the cult of the goddess has not only been a 'major integrating device' in Hinduism but also has served as a 'refuge for the dispossessed and insecure elements of Indian society' (1980, 90). The shades of Durkheim and Marx thus still resonate within anthropological writing.

Although shakti is one of the forms of the goddess, and usually refers to female power within the universe with connotations of energy, strength, and vigour, Susan Wadley suggests that such power is not specifically feminine. It rather refers to a kind of spiritual power or force that inheres within all living things. But some beings – specifically deities and spirits – have more powers than others, and she therefore writes of these spiritual agencies not as personages but as 'power-filled beings' (1985, 55–8). In her ethnographic study of religious life in the village of Karimpur in Uttar Pradesh, Wadley gives a complex analysis of the different kinds of 'powerful beings' ranging from male deities [*bhagvan*] who are the focus of rites of salvation, to the goddesses such as Sita, Lakshmi, and Sitala [*devi*] who are less concerned with salvation but have a 'role' in 'rescuing' people from physical distress, to purely malevolent beings who are not conceived of as deities [*deva*] at all. Importantly, in the village, the goddesses, unlike the male deities [*bhagvan*], are seen essentially as ambivalent beings and are not usually the focus of devotion or enduring relationships. Often the goddesses, she writes, are 'really feared' (Wadley 1985, 116–23).

Although not specifically focussed on temples devoted to the goddess, we may nonetheless conclude this section with a brief mention of pilgrimages. For throughout India, the pilgrimage to specific temples or sacred sites has always been an intrinsic and vital part of popular Hinduism. Having myself undertaken pilgrimages to the temple of Venkateshwara (Vishnu) at Tirupati in Andhra Pradesh and to the Aiyappan temple at Sabarimalai in the Ghat Mountains of Kerala, I can but affirm their crucial social and religious significance. At some of the more famous pilgrimage centres, which are usually associated with the more important deities such as Shiva (in various forms), Krishna, and Rama, millions of pilgrims may assemble, to join in the many rituals and festivities, to bathe in the river, or simply to get a glimpse of the deity in the inner sanctum of the temple. The pilgrimage is seen as a 'crossing' [*tirtha*, ford] or journey [*yatra*] to a holy place, and the pilgrim in essence becomes a 'renouncer'. Thus, prior to the journey, the pilgrim may observe dietary restrictions, become celibate, or may learn devotional songs or hymns, and during the pilgrimage itself may wear special clothing or necklaces and go barefoot. Collective rituals undertaken on the pilgrimage and the constant singing of hymns generate a real sense of group or collective identity, but it is questionable whether this experience overrides gender or caste identity. Victor Turner's notion that pilgrimages exemplify 'communitas', in which relationships are spontaneous, immediate, concrete, and unmediated, and express a 'sentiment for humanity' (1974, 274) is problematic, and has been extensively criticized by anthropologists (Morris 1987, 256–60; Fuller 1992, 212–3).

What is crucial for the pilgrims, however, is making contact with the deity – even becoming identified with the divinity – and thus receiving what is commonly described in India as a 'boon' – blessing, support in overcoming many of life's problems, even the promise of liberation from the endless cycle of rebirths (for useful studies of pilgrimages in India, see Bharati 1963; Bhardwaj 1973; Daniel 1984; 245–87; Morinis 1984; Gold 1988; Fuller 1992, 204–23).

4.5. BHAKTI CULTS

The various Bhakti or devotional movements that flourished during the Middle Ages centred mainly around the deities Vishnu and Shiva, who, along with various forms of the mother-goddess and other lesser gods and spirits, feature prominently in the Epics. The Bhakti cults were particularly associated with Tamilnadu, the writings of Ramanuja, an important theistic philosopher of the eleventh century, being particularly influential. For Ramanuja, the deity was a personal being who should be approached with love and devotion. Unlike in the Vedanta doctrine, the phenomenal world, he felt, was real, and the human soul and god eternally distinct. In salvation, the soul is united but not identified with the deity and thus conscious of the joyous experience. The Vaisnava movement was also conspicuous in Bengal, where the fifteenth-century devotee of Krishna and Radha, Chaitanya, also had an important influence. Both Ramanuja and Chaitanya were Brahmans, and they maintained a theistic conception of deity and stressed that salvation is attained only through devotional practice. The chants associated with the contemporary Hare Krishna cult were first sung by the followers of Chaitanya over 400 years ago. Women played an important part in these Bhakti movements, which were in essence opposed to caste distinctions. At least, it has generally been recognized that the early Bhakti movements, by putting a focal emphasis on personal devotion [*Bhakti*] to the deity, elevating this path above that of contemplative knowledge [*jnana*] and action [*karma*], provided a 'charter for egalitarianism' for the society as a whole (Fuller 1992, 158). Yet, for most of their history, the Bhakti cults have accommodated themselves to the institutionalized inequality inherent in the caste system, and this is particularly evident in the two contemporary movements we shall explore in this section: the Radha-Krishna Bhajanas of Madras and the Hare Krishna movement.

The Radha-Krishna Bhajanas is a form of collective devotional worship associated with groups of middle-class professionals and Smarta Brahmans in the suburbs of Madras City. Although in the past the Smarta Brahmans were largely followers of Shankara and Advaita Vedanta, with its non-theistic theology, in more recent years, Milton Singer (1968) records, Bhakti-type cults have become increasingly popular among the middle classes. Linking temple and domestic worship, the basic unit of the Bhajana social organization is a local neighbourhood group that meets regularly, usually in an evening, to conduct hymn singing and other rituals – Bhajana essentially referring to a 'devotional song' or prayer.

Although nominally open to all castes, the Radha-Krishna cult draws its leadership and its support mainly from Smarta Brahmans and only some twenty per cent of its members are non-Brahmans. Equally important, the organizers and main participants of the cult rituals tend to be adult males (Singer 1968, 102). Throughout the year, the Radha-Krishna cult performs many types of ritual, all of which usually involve the making of religious offerings, food, flowers, or the lighting of a camphor lamp to the deity [*puja*] and the singing of devotional songs [*bhajana*]. The songs often relate in particular to the deity Krishna's activities and 'sports' [*lilas*] with the *gopis*, or milkmaids. Each year a large festival is held, involving the ritual marriage of Krishna to Radha, his favourite gopi. The marriage is usually conducted by a professional Vedic priest [*purohita*]. Formal leadership within the Bhajana groups is expressed mainly through the guru–disciple relationship, which, Singer suggests, 'operates as the very lifeline of the culture and the social structure' (1968, 117).

Milton Singer suggests that the Radha-Krishna devotional cults perform two kinds of social function. On the one hand, Bhakti-type devotions to the deity provide an easier path to salvation in an urban context – in contrast to the paths of ascetic withdrawal or esoteric religious knowledge [*jnana*]. On the other hand, Singer suggests that the Bhajana rituals have an integrative function and help to reduce caste consciousness – particularly in the context of Tamilnadu where there has been a strong anti-Brahman political movement (which Singer mentions but does not explore). Many cult participants suggest that 'there is no caste in the world of devotion', and Singer concludes that the Bhajana cults as neighbourhood groups provide 'forms of sociability and intimacy in an urban setting that transcend kin, caste, sect and region' (1968, 123). He emphasizes, however, that the Radha-Krishna Bhajanas are not merely a 'survival' of an old Bhakti tradition but are adaptations to contemporary city life (1968, 122–3).

The emphasis that Singer puts on the 'integrative function' of the Radha-Krishna devotional cults and his suggestion that the rituals are 'dramatizations of the ideals of social equality' (1972, 239) are, however, as Fuller argues, contradicted by his own ethnography. For, as we have seen, only men are normally active devotees, and membership of the cult is drawn mainly from the Smarta Brahman community. Class and gender inequalities tend therefore to be entrenched in the hymn-singing sessions, and the cult associations tend to express Brahmanic middle-class status rather than any egalitarian ethos (Fuller 1992, 161–2).

Let us now turn to the Hare Krishna cult, which also follows the Bhakti tradition but has a much wider appeal, and I draw on my own earlier writings (1979).

The Hare Krishna movement is well known, for its devotees dressed in saffron robes and with shaven heads are common sights on the streets of London and San Francisco, chanting their mantras. The movement was founded by A.C. Bhaktivedanta, a wealthy Brahman and a Sanskrit scholar, who was born in Calcutta and spent most of his life as a manager of a chemical firm. In 1959, shortly after his retirement, he became a *sannyasin*, a religious mystic who renounces the world, and six years later, at the age of seventy, he sailed for America. The trip was financed by Srimati Morarji (reputedly the richest woman in India) and was specifically to fulfil a promise Bhaktivedanta had made to his spiritual master, namely, to propagate the cult of Krishna in the English-speaking world. On his arrival in New York, Bhaktivedanta began chanting the names of Krishna while sitting under trees in Tompkins Park, and he soon gathered around him a group of devotees, mostly hippies. From this small beginning, the movement has grown apace, and there are now cult centres of the International Society for Krsna Consciousness (formally incorporated in 1966) in many parts of the world. In fact, although Bhaktivedanta died in 1977, the cult is still expanding, and the books and translations of the founder have found a wide and ready market. The most useful outline of its ideas is Bhaktivedanta's *The Science of Self Realisation* (1977).

The theology of the cult stands firmly in the Hindu Bhakti tradition. It accepts the doctrine of reincarnation [*samsara*] and the idea that the human soul passes through a cycle of rebirths; but, unlike other Hindu sects, it holds to the view that salvation [*moksha*], or release from this rebirth cycle, comes not from the union [*yoga*] of the individual soul with an impersonal absolute (as expressed by the Vedantist philosopher Shankara and by mystics generally) or through action [*karma*] or knowledge [*jnana*] but through devotion [*bhakti*] to God, conceptualized in highly anthropomorphic terms. It is therefore rigidly theistic, equating God with the personality of Krishna (as depicted in the Hindu scriptures), as well as expressing a kind of double dualism. For besides postulating a rigid dualism between spirit (God) and matter, it suggests an eternal paradox, namely, that the human soul is an aspect of God and yet at the same time is an individual. Thus even on attaining a state of salvation, the soul retains enough individuality to realize the bliss of the union with God.

Hence, the doctrines of Hare Krishna cult differ from other forms of mysticism, which, as Aldous Huxley and others have noted, tend to see the human soul as a manifestation of the divine reality, and it is even more at variance with the central doctrines of classical Buddhism. The latter religion – disparagingly described by Bhaktivedanta as the 'philosophy of the void' – is, of course, essentially atheistic, and one of its central tenets is the emphatic denial that there is any permanent soul.

Given this theistic bias, the Hare Krishna cult puts a focal emphasis on the scriptures and on devotional practice. With respect to the former, the cult, following Bhaktivedanta, takes the Vedic scriptures as infallible and authoritative sources, but it specifically takes its guidance not from the classical Vedic texts but from the later Bhavagad Gita (which forms part of the Mahabharata epic) and from what has been described as a kind of 'New Testament of Vaishnavism' – the Bhagavata Purana, compiled in the ninth or tenth century C.E. These two texts contain the various 'legends' relating to the god Krishna who, though traditionally reported to be an incarnation of Vishnu, one of the members of the ancient Hindu pantheon, is seen by the Hare Krishna devotees as the supreme spirit. Whether as a charioteer giving instructions to Arjuna or as a youthful hero cavorting with the cowherd's daughters [*gopis*] who were distraught by their love for him or as the king of Mathura (who apparently had more than 16,000 wives), Krishna embodies for the devotees all aspects of an extremely personal divinity.

Devotion to Krishna expressed through a loving and selfless dedication to the spirit and through cultivating a conscious awareness that one is eternally related to him (Krishna) are the basic premises of the cult. Ritually, this implies making sacramental offerings [*puja*] to the deity, represented in typical Hindu fashion as anthropomorphic icons, and the constant chanting of the holy names of God. The 'Hare Krishna' chant that one associates with the cult, and that was first sung by Chaitanya over 400 years ago, is believed to awaken within the person an awareness that we are eternally related to God and that one's material body is distinct from the real self (soul).

What all this implies, of course, is an extremely negative attitude towards the natural world (including one's own body), which is seen by Bhaktivedanta as unreal and polluting – even as a 'prison' for the soul. The Hare Krishna devotees, as Francine Daner writes in *The American Children of Krsna* (1976), believe that identifying with one's material body is one of the greatest pitfalls, and that the aim of human life is to 'free' the soul (through devotion to Krishna) from 'material contamination'. In spite of their advocacy of non-violence and vegetarianism, it would be difficult to find a philosophy that is more anti-ecological. Even a cursory reading of any ecological text would demonstrate for the devotees the complex – and *necessary* – interrelationship between life-forms and the material world, and the assumption that life (as we normally understand the term) is inconceivable apart from nature. They admit that the body is subject to the laws of material nature, but life is seen as somehow independent, as an aspect of an eternal realm. The fact that this contradicts the senses and that non-attachment to the world (salvation) could not be achieved in this lifetime does not, however, trouble their logic.

The members of the Hare Krishna cult see themselves as a challenge to the old dogmas of evolutionism, but in reality they represent and advocate the pre-Darwinian idea that human beings are not a part of nature but an aspect of the divine. Bhaktivedanta Swami Prabhupada made it clear that 'real life' meant following the Bhakti tradition, devotion to Krsna [*God*]. None of the followers of jnana, yoga, and karma can know God, he argued – only the bhakta [devotee]. He quotes from the Gita: 'only through the process of bhakti can one understand God' (1977, 13). Such understanding and devotion implied the 'severance' of the roots that bind us to material existence and 'to renounce everything related to the material conception of life' (Gita 8). Through devotion to Krsna, 'we come to realise that we are part and parcel of God' and this realization involves an evolution – 'back to Godhead'. And he continues:

> We consider that we are born and that we die. Such thinking is called maya, or illusion, and as soon as we get out of this illusion of the soul with the body, we attain the stage of Brahma-Bhuta. When one realises 'I am not this body; I am spirit-soul, part and parcel of the Supreme Brahman' he attains what is called Brahman realization. (1977, 237)

The notion that the self is not to be identified with the body but is an immortal soul is also a key feature of the Brahma Kumari sect, a strongly millenarian movement founded by the Sindhi businessman, Dada Lekhraj, in the 1930s (see Babb 1986, 110).

The social aspects of the Hare Krishna cult are also less progressive than many people have realized. In the Bhagavad Gita, divine justification for the caste [*varna*] system is given in the words of Krishna: 'The four orders of men arose from me, in justice to their natures and their works. Know that this work was mine, though . . . I am in eternity'. The four orders, of course, are the Brahmans [priests], Kshatriyas [political rulers], Vaisyas [merchants], and Sudras [workers]. Bhaktivedanta not only takes this feudal hierarchy to be a universal form of social organization – thus showing a limited anthropology – but advocates it as an ideal (and seemingly necessary) form of human society. Significantly, this caste system – like that in Plato's *Republic* – is based, according to Bhaktivedanta, not on ascription but on intrinsic worth and education. Whereas the medieval Bhakti movements were in essence against the caste hierarchy, the Hare Krishna cult supports hierarchy and inequality, and its devotees see themselves as a new intellectual elite. Although open to anyone, the cult nonetheless represents a new priestly order, modelled on that of the Brahman caste. This is evident from Bhaktivedanta's writings and the theology and rituals of the cult, as well as from its advocacy of a Brahmanic lifestyle. As the founder put it, cult propaganda 'is meant for creating Brahmanas all over the world because the Brahmana element is lacking'. And like the priests of old, they would no doubt – as Bhaktivedanta mentions – give advice to the political rulers. The whole conception is a feudal one – adapted to modern conditions. It is not surprising therefore that Bhaktivedanta should describe most human beings as uncivilized, that he should think of his own devotees as a new intelligentsia devoted to Krishna, and that he should look on that other rival intellectual elite – the scientific community – as a lot of rascals.

Within the movement itself there is the same stress on hierarchy. The social organization of the Hare Krishna temple, as Daner describes it, follows the pattern of a 'total institution', and Bhaktivedanta's remarks on women are far from enlightening. Celibacy is enjoined for all, and sex is permissible only for the purposes of procreation. Although suggesting that no distinctions are made on the basis of sex and that Krishna consciousness is available to both men and women, it is held that 'a woman's physical and psychological constitution make it natural for her to accept the guidance and protection of a man'. The women's liberation movement is significantly seen as a ploy by men, and Bhaktivedanta asks: 'Which is real independence – to remain under the care of a husband or to be enjoyed by everyone?' He seems to be unaware that there may be other alternatives open to women.

Bhaktlvedanta apparently was in his younger days a member of Gandhi's movement. But the founder of the Hare Krishna cult had neither the humility nor the libertarian sentiments that Gandhi expressed. Whereas Gandhi was a political activist and advocated social reconstruction – indeed, Bhaktivedanta criticized him for being intoxicated with material life! – and yet attempted to live a simple life, Bhaktivedanta castigates materialism, but as God's representative on earth he allowed himself to be treated as if he were a God. Thus he was always driven around in a luxurious car and as a spiritual guru, his every whim was catered for by disciples. It wasn't beneath Gandhi's dignity to clean public toilets, but one can hardly imagine the founder of the Hare Krishna cult doing such menial tasks.

I have said enough to question whether religious movements like the Hare Krishna cult can be deemed progressive in any way. If the 'counterculture' may be described as an inchoate attempt to challenge inequality and authoritarian patterns of social organization, and to propagate an ecological attitude towards the natural world, then the Hare Krishna cult might well be described as the *counter* counterculture.

As the Hare Krishna movement in the United States seemed to appeal particularly to young and affluent middle-class Americans in the late 1960s, it has always been linked to the 'counterculture' movement. The latter movement was especially associated with the widespread use of 'psychedelic' drugs to achieve radical visions. The Hare Krishna movement specifically targeted such educated and privileged youth, whom Daner (1976, 6–14) suggested were culturally isolated and alienated and engaged in a 'search for identity' and self-affirmation. Thus, given this 'crisis of meaning', Hare Krishna posters specifically suggested that one could 'stay high forever' and achieve 'transcendental ecstasy' not through drugs but through chanting and devotional rituals (Johnson 1976, 36; Bainbridge 1997, 194). Nevertheless, as just suggested, the Hare Krishna cult was opposed to most of the tenets of the radical counterculture movement, in being anti-feminist and anti-ecological. It was equally against the countercultural movement in not only being world-rejecting but also in its absolute opposition to the pursuit of personal pleasure and material enjoyment. The Hare Krishna cult offered an alternative spiritual identity that advocated a life of self-imposed poverty and ascetic denial – a complete rejection of the prosperous middle-class homes from which most of the devotees came (Johnson 1976, 39). This meant that when a person became a devotee, all aspects of that person's prior identity was surrendered, and the initiate to the Hare Krishna cult adopted a Sanskrit name. They also followed a complete ascetic regime, with a strict set of prohibitions – no drugs, no sex outside marriage, with celibacy the ideal, no meat-eating, no gambling, and all intoxicants forbidden. Relationships within the movement were focussed around Bhaktivedanta's absolute spiritual authority. No wonder Daner considered the Hare Krishna temple as akin to what Goffman defined as a 'total institution' (1976, 14). Johnson, in contrast, sees the emergence of the Hare Krishna cult as exemplifying in San Francisco the 'failure' of the counterculture movement.

Over the past two decades, the Hare Krishna movement has gone through a period of turmoil, internal conflicts, and a high attrition rate of members – as well as some scandals. But as the headquarters of the movement in Britain, Bhaktivedanta Manor in Hertfordshire, has become a major temple and during the important Hindu festivals is visited by thousands of British Hindus, there is a sense in which the Hare Krishna movement has now become integrated into the wider Hindu community (Barrett 2001, 283–9; on the Hare Krishna movement, see also Judah 1974; Singh 1975, 73–94; Carey 1987; Bromley and Shinn 1989; on Bhakti and other devotional movements, see also Dimock 1968; Williams 1984; Van der Veer 1988).

4.6. GURUS AND HINDU NATIONALISM

During the past two decades, politics in India has been transformed with the emergence of a strident form of Hindu nationalism, a militant and violent form of Hindu ideology that equates Indian national identity with Hinduism. This chauvanistic anti-minority ideology of Hindu 'supremacism', as Chetan Bhatt (2001) describes it, is closely linked with two other important developments in the political economy of India: the expansion of transnational capitalism and the development of nuclear missiles, so that India has now become a nuclear superpower. The promotion of a neo-liberal capitalist economy, along with state subsidies for private corporations and large landowners, has had serious social and ecological costs, leading some scholars to suggest that one third of India's population are now refugees in their own country (Gadgil and Guha 1995). This neo-liberal economic strategy has tended to complement Hindu nationalism, and it was a government led by the Bharatiya Janata Party (BJP), which is closely associated with Hindu nationalism, that heralded India's emergence as a nuclear power. The name given to India's ballistic missile was Agni, the Vedic God of fire, and the nationalist organization Vishva Hindu Parishad (VHP: World Hindu Council) called for a temple dedicated to the goddess Shakti to be built near the site of the nuclear tests to symbolize Hindu power (Bhatt 2001, 1). And it was largely through the instigation of the BJP that Hindu militants destroyed the old mosque of Ayodhya in Uttar Pradesh in December 1992. During the past decades, there have been sporadic outbreaks of Hindu–Muslim violence, mostly in urban areas, and, in Gujerat, the rallying cry of the early Hindu nationalist, Vinayak Savarkar, 'Hinduise all politics and militarise all Hindudom' (McKean 1996, 71), seems to have been enacted during the past decade. It is well beyond the scope of the present study to discuss in detail Hindu nationalism, and I have no wish to enter the 'labyrinthine morass' of modern Indian politics: instead, drawing on Lise McKean's seminal study, '*Divine Enterprise*' (1996), I focus on the role of gurus in the Hindu nationalist movement.

With the expansion of global capitalism in India and the growing support for Hindu nationalism, religious gurus, along with their associations and establishments, have become key players, McKean suggests, in the business and politics of 'spirituality'. While Hindu nationalist ideology has become more pervasive and powerful, serving to legitimate the power and to mask the interests of India's ruling classes, so gurus have become increasingly important in the propagation of Hindu nationalism. Taking a critical Marxist perspective, McKean essentially propounds two interrelated theses. The first is that 'Hindu nationialism in militant or modulated forms has become a major ideological weapon and political strategy for consolidating the power of India's ruling classes' (1996, 39). Second, ideas concerning spirituality are embedded in Hindu nationalism, and thus gurus and other religious professionals, especially through the organization VHP, have become a 'potent political force' in the promotion and consolidation of militant Hindu nationalism in India (1996, 26). Her study, in fact, based on ethnographic research at the important pilgrimage centre Hardwar, Uttar Pradesh, is essentially concerned with exploring the political uses of spirituality in contemporary India. Her central argument is thus that the 'spiritualism' promoted and organized through religious gurus and their associations provides formidable aesthetic and intitutional support in the making of Hindu nationalism into a powerful political force (1996, 27). McKean is thus critical of early anthropological studies of Hindu religious organizations that tended to ignore their political functions. For example, Lawrence Babb (1986) has written a detailed and perceptive study of three religious organizations in Delhi – the Radhasoami movement, the Brahma Kumari millenial sect, and the network of devotees that follow the cult of the world-famous guru, Sathya Sai Baba. Although acknowledging the diversity of Hinduism and suggesting that there is 'no such thing as a Hindu world view' (1986, 5), Babb's main concern in the study is to focus on the Hindu religious imagination and to delineate enduring Hindu images and motifs, thus privileging continuity and unity over historical specificity. His aim was to explore the 'distinctive spiritual disposition' of the Hindus and their capacity to invest the world with 'religious meaning'; he therefore, as McKean suggests, tended to ignore the political and economic aspects of these three movements (1996, 20).

Addressing what she perceived to be a neglected topic in anthropological studies of Indian society – the political economy of spirituality – McKean firmly argues that religious activities focussed around gurus form a crucial part of the 'magnetic core' that attracts individuals and groups to the Hindu Nationalist Movement. It operates, she writes, 'as a populist and democratic façade for the militant and authoritarian infrastructure of the Hindu Nationalist Movement' (1996, 12).

Hardwar and Rishikesh, the two North Indian towns where McKean conducted her fieldwork, are important pilgrimage centres seemingly awash with gurus, ascetics, temples, and ashrams. Here one finds a rich array of religious activities associated with pilgrimages – the worshipping of various deities in temples, meditation retreats, bathing in the sacred waters of the Ganges, performing life-cycle and mortuary rituals. But, importantly, the two towns are closely associated with the Hindu Nationalist Movement, for the early Hindu nationalist organization, the Hindu Mahasabha, held its first meetings in Hardwar, and the town's ashrams are important sites for Hindu nationalist activism. The VHP, founded in 1964, often holds rallies in Hardwar, which is only five hours by road from Delhi. Pilgrimage is indeed business in Hardwar, and McKean concludes that business, religion, and politics in the town make it an important site for the institutional formations of both Hinduism and the nationalist culture with which it is identified (1996, 64).

Two key figures are seen by McKean as crucial in the rise of Hindu nationalism as a political force. The first is the well-known guru, Swami Vivekananda (1863–1902), who was a devotee of the Bengali mystic Ramakrishna and who has been seen as representing the 'high noon' in the revival of Hinduism at the end of the nineteenth century. Vivekananda propagated Advaita Vedanta as a universal religion and as the 'timeless spiritual essence of India's superior culture and society' (McKean 1996, 285). Denouncing the materialism of western civilization and suggesting that Indian culture was inherently spiritual, Vivekananda became the leading exponent and organizer of a 'religiously infused national identity', the spirituality of Advaita Vedanta being equated with both Hinduism and Indian national culture. Vivekananda, the 'warrior–monk', particularly appealed to urban, educated, high-caste Hindus and has been interpreted as a key figure in both the 'modernization' of Hinduism and in invoking a kind of 'spiritualized' Hindu nationalism (McKean 1996, 280–5; for useful studies of Vivekananda, see Williams 1981; Radice 1998).

The second important figure in the rise of Hindu nationalism is Vinayak Savarkar (1883–1966), who was a revolutionary nationalist during the colonial period. Born in Maharashtra into a Brahman family, he is now celebrated in contemporary India as a romantic hero who, unlike Gandhi, was dedicated to violent and revolutionary insurrection against British colonial rule. In fact, he spent many, many years in prison before becoming president of the Hindu Mahasabha in 1937. The Hindu Mahasabha was founded around 1914 at Hardwar to promote and protect Hindu interests, initially in loyal co-operation with the government. What Savarkar did during his presidency (1937–1944) was to transform the Hindu Mahasabha from a religious and social movement into a political force of Hindu nationalism – opposed to both the Congress Party and the Muslim League. Savarkar systematized and popularized the militant ideology of Hindutva, the essence or 'beingness of a Hindu' (Bhatt 2001, 77). An admirer of fascism, Savarkar's concept of Hindutva conflated race, culture, and religion, and advocated militarism, the establishment of the theocratic Hindu nation–state that excluded Muslims and Christians, and the promotion of industrial capitalism. Although encouraging the absorption of tribal people and 'untouchables' into the Hindu fold, Savarkar, McKean writes, had little sympathy for the impoverished people of India (1996, 90). As the person who assassinated Gandhi, Nathuram Godse, was a close friend and ally of Savarkar, both Savarkar and the Hindu Mahasabha lost political influence in the years immediately after independence (on Savarkar, see Keer 1988; McKean 1996, 71–96; Bhatt 2001, 77–111).

The ideology of Hindu nationalism took a new lease of life in 1964, with the formation of the VHP, although it was not until the 1980s that it really began to flourish. Because of dismay at the lack of unity among Hindu religious leaders, it was instigated by Madhav Golwalker, and Swami Chinmayananda became its first president. It advocated the ideology of militant Hindu nationalism earlier systemized by Sarvarkar and promoted by the militaristic Rashtriya Swayamsevak Sangh (National Volunteer Corps), which was initially formed in 1925 and, though devoted to physical exercise, weapon training, and military drill, as a nationalist organization it was not in its early years involved in anti-colonial struggles (Bhatt 2001, 119–23). Through the VHP, Hindu gurus and other religious figures have organized themselves into a substantive political force, and McKean argues that they have become the leading protagonist of militant Hindu nationalism in India. The movement has been concerned with reinterpreting the meaning of secularism – to imply state support for religion and to suggest that because Hinduism emanates from universal spiritual values, it is uniquely tolerant of other religions – which in reality belies its actual practices. Describing itself as a worldwide religious and cultural movement that aims to protect and disseminate Hindu ethical and spiritual values, the VHP has been involved in a number of key activities; to incorporate tribal and 'untouchable' communities into Hinduism; to 'reconvert' [*shuddhi*] those 'lost' to Christianity and Islam; to encourage the adoption of the Bhagavad Gita as the sacred book of the Hindus; and to popularize the worship of Bharat Mata [mother India] as the goddess central to the cult of the Hindu nationalists.

In her study, Lise McKean essentially focusses on two important religious gurus who are associated with the VHP and who have had an important influence in the consolidation of Hindu spiritual nationalism. The first is Swami Satyamitranand Giri. Born in 1932 in Agra, and from a Brahman family, Swami Satyamitranand spent his early life as a wandering ascetic, and, inspired by Vivekananda and belonging to an order founded by Shankara, he eventually formed his own religious organization, Samanvaya Parivar [Family of Harmony]. His ashram at Hardwar became the headquarters of Swami's organization. But Satyamitranand also participated in the founding of the VHP and during the early 1980s played the key role in the founding of the huge Bharat Mata temple in Hardwar. Consecrated in May 1983, the temple became, as Bhatt writes, a key 'Hindutva symbol', particularly serving the hegemony of urban upper-caste Hindus (2001, 187–8). The temple contains not only religious icons to the major Hindu deities, particularly the mother-goddess, but also images and statues relating to a diverse number of ascetics, saints, and nationalist 'heroes' – including Mahatma Gandhi, Vivekananda, Savarka, and Annie Besant. The Bharat Mata is thus a monument that both enshrines and popularizes Hindu nationalism (McKean 1996, 144–63).

The second important guru discussed by McKean is Swami Shivananda Saraswati, who founded the Divine Life Society. Like Satyamitranand, Swami Shivananda (1887–1963) was a high-caste Brahman and an advocate of Shankara's Advaita Vedanta. Born near Pattamadai in Tamilnadu, Shivananda spent his early life in Malaya, working as a medical doctor on a rubber estate. Returning to India in 1923, at the age of thirty-six, he become a wandering ascetic but spent much of his time living on the banks of the River Ganges near Rishikesh. Here he established an ashram and medical dispensary, and eventually, in 1936, the Divine Life Society. He gave an astonishing amount of lectures and addresses, both in Hindi and English, and, like Rajneesh, almost every word that Shivananda delivered to his coterie of disciples was dutifully recorded. He thus published numerous books and pamphlets on yoga and on Advaita Vedanta philosophy, and emphasized, like his contemporary Sarvepalli Radhakrishna, the universal 'practical spirituality' of Hinduism. What is important is that Swami Chinmayananda, one of the founders of the VHP, was an early disciple of Shivananda, and that Swami Chidananda, who became president of the Divine Life Society in 1963 on the death of Shivananda, has important ties with both the VHP and the Bharat Mata temple. What McKean suggests, therefore, is that Hindu spirituality, as propagated by these gurus, became an essential and defining characteristic of Indian national identity and thereby an essential force in the emergence of a militant and aggressive Hindu nationalism. But although advocating 'tribal uplift' and the unity of all Hindus, the spiritual teachings of these gurus tended to ignore, McKean suggests, the exploitation and the hardships endured by the working classes under industrial capitalism (1996, 142). She also emphasizes the subordination inherent in the relationship between the gurus and their devotees and the fact that 'spirituality' in the Indian context is often an instrument of domination. There is therefore an intrinsic and dynamic relationship between religious authority expressed by the guru and political power, particularly in the context of a militaristic Hindu nationalism. But, as Fuller suggests, although Hindu nationalism is now an important aspect of contemporary politics in India, the majority of Hindus in most parts of India are not particularly aggressive about their religion, and, of course, the more secular testaments of Gandhi and Nehru still have some influence (Fuller 1992, 260; for studies of Hindu nationalism, see Van der Veer 1994; Madan 1997; Corbridge and Harriss 2000; on the other well-known guru, Sathya Sai Baba, see White 1972; Singh 1975, 1–6; Ruhela and Robinson 1985; Babb 1986, 159–201; Taylor 1987).

5

Christianity and Religion in Africa

5.1. THE CHRISTIAN TRADITION

Christianity is reputed to be the largest of the world's religions and is found, in one form or another, throughout the world. It is estimated that around thirty-two per cent of the world's population is Christians – around 2 billion people, half of whom are adherents of the Roman Catholic faith. Still an important influence in Western Europe and North America, Christianity has always had a strong missionary impetus and since the sixteenth century has spread throughout much of what is now described as the 'developing' world – Asia, Latin America, Africa, and Oceania. Christianity has thus been closely implicated in both the rise and the spread of capitalism and in the 'colonial encounter' itself. Although Christianity is claimed as a transcendental truth of universal significance, it has been communicated in diverse historical and socio-cultural contexts and has thus given rise to a bewildering number of different denominations, sects, churches, and movements. Besides the Roman Catholic Church and the Eastern Orthodox Church (which has more than 200 million adherents), and such established Christian churches as the Anglican, Methodist, Apostolic, Lutheran, and Baptist churches, there exist throughout the world many thousands of different independent Christian churches. With the resurgence of charismatic and pentecostalist forms of Christianity, there has been, in recent decades, a huge expansion of Christianity in many parts of Africa, Asia, and Latin America – as we shall later note.

Christianity had its origin in Palestine, specifically in the region of Judea, and is centred on the life and work of one Jesus of Nazareth (5 B.C.E. – 30 C.E.), a Jewish spirit-healer and exorcist. It is debatable whether Jesus intended to establish a new religion, but in an important sense Christianity is a continuation and development of Judaism – though the relationship is a complex one. Born in a stable, baptized by John the Baptist in the River Jordan, Jesus during his life went around the countryside engaged in spirit-healing, exorcising evil spirits that were possessing people, raising people from the dead, propagating his message in parables, and proclaiming himself the 'son' of God. With twelve disciples, he formed a communion of believers and was executed by crucifixion by the order of Pontius Pilate, the Roman governor of Judea, seemingly for causing political and religious unrest. Believed by his followers to have risen from the dead, Jesus became the focus of a cult that spread thoughout the Meditteranean region. The apostle Paul, converted to Christianity by a vision of Jesus on the road to Damascus, was especially important as an early missionary.

Around the year 313, the Roman Emperor Constantine espoused the Christian faith and established Christianity as the official religion of the Roman Empire. A decade later, at the Council of Nicaea (325), convened by Constantine himself, the basic doctrines of the Christian Church were established. Of central importance was the doctrine of the trinity, which held that the godhead consisted of three persons, though of one substance – God the father, creator of heaven and earth; Jesus the son of God; and the holy ghost, which unites the believer with God – the term *charism* referring to an individual being possessed by the holy ghost or holy spirit. In the writings of St. Augustine of Hippo (354–430), reputed to be the greatest and most influential theologian of the Christian tradition, some further basic tenets of the Christian faith were established: the authority of the Bible, which incorporates both the Hebrew Bible and the New Testament; the idea that God created the world *ex nihilo* [out of nothing], thus countering the Neoplatonist idea that the world was an emanation of god; the concept of 'original sin' inherent in humans and thus the need for salvation – acknowledging the sacrifice of Jesus for the redemption of all humanity. The name of the religion in fact is derived from *christos*, Greek for 'anointed', which refers to Jesus as the messiah. Unlike in Judaism and Islam, Christians hold that Jesus is more than a mere prophet: He is unique in being both human and God – God incarnate.

Within Christianity ethical principles and authority derive from several sources: namely, human reason, religious tradition as expressed through the church and the sacraments, the Christian Bible, and the gifts expressed through the holy spirit. Whereas the Roman Catholic and Eastern Orthodox Churches place a great emphasis on the authority of the church and on Christian tradition (as expressed through the sacraments), Protestant churches have historically placed more emphasis on the authority of the Scriptures. But what is of interest is that in recent decades, accompanying the expansion of global capitalism, there has been a tremendous upsurge of pentecostalism or 'charismatic' Christianity. This has entailed a number of key features: an emphasis on conversion and salvation through Jesus Christ; an acknowledgement of the Bible as a unique source of authority; a belief in the second coming of Jesus; an affirmation of the value of the nuclear family and thus an intolerant attitude towards feminism and homosexuality, as well as towards the theory of evolution; and finally, and most important, an emphasis on possession by the holy spirit and thus on spirit-healing, in the widest sense. With regard to gender relations and the subordination of women, the pentecostalists and the charismatics have affinities to the more orthodox Christian churches, for neither the Eastern Orthodox Church nor the Roman Catholic Church allow the ordination of women as priests (for a useful overview of Christianity, see Woodhead 2002, 153–81).

It is important to note that some of the key concepts utilized in the anthropological study of religion – belief, charisma, spirit, sacrifice, symbol, ritual, the sacred, as well as the concept of religion itself – are derived essentially from Christian theology. Such concepts therefore, as many have noted, carry a good deal of cultural baggage: But this is no reason for the wholesale repudiation of such concepts, as suggested by some postmodern theologians who have just discovered Derrida.

This chapter in not specifically focussed on Christianity within Africa or with the activities of the Christian missionaries per se; it rather explores the important dialectic between Christianity, as introduced by the European missionaries, and African religious traditions and practices – specifically with regard to such independent religious movements as Kimbanguism (Zaire), the Lumpa Church of Alice Lenshina (Zambia), and the Zionist churches of South Africa – although I have tried to situate these movements within their socio-historical contexts. It is important to note, of course, that Islam has long had an important presence in Africa, as indicated in Chapter 3. But first some reflections on the religious traditions and practices of sub-Saharan Africa.

5.2. PROLOGUE ON AFRICAN RELIGION

African culture and religion – in contrast to those of China and India – have often been despised, ridiculed, even dismissed by European scholars. Worse: It has sometimes been completely ignored or seen as unhistorical. Hegel, as is well-known, saw African and tribal cultures generally as outside history, as 'undeveloped spirit', a viewpoint still implied by many historians. The well-known historian Arnold Toynbee, for example, in his study *Mankind and Mother Earth* (1976), barely mentions the African continent, and it is significant that one rarely finds books on Africa in New Age bookshops. Over the past half century, however, anthropological research has provided us with numerous ethnographic studies, both of specific religious traditions, exemplified by such classic studies as Evans-Pritchard's *Nuer Religion* (1956) and Meyer Fortes' *Oedipus and Job in West African Religion* (1959), as well as of religious movements in Africa and their impact on social and political life (see, for example, the lucid review by Ranger 1986).

Although some African scholars have seen such ethnographic studies as biased and anachronistic, as based on a limited understanding of the local language, and as marred by deep-rooted western 'prejudices', it is rather churlish to deny the pioneering intellectual efforts of such scholars as Evans-Pritchard, Fortes, and Monica Wilson. They have indeed, as Maxwell Owusu (1997) admits, bequeathed to Africa an important scholarly legacy, even though, as social scientists, they may have got some of their social facts wrong, and their interpretations may be open to question.

The peoples of sub-Saharan Africa, with a population of over 600 million, are characterized by a great diversity of religious beliefs, concepts, and ritual practices.

They have long felt the impact of what is now described as 'modernity', and both Islam and Christianity have long historical trajectories in Africa; both these 'world' religions are now an intrinsic part of the religious consciousness of people in many parts of Africa. But local expressions of religion are often identified by such terms as 'traditional' and 'indigenous', and there has thus arisen a welter of books that attempt to outline what is thought to have been African traditional religion, usually seen as a 'worldview' or as an 'underlying cultural unity' (see, for example, Mbiti 1969; Idowu 1973; Zuesse 1979). These texts are often written by priests or religiously inclined scholars and thus tend to equate – as elsewhere – African culture and thought with specific peoples' religious cosmologies. Whether it is feasible to speak of an *African* philosophy or religion has long been the subject of debate, particularly among African scholars, but many assume that there is a corpus of beliefs and practices that are common and widespread throughout Africa and, to some degree, constitute an underlying *Weltanschauung* or worldview. As Ivor Kopytoff expressed it: Sub-Saharan Africa exhibits to a striking degree 'a fundamental cultural unity' (1987, 10). This viewpoint, however, has been challenged by Paulin Hountondji (1983), who considers the idea of an African religious worldview or philosophy to be a fiction, an imaginary construct of scholars eager to satisfy the western craving for exoticism. Kwame Appiah expresses a similar view, arguing that there is no cultural unity in Africa and that Africans do not share a common religious culture (1992, 41). Nevertheless, as Kwame Gyekye writes, although there is undoubted cultural diversity within sub-Saharan Africa, 'threads of underlying affinity do run through the beliefs, customs, value systems and sociopolitical institutions and practices of the various African societies' (1987, 192).

With regard to African religious conceptions and practices, there are five elements or components that go into the making of this religion: a belief in god, cults associated with various divinities or nature spirits, rituals and beliefs focussed around ancestral spirits, a belief in magic and the efficacy of medicines, and the fear of witchcraft. We briefly discuss each of these in turn.

5.2.1. God

A central aspect of African religion was the idea of god, which was invariably linked to the sky, and associated with such phenomena as lightning, rainfall, and thunder. As Mbiti writes, 'practically all African peoples associate God with the sky, in one way or another' (1969, 33). Thus, god is often seen as a transcendental being, remote from daily life, and is not usually associated with specific rituals. But god is also seen as immanent, or manifested in natural objects or phenomena. Thus, African scholars suggest that god is conceived both as a pervasive presence, a real being immanent in the world, and as a spirit somewhat remote from human affairs. Although conceived of as essentially an anthropomorphic being, Mbiti affirms that as far as is known, 'there are no images or physical representations of God by

African peoples' (1970, 23). But the attributes and manifestations associated with the divinity – as creator, guardian or protector, moral adjudicator, and so on – are extremely variable among African peoples. Yet there is a general sense in which people's relationship with god is, as Mbiti writes, 'pragmatic and utilitarian rather than spiritual or mystical' (1969, 5). Not surprisingly, African conceptions of deity have been variously interpreted: as a form of pantheism (Mazrui 1986), deism (Kalilombe 1980), and monotheism (Idowu 1973). (For important studies of conceptions of god in Africa, see Danquah 1944; Idowu 1962; Daneel 1970; Mbiti 1970.)

5.2.2. Divinities

Although not universal, African religious conceptions invariably entail, as with the Greeks, a belief in a variety of divinities or spirits associated with specific natural phenomena, and often with clearly defined functions. They are often contacted through spirit-mediums and may be the focus of elaborate cult rituals. The Ashanti, for example, have a pantheon of spirits, known as *abosum*, which are thought to derive their powers from god and are usually associated with lakes and rivers. Many of these divinities have wide significance, and elaborate rituals are held in their favour. A priest or priestess acts as a medium for the spirit, and the spirits' help is sought to cope with misfortunes and afflictions (Gyekye 1987, 73–4).

5.2.3. Ancestral Spirits

Throughout Africa, cults and rituals associated with ancestral spirits or spirits of the dead play an important role in the social and cultural life of local communities. Contacted through dreams or rituals, the ancestral spirits are intimately concerned with the health and well-being of their living kin and centrally involved in upholding the moral order. As Monica Wilson writes, African people generally have a 'very lively sense of the presence of the dead', to whom regular offerings are made (1971, 29). To express this intimacy, Wilson refers to the spirits as 'shades'; Mbiti as the 'living-dead' (1969, 83). Although of crucial importance, the cults of the ancestors do not constitute African religion per se, nor do people 'worship' their ancestors in any meaningful sense. What is clearly evident, however, is that African people tend to make a clear distinction among the deity, divinities, and the ancestral spirits. In specific contexts, cults associated with the spirits of dead chiefs become important, and, as we shall see, foreign spirits may become the focus of elaborate spirit-possession cults, or cults of affliction.

5.2.4. Medicine

The fourth component of African religious culture was the belief that vital power resided in certain material substances, particularly woody plants, but also animals, including human flesh and blood. Such medicines were employed for a variety of purposes extending far beyond the therapeutic context, for good luck charms, for assistance in a variety of activities and concerns (hunting, friendship, employment, marriage, agriculture, court cases), as protecting medicine against witches, at all important initiations, for potency and reproductive purposes, as well as herbal remedies for a wide variety of ailments. Apart from writers like Idowu (1973, 199) and Janzen (1992, 149), who seem to think that medicines only have efficacy if 'spirits' are invoked or if they become 'metaphors' through song or rite, most anthropologists writing on African cultures have stressed the widespread belief that medicines have intrinsic powers. Audrey Richards, for example, writes of *bwanga* (which, like many early anthropologists, she translates as 'magic' though 'vital power' would perhaps be more appropriate), that it is for the Bemba the force 'contained in the leaves, roots, or bark of various trees and shrubs and a number of activating agencies [*fishimba*] such as the parts of animals and human beings' that are used by the Nganga for a variety of purposes (1956, 29). Writers on Zulu medicine have also stressed the powers [*amanda*] inherent in material substances [*imithi*], Ngubane noting (1977, 109) that many medicines are believed to contain potency in themselves, independent of any ritual context (see Morris 1998, 214–21). Needless to say, medicines can also be used for destructive or malevolent purposes and are thus associated with sorcery and witchcraft. The *nganga* [herbalist–diviner] is thus an important ritual practitioner in most African societies and is mostly concerned with countering witchcraft.

5.2.5. Witchcraft

Although witchcraft is usually seen as distinct from religion – and is often bypassed completely in many texts on African cultural knowledge (cf. Mudimbe 1988) – it nevertheless forms a constituent part of African religious culture. Occult power, whether derived from the spirits or medicinal substances, is intrinsically ambivalent, in Africa as elsewhere, and thus can be used for either good or malevolent purposes. But the witch or sorcerer is invariably seen as a person who, motivated by jealousy or envy, has an innate power to cause harm, or even kill, other people. The witch, as Monica Wilson puts it, is the 'embodiment of evil in Africa' (1971, 35), and represents the antithesis of moral personhood. (For useful studies of African witchcraft during the colonial period, see also Krige 1947; Middleton and Winter 1963; Crawford 1967; Gelfand 1967; Bourdillon 1991, 187–213; for an interesting cross-cultural survey of witchcraft, see Sanders 1995; on witchcraft in contemporary Africa, see Rowlands and Warnier 1988; Jackson 1989, 88–101; Auslander 1993; Abrahams 1994; Geschiere 1997; Moore and Sanders 2001. For useful general texts on African religions, see Ray 1976; Bourdillon 1991; Gore, 2002.)

Each of these components is discussed in the present chapter, but it must be stressed that they all form an integral part of a religious cosmology that can be understood only within a specific socio-historical context. The literature on religion in sub-Saharan Africa, in all its diversity, is now vast, and it would be impossible to review this literature here. I therefore in this chapter focus the discussion on some key ethnographic texts that have attempted to go beyond a narrow hermeneutical approach and to explore specific African religions within their socio-historical context.

In the next two sections, I explore Kongo religion and prophetic movements within Lower Zaire, focussing on the ethnographical studies of Wyatt MacGaffey. In Section 5.3, I describe Kongo religious cosmology as expressed in the pre-colonial period – the world of Kongo belief as Simon Bockie (1993) describes it – that essentially has two dimensions or models, one reflecting a 'reciprocating universe' between the living and the dead, the other an encompassing 'spiral universe' that incorporates a hierarchy of spiritual beings or mystical powers. These fall under five broad categories, which I describe – god [*nzambi*], ancestral spirits [*bakulu*], local spirits [*bisimbi*], witches [*ndoki*], and consecrated medicines [*min'kisi*]. In the following section, I focus on prophetic movements in Lower Zaire, particularly on the independent church associated with Simon Kimbangu, and its distinction from other prophetic movements known as Ngunzism, which put more emphasis on ecstatic rituals and spirit-healing.

The next two sections focus on Zambia, and the seminal studies of Wim Van Binsbergen (1981). Writing from a Marxist perspective, Van Binsbergen explored religious change in Zambia from the beginning of the nineteenth century, attempting to relate religious transformations and innovations to changes in Zambia's socio-economic life. In Section 5.5, I describe Van Binsbergen's approach to anthropology and outline what he describes as the 'primordial village religion', which, as in Lower Zaire, essentially consisted of four ritual complexes or forms. These were the notion of a high god, ancestral spirits, witchcraft and sorcery, and rituals focussed around territorial spirits. During the nineteenth and early twentieth century, profound socio-economic changes in Zambia – the Atlantic slave trade, the rise of chiefdoms, the penetration of the capitalist economy, and the establishment of the colonial state – gave rise to what Van Binsbergen describes as 'religious innovations'. These innovations are the subject of Section 5.6, which deals specifically with the four main forms – cults of affliction that focus around women and spirit-possession; prophetic cults; watchtower and witch-cleansing movements, with a specific focus on the Mwana Lesa movement; and finally, the independent churches in Zambia, specifically the Lumpa Church of Alice Lenshina. The section concludes with a discussion of the ministry of Archbishop Milingo of Lusaka, who attempted to introduce spirit-healing into the Catholic Church in Zambia.

The chapter concludes with an extensive discussion of another classic ethnography, Jean Comaroff's *Body of Power, Spirit of Resistance* (1985). Like both MacGaffey and Van Binsbergen, Comaroff is an advocate of historical anthropology, her work combining ethnographic analysis with a historical perspective. Thus, Section 5.7 is devoted to the religious cosmology of the Tshidi Barolong, a marginal community of South Africa, as this was expressed in the early nineteenth century. Comaroff suggests that this cosmology formed a cultural logic that mediated between socio-cultural structures and everyday social practice. As Comaroff is centrally concerned with the dialectic between the Tshidi and the wider political economy – specifically the expanding capitalist economy – the final section explores the cultural logic of the Methodist missions during the colonial period – seen as involving the 'colonization of consciousness' – and the sociology of the Zionist churches in South Africa, the latter being interpreted as a form of cultural 'resistance'. The chapter closes with a brief note on the pentecostalist movement in Africa.

5.3. THE WORLD OF KONGO BELIEF

The title of the present section is derived from a very readable and personal account of the spiritual beliefs of the Bakongo of Lower Zaire by Simon Bockie (1993), himself a native of the region. Bockie clearly felt that 'belief' was not a pejorative term. Nor for Bockie, and other anthropologists using the concept, did it imply that they failed to acknowledge that the gods, spirits, and witches have a reality for many African peoples. No anthropologist, as far as I am aware, has ever doubted that spirits, deities, and witches have a reality for many of the people they study and that such beliefs may be considered a form of cultural knowledge (E. Turner 1992; Morris 2000, 223). Bockie, in fact, dedicated his book to the spirits.

But here I want to focus on the studies of Kongo religion by Wyatt MacGaffey, an apprentice (as he puts it) to Kongo culture for more than twenty years. MacGaffey's study (1986) is salutary in attempting to situate Kongo religious culture in its socio-historical context, and to this end he incorporates into his analysis ethnographic material collected by earlier scholars, particularly that of the Swedish missionary Karl Laman who between 1912 and 1919 collected around 400 ethnographic note-books written by Kongo catechists in response to detailed questionnaires. But this makes it difficult at times to ascertain to what extent the religious beliefs and ritual practices described in the book have salience in the contemporary setting. Bockie, however, is quite affirmative in suggesting their continuing relevance:

> In spite of the enormous – and destructive – impact of the west, the social fabric of life in the Kongo is still held together by its traditional beliefs and spiritual practices. (1993, ix)

The Kongo people inhabit the central African coast on both sides of the Zaire River and are described by Bockie as an 'ancient culture' whose original home was in Northern Angola, Mbanza Kongo being the capital of the earlier Kongo Kingdom. As in many other African societies, there was a marked gender division during the nineteenth century, women being the main subsistence cultivators – principally of manioc, peanuts, and beans – and the men engaging in hunting and trade.

Men and women are still said to live in two distinct and separate worlds (Bockie 1993, 5). There was thus a distinction between the subsistence and prestige spheres of the economy, and correspondingly between what MacGaffey describes as 'two models' of social life – egalitarian and hierarchical. The matrilineal clan [*luvila*] was the basis of social organization, but the descent groups were not corporate – being neither local groups nor units of production. MacGaffey's study is primarily concerned with describing the religious life of the Kongo people as it was in the nineteenth century (1986, ix).

Central to Kongo religious cosmology was a two-world theory that suggested the existence of an alternative 'spiritual universe' – a world or community of 'invisible powers' that gives order and direction to all earthly life. This 'two-world' cosmology is seen as implicit in all Kongo myths and rituals, and, according to MacGaffey, people speak of these two parts of the cosmos as *this world* [*nza yayi*] and *the land of the dead* [*nsi a bafwa*]. In myth, the worlds are often separated by a body of water, traditionally called *kalunga* or *nzadi* [great river]. The term *nsi* means underneath or 'down below', although the land of the dead is also associated with the forest [*ku mfinda*]. The worlds of the living and the dead form together what MacGaffey refers to as a 'reciprocating universe', which is 'not static', as he implies, but cyclic, and the human life-cycle is in essence an oscillatory or cyclic movement between the two worlds, death being merely a 'transition in the process of change' (1986, 43–4). MacGaffey thus sums up Kongo thought by suggesting that 'human life is a progress in space and time from the other world, through this world, and back again' (1986, 12). This notion of a 'reciprocating' universe still has contemporary relevance. Although it is continually implied that African people do not make a distinction between the empirical and the mystical, or between the secular and the spiritual (MacGaffey 1986, 42; Bockie 1993, 1), this 'two-world' cosmology seems to imply such a distinction. (On the notion that life and death are both aspects of a single cyclic process, see Morris 2000, 165, with regard to the matrilineal people of Malawi.)

But MacGaffey suggests another version of Kongo cosmology, which he refers to as a 'spiral universe': it suggests a 'spiritual hierarchy' that encompasses the aforementioned division of the universe into 'two worlds', the living and the dead. This second cosmological schema essentially consists of four classes of what MacGaffey describes as 'the dead', four different kinds of 'occult power' [*kindoki*], and correspondingly four holders of what are described as a 'religious commission' – ritual practitioners such as the chief, priest, magician, and witch. MacGaffey's penchant for presenting the ethnographic data in the form of a quadrant, based on the distinctions public–private, benevolent (life)–destructive (death), is, however, somewhat overdrawn at times. It is suggested that the Kongo do not have clearly defined religious concepts, are rather vague in how they characterize status designations, and use verbal labels rather loosely and interchangeably (MacGaffey 1986, 64–5); nevertheless, their religious life can be broadly discussed under five relevant categories: god [*nzambi*], the ancestors [*bakulu*], local spirits [*bisimbi*], witches [*ndoki*], and consecrated medicines [*min'kisi*]. I discuss each of these in turn.

5.3.1. *God*

In the 'spiritual hierarchy', *Nzambi*, usually translated as 'god', is generally considered to be the highest spiritual form, and as the creator of the universe and human life, *Nzambi mpungu*, 'the highest Nzambi', was identified with the Christian god, and Bockie suggests that it is an 'all-pervasive power' that permeates all things – trees, rivers, stones – and yet is detached from day-to-day involvement in human affairs. Thus the ancestral spirits [*bakulu*] are said to serve as mediators between the deity and humans. But although Nzambi may be addressed at times of crisis, there were no organized cults or shrines associated with god, and Bockie suggests that the idea of god's presence could be confined to a specific place or object was alien to Kongo thought (1993, 134–5).

5.3.2. *Ancestral Spirits (Bakulu)*

What we call 'spirits', MacGaffey suggests, are for the Kongo human beings who after death exist in other forms or 'bodies'. The most important of these spirits were the ancestors, and, as in other African societies, the cult of the ancestors was extremely important in early Kongo society and was intrinsically associated with various forms of chiefship. Although a matrilineal society, the chief [*mfumu*] was invariably a man, who had authority, both ritual and political, over a particular subclan [*kanda*] and was, according to Bockie, chosen by the ancestors for his good character and qualities. He was thus seen as the 'embodiment' of ancestral power, and the well-being of the community, the fertility of the soil, and individual success and failure depended specifically on 'ancestral blessings'. The chief was therefore a key figure in mediating between the living members of the matrilineal kin group and the ancestors, and any misfortunes that befell the community was put down to a breaking of the 'covenant' between humans and these spiritual beings. To restore harmony, the chief, on behalf of the community, would therefore make a sacrifice of a goat or oblations of palm wine, thus placating the ancestors. As with the Lugbara, the chief was therefore an important ritual figure (Bockie 1993, 7–19). The ancestors were in general 'benevolently disposed', as MacGaffey puts it, and they were expected to provide their descendants with good hunting, abundant crops, children, and long life and health (1986, 67). As representative of the ancestors, the chief had a role that was therefore primarily that of guardian or protector of the kin group – or wider polity – and was not purely concerned with 'death' nor 'destructive', as MacGaffey seems to stress. Significantly, territorial chiefs, as distinct from local village headmen (the distinction is important), had to be invested by the priest [*nganga mbangu*] of the spirit associated with a particular territory [*n'kisi nsi*] (1986, 69).

5.3.3. *Local Spirits (Bisimbi)*

The 'invisible world' (Bockie) or 'land of the dead' (MacGaffey) contains not only the ancestral spirits [*bakulu*] but also a multitude of other spirits that are associated with specific localities or natural phenomena. Most of these spirits are benevolent, but some, as active forces, may be considered evil and held responsible for misfortunes, and they intrude on the world of the living in many different ways. Some regional spirits, such as *bunzi*, are associated with storms and lightning; other local or earthly spirits [*n'kisi nsi*] are associated with consecrated medicines (usually described as *min'kisi*), but the most familiar of the local spirits are known as *bisimbi* (also called *nkita*). These spirits are located in particular natural phenomena, certain rocks or pools, termite mounds, or rivers, and are often divided into those 'of the water', 'of the sky', and 'of the land'. Such spirits take various forms or manifestations and are particularly associated with fertility, metalworking, and healing rites. Significantly, twins [*nsimba*] are regarded as a 'sort of incarnation of bisimbi' and as thus having occult power [*kindoki*] (MacGaffey 1986, 77–88).

5.3.4. *Witches [Ndoki]*

Witches are not spiritual beings for the Kongo but living people who use occult or mystical power [*kindoki*] to harm other people. As Bockie puts it, there is a belief that 'ndoki destroys his victims by eating them'. The term *kindoki*, although derived from the Kikongo verb *loka*, meaning *to bewitch*, has a wide meaning and does not necessarily imply something malevolent or evil; it essentially signifies a mystical power or force. A chief, a successful farmer or trader, or a lineage elder may all be considered ndoki and as possessing this occult power. But its usual meaning denotes this power as harmful or evil, and throughout his text, Bockie employs the term *ndoki* to signify a living individual who practices maleficium, causing harm, misfortunes, or even death to kin or neighbours. MacGaffey also describes witchcraft as a 'negative cult of the dead'. Although many Christians in Lower Zaire profess not to believe in witchcraft [*kindoki*], Bockie confidently affirms that although such Christians may reject such beliefs in public, they often privately acknowledge its effects. People may be unconscious of the fact that they are witches, and Bockie suggests that they mainly attack their own kin. Any person convicted of being a witch [*ndoki*] was liable to being publicly denounced and expelled from the village or even beaten or stoned to death. As in other African societies, the Kongo attribute witchcraft, whether conscious or unconscious, to jealousy [*kimpala*], and witches may assume the form of harmful mosquitoes or wild animals or send animals as familiars to destroy crops or livestock.

By killing a person, the witch may accumulate witchcraft substance [*kundu*], which makes the witch even more powerful. Again, as in many other African societies, a poison ordeal was often administered with the bark of the n'kasa tree (*Erythrophleum suaveulens*) in order to identify suspected witches. But in normal circumstances, the detection of witchcraft and countermeasures are the main concerns of diviners [*nganga ngombo*].

During the 1950s, a witch-finding movement, called *Munkukusa* – derived from the verb *kukusa* [to confess, purify] – swept through the Lower Zaire. It was not specifically anti-Christian or anti-European, but it involved confession and the taking of special anti-witchcraft medicines. Those who refused to take part in the rituals were treated as if they were witches [*ndoki*], which could lead to their being stoned to death as suspected witches (MacGaffey 1986, 160–7; Bockie 1993, 40–61).

Witches on their death did not become ancestors but ghosts [*min'kuyu*], who thereafter were condemned to wander aimlessly in the infertile grasslands between the cultivated valleys and the forests. The min'kuyu were not the focus of any cult rituals and were usually deemed malevolent, to be exorcised, not supplicated. Bockie describes the *bankuyu* as the 'evil dead' who were engaged in witchcraft during their lifetime and are now 'the nomads of the other world' (MacGaffey 1986, 73; Bockie 1993, 131).

5.3.5. Consecrated Medicines [Min'kisi]

As in other African societies, medicines play a crucial role in all aspects of Kongo social life, both religious and secular. But what is of particular significance among the Kongo is that specific medicines or material objects – whether animals, plants [*min'ti*], skins, shells, stones, or artefacts – are conceived as embodying spiritual power. They may thus be viewed as animate and as having personalities. In the past they were described as 'fetishes', but MacGaffey describes them as 'charms' [*min'kisi*], *nkisi* essentially referring to the spirit they embody. Thus min'kisi are essentially material objects, whether natural or artificial, that are said to 'embody' or 'incorporate' the spirits [*nkisi*] and are thus essentially consecrated medicines (charms) or religious icons. The charms are utilized for a variety of purposes – as protective amulets, as healing medicine for various ailments and to facilitate childbirth, for hunting success, as well as being key items in divinatory rites.

Two ritual practitioners are particularly associated with consecrated medicines, both described as *nganga*. As elsewhere, *nganga* is a term that has a wide range of meaning and in different contexts can denote a herbalist, physician, diviner, spirit-medium, priest, or visionary.

(For an interesting discussion of the nganga paradigm, see Schoffeleers 1994, although it is important to stress that Jesus Christ was essentially a spirit-healer and exorcist, while the use of medicines, whether or not consecrated, is a key part of the role of the African nganga.)

Prototypically, *kinganga* combines a focus on both medicines and spirits, and *ngang'a mbuki* (or *ngang'a nkisi*) refers to a herbalist whose healing rituals may entail spiritual-healing but whose practice essentially involves individual clients. On the other hand, *ngang'a ngombo* – the term *ngombo* refers to the consecrated material object that embodies or is the 'incarnation' (according to Bockie) of a tutelary spirit – is essentially a diviner. The ngang'a ngombo is particularly concerned with identiying the specific cause of a misfortune, illness, or death, and, with the help of the spirits [*nkisi*], ascertaining whether these are due to a malevolent spirit or to a witch (Bockie 1993, 66–71). Of interest is that in recent years, few people admit to being an ngang'a n'kisi, given the influence of Christianity and the association that is often made between medicines and witchcraft. Healers thus present themselves as essentially herbalists. MacGaffey gives a rather disparaging account of one such urban magician [*ngang'a*] (1986, 220–6).

In the nineteenth century, MacGaffey suggests, two kinds of ngang'a were recognized: those associated with personal afflictions and the 'true ngang'a' – the *ngange mbangu*, whose primary function was that of a priest and who essentially performed public rituals.

Although I think the analysis is somewhat strained, using the distinctions between public and private interests or ends and between benevolent and destructive effects, MacGaffey (1986, 172–3) suggests the following four primary 'religious' roles or commissions.

	Public	**Private**
Destructive	Chief [*mfumu*]	Witch [*ndoki*]
Benevolent	Priest or diviner [*ngang'a mbangu*]	Magician [*ngang'a n'kisi*]

Although these two distinctions probably have wide cross-cultural reference in Africa, this formal schema has a heuristic rather than any explanatory significance.

In a Durkheimian analysis, MacGaffey suggests that Kongo religion 'finds its place in the political dimension of public life', and that there is an evident 'isomorphism' between their cosmology and their social organization. Thus the hierarchical organization of society, focussed around the chiefs and official relations, is the 'model', he writes, for the 'hierarchy of spirits that formed the core of the spiral universe', and with the collapse of this political structure during the colonial period, so the 'spiritual hierarchy' also collapsed, and thus has little relevance in the contemporary setting (1986, 100–2). On the other hand, beliefs and ritual practices that focus around witchcraft and the magician [*ngang'a n'kisi*] represents the egalitarian model of society, although MacGaffey suggests an equation between this egalitarian model – which is intrinsically linked to matrilineal kinship, the village community, and systems of mutual aid – with the individualism expressed by the Bakongo, who have always been, he noted, 'entrepreneurs anxious to make a profit' (1986, 174). This equation, however, seems to be problematic.

In the concluding part of the study, MacGaffey has a brief account of prophetic movements in Kongo religious history. But the role of the prophet [*ngunza*] and particularly a discussion of the most famous prophetic movement in Zaire, the independent church associated with Simon Kimbangu, are the subjects of the next section.

5.4. PROPHETIC MOVEMENTS IN LOWER ZAIRE

In an article on Kongo religion, Wyatt MacGaffey is critical of the concept of 'syncretism', for not only does it have pejorative connotations, particularly in the hands of some theologians, but syncretism of some kind is a 'universal property of culture'. In fact all religions are to some degree 'syncretic' (1994, 241–5). He was also at pains to stress that the religious system of the Bakongo, as described by earlier ethnographers, was in no sense 'traditional' but largely a political artefact of colonial rule. So-called 'modernity' is not therefore some recent phenomena in Africa but has a long history. For with regard to the Congo region, the impact of capitalism and the Atlantic slave trade, literacy, bureaucratic forms of government through the colonial state, and the activities of Christian missionaries all go back many centuries. From the end of the seventeenth century, a series of European trading depots was established, and in 1645 Capuchin missionaries sent from Rome arrived in the Congo. All this had a profound impact on the social and political life of the Bakongo, leading to a severe disruption of their social life and the demise of the Kongo kingdom. One of the responses to these events was the emergence of what has been described as 'prophetic' religious movements, which in a sense reflect a reaction and a form of resistance to both missionary activity and colonial rule. One of the earliest of these prophetic movements was focussed around the prophetess Donna Beatrice.

In 1704, a young Kongolese woman, Kimpa Vita, who was given the name Beatrice on her baptism, experienced a series of visions and dreams. She had become seriously ill, and during her illness a Capuchin monk had appeared to her and revealed himself as St. Anthony, a saint who was particularly venerated by Catholics in the Congo. She thus came to see herself as an incarnation of St. Anthony. Announcing that the day of judgement was at hand and that Christ was born as an African in Sao Salvador, she led a movement of spiritual and religious renewal that represented a 'massive protest' against the Catholic Church. The movement she founded was known as Antonism, and it attracted a huge following. Her closest followers were called 'angels', who travelled the country proclaiming her message. With regard to her own preaching, three elements are of particular interest. The first is that she not only repudiated consecrated medicines [*nkisi*] but also burned all crosses and images of the crucified Christ, and preached against missionaries and their sacraments. She was thus seen by the Catholic Church as an 'enemy of the cross'. Second, she identified Christ as an African and preached that not only Jesus but also his apostles, the Madonna, and St. Francis of Assissi were all black. And finally, her prophecy had a millennial and political aspect in that she envisaged the restoration of the ancient kingdom of Kongo under a new monarch and the coming of a kind of paradise on earth. It is hardly surprising that she aroused the extreme hostility of both the Catholic missionaries and the colonial authorities and that she was accused of both 'heresy' and 'sedition'. Her cause was not helped by the fact that, while she preached chastity, she gave birth to a son, the father being a close 'angel' – 'Saint John'. She claimed, however, that she had conceived the child by the holy spirit. The outcome was that Beatrice was arrested in 1706 and burned at the stake as a heretic, along with her young son (Martin 1975, 14–17; MacGaffey 1986, 208–11).

Such prophetic or messianic movements occurred throughout the colonial period in the Lower Congo, as well as throughout much of Africa. But one of the most renowned is that associated with the prophet Simon Kimbangu, whom Bryan Wilson described as 'one of the great prophets of the twentieth century' (in Martin 1975, xiv). Kimbanguism has been described as both a new Christian movement and as drawing heavily on Kongo 'spiritual traditions'. It is now a well-established independent church in central Africa: the 'Church of Jesus Christ on Earth Through the Prophet Simon Kimbangu', having been established in 1956. It now has a membership of over 3 million people.

Towards the end of the nineteenth century, colonial rule was firmly ensconced in the Congo, with the Congo Free State being established in 1885 – to become the Belgian Congo in 1908 – and this was accompanied by the intensification of missionary activity. In 1878, the British Baptist Missionary Society established itself at Mbanza Kongo, and in the following decades other Protestant groups began mission work in the region, including the Plymouth Brethren. Given this missionary influence, within a few decades most people in the Congo came to describe themselves, at least nominally, as Christians. But the combined effects of colonial rule and missionary activity – with its strident evangelism – led to what has been described as a 'prophetic reaction'. The key figure in this response to the various social discontents was the prophet Simon Kimbangu (Martin 1975, 20–38; MacGaffey 1986, 214–15).

Simon Kimbangu was born in the small village of Nkamba in the Lower Congo in 1889. Both his parents died when he was a child, and he was brought up by an aunt. He became a member of the local Baptist Church and was married with three young boys – the youngest, Joseph Diangienda, eventually becoming head of the Church. He was for a while a teacher at a mission school and by all accounts a likeable and modest man, intelligent, with a strong personality, and he had a very good knowledge of the Bible. He worked for a period as a labourer in Kinshasa, and then, around 1918, during the influenza epidemic, he began to hear voices, calling him to the ministry. By 1921, he had become renowned as a prophet [*ngunzi*], healing the sick by the laying on of hands, curing a blind person by using soil and saliva, and performing miracles, including resurrecting the dead. Kimbangu saw his power as deriving from god and the holy spirit, and the spirit-healing that is attributed to him and his later suffering are seen as re-enactments of the life and ministry of Jesus. Speaking in tongues and repudiating the use of consecrated medicines, Kimbangu used, spring water at Nkamba as a blessing. He emphasized purity, faith, and repentance; spoke against dancing and polygamy; and taught obedience to those in authority. In her study of Kimbanguism, Marie-Louise Martin suggests that Kimbangu was a true Christian prophet who healed in the name of Jesus and that his message was neither anti-European nor anti-missionary. Here, she wrote, 'was an outpouring of the Holy Spirit in the middle of Africa, and Nkamba became the "New Jerusalem"' (1975, 42–8). As a Christian theologian, she describes all other prophets as 'false prophets' and their movements as being, unlike that of Kimbangu, a form of syncretism. Although Kimbangu's evangelism was essentially Christian, other scholars have suggested that his preaching had an unmistakable nationalistic tenor. Thus Lanternari writes that Kimbangu

> prophesised the immanent ousting of the foreign rulers, a new way of life for Africans, the return of the dead, and the coming of a golden age. (1963, 26)

Kimbangu's prophecy and healing soon became widely known, and he gathered around him a large following, Nkamba attracting many pilgrims. Afraid that Kimbangu and his followers would become a political, anti-colonial movement, the Belgian authorities, urged by many Catholic priests, decided to arrest Kimbangu. In June 1921, an attempt to capture him at Nkamba failed, and Kimbangu for some three months went into hiding. Then, hearing god's voice telling him to return to Nkamba to be arrested, Kimbangu in September 1921 gave himself up voluntarily to the colonial authorities. In October, he was tried in a military court for sedition and hostility towards Europeans – he had no legal counsel – and he was found guilty and sentenced to 120 lashes of the whip and to be put to death. The trial was, as Wilson remarked, a 'travesty of justice'. His sentence was later commuted to life imprisonment, and at the age of thirty-two Kimbangu was transported to a prison at Lubumbashi, thousands of kilometres from his home village of Nkamba. He never saw his family again and spent the next thirty years of his life in prison, mostly in solitary confinement. He died in October 1951 (Wilson 1973, 367–71; Martin 1975, 52–63).

In the decades following Kimbangu's imprisonment, the followers of the prophet continued to be active, and many other prophetic movements sprang up throughout the Congo. These 'prophetic disturbances' were strongly opposed by the Belgian authorities, and harsh measures were enacted to suppress them – persecution, imprisonment, and the massive deportation of people to 'concentration camps'. The Kimbanguist movement, which was not confined to the Bakongo but had spread throughout the region, was seen by the authorities as seditious and as constituting a threat to the colonial state. Nevertheless, the repressive measures and the generally hostile attitude of the missionaries only served to drive the prophetic movements underground, to intensify anti-white feelings, and to force these movements beyond Protestant control (Wilson 1973, 372).

There is a good deal of overlap between the followers of Kimbangu and other prophetic movements, but scholars have tended to make a distinction between Kimbanguism and various other movements that are seen as more 'syncretic' – incorporating elements of Kongo religion – and that are described as Ngunzism. The term *ngunza* in Kikongo means 'prophet' and essentially refers to the Nganga who is both a prophet and a spirit-healer. Most Ngunza draw a sharp distinction between themselves and the *nganga n'kisi* [herbalist–diviners] who are seen as 'peddlers' (MacGaffey uses this rather derogatory term) of medicines, and whose beliefs and practices are associated with the pursuit of personal profit (MacGaffey 1994, 252). Kimbangu was known as a Ngunza. But Marie-Louise Martin describes the Ngunzist movement as quite distinct from that of Kimbanguism and as being led by 'false prophets', who urged people to withhold taxes, preached hatred of Europeans, and encouraged resistance to the forced-labour schemes of the colonial state. In contrast to Kimbanguism, the Ngunzist movement is seen as essentially a political as well as a religious movement; as consisting of small groups led by a local prophet without any ecclesiastical structure; as putting more emphasis on ecstasy and the beating of drums than on Christian hymns, prayers, and Bible-reading; and as primarily engaged in spirit-healing, exorcism, and in countering witchcraft [*ndoki*]. Ngunzism was also seen as having a messianic emphasis, advocating the restoration of the Kongo kingdom, and being 'syncretic' – Martin using this term in a pejorative sense. Thus she interpreted the movement associated with Simon Kimbangu as a 'true' Christian movement based on faith, prayer, and intercession (1975, 72–8).

Another figure who was influential and important in relation to the prophetic movements during the latter part of colonial rule was Simon Mpadi. Like Kimbangu, Simon Mpadi was originally a Baptist and worked for a while as a village schoolteacher. Dismissed by the American Baptist Mission for adultery – around 1937 – Mpadi joined the Salvation Army. The arrival of the Salvation Army in the Congo in 1935 apparently produced an extraordinary effect among the people of the Congo. The uniforms, the ceremonies accompanied by martial hymns and the rhythm of drums, the emphasis on handshakes and joyous expression – all had a great appeal for local people. It appears that even the letter 'S' displayed on the Salvation Army uniform was interpreted as a sign for Simon (Kimbangu). Thus people began to abandon the missions in large numbers and to attach themselves to the Salvation Army with its easy confession and emphasis on salvation. Dismissed in turn from the Salvation Army, Simon Mpadi, in 1939, founded the Mission des Noire – Mission to the Blacks, which afterwards became known as the Khaki movement on account of its khaki uniforms. This movement had a complex hierarchical structure, Mpadi seeing himself as chief of the apostles of Simon Kimbangu, and its emphasis was on ecstatic rites and in countering the malevolent influences of witchcraft. Mpadi drafted a 'creed' for the Black Church that outlined the twelve 'personalities' of Simon Kimpbangu, who is described as a priest [*nganga*] and as the saviour [*mvulusi*] of black people, and as manifested in various icons (Lanternari 1963, 29–32; Martin 1975, 91–2; MacGaffey 1986, 113–16).

During the colonial period, all religious movements in the Congo had been suppressed, often quite brutally, and the founding of churches outside the Protestant and Catholic missions was declared illegal. But the followers of Kimbangu often met secretly, singing their hymns and conducting services, and many went on pilgrimages to the Nkamba shrine. In the last years of colonial rule, the political situation became less intolerant, and Joseph Diangienda, the son of Kimbangu, supported by his two older brothers, began to organize the followers of Kimbangu into a unified church. In 1956, the movement drafted a memorandum demanding an end to colonial rule, and in that same year Diangienda gathered the various local groups together to found the Kimbaguist Church. It was called 'The Church of Jesus Christ on Earth Through the Prophet Simon Kimbangu'. In 1959, the year before independence, it was recognized by the Belgian colonial government as an independent church, placing it on the same footing as the Catholic Church and the various Protestant churches. In 1960, the mortal remains of Simon Kimbangu were transferred from Lubumbashi to Nkamba, his home village, and placed in a simple mausoleum. Nkamba was thus finally established as the 'New Jerusalem'.

The church essentially followed the original doctrines and rituals established by Simon Kimbangu and thus, as Martin emphasizes, saw itself as a thoroughly Christian church. It has an ecclesiastical structure, and a constitution, drafted by Diangienda as head of the church, stresses that it is founded on the Christian faith, working through the power of the holy spirit. It acknowledges the Christian message as revealed in the Bible and advocates the separation of spiritual (i.e., ecclesiastical) and secular (i.e., state) authority. Although Kimbangu is often heralded as a 'nationalist' hero, it is significant that Kimbanguism did not become the state church of Zaire. But the church did advocate 'obedience to state authority' in accordance with Romans 13: 1–3. The Kimbanguist Church also distanced itself from many aspects of Kongo culture, demanding that its members neither indulge in alcohol, polygamy, or dancing nor engage in 'fetishism', that is, have any dealings with consecrated medicines. Public rituals focus on prayer, hymn-singing, and sermons, with little ecstatic emphasis, and the rite of healing by the laying on of hands is restricted to the head of the church (Martin 1975, 130–5). All this contrasts with other prophetic movements, such as the Church of the Holy Spirit (Ngunzist), whose rituals usually consist of two phases – an ordinary Protestant service with hymns, Bible-reading, prayers, and a sermon, and a second phase involving spirit-possession, ecstatic healing, and divination. MacGaffey suggests that after

1960, the Kimbanguist Church lost much of its popular support by curtailing ecstatic and healing practices – in its effort to develop a bureaucratic structure. Thus there is a sense in which the prophet's charisma has been routinized, with the development of an ecclesiastical structure, and the element of political protest has been lost (Banton 1970, 224; MacGaffey 1994, 246–252; for other studies of Kimbangu and prophetic movements in Lower Zaire, see Andersson 1958; Chomé 1959; MacGaffey 1983).

5.5. RELIGIOUS CHANGE IN ZAMBIA

Around the 1970s, there was within anthropology a marked reaction against structural functionalism, the kind of analysis exemplified by Middleton's study (1960) of the Lugbara, even though many scholars within this tradition had produced some excellent pioneering ethnographic studies. Besides structuralism and interpretive anthropology, advocated respectively by Levi-Strauss and Geertz, a plethora of other theoretical strategies was then being broached: games theory and generative models; cultural ecology; cultural materialism; the 'new' ethnography (cognitive anthropology); network and transactional analysis; and various forms of 'symbolic' or hermeneutic understanding. But one important theoretical tendency involved a resurgence of interest in the relationship between Marxism and anthropology and the attempt by a number of scholars to explore the possibility of interpreting pre-capitalist societies in terms of a Marxist paradigm. Apart from Godelier, whose work I have discussed elsewhere, Marxist anthropology tended to focus on kinship organization and the political economy and largely ignored religion. Eric Wolf's magisterial study, *Europe and the People Without History* (1982), for example, hardly mentions religion in the entire text. One scholar, however, who has explicitly attempted to apply the theoretical concepts derived from Marx to a study of African religion is Wim Van Binsbergen (1981), and the present section and the following section are devoted to a discussion of his seminal essays on religious change in Zambia (for useful discussion of Marxist anthropology, see Kahn and Llobera 1981; Bloch 1983; Morris 1987, 319–28).

Although Van Binsbergen describes his work as 'exploratory' and as a case of rushing in 'where angels fear to tread' (1981, 286), his study is nevertheless a stimulating attempt, within the social scientific tradition, to both interpret and explain religious change in Zambia. As a Marxist analysis, Van Binbergen utilizes two key conceptual ideas derived from Marx, namely, the distinction between a society's superstructure and infrastructure and the concept of 'mode of production'. The term *superstructure* refers to the mutually shared ideas concerning the universe and the place of humans within it that are held by members of a society. It provides a 'central repository of meaning' for such members, and these ideas are reinforced by ritual and supported by implicit and often unconscious cognitive structures.

Contrasting with the base or infrastructure, the organization of productive activities on which people's lives depend, the superstructure is akin to what other scholars have described as the 'symbolic order', 'ideology', or the 'cultural system'. Van Binsbergen emphasizes the dialectical relationship between the superstructure (which includes religion) and the infrastructure, eschews economic determinism, while suggesting that a religious ideology has only a 'relative autonomy'. Thus, although religion is important in influencing and shaping social life, it is neither an autonomous realm nor simply a reflection of material or economic processes (see Williams 1980, 31–49, for interesting reflections of the base–superstructure metaphor; and Comaroff 1985, 170, on Van Binsbergen's use of it).

Thus Van Binsbergen argues that only a 'highly contextualized' approach to African religion is appropriate and meaningful. On the other hand, Van Binsbergen is critical of the classical Durkheimian approach that tends to treat society as a bounded, internally integrated whole, divorced from its socio-historical context and that sees the relationship between religious beliefs and practices and the social structure as essentially one of correspondence or isomorphic. This correspondence theory is particularly evident in the work of Mary Douglas (1970), Geertz (1975), and in Middleton's study (1960) of Lugbara religion (Van Binsbergen 1981, 60–1).

For Van Binsbergen, neither the ideological 'superstructure' nor the economic infrastructure of a society is monolithic, for the superstructure is seen as constituted by various religious 'forms', and the infrastructure itself in contemporary Zambia is interpreted as an 'articulation' of distinct modes of production. A mode of production, as both Eric Wolf and Van Binsbergen describe it, is a specific historically occurring set of social relations through which labour is organized by people in order to produce the basic necessities of life. This often crucially entails a differential distribution of power and resources. Both scholars refer to three modes of production: the *domestic* or kin-ordered mode of production, which essentially revolves around subsistence agriculture, the dominance of the senior generation, reinforced by the gender division, and in which the political economy is largely organized through kinship; the *tributary* mode of production, which is linked to the rise of chiefdoms and the emergence of long-distance trade and which involved the extraction of surpluses from the village community through tribute; and finally the *capitalist* mode of production. Van Binsbergen makes a further distinction between mercantile capitalism, which flourished in the nineteenth century, and industrial capitalism, which emerged in Zambia around 1900 with the establishment of the colonial state (1981, 43–9; Wolf 1982, 75–100).

Van Binbergen's study is not focussed on religion and ritual symbolism per se, but on the relationship between social structural change in Zambia over the past two centuries and the emergence of specific religious 'forms' or movements. He is reluctant, however, to define religion 'as such' but takes a commonsense approach, focussing on those beliefs, rituals, and cults that relate to what he describes as 'non-empirical beings and forces' or 'invisible entities'. In sum, Van Binsbergen's study is historical, synthetic, and comparative in approach, drawing not only on his own fieldwork experiences among the Nyoka of Western Zambia (undertaken mainly between 1972 and 1974) but also on archival material and on the exemplary ethnographic studies by such fine scholars as Monica Wilson, Victor Turner, and Audrey Richards (Richards 1939; Turner 1967, 1968; Wilson 1971).

As a kind of 'baseline', Van Binsbergen outlines what he describes as the 'primordial village religion', which he suggests characterized the peoples of Western Zambia around the turn of the nineteenth century. He notes that these people lived in a common savannah environment; practised shifting cultivation, hunting, and gathering and small-scale animal husbandry; and had a striking social structural homogeneity – depicted as the domestic mode of production. They also shared a common cultural heritage that in its religious aspects consisted of four ritual complexes, relating to the high god, ancestral spirits, witchcraft, and land spirits.

Of crucial importance to the people of Western Zambia was the notion of a *high god* who was considered the ultimate creator and associated with the sky and atmospheric phenomena, especially rain, so vital to subsistence cultivators. But although territorial cults were sometimes associated with the divinity, in early times, Van Binsbergen writes, god was hardly ever approached directly through ritual or identified as the cause of misfortunes. He even suggests that in Western Zambia, people did not explicitly ask the dead – the ancestral spirits – to intervene with god on their behalf, or if they did, this was mainly due to Christian influences (1981, 139–41).

The second important religious 'form', or cult, was that associated with the *ancestral spirits*. Misfortunes and illness were often interpreted as being due to the wrath of an ancestral spirit, and treatment usually involved both specific medicines and the use of divination to ascertain the cause of the misfortune, and the necessary ritual steps to be taken to appease the spirits. Village and neighbourhood shrines were particularly associated with deceased kin; additionally, there were individual shrines relating to specific skills such as hunting, honey-collecting, and iron-smelting (1981, 104–5).

The third ideological dimension relating to the 'primordial' village religion was the beliefs and rituals associated with *witchcraft and sorcery*, for illness, misfortune, and even death were often interpreted as the result of human malice. Van Binsbergen highlights three themes relating to witchcraft and sorcery: that while illness relating to the ancestors was often of a debilitating or chronic nature, the symptom pattern relating to witchcraft was a violent and rapidly deteriorating illness that often led to death; that witchcraft involved a human agent who expressed malice towards neighbours and kin and practised cannibalism, feeding on human flesh; and finally, that while witchcraft often reflected interpersonal conflict and social tensions, it was also felt that anyone achieving high status or power inevitably had access to powerful medicines, especially those derived from a human corpse.

As Van Binsbergen writes,

It is highly significant that medicine prepared out of human remains is considered to be essential for the attainment and maintaining of precisely the few elevated statuses existing in the society of central Western Zambia: the hunter, the doctor (nganga), the commercial entrepreneur, and especially the chief. (1981, 142)

The final dimension of the earlier religious system of Western Zambia is related to the existence of *territorial cults*, which had important ecological functions. Matthew Schoffeleers – cited by Van Binsbergen – had tentatively defined the concept of territorial cult as 'an institution of spirit veneration, proper to a land area, whose primary concern is the material and moral well-being of its population, archetypically represented by its rain-calling function, and whose immediate control is institutionally limited to an elite' (1981, 100). The shrines of the territorial cults were associated with local spirits, had a regional focus, were normally under the control of priests, and aimed at ensuring the success of ecological activities – agriculture and hunting in particular – and the overall social well-being of the people of a particular territory. With the emergence of the tributary mode of production, long-distance trade, and development of chiefdoms, the shrines associated with the chiefdom became increasingly important. Containing the graves and relics of deceased chiefs, these territorial or royal shrines were associated with chiefly cults that enabled the chiefs to claim ritual suzerainty over a particular territory. What was of especial importance was the land's fertility, the availability of rain at crucial times, and the control of epidemics and locust plagues. Thus Van Binsbergen emphasizes that the main function of these chiefly shrines was as a source of political legitimation for the chief (1981, 104). (For an important study of territorial cults in Central Africa, see Schoffeleers 1979; and for regional cults more generally, see Werbner 1977.)

From the end of the eighteenth century, two socio-economic changes had a profound impact on the religious life of the people of Western Zambia. The first consisted of the increasing involvement of local communities in a new mode of production, the tributary mode, that was based on the long-distance trade that had penetrated the area. The second important infrastructural change was the penetration of capitalism, initially in its mercantile form, with the increasing imposition of the Atlantic slave trade, as well as the ivory trade towards the end of the nineteenth century. With the imposition of colonial rule around 1900, industrial capitalism then penetrated the region through labour migration and the introduction of manufactured commodities. This also involved the destruction of pre-existing networks of trade and tribute, the imposition of hut tax, and the transformation of local chiefs into petty administrators for the colonial state (1981, 276). These profound socio-ecomonic and political transformations led to the emergence of several distinct religious forms, or what Van Binsbergen describes as 'religious innovations', and four are worth noting: the various cults of affliction that emerged in the late nineteenth century; the prophetic cults; the watchtower and witch-cleansing movements; and the independent churches, all of which emerged from the 1930s onwards. These four cults or religious innovations are discussed in the next section.

5.6. RELIGIOUS MOVEMENTS IN ZAMBIA

The impact of capitalism in Zambia and its articulation with other modes of production gave rise, Van Binsbergen suggests, to essentially four religious movements. Each of these I discuss in turn, relating them to their specific socio-historical context.

5.6.1. Cults of Affliction

The cults of affliction that emerged in the late nineteenth century and the early twentieth century were in essence spirit-possession cults that offered new interpretations of physical and mental disorders. Illness, disease, and infertility were thus no longer attributed to ancestral spirits but to foreign spirits, or what Van Binsbergen describes as 'abstract impersonal principles'. Among these new cults were Songo (after the Songo people of Angola), Bindele (referring to white people or Swahili traders), and Ndeke (aeroplane), as well as such cults as Mashawe, Chimbandu, Vimbuza, Kayongo, and Kasheba. These terms refer to the disease, the cult, and the offending spirit, and the idea common to all these cults, Van Binsbergen writes

> is that one could contract such a disease from strangers, particularly in situations of trade, slavery and labour migration. (1981, 151)

In the early twentieth century, such cults were prolific and, though developing directly out of the nganga tradition of medicine and healing, they were always explicitly associated with foreign spirits (or groups) and were usually named after them. The leaders of the cults were usually elderly women, and the cults themselves consisted of an informed grouping of loyal adepts, mainly women, grouped around a cult leader. Modern spirit-mediums are described by Van Binsbergen as predominantly 'ritual entrepreneurs' (1981, 191). The cults focussed on the individual, whose physical affliction or mental distress was interpreted as possession by a foreign spirit, whilst treatment consisted mainly of initiation into the cult venerating the spirit.

Like Ioan Lewis, Van Binsbergen emphasizes that the cults of affliction had connotations of impersonality and alien-ness, and interpreted the ailments as due to amoral foreign spirits, rather than as due to a moral breach of kin relations or sorcery. As he writes, 'These cults are concerned with suffering, and not with morality. Their frame of reference features patients afflicted by essentially unpredictable, non-human agents' (1981, 186).

But Van Binsbergen does not interpret these cults of affliction as a form of protest and is critical of the 'deprivation hypothesis' as an explanation for such movements (1981, 87; on the use of relative deprivation to explain recent religious movements, see Glock 1964; Hamilton 2001, 240).

Although spirit-possession cults are still flourishing in Zambia, in both the rural and the urban contexts, Van Binsbergen suggests that while they appeared prior to the prophetic cults and healing churches, as well as other forms of organized Christianity, they 'now seem to be losing ground to the latter' (1981, 161).

But what is of particular interest is that Van Binsbergen describes these modern cults of affliction in Zambia as 'cults of egotism par excellence' and, like Lewis, suggests that they serve as a way that women may demand and receive male support in urban situations where they are seriously disadvantaged. Van Binsbergen even suggests that the theme of a woman in town seeking redress for a breach of conjugal relationship through the spirit-possession cult is a recurrent one (1981, 238–46). What is also of interest is that not only in Zambia but throughout Africa, cults of affliction – spirit-possession cults – are in fact proliferating and are intrinsically related to what has been described as the 'experience of modernity', the increasing penetration of global capitalism and bureaucratic state power into local communities. Why this upsurge of religious fervour should come as a surprise to postmodern anthropologists is hard to fathom – at least to anyone who has read Marx! Yet while this has been happening, many of these anthropologists have been abandoning sociological analysis for hermeneutics – content to describe the aesthetics of ritual. As with spirit-possession cults in relation to Buddhism and Islam, cults of affliction in Africa are complex social phenomena and are not only intrinsically related to politics, gender issues, and healing, but – to state the obvious – are also a form of entertainment, have an aesthetic dimension in relation to dance and music, and offer a social critique by providing 'a discourse about otherness' – to use postmodern jargon. Dismissive of earlier sociological approaches, Heike Behrend (1999, 138–42) emphasizes that spirits have agency and are represented as external, alien powers – which is hardly news to scholars like Lewis and Van Binsbergen!

(For further studies of spirit-possession cults [or cults of affliction] in sub-Saharan Africa, see Turner 1968; Beattie and Middleton 1969; Fry 1976; Devisch 1993; Ben-Amos 1994; Janzen 1994; Behrend and Luig 1999; Morris 2000, 235–50.)

5.6.2. Prophetic Cults

By the 1930s, cults of affliction had become well established in Western Zambia, but around that time a new type of cult of affliction emerged, which Van Binsbergen describes as a 'prophetic regional cult'. He describes in detail three such cults. The first was associated with a man, Mupumani, of humble origins and a leper, who around 1913 had a serious illness in which he 'died', to be resurrected and to claim that he had received a message from god, identified with Mulengachika (the creator of pestilence). The message entailed a denunciation of mourning rituals, central to the ancestor cult, particularly the sacrifice of cattle, and the creation of a shrine with two white poles dedicated to the deity. Mupumani's vision met with a 'phenomenal response', and Van Binsbergen suggests that labour migration facilitated the rapid spread of this prophetic movement. There was, however, a dialectical relationship between the prophet's vision and the popular response, and soon it was suggested that, through devotion to god, primordial times would return with good harvests, plenty of game, the denial of death, and the absence of witchcraft. Mupumani's message thus became a millennial movement. Mupumani travelled widely spreading his message, but his movement was short-lived, for in 1914 he was arrested and imprisoned by the colonial government for vagrancy and false pretensions. Thus people's expectations led to a swift disillusion, and, as Van Binsbergen writes:

> The primordial times were evidently not restored, the prophet's medicine turned out to be useless, his supernatural powers were ineffective against those of the district officer who committed him to prison; and the movement died out as quickly as it had arisen. (1981, 147–50)

The second prophetic movement, known as the Nzila cult or 'Twelve Society', was founded in 1944 by a Luvale man from Angola, Rice Kamanga. Like Mupumani, he too was a leper. Initially interpreted as suffering from the Bindele affliction, Kamanga appears to have gone into the bush and had a visionary experience of a white spirit, which not only cured him of his Bindele ailment but also instructed him to acknowledge god and to preach and heal in god's name. He was commissioned by the spirit to treat this affliction and to found a church from the first twelve patients he cured, who were to become doctors. His subsequent healing powers were thus closely identified with god, and his method, as Van Binsbergen writes,

> involved the erection of a shrine, daily ablutions in this shrine with water medicated by selected herbs, and nocturnal ritual dances. (1981, 200)

A strong emphasis was put on spiritual cleansing, on moral teaching, and on Saturday church services. The term *Nzila* means *path*, acknowledging the shift of emphasis away from Bindele affliction, and Kamanga subsequently came to call himself Chana. He was to remain a member of the Seventh-Day Adventist Church all his life.

Although the Nzila prophetic movement initially appealed to Luvale immigrants in Western Zambia, it subsequently spread during the 1950s to most areas of Zambia, even reaching Bulawayo. A cult centre was erected near Mongu, and in 1966 the movement was registered as the Zambia Nzila Sect. It then had a membership of around 100,000.

Beginning as a charismatic movement, the Nzila cult developed over time into a large independent church with a formal organization, an annual convention, explicit regulations, and ritual paraphernalia that was strictly controlled by the central administration. It also developed strong links with Christian churches and adapted itself to the urban context. While Wilson describes it as a local 'syncretic' movement, Van Binsbergen emphasizes that through its formal organization, the Nzila sect has routinized and channelled the founder's charisma into a stable church (1981, 200–6; Wilson 1973, 92–3).

The third prophetic movement described by Van Binsbergen, the Bituma cult, has been 'much less of a success story'. Developing as a prophetic regional cult in the 1930s, the Bituma cult was to fragment on the death of its founder and then took the form of essentially another spirit-possession cult. The Bituma movement was founded by the prophet Simbinga, who belonged to the Mbunda ethnic group and was, like Chana, an immigrant from Angola. He settled in the Kaoma (Mankoya) district in the 1930s and began to experience visions, which he interpreted as manifestations of an angel [*angelo*] sent by god. He had initially been an evangelist of the fundamentalist South Africa General Mission and had travelled to South Africa as a labour migrant. When he returned, he brought back with him an elaborate collection of ritual paraphernalia and began spirit-healing, treating the affliction that became known as *bituma* [*sent him*], relating it to the angel as a messenger of god. Simbinga built a shrine, offered a theistic interpretation of the affliction, and, like Chana, emphasized a rather puritanical moral teaching. Although it developed a following, mainly in rural areas, on the death of Simbinga in 1960 – in suspicious circumstances while he was out hunting – the cult fragmented. Since then the Bituma ritual has been practised by individual cult leaders on a very independent basis, and there is no formal organization linking the various cult groups. Van Binsbergen suggests that these groups cater to a 'stagnated peasantry', particularly Nkoya people living in Lusaka. In fact, its membership largely consists of Nkoya, although Van Binsbergen interprets this cult movement not as an expression of Nkoya ethnic identity but rather as the outcome of the 'articulation' between the domestic and capitalist modes of production (1981, 238–63).

5.6.3. *Watchtower and Witch-Cleansing Movements*

Another form of religious movement that came into prominence in Zambia during the colonial period was the African Watchtower, which in itself was derived from the North American religious movement, now called the Jehovah's Witnesses. Van Binsbergen suggests that the watchtower movement, locally known as *Kitawala*, belongs essentially to the 'proletarian context', although during the colonial period, prior to the Second World War, it was propagated on a large scale in rural areas throughout Central Africa (1981, 284; Fields 1985, 91–127).

Witch-cleansing movements, in fact, were common in Zambia throughout the colonial period, but perhaps the most famous of these, and certainly the most extreme example of a watchtower preacher, is what has come to be known as the Mwana Lesa movement, for it centred around the 'sinister figure', as Karen Fields describes him, of Tomo Nyirenda (1985, 163).

A literate Tumbuka from the Karonga district in Malawi (then Nyasaland), Tomo Nyirenda had been educated for some six years at the Livingstonia Mission of the Free Church of Scotland at Bandawe. He then moved to Broken Hill (Kabwe) in Zambia and worked as a cook, and in February 1925 he was converted to the Watchtower Bible and Tract Society by a fellow Nyasa, Gabriel Phiri. Better known later as the Jehovah's Witnesses, a church founded by Charles Taze Russell in Pennsylvania in 1884, the watchtower preached a millennial message, the imminent second coming of Christ and the setting up of a heavenly kingdom on earth, and baptism by complete immersion that would signify entry into a special community that alone would be saved. In April, Nyirenda took up preaching the gospel, and by all accounts he was highly regarded – charismatic, articulate, educated, enthusiastic. Declaring himself to be Mwana Lesa, the son or child of god, he went among the Lala of the Serenje and Mkushi districts preaching the millennial message of the watchtower, calling on people to repent, emphasizing that the second coming was at hand, and suggesting that those baptized would be saved. The coming millennium would involve the arrival of Americans, an end to taxation, the bestowal of wealth on the faithful, and an end to white rule. He urged his followers to love one another, to refrain from adultery and stealing, and to be hospitable to strangers. He also told people to renounce witchcraft and to give up their medicines and charms. Much of this was simply an echo of watchtower teaching, but gradually Nyirenda's message and practice changed, and he began to detect witches, and became involved in witch-cleansing ritual practices. Baptism by complete immersion, 'dipping', was the crucial ritual of the watchtower, but Nyirenda began to denounce the unbaptized as 'worthless' and as witches, and he saw the immersion as a kind of ordeal for detecting witches. As Rotberg writes, Nyirenda's ability to divine witches 'set him apart from the usual apocalyptic advocates'. Soon Nyirenda became widely known as an evangelist, prophet, and witchfinder, able to detect witches simply because they could not be completely immersed (1965, 144).

Having an established reputation as a witchfinder, Nyirenda was asked by a local Lala chief, Shaiwila, to rid his country of witches, and he authorized him to baptize all his people and to kill – not simply cleanse – all those who proved to be witches. Between May and June 1925, Nyirenda drowned or otherwise killed around sixteen Lala villagers – as well as more than a hundred people in neighbouring Zaire. During his witch-finding crusade, assisted by several young men, Nyirenda is described as displaying 'excessive zeal', and thus his movement came to the attention of the colonial authorities. On his return from Zaire, he remained in hiding for a while, receiving food and shelter from local villagers, for Nyirenda was believed by local people to have killed witches [*afiti*], not people. He was eventually captured in September. Unfortunately, his captors bound his arms too tightly, gangrene set in, and he had to have both arms amputated. After a two-day trial in February 1926,

Nyirenda, along with Chief Shaiwala, was sentenced to be hanged – thus removing, it is said, a serious threat to the colonial order (Rotberg 1965, 146).

In his seminal essay on the Mwana Lesa movement, Terence Ranger (1975) stressed that Nyirenda saw himself as pre-eminently a Christian evangelist and that in a 'witch-dominated spiritual economy' (as he described Lala culture), Nyirenda probably believed in the benefits of his witch-cleansing crusade. Certainly his defence counsel at his trial defended Nyirenda on these grounds (Fields 1985, 171). Ranger, however, views Nyirenda neither as a monster nor as a victim, but he does suggest that, unlike other leaders of witch-finding movements, Nyirenda did not simply 'cleanse' those guilty of witchcraft, rather 'he purged society of them' (1975, 68). Thus his actions are not explicable simply in terms of cultural beliefs about witches. Also significant is the fact that no elders played a prominent role in the Mwana Lesa movement: The movement rather gave opportunities to educated ambitious young men, who had experienced a world beyond the village (Fields 1985, 188). Important too is the 'syncretic' nature of the movement, which was formed through the interaction of watchtower millennial teaching and Lala religious beliefs – particularly about witches (Ranger 1975, 53).

In Central Africa during the colonial period, there were many other movements like that of Mwana Lesa, emphasizing witch-cleansing, forms of baptism, and millennial expectations. Some were anti-colonial and thus attracted the attention and hostility of the colonial state.

(On the politics of the watchtower movement in Zambia, see Meebelo 1971, 133–85; on witch-finding movements, see Richards 1935; Marwick 1950; Willis 1968.)

Jehovah's Witnesses still play an important role in Zambia society, and among people such as the Lala and Luapula they are usually the better-educated members of the society. Petty capitalists and wealthy commercial farmers are often Jehovah's Witnesses, and they tend to live in small nuclear families and to rely on each other for moral and economic support. They often separate themselves socially from other members of the community, forming a tightly organized and exclusive group, and see themselves as the 'chosen people' who have the task of warning others of the coming destruction. The ideology of the witnesses emphasizes a disciplined and orderly life, Bible study, and a millennial witness, the belief in the coming Armageddon. Karla Poewe suggests that, to affirm a separate identity and to reduce the pressures of kinship and sharing and the duress of witchcraft, petty capitalists among the Luapula adopt the ideology of the Protestant ethic – especially that of the Jehovah's Witnesses (1981, 80; Long 1968, 200–36; for sociological studies of the Jehovah's Witnesses, see Beckford 1975; Bainbridge 1997, 96–101).

It has to be noted that in both Zambia and Malawi in the years immediately after independence, the Jehovah's Witnesses suffered horrific and sustained persecution by the post-colonial state, mainly because of their refusal to engage in party politics (see Hodges 1976; Fiedler 1996).

5.6.4. *Independent Churches*

There are many independent churches in Zambia but perhaps the most famous, and the one discussed at length by Van Binsbergen, is the Lumpa Church of Alice Lenshina. It owes its fame to the dramatic conflict that took place in 1964 between the Lumpa Church and the Zambian government, immediately prior to independence. It is estimated that around 1,500 people died in the conflict.

The prophet of the Lumpa church, Alice Lenshina, described as a 'simple woman', was born around 1920. The daughter of a Bemba villager and growing up near the Lubwa mission of the United Church of Central Africa, she was not a baptized Christian when, around 1953, she began to experience visions. She claimed she had died and been to heaven, but that god had sent her back to earth to preach the 'good news', giving her a book of hymns. As her husband worked as a carpenter at the nearby Lubwa mission, she contacted the white missionary-in-charge, who took her seriously, baptized her, gave her Bible lessons, as well as the name Alice. When she left the mission, Lenshina began, from 1955 onwards, to preach her own message, and, as her revelation and teachings became widely known, hundreds of people came to attend her services. She thus came to establish her own independent church, the Lumpa church – the term *lumpa* meaning to excel or surpass. By 1958 she had a huge following, estimated at around 65,000, mostly people from her own district, but thousands of pilgrims came from elsewhere, flocking to Lenshina's village, Kasomo, which was renamed *Sioni* [*Zion*]. Many people came to settle there, and a large cathedral was built. Inevitably, Lenshina's fame had an impact on the surrounding Christian mission churches, with many people deserting the missions, not only the Lubwa mission but also the large Roman Catholic Mission at Ilondola under the White Fathers. Many of her followers were in fact Catholics.

Compared with earlier religious movements in Zambia, the Lumpa Church, Van Binsbergen suggests, did not offer anything particularly original in its combination of symbolic themes. It was a form of Christian evangelism that highlighted God and Jesus and put an emphasis on baptism and healing. Lenshina denounced local medicines and charms, as well as the veneration of the ancestors and other spirits. But baptism and the relinquishing of medicines and charms was specifically linked to the eradication of witchcraft, and the Lumpa Church has indeed been described as conducting a 'holy war' against witchcraft (Wilson 1973, 98). Lenshina was apparently held in 'great awe' by her followers and thus in many respects came to assume the status of a chief. Not surprisingly, Lenshina aroused the hostility not only of the Catholic Church but that of the local chief Nkula, who saw the Lumpa Church as a rival claimant to his own authority (Wilson 1973, 96). The Lumpa Church was not in its origin 'anti-white', though it was critical of the missionaries and colonialism, nor was it, in contrast with the watchtower preachers, specifically millennial in its teaching. But 'eschatological overtones' did become dominant in the months prior to the final conflict with the state (Van Binsbergen 1981, 289).

Assisted by her husband, Lenshina had established by around 1960 a viable independent church with a hierarchy of priests, carefully regulated by Lenshina. It was also coming more and more to define itself as an exclusive peasant movement, with absolute control over its members and over the land. As Van Binsbergen writes, it envisioned a new society that 'was to be a theocratic one, in which all authority had to derive from God and his prophetess Lenshina. The boma [government], chiefs and local courts, as they had no access to this authority, were denounced and ignored' (1981, 291).

This inevitably led to a conflict with local chiefs and the government with respect to the control over land and with the United National Independence Party (UNIP), then in the process of creating the post-colonial state. They had no wish to see an exclusive peasant church, opting out of state control – a 'state within a state'. In fact, as a theocratic rural enclave, the Lumpa Church is seen by Van Binsbergen as more 'radical' than the UNIP who supported the incorporation of the rural communities of Zambia into the capitalist economy and the post-colonial state (1981, 296). The eventual confrontation between the Lumpa Church and the forces of the state led to hundreds of casualties, the exodus of thousands of Lumpa devotees from Northern Zambia, and the banning of the church by the Zambian government.

Although Van Binsbergen described the Lumpa Church as the largest and most powerful peasant movement Zambia had seen, and the conflict between the church and the UNIP as a form of 'class conflict', nevertheless he emphasizes that the Lumpa Church was a form of 'religious innovation' that was far from unique in Zambia. (On the Lumpa Church, see Rotberg 1961; Taylor and Lehmann 1961, 248–68; Roberts 1970; Wilson 1973, 94–100; Van Binsbergen 1981, 266–316.)

Despite differences in idiom, ritual, and organization, each of these four 'religious innovations' just described – cults of affliction, prophetic cults, watchtower and witch-cleansing movements, and the Lumpa Church – are aspects, Van Binsbergen argues, of a much broader process of religious change in Zambia. Intimately related to the socio-economic and political changes that have occurred during the twentieth century, this process of superstructural change is seen as having five crucial dimensions. First, whereas the early religious system was largely geared to the annual ecological cycle, and thus the dominant conception of time was that of a 'cyclical present' – akin to the concept of 'reciprocating universe' described by MacGaffey with regard to Kongo religion – this has given way to a linear time perspective. Contemporary religion thus emphasizes historical development and personal careers, and even eschatological notions as expressed by the watchtower-type preachers. Second, ecological concerns of the early religious system are no longer prominent and with prophetic cults and the watchtower movements, we do not encounter, Van Binsbergen suggests, the 'slightest trace of a concern for land'. The economic significance of the natural world is thus downplayed. Third, the importance of the 'village dead', the spirits of the ancestors, has given way to an increasing emphasis on god. As Van Binsbergen writes, 'what is new here is not the conception of the High God itself, but the attempt to endow this conception with so much splendour, power and immediate relevance' (1981, 159). The prophets Chana, Mwana Lesa, and Lenshina all emphasized rituals focussed around the deity. Fourth, the communal basis of the earlier religious system, focussed around the ancestral cults and collective rituals, has given way to a counter-ideology of individualism, with a strong emphasis on the 'suffering individual' and the downplaying of kinship obligations and morality. Finally, religious change during the twentieth century, expressed by these various innovations, has attempted to formulate alternatives to witchcraft. Although continuing to accept the reality of witchcraft, prophetic movements, watchtower, and independent churches all attempted, in various ways, to eradicate witchcraft once and for all and to establish new forms of community (Van Binsbergen 1981, 160–6).

To conclude this section, a brief mention may be made of the controversy that surrounded the archbishop of Lusaka, Emmanuel Milingo, who attempted to introduce 'African spirituality' into the Roman Catholic Church. Of humble origins and an Ngoni from Chipata, Milingo was ordained to the priesthood in 1958. After studies in Rome and Dublin, he was appointed archbishop of Lusaka in 1969, at the early age of thirty-nine. Four years later, having acquired the gift of healing from God and influenced by the worldwide charismatic renewal movement, Milingo came to interpret his ministry as akin to that of Jesus – one of spirit-healing. He emphasized that in many African traditions, the attributes of motherhood were given to God, gave Jesus the title of supreme ancestor, and stressed the reality of the ancestral spirits [*mizimu*], whom Milingo saw as essentially benign spirits and as a 'world in between', mediating between humans and God. Acknowledging that illness, misfortune, and social distress were caused by 'evil spirits' – such as *mashawe, vimbuza, ngulu,* and *chimbandu* – that possess people, Milingo came to see his role as a spirit-healer and exorcist – driving out the evil spirits. As Milingo put it, through the power of the 'holy spirit' and exorcism people are 'redeemed and liberated from the tyranny of demonic oppression'. Milingo's healing rituals drew vast crowds, and often over a thousand people attended his sessions. Although his ministry was aimed at both men and women, the sessions seem to have been attended mainly by women, who, possessed by spirits, went into trances, spoke in tongues, and expressed other manifestations of ecstatic behaviour. Milingo always thought of himself as a devout Catholic and spirit-healing as an essential part of the Christian ministry. The Catholic Church thought otherwise. In 1974 he received a letter from the Vatican urging him to stop the spirit-healing, and later he was accused of unorthodox teaching and neglecting his pastoral duties as archbishop. In 1982 Milingo was mysteriously summoned to Rome, forced to resign as archbishop, and thereafter lived and worked in Rome. Until, that is, the year 2001, when this rather maverick archbishop at the age of seventy-one married a South Korean doctor, Maria Song, almost thirty years his junior, at a collective wedding ceremony in New York – having been 'called by God' to become a member of the Unification

Church (whose adherents are known as the Moonies). He was thus finally excommunicated from the Catholic Church (on his ministry, see Milingo 1984; Ter Haar 1992).

The controversy that surrounded Archbishop Milingo illustrated the tense and complex relationship that has always existed between the Roman Catholic Church and African religious culture, although in recent years a sustained attempt has been made, through the process of 'enculturation' to render the Catholic faith more receptive to African religious culture (on the theology of enculturation, see Shorter 1988, 1996; and for a lucid summary, see Ott 2000, 21–71).

5.7. TSHIDI BAROLONG COSMOLOGY

In this chapter, I have largely focussed not on the hermeneutics and aesthetics of African religious movements and rituals but rather on studies that have attempted to understand African religious culture by situating it within its socio-historical context. To conclude this chapter, I briefly examine a further exemplar of this approach, one that has now become something of an anthropological classic, Jean Comaroff's study *Body of Power, Spirit of Resistance* (1985). A student of Monica Wilson, Jean Comaroff, along with John Comaroff and Van Binsbergen, has long been an advocate of a Marxist-inspired historical anthropology, which envisions an anthropology of Southern Africa as being centrally concerned with local people's *Reaction to Conquest* – the title of Wilson's (1936) seminal and exhaustive study of the Pondo of South Africa. Jean Comaroff's study is therefore focussed on the historical relationship between a Southern Tswana people, the Barolong Tshidi, and the expanding Southern Africa political economy since the beginning of the nineteenth century. Thus, like both MacGaffey and Van Binsbergen, Comaroff takes a dialectical approach and views the study of social systems as implying an engagement between anthropology and history, combining ethnography with a historical imagination (Comaroff and Comaroff 1992).

Ethnography in this context does not imply a naïve empiricism, nor the reduction of anthropological research to hermeneutics, dialogics, and 'intersubjectivity'; still less does it entail making a fetish of cultural differences. For Comaroff, ethnography is an exercise in dialectics and is a 'historically situated mode of understanding historically situated contexts', each with its own focus of subjectivity, culture, and social life. Ethnography thus does not speak for others: it is *about* them (Comaroff and Comaroff 1992, 9). As for historical understanding, the Comaroffs suggest that history is not simply about structural change and the 'cyclic dynamics' of social systems (as described by Middleton (1960) for example) but is also crucially involved in understanding two interrelated processes or perspectives – one is the internal dynamics and historicity of all societies, for, as Edmund Leach remarked, 'every real society is a process in time' (1954, 4); the other is the historical encounter or dialectic between a particular society or 'local world' and encompassing social processes, structures, or agencies – whether regional or global like capitalism (Comaroff and Comaroff 1992, 95–8).

In her ethnography, Jean Comaroff makes an important distinction among three socio-cultural domains or levels of analysis – identified by the terms structure, practice, and symbolic. The first level focusses on the 'determining force of socio-cultural structures' – the prevailing structural principles and constraints that characterize a 'socio-cultural order'. This is the *structure* of a social system or process and clearly relates to the political economy, the material relations of production and power. The second level of social life relates to the 'transformative practices of human actors' – to the social practices that are embedded in social relations and that blend together both pragmatic (material) and semantic (communicative) dimensions. *Practice* therefore relates to the 'flow of everyday life' and to human agency (1985, 118). An adequate account of human agency, Comaroff suggests, thus implies a complex dialectic between structure and social action (practice) (1985, 4). But this dialectic she sees as 'mediated' by what she variously describes as 'signifying practices' or as a 'coherent *symbolic* order' (1985, 253). Whether describing the pre-colonial cosmology of the Tshidi or Zionist religious culture, this coherent 'symbolic order' is seen as 'mediating' between both the socio-cultural order and human practice and between the Tshidi and the dominant political economy associated with European colonialism and capitalism (1985, 252–3).

Importantly, these 'symbolic schemas' are seen as embedded both in forms of everyday practice and in the imaginative conceptions of ritual and cosmology. Through the process of socialization, these symbolic schemas are also focussed, Comaroff emphasizes, on the body, 'the medium through which the meanings and values of any social system become internalized as categories of individual experience and identity' (1985, 124). This 'embodiment' of cultural categories and values is, she argues, a universal process. The logic of social action and cultural life more generally seem to be vested, she writes, 'more in corporeal signs that in conceptual categories' (Comaroff and Comaroff 1992, 71). But like many postmodern scholars, Comaroff often enters the dizzy realm of conceptual abstractions herself, suggesting, for example, that the body 'cannot escape being a vehicle of history, a metaphor and metonym of being – in – time' (1992, 79) – thus reifying the body.

Jean Comaroff's book is divided essentially into three parts, dealing respectively with the socio-cultural order and religious cosmology of the Tshidi in the early nineteenth century (circa 1800–1830); the cultural logic of the Methodist missionaries, which is interpreted as an ideological precursor of capitalism; and an account of Zionist churches in Mafeking – which in the pre-colonial period was the capital of the Tshidi chiefdom. As with MacGaffey and Van Binsbergen, Comaroff thus attempts to explore religious change in an African community over a span of 150 years, specifically focussing on the dialectical engagement between the Tshidi social system and the South African political economy and on the mediatory role of religious symbols in the process of structural transformation. In this section, I focus on the religious cosmology of the pre-colonial Tshidi and discuss contemporary Zionist churches in the final section of the chapter.

During the early nineteenth century, the Tshidi emerged as an independent, highly centralized chiefdom, although there was always a tension – indeed, an oscillation – between two contradictory tendencies: one towards centralization and hierarchy, the other towards decentralization and the atomatization of the social universe into more or less autonomous villages (see Mann 1986, 63–70, on the instability and cyclic process relating to the early chiefdoms). The political economy of the Tshidi also expressed contradictory tendencies, being based on both agriculture and pastoralism, augmented by hunting and gathering. Agriculture was essentially a female occupation, women holding land in their own right, and it provided the bulk of everyday subsistence requirements. Agriculture was metaphorically linked to human procreation and was seen as 'an inherently risky enterprise' (Comaroff 1985, 67). Pastoralism, in contrast, was associated with men and was more controlled, and livestock provided security in the face of crop failure, as well as playing an important role in ritual and in the wider political economy, as an important item of trade and as an icon of the symbolic order. The politics of rank were largely conducted through the medium of cattle, and the essence of chieftainship was in the holding of a large herd of livestock. Women were, in fact, debarred from any physical contact with cattle. As elsewhere in Africa, cattle for the Tshidi embodied both material and symbolic value (1985, 60–74).

A second related aspect of the Tshidi socio-cultural order – the political economy – was the contrast between agnation and matrilaterality. Although the household was the major unit of landholding and production, there was a 'thoroughgoing' distinction between agnation and matrilaterality, which roughly corresponded to the gender division. Whereas agnation was associated with hierarchy, masculinity, public space, and political processes, matrilaterality had opposite connotations – equality, female-centred relations, and the privacy of the household. Agnation, in a sense, encompassed the domestic unit into a high-order collectivity (1985, 47–9).

Mediating between this socio-cultural system and everyday life was a cosmological order that Comaroff describes as a symbolic schema of 'hidden meanings' that shaped people's everyday practices and perceptions – particularly of space. It implied a concentric model and a symbolic opposition between the settlement [*motse*] and chiefly court, and the bush [*naga*], mediated by the homestead, and, as elsewhere, a symbolic equation was made between the female body and the house. Moreover, women were associated with the repetitive cycles of nature, seasonal production, transience, and heat – which had negative connotations of pollution and ill health, while men were associated with cattle, the ancestral spirits [*badimo*], permanence, enduring social values, and coolness. The term 'to cool' also meant 'to heal' (1985, 68). Thus, in common with other Southern Bantu peoples – Nguni, Venda, and Sotho – the Tshidi expressed a hot/cold symbolism that tended to correlate with gender. The central oppositions were the following:

Female	**Male**
Hot [*bothitho*]	Cool [*tsididi*]
Red	White
Menstrual blood	Semen
Lightning	Rain
Witches (causing sickness and sterility)	Ancestors (causing health and fertility)

But as Adam Kuper indicated, the meanings of this hot–cool symbolism is not gender-specific but varied according to the social context. Men who have recently had sexual relations are 'hot' while pre-pubescent girls and elderly women are 'cool', and the former were often favoured for conducting rain-making rituals among the Nguni. Comaroff, however, tends to see women as having 'innate physical heat' (1985, 96; Kuper 1982, 18–20; Berglund 1976, 340; see Morris 2000, 78–82, on the contrasting hot–cool symbolism of other African peoples where there is a more balanced polarity).

Comaroff continually refers to the Tshidi as having a cosmology that is coherent and as forming a 'total symbolic order', as if it were a totalizing system of meanings that structures and shapes everyday experience. But Bloch (1989, 106–17) and Bourdieu (1990, 11) have rightly questioned the limitations of such logical models, which, though aesthetically pleasing, may be too Procrustean to capture the fluidity and flexibility of social life – as expressed in social practice. But Comaroff also suggests that a 'superhuman realm' forms apart of this symbolic order, representing its logic. As in other African societies, three 'superhuman' entities are primarily associated with this realm: the ancestors [*badimo*], the supreme being [*modimo*], and the witch or sorcerer [*sorcery, boloi*].

Comaroff is insistent that the 'conceptual schemes' of the pre-colonial Tshidi were 'implicit' in their social practices and rituals; they thus had no 'beliefs', no reflective thought, and no formal knowledge – although it is unclear why the concept of 'belief' should imply a reification of social phenomena. Every divination ceremony surely makes explicit peoples' beliefs about witches, ancestral spirits, and deities? In reacting against the Cartesian notion of a 'disembodied mind' and the long-standing bias of theologians favouring mentality and formal beliefs, many anthropologists like Comaroff seem to have gone to the other extreme: They thus make the body into a cultural fetish and seem to deny that people have any formal knowledge or beliefs at all. But the Tshidi seem to believe, or at least to explicitly conceptualize, the notion that on death the spiritual component of a human being [*moya*, literally *breath*] is transformed into *dimo*, a superhuman power. Yet the ancestors [*badimo*] seem to have had only a collective identity for the Tshidi and were largely the concern of the domestic group. They were an important force in the economy of everyday life, tended to uphold the moral order, and were mainly contacted through the rites of sacrifice. People who had died 'unnatural' deaths never became a part of the collectivity of ancestors and were associated with the wild 'bush'. There were also important collective rituals focussed around the chiefly ancestors (1985, 82–3).

The supreme being [*modimo*] seems to have been a rather remote figure, and Comaroff suggests that there was no explicit connection between this deity and the creation of the Tswana universe. In fact, she writes that 'Modimo did not participate in the flow of everyday events and was inaccessible through ritual, featuring as a residual referent in the margins of experience and cultural control' (1985, 83–4).

Whether Tshidi conceptions of divinity were quite that otiose is perhaps debatable.

A key figure of pre-colonial Tshidi society, however, was the *ngaka*, a ritual expert who combined the roles of herbalist and diviner, and who was particularly associated with medicines [*ditlhare*] that, as in other African societies, was a polysemic term meaning both 'wood plant' and 'medicine' – 'substances which bring activating natural force to bear upon human beings' (1985, 89; see Morris 1998, 209–22, for a discussion of medicines and empirical herbalism).

What was crucial for the Tshidi was that a clear distinction was made between the work of the ngaka, which was seen as beneficent, and sorcery [*boloi*]. It was the role of the ngaka to ascertain whether a particular affliction was due to sorcery, the ancestors, or a breach of ritual prohibition, Comaroff suggesting that these were normally associated with offences against the 'normative order' (1985, 84).

Comaroff's account of the religious life of nineteenth-century Tshidi Barolong society is, however, largely given over to a detailed account and analysis of the boy's initiation ritual [*bogwera*], as well as the less elaborate girls' initiation [*bojale*] (1985, 85–120), drawing mainly on the earlier studies of Willoughby (1928) and Schapera (1971). These initiations, like initiation rites throughout Africa, were complex and multifaceted, and Comaroff's study highlights some of the following themes:

- The initiations, as Van Gennep (1960) described, consisted essentially of three phases – the 'chopping' or preliminary phase; a liminal phase involving circumcision; and rites of aggregation when the boys returned from the 'wild'.
- The boys' initiation was coordinated throughout the chiefdom and was held at roughly four-year intervals.
- The initiation of boys was undertaken in a grass lodge in the bush, usually near water, and thus contrasted with that of the girls' initiation, which took place in the homestead on the margins of the town.
- The hot–cool symbolism; the use of animals as social metaphors; and the colour triad of red, black, and white all played a symbolic role in the rituals, which were essentially concerned with the social construction of gender and

adulthood and the 'collective appropriation of natural procreative powers' (1985, 116).
- The boys' initiation facilitated not only the ritual construction of male sexual potency but was also crucial to the reproduction of a vital and enduring social order.
- Thus, although the initiation rituals were not simply univocal and conservative, they nevertheless played a major role in 'reproducing established structures of inequality and in managing the tensions they embodied' (1985, 119).
- The initiations were therefore important both as a transformative rite in the creation of individual social beings and as a means of establishing and sustaining the social collectivity. They were thus a form of hegemonic power – hegemony referring to those aspects of a society's culture or ideology that have come to 'naturalize structures of inequality' (Comaroff and Comaroff 1992, 29).

Comaroff's analysis of initiation rites is thus similar to that of Jean La Fontaine, who emphasizes that these rites have a 'many-textured quality' and must be understood in terms of their total social context. La Fontaine stresses that initiations not only serve to transform individuals, and thus have a psychological dimension, but also have the effect of demonstrating the power of local knowledge to 'legitimize a continuing social order' (1985, 179; for illuminating essays that also emphasize the crucial relationship between ritual and ideological [or hegemonic] power, see Bloch 1989; for further useful studies of initiation rites in Africa, see Richards 1956; Turner 1967, 151–279; Droogers 1980; Ottenberg 1989; Beidelman 1997; Morris 2000, 69–131).

5.8. ZIONIST CHURCHES IN SOUTH AFRICA

The second part of Jean Comaroff's seminal study of the Barolong Tshidi deals with the impact of colonialism on this society. As earlier noted, two topics are involved: the first is the 'cultural logic' of the Methodist missionaries and its relationship to Tshidi culture; the second is the ritual practices of contemporary Zionist churches in Mafeking. I discuss these two topics in turn.

The Comaroffs describe the history of Southern Africa as one involving a 'symbolic struggle', a bitter contest involving conscience and consciousness. Although they do not deny the coercive nature of colonialism, and the violent class struggles and racial inequality that the impact of capitalism and the bureaucratic state involved, their focus is essentially on cultural symbolism and consciousness – not on the 'brute material dimensions' of the colonial encounter. They write about the 'colonization of consciousness' and the 'consciousness of colonization'. Their central argument is that the colonization of South Africa began with 'an ideological onslaught on the part of the Christian missionaries' and that the evangelical protestant missionaries were 'cultural agents' of capitalism and the empire (1992, 235–6).

The Christian missionaries that came into contact with the Barolong Tshidi in the early nineteenth century came largely from the British Protestant tradition and were particularly associated with the London Missionary Society and the Wesleyan Methodist Missionary Society. They arrived at a time when local people were already experiencing severe social upheaval because of the Defikane, the rise and expansion of the Zulu chiefdom under Shaka around 1823, which caused severe dislocation among agrarian peoples throughout Southern Africa. The missionaries were mainly Methodists, and their church became the dominant context of Christian conversion among the Tshidi throughout the nineteenth century.

Jean Comaroff thus devotes some discussion to the ethos and 'cultural logic' of the Methodist mission to South Africa. Methodism was a Christian denomination founded by John Wesley in 1739 as an evangelical revivalist movement within the Church of England. It became a separate body at the end of the eighteenth century. Stressing the importance of the holy spirit, Methodism replaced the priestly hierarchy and sacramental rituals of the established church with a subjective spiritualism, an emphasis on a close personal relationship with God, and the certainty of the scriptures. Methodism has been seen as the product of the industrial revolution in Britain, and Jean Comaroff outlines certain key features of its cultural ethos – a dichotomy between church and state, an individualism that was both emotive and utilitarian, and a stress on the values of discipline and self-realization through work. Following the studies of Hobsbawn (1957) and Thompson (1963), Comaroff emphasizes the ideological role of Methodism in Britain in the early nineteenth century, in channelling the political energies of the working classes into a more conservative direction, thus being supportive of the status quo and the development of industrial capitalism (1985, 129–35). In its role as a missionary enterprise, Methodism is seen by the Comaroffs as having made a similar impact in South Africa. For although there were obviously many factors involved in the dispossession and domination of the Tshidi, the Methodist missionaries certainly contributed, both materially and culturally, 'to the entry of these peoples into a cycle of peasant (under-) production and wage labour. For they toiled hard to introduce an appreciation of money, time, work discipline and the other essential features of industrial capitalism' (1992, 250).

The Comaroffs suggest that the Methodist missionaries saw their 'civilizing' mission as involving both the personal transformation of the 'heathen' and the establishment of a new social order – which, given their own background, they tended to envisage as an agrarian society of free yeomanry. The irony was that the missionaries helped to prepare the ground not for an 'independent peasantry' but for the establishment of industrial capitalism, with its population of peasant proletarians 'snared in a web of economic dependency'. All this happened before the enactment of coercive colonial policies that sought to enforce the Tshidi and other peoples into the wage-labour economy (1992, 249).

Jean Comaroff recognized that the dialectic between the Tshidi and other Tswana peoples and the 'colonial venture' – the expanding capitalist economy – was a long, complex, and protracted process, involving domination and resistance, as well as the imposition of cultural hegemony and various forms of protest. But her central focus is on the 'confrontation' of two cultural systems, embodied in the contrasting terms *setswana* and *sekgoa*, standing respectively for Tswana and European ways of life, Tswana ethnic identity being largely a product of the colonial encounter. In a classic article, the Comaroffs offer an interesting discussion on the politics of water and on the introduction of plough agriculture – which had important social and economic consequences, particularly in leading to the emergence of a class of commercial farmers among the Tshidi, and growing inequalities and impoverishment. They also discuss the missionary opposition to the local culture, particularly initiations and rain-making rituals, and the cultural implications of Reverend Robert Moffat's translation of the Bible into Tswana, which, for example, misleadingly conflated the Tshidi concept of *badimo* [ancestors] with the Christian concept of 'demons' (1992, 240–52).

Although the Methodist missionaries clearly played an important part in promoting the ideology of bourgeois individualism, it is unhelpful to equate (as Comaroff does) the culture of capitalism and the ideological concept of possessive individualism with the personhood of western epistemology and culture, in all its diversity. Indeed, the Comaroffs tend to exaggerate the ontological differences between the 'worlds' of the setswana and sekgoa, portraying the Tshidi in terms similar to that of the early Christian missionaries, as lacking reflective thought and formal knowledge and as failing to make any distinction between words and things. Like some postmodernist scholars, the Tshidi are seemingly endowed with the capacity to construct reality by means of language!? (1992, 255).

Magical thought and the 'magical power of words' surely relate not to Tshidi thought generally, but to specific ritual contexts.

The Tshidi social world that Jean Comaroff experienced during the 1970s, when she undertook fieldwork in Mafeking (pop. around 25,000), reflected a community that had long been subject to progressive impoverishments. This was the result of increasing soil erosion and the dependency of people on an exploitative migrant labour system. The Tshidi were thus experiencing poverty and acute alienation and had become part of what Comaroff describes as a 'black rural periphery' (1985, 161).

Although the original Methodist Church still stood in the middle of Mafeking and still represented Christian orthodoxy, Comaroff's researches revealed the existence of some fifty-six distinct religious movements or churches [*dikereke*] in the district, with several hundred congregations. These churches, focussed around an inspired leader, were collectively known as 'Zionist' or 'spirit' churches, and their rituals were centrally focussed around spirit-healing. These 'flamboyant' Zionist sects, however, were by no means a new phenomenon in South Africa, and Comaroff pays warm tribute to the pioneering study of independent church movements among the Zulu by Bengt Sundkler – *Bantu Prophets in South Africa* (1948).

Sundkler, Comaroff suggests, was sensitive to the way in which these 'syncretic movements' or independent churches were novel religious forms that constituted a mode of resistance to the culture of colonial domination. In fact, Sundkler described the separatist churches among the Zulu as a 'reaction to conquest' (1948, 179). But Sundkler also stressed the 'creative interplay' between the prophets as religious innovators and the forms of mission Christianity, thus emphasizing that the independent churches, such as that of Isaiah Shembe's Nazarite Church, were 'complex symbolic systems' (Comaroff 1985, 168). Sundkler recorded around 800 independent churches and suggested that they could be divided into two main types.

The first type, the Ethiopian churches, were largely offshoots of the mission churches, and their church organization and biblical interpretation largely followed that of the Protestant churches. But they had seceded from the missions largely because, as Sundkler puts it, of the 'colour issue' (1948, 106).They therefore combined an incipient African nationalism and an emphasis on 'Africa for Africans' – which was particularly identified with Ethiopia and the idea of a Christian African kingship – with the symbolism of what Comaroff describes as a 'biblically indexed millennium' (1985, 175; Sundkler 1948, 54–8). Even though the Ethiopian-type independent churches rejected the political hegemony of the mission churches, their protest was largely expressed through Orthodox protestant ideas and theology, and they did not, Comaroff writes, 'contest the structure of the colonial order; rather, they debated the place within it of the aspiring black Protestant elite' (1985, 176).

The second type of independent church Sundkler describes as Zionist, which includes movements that call themselves by such terms as 'Zion', 'Apostolic', and 'Pentecostal'. Historically they have their roots in the Christian Catholic Apostolic Church, founded in 1896 in Zion City, Illinois, by John Alexander Dowie. It emphasized 'divine healing' and held the conviction that the 'second coming' of the Lord was 'near at hand'. The teachings of this church were introduced into South Africa in the first decade of the twentieth century, to be called the Zion Apostolic Church (Sundkler 1948, 48). Theologically, Sundkler describes Zionism as a 'syncretistic Bantu movement with healing, speaking in tongues, purification rites and taboos as the main expressions of their faith' (1948, cit 55). The leadership of these movements was focussed around healing prophets, such as Isaiah Shembe, who achieved a wide reputation as a spirit-healer among the Zulu in the early part of the twentieth century, preaching and driving out demons by means of the holy spirit (Sundkler 1948, 110). Centred on the image of Zion, the Zionist movement attempted to construct a symbolic order that directly opposed Protestant orthodoxy and, like the Lumpa Church of Alice Lenshina, to reconstruct a 'holistic' (theocratic) community within which 'the impact of industrial capitalism could be resisted' (1985, 176).

Applauding Sundkler's classic study, Comaroff is critical of later studies of African independent churches, such as those of Peel (1968) and Horton (1971), suggesting that they offer a rather idealist approach to religious movements by ignoring their embeddedness in social and cultural systems (1985, 169).

In giving an account of the original Christian Catholic Apostolic Church in Zion, which under Dowie founded Zion City near Chicago in 1896, Comaroff elicits what she describes as its 'cultural logic'. This church appealed mainly to poor and working-class people in Chicago and attempted to counter industrial capitalism by the formation of a theocratic-bounded community that put a focal emphasis on spirit-healing – and was thus opposed to secular medicine. It was millennial in ideology, puritanical in ethos, and obsessed with the intrusions of Satan into mundane affairs. The healing of afflictions, Comaroff writes, was the most 'pervasive metaphor' of the culture of the Zionist church (1985, 177–85). Both charismatic authority and spirit-healing are thus the two central themes of the Zionist churches, and Comaroff writes that such churches entered the Tshidi world largely though returning labour migrants and lone itinerant 'prophets' who were in search of a local following. As among the Zulu described by Sundkler, 'prophets' often seem to be outsiders (1948, 96).

The Tshidi became, during the colonial period, mainly nominal converts to Methodism, and the Methodist Church during the 1970s still remained the 'official' denomination of the Tshidi, representing orthodox Protestantism. It had a membership of around 5,000. The Roman Catholic Church had around 800 members, while the largest of the independent churches, the African Methodist Episcopal (AME) Church had a congregation of similar numbers and still retains its links with the black North American church of the same name. Comaroff enumerated that almost 4,000 Tshidi were members of Zionist churches, and both their leadership and followers were mostly poor and uneducated; none of the petite bourgeoisie were formal adherents of Zionism. What is significant, however, is that there has been a 'polarization' of two forms of religious expression that is clearly related to the dynamics of class formation and increasing social inequalities. This is reflected in the dichotomy between orthodox Protestantism, the 'churches of the law' [*dikereke tsa molao*] associated particularly with the petite bourgeoisie, and Zionism, the 'churches of the spirit' [*dikereke tsa moya*], mainly supported by Tshidi 'peasant-proletarians' cut off from the mainstream culture. Thus African independent churches, prominent in the early part of the twentieth century, have been losing ground in recent decades in a community that has been increasingly polarized, both economically and culturally (1985, 187–92).

Describing the situation in the 1970s in Mafeking as a 'neo-colonial context', Comaroff suggests that the Tshidi response to the 'stark contours of oppression' – the brutal mine compound, racial segregation under Apartheid – often took a highly coded form. She thus suggests that rituals often provide a medium through which the oppressions of a 'contradictory world' (capitalism) may be addressed and modified. This leads her to give a detailed description and analysis of the social organization and ritual forms of two Zionist churches – the Full Witness Apostolic

Church in Zion and the Zion Christian Church. Although the prophetic leaders of the churches are usually men, membership of the churches focussed mainly around women from female-headed households. Church rituals centre on baptism as an initiatory rite and on healing rites that involve possession and the summoning of the spirit [*go bitsa*], and both the drum and the symbolism of water play an important role in Zionist rituals. Members of the churches have distinctive uniforms; the men of the Zion Christian Church, for example, wearing black-peaked caps and large white boots, with which they can 'stamp evil underfoot' (1985, 202–51).

Although the Comaroffs (1991, 1992) stress that a *dialectical* relationship pertains between socio-cultural structures and symbolic forms and continually emphasize the coercive nature of the South African state and the intrusive capitalist economy, they have surprisingly been criticized for adhering to a 'Cartesian dualism' and for downplaying the violence inherent in European colonialism. They have also been accused of not providing a 'link' between objective social realities and subjective meanings (Reyna 2002, 35–9). Given their emphasis on dialectics and practice, such criticisms seem to me somewhat exaggerated.

A final note: In recent years there has been a resurgence and expansion of pentecostalism throughout much of Africa, associated with such churches as the Apostolic Faith Mission, Assemblies of God, and various pentecostalist and evangelical churches. In fact, Africa is now besieged with foreign missionaries, mostly of Baptist or pentecostalist persuasion, for the pentecostalist movement has now become perhaps the largest Protestant denomination. Pentecostalism is, of course, in many ways an extension of Methodism and the contemporary expression of a recurrent evangelical revivalism within Christianity. Such pentecostalist churches in Africa put a focal emphasis on spirit-healing – through the holy spirit – and tend to denigrate local culture, all folk medicine being equated with witchcraft and local spirits interpreted as demons. Among pentecostalists there is often an obsession with the devil and a dualistic metaphysic expressed that entails a 'spiritual warfare' between the divinity and the devil, such that healing or salvation involves the exorcism of evil spirits through the power of Jesus or the 'holy spirit'. Thus pentecostalism involves what Birgit Meyer describes as the 'diabolisation' of African religion (1999, 110). Pentecostalism also emphasizes salvation through Jesus and his imminent second coming and affirms the pre-eminent values of the nuclear family, and is thus hostile to both homosexuality and feminism. It is worth noting, of course, that the Lumpa Church of Alice Lenshina, the churches associated with Isaiah Shembe and Simon Kimbangu, the Aladura Church in Nigeria (Peel 1968), as well as Zionist churches are all pentecostalist-type movements (Woodhead 2002, 170–5; for further studies of independent churches and charismatic or pentecostalist movements in Africa, see Peel 1968; Jules-Rosette 1975; de Craemer 1977; H. W. Turner 1979; Gifford 1991; Anderson 1993; Fabian 1994; and Martin 2002, 132–52).

6

African-American Religions

6.1. PROLOGUE

> The slave-ships carried not only men, women and children, but also their gods, beliefs, and traditional folklore.
>
> So wrote the pioneering French Sociologist, Roger Bastide (1971, 23).

When Columbus reached the Caribbean Islands in 1492, the American continent was populated by human communities whose social institutions and cultural patterns showed a remarkable diversity ranging from nomadic foragers like the Shoshoni and Paiute to complex theocratic states and civilizations – in its original sense – like the Aztec, Maya, and Inca (Farb 1969). The pattern of cultures that pre-existed the penetration and colonization of the American continent by European peoples, along with the developing market economy, to a large degree structured the subsequent division of the continent into what has been described as the 'three Americas' (Harris 1964). The temperate regions of the Americas, peopled largely by hunter–gatherers or shifting cultivators, were colonized by Europeans and now constitute 'white' America. In these regions, in countries such as the United States, Chile, and Argentina, the Native American population was largely eliminated through disease, forced labour, and genocide, and the majority of the population are now of European descent. In parts of Central and South America, however, the locus of the theocratic states of the Incas and Aztecs, the Native American population was high, and the Spanish and Portuguese colonizers, having conquered the region, simply supplanted the traditional elite and proceeded to rule these areas as imperial domains. This region was termed by Harris as 'Indian' America, and it is here that a syncretic form of folk Catholicism developed, incorporating many elements of Native American culture into the ritual system. (For interesting studies of the religions of Mexico and the Andes region, for example, see Bastien 1978; Taussig 1980; Sallnow 1987; O'Connor 1997; Dow and Sandstrom 2001.)

In the more tropical areas of the Americas, particularly the Caribbean Islands and the Atlantic coast of South America, the European colonizers were unable initially to exploit the region, as the original inhabitants of these regions, Native Americans such as the Arawak, were soon eradicated through the ravages of disease and the ill effects of forced labour during the early days of European settlement.

On many Caribbean Islands, as well as in the southern region of the United States, there is today little evidence of the original inhabitants. To exploit these regions and to establish a plantation economy, the European colonists began the importation of human labour from elsewhere. Thus began the infamous Atlantic 'slave trade', European planters acquiring their labour from the West African coast and exporting tropical produce – mainly tobacco, cotton, and sugar – to Europe. It is difficult to assess the number of slaves that were shipped to the 'New World' from Africa, but it is estimated that at least 11 million Africans crossed the 'Middle Passage', as it was called by the European slave owners. Around fifteen per cent died on the voyage. The term *trade* for this system is something of a misnomer, for it was based on political domination and social violence, the slaves being legally considered 'property'. The importance of the slave trade as a factor in the development of industrial capitalism in Western Europe, in the underdevelopment of Africa, in the emergence of the Dahomey state as a powerful kingdom that controlled large reaches of the internal slave trade, and in changing consumption patterns of European peoples has been discussed by many scholars. Such issues are beyond the scope of the present study. (For important classic studies of the Atlantic slave trade, see Williams 1964; Patterson 1967; Rodney 1972; Galeano 1973; Walvin 1992.)

But there are two points that need to be stressed.

First, as it was based on forced labour, conflict was integral to the plantation economy, and the African slaves resisted this 'dehumanizing' system at every opportunity. They attempted to avoid their slave status on the Middle Passage, even leaping overboard into the sea, and slave revolts and many other forms of protest and rebellion were a constant feature of slavery – whether aboard the slave ships or on the plantations. In the 'New World', many escaped to form 'maroon' communities. Later, this resistance was expressed through cultural forms, particularly religion.

Second, as Bastide intimated, the Africans who were transported to the Americas took many of their cultural beliefs and social attitudes with them, and long ago Melville Herskovits wrote a detailed critique of the *Myth of the Negro Past* (1958a). This myth implied that Africans were naturally childlike, and readily adjusted to the most inhumane conditions, and as they lacked any civilization of their own, they also readily embraced and acknowledged the superiority of European culture. Thus Africans in the Americas were 'people without a past' (1958a, 1–2). A long line of scholars after Herskovits have emphasized the creativity and the social innovations of the African slaves as they adapted themselves to the new conditions in the Americas. As Mintz and Price wrote in a well-known essay, 'the organizational task of enslaved Africans in the New World was that of creating institutions – institutions that would prove responsive to the needs of everyday life under the limiting conditions that slavery imposed upon them' (1976, 19).

Such social institutions related, for example, to the folk economy, to kinship and family life, as well as to religion, cultural forms simply being an aspect of these social institutions, the latter defined as enduring and normative patterns of social relationships. Thus, although drawing on various religious beliefs and practices that they brought with them from Africa – and Herskovits emphasizes the importance of spirit-possession rituals involving song and dance (1958a, 214–15) – which may themselves have had an ethnic or regional significance, African peoples in the Americas created new social institutions, new languages, and new cultural forms.

Although both Herskovits (1958a) and Bastide (1971) recognized, and stressed, the crucial importance of what was termed 'Africanisms' – African culture – in the religious life of Africans in the New World, they did not see such African religious patterns as simply a 'survival' of an earlier pristine culture. Herskovits wrote that while the impulses of a 'traditional past' played their part in influencing such phenomenon as revivalism, nevertheless, what was also crucial was the institutional context of the New World, the current situation, and the creation of *new* religious forms (1958a, 225). Herskovits was to employ the concept of 'syncretism' to express the way in which African people, during the early years of slavery, combined aspects of both African and European culture to create new and distinctive religious forms (Herskovits 1958b; Greenfield and Droogers 2001, 24–7). The myriad new religious forms that emerged in what Harris called 'Black' America have been described in many texts; they include the Winti or Creole religion of Surinam (Van Wetering 2001); Myalism, Revivalism, and Rastafari in Jamaica; Vodou in Haiti; Santeria in Cuba (Barnet 1997); Candomble, Macumba, and Umbanda in Brazil; and Xango (Shango) in Trinidad (Simpson 1962). In this chapter I make no attempt to cover all these African-derived religious traditions but focus instead on three specific contexts – Haiti, Jamaica, and Brazil.

In the next two sections I discuss Vodou in Haiti. In Section 6.2, I describe the social and historical background of Vodou as a form of folk religion that is embraced by the majority of the Haitian peasantry, even though they consider themselves good Catholics. I outline the beliefs relating to the Lwa spirits and the three other spiritual agencies that have significance for the Vodou devotees – spirits of the dead, sacred twins, and Le Bon Dieu – god. In the following section, I discuss Vodou rituals, particularly the spirit-possession rituals that play such a vital role in Vodou religion, which Metraux indeed described as a 'danced religion'. I conclude the section with a discussion of Karen Brown's well-known spiritual biography of a Vodou practitioner in Brooklyn.

In the following three sections (Sections 6.4–6.6), I discuss the religions of Jamaica, focussing specifically on Revivalism and Rastafari. In Section 6.4, I discuss the history of Jamaica, emphasizing its long and bitter history of exploitation and oppression, and the important role that religion has played as a form of resistance. In the section, I focus on Revivalism, which writers like Chevannes have seen as the syncretic folk religion or 'worldview' of the Jamaican peasantry. In Section 6.5, I discuss the history of the Rastafari movement: the important role and inspiration of Marcus Garvey, the acceptance of Haile Selassie as the black redeemer by the emerging Rastafari groups of the 1930s and 1940s, and the adoption of two key symbols of the movement – the smoking of ganja and the wearing of dreadlocks. I conclude the section by discussing various conventions and events at the end of the 1950s when 'back to Africa' millennial tendencies were expressed and their opposition to the colonial state led to open conflict between the Rastafari and the government. I conclude the section by outlining some of the general characteristics of the Rastafari movement. In Section 6.6, I discuss their beliefs and practices in more detail. These include the notion that Haile Selassie is the true and living god; the millennial idea of repatriation to Africa; the use of the Bible as a book of symbols and the idea that the Rastafari are the true Israelites; their communitarian ethos that goes hand-in-hand with an emphasis also on charisma and patriarchy; and, finally, the importance of rituals focussed on the body – the smoking of ganja, the wearing of dreadlocks, and the adherence to certain food prohibitions. I conclude the sections with a discussion of the politics of Rastafari.

The final section of the chapter is focussed on the religions of Brazil. I give, in broad outline, an account of the religious traditions of Brazil, a country where the majority of the population live in cities on the Atlantic coast. Noting that what has emerged in Brazil in recent decades is something akin to a 'religious marketplace' and that the relationship between the devotee and the saint in folk Catholicism takes a form that is analagous to a patron-driven relationship, I give accounts of two important syncretic religious traditions. These are Catimbo, which is focussed around Native American spirits (Caboclo), and the African-derived religion, Candomble, which is centred on the Orixa spirits of Yoruba origin. Drawing on the ethnography, *Spirits of the Deep*, I discuss in detail one African-based spirit-possession cult in Belem city. I conclude the section with a discussion of the concept of syncretism as it relates to African-derived religions.

6.2. VODOU IN HAITI

Perhaps the most renowned of the African-based religions of the Americas is Vodou. The term Vodou (or Voodoo) is widely used to describe the religious beliefs and practices of the majority of people of Haiti. It is commonly and rather misleadingly seen as a strange and exotic cult. Even worse, Vodou has been regarded as something puerile and depraved and identified with bizarre and orgiastic rituals, sorcery, zombies, and cannibalism. It has often been – and still is by many Christian evangelists – interpreted as a form of Satanism. 'Voodoo is the MOST bestial, cruel and depraved of all religions', wrote one commentator (Metraux 1959, 10), and the American writer William Seabrook (1929), during the American occupation of Haiti (1915–1934), described the cult in such terms as to stress its more magical and esoteric aspects. But as the studies of Maya Deren (1953) and Alfred Metraux (1959) long ago indicated, the essential tenets and rituals of Vodou have similarities with other religions: There is nothing unique or bizarre about Vodou as a religious system. It is, as Lucy Mair wrote, 'simply a folk religion' (1969, 235). Even so, given the sensational media coverage that surrounds Vodou, some scholars still feel the need to emphasize that Vodou is a legitimate religious practice. For example, describing Vodou as the 'most misunderstood' and 'most maligned' of all the world's religions, Karen Brown's spiritual biography of a Vodou priestess in Brooklyn, *Mama Lola*, seems to be motivated at least partly by the need to counter some of the widespread cultural prejudices against Vodou practitioners (1991, xvii).

The history of Vodou begins, as Metraux writes, with the arrival of the first batch of slaves at Saint Dominique – then a French colony – in the second half of the seventeenth century. Most of the slaves were from Dahomey and Nigeria and by the end of the eighteenth century, Saint Dominique had become one of the wealthiest colonies of the French Empire – the 'richest jewel' in the French crown (1959, 44). The greatest individual market for the Atlantic slave trade, the colony supplied two-thirds of the overseas trade of France – trade particularly focussed around sugar and indigo. There were then around 800 sugar plantations on Saint Dominique. It was estimated that at the end of the eighteenth century, the slave population of the island totalled around 400,000 slaves, greatly outnumbering the French planters (pop. 40,000) and the free blacks and mulattoes (25,000). Although the winds of rebellion never ceased to blow on Saint Dominique, the French Revolution of 1789 had a profound impact on the island; for the spirit of freedom and independence went far beyond the planter class and soon spread to the slave population (Hurbon 1995, 41–2). The outcome was what C. L. R. James, in his pioneering study *The Black Jacobins*, described as 'the only successful slave revolt in history' (1938, ix). But James' classic account of the slave rebellion on Saint Dominique and the establishment of the independent state of Haiti devotes little discussion to the role that religion played in the revolt. The evidence suggests, however, that religion did indeed play a crucial part in the revolt, for a former slave and Vodou priest, named Boukman, organized a spirit ritual involving a pig sacrifice, which initiaily triggered the rebellion among the plantation slaves (Laguerre 1989, 60–7).

With the establishment of the independent state of Haiti in 1804, the plantation economy was largely destroyed, and the country became a land of peasant smallholders. More important, the ties with Africa were severed, and for about sixty years – until the Haitian government made a concordance with the Catholic Church in 1860 – the country also remained outside the framework of the Christian church. It was, as Metraux puts it, 'sealed off hermetically' from the outside world (1959, 44). Initially a 'plantation based institution' (Laguerre 1989, 33), Vodou during the nineteenth century, as the religion of ex-slaves, was free to evolve in its own fashion. Vodou, as we have come to know it, was the result.

In contemporary Haiti, Vodou is a folk religion of the rural peasants and urban poor who constitute the majority (around ninety per cent) of the population and speak a Creole language. The official state religion is the Catholic Church, which is more strictly adhered to by the educated elite, French speakers, many of whom look on Vodou as a distasteful and evil superstition. Maya Deren explicitly affirmed that she did not share the 'distaste' of the 'educated' Haitian for Vodou (1953, 23). It is, of course, worth noting that Haiti, with a population of around 6 million, is one of the poorest countries in the world, and the majority of its people are poverty-stricken peasants.

Throughout its long history, there has been a complex relationship between Vodou religion and politics in Haiti, whether local or state politics are involved. It is thus rather narrow and misleading to interpret Vodou as simply a benign 'healing art'. On independence in 1804, the first head of state, Jean-Jacques Dessalines, who significantly took the title of emperor, besides forcing the people back into virtual slavery, also expressed hostility towards Vodou rituals, and he even executed many of its adherents (Metraux 1959, 53). He was assassinated two years later and now, as a spirit [*lwa*], has rather ironically become a part of the Vodou pantheon. In contrast, Faustin Soulouque, head of state and then emperor of Haiti between 1847 and 1859 was a Vodou practitioner, and under his own implacable dictatorship, Vodou became almost the established religion of the state (Metraux 1959, 54; Laguerre 1989, 86–8). It was after his fall from power that an agreement was signed with the Vatican, making Catholicism the official religion of Haiti. Henceforth, at various intervals, both the government and the Catholic Church have made attempts to stamp out the Vodou cult, and Metraux describes in detail the events surrounding one 'anti-superstition' campaign in the early 1940s (1959, 343–50). Thus, to 'cleanse' the country of 'abominations' and 'superstitions', the government and the Catholic Church came together to destroy Vodou temples [*ounfo*]; burn various cult icons, drums, and sacred objects; and imprison recalcitrant Vodou priests [*oungan*] and priestesses [*manbo*]. During the campaign described by Metraux, every Catholic was enjoined to take an 'oath of rejection' and to publically repudiate Vodou practices as satanic (Hurbon 1995, 57).

The pendulum swung to the other extreme during the dictatorship of François 'Papa Doc' Duvalier (1957–1971), who used Vodou to bolster his own repressive regime. A former country doctor and anthropologist – he had published several articles emphasizing the need to restore Vodou politically – Duvalier was also a Vodou priest, and his quest for power emphasized that Vodou was the 'authentic soul' of the Haitian people. He thus presented himself as the zealous defender of the African aspects of Haitian culture. When in power, he had many Vodou priests serving as his advisors, and Vodou devotees were allowed to practise their religion openly with state support and protection. A symbiotic relationship was thus established between the state administration and influential Vodou priests, and the priests often acted both as political brokers and as agents of control, to intimidate people as the infamous Tonton Macoutes – the secret local militia. The term derived from the 'bogeyman' of Haitian folktales – the uncle [*tonton*] carrying off a misbehaving child in his straw shoulder bag [*macoute*] (Davis 1986, 303; Laguerre 1989, 103–9; Hurbon 1995, 118–19).

Since the fall of the Duvalier regime in 1986, Vodou religious practices have again come under attack, this time from Protestant missionaries – particularly Pentecostalists, Baptists, and Evangelists – who, as with Pentecostalists in Africa, have interpreted Vodou as satanic and a form of 'devil worship' – and an emphasis is put on repentence, confession, and the removal of the possessing lwa spirits by exorcism.

Members of the bourgeois elite and Catholic priests often make a clear distinction between Catholicism and Vodou: For the ordinary peasant in Haiti, however, there is no antithesis between the two religious systems, and Metraux speaks of a 'symbiosis' between the two cults, although it would appear that there is a 'parallelism' of two forms of ritual rather than a syncretism. Nonetheless, Vodou spirits [*lwa*] and the Catholic saints [*sen-to*] are often equated, and members of the Vodou cult always look on themselves as true Catholics and participate in the true Catholic rites – baptism, marriage, and communion. Indeed, one peasant remarked to Metraux that 'to serve the loa (lwa) you have to be a Catholic' (1959, 322). In fact, 'to serve the spirits [*lwa*]' is how the Vodou devotees themselves describe their own religion. The Vodou cult in many ways exemplifies what Lewis (1971) describes as a peripheral possession cult, when set in its political context – for the ruling elite tend to be Catholics – even though the lwa spirits have an important moral aspect.

The term *Vodou* (or *Vodoun*) comes from the Fon word meaning spirit, deity, or 'mystical force': This clearly signifies that the Vodou cult is to be seen positively as a form of religion rather than as a system of magic or the worship of 'fetishes'. Indeed, both Maya Deren (1953, 78–9) and Serge Larose (1977) stress the opposition, expressed in Haiti, between Vodou and magic [*maji*]. The religion itself is focussed around the lwa spirits – the term *lwa* (or loa), of Kongo derivation, also meaning 'god' or 'spirit'. These spirits are seen as being created by god and are referred to also as the 'Saints', the 'mysteries' [*miste*], or 'invisibles' [*envizil*]. As elsewhere, they are often associated with air or the winds. These spirits form a complex pantheon, but there is no agreement as to their number, and there is much variation, in terms of the importance of specific spirits, from one locality to another. As in Hinduism, the lwa spirit may take many different forms or manifestations, which in turn may be regarded as distinct spirit entities. They thus have multiple emanations, and Joan Dayan declares that there 'are thousands of gods in Haiti' (1997, 16). In an important sense, the lwa spirits are looked on as distant ancestors who are associated with African Guinea, where they now reside – although Guinea is looked on as a sort of Valhalla and has no real geographical meaning. Thus the lwa are classified into groups or nations [*nanchon*], reflecting the various ethnic affiliations of the early slaves – Ibo, Kongo, Bambara, Nago (Yoruba), Mondongue, and the like (Metraux 1959, 86–92; Larose 1977, 100–1).

But the important division is between the Rada and Petro (Petwo) spirits. The *rada* spirits – the word *rada* being derived from the town of Arada in Dahomey – are essentially intimate, benevolent, and dependable spirits associated with Guinea, specifically the lwa of Dahomey and Nigeria. In fact, a devotee speaking of the lwa of 'Afrique Guinin' generally means the Rada lwa. The Petro lwa, on the other hand, are associated with sorcery and looked on as essentially, or at least potentially, malevolent. They are described by Brown as 'hot-tempered and volatile' spirits, who must be handled with care (1991, 101). The name derives from one Dom Petro, a historical figure who lived in the middle of the eighteenth century. The Petro spirits are looked on as of Caribbean origin, and Maya Deren argues that these spirits, with their aggressive nature, represent the Amerindian contribution to the Vodou cult (1953, 70–1). Noteworthy is the fact that an important Petro spirit, Baron Samdi, derives its name (like zombi) from the Native American term *zemi*, which connotes the spirits of the dead. The rites associated with the Petro and Rada spirits are always kept distinct (Deren 1953, 65–73; Metraux 1959, 88–91).

The lwa spirits have a complex symbolism associated with them. They have their own symbolic drawings or *veve*, which are material representations of the deity, made from tracing an outline with flour and ashes on the ground. Each veve incorporates specific symbols of the spirit and has a sacred or magical quality that invokes the lwa at Vodou ceremonies. Joan Dayan suggests that the lwa 'do not correlate with objects in the natural world nor with specific human activities' but receive their identity specifically in relation to their devotees (1997, 21). Although the symbolism associated with the lwa is complex and variable, in fact each of the more important spirits has specific plants, colours, days of the week, personality or social types, drumbeats, rituals, and regions associated with that spirit. Thus, although on the surface Vodou religion appears to be ad hoc and variable, an underlying symbolic logic is discernible – perhaps deriving from Dahomey where complex divinatory systems are found. Maya Deren, who, as a film-maker and artist, pleads a lack of scientific detachment in her approach to Vodou, nonetheless writes perceptively about this aspect of the religion – even though, like contemporary postmodern scholars, she misleadingly equates detachment and objectivity with Cartesian metaphysics (1953, 17). Thus, Deren stresses that there is a 'metaphysical logic' implicit in Vodou beliefs and rituals, and in ways that anticipate the theories of Levi-Strauss (1966) and his 'science of the concrete', she suggests that through religion there is an 'organization of experience with a meaningful pattern' – which is essentially a function of the human mind. Vodou beliefs, therefore, Deren writes, are consistent with the idea that 'The universe is completely integrated and entirely logical, however devious and obscure that logic may sometimes seem' (1953, 90–2).

But Deren also argues that Haitian people are realists and pragmatists and have extensive empirical knowledge of the natural world. They therefore think of their religion in 'working terms' and to ask devotees whether they 'believe' in the spirits is to pose a rather irrelevant question, as the existence of the spirits as 'realities' is taken for granted (1953, 77). But her own attempt at the classification of the lwa simply relates to their ethnic affiliation and to what she describes as archetypal or cosmic principles – sea, fire, female, the earth, crossroads (1953, 85).

The major Vodou spirits may be briefly denoted. *Legba*, the 'master of the crossroads', is the guardian of boundaries and of roads and paths. He is especially seen as the link between humans and spirits, and is always the first lwa to be saluted at ceremonies. Legba is represented as a feeble old man in rags, leaning on a crutch and with a pipe. His sacred plant is *Euphorbia jatropha*. A trickster figure, he is identified with St. Lazarus, and, like Prometheus in the Greek myth, Legba stole gods' secrets and gave them to humanity. *Agwe* is a lwa associated with the sea, and a miniature boat or trident are among his emblems. He is invariably represented as a fair-skinned naval officer, and, as Deren writes, the 'lord of the sea' has 'royal habits' (1953, 120). Blue and white are his sacred colours. Rituals associated with Agwe, who is identified with St. Ulrich, are often held near the sea.

Dambala Wedo is a serpent spirit, and people possessed by this lwa crawl on the ground, moving like a snake, and hiss. He is associated with the rainbow and with river haunts, springs, and marshes. White is his colour, and as silver is seen as a 'white' metal, Dambala is associated with treasure. Metraux speaks of a mystical correspondence between treasure and the rainbow (1959, 107), while Deren writes that this lwa, together with his consort *Ayida Wedo*, represents the cosmos or sexual totality (1953, 114). Dambala is one of the most ancient of the ancestral spirits, and is associated with the bouganvillea plant and with St. Patrick. The term *da*, it is worth noting, is a Dahomean word referring essentially to 'life force' or fecundity (Deren 1953, 113).

Simbi is the 'patron of the rains' and is associated with magic [*maji*], whether it be protective, medicinal, or malevolent. Rituals and feasts for Simbi are usually held near springs, and while Dambala is seen as a positive force, in many regions Simbi is predominantly associated, as a Petro spirit, with malevolence, as well as with clairvoyance. He is associated with the colour black and the Magi.

Ogou belongs to the same classical tradition as the Greek Zeus and is a sky divinity associated with thunder, fire, and power. This lwa is the patron of warriors and blacksmiths. People possessed by him wrap pieces of red cloth about themselves and wave a sabre or machete – for these are his sacred emblems. The mango tree is associated with this lwa, and he is identified with St. James. The 'deity of fire', he has red as his colour. Embracing the Vodou faith to affirm her intimacy with her informants, Karen Brown was united in marriage to this brave and assertive lwa (1991, 133–9).

Loco is the spirit of vegetation, especially trees. It is this lwa who gives healing power to plants, and he is the patron of herbalists. He is particularly associated with the silk cotton tree [*Ceiba pentandra*]. Loco as a possessing spirit is recognized by his pipe and stick.

Azaka is associated with crops and agriculture and is an 'inarticulate, gauche peasant Pan', as Deren puts it, for he is represented in possession rites as a peasant with a straw hat and blue denim shirt, a clay pipe in his mouth and with a rustic speech (1953, 109). He thus represents the typical peasant farmer in Haiti, although Metraux refers to him as the 'minister of agriculture' in the world of spirits (1959, 109). He is associated with the colour green, St. Isidore, and the banana plant.

Ezili is a spirit who is reminiscent of the Greek deity Aphrodite and has 'all the characteristics of a pretty Mulatto; she is coquettish, sensual, pleasure-loving and extravagant' (Metraux 1959, 112). Devotees possessed by Ezili display provocative and seductive behaviour and express a desire for perfume. Described by Deren as the lady of 'sublime luxury' (1953, 134), she is associated with the basil plant and the Virgin Mary. But Ezili may take many forms: As Ezili Danto she is a dark-skinned, hard-working, independent mother associated with Africa, who can at times be malevolent; while as Ezili Freda, she is a white woman, sensual, seductive with a love of fine clothes and jewellery (Brown 1991, 220–47).

Gede is a family of lwa, including both Rada and Petro spirits, who are essentially conceived as spirits of the dead and are associated with death and cemeteries. Although taking many different forms, the Gede have been described as the 'Vodou spirit who presides over the realms of sex, death and humour' (Brown 1991, 360). Such spirits are represented as drunken vagabonds, who dance erotic or obscene dances, and have voracious appetites. Gede are archetypal gluttons, stuffing food into their mouths with both hands. Having the license to break all social rules, the Gede also use obscene or provocating language and often play tricks on people. In some Vodou temples [*ounfo*], the altar sometimes displays a huge wooden phallus that is taken up by those 'possessed' by the Gede. The lwa Baron Samdi, the head of the Gede, is seen as the guardian of the cemetery and is the best-known representative of the family. For many problems of daily life, this is the spirit whose help is most often sought. He is associated with the cross and the colour black. It is the Gede spirits who, on All Saints' Day, publicly possess their devotees, often in a spontaneous fashion.

(For detailed accounts of the lwa spirits from which the preceding notes have been extracted, see Deren 1953, 96–144; Metraux 1959, 103–15; on the classificatory symbolism relating to the main spirits, see Hurbon 1995, 140–3.)

Unlike many scholars writing about African cosmologies (earlier discussed), Karen Brown suggests that Vodou 'does not assume the existence of a two-storey universe'; rather, god and the lwa spirits operate in ways that permeate ordinary human life (1991, 347). But although the lwa spirits are the principal 'supernaturals', three other categories of spirits are also important to Vodou devotees – the spirits of the dead [*lemo*], the sacred twins [*marassa*], and the supreme deity [*bondye*].

Vodou devotees make a clear distinction between the 'souls' of the dead [*lemo, Les Morts*] and the lwa, the mysteries [*miste*]. The relationship between the souls of the dead and the lwa spirits, including the Gede, is, however, extremely complex and by no means easy to determine. In Haiti the individual person is thought of as consisting of three parts. The first part is the body, the gross physicality of the person, and it is this that is buried on the death of the individual. During life it is animated by two principles or souls: the *gros-bon ange* [*anj*], 'big good angel' and the *ti-bon ange*, or 'little good angel'. The 'big angel' is the seat of consciousness, emotions, and sentiments and is the source of all mental and physical energy. It roughly represents the personality of the individual; Larose writes that it is the spiritual essence that leaves the body at night, thus accounting for dreams (1977, 92). During possession rituals, the lwa temporarily displaces the 'big angel' of a living person and thus becomes the animating force of the physical body. Often there is a struggle between the lwa and the 'big angel', which the spirit invariably wins, and the 'big angel' is sent to wander during the rite (Brown 1991, 61). It is the 'big angel' that is liable to be captured – especially at the point of death – by a sorcerer [*Boko*] and used for malevolent purposes. The 'little angel', on the other hand, is immune from mystical attacks and represents the individual conscience or spiritual energy, and though distinct from the lwa – which is always seen as external to the individual person – it is this aspect of the person that survives death. At death, Larose writes, the 'little angel' is sent 'under the waters' – meaning Guinea – and here the soul of the dead remains for about a year (1977, 94). Then a complex ceremony is performed to retrieve the spirit (or soul) from the waters, at the end of which it is placed in a red clay pot [*govi*]. From then on, the spirit may be looked on as a tutelary deity, a kind of minor lwa who looks after the welfare of its relatives, and who, in return for sacrifices offered to it, responds to appeals for advice and protection (Metraux 1959, 262). Hurbon refer to these spirits of the dead as 'family ancestors' (1995, 83). The souls of the dead and the lwa spirits are therefore, as Deren writes, 'but different stages of the same essence' – and both the dead and lwa are kept in clay pots and both are referred to as *spirits* [*esprit*] (1953, 252). But the human 'soul' is quite distinct from the *nanm*, which is a 'spiritual essence' or power that Haitians may attribute to many natural phenomena – for example, the sun and earth and many plants that have medicinal properties. The nanm of the silk cotton tree is of especial importance (Metraux 1959, 154).

The second category of spirits, the Marassa or sacred twins, has a special significance in Vodou for they are reckoned to be more powerful than the lwa. They are therefore invoked and saluted at the beginning of a ceremony immediately after Legba. Maya Deren suggests that the notion of Marassa has a vestigial reference to ancient African origin myths and contains the idea of the segmentation of some original cosmic unity. Thus, although the divine twins are considered distinct from the lwa, they are in essence the first ancestral lwa and the origin of all the lwa (1953, 44–7). The Marassa belong, like the lwa, to different nations [*nanchon*] and are regularly given food offerings called *mange Marassa* [feast of the twins] – usually involving the sacrifice of a goat or chicken (Metraux 1959, 146–52).

The third spiritual being important in Vodou is the supreme being or god [*bondye*]. Like the Christian saints, the lwa are considered to have been once humans and though the immediate guardians and protectors of people, in relation to god their powers are limited. The lwa have powers only if 'god is willing' and God is seen as having created the spirits (Deren 1953, 60). Thus God [*bondye*] is supreme in Haitian Vodou, and this conception of divinity has its roots in both the Christian God and the high God of African religious traditions. Yet, as in the African context, God in Vodou rarely gets involved in everyday human affairs of the devotees, even though they consider themselves good Catholics. As Brown writes, dealing with the everyday concerns of human life is not the work of god but of his angels – the Vodou spirits (1991, 111). In fact, god is hardly mentioned in the classic studies of both Deren and Metraux. Thus the Vodou devotees' approach to the divinity is very different from that of more 'orthodox' Catholics, for, as with many Africans, god is not viewed as being involved in personal issues or everyday social life. As Joan Dayan writes, 'Although all practitioners of Vodou will tell you that they believe in a supreme God, Le Bon Dieu, that singular power is surely absent from the pressing concerns of the Haitian rural communities' (1997, 23–4).

It is to the lwa spirits that Vodou adherents turn when in need of help and support. So much for Vodou beliefs – recognizing that 'beliefs' (epistemology) and 'existence' (ontology) are not antithetical concepts, as some postmodern anthropologists seem to assume! I turn now in the next section to Vodou ritual practices.

6.3. VODOU RITUALS

In discussing Vodou rituals and their social context, I draw on the excellent ethnographic study of Alfred Metraux (1959) whose work is an early example of historical anthropology. Nowadays such work is nonchalantly dismissed and denigrated by literary scholars as 'detached' or 'objectivist', although it is clear to anyone who reads the text that Metraux combines intimacy and detachment, subjectivity and objectivity, participation and observation, and incorporates an engaged hermeneutics into a social scientific perspective. Sidney Mintz in his preface to a later edition of the text (1974) gives a much more balanced assessment of Metraux's study of the religion of the Haitian peasantry – Vodou.

As with many other African religions, Vodou is essentially a 'practical and utilitarian religion'. Both Deren and Metraux stress this. The former scholar indeed suggests that life in Haiti for the ordinary peasant is too pressing and 'hopeless' and too critical to permit the luxury of idealism or mysticism, and that folk beliefs provide therefore not so much a reason for living but a *means* of living. The Haitian, she writes, thinks of his or her religion in working terms, as a 'practical methodology', not as an irrational hope. Vodou is thus 'la science des mysteres' [the science of the mysteries] (1953, 76–7). Karen Brown stridently affirms that 'there is no Vodou ritual . . . which is not a healing rite' (1991, 10). This is something of an exaggeration, without 'healing' is a term used to cover securing needed employment or a love relationship, help in problems of subsistence, sacrifices, initiations, and divination, as well as support in political disputes and family quarrels, but she nonetheless emphasizes an important point: For it is in relation to misfortunes and their treatment that lwa spirits have particular relevance. Moreover, it is in terms of the here and now, rather than in terms of a past golden age, or a future millennial dream, or even a future heaven, that the lwa spirits are primarily concerned. They thus give support and address problems that relate to a life that for most Haitians, Brown writes, is filled with struggle and suffering (1991, 345).

Illness and misfortunes, especially of a serious or enduring kind, are frequently interpreted in Haiti as being caused by the lwa, or by the spirits of the dead, or possibly by sorcery. As the lwa are said to 'seize' a person who has offended them either through neglect or the transgression of some social rule, they are essentially moral agents closely involved in upholding the norms and welfare of a group. There is therefore in Haiti a contrast between the lwa, specifically identified with Guinea, and other agents of misfortune. Contact with the lwa, who are described as being 'served' by their devotees, can be made through dreams, but the most important mode of communication is through possession rites.

The explanation given for mystic trance is fairly straightforward; invoked in a ritual setting, the lwa moves into the head of a person and in doing so displaces the individual's 'big angel'. The eviction of the soul is held responsible for the tremblings and convulsions that accompany the initial possession, and once the 'big angel' has gone, the individual experiences a feeling of emptiness. Possessed by the lwa, the person becomes in fact the deity and makes the appropriate responses and is addressed by others as if she or he were the spirit. The relationship between the lwa and the person possessed is compared to that between a rider and a horse [*chwal*]. That is why a lwa is spoken of as 'mounting' his horse – the person. The spirits, whatever their sex, incarnate themselves in men or women as they please. The possessed devotees indicate by dress or manner the spirit that is incarnating them, for, as has been noted, the principal lwa are symbolized by fairly clearly defined social stereotypes. The possession rite, as Metraux stresses, therefore has a theatrical aspect. It may also have, as Francis Huxley noted (1966, 201), a sexual element – expressed particularly through the lwa Ogoun and Ezili – but although allowing for a good deal of abandonment and emotional release, possession is a fairly controlled ritual event. The possessed person is protected from the possible effects of their own frenzy by other members of the cult group, they are prevented from hurting themselves, and their modesty may be shielded to save embarrassment. Metraux suggests that it is this sympathetic concern expressed by members of a group that creates 'an atmosphere of moral and physical security which is conducive to total abandon in the state of trance' (1959, 123).

Several writers have given detailed accounts of the possession trance (Metraux 1959, 126–7; Huxley 1966, 108–10), but perhaps the most interesting is Maya Deren's own account of her possession by the lwa Ezili (1953, 236–45). Significantly, the individual in a trance state is not held responsible for his or her own actions and words, and when they have emerged from the trance can remember nothing of what they said or did while possessed. Equally important is that in Vodou, a very clear distinction is made between possession by lwa, which is sought after and desired, and possession by evil spirts [*baka*].

Two interesting questions have frequently been posed regarding such trance states. The first is whether or not the possession is faked or simulated or whether there is genuine dissociation. Clearly, many individuals do appear, as many observers have noted, to simulate possession – even though they may categorically deny it. However, this issue is not resolved by scrutinizing the authenticity of the devotee but to realize that possession is a culturally prescribed pattern of behaviour and that although initial possession may be uncontrolled, what happens is that an individual learns how to lapse into a controlled trance state. Some devotees, for personal reasons, may never learn how to achieve this, but the majority do. They are thus able to give a *controlled* 'performance' and yet are *not* conscious of what they are doing. Maya Deren's account (1953, 288–9) of her own trance experience, substantiates this.

The second question, namely, whether possession trances are comparable to cases of hysteria or other forms of neurosis, has often been posed and was discussed in Chapter 1. Deren's study confirms the suggestions of Metraux (1959, 137), and she quotes at length from Herskovits' study of Haiti (1937, 153) to the effect that Vodou cannot be understood either as a form of magic or as pathological hysteria (1953, 285).

An important aspect of Vodou ritual is that trance states are induced not by hallucinogenic drugs but by rhythmic drumming and dancing. Indeed, it is difficult to overestimate the importance of dance and of the drumming in Vodou, so crucial and central are they to the rituals. Many of the drums in fact are deemed sacred and are thought to possess spiritual power. 'Beating the drum' is a virtual synonym for Vodou religious activities and in possession states, the spirit is referred to as 'danced' or being 'beaten' into the head of his devotee. Metraux regards Vodou as a 'danced religion', for dancing is a ritual act that, together with the drum rhythms, has a power to attract the lwa spirits. Importantly, the drummer himself never becomes possessed by the lwa (1959, 178–89).

Although in an important sense Vodou is a family-based religion, and the lwa are looked on as distant ancestors, the cult itself is mainly organized through cult associations under the leadership of a ritual specialist. The temple or cult house [*oumfo*], often attached to the domestic household, consists essentially of a covered area or shed where dances and ceremonies are held. The centre post [*poteau mitan*] of the main building or peristyle has a special ritual significance and adjacent to this in a smaller building there is an inner sanctuary that contains an altar and houses the ritual paraphernalia. Of especial significance are the *Govi*, the red earthen pots in which the lwa or the spirits of the dead are kept. Each sanctuary is associated with a particular Vodou priest or priestess [*oungan or manbo*] who is the leader of an autonomous sect or cult group, for there is no clerical hierarchy in Vodou. Under their leadership are a number of cult initiates [*ounsi*], a term that means 'wife of the spirit'. The majority of cult members are women; even so, the term is often applied to men. To join the cult, novitiates go through a complex initiation ceremony [*kanzo*] that is expensive and demands many personal sacrifices. The initiation involves the observance of certain moral taboos, a forty-one-day period of seclusion, and – most important – a possession rite in which a person is initially conjoined with a specific lwa that thereafter becomes a kind of guardian spirit known as *maittete* – the 'master of the head' (Metraux 1959, 192–212). On the death of a person, there is an equally important ceremony known as *dessounen* – a part of the funerary rite – which is specifically designed to separate this lwa spirit, as well as the 'big angel', from the body of the deceased (Metraux 1959, 244).

The oungan or manbo, assisted by a number of cult officials, organizes the cult activities. Besides the possession rite, there are a number of other associated rituals that are worth mentioning. First, there is a ceremony that frequently precedes possession known as *manje*–lwa [feeding the loa]. This is a form of sacrifice, the purpose of which is to feed and strengthen the lwa, thus ensuring 'the constant flow of psychic energy' (Deren 1953, 198). The animal to be sacrificed, a chicken or domestic animal – chosen according to the preferences of the lwa (e.g., a white animal is offered to Dambala – Wedo) – is first consecrated by means of a ceremonial bath, or cleansing rite. The animal is then given some food, and its acceptance of this signifies that it is also acceptable to the lwa, and indeed it becomes the property of the spirit and partakes of the divinity. Often at this point, the person who is to perform the sacrifice becomes possessed by the lwa for whom the animal is to be sacrificed. Sometimes the sacrificial animal may be ridden by the devotees in a manner similar to that recorded among the Zar cults of the Sudan. After being killed, the blood of the animal is collected in a calabash and, mixed with various condiments, is made into a beverage that is drunk by the participants. It is the essence of the food that is consumed by the lwa, and though some of the sacrifice may be placed for them on the altar, or scattered in the direction of the cardinal points, most of the meat is cooked and later eaten. Offerings of fruit, vegetables, and drinks are also made to the lwa; indeed, a devotee seldom communicates with the spirits without first inviting them to partake of food. Deren stresses that the idea of animal sacrifice to the Haitian peasant carries with it no emotional repugnance, nor do they have any sentimentality towards animals (1953, 198–202).

Another important and interesting ceremony is the 'mystical' marriage, which involves the union of a devotee to some particular lwa (Metraux 1959, 212–19). It is often a spirit like Ezili who initiates the partnership.

The oungan, however, is much more than just a priest, for the cult group performs many different social functions. As Metraux writes,

A good Oungan is at one and the same time priest, healer, soothsayer, exorcizer, organizer of public entertainments, and choirmaster. His functions are by no means limited to the domain of the sacred. He is an influential political guide, an electoral agent . . . and . . . the accepted counsellor of the community. (1959, 67)

Of particular importance is his role as healer, for as in many other societies, the Vodou ritual specialist has both a medical and a religious function. Deren stresses the importance of herbal knowledge and the unnecessary and shameful prejudice that has been levelled in the past against the 'oungan'. There is a need, she suggests, to abandon the image of the esoteric 'witch-doctor', and to break down the barriers between folk and scientific medicine. In the Haitian context, the oungan (or manbo) is a known and trusted individual who, given the poverty and lack of medical facilities on the island, has an important and beneficent role as a healer and therapist (1953, 154–63). Vodou cult groups therefore are more than simply religious associations: They have important social and welfare functions. Needless to say, though initiation into the priesthood is a lengthy and costly business, oungans and manbos often enjoy a wide influence and a lucrative income as the leader of a cult association (Metraux 1959, 78).

Deren's study focusses on the more positive aspects of Vodou religion, and in many ways she is an apologist for the cult. But though the Haitians themselves make an important distinction between the 'guinea' (Vodou) and magic, it is important to realize that there is no clear demarcation between the lwa spirits and those ritual activities associated with magic and sorcery. For in the Haitian context, the sorcerer [*boko*] may be an oungan who 'serves with both hands'. Indeed, Larose writes that the majority of oungans have two cult houses, one devoted to the beneficent family loa, the other where they keep their 'points' and zombies (1977, 115).

A boko, in contrast to the oungan, is one who practices evil magic. They are not necessarily wayward oungans, but as oungans must know the techniques of sorcery if they are to counter such influences, they are naturally prone to indulge secretly in magic. The boko causes harm or even death in a number of ways. They have, for instance, the ability of 'sending the dead' – though the success of this rite depends on the goodwill of the spirit Baron Samdi. They may also employ magical charms [*wanga*] – objects or points endowed with condensed magical power that are used for malevolent purposes. Equally important are the zombies, a term applied either to the 'living dead', the bodies of individuals whose soul has been captured by a boko or to the disembodied soul of a dead person (Brown 1987, 300). The researches of the ethnobotonist Wade Davis (1986, 1988) have, however, indicated that specific poisons are used by means of which an individual may lose the faculties of speech and willpower though be able to act and move (1986, 253). Davis links the zombies to certain secret societies, like the Bizango, which enforce social rules within a particular locality. Disembodied souls together with the lwa who have been 'bought' are often believed to be used by sorcerers for evil purposes and are collectively known as *baka* [evil spirits]. Such spirits often take the form of animals. The term *point* refers, in a wide range of contexts, to these various malevolent powers, all associated with situations in which a person – the boko – is motivated by the desire for personal wealth or gain. There is a belief that sorcerers meet together at night at crossroads or in cemeteries, and that they take the form of *zobops*, grotesque monsters who are organized into secret 'red sects'. Werewolves [*loup garou*], on the other hand, are mainly thought to be women, a sort of female vampire who makes small children die by sucking their blood. Women often commit such deeds unknowingly, and Haitian ideas about werewolves have a similarity to beliefs about witches elsewhere (Metraux 1959, 291–9).

In the Haitian context, therefore, the usual analytical distinction between religion and magic – the latter being seen as the conscious manipulation of occult forces – is misleading. For the distinction that is important in Vodou is between the lwa spirits associated with Guinea and the 'points', the spirits and magical powers that are essentially malevolent. The rites focussed on the lwa are collective and their purpose beneficent, while the rites associated with the 'points' are performed in private for an individual and their purpose is usually immoral. Although Vodou is a peripheral possession cult, the lwa spirits are in essence ancestral or family deities whose function is to uphold the social structure, tradition in Haiti being equated with and defined in terms of a mystical past – African Guinea (Larose 1977, 106–12). But as Bastide writes, the fact that Haiti won its independence at the beginning of the nineteenth century inevitably meant that Haitian culture was isolated from Africa. There was in fact a period of 'religious anarchy' (1971, 131) lasting more than sixty years, during which time Vodou developed as a 'living religion', adapting to the changing circumstances. One result of this is that Vodou lacks any centralized religious authority, although some scholars often refer to the 'Vodou church' (e.g., Laguerre 1989).

In recent decades, the poverty, high unemployment, and political repression in Haiti have led many Haitians to seek a better life elsewhere. There has thus been a massive immigration into the United States, many people arriving there as 'boat people'. Almost half a million Haitian people now live in the New York area, and Karen McCarthy Brown's study, *Mama Lola* (1991), is a fascinating account of one Vodou priestess in Brooklyn. It is less an ethnography than a 'spiritual biography' of a spirit medium and her family. Heralded as an exemplary 'postmodern ethnography' and showered with accolades, the book is crucially focussed on hermeneutics and dialogics. There are thus lyrical descriptions of places, events, and people, focussed around Mama Lola and her family – their personalities and oral histories – and pages upon pages of memorized conversations. These no doubt have an aesthetic value, particularly to hermeneutic scholars and literary critics, and, like Wade Davis', *The Serpent and the Rainbow* (1986), it makes for a good read. But the more illuminating parts of the study come when Brown abandons her lyricism and engages in sociological and political analysis, when she adopts in fact an 'objectivist perspective' – 'objectivism' being the current derogatory term for social science, despised and denigrated by postmodern scholars with whom Brown aligns herself. Thus scattered within the lyricism and dialogics of the book, some important sociological observations are made by Brown that are worth noting. One is that although Vodou is not an 'agrarian religion' there is still, even within urban areas, an important emphasis made through the lwa, of peoples' roots in the land. Brown emphasizes also that women have tended to be more adaptable than men in coping with urban living, given their skills in small-scale trading, and although the priestesses [*manbo*] do not challenge the religious hegemony of the rural male, at least half the Vodou leaders in the urban context are women (1991, 221). But Brown has little discussion of the oungan or even of Vodou as a religious system within the urban context, and the only Vodou priest she describes is dismissed as a misogynistic, money-grabbing charlatan, who is linked with sorcery and the Tonton Macoutes (1991, 185–7). What she emphasizes, however, is important, even though much of her discussion simply replicates that of Deren and Metraux; namely, that Vodou has integrity as a religion and serves as a 'repository of wisdom' accumulated by people who have endured through the centuries slavery, hunger, disease, repression, corruption, and violence (1991, 98); that Vodou is a 'religion of survival', particularly associated with the poor and the 'oppressed', and largely serves to 'empower' women to a degree much greater than in the majority of the world's religions (1991, 220); and, finally, that for many women healers [*manbo*], relationships with the spirits [*lwa*] often replace those with men, for the spirits are seen as providing security, guidance, and support. As she writes,

> To work for the spirits is to see it as an alternative to inadequate love relationships, Vodou spirits are ideal lovers – protective, constant, powerful, and, if treated right, benevolent.
>
> To serve the spirits is thus to stop serving men, and the relationship between the Manbo and the lwa becomes one of 'exchange partners'. (1991, 167–84)

A covert functionalist and Marxist when she leaves aside the hermeneutics and dialogics, Brown affirms that it is a universal instinct 'to turn to religion in times of crisis' (1991, 253), and she concludes that

> the strength of religious belief in Haiti can be accounted for, in part, by the poverty and political oppression that have characterized life for most Haitians from independence to the present. (1991, 5)

But the link between Vodou and politics is never explored in the text – she dismisses the issue by simply acknowledging that Vodou has often been 'misused by tyrants and scoundrels alike' (1991, 109).

The moral purity of religion as a social phenomenon is thus affirmed.

Brown assumes that participation and empathy with the subjects of study, which anthropologists, of course, have been practising since the 1920s, involve embracing the Vodou faith. This is seen as validating her 'intimacy' with her informants and the 'authenticity' of her study. Following this logic, presumably if she had studied a pentecostalist preacher in Haiti, rather than Mama Lola, Brown would have gone around denigrating the Vodou cult and engaged in rites of exorcism to drive out the evil lwa spirits!

(For other studies of Vodou, besides those already cited, see Hurston 1981; Rodman and Cleaver 1992; and for an interesting account of a Haitian oungan and flagmaker, see Wexler 1997.)

6.4. RELIGIONS OF JAMAICA

Jamaica, like Haiti and other Caribbean Islands, has, as Orlando Patterson (1967) suggested, a unique history. For it was a rare example of a human society artificially created for the sole purpose of profit-making, within an emerging capitalist economy. When it was captured by the British in 1655, it was virtually a 'clean slate', for the indigenous Arawak peoples of Jamaica, estimated at around 60,000, had become extinct during the preceding century because of disease, brutal exploitation, and genocide. The colonial system of slavery that was instituted in the interests of the slave-owners has thus left an important legacy for the island, namely, a severe maldistribution of land and wealth, for prior to independence about sixty per cent of the land was held by one per cent of the population, mostly absentee landowners. The history of Jamaica, as Barrett writes, 'is one long tale of exploitation by a few rich families whose privileges were never questioned' (1977, 13).

Unlike in Haiti, where the influence of the Catholic Church was pronounced, the English planters in Jamaica adamantly refused to share their religion with the slaves, fearing that the Christian message might incite rebellion. Thus, until the end of the eighteenth century, one of the striking features of Jamaican society was that almost the entire slave population remained ignorant of the religion of their masters. Left to themselves, the slaves therefore developed certain aspects of the religion of their homelands – the West African coast. The slave religion that developed focussed around two important concepts. The first was a belief in *obeah*, or witchcraft, the term itself derived from the Twi (Akan) word for sorcery, *obayi*. It is used to designate a person who harms others by psychic means through either the evil eye or cursing or by use of medicines (Barrett 1976, 73–4). The second is the notion of *myalism*. This was essentially a cult phenomena focussed around possession rites, and in a sense was an anti-witchcraft movement as Patterson (1967, 188) implied. Central to this cult was a possession dance involving the ancestral spirits, which has come to be known as *kumina*, derived from the possession rites of the Ashanti people of Ghana (Twi, *akom* [to be possessed], *ana* [an ancestral spirit]). Ernest Cashmore suggests that the African–derived *obeah-myal* belief system, in perceiving evil as lying in the realms of the spiritual, posed little threat to the social order and had essentially a conservative function (1979, 15). It is worth noting, however, that rebellion, or the threat of it, was almost a permanent feature of Jamaican society during the colonial period, and independent Maroon communities had long established themselves in various parts of the island. Eventually, after the Maroons had resisted many attempts to reenslave them, a peace treaty was signed (in 1738) between these communities and the British planters, and the former became, as Cashmore puts it, the 'mercenary puppets of the colonial authorities' (1979, 14).

The introduction of Christianity by missionaries at the end of the eighteenth century, however, had an important and crucial impact on Jamaican society, particularly through the Baptist missionaries, who were the most successful in converting the slaves to Christianity. One of the first preachers was George Liele, an American ex-slave who came to the island in 1782. Along with several other preachers, who started thriving Baptist missions on the island, Liele was instrumental in the development of a new religious form that combined or rather grafted Christianity onto the African-derived slave religion. This not only laid the foundation for modern Jamaican revivalism (Beckwith 1929) but, as Barrett writes, this new 'spiritual combination' took a millennarian fervour and 'became the energizing force behind the slaves in their demand for freedom as command from God' (1977, 40). Charismatic Baptist ministers, such as Sam Sharpe, played a prominent role in the rebellion of 1832, the groundwork for the rebellion being laid in prayer meetings. Sharpe, an authority on the Bible, proclaimed the equality of all humans. Known as the 'Baptist war', the insurrection was violently suppressed, and thousands of slaves were put to death after trial by court martial. Sharpe himself was executed in Montego Bay in 1832. Another rebellion in 1865 – the Morant Bay rebellion – also involved Baptist preachers, Paul Bogle and George Gordon being the prominent leaders. They spoke out against the poverty and the lack of freedoms, and Gordon, in messianic tones, preached self-government by the blacks. This rebellion was crushed with equal severity, and many thousands were killed, including Bogle and Gordon, the Maroons ironically supporting the crown. (For useful accounts of the history of Jamaica and the slave rebellions, see Ragatz 1963; Patterson 1967; Barrett 1977, 29–63; Morrish 1982, 25–39; Chevannes 1994, 1–16.)

Such is the historical background, and it is against this background that the Rastafari Movement of Jamaica has to be set. It is, as Barrett writes, 'the most recent religious expression of a people who have experienced a bitter history of exploitation and oppression'. It represents a reaction not only against orthodox Christianity but also against the Christian revivalist and pentecostelist movements within Jamaica (1977, 28).

Jamaica, a small Caribbean island with a population of just over 2 million people, had, as has been noted, a long tradition of revolts and rebellions against colonial slavery. Equally important, there has been an important tradition of cultural resistance, and this was largely expressed through religion – the latter being not only a belief system or 'worldview' but also a cultural system with its social institutions and patterns of social organization. The majority of people of Jamaica, some ninety per cent, are of African origins or of Afro-European descent (Barrett 1977, 4). The country has been described as a 'museum of religions' – although such a depiction might well apply to many other countries throughout the world. During the 1970s, Ivor Morrish recorded over a hundred Christian denominations, sects, and independent churches, and, according to the 1970 census of Jamaica, the Anglican and Baptist Churches comprised around fifteen per cent and eighteen per cent, respectively, of the total population. The Roman Catholic Church had a membership of around eight per cent (Morrish 1982, 92–4). A decade later, around thirty per cent of the population were noted as affiliated to the established churches – Anglican, Roman Catholic, Methodist, Baptist, Presbyterian – that mainly established themselves as mission churches during the nineteenth century and that are particularly associated with the middle- and upper-class Jamaicans who have wealth and power. Around thirty-three per cent of the population in the 1982 census were affiliated to the non-conformist churches that had established themselves in the twentieth century, and these included the American-inspired Pentecostalist, Church of God, Seventh-Day Adventist, and Revivalist Churches, including the AME Zion Church. These churches have increased their membership considerably over the past two decades. But there is a third category of religions that is hardly mentioned in the census and has what Barry Chevannes describes as a 'sort of underground existence': These are the African-derived religions that have been described as 'Revivalism' and 'Rastafari'. He notes that because of the power and influence of the established churches, and the colonial efforts to suppress African religious traditions, many people in Jamaica, particularly rural peasants and the urban poor, have a 'dual membership', nominally belonging to one of the established churches while being actively engaged in 'revivalist' religious practices (Chevannes 1995, 2–3).

Indeed, Leonard Barrett suggests that many Jamaicans, like himself, identify themselves as a 'people of two cultures': 'first, African and a part of our identity, the second, a thin layer of the European Slavemaster's culture that filtered down to us through the churches and the mission schools' (1976, 13). This 'underground', African-derived religious culture Chevannes describes as Revivalism, or as Revival Zion. What earlier writers had described as distinct belief systems – myalism, Revivalism, Bedwardism, Pukumina, Zionism – and recognizing that it was difficult to see where they began and ended (Morrish 1982, 51), Chevannes links them all together as a single 'coherent worldview' that he describes as Revivalism. Moreover, this is seen as the 'world-view of the Jamaicans' (1995, 22–6). In fact, in Chevannes' writings, 'Revivalism' becomes a virtual synonym for the folk culture of the Jamaican peasantry and even encompasses folk herbalism, which is essentially a secular healing tradition focussed around 'root doctors' and 'balm yards', with its own internal logic and coherence, even though herbal medicine is also utilized by spirit healers, magicians, and the Rastafari – indeed, most of the Jamaican peasantry (Laguerre 1987).

Revivalism is essentially a syncretic movement combining Christianity and African religious forms, and its development as a religious tradition went through a number of distinct phases – if one assumes that it is a single religious tradition or 'worldview' that develops in rather linear fashion.

Initially, revivalism is seen as growing out of myalism, which, as we have noted, is a term used to describe the religion of the plantation slaves – and was not specifically ethnic but rather 'pan-African', at least in relation to the cultures of West Africa. According to Barrett, the term *myal* refers to a class of ritual specialists who through spirit-possession rites [*myal*] can detect the malevolent influences of *obeah* or sorcery (1976, 70). It largely derives from the religion of the Ashanti, most Jamaican slaves coming from Ghana (Ashanti – Fanti) or Nigeria (Yoruba [Nago] – lbo) (1976, 16). The emphasis in myalism was on spirit-healing through possession rites, and it was, as Chevannes describes it, 'very anti-obeah' – *obeah* in this context essentially referring to sorcery, the use of symbols, or medicines to inflict harm on other people. This is an aspect of folk religion in Jamaica that still has resonance among the peasantry, and it is associated with tensions, jealousy, quarrels, and frustrations – and the general 'malaise of uncertainty' (Barrett 1976, 73–6). There is no religion in Jamaica today, Chevannes writes, to which the name *myal* applies, but the term still has currency in relation to the possession ritual known as *kumina*. For the term *myal* is used to describe the stage in the ritual when the person becomes possessed by the ancestral spirit. The person is then described as 'getting myal' (Barrett 1976, 25; Chevannes 1995, 7).

At the end of the eighteenth century, under the aegis of Methodist revivalism, myalism was transformed. For with the advent of Christianity in Jamaica, largely through black American Baptist preachers who came over as slaves in 1782 – prominent among these were George Liele, Moses Baker, and George Lewis – there was also a resurgence of rituals focussed around spirit-healing and spirit-possession. The establishment of native Baptist churches in the early nineteenth century heralded a mingling of the beliefs and rituals associated with myalism and Christian observances – a particular stress being put on Baptism. Both evangelical Christianity and myalism also placed an important emphasis on the spirit and on religious experience, and, as Chevannes writes, 'Possession by the spirit thus became the quintessential experience of the myalized Christianity, replacing prayer and hymn singing' (1994, 19).

The folk religion of Jamaica, earlier known as myalism, underwent a further transformation around the 1860s with the arrival in Jamaica of what has been described as the 'Great Revival' (1860, 61), which spread throughout Britain and the United States and is particularly associated with the figures of Dwight Moody and Ira Sankey. The 1860 Revival also had an impact in Jamaica, giving rise to two syncretic cults that became known as Revival Zion and Pukumina (Barrett 1976, 54). The term *Pukumina* essentially refers to a style of Jamaican religion that combines (or is a syncretism of) Kumina (the spirit-possession rites associated with the African – based religion, myalism) and Christianity – particularly the more emotional and ecstatic aspects of evangelical Christianity (Barrett 1976, 27).

From the 1860 'Great Revival', two religious traditions thus emerged – Zion Revival and Pukumina; the latter cult is seen as closer to 'traditional' African religions, with more emphasis on spirit-possession and less emphasis on the Bible and the notion of Satan. Both are seen as variants of Revivalism, which emerged at that period (Chevannes 1994, 20–1). Equally important in the final emergence of Revivalism as a coherent folk religion was the prophetic career of Alexander Bedward. Born in 1859, Bedward had an early visionary experience that he claimed derived from God, and he came to see himself as an incarnation of Moses and John the Baptist. Originally a member of the Jamaican Native Baptist Church, he had travelled to Panama as a migrant worker, and in 1895 he established his own Baptist Church in August Town, near Kingston. He soon became widely known as a charismatic preacher and spirit-healer, and in that year he was arrested briefly for sedition. On release, he continued his activities, and during the early years of the twentieth century became famous throughout Jamaica as a great revivalist preacher and healer, and around Bedward there formed a loose network of revivalist groups. In 1920, Bedward proclaimed himself the messiah, and in December of that year, a large crowd gathered at Mona, near Kingston. It was to be the occasion when Bedward would fly to heaven like Elijah. His ascension did not materialize, and when later he led a march to the city 'to do battle with his enemies', he and around 800 of his followers were arrested. Bedward was committed to a mental hospital, and there he died in 1930. There is a strong suspicion that his arrest and confinement were politically motivated (Morrish 1982, 49–51; Chevannes 1994, 39).

Three aspects of Bedward's prophetic career are noteworthy, which have parallels in many other contexts – his preaching that blacks should rise up and overthrow European domination; his apocalyptic vision that the end of the world would come, and all true believers would go to heaven; and finally, the important stress he placed on baptism with water as the main form of healing and salvation (Chevannes 1994, 80; 1995, 9). The charismatic movement associated with Bedward continued to flourish after his death, known as Bedwardism, and many of its members were important in the origins of Rastafari.

Revivalism as a religious worldview acknowledges God as the creator (Big Maasa). Associated with lightning and thunder, God seems, as in other African religions and Vodou, to play little part in the everyday life or rituals of the Jamaican peasantry. He thus has little role in the revival complex. But whereas God is distant, the spirits are real and close, and the spirits – of which there is a whole pantheon – occupy a prominent role in the beliefs and rituals of Revivalism. Jesus is the most important spirit, the one most frequently invoked in rituals, but also of significance are angels, archangels, prophets (especially John the Baptist), the Apostles, and the spirits of the dead, known in Jamaica as *duppies*. While the Revival Zionists conceive of the spirits as essentially good, they acknowledge the existence of Satan: But they are little concerned with the spirits of the dead. The duppies, however, disembodied spirits that linger around the community after the death of a person, play a more important role in the Pukumina cult and can be utilized by sorcerers to harm people. In both cults, spirit-possession rituals are the main form of communication with the spirits. Chevannes stresses that nature, humanity, and the spirits are interdependent and form an essential unity in the Revivalist worldview and that folk healing is an important part of this tradition. But while acknowledging the distinction between two levels of healing, the natural and the spiritual, he emphasizes the priority of the spiritual over the material in Revivalism and that the most well-known folk healers are charismatic spirit-healers rather than simple herbalists or obeahmen (Chevannes 1994, 22–32; 1995, 23–5).

It is important to note that the term *obeah* in its original sense meant a man or woman who was essentially a magical practitioner, combining herbalism, divination, and spirit-healing. He or she was able to summon up both the good and bad spirits on behalf of the client. As Ndoki among the Kongo, *obeah* thus originally meant a spiritual power that could be accessed through spirit-possession or myal, and harnessed for both positive (healing) as well as for malevolent purposes (Hall 1985, 278; Besson 2002, 242). In the hands of the myalist and native Baptist priests, the term *obeah*, however, came to be identified with sorcery and malevolent practices.

In the 1970s, Chevannes (1978) considered that Revivalism was a 'disappearing religion' in Jamaica and was no longer an important factor in the religious life of the people. But in recent years, both in rural and urban areas, there has been something of a resurgence of 'Revivalism', yet it is mainly in the form of Revival Zion, which repudiates the more African elements of Revivalism. In her excellent ethnographic study of Martha Brae, Jean Besson recorded that 'Baptist Christianity' and Revival ideology coexisted and were often complementary but though the latter had important healing functions, it was hardly a flourishing cult. During her fieldwork over thirty years, only three Revival tabernacles existed, and by the 1990s, two of these tabernacles had declined. Moreover, Revivalism in the village was in the form of Revival Zion, and there was, as with African pentecostalists, an emphasis on healing through the holy spirit and a repudiation of both obeah (equated with sorcery) and Pukumina, with its emphasis on the spirits of the dead (the ancestors). It seems to have taken on the role of an anti-witchcraft cult and tended to 'demonize' African religious forms as being opposed to the divine spirit. Revival Zion is thus a form of Christianity, with an emphasis on spirit-healing and spirit-possession. Besson emphasizes that Revival Zion reflects a mode of 'culture-building' and represents, like the Baptist Church and Rastafari, a 'culture of resistance' in opposition to "Euro-American hegemony" (Besson 2002, 240–75). 'Culture-building', of course, is not unique to the Jamaican Revivalists but is a capacity of humans, expressed throughout history, as Herskovits (1958a) long ago stressed; and Besson offers little illustration of how Revival Zionism actually challenges western hegemony, especially as expressed through Christianity, the capitalist market economy, and the post-colonial state. It seems to oppose, rather, much of its own African legacy. (On the Revivalist tradition, see also Simpson 1956; Schuler 1979.)

Chevannes tends to see Rastafari as the latest manifestation of Revivalism or, as he puts it, Revivalism has 'remained alive in the Rastafari movement' (1994, 21). But what is important about Rastafari is its distinctiveness as a religious movement, distinct from both Christianity and the folk religion of the Jamaican peasantry while having its roots in both. But let me turn now to the Rastafari as a new religious movement.

6.5. THE RASTAFARI MOVEMENT

Although as a religious movement Rastafari is difficult to encapsulate, it is often depicted as a messianic movement based on the notion that life in Jamaica is a kind of exile. Its emergence has been closely linked, by many observers, to the extreme poverty in Jamaica and to the low status, deprivation, and racial denigration experienced by the majority of the Jamaican peasantry. It has its roots, however, in the slums of Kingston. The novelist V. S. Naipaul gave a succinct, early impressionistic account of the movement when he wrote this:

> The sects known as Rastafarians or 'Rastas' have developed their own psychology of survival. They reply to rejection with rejection. They will not cut their hair or wash; and for this neglect of the body, this expression of profound self-concept they find Biblical sanction. Many will not work, turning necessity into principle; and many console themselves with marijuana, which God himself smokes. They will vote for no party, because Jamaica is not their country and the Jamaican government not one they recognize. Their country is Ethiopia, and they worship Ras Tafari, the Emperor Haile Selassie. They no longer wish to be part of that world which has no place for them – Babylon. (1962, 216)

The acknowledged forerunner and the guiding inspiration of the Rastafari movement was the radical reformer Marcus Garvey (1887–1940), who was born in Jamaica – though the exact connection between Garvey and the early 'Rastas' is somewhat unclear. Widely travelled, Garvey organized in 1914 the Universal Negro Improvement Society in Kingston. Critical of the colonial system that had dispersed, exploited, and humiliated African peoples, Garvey's political aims were essentially threefold: to restore the political integrity of Africa (Ethiopia) as world power; to develop educational and cultural institutions that would enhance the self-esteem and thus 'uplift' the stature of black people; and to create the conditions and facilities for the return of black people to Africa. Garvey's appeal was psychological as well as political, for he advanced a plebian form of capitalism and endeavoured to challenge and supplant what Nettleford has described as 'the persistent denigration of the African presence' in Jamaica (Owens 1976, ix).

Although Garvey's 'Back-to-Africa' schemes never materialized, and when he died in 1940 many of his dreams remained unfulfilled, the 'ethos' of his movement was sustained in Jamaica.

In his writings and speeches, Garvey proclaimed the cultural integrity, indeed the superiority, of African civilization. Ethiopianism, a term first adopted in 1784 by George Liele in founding the first Ethiopian Baptist Church, thus became a watchword and a messianic call to the glory of things to come, although it is worth noting that Garvey never visited Africa, and his knowledge of the continent was biblically based (Barrett 1977, 79).

Much has been written on the life and politics of Marcus Garvey and his relationship to the Rastafari. He was a strange kind of radical who preached racial purity, and preferred the Ku Klux Klan to black radicals like W. E. B. Dubois, and described himself as the 'first fascist'. Although born a Catholic, he sought to create an autonomous religious institution, the African Orthodox Church, which emphasized that Africans should worship God in their own image – as black. His 'Back-to-Africa' scheme was not so much an advocacy of a mass exodus of black people to Africa but rather a scheme to 'civilize' the 'backward tribes' of Africa and to strengthen the independence of African states (Wilson 1973, 64; Mackie 1987, 19).

In his discussion of Garvey's movement, Chevannes emphasizes a number of key themes: the notion of 'Africa for the Africans' – which under the name of Ethiopia represented both a homeland and a source of identity; Garvey's advocacy of a 'Back-to-Africa' scheme, which implied a stress on the decolonization of Africa; an emphasis on racial consciousness and the unity of African peoples; and, finally, a stress on self-reliance and self-respect and a repudiation of all acts of deference or subservience towards whites (1994, 91–9). But Chevannes, noting the many myths that surround Garvey, suggests that whatever his shortcomings, Garvey did not regard himself as either divine or an inspired visionary (1994, 99).

There are few figures of the last century, Liz Mackie writes, who can be said 'to have envisaged so much, completed so little, and inspired so many' as Marcus Garvey (1987, 9). For although his 'Back-to-Africa' scheme failed, and his many other economic enterprises floundered, and his many years of involvement in Jamaican politics bore precious little fruit, nevertheless it is difficult to find a black political activist who influenced and inspired so many peoples of the African diaspora as Garvey, as well, of course, as influencing such African Nationalists as Kenyatta and Nkrumah. Even his harshest critics, like C. L. R. James and W. E. B. Dubois, celebrated Garvey's contribution – particularly as a propagandist – to what Horace Campbell describes as the 'struggles for black liberation' (1985, 53–65; Chevannes 1995, 29; for further studies of Garvey, see Cronon 1962; Burkett 1978; Stein 1986; Lewis 1987).

But what is crucial in the present context is that Garvey's movement provided 'one of the ideological foundations of the Rastafari religion' (Chevannes 1994, 87).

Scattered groups of Marcus Garvey's followers were to be found throughout Jamaica when, in 1930, Rastafari was crowned emperor of Ethiopia and took the name *Haile Selassie* [power of the trinity]. He also took the title 'king of kings, conquering lion of the tribe of Judah, Elect of God and Light of the World'. This event, which was taken to have a crucial significance among many such groups, also recalled a statement that Garvey was supposed to have made on leaving for America: 'Look to Africa for the crowning of a Black King, he shall be the redeemer' (Barrett 1977, 81; Chevannes 1994, 42). Three men in particular, all ministers – Leonard Howell, Archibald Dunkley, and Joseph Hibbert – independently of each other began claiming to have received the revelation that the newly crowned king of Ethiopia was the Messiah of the black people. Thus the Rastafari movement began – initially in the slums of Kingston. The majority of the early Rastafarians came from the landless and small-scale peasant cultivators who had migrated into Kingston during the 1930s, and they adopted the social ethos of the peasantry. This entailed an emphasis on self-employment and independence and a reluctance to engage in wage-labour – although employment opportunities were then generally scarce (Chevannes 1994, 44–77).

Leonard Howell has been described as the very first preacher of Rastafari and the first to introduce the notion that Ras Tafari was the 'living god'. Born in Jamaica in 1898, he had travelled widely, serving as a soldier in both Panama and West Africa before being discharged from the U.S. Army in 1923. Howell returned to Jamaica in 1932, having earned a living running a local bakery. Coming under the influence of the black nationalist George Padmore, he was fiercely anti-colonial, and he began his ministry in the slums of Kingston and immediately drew a following. He went around selling photographs of Haile Selassie, stressing his divine status – and was in 1934 arrested for sedition, along with Dunkley and Hibbert. He was sentenced to two years' imprisonment. On his release, Howell formed the 'Ethiopian Salvation Society' and around 1940, in order to avoid police harassment, formed a commune at Pinnacle, in the parish of St. Catherine. A charismatic figure, Howell formed a community of believers, and it was here that the smoking of *ganja* [marijuana or *Cannabis sativa*] began as a religious rite. Indeed, Chevannes describes Howell as both autocratic and the first 'ganja farmer'; he was also reputed to have thirteen wives. It was here too that male members of the Rastafari cults began to grow their hair in locks – now known as 'dreadlocks'. Howell and members of the commune were continually harassed by the police and often imprisoned. In 1954, the police yet again raided the Pinnacle commune and arrested Howell, along with about 160 of his followers. Howell this time was acquitted, but members of the commune were dispersed and the commune itself destroyed. Having suffered much from the colonial state, Howell spent the remainder of his life in seclusion, only a few miles from the Pinnacle estate (Barrett 1977, 81–8; Chevannes 1994, 121–4).

Although the occulist Joseph Hibbert and Archibald Dunkley – who expressed a strong aversion towards the Revivalist practice of spirit-possession – were important in the emergence of Rastafari (Chevannes 1994, 124–6), it was Howell who was the 'real hero' in the establishment of the movement (Barrett 1977, 91). Also important was Robert Hinds, a follower of both Bedward and Garvey, who founded the King of Kings Mission, which was organized like a Revivalist group. Regarded by his followers as a prophet, Hinds' mission in its heyday had over 800 members, including many women, and put a focal emphasis on fasting and baptism. But when he died in 1950, Hinds had not one single faithful devotee left to attend him, and he was given a pauper's funeral (Chevannes 1994, 126–42).

By the 1950s there existed several groups of Rastafari in Kingston, all of which emphasized the key features of the new movement – the recognition of Ras Tafari (Haile Selassie) as the true and living god, the smoking of ganja, the wearing of dreadlocks, and the utilization of Rasta-talk. They also expressed their opposition to the colonial state and advocated, as a basic human right, repatriation to Africa. In 1958, under the leadership of Prince Emmanuel Edwards, a large convention [*nyabinghi*] of Rastafari was held at Back-o-Wall, one of the slum areas of Kingston. Around 300 Rastafari attended. The meetings consisted of dancing and drumming and the ritual smoking of ganja but at the end of the two weeks, hundreds of Rastas marched to the Central Square of the city, planted a flag, and symbolically 'captured' the city in the name of Haile Selassie. The convention and this episode gave the Rastafari much publicity and in the ensuing months there was much tension between the government and the Rastafari. Many Rastafari were arrested for using ganja, and Prince Emmanuel Edwards' camp in Back-o-Wall was burnt to the ground by the police. Chevannes notes that many Rastafari had sold off their belongings, expecting to be transported to Africa at the end of convention. Given police harassment and loss of support among the Rastas, Prince Emmanuel retreated with his followers to form a small utopian community on a hill some nine miles east of Kingston, an autonomous group known as the *Bobos* (Chevannes 1995, 12–13).

A year after the convention – in 1959 – another millennarian episode took place, instigated by a visionary, Claudius Henry. Jamaican by birth, Henry had lived for many years in the United States and had been involved in the Ethiopian World Federation. In 1958, he returned to Jamaica and quickly established himself as the leader of a Rastafari church, the African Reform Church. He announced himself as god's prophet, setting himself up as the 'Moses of the Blacks' and began selling blue cards, at the price of one shilling, that would guarantee the buyer a return to Africa – the promised land. In October 1959, hundreds of Rastafari brethren flocked to Kingston in anticipation of their repatriation to Africa – but the promised emigration to Ethiopia did not take place. The prophecy failed. Henry was later arrested, but he was seen more as a religious fanatic than a political agitator and was bound over to keep the peace and fined £100. But a year later, an arms cache was found in his church in Kingston, along with letters to Fidel Castro, and Henry, together with several of his followers, was charged with treason and, after a long and stormy trial, sent to prison for six years – but not before events took a more violent turn, for Henry's son Ronald returned from the United States and is alleged to have set up a guerrilla base in the Red Hills overlooking Kingston. During the police raid in June 1960, two British soldiers were killed, and subsequently Ronald Henry and four of his men were captured and sentenced to death (Barrett 1977, 95–9; Morrish 1982, 73–5).

These tragic events had a profound impact on the Rastafari movement, as well as on the Jamaican public, who came to perceive the Rastas as 'violent cultists' (Campbell 1985, 103). This led the government, at the request of the Rastafari, to set up an independent study into the Rastafari movement. The result was the famous 'Report on the Rastafari Movement in Kingston' – one of the first scholarly treatments of the Rastafari in Jamaica (Smith, Augier, and Nettleford 1960).

During the 1970s, when many scholars were conducting ethnographic research on the Rastafari, there were many different and rather independent groups identifying themselves as Rastafari. Indeed, Ivor Morrish suggests that there was no single Rastafari Movement, but rather a heterogeneous collection of different religious groupings, and that they exhibited many different shades of political opinion. Many claimed to be non-political and non-subversive, although they had no wish to co-operate or compromise with the government. Others, such as the Rasfarian group of Samuel Brown, actively engaged in electoral politics (Morrish 1982, 76–80). In giving an account of two Rastafari groups, the Bobo community associated with Prince Emmanuel Edwards and the Hola Coptic Church, Chevannes tends to stress not their distinctiveness as Rastafari but their affinities with Revivalism (1994, 171–96).

The general characteristics of the Rastafari membership were summarized by Barrett, who suggested that in the early 1970s the membership, including sympathizers, numbered around 70,000; that most of the members were male, aged between seventeen and thirty-five, and that women tended to play a minor role in the Rastafari Movement; and, finally, that membership was essentially lower class and almost a hundred per cent of African background. Although the Rastas considered Jamaica as a land of oppression – Babylon – and could be considered 'products of the slums', from 1965 the Rastafari came to be particularly associated with the youth of the educated middle classes and were often frustrated young people from the secondary school and the university (Barrett 1977, 2–3).

The subsequent history of the Rastafari Movement – its relationship with the Jamaican government, its response to the death of Haile Selassie in 1975, its profound and creative impact on Jamaican culture (music, arts, and literature), and finally, its spread among black communities in Britain and elsewhere – has been the subject of numerous studies and so need not be outlined here. Particularly significant has been the impact of reggae music and 'dreadlocks' as a hairstyle among urban youth worldwide. Indeed, reggae music, associated particularly with folk hero Bob

Marley, has been a powerful medium in communicating the spirit and message of Rastafari outside Jamaica. In many ways it has countered the negative image of Rastafari as being associated with street gangs, violence, and crime (Barrett 1977, 185–97; Chevannes 1994, 273; Savishinsky 1999; Zips 2001). But it is worth exploring, however briefly, some of the essential characteristics and tenets of the Rastafari Movement, drawing particularly on the writing of Barrett (1977) and Chevannes (1994). This is the subject of the next section.

6.6. RASTAFARI BELIEFS AND PRACTICES

The key tenet of all Rastafari is the belief that Haile Selassie is the true and living god – a messiah of the black people. And it will be through his living presence that the African people will be redeemed and returned to their homeland – Ethiopia. God is black and immanent in both Ras Tafari, the emperor of Ethiopia, and in every person. As Cashmore put it, for Rastafari 'God is both a deity and inherent in all men' (1979, 6). The name Rastafari is thus applied by the brethren both to God (Ras Tafari) and to themselves and, when asked their name, many Rastas simply reply 'Rastafari' and nothing more. There is thus a conviction that a person is an aspect of god [*jah*] (Owens 1976, 130). In this emphasis on God, the Rastafari differ fundamentally from Revivalists and African religions generally and have affinities to esoteric Christianity. But with its messianic message, repatriation of Rastafari exiles is ensured. As Owens writes in his sensitive study of Rastafari, 'The continent of Africa is the promised land in the Rastafarian proclamation of redemption' (1976, 222). Many observers have stressed that Rastafari was a messianic movement, neither a flight into mysticism nor an explicitly political movement, but rather a 'politico-religious messianic movement' (Hurbon 1986, 174). Indeed, Barrett begins his account of the Rastafari cult by suggesting that it is 'a messianic movement unique to Jamaica' (1977, 1).

In recent years, however, the imminent nature of this repatriation has been less emphasized and thus its millennial tendency has become less pronounced. Whether the movement will eventually develop into a separatist sect or church, it is difficult to say, but Barrett suggests that the establishment of a Rastafari church is a possibility (1977, 219) – although in fact nothing has yet emerged. Hurbon, however, was struck by the similarities between Rastafari and Kimbanguism (1986, 163). Many Rastafari became associated with the Ethiopian Orthodox Church when it was established in Jamaica in 1969, although many Rastas repudiated its emphasis on baptism and death and its ecclesiastical structure. The fact that the Ethiopian Orthodox Church had nothing to say about the divinity of Haile Selassie gave it even less appeal to many Rastafari (Barrett 1977, 206-7).

As with many other millennarian–type movements, Rastafari has been interpreted as a creative response, or reaction, to the grinding poverty and deprivation experienced by the Jamaican peasantry and slum dwellers. As Barrett puts it, 'the movement was born in colonial oppression and structured itself in the slums' (1977, 110).

Although in many ways reacting against pentecostalism and orthodox Christianity, Rastafari nonetheless use the Bible as a key scripture; but they mainly use it as 'book of symbols' to be interpreted. Many of the basic tenets and practices of the movement have their sanction in scriptural quotations, particularly drawn from the books of Isaiah and Revelation. Indeed, Joseph Owens suggests that the Bible has a pre-eminent place in the religious life of the Rastafari because they look on the Bible as written by and for black people, identifying themselves as the ancient Israelites. According to the Rastafari, God's chosen people are black and Europeans, after enslaving Africans, simply appropriated the sacred scriptures. The brethren's reliance on the Bible gives them scope to interpret and understand the present world (Owens 1976, 30–44). And through the use of biblical imagery, contemporary Jamaican society is conceived as Babylon – a land of violence and oppression that is beyond redemption. They thus make a radical dichotomy between Babylon, identified with oppression and exile in Jamaica, and Zion, the promised land. This critique is extended to western culture itself. Basing their interpretation on the prophecy of David, many Rastafari believe that whites are destined to destroy themselves, either through ecological degradation or with nuclear weapons, after which blacks will rightly and justly inherit the earth. In many ways they simply echo and appropriate the western ecological critique of capitalism. As with Christianity, the Rastafari base their teachings and practices on the Bible, but they interpret the Bible as containing hidden truths and see it essentially as a history of the black people (Chevannes 1994, 116–18).

The Rastafari express very strongly a communitarian and egalitarian ethos. The movement has always been loosely structured, without hierarchy, and it is only in the concept of 'I-am-I' and the belief that God is inherent in all humans that the Rastafari have articulated any structure to what has essentially been an amorphous cult movement. Cashmore even eschews the term 'Rastafarianism' as the 'ism' gives the movement a coherence in doctrine and organization that it does not possess (1979, 8–9). But the concept 'I-am-I' does create contradictions with respect to the notion that black people are God's anointed. However, in its openness to whites, in its non-violent creed, and in its universal character, the Rastafari movement has been seen as generous and exemplary. Barrett has suggested that the 'brotherhood' denoted by 'I-am-I' goes beyond the personalism of Martin Buber and the Quaker doctrine, as well as introducing the idea of socialism into Jamaica – which is debatable (1977, 144–5). But the Rastafarian concept seems to reflect a viewpoint that has been expressed throughout history by communitarians and religious anarchists (see Rexroth 1975). In many respects, the Rastafari have affinities to the religious anarchists, although charismatic authority is an essential ingredient of the movement. Moreover, the Rastafari have a strong patriarchal emphasis, and the subordination of women to men is a general characteristic of the movement and was especially so during the early period. Morrish asserted that it was a 'predominately male cult' (1982, 83). Many writers have thus discussed this emphasis on male supremacy and stressed the 'pecularity' of the Rastas in their ideological and ritual subordination of women, which is linked to beliefs about women's natural inferiority and power to contaminate men. The Bobo dreadlocks described by Chevannes certainly emphasize charismatic authority and gender inequality – women in the commune being confined to looking after children and performing household chores, and they were expected to show deference towards men (1994, 176–7). Some scholars have seen this emphasis on patriarchy, and the facts that women play little part in rituals and must show such deference, as a reaction against the matrifocal emphasis of the Jamaican peasant family. Although in recent years Rastafari women have become increasingly vocal in challenging their subordination, nevertheless Rastas express a general antipathy towards feminism, as well as towards homosexuality and birth control (Cashmore 1979, 78–9; Chevannes 1995, 15; on the role of women in the Rastafari Movement, see also Kitzinger 1969; Rowe 1980; Campbell 1985, 199–200).

It has been said that there is a dearth of religious ritual among the Rasta Fari compared, that is, with Christianity and Revivalism. The most important ceremonial occasion is the Nyabinghi, which is held to commemorate events that are sacred to the Rastafari. The term is derived from *Nyabinghi*, which was a religio-political cult that resisted colonial domination in Uganda in the last decade of the nineteenth century. It was also a term that came to suggest a secret organization, Nyabinghi, that swore on oath 'death to the whites' (Chevannes 1994, 167). But in the contemporary setting, it essentially refers to Rastafari ritual meetings, otherwise known as *groundation*, a conflation of the words 'ground' and 'foundation' (Morrish 1982, 83). The typical Nyabinghi meetings were held monthly or on specific occasions, such as to mark the coronation or birthday of Haile Selassie. They began in the early evening and would last for an entire night or extend for several days with prayers, readings from the Bible, dancing, the smoking of ganja, and feasting. The meetings brought together brethren from all parts of Jamaica. The other kind of ritual is more informal and consists of a small gathering of brethren who share the smoking of the sacred weed, ganja, and engage in what is described as 'reasoning' (Chevannes 1995, 17). Morrish compares this communal ganja smoking to the smoking of a 'peace pipe' among Native Americans (1982, 83). Yet although there is very little in the way of formal rituals among the Rastafari – and they repudiate baptism and funerary rituals – nevertheless there are crucial rituals focussed around the individual person and the body. These relate to the growing of dreadlocks, the smoking of ganja, and certain food prohibitions.

Rastafari are easily recognized by their beards and long hair – grown to form dreadlocks. According to Owens, beards and locks were cultivated by the Rastas because they were seen as the fullest expression of a natural lifestyle: 'The locks and beards are a sign of the anciency of the ways of the Rastafarians' (1976, 155).

The cultivation of dreadlocks was seen as sanctioned by the Bible (e.g., Leviticus 21:5, Numbers 6:5). Chevannes suggests that the wearing of dreadlocks came into prominence particularly in the 1940s with the Youth Black Faith, and thus Rastafari became synonymous with bearded men. The Youth Black Faith wore dreadlocks to symbolize their rejection of society, as well as to express a revolt against the Revivalist tradition. It was believed that only those who wore beards would be repatriated (1994, 154–7) (for an interesting discussion of the symbolism of dreadlocks in Jamaica, see also Chevannes 1995, 97–126).

The smoking of ganja (*Cannabis sativa*) was also a key element of Rastafari religion; and the sacred nature of the ganja herb was accepted by all Rastafari. The herb was either smoked as a pipe or drunk as an infusion – and was considered to be both a refreshment and a healing remedy. Ganja was also believed to induce wisdom and understanding, to help communing with the brethren by provoking tranquillity and peacefulness, as well as being of assistance in what was described as 'reasoning'. For the brethren placed much emphasis, indeed esteem, on the powers of the intellect and on reasoning. Owens suggests that their 'reasoning sessions', involving the communal smoking of ganja, was the Rastafari 'prime mode of worship' (1976, 157–62, 185–7). Needless to say, it was the smoking of ganja that brought the Rastafari continually into conflict with the Jamaican government.

The third aspect of Rastafari personal rituals is the emphasis on *I-tal* [natural] food and the ritual avoidance of many foods that were not considered natural. The Rastafari, in varying degrees, refrain from drinking alcohol (which is associated with aggression), using salt in their cooking, eating meat (which is associated with sexuality), and even express a revulsion for chickens and goats that, like the pig, are associated with scavenging (Kitzinger 1969, 241). All this is linked by Owens to the concern of the Rastafari 'for fidelity to earth and nature', but it also indicates a repudiation of African cultural traditions, which puts a crucial emphasis on beer-drinking and animal life (Morris 2000). Owens goes on to suggest that the Rastafari express a viewpoint that is essentially naturalistic and ecological, for like the early romantics, they take a positive attitude towards nature and organic life. Being largely a verbal culture, Rastafari have few theoreticians to articulate their philosophy; but in their discussions with Owens, they appear to view themselves as the 'ancients', and they acknowledge an urgent need to develop a culture that will restore to them the intimacy with nature that people knew in the 'ancient days'. Even their dreadlocks are seen as a sign of their ancient longings. Nature, Owens concludes, 'is a basic concept in the Rastafarian creed', and the Rastafari see themselves as a people devoted to nature and the good earth, who emphasize the need for a piece of land to cultivate and are against the private ownership of land, allowing only usufruct rights (Owens 1976, 144–52, 166–7). But the Rastafari relationship to land is more spiritual than ecological, for they deny that predation and scavenging are a part of nature. Yet though affirming that they are vegetarians and non-violent, the key image that they promote of themselves is, ironically, that of a lion – aggressive, proud, dominant, dreadful, and they 'simulate the spirit of the lion in the way they wear their locks and in the way they walk' (Barrett 1977, 142).

There has been much debate on the political dimension of the Rastafari Movement, and whether it was essentially apolitical and offered simply spiritual redemption or whether it was a revolutionary movement. Morrish suggests it was more of an 'escapist movement' than a revolutionary one (1982, 84). Some scholars have suggested that in the 1960s, during a third phase in the development of the movement, Rastafari became 'politicized'. But it is worth noting that the 1960s was a time of widespread radical political engagement – with the counterculture movement that culminated in the Paris uprising in 1968, the nationalist struggles for political liberation in Africa, and the civil rights movement in the United States. The diffusion of Rastafari within Jamaican lower-class culture coincided with this 'great awakening' or upsurge in radical politics, and Stuart Hall suggests that Rastafari provided the form for an indigenous – Jamaican – black cultural nationalism, and so functioned as a 'revolutionising ideological force' (1985, 289). The notion that in the 1960s the Rastafari underwent a 'metamorphosis into a revolutionary force' has, however, been questioned by other scholars, who stress the diversity of political opinions within the Rastafari movement (Cashmore 1979, 35–6). Although many Rastas were consistently anti-state politically, and often refused to associate themselves with revolutionary political movements (Kitzinger 1969, 248), nevertheless, as Campbell (1980) has argued, the Rastafari, as with the Zionist churches in South Africa, can clearly be interpreted as a 'culture of resistance'. For in their repudiation of white supremacy and white racism, in their anti-colonial and anti-imperialist stance, and in their critique of contemporary capitalist society in Jamaica (as Babylon), the Rastafari offered a radical critique of existing institutions, even though expressed in religious form.

As a form of socio-political protest, Rastafari has since the 1970s spread throughout the world, greatly facilitated by the commodification of culture and the global expansion of transnational popular music, particularly in relation to the appeal of reggae. The wearing of dreadlocks, the smoking of ganja, listening to reggae music, and socio-political protest now have a widespread appeal – although they do not necessarily imply an adherence to Rastafari. In the process, the deification of Haile Selassie and the idea of repatriation to Africa have tended to be downplayed. But Savishinsky rightly notes the similarities between the Rastafari and many of the new religious movements in Africa – such as Kimbanguism and the Zionist churches in South Africa – for many of these groups 'expressed a belief in a black God; prophesied the coming of a black messiah who would usher in the kingdom of God and a golden age of prosperity free from domination; identified their group with the Biblical Hebrews; and finally were highly critical of European civilization and the destructive elements introduced into their societies by the white man' (1999, 358).

Important with both the Rastafari and the new religious movements in Africa is their syncretic nature and their repudiation of many aspects of indigenous African belief and practice. Although Chevannes continually emphasizes the affinities between Rastafari and Revivalism, stressing their continuity, it is clear from his own account that the Rastafari express a radical break with the earlier African-based folk religion – Revivalism. As he writes, the emergence of Rastafari in Jamaica marks 'a radical departure from the African tradition' and all that had gone before it (1995, 29–30) – as well as from Christianity. For the Rastafari put a central emphasis on God [*jah*]; express little concern for the spirits of the dead (ancestors); repudiate animal sacrifices, beer-drinking, and spirit-possession (all of which are key aspects of African rituals); and do not engage in either baptism or funerary rituals (so central to Revivalism). He writes of the Rastafari as constituting a 'revolt' against the Revivalist tradition (1994, 154). Rather oddly, Jean Besson, following Chevannes, suggests that the Rastafari can be regarded as the 'fulfilment of Revival' through the 'rejection' of it (2002, 273). Paradoxically, of course, while repudiating many aspects of African religious culture, the Rastafari have been interpreted as forging a new African identity for the working people of Jamaica and other Caribbean Islands (Hurbon 1986, 164). (For other studies of Rastafari not mentioned in the text, see Nettleford 1970; Clarke 1986; Lewis 1993; the essays in Chevannes 1995; and Legesse' interesting discussion [1994] of Rastafari as a prophetic movement without a prophet.)

6.7. RELIGIONS OF BRAZIL

Brazil is the fifth largest country in the world, with a land mass larger than that of Europe. At the end of the nineteenth century, it had a population of around 17 million: It is now more than 170 million, the majority of Brazilians – around eighty per cent – living in the crowded cities of the Atlantic coast – Belem, Sao Luis, Recife, Salvador, Rio de Janeiro, and São Paulo. The massive influx of rural migrants into the urban areas last century began before the development of industrial capitalism and as this was capital rather than labour-intensive, in the Brazilian cities there is now high unemployment, extensive poverty, and extreme social and economic inequalities. In 1995, for example, the poorest twenty per cent of the population – some 32 million people – received only 2.5 per cent of the national income. Thus, as Sidney Greenfield writes, 'vast and ever-growing numbers of people live in squatter settlements, generally known as favelas', without adequate housing and transport, water, sewage, or the means of basic livelihood. Endemic and chronic diseases are thus rife (2001, 55–8). Under these conditions, rather than seeing the decline of religion in Brazil, as suggested by early modernization theory, in recent decades there has been a great upsurge and diversification of religious traditions in the country. What has thus emerged, Greenfield suggests, is something akin to a 'religious marketplace' where different religious groups compete – each offering material or spiritual rewards to its devotees and potential members. A situation of 'religious pluralism' is thus now characteristic of Brazilian social and cultural life (Willems 1969; Greenfield 2001, 56).

The dominant religion of Brazil is the Catholic Church, and although only about fifteen per cent of the population are practising Catholics, most Brazilians – apart from those who adhere to the strict Protestant sects – think of themselves as Catholics. It has the status almost of an established church, and Emilio Willems suggests that Catholicism has historically been bound up with Brazilian nationalism. During the nineteenth century, Roman Catholicism became almost the 'state church' and was associated particularly with the upper classes, who saw themselves as carriers of the national culture (Willems 1969, 196–201). But although opposed by the Catholic Church, Protestant sects began to emerge and flourish, particularly after the Second World War, and by the 1960s there were over 4 million Protestants in Brazil (Willems 1969, 203). They represent now about ten per cent of the population, the majority being Pentecostalists (Hess 1991, 14).

On Brazil's becoming a republic at the end of the nineteenth century, the Catholic Church lost its monopoly of religious expression, and the practice of other religions in Brazil – the African-derived candomble (in its many forms), spiritism, and the Protestant sects – was legally recognized. Nevertheless, these other religions were subject to varying degrees of official opposition and disapproval, as well as informal harassment, disparagement, and repression, until well into the twentieth century (Willems 1969, 196; Greenfield 2001, 62). During the Vargas dictatorship (1930–1945), when President Vargas formed a close relationship with the Catholic Church, there was widespread police repression of all the religions that involved spirit-mediums 'from the most African of the Candomble Terreiros to the most European of the spiritist centres' (Hess 1994, 74).

But during the past half century, as noted, practitioners of non-Catholic religions have greatly increased, and the number and variety of religious groups–movements in Brazil have also grown apace. Greenfield suggests that the emergence of these various religions represents an 'adaptive strategy' with regard to the poverty, insecurity, and suffering experienced by many Brazilians in urban areas. It is, however, important to note, as the pioneering sociologist Roger Bastide (1951) described, that Catholicism as practised by ordinary people in Brazil was distinct from the formal Catholicism of the Church. For it was a form of folk Catholicism that put a focal emphasis on the cult of the saints, miracles, processions, and pilgrimages. It was a form of propitiatory ritualism with therapeutic aims, and the relationship of the devotee to the saint was one of exchange and was akin to patron–client relationships in the wider society. Thus in return for acts of penance, prayers, and devotion, the saint was expected to offer the devotee help and support in seeking, for example, employment or overcoming an illness.

Roger Bastide long ago suggested that the situation in Brazil with regard to African-derived religious movements was complex and diverse, and that there were in fact 'three different Brazils' – white, black, and Indian or Caboclo (1971, 19). The religious cults that have emerged in Brazil, though largely syncretic, show therefore a wide variation in their cultural content and rituals, according to the locality in which they are found. Although in many ways there is a continuum in these different religious forms, anthropologists have generally recognized four distinct types of religious cults or movements in Brazil – distinct, that is, from both the Protestant sects and Catholicism. These are Catimbo, Candomblé, Umbanda, and Spiritism. I discuss only the first two movements, although in making this typology, anthropologists do not intend the reification of such social phenomena. Yet one can but concur with Bryan Wilson that the diversity of religions in Brazil and the mutations and variants of their practices and beliefs make any systematic categorization rather problematic (1973, 11). But it is worth emphasizing that in each of these four religions, spirit rituals involving possession are of focal importance, and all put an emphasis on the healing of afflictions. They thus have affinities to the cults of affliction found throughout Africa and that Lewis (1971) described as peripheral possession cults – although, with regard to the Umbanda and Spiritism, they are hardly 'religions of the oppressed' (Lanternari 1963). In this final section, I focus on Catimbo and Candomblé religious forms. (On Umbanda and Spiritism, see Brown 1979, 1986; Hess 1991, 1994; Motta 2001.)

Catimbo

A syncretic religion found in Northeast Brazil, Catimbo is one of the most widespread religions of the region, in spite of being officially banned for many years. It derives its name, Catimbo, from the pipe that is used to smoke tobacco as it is through the use of tobacco, usually shunned by other forms of African–Brazilian worship, that devotees of Catimbo make contact with the spirits. Whereas among African–Brazilian cults a state of trance is usually induced by drumming and dancing, in Catimbo the smoking of tobacco is important as a ritual stimulant (Bastide 1971, 83). Tobacco smoke is also used as a form of ritual blowing, as with the Akawaio, in the simplest form of healing ritual. Catimbo is reckoned to be the oldest and most widespread of the popular religious cults of Brazil, having emerged some three centuries ago in the villages [*aldeia*] of the Native Americans, who had been converted, at least nominally, by the Portuguese. Since then it has spread to such cities as Recife, Salvador, and Rio de Janeiro.

Catimbo is focussed essentially around Native American (Indian) spirits, the Caboclo, a term that has many different meanings. Usually it is used to refer to a Brazilian peasant, a *mestizo* from mixed white and Native American parentage, but in Brazilian religion its specific reference is a category of spirit entities – healing spirits of supposedly Native American, or at least Brazilian, ancestry. Although the Caboclos, as time-honoured spirits, are also venerated in other African–Brazilian ritual centres, such as those of Candomblé and Umbanda, they are of central importance in Catimbo, and their ritual practitioners [*catimbozeiros*] generally look on their rituals as specifically Indian or Caboclo (Motta, 2001, 73). Nevertheless, they generally incorporate into their rituals various other spirits, such as mestres, gypsies, and spirits of African origin. Although their rituals seem to exclude drumming, Catimbo ceremonies involve invocations to the spirits, singing and dancing, and possession rites, the spirits through the medium giving support and redress in relation to problems concerning health, employment, and general well-being. Catimbo groups are focussed around a spirit-medium and are generally small, with little formal organization. Roberto Motta interprets them as quintessential 'peripheral' possession cults (2001, 73-4).

Candomblé

The plantation zone in Brazil is largely focussed around the north-eastern region, and thus in places like Salvador (Bahia), the historic first capital of Brazil and the centre of the slave 'trade', some seventy per cent of the population are of African origin. Here an African-American religious cult, Candomblé, was established in the early nineteenth century and was particularly associated with an economic system based on slave labour and large plantations of sugar. The religion subsequently spread to the larger cities, São Luis, Maceio, Recife, and Rio de Janeiro, and became essentially an urban phenomena, its adherents being mainly poor and marginal people of African origin. As an African-derived religious movement, it flourished in many of the cities of Brazil, and as a religious syncretism, the cults associated with the movement took various names – in Salvador (Bahia), it was known as Candomblé; in São Luis, Tambor de Mina; in Maceio and Recife, it was called Xango; in Rio de Janeiro and São Paulo, Macumba. All these cults have much in common, particularly the rituals centred around the possession of African deities or ancestral spirits, the Orixas (Orishas), derived specifically from the Yoruba of Nigeria.

Candomblé has been described as the 'classical' form of African–Brazilian religion and as the 'epitome of syncretism' (Sjørslev 2001, 132). For although the religion is based on or focussed around the worship of African deities, the Orixas, these spirits are syncretized or mixed with the saints of popular Catholicism, Native American spirits (Caboclos), and such possessing spirits as sailors and prostitutes, trickster figures, gypsies, and old slaves (Sjørslev 2001, 131). Many have seen Candomblé as essentially a syncretism or mixing of two religious traditions – West African religion and folk Catholicism, as with Vodou. And, like folk Catholicism, it has not been regarded as an ethical religion but rather as based on the notion of contract or exchange between the devotee or practitioner and specific deities or spirits. As Roberto Motta puts it,

> In exchange for gifts, sacrifices, and other offerings . . . the believer receives support and protection in his daily life, especially in periods of crisis. (2001, 75)

Regarded as the antithesis of rational religion (as described by Max Weber) and as not being centred on salvation, Candomblé has thus been described as being concerned with 'survival in this world'. Focussed around the feast and possession rites, singing and dancing, the essence of the religion, Motta continues, is 'the sight and smell of blood, the heads of sacrificed animals, libations of rum and joy, leading to ecstasy' (2001, 75). For as with Vodou, animal sacrifices and possession rites form the core of Candomblé religion.

The typical Candomblé group is more formally organized than that of the Catimbo and has a hierarchical structure focussed around a small ritual shrine or temple [*terreiros*]. Each temple is headed by a spirit-medium, usually described as *Pais De Santo* [father in sainthood] or *Mais De Santo* [mother in sainthood], and spirit-mediums in Candomblé are mostly women. Each Candomblé group tends to represent a particular African ethnic group or *nacio* [nation], but generally speaking, as Roberto Motta writes, 'the Yoruba tradition has dominated the beliefs and ritual practices of Brazilian Candomblé' (2001, 76).

There seems to be no such thing as a typical African–Brazilian or Candomblé religious cult as there is no centralized church and wide regional or even local variations in their constituent beliefs and ritual practices: It might therefore be useful to focus specifically on one illustrative ethnography. I thus focus on Seth and Ruth Leacock's (1975) lucid and interesting account of an African-derived religious cult in Belem, based on researches undertaken in the 1960s, even though this cult has been much influenced by Umbanda.

The city of Belem, a seaport on the Amazon, was once the 'smuggling capital' of Brazil, and its development as a city has been closely linked with the river. It has always served as an administrative and commercial centre of the Amazon Basin. But, like many other cities in Latin America, it has in recent years attracted rural migrants, and the population of the city has doubled in the past decades. To some degree isolated from the other urban centres of Brazil, Belem did not have, until the beginning of the present century, any religious movement of a specifically African origin. This is because, compared with other parts of north-eastern Brazil, the number of African slaves introduced into the state of Para was comparatively small – probably not more than 30,000. Whereas elsewhere in Brazil, African-derived religions developed wherever a large slave population was concentrated and by the early nineteenth century well-developed cults were flourishing in the larger cities, in Belem no such cults emerged – given that lower-class culture was predominantly Native American. The influx of rural migrants has changed this, and today in the lower-class neighbourhoods of Belem – many urban slums – an Umbanda-type cult flourishes, with about 140 registered cult centres.

Umbanda first appeared in Rio do Janeiro after the First World War. It was essentially the product of a combination of certain beliefs of the spiritist movement with the basic rituals and concepts of Macumba, the African-derived cult dominant in Rio at the time. Contemporary cults in Belem involve a synthesis of Umbanda with a highly syncretized cult that developed among ex-slaves in the city of São Luis, the capital city of Maranhao. The latter cult, based largely on religious practices of Dahomean and Yoruba origin, was introduced to Belem about seventy years ago. Thus contemporary Belem cults are highly syncretic and may be referred to by various names: Macumba (by outsiders), Nago (derived from the name given to the Yoruba) or Umbanda; the Leacocks use a more neutral term, Batuque, to describe this cult. The term itself is used to denote their public ceremonies.

As in Vodou, the supernatural beings that make up the Batuque pantheon are numerous and, equally important, they are of diverse origins. There are first the deities and spirits associated with the Christian Church. Batuque members accept Catholic teachings on most matters but god is looked on as a somewhat remote figure in heaven, having little interest in the petty concerns of ordinary men and women. The saints [*santo*] who once lived on earth, but who now live in heaven with God and the angels, are more inclined to notice people's problems. Each person therefore has a particular saint or several saints whom he or she is said to 'adore' and with whom a 'dyadic contract' is established: 'In return for prayers, candles and respect, each of these saints is expected to provide long-term and continuous surveillance over the well-being of his devotee' (Leacock and Leacock 1975, 58).

Among the more important saints in Belem are Our Lady of Nazareth, St. Sebastian, and the Patron-Saint of African – Brazilian cults, St. Barbara.

Unlike in Vodou, a clear distinction is made between the saints and the next category of spirits, the *encantados* [the enchanted ones]. The saints are of higher status, live in heaven, and never descend to earth to take possession of human beings. But it is the encantados that form the core of the Batuque pantheon. Sometimes referred to as *Vodun* or *Orixa* (the Dahomean and Yoruba terms for *deity*), these encantados are thought to live under the earth or in the seas and to be 'living' spirits. The nature and the location of their dwelling place vary with the type of encantado. They are equivalent to the lwa spirits in Vodou. There are many different types, and though there is a plurality of names, they are essentially organized into 'families' and 'lines'. And in their names and attributes they incorporate cultural elements drawn from many sources.

The Rei Turquia spirit family is associated primarily with the Middle East, even though several of these encantados are identified with animals and birds that were important in Native American shamanism – the macaw and jaguar, for instance. Rei Sebastiao is linked specifically with an historical figure, a Portuguese king who died in 1578 whilst on a holy crusade in Morocco. The members of the Japetequara family are the descendents of a Native American king, and these spirits are dark-skinned and live in dense forest. They are recognized by their wild and abandoned dancing. There are also many encantado spirits of African derivation, Ogun, Xango, Oxossi, and Oxala for instance. An equally important class of encantados is the *exu*, malevolent spirits who are too dangerous to cultivate. These various spirits are further subdivided into two classes, the *senhores* or high-status encantado and the caboclos. Besides referring to specifically Native American spirits, the latter term denotes encantados of lower status, who are considered rough, frank, uneducated, and lacking in sophistication.

And finally, 'at the bottom of the supernatural ladder' are the souls of the dead. Although these spirits can contact living people, they are believed to have little power and are thus not considered very important. Possession by the spirits of the dead is considered highly undesirable (Leacock and Leacock 1975, 90–2, 125–68).

As in Vodou, possession rites (focussed around the encantados) form the central aspect of the Batuque cult. According to their basic doctrine, it is the encantado who initiates a relationship with a human being, a medium being 'seized' by the spirit. Every person is a potential medium, but many devotees of the cult never become possessed and their attitude towards the spirit is similar to that towards the saints. The relationship between the encantado and a medium is likened to that between a parent and child, and the spirit is referred to as *pai* [father] or *mae* [mother].

'Encantados', write the Leacocks, 'are believed to induce rich people to make contributions to terreiros (cult houses), to cause employers to offer jobs to the faithful, to force philandering husbands to return to their families – in all cases, of course, without the coerced person recognizing that he is being manipulated' (1975, 55).

Most cult members have a shrine to their encantados in their own homes and make periodic offerings. The spirits therefore are generally looked on as beneficent supernaturals who protect and look after the welfare of their devotees. But they may also inflict misfortunes. Although, as the Leacocks suggest, the connection between the spirits and morality is somewhat tenuous, the encantados are essentially concerned with maintaining harmony within the family household and with upholding the moral precepts of the cult group. As they write, 'When adversity strikes, cult members are inclined to first consider the possibility that they have in some way offended their encantados and are consequently being punished' (1975, 74).

Batuque religion, as with Vodou, is focussed around a cult leader, who may be of either sex and who is head of a permanent cult association consisting of about thirty mediums. For the most part, people who participate in the Batuque cult are extremely poor and live difficult, sometimes desperate, lives; the mediums inevitably come from the lower class and are mainly women. But public ceremonies, which are primarily designed to enable mediums to receive their spirits, are attended by many outsiders and often constitute a public spectacle – with dancing, music, colour, excitement, and mystery. Spirit-possession plays a dominant part in these ceremonies for, as the Leacocks write, the whole belief system of the Batuque 'centres around the concept of possession . . . and is the ultimate proof that encantados really do exist'. They write perceptively and at length about these possession rites (1975, 170–217), stressing that possession is not some frenzy of uncontrolled behaviour but is something that has to be learned. Thus the ability to control oneself during trance and to behave properly as an encantado or as a specific encantado is the end-product of a development process that may take several months, or even years, to attain. During the trance state, individuals must behave in appropriate ways in order to prove that they are possessed, and there are, too, appropriate ways in which to enter and leave a trance. Their observations largely confirm what we have noted earlier, namely that mediums are relatively well-adjusted individuals, and that the essence of possession is enacting a role that although similar to hypnotism is not in itself pathological.

Again in ways similar to Vodou, Batuque cult leaders hold important curing rites, and may become implicated – given the rivalry and competition between cult leaders – with sorcery activities. Sorcery in the Belem context involves the use of magic and appealing to the malevolent exu spirits to inflict misfortunes, induced by a suitable offering (Leacock and Leacock 1975, 276).

The Leacocks stress that, compared with the Candomblé, Tambor de Mina, and Xango cults, which tend to place more emphasis on African-derived beliefs and rites, the Batuque cult is less group-oriented – divination is not so prominent, and there is less involvement in complex initiation and sacrificial rites among the Belem cults. Thus although there are many elements in the Batuque cult that have their origin in Africa, the Leacocks conclude that this cult has been 'Brazilianized', and that it represents an independent, coherent religious system that has emerged as the creative synthesis of belief and rites drawn from many diverse sources. It was thus not a 'watered-down version' of Candomblé, and its hierarchy of spirits tended to reflect the Brazilian class structure. They also emphasize the individualism expressed in the cult, the respect and deference shown towards the upper-class spirits – modelled on that of patron–client relations – and suggest they could find little evidence that the Batuque was a protest movement of any kind (1975, 316–23).

A different ideology seems to have been expressed by the Candomblé cults in Salvador (Bahia), particularly the Candomblé Nago, which emphasizes African origins and ritual practices. Within the city, there are many types of Candomblé, identified by reference to ethnic categories or 'Nations' – Gege (identified with the Ewe of Benin), Angola, Congo, Caboclo, and Nago (Yoruba). The Caboclo Candomblé, as the name suggests, are largely focussed around Native American or Brazilian spirits [*encantados*] although also incorporating African spirits and deities (Bastide 1971, 83–6). Candomblé Nago, on the other hand, which are the most numerous and most influential of the Candomblé religious associations in Salvador, are largely devoted to the preservation of 'pure' African ideas, particularly the beliefs and practices of the Yoruba (Nago). As in Vodou, there are elaborate initiation rites associated with the cult, involving animal sacrifices, the 'localizing' of the orixa spirits in specific material objects, periods of seclusion, and the induction of the cult initiate, through possession trance, into the ways of the orixa – for each spirit, such as ogum, xango, oxum, or exu, is associated with specific personality types and characteristic modes of behaviour. Each orixa also has its own specific drum beat and dances, as well as being related, as with the lwa in Vodou, to a complex system of symbolic associations (Omari 1994, 137–47). As with other Brazilian spirit-cults, the possession trance, whereby the spirit-medium is possessed and serves as a vehicle for an orixa, forms the central nexus of Candomblé Nagos religion. Emphasizing the continuity between Yoruba religion (of past centuries) and Candomblé, Mikelle Omari suggests that its membership largely consists of poor, marginal people of low economic status and of 'clear African descent' – identified with extreme curly hair and dark skin colour (1994, 157). But she also suggests that Candomblé Nago inverts the values of the Brazilian economic elite in putting an emphasis on African descent and culture and in affirming that black skin is prestigious. As a religious system, Candomblé Nago thus forms a pre-literate 'religious microcosm' that affirms African social and religious values – such as the emphasis on community – and operate as 'centres of cultural resistance' against the wider Brazilian society within which they seem to perceive themselves as 'powerless'. Thus participation in Candomblé provides its devotees with a sense of order and meaning and hope and control in what is otherwise a pattern of 'persistent adversity' and socio-economic and political marginality (Omari 1994, 147–56).

In recent years, among both Candomblé spirit-mediums and scholars, there has been a rejection of the concept of syncretism and the affirmation that Candomblé represents a 'pure' and 'authentic' form of African spirituality derived from the Yoruba. It thus reflects a continuation, indeed the 'survival', of Yoruba religious beliefs and practices in their 'pristine purity'. Candomblé is thus seen as 'purely African'. This view, however, has been challenged by recent scholars. On the one hand, they have reaffirmed the importance of the concept of syncretism – involving the intermixing, through convergence, linkage, or juxtaposition, of different religious cultures. They have thus suggested that although syncretism lacks any explanatory power, it is still a useful concept, for it has a descriptive value in referring to what happens concretely when peoples and cultures meet (Greenfield and Droogers 2001). On the other hand, various scholars have indicated in their ethnographic studies that the beliefs and rituals of African–Brazilian cults in such cities as Recife (Candomblé – Xango) and São Luis (Tambor de Mina) are indeed syncretic. For such cults focus not only on the orixa spirits of the Yoruba but also incorporate Catholic saints and many non-African spirits – Caboclo spirits of Native American origin, Turkish spirits, the spirit of the Portuguese king Dom Joao, as well as specifically Brazilian spirits, such as the cowboy (boiadeiros) (Ferretti 2001; Motta 2001). Thus Candomblé, according to Greenfield, is not a survival or continuation of some pristine Yoruba religion but is a syncretic religion that indicates how people of African descent selected and adapted 'the beliefs and practices of their ancestors to the social and political circumstances in which they found themselves in Brazil' (2001, 122).

In recent years there has been something of a 'revival' of Candomblé, given its emphasis on African rather than Brazilian identity. But rather paradoxically, though it has become a movement of ethnic fundamentalism emphasizing its pure and authentic African origins, its appeal in the 'religious marketplace' has been to consumers who are primarily white and of European descent (Motta 2001, 81).

To conclude this chapter, a brief mention is made of the striking upsurge in evangelical Christianity, particularly Pentecostalism, in Brazil over the past few decades. A study recently conducted in Rio de Janeiro concluded that around fifteen per cent of the population were evangelical Christians, mostly Assemblies of God, Baptists, Pentecostalists, and the recently expanding Brazilian church, the Universal Church of the Kingdom of God (Martin 2002, 100). Most Pentecostalists came from the least educated and poorest sections of Brazilian society. Although the Pentecostalists tend to repudiate African–Brazilian cults, branding them as work of the devil and interpreting the orixas as demons, they nevertheless have much in common with Candomblé and Umbanda. For they place a fundamental emphasis on possession by the holy spirit and on spirit-healing, though they also emphasize the authority of the Bible and place a pre-eminent value on the nuclear family. The stress that is placed on charisma and the fissiparous nature of their social organization also has affinities with the African–Brazilian religions.

7

Religions of Melanesia

7.1. PROLOGUE

In this chapter, I focus on Melanesian religion, but it is well to recall that many of the early pioneering ethnographic studies in anthropology were in fact undertaken in the Pacific region. Bronislaw Malinowski's early researches in the Trobriand Islands, Margaret Mead's classic writings on Samoa and Manus, Gregory Bateson's stimulating study of the Naven ritual among the latmul, and Raymond Firth's exemplary studies of the people of Tikopia are all well known and noteworthy (Malinowski 1922, 1974; Mead 1928, 1930; Firth 1940; Bateson 1980).

It is beyond the scope of the present study to discuss the religions of Oceania, which includes both Australasia and the Pacific Islands, a region of the world that was once romantically known to Europeans as the 'South Seas'. Anthropological studies of the region were influenced by both the colonial encounter and this fascination with the strange and exotic, and local cultural concepts such as mana and tapu soon became a constituent part of the comparative study of religion. Durkheim's monumental study, *Elementary Forms of the Religious Life* (1915), was also based on ethnographic data derived from the Australian Aborigines. But in this chapter, I focus specifically on Melanesia. (For useful studies of the religions of Australia and Oceania, more generally, see Goldman 1970; Berndt 1974; Elkin 1977; Charlesworth, Morphy, Bell, and Maddock 1984; Swain and Trompf 1995; Mageo and Howard 1996).

In contrast to both Australian Aboriginal and Polynesian religions, the 'dominant motif' of Melanesian religious systems has been described as the 'maintenance of collective material welfare' (Swain and Trompf 1995, 121). This does not imply a disinterest in mythology and the cosmic order, but it does suggest that Melanesian people have a very pragmatic orientation with respect to their religious beliefs and practices. As we shall see, this pragmatism is emphasized in the studies of both Keesing and Rappaport. As Lawrence and Meggitt suggest, Melanesian people tend to view the cosmos as a unitary physical realm with few transcendental attributes, and the 'prevailing attitude towards religion is essentially pragmatic and materialistic. Religion is a technology rather than a spiritual force for human salvation' (1965, 18).

Melanesian societies before the colonial impact were tribal societies, lacking centralized, coercive (state) institutions, and they generally lived in small villages or hamlets, the local groups based on kinship. It is, however, important to note that in pre-contact times, chiefdoms emerged on such islands as Fiji and the Trobriand Islands. They were mainly horticulturalists but hunting was important, and in coastal areas, fishing was a key occupation. Pig husbandry was also significant, and their political system focussed around 'big men', and periodic ceremonial exchanges involving pigs and shell valuables. In relation to such 'big men', there was a widespread emphasis on physical aggression, florid oratory, and the accumulation of pigs, and in many Melanesian societies there was a marked gender division. In pre-contact times, feuding between the local groups seems to have been endemic. The socio-economic life of Melanesians, and thus their religion, focussed around the fertility of people, crops, and pigs, and success in the manufacture and use of artefacts. The men's house, which often contained sacred ritual objects, was a key institution in many societies. There was a marked contrast between the people of the coastal regions that had long been in contact with the outside world, through missions, the colonial administration, and a migrant labour system – and most coastal people soon became nominal Christians – and the people of the highland region of New Guinea. Many people in the highlands were not contacted by Europeans until the 1930s.

Although there is a great diversity among Melanesian people with regard to both language and religious culture, there are patterns of beliefs and practices that are widely shared in the region. Trompf describes them as 'recurrent motifs or themes' (1991, 12). Beliefs relating to occult forces can be roughly classified into five categories, although it is worth emphasizing at the outset that all spiritual beings – gods, ghosts, ancestors, malevolent spirits, or totems – are generally described as living on the earth, often close to human settlements. And though more powerful than humans, they too often assume corporeal form (Lawrence and Meggitt 1965, 9).

The first category relates to autonomous spiritual beings, such as deities or culture-heroes, who may be conceived as creative or regulative, or sometimes both. There is wide variation in the number and significance of these spirit-beings with respect to different ethnic communities, but even though some spirits may be associated with the sky, such as among the Mae Enga and Kyaka, they are not usually conceived as transcendental. Culture-heroes are often depicted in myths as creating the cosmos, as among the Wogeo. Many ethnic communities, however, have little interest in creator-spirits and assume that the earth has always existed.

Second, there are autonomous spirits who have little creative or regulative functions and often take a malevolent form – as forest spirits, demons, or tricksters.

Third, there are the spirits of the dead, whether of the recent dead (ghosts) or ancestral spirits. While people in the highlands of New Guinea generally make a clear distinction between these two types of dead, coastal communities tend to have little regard for the more remote ancestral spirits, although this dichotomy has been questioned by some scholars (Trompf 1991, 15). Totems are often associated with the spirits of the dead but again, many communities, like the Wogeo and Tangu, have no totemic beliefs. The importance of the ancestral spirits in the religious life of Melanesians has been emphasized by many scholars, and Lanternari indeed suggested that the fundamental feature of Melanasian religion is the 'cult of ancestors' (1988, 85; Trompf 1991, 14).

Fourth, although Melanesians do not make a radical distinction between religion and magic – the harnessing of occult power for instrumental purposes – there is a general acceptance that occult forces can be controlled and utilized through sympathetic magic. But such occult forces are conceived as purely earthly powers.

Finally, among both the highland and the coastal people of Melanesia there is a widespread acceptance of sorcery – which is 'any ritual designed to kill or harm people'. The powers of magic may either lie in the ritual object or activity itself or be derived from some spirit-being (Lawrence and Meggitt 1965, 8–11).

There is little emphasis in Melanesia on formal beliefs or doctrines or on speculative knowledge for its own sake. As Robertson Smith long ago emphasized with respect to tribal religions generally, the religious conceptions and cosmological notions of Melanesians are largely expressed through rituals. The most important rituals include initiations and puberty rituals, funerary rites, fertility rites, divination, magical rites, and a host of rituals relating to ceremonial exchanges and to political relationships with other local groups. It is of interest that although boys' initiation rites play a crucial role in many Melanesian societies and are prototypical in their revelatory function – the disclosure of sacred knowledge – there is no mention of initiations in the ethnographies of Keesing and Rappaport, which we discuss later in the chapter (on initiation rites in Melanesia, see Allen 1967; Hogbin 1970; Barth 1975; Poole 1982).

There has been much debate among scholars regarding the degree to which Melanesian cosmology or religious 'order' may be viewed as a coherent integrated and stable intellectual system. This long-standing debate was evoked by a well-known article by Ron Brunton (1980), which suggested that anthropologists had greatly exaggerated the orderliness of Melanesian cosmology. In offering reflections on this debate, Harvey Whitehouse suggests that a distinction must be made between the degree of order that may be evident in specific cultural contexts in respect to the informant's 'mental representations' – which may be variable – and the order and coherence expressed by the anthropologists' own analytical models. In regard to Melanesian ethnography, these models either are derived from psychoanalysis or reflect the structuralist approach to religious symbolism – which has continually been critiqued by Frederick Barth (Gell 1975; Barth 1975, 1987; Juillerat 1992). Whitehouse seems to suggest that 'well-ordered religious traditions' are characteristic of a mode of religiosity he defines as 'doctrinal' and is exemplified by Christianity, and by such Christian-influenced religious movements as the Pomio Kivung and the Paliau movement. He thus comes to set up a rather misleading radical dichotomy between 'analogical coding', expressed in the 'multivocality of ritual symbolism' that is characteristic of the iconic or 'imagistic' mode of religiosity (exemplified in the 'fragmented' ritual traditions of small-scale societies) and 'digital coding' that he identifies, in the context of exegesis, with the symbolic binary oppositions of structural analysis and the 'doctrinal' mode of religiosity (Whitehouse 2000, 81–98). But whatever the validity of Whitehouse's dichotomy, two 'ideal-type' forms of religiosity – doctrinal and imagistic, which are discussed in Section 7.6 – it must be stressed that 'analogic' (multivocal symbolism) and 'digital' (symbolic binary oppositions) are interdependent, and both exist, as we shall observe, in the Melanesian context. In fact, the structural pattern of symbolic binary oppositions implies an implicit logical integration and thus entails that all key symbols are multivocal. The opposition between analogical and digital coding is thus a false opposition.

This chapter consists of five sections. In the first two sections I focus, in turn, on two classical ethnographies of Melanesian religion by, respectively, Roger Keesing and Roy Rappaport.

Section 7.2 is thus devoted to a discussion of Keesing's study of *Kwaio Religion* (1982), a group of 'cultural conservatives' living in the mountains of Malaita. I outline the four aspects of their religious culture – their beliefs regarding the ancestral spirits, which play a predominant role in Kwaio religion, the cosmological schema and ritual prohibitions that structure their environment, their ritual magic, and the various rituals around which much of Kwaio social life is focussed. I emphasize Keesing's suggestions regarding the pragmatic orientation of Kwaio religion, the people's general disinterest in exegesis and metaphysics, and the role that religious culture [*kastom*] plays in affirming Kwaio identity and cultural resistance. I conclude the section with a discussion of the recent incorporation of alien spirits into their religion, which reflects their contemporary concerns regarding external socio-economic forces and constraints.

Roy Rappaport's well-known ethnography, *Pigs for the Ancestors* (1968), is the subject of Section 7.3. After some reflections on Rappaport's theoretical approach to socio-cultural life, which has been described as 'ecological rationalism' – particularly focussing on the levels of understanding and meaning that he postulates – I critically examine the role that ritual plays in regulating ecological and social relationships among the Tsembaga of New Guinea. I discuss, in turn, Tsembaga spirit beliefs, cosmological ideas, their ritual cycle – which is intrinsically related to intergroup conflict – and I give an account of the 'functions' of these rituals as suggested by Rappaport. I conclude the chapter with some critical reflections on Rappaport's theory of ritual.

The second part of the chapter (Sections 7.4–7.6) is devoted to a discussion of millenarian or cargo-cult movements that sporadically erupted in Melanesia throughout the colonial period. Section 7.4 is focussed on Peter Worsley's pioneering survey, *The Trumpet Shall Sound* (1957). I outline the meaning of 'millenarianism' and Worsley's Marxist–inspired approach to anthropology and then go on to briefly describe two religious movements that emerged during the early colonial period – the Taro cult (1914–1928) and the so-called 'Vailala Madness' (1919–1923). In the following section (Section 7.5), I focus on an exemplary ethnographic account of one such 'cargo' movement, Peter Lawrence's study, *Road Belong Cargo* (1964). This study gives a graphic account that I outline of the cargo movement associated with the prophet Yali, which flourished in the South Madang district of Papua, New Guinea, at the end of the Second World War.

In the final section, I discuss the various interpretations of millenarian and cargo-type movements that have been suggested by sociologists and anthropologists. I thus critically examine a number of different interpretive strategies and explanations, namely, theories that have seen such movements as forms of cultural revitalization, as religions of the oppressed or 'crisis cults', as charismatic or proto-nationalist movements, and as providing scope for the emergence of new political leaders or 'big men'. I conclude the chapter with a brief discussion of Harvey Whitehouse's 'ideal-type' theory of two types of religiosity.

7.2. KWAIO RELIGION

The Kwaio of Malaita, one of the Solomon Islands, is a small, remote community of around 2,000 people. They are described by their ethnographer Roger Keesing as 'diehard cultural conservatives', for living in the mountains of the interior, these stubborn pagans 'still sacrifice pigs to their ancestors, still carry bows and arrows and clubs, still give mortuary feasts using strung shell valuables, still subsist on food they grow in rain forest swiddens' (1992, 3).

Yet only seventy-five miles away, on Guadacanal Island, is the prosperous, bustling, and cosmopolitan city of Honiara, the capital of the Solomon Islands. Inhabiting what Keesing describes as a 'beleaguered enclave', the Kwaio people of central Malaita have long had to contend with a government committed to western-style development and values, both colonial and post-colonial; with the instrusions of a market economy that early instituted a migrant labour system – a 'traffic in human cargo' – in the establishment of sugar plantations in Queensland and Fiji; and, finally, with the input of Christian missionaries and evangelists whose 'weapons of conversion' included not only education but also modern medicine, hospitals, and aeroplanes (Keesing 1982, 1).

The Kwaio and other people of Malaita have long resisted these intrusions, a struggle that has involved both armed resistance and millenarianism, even though the island was eventually 'pacified' by a massive punitive expedition in 1927 – which led to the death of more than a hundred people and the systematic desecration of the ancestral shrines. At the end of the Second World War, an anti-colonial movement, which had millenarian overtones, erupted in the Solomon Islands, and most Kwaio joined the movement – the Marching [*Maasina*] Rule (Keesing 1982, 23–5). Thus the conservatism of the highland Kwaio, and their tendency to follow ancestral ways, was born of struggle; it was not because they have been isolated from the wider world (Keesing 1982, 2).

Like other people on Malaita, with whom they share a common cultural heritage, the social life of the Kwaio is focussed around local agnatic descent groups. These are linked to specific territories through 'ancient shrines', where the ancestral spirits are propitiated. Thus local descent groups form ritual congregations that are centred around specific shrines, the tract of land associated with a founding ancestor being known as *Fanua*, or shrine territory. But though the emphasis was on agnatic descent, cognatic and affinal relationships were also important. Local descent groups were generally small, consisting of only around ten adult males. Three types of leaders were evident among the Kwaio, essentially reflecting the economic, political, and ideological aspects of their social life. These were the entrepreneurial 'big men', whose power focussed around a 'prestige economy' involving the exchange of pigs and shell valuables and the giving of feasts; the warriors [*lamo*], who were, in the past, specifically associated with blood feuds and bounty hunting; and shrine-priests [*fataabu*]. The economy of the Kwaio was focussed around the cultivation of taro and yams and the breeding of pigs, and both shell valuables [*bata*] and pigs were intrinsic to the prestige economy, the organization of mortuary feasts, and marriage transactions (Keesing 1982, 13–20).

The Kwaio, like most pre-capitalist societies, do not conceptualize 'religion' as a separate cultural domain. This does not imply that they do not have any religious beliefs and practices; Keesing thus utilizes the term 'religion' as an analytic category to cover beliefs and rituals that relate to the ancestral spirits, the spirit-beings that are of such crucial importance in Kwaio daily life. Indeed, Keesing makes little mention of any other spirits or deities. Kwaio religious culture consists essentially of four aspects, relating to the ancestral spirits, cosmological schemas, and ritual prohibitions; and ritual magic and the various kinds of rituals that relate either directly or indirectly to the ancestral spirits. We discuss each of these in turn.

7.2.1. The Ancestral Spirits

The spirits of the dead (*adalo* is the generic term for spirits) have an immediate 'unseen' presence for the Kwaio and they relate to and impinge on Kwaio social life in many and varied ways. The spirits are all-seeing and all-knowing and are seemingly everywhere, 'like the wind'. The cries of some birds and the appearance of certain animals, such as the grasshopper or a variety of snake, are interpreted as messengers of the spirits. Seen as having originated from the earth, the spirits, if displeased, can inflict death or misfortune on the living, and what particularly displeases them is the violations of ritual prohibitions. But they also protect and support their living kin, and of particular importance are the ancestral spirits [*walafu*]. The ancestors, as spirits, value what human beings value – shell valuables, pigs, coconuts, areca nuts, and taro pudding. In the land of the dead [*Anogwa'u*], identified with Ramos Island (which lies between Malaita and Santa Isabel), the spirits live a life much like that of living humans; they live in villages, cultivate taro, and raise pigs (Keesing 1982, 110). The ancestral spirits epitomize the social and moral order of the Kwaio, and, like living people, they have personalities, moods, and jealousies and are emotionally attached to their descendants (Akin 1996, 151–3). In contrast with the ancestral spirits, however, are the spirits marginal to the community and associated with the wild [*kwasi*]. These are usually seen as malevolent and include such spirits as *funu*, small hairy spirits; *buru*, who impersonate the ancestors; and *fele*, who are the spirit familiars of sorcerers (Keesing 1982, 35). Sorcery, like the wild spirits [*adalo kwasi*], is particularly associated with marginal areas (1982, 52).

There is a close association of the spirits with pigs, for pigs are often consecrated to the spirits and bear the ancestor's name, and the spirits are propitiated through the sacrifice of pigs on all important ritual occasions. For in an important sense, 'it is in the nature of the Adalo to visit misfortune upon the living or to protect them from it' (Keesing 1982, 45). Thus pigs are raised and consecrated to the ancestors, specifically to solicit ancestral support and protection, and the concept of *nanama* (*mana*) is less the attribute of some entity than the process whereby the ancestors confer blessing and protection on humans and on their work and activities (1982, 46–7). The *adala*, the spirits of the dead, like humans 'crave pork', and thus a man may normally 'keep' from eight to fifteen consecrated pigs [*fo'ota*], dedicated to the spirits (1982, 81).

Throughout the forest landscape are specific shrines [*ba'e*] associated with the spirits, specifically with the founding ancestors; and these are used for important rituals. Keesing emphasizes a close association between the sociology of the living with that of the dead, for the shrines and the sacrificial rites provide a kind of mapping of the history of social relationships. Thus 'ancestors serve as crucial points of reference in terms of which the living trace their relationships to one another and to land' (1982, 84).

People who sacrifice together form a 'ritual community', and each descent group normally has one priest, the 'shrine-man' [*wane naa ba'e*], who conducts rituals, particularly sacrifices, on behalf of the group. He is normally a senior man, and agnatically descended from the founding ancestors – but he is not a full-time ritual specialist. Although women are often knowledgeable about ritual procedures, and senior women may perform important roles in the religious life of the community, they do not act as ritual officiants (1982, 87–93).

7.2.2. Kwaio Cosmology

The second aspect of Kwaio religious life is a cosmological or symbolic schema that structures not only ritual practices but also everyday life, especially in relation to spatial organization. It focusses essentially around two contrasting concepts: that of *abu* (in eastern Oceania, *tapu*), which refers to something being forbidden, sacred, separate, or, as Keesing puts it, 'off limits'; and *mola*, which refers to the ordinary, everyday, secular, permitted, mundane. Keesing emphasizes that the sacred [*abu*] or sanctity is relational, and that it is not an attribute or quality that inheres in a place, event, or object – although the tendency to set up a dichotomy between things and relations is misleading and undialectical. Both 'hard' and 'hot' are relational concepts, but that does not forbid us from speaking of a hard rock or a hot bath! In specific contexts, people, things, and activities are in fact deemed to be *abu* [taboo]. This arises from the idea that there are what Keesing describes as 'invisible lines' that structure social life and particularly the layout of settlements or hamlets within the forest clearings. At the upper margin of the clearing is the men's house [*tau*], where men and boys often sleep and eat and that is surrounded by many plants of ritual significance. Nearby there is often the priest's house, associated with the spirits and where consecrated ritual objects are kept. In the middle of the clearing are the dwelling houses, and below these are one or more menstrual huts [*bisi*], situated in the woman's or menstrual area [*kaakaba*]. Importantly, 'only men (and boys) can enter the men's houses and shrines; only women (and infant boys) can enter the Kaakaba (menstrual area) and Bisi (menstrual hut)' (1992, 23).

Thus the men's house is abu for women, and the menstrual area is abu for men – the middle area containing the dwelling houses being profane [*Mola*]; there is thus a symbolic schema focussed around the gender dichotomy:

Female	**Male**
Down	Up
Menstrual hut	Men's house
Realm of reproductive powers	Realm of ancestral powers
Childbirth	Death
Flesh	Bone

Although a triadic symbolic schema is also implied, as the dwelling houses (family) are mola and mediates these two domains, Keesing emphasizes the gender contrast. Thus woman are associated with menstruation, childbirth, and life-giving powers; men with sacrifices, the ancestral spirits, and death – for men give birth to ancestral spirits through rituals that are abu to women. Keesing stresses that transitions between the states of sacred [abu] and profane [moea] is always ritualized, involving either purificatory or desacralizing rituals. Another symbolic schema draws a contrast between the settlement and the surrounding forest [*kalona*]:

Culture	**Nature**
Ancestors	Wild spirits
Settlement	Forest
Controlled	Uncontrolled
Centre	Periphery
Human	Non-human

But crucial to their cosmology is the distinction between the ancestral spirits and living humans, which Keesing identifies with the contrast between the noumenal (invisible) and phenomenal (visible) realms of existence (1982, 58–73).

7.2.3. Ritual Magic

The third aspect of Kwaio religious life is magic – the use of material objects or medicinal plants and the invocation of verbal formulae to control and manipulate events and the surrounding world. Magic is distinguished conceptually by the Kwaio from other activities and other forms of knowledge, and though some types of magic are open to the community, magical knowledge constitutes individual 'property' and can be bought and sold. As magic generally involves communications with the ancestral spirits, it could be viewed as a mode of religious expression, and it is utilized for a variety of different purposes – protection from malevolent influences, curing, to obtain abundant yams and taro crops, in fighting and feast-giving, as well as to generally sustain prosperity and well-being. Magic can also be used for destructive or malevolent purposes – as sorcery (*gelema*, a term that is also applied to certain forms of love magic) (Keesing 1982, 50–6).

7.2.4. Kwaio Rituals

Almost all rituals contain a series of magical acts, and it is these rituals that comprise the fourth aspect and indeed form the core of Kwaio religion. Keesing emphasizes, however, a seeming contradiction – namely, that there is a complex elaboration of ritual procedures without any developed mythology and 'without an elaborated view of the cosmos, and without an accompanying exegetic tradition' (1982, 112). For he stresses throughout the text that the Kwaio take an extremely 'pragmatic attitude' towards life, living as they do in an uncertain world, and they have therefore a general disinterest in metaphysics. The Kwaio, he writes, 'are more concerned with acting in the world than creating an all-embracing metaphysical system . . . [they] are more concerned with means than with meaning, with results than with reasons, with controlling than with explaining'. Having little interest in ultimate origins or systematic theology, Kwaio religion is thus less a spiritual metaphysics than a 'pragmatic philosophy' (1982, 48–9).

The Kwaio are therefore concerned essentially with the immediacies of life, and their rituals express these concerns. Almost all the rituals involve communicating, in some way or other, with the ancestral spirits, and the main ritual forms are described at length by Keesing. They include *divination*, during which the ancestors reveal to people the cause of some misfortune and the corrective action needed; *curing rites*, which focus on the symptoms of a disease – more elaborate rituals involving sacrifice are necessary to treat the causes of an affliction; *first-fruit ceremonies*, centred essentially around yams and taro; and the rituals focussed around *childbirth*. As with menstruation, childbirth, Keesing argues, is ill understood in terms of pollution or as being 'unclean'; but rather the rites express the collective concerns of the community, with the emphasis on the ritual isolation of the 'woman's powers' from the menfolk. Finally, there are the *mortuary rites*, which particularly focus around men, especially if it involves the death of a priest (1982, 112–27, 143–67). Interestingly, Keesing makes no mention of initiations.

But the key ritual, and a central aspect of Kwaio religion, is the sacrifice of pigs. This is essentially an expiatory or purification ritual – *Suina* means 'washing' – which is an atonement or to make amends for some wrongdoing or the violation of some ritual prohibition. The pig is killed either through suffocation or is cremated; the ritual is not undertaken in a tone of reverence; and in addressing the spirit, the emphasis is on the payment of 'compensation' rather than a solicitation of patronage.

(The interpretation of sacrifice has long been a topic of interest among anthropologists and students of religion; see, for example, Hubert and Mauss 1964; Burkert, Girard, and Smith 1987.)

The rituals emphasize the fact that the ancestral spirits and living humans are 'co-participants' in the everyday world, and they address the basic concerns of the Kwaio. The rituals emphasize gender relations; they also affirm group identity, for the rituals provide 'a collective dramatization of who one is, with whom one stands, and where one's strongest interests and deepest ancestral attachments lie' (Keesing 1982, 170).

In reflecting on the symbolism of Kwaio ritual, Keesing is rather sceptical of the quest to find order and coherence in the categories of religious thought, in a tradition he describes as 'cultural theology' (Levi-Strauss 1963; Needham 1973; Douglas 1975). This, he feels, leads to 'over-interpretation' or to a 'misconstrued order' and thus tends to downplay both individual variations in beliefs and the pragmatic significance of rituals and symbolic systems (see Schieffelin 1976, 104; Brunton 1980). We need, Keesing suggests, to resituate these symbolic schemas within the everyday life and experience of the people, for the Kwaio, he argues, live, 'pragmatically with their ancestors' (1982, 184). Keesing also emphasizes that people vary widely in the extent of their knowledge of rituals and symbolic schemas and often interpret such shared understandings in divergent ways. Humans are not simply an 'effect' of their culture (1982, 223).

Keesing's study of Kwaio religion is an exemplary text in that he sought to understand this religion not simply as a 'system of meanings' but also as an ideology that is rooted in 'earthly' economics and politics. Thus he writes that we need to work towards a theory

> that takes into account the way cosmological schemas operate to infuse human life with meaning, and preserve a logical structure, but at the same time shows how these schemas are anchored in political and economic realities and serve ideological ends (1982, 142, 219).

An anthropology of religion therefore requires a delicate balance between these 'two perspectives' – hermeneutics and critical social science. An emphasis on the religious system as an autonomous realm of collective symbols floating above and beyond both the diverse subjective experiences of individuals and the political and economic interests of groups and classes is seriously inadequate and misleading. This is the approach of many religious phenomenologists and interpretive anthropologists. On the other hand, to go in the opposite direction and to see religions as simply 'mystifying ideologies' and to completely ignore their symbolic coherence and the subjective meanings of religious phenomena – the strategy, Keesing suggests, of 'vulgar Marxists' – is equally unhelpful and narrow. What is needed is an approach that combines both hermeneutics and a critical social science (see Morris 1997; Bloch 1998, 39–42, for a defence of this approach).

Although acknowledging that senior Kwaio men rely on the control of the sacred knowledge and rituals to maintain their control over 'earthy politics' – for they dominate the prestige economy and exploit women's labour fairly effectively – nevertheless, gender relations among the Kwaio, Keesing suggests, are complex and far from one-sided. The relationship between men and women is dialectical and is not simply a reflection of religious ideology; to understand gender relationships, it is necessary therefore to go beyond the symbolic schemas and to understand the 'texture of actual social relations, in the way real humans live their lives' (1982, 224). Kwaio women, he thus concludes, are not radically subjugated or exploited (1982, 225).

Equally important, Keesing stresses that Kwaio religious ideology, with its emphasis on sacrificing to the ancestors, not only constituted a 'way of life' but was also a 'mode of political struggle'. Their resistance to Christianity and the commitment of the Kwaio to the 'ancestral ways', depicted as *kastomu* [custom], were thus important in affirming their cultural autonomy and identity, in their struggles against an encroaching western culture and a post-colonial state (1982, 240; 1992, 5).

It is of interest that Keesing's study of Kwaio religion – and he undertook most of his ethnographic researches between 1962 and 1979 – is focussed almost exclusively on the ancestral spirits and the rituals and rules that surround them. But in a recent study of the same community, David Akin (1996) has indicated that although the mountain Kwaio still have a 'siege mentality', expending much effort in an attempt to keep 'unwanted alien influences out of the mountains', nevertheless, foreign spirits have become increasingly important in their religious life.

There are around 10,000 Kwaio speakers in Malaita, but the majority live in large coastal villages and are Christians – whether Catholics, Seventh-Day Adventists, or members of the South Sea Evangelical Church. But the 2,000 Kwaio who live in the mountains of the interior – the subject of Keesing's book – still attempt to maintain their cultural autonomy. They oppose the entry of Christians into their community, prefer to use their own shell money instead of cash, and openly resist government control (Akin 1996, 147). They therefore tend to be denigrated and despised, and even feared, by Europeans and Solomon Island Christians (Keesing 1992, viii). They, in turn, are critical of European culture, Christianity, and capitalism, which they see as immoral and demeaning and as undermining Kwaio sociality and sense of community, as well as their own culture [*kastomu*]. But a deep tension runs through Kwaio society, for although there is a public advocacy of 'cultural conservatism', the outside world has had an impact on Kwaio society in many different ways, and no highland Kwaio is simply content to follow the ways of his ancestors (Akin 1996, 168–70). Reflecting the crucial tensions or contradictions of the heart of contemporary Kwaio society has been the 'importation' or incorporation of alien spirits into their belief system.

In the past, as Keesing described, the ancestral spirits were pre-eminent and a symbol of the kin groups' identity, continuity, and place. Their powers were harnessed through both rituals and magic. But increasingly, buru spirits have become an active and growing force in Kwaio social and religious life. As noted earlier, they are associated with the 'wild' and are often identified with the kwasi spirits. These spirits are socially unconnected either because they are foreign or because they have lost all their descendants to death or Christianity. The buru spirits are female over whom living people have little influence or control, and they frequently possess women. Such spirit-possession frequently manifests itself as a serious or chronic illness, which is generally unresponsive to treatment and may lead to suicide. The buru spirits also chase away the ancestral spirits, thus leaving the local community unprotected; the presence of a buru spirit is often indicated by the fact that the ancestral spirits have been unresponsive to people's prayers and ritual sacrifices. These beliefs about alien spirits are clearly a reflection, David Akin suggests, of contemporary Kwaio concerns, and their fears that their cultural autonomy and social well-being are being undermined by 'alien forces' – the market economy, Christianity, and the post-colonial state (Akin 1996, 154–67; for a further study of religion in the Solomon Islands, see Burt 1994).

7.3. RELIGION AND ECOLOGY

Nature is seen by humans through a screen of beliefs, knowledge, and purposes, and it is in terms of their images of nature, rather than the actual structure of nature, that they act. Yet, it is upon nature itself that they do act, and it is nature itself that acts upon them, nurturing or destroying them. Disparities between images of nature and the actual structure of ecosystems are inevitable.

So wrote Roy Rappaport in his seminal essay, 'On Cognized Models'(1979, 97). Drawing on insights and perspectives from Marxism, anthropology, and ecology – although he hardly ever mentions Marx – Rappaport offers an approach to the study of religion and social life that combines realism, naturalism, and dialectics. Strongly influenced by the work of Gregory Bateson (1972), Rappaport also emphasizes both the systematic and processual nature of social life and advocates a holistic approach to anthropology that combines humanism (hermeneutics) and naturalism (social and natural science). Anthropologists should therefore, he suggests, be concerned with the relationships between the subjective aspects of human life – motives, purposes, understandings, culturally constituted meanings – and the objective domain of nature – rocks, water, trees, animals, metabolism, mutation, growth, decay, entropy (1979, 82). They should thus relate the 'Cognized Model' – a description of a people's knowledge of their environment and their beliefs concerning it – to the 'operational model', a description of the ecological system, including people, in accordance with the assumptions and methods of the objective sciences, Rappaport having a particular fondness for the science of ecology (1979, 97).

In his advocacy of an ecological anthropology and his emphasis on combining humanism and science, Rappaport was not offering anything unique or unusual (Benedict 1948; Harris 1980; Morris 1997; Bloch 1998, 39–42), but his approach nonetheless is a far cry from the subjectivism, relativism, and idealism of much contemporary interpretive and postmodern anthropology. Yet Rappaport, along with Marvin Harris, has been critiqued as a 'vulgar materialist', the suggestion being that he treats cultural and social forms as merely 'epiphenomena' of technologies and the economy (Friedman 1974). Rappaport stridently counters this misrepresentation of his approach (1979, 43–51). It is beyond the scope of the present study to discuss in full Rappaport's theoretical trajectory, as he came in later years to embrace a more theological perspective. Indeed, he has recently become something of a 'cult figure' and, like Foucault and Derrida, is lauded as a 'prophet' and 'visionary', ironically even by hermeneutic scholars who repudiate social science! (Messer and Lambek 2001). I want rather, in this section, to introduce Rappaport's ideas on levels or structures of understandings and meaning and then to focus the discussion on his classical ethnography on the cultural ecology of the Tsembaga, *Pigs for the Ancestors* (1968).

In reflecting on his ethnographic writings, Rappaport suggested that 'liturgical orders', that is, a cycle of rituals, encode a hierarchical organization of 'understandings' – although such understandings are by no means restricted, as he often seems to imply, to the ritual context. As aspects of a 'conceptual structure' or 'Cognized

Model', such understandings relate essentially to four levels, which Rappaport suggests form a value hierarchy – relating to religion, cosmology, social rules, and empirical knowledge.

At the 'apex' of the conceptual structure or hierarchy are what Rappaport describes as 'ultimate sacred postulates' that for people like the Tsembaga relate to the existence of spirits, particularly the deceased ancestors. This is equivalent to the Sioux beliefs relating to the great spirit [*Wakan-Tanka*] or the Islamic credo 'there is no God but Allah, and Muhammad is the messenger of God'. The sacred, for Rappaport, is a property of religious discourse, and such 'ultimate sacred postulates' are not derived from ordinary experience; in fact, they are often counterintuitive, and 'out of the ordinary'. These understandings, relating to deities and spirits, are devoid of material significata, and therefore beyond empirical falsification as well as beyond logical refutation. Such postulates are taken to be 'unquestionable', that is, regarded as absolute truths. Indeed, Rappaport defines the sacred as a discursive concept that implies absolute certainty. Sacred knowledge or understanding is thus by definition ultimate as well as being 'immutable and eternal' (1979, 117; 1999, 277–81). As Durkheim does, Rappaport makes a radical dichotomy between the sacred and the profane, but then suggests that the ultimate sacred postulates provide a source or 'font' from which 'sanctity flows', and people, material objects, actions, and discourses thus become 'sanctified' through ritual (1999, 315).

The second level or class of understandings relates to cosmological axioms or structures. Rappaport makes a clear distinction between religion as expressed in sacred postulates relating to spirits and what are generally described as 'symbolic schemas'. These cosmological or symbolic schemas refer to the assumptions concerning the fundamental structure of the world and are constituted, for peoples like the Kwaio and Maring, by a series of symbolic oppositions: hot–cold, high–low, dry–moist, domestic–wild, women–men. Although Rappaport suggests that the spirits, as ultimate sacred postulates, are devoid of materiality and are regarded as 'external verities' (1979, 119) – thus implying a Platonic transcendental realm – the spirits in fact are incorporated into the symbolic schemas (cosmos) and are seen by the Tsembaga as spirit-beings existing in the world. As Rappaport himself suggests, the Tsembaga regard the spirits [*raua*] to be significant components of their environment, not simply transcendental beings (1968, 38). It is thus questionable whether they regard the spirits as eternal or as conveying absolute truths.

The third and, for Rappaport, 'lower' level of understandings relates to social rules that govern the behaviour of everyday life, though Rappaport tends to conceive these as 'rules and taboos' that are expressed in ritual and 'informed' by the understandings of the cosmological structures. He also posits the incorporation into ritual of 'information' derived from the material and social conditions of everyday life as constituting a further 'level' of 'understanding'.

But the final level of understanding relates to the secular knowledge of the everyday-life world: empirical knowledge relating to secular understandings of the material world, its people, its organic life, its places, and its processes. Thus the 'lowest' level of understanding is acknowledged as more or less completely 'external' to the ritual context. But replicating the religious ideology, religious beliefs, and rituals is seen by Rappaport as having priority, for 'religion', and not people's empirical relations with the natural world, 'has been the ground upon which human life has stood since humans first became humans' (1979, 121; 1999, 407). This reflects rather idealist metaphysics.

Rappaport also suggests three types or levels of meaning, which in many ways match the levels of understanding, though he presents them in reverse order, beginning with the empirical and ending with the mystical. The first 'lower-order' level of meaning relates to meaning in its everyday semantic sense, such as expressed in folk classifications and everyday conversations. Second, there are the 'middle-order' meanings expressed in art, poetry, and symbolic schemes. And, finally, there are the 'higher-order' meanings that are 'grounded in identity or unity, the radical identification of self with other' (1979, 127). This form of meaning is experiential rather than intellectual and is expressed in mystical states or religious rituals, in acts of love, and in the experience of 'pure being'. This type of meaning is ineffable and beyond language. That such experiences may have nothing to do with religion or ritual is not seriously explored by Rappaport. Neither can unity and identity be equated. But Rappaport sees each level of meaning as roughly corresponding to the three forms of signs discussed by Peirce – symbol, in which the relation between the sign and signified is conventional or arbitrary; icon, in which the relationship is based on resemblance; and finally, the index, in which signs are a part or an effect of that which they signify (1979, 126–7; 1999, 70–2). Thus we have Rappaport's triadic symbolic schema:

	Lower	**Middle**	**Higher**
Understanding	Empirical	Cosmological	Religious (sacred knowledge)
Meaning Sign	Semantic symbol (distinction)	Symbolic icon (similarity)	Mystical index (identity)
Truths	Empirical	Conventional	Absolute

Let us now turn to Rappaport's ethnography of the Tsembaga, a small population of 'tribal horticulturalists' living in the highlands of New Guinea. Belonging to the Maring group, they numbered around 200 individuals when Rappaport undertook his ethnographic researches during the years 1962–1963. Swidden cultivators, the main crops grown by the Tsembaga are taro, sweet potato, and yams, and pigs form an important part of the domestic economy. All male pigs are castrated when around three months old, for boars are considered dangerous, and pregnancy is the result of the union of the domestic sows with feral males. The pigs are domiciled and fed in the women's houses but tend to wander freely during the day. Besides providing meat, they form a useful function in keeping residential areas clean, eating garbage and human faeces. The Tsembaga almost never eat pigs outside the ritual context, and, as we shall see, the Tsembaga ritual cycle is closely bound up with pigs (1968, 56–9; 1979, 32–3).

The Tsembaga have complex political relations, highly ritualized, with neighbouring local groups, other Maring groups such as the Tuguma and Kundagai. In the past, warfare was endemic between these groups, although it was small scale, and feuding is perhaps a better term to describe these conflicts.

We may discuss Tsembaga religion in terms of four topics – namely, their spirit beliefs, cosmology, the ritual cycle, and the functions of these rituals as interpreted by Rappaport.

7.3.1. Spirits

Two contrasting sets of spirits [*raua*] 'inhabit' (as Rappaport puts it) the world of the Tsembaga; one set is associated with high altitudes, the other with the low. Those dwelling in the upper regions include two important spirits, the red spirits [*raua mugi*] and the smoke woman [*kun kase ambra*]. The red spirits are ancestral spirits, associated with particular patrilineal clans, and they reside in the clan's high-altitude forest. They are especially identified with those who have been killed in warfare and are associated symbolically with heat, dryness, strength, hardness, masculinity, and the epiphytic orchids that grow in the high-altitude forests; arboreal marsupials are said to be their pigs. They may cause afflictions relating to the head and chest. All rituals relating to warfare are addressed to the red spirits, and they also enforce the ritual prohibitions associated with the ritual cycle that in turn is intrinsically linked to the ebb and flow of intergroup conflicts.

Smoke woman, on the other hand, is not considered to have been human but is conceived of as a female. She is not specifically associated with women [*ambra*], nor with fertility, and the term *kun kase* refers to the technique by which shamanic ecstasy is produced. This involves the use of tobacco. Thus shamans [*kun kase yu*], who are always men, communicate with the smoke woman through séances conducted at night in the men's houses. These consist of inhaling tobacco, the spirit entering the shaman's head through the nose. Through possession, the 'smoke woman' informs the living of the wishes of the dead, and Rappaport therefore suggests that the female spirit acts as an intermediary between living people and all other categories of spirits (1979, 103–4; 1999, 237–8).

There are two categories of spirits associated with the lower regions, which are collectively known as *raua mai*. The term *mai* suggests what comes before or is antecedent in a biological sense. The two important spirits are *koipa mangiang* and *raua tukump*. They are little associated with warfare, their major concern being fertility, and rituals concerned with fertility are mainly addressed to them. As Rappaport writes, 'The spirits of the low ground are concerned with growth and fertility. It is they who look after the increase and growth of people and pigs, and the productivity of gardens and groves' (1968, 38).

Koipa mangiang was never human and is often associated with streams and pools, and he could be malevolent. Conceived as a male, he is said to have eels as his pigs. Rava tukump – *tukump* in other contexts refers to the mould that grows on plant artefacts and hence Rappaport describes them as 'spirits of rot' – are seen as the spirits of the Tsembaga who have died through illness or accident. Both these spirits are associated with 'coldness' [*kinim*] – the cold and wet conditions that induce decay and the dissolution of organic matter. Thus in Maring culture, there is a close association between fertility and death (decay), and, as Rappaport writes, 'both hotness and coldness, both strength and fertility are, in the Maring view, qualities necessary for survival – to the successful defence of the land and the successful cultivation of the land defended' (1999, 239).

7.3.2. Cosmology

Implicit in the spirit beliefs of the Tsembaga, as well as in their rituals and everyday life, is a symbolic schema or cosmology that is essentially focussed around the gender division. It has affinities with that described by Keesing with respect to the Kwaio and by many other scholars elsewhere (see Needham 1973; Willis 1975; Morris 1987, 225–6, 293–6). They are often depicted as 'dualistic' symbolic classifications, but they are less of a dualism than a coherent set of complementary structural oppositions. The symbolic schema implicitly suggested by Rappaports' ethnographic account of the Tsembaga is as follows:

Male	**Female**
High	Low
Red spirits [raua mugi]	Spirits of rot (*raua tukump*)
Head	Legs
Arboreal marsupials	Eel
Warfare	Agriculture
Hot	Cold
Dry	Wet
Strength	Fertility

As with the Kwaio, the Tsembaga also make an important symbolic opposition between the domestic [*t'ip wombi*] and the wild [*t'ip demi*], and the latter is not only associated with what is wild and dangerous, but also with malevolent spirits and enemies.

7.3.3. The Ritual Cycle

The ritual cycle of the Maring, which is intrinsically connected with political relations between local groups, has been explored at great depth by Rappaport and subjected by him to a plethora of interpretation. Here I only briefly and schematically outline the main rituals.

The ritual cycle may be usefully conceived of as beginning with the outbreak of hostilities between two Maring local groups or communities. What prompts hostilities may be variable, some serious grievance or homicide, but with respect to homicide, the principle of 'balanced reciprocity' pertains, and the spirit of every person killed demands to be avenged with the life of a person from the enemy group. A state of 'war' is declared or affirmed by an elaborate ritual that involves the hanging of 'fighting stones' [*bamp ku*] from the centre post of a ritual house [*ringi yang*]. During the ritual, in which only men participate, men – as warriors – are possessed by the red spirits, and their support in the ensuing conflict is requested. From then on, a whole series of ritual prohibitions is activated; there is thus an explicit separation made between the various symbolic oppositions implied in the cosmic schema. The spirits of the high altitudes are segregated from the 'spirits of rot'; sexual intercourse is prohibited; and men have to avoid contact with any substances that are cold, wet, or soft. Eels may therefore be neither trapped nor eaten, as this would be inimical to the man's strength.

At the termination of warfare, the 'reintegration' of the universe or cosmic order, as it were, begins. An agreement having been made by the respective antagonists to cease fighting, everyone in the local group – men, women, and children, as well as allies – assemble in preparation for the planting of the *rumbim*, a red-leafed variety of *Cordyline fruticosa*, which is a small tree widely used throughout Melanesia for ritual purposes (see Hogbin 1970, 67; Keesing 1982, 113). A sacrifice of pigs is made, mainly as an offering to the spirits of the low ground, and the pork given to the allies. A special earthen 'oven' [*pubit*] is prepared, made out of bark, and in this is cooked all possible varieties of edible wild animals (marsupials, snakes, lizards, frogs, rats, insects, grubs, birds), as well as wild greens and the fat from the belly of a female pig. This oven is interpreted by Rappaport as not only representing the 'fruitfulness of nature' and a primeval 'pre-cultural state' but also a vagina through which the fruits of the earth come forth. When the feasting is finished, the women are sent away, and the men plant the rumbim tree in the middle of the emptied oven, each man of the local group placing his hand on the tree as it is planted. The *min*, the shadow or life-force, of the man is said to enter the rumbim plant. The ritual planting of the rumbim indicates the successful defence of the local group's territory, an end to the ritual prohibition of sexual intercourse and the forbidden foods, and the beginning of a period of truce. The planting of the rumbin is essentially a 'truce ritual', and the peace that follows the planting one of truce only. Rappaport suggests that, like the mudyi tree of the Ndembu, the rumbim plant is a multivocal symbol with many references and associations – agnatic kinship, red spirits, men, hardness, strength, territory, spirituality, and immortality.

The length of the truce, and thus the ritual cycle, depends largely on the demographic fortunes of the Tsembaga pig husbandry. The main thrust, during the period of sanctified truce, is to build up the pig population in order to repay debts to the red spirits and to allies that were incurred during the period of conflict. During the period of truce, which may take a decade or more, people, as Rappaport writes, 'will devote themselves primarily to raising pigs until they have accumulated a sufficient number to discharge the debt to ancestors (and allies) properly' (1999, 243).

When sufficient pigs have thus been raised, largely through the labour of women, a year-long festival, *kaiko*, is held and thus culminates the ritual cycle. During the festival there are rituals involving the uprooting of the rumbim; the marking of local group boundaries, which may involve the annexing of enemy land; and community-wide rituals involving dancing, feasting, and the sacrifice of 'pigs for the ancestors'. Besides bringing the entire ritual cycle to a climax, the kaiko festivities indicate that debts to both the living and ancestral spirits have been repaid, and that the local group is again free to initiate warfare (Rappaport 1968, 146–220; 1979, 106–16; 1999, 237–51).

7.3.4. The Functions of Rituals

In his magnus opus, *Ritual and Religion in the Making of Humanity* (1999), which is a summation of his earlier writings, Roy Rappaport, in rather scholastic fashion, is primarily concerned with semiotics and with the formal definition of ritual. He defines ritual as 'the performance of more or less invariant sequences of formal acts and utterances not entirely encoded by performers' (1999, 24). Although he acknowledges that the economic and ecological functions of many rituals are reasonably well founded and that rituals have important communicative functions – the kaiko festivities, for example, indicate the political strength and prestige of the local group (1999, 82–5) – nevertheless, Rappaport denies that rituals, in general, necessarily have ecological or political functions (1999, 27–8). But his ethnographic study, *Pigs for the Ancestors*, which has eulogistically been described as a work of 'intellectual daring and beauty' (Gillison 2001, 291), is a classical account of cultural ecology, and Rappaport's interpretation of the Maring ritual cycle is an exemplary functionalist analysis. The book, in fact, evoked a plethora of criticism on this account not only from Marxists (Friedman 1974; Bloch 1986, 5–6) but also from die-hard cultural anthropologists. Marshall Sahlins, for example, described Rappaport's functionalist mode of analysis as leading to 'conceptual impoverishment' and as a form of 'ecology fetishism' (1976, 87–8). One could equally well suggest that Sahlins himself makes a fetish out of culture, and he has indeed been described as a 'crusading cultural determinist' who implies that all Marxists and functionalist anthropologists are either vulgar materialists or crass utilitarians (Kuper 1999, 199). Neither of these labels describes adequately or fairly Rappaport's style of cultural ecology, which while recognizing the autonomy of culture and the important role that symbolism uniquely plays in human life, nevertheless aimed to preserve a view of humanity as an intrinsic part of the natural world.

The focus of Rappaport's ethnography was on the systematic role that the ritual cycle played in Tsembaga social and cultural life. In fact, he regarded the rituals as a set of mechanisms that regulated some of the relationships of the Tsembaga with their surrounding environment. He suggested that this regulation

> helps to maintain the biotic communities with their territories, redistributes land among people, and people over land, and limits the frequency of fighting. In the absence of authoritative political statuses or offices, the ritual cycle likewise provides a means for mobilizing allies when warfare may be undertaken. (1979, 28)

Rappaport also suggests that ritual functions regulate the conservation of marsupial fauna and provide a mechanism for the redistribution of surplus pigs, thus ensuring that people receive an adequate supply of high-quality protein, as well as helping to prevent the degradation of the environment. As there is an absence of power vested in discrete authorities among the Tsembaga, Rappaport suggests that compliance with cultural conventions is ensured, or at least encouraged, by their being sanctified through ritual. Thus sanctity 'is a functional alternative to political power among the Maring' (1968, 237). Thus Rappaport concludes with this suggestion:

> The ritual cycle is a sacred structure within which productive and reproductive activities (ecological, biological, and social) proceed, and in terms of which social, political and ecological relations are defined and given meaning. (1979, 73)

Indeed, ritual is defined as 'humanity's basic social act' (1999, 107).

All this is something of an exaggeration and rather topsy-turvy, for religious rituals are only an aspect of socio-cultural life and are by no means all-encompassing, even in tribal contexts like that of the Tsembaga. Moreover, rituals tend to affirm or publicly validate social arrangements and states of affairs that have already been enacted, rather than creating these events. Functional analysis, as Bloch argues, tends too easily to confound effects with causes (1986, 5). It is, however, of interest that, while Rappaport is offered panegyrics by many anthropologists and theologians, he seems to be completely ignored by scholars focussing on Melanesian religion (e.g., Trompf 1991; Mageo and Howard 1996; Whitehouse 2000).

The observations of Catherine Bell on Rappaport's ecological rationalism are perhaps apposite: She suggests that in overemphasizing what ritual 'does', he ends up mystifying the phenomenon (1992, 108–9).

7.4. MILLENARIAN MOVEMENTS IN MELANESIA

Millennial–type movements have occurred in diverse cultural settings and throughout history – at least since the emergence of centralized states. Indeed, several anthropologists have suggested that many 'world' religions have begun as millennial sects, which have subsequently been institutionalized. This is in line with

Max Weber's idea that under specific social conditions, a charismatic figure may emerge and as a 'prophet' articulate a radical 'break' with the established 'church' or culture (1965, 46–59). In broadest terms then, millenarian movements are religious movements in which the imminence of radical or 'supernatural' change in the social order is prophesied or expected. In his pioneering study of 'cargo' cults in Melanesia, Peter Worsley noted that in such movements 'a prophet announces the imminence of the end of the world in a cataclysm which will destroy everything. Then the ancestors will return, or God, or some other liberating power, will appear, bringing all the goods the people desire, and ushering in a reign of external bliss' (1957, 11).

The original meaning of the term *millennial* is, however, more precise and narrow, and derives from the Judeo–Christian tradition. It referred to the belief, based on the Book of Revelation (Chapter 20), that after his second coming, Christ would establish a messianic kingdom on earth and would reign over it for a thousand years before the last judgement (Cohn 1957, 13). Described as a 'surrealistic text', the Book of Revelation thus suggests an apocalyptic vision regarding the 'end of time' and the advent of a 'new heaven and a new earth' at the end of a thousand years (Thompson 1996, 3–55). In his classic study of millenarian cults in medieval Europe, Norman Cohn (1957) suggests that these cults had three essential characteristics: redemption was *collective* rather than individual and related to deliverance in this world, rather than in some future afterlife; the millennium was *imminent*, and would take place in the near future; and, finally, salvation would come through some *supernatural* agency. Such movements usually were instigated by a person who claimed divine inspiration or authority.

In this section I want to focus on Peter Worsley's important study of 'cargo' or millenarian cults in Melanesia, *The Trumpet Shall Sound* (1957), and briefly discuss two earlier movements – the 'Taro cult' (1914) and the 'Vailala Madness' (1919–1922). The following section (Section 7.5) is specifically devoted to Peter Lawrence's ethnographic study of the 'cargo' movement associated with Yali, which sprang up in the Madang district at the end of the Second World War, and I conclude the chapter with a discussion of the various interpretations of cargo cults that have been suggested by anthropologists.

Peter Worsley, like Keesing, is a Marxist – an inspired anthropologist who is critical of those cultural anthropologists who focus exclusively on the coherence of religion as a symbolic system, divorced from socio-economic life, and the wider historical context. He suggests that academics have a natural tendency to project a 'spurious unity' onto other people's belief systems and not only to 'oversystematize' these beliefs but also give them philosophical and cosmological priority – viewing religion as somehow 'primary' or 'higher' (as does Rappaport). Worsley follows Melford Spiro in defining religion as 'an institution consisting of culturally patterned interaction with culturally postulated superhuman beings' (Spiro 1987, 197) but suggests that it might be better to speak of a superhuman 'realm' or of 'powers'.

But like Spiro, Worsley emphasizes that religion is not simply a set of beliefs but is a cultural system or institution and that religious beliefs are '*used* in day-to-day social activities' (1957, xxix). Although Worsley argues that pre-literate people are realists and readily acknowledge that the world around them exists and that it has its own regularities and operations, and though Worsley also suggests that a distinction can be made between the 'empirical' (or mundane) and the mystical (or magical), he nevertheless emphasizes that this is an analytical distinction and that pre-literate people are not metaphysical dualists. They do not operate, he writes, 'with a model of "two worlds"'. Worsley thus suggests that pre-literate people have a conception of the world as a 'single order of reality' of which both humans and spirits are a part, and that people have essentially a 'practical' attitude to life and tend to be generally uninterested in metaphysics. He thus, like Keesing, views Melanesian religion as essentially a practical enterprise (1957, xxv–xxvii). Worsley also notes several other telling observations, namely, that it is misleading to assume that ethical values and moral behaviour is always interwoven with religion; that religious institutions, though potentially innovatory, may serve either conservative or revolutionary interests; and finally, that 'individual' religious experiences are always highly social phenomenon (1957, xxix–xxxv).

In his study of 'cargo' cults in Melanesia, Worlsey discussed in detail numerous examples of similar kinds of cults or movements that emerged spontaneously during the colonial period – the Tuka movement that had flourished in Fiji towards the end of the nineteenth century; the John Frum cult on the island of Tanna in the New Hebrides (1940–1941); and the Marching Rule movement that broke out in 1944 in the Solomon Islands are examples – and he attempted to situate these movements in their political and socio-historical context. Since then, a wealth of ethnographic and historical studies of 'cargo' cult movements has emerged, but here I briefly describe only two such movements: the Taro cult and the 'Vailala Madness'.

7.4.1. The Taro Cult

In early 1914, among the Orokaiva people of Northern Papua a man named Buninia, who had no particular reputation as a prophet or magician, went around the villages proclaiming that he had been possessed by the spirit of taro – taro being the staple crop of the area. He had, it appeared, become suddenly 'struck down' by the spirit while working in his garden. There is some dispute about the initial possession, as a missionary reported that he had been visited by his father's spirit. Whatever the case, Buninia proclaimed that the existing methods of agriculture were slow and should be abandoned, and he announced a special ritual to be applied to gardening activities. Nobody took much interest in Buninia or the rituals he advocated; then in late 1914, a girl from a neighbouring village was suddenly 'struck down' by the spirit of taro and, singing Buninia's ritual song, went into a trance. In other villages, other cases of 'sickness' occurred, and soon whole village communities were spontaneously experiencing these shaking fits [*Jipari*]. The trances themselves were believed to have a beneficent effect on the taro crop. Taro 'priests' became prominent in the area, organizing cult activities and treating spirit-caused illness. Special platforms were built and offerings made to ancestral spirits. A ritual feast [*Kasamba*], involving drumming, singing, and possession rites, was a central aspect of cult activities, and the cult leaders, the taro men who organized the feasts, were believed to be possessed by the taro spirit or the spirits of the dead (Worsley 1957, 59–63).

Although many 'traditional' cultural elements were incorporated into cult activities, the taro cult, as Worsley suggests, was not an attempt to 'revive old customs.' Nor was it specifically a millennial movement. But it contained elements that were quite distinct from Orokaiva traditional religion. It was implicitly anti-white, and cult members firmly disassociated themselves from the Christian missions in the area. It was also pan-tribal, for the cult spread over a wide area. Finally, it was forward-looking for certain members of the taro cult believed that the ancestors would come by steamer and canoe and bring European trade goods (1957, 69).

In his account of this cult, Worsley suggests that although there was a focus on traditional and still vital interests (crop fertility, curing rites, and ancestral spirits), and although there was little millennial emphasis, the cult exhibited many of the features characteristic of millenarian movements.

Some of these characteristics are worth noting. The first is that the taro cult seems to have been, as noted, pan-tribal and to have spread widely and rapidly, so that it soon came to the attention of the colonial administrators. Although it had a 'sort of hierarchy', as F. E. Williams expressed it (1928, 32), and there was evidence of a political structure, the movement was highly fragmented and sporadic. It was divided into numerous sects, which tended to be focussed around a particular variety of taro, and there were wide variations in the cult objects, incantations, ritual prohibitions, and beliefs associated with each sect (Worsley 1957, 68–9). The kasamba ritual, which involved feasting, singing, and drumming, and which involved the whole community and the jipari spirit-possession rites associated with the taro and ancestral spirits, seem to have been the key observances shared by all members of the taro cult. Yet Harvey Whitehouse emphasizes that the spread of the cult tended to be spontaneous and by means of ritual 'contagion', for the movement had little in the way of explicit doctrine, and the movement did not spread by 'direct proselytism' – as with the later Paliau movement in and around the island of Manus (1946–1950) (2000, 72). It was not a highly integrated movement, Worsley notes, with a unitary authority structure (1957, 68).

Second, the taro cult placed a significant emphasis on material well-being, but in the early period of colonial rule, the focus was not on 'cargo' per se (European trade goods) but on the successful planting and harvesting of the taro crop. Many of the ritual prohibitions associated with the cult – which tabooed the eating of certain marsupials or certain species of frog – were analogically linked to the taro plant. Special magical rites were also performed by the Taro men [*ba embo*] to ensure a good taro crop (Williams 1928, 45–6; Worsley 1957, 62; Whitehouse 2000, 72).

And finally, although the taro cult dissociated itself from the Christian missions, it nevertheless had a syncretic aspect, for it incorporated many Christian elements in its rituals and invocations. Even more significant, many of the cult leaders were ex-policeman, as was the prophet Yali, who is discussed in the next section (Worsley 1957, 68–9; for an interesting discussion of contemporary Orokaiva religion, see Iteanu 1995; a summary of the taro cult is given in Lanternari 1963, 163–5).

Less radical and millenarian than other religious movements of the period, the taro cult seems to have persisted until around 1928.

7.4.2. Vailala Madness

Described as an 'extraordinary phenomena', the so-called 'Vailala Madness' was a religious movement that emerged along the Vailala River during the period 1919–1923. It occurred in the Gulf of Papua among the western Elema people (Swain and Trompf 1995, 176). The classic account of this cult was by F. E. Williams (1923, 1976), but this ethnography has been summarized by many other writers on millenarianism and 'cargo cults'.

The cult was characterized by a certain mode of behaviour referred to as *kavakeva* [madness] or 'head-he-go-round', a type of possession seizure that often affected whole villages. Individuals would be subject to uncontrolled behaviour and would stagger about and gesticulate and utter meaningless phrases. Although a narcotic 'mushroom madness' has been recorded from the Highlands of New Guinea (Reay 1960), the Vailala Madness of the coastal region has been considered to be purely a cultural phenomenon. The 'madness' appears to have originated in an old man, Evara, who, though described as 'brisk and intelligent', appears to have been subject to epilepsy or trance states. One day, out hunting alone in the bush, he is reported to have fallen into an unconscious state. The villagers searched in vain for him when he did not return to the village, but after four days he eventually made his way home. Some time later, after the death of his father and younger brother, Evara again went into a trance state, and his 'madness' quickly seems to have affected other villagers. But it wasn't only his seizures that were significant, for Evara also prophesied the coming of a steamer, carrying the ancestors and dead relatives on board, who would bring with them the 'cargo'. The latter consisted of gifts of tobacco, axes, calico, knives, and such like commodities. The spirits had revealed that these trade goods rightfully belong to the Papuans, but the steamers had been intercepted by Europeans. There were stray elements of European and mission culture incorporated into the cult as it developed; the adherents referred to themselves as 'Jesus Christ' men; there was an imitation of plantation or police discipline, with parades and whistleblowing; each village had a cult house and a flagpole that was the medium of communication between the living and the dead; and besides insisting that villagers keep the Sabbath and refrain from committing adultery, the ancestors urged them to abandon traditional ornaments and many of the traditional rituals. The ethnographer Williams was dismayed to see many members of the cult destroying their sacred masks and denouncing the traditional dances as 'wicked' – in the same tenor as the missionaries. The cult articulated a kind of 'ascetic Puritanism' and, as Worsley notes, represented a 'sharp break with the old morality'. Significantly, the majority of the cult followers seemed to have been, at one time, indentured labourers on the European plantations. But the cargo to be brought by the ancestors never arrived and by the mid-1930s, the movement had died out (Williams 1923; Worsley 1957, 75–92).

Such in brief outline was the Vailala Madness. Unfortunately, the early ethnographer F. E. Williams had a very negative attitude towards the cult and tended to pay special attention to its psychological aspects. Thus the spirit-mediums were described as 'automaniacs', the speaking of apparently unintelligible words was labelled 'gibberish' rather than glossolalia, and the whole phenomena was seen as exemplifying 'mass hysteria'. Thus Williams, as Worsley writes, tended to ignore the social, political, and organizational aspects of the cult and to view it as a form of pathology. Both Worsley and Cochrane therefore emphasize the impact of the colonial economy and of the European missionaries on the social life of the Elema. The discovery of oil near the Vailala River in 1911 led to intensified European penetration, and in 1918 compulsory taxation was introduced and the Elema forced to cultivate rice and plant coconuts. Men were recruited for work on overseas plantations, and Worsley notes that the majority of the more active members of the Vailala Madness were returning indentured labourers (Worsley 1957, 79; Cochrane 1970, 52–3).

Although there was continuity between the Vailala Madness and pre-contact Elema culture – the cargo was to be brought by the ancestral spirits and significantly it did not include 'money', and Cochrane describes the cult leaders as new 'big men' – there were important elements of European culture. Indeed, the new ceremonies of the Vailala Madness are interpreted by Cochrane as 'an eclectic mixture of European and Elema culture involving a blending of new ideas with the old in the light of epistemological assumptions about the nature of European power' (1970, 62–3). The main ceremony itself involved cult temples that were called the 'office' or *ahea uvi* [literally hot houses], tables were set up, and offerings of betel, rice, and flowers were made to the spirits of the dead; a painted village flagpole had an important ritual significance in communicating with the spirits.

Initially, the movement spread 'like wildfire' and, by 1923, had spread over a wide area in the Gulf of Papua. By 1930, the Vailala Madness is said to have finally died out. Even so, the colonial administration took repressive measures against the cult, and a number of its leaders, the new 'big men', were imprisoned. Worsley concluded that it 'expressed powerful native resentment of their social and political position in the new order of things' and represented a mechanism for dealing with the new colonial economy. Cochrane felt that Vailala Madness ultimately failed because Europeans continued to treat the Elema as 'rubbish men' (Worsley 1957, 89; Cochrane 1970, 66; for other discussions of Vailala Madness, see La Barre 1972, 239–44; Wilson 1973, 317–22).

The literature on 'cargo' cults and religious movements generally in Melanesia is now extensive. With respect to some of the key movements, the following studies are noteworthy:

- The Tuka movement of Fiji (1883–1885): Worsley 1957, 17–31; Lanternari 1963, 192–3; Burridge 1969, 49–53. Martha Kaplan's (1995) important study of the movement suggests that the Tuka movement was never primarily about European goods – 'cargo' – and did not exist as a 'cult': It seems, however, to have had existence as a 'new ritual system'. Following postmodern idealist fashions, the colonial state, she also informs us, did not exist in Fiji!
- The Paliau movement on Manus (1946–1954): Mead 1956; Worsley 1957, 183–92; Schwartz 1962; Otto 1992.
- The John Frum cult on the island of Tanna in the New Hebrides (Vanuatu) (1940–1947): Guiart 1951; Worsley 1957, 152–60; Wilson 1973, 322–6; Parsonson 1975.
- The Marching Rule [*Maasina*] movement in the Solomon Islands (1944–1954): Worsley 1957, 170–82; Cochrane 1970, 67–96; Wilson 1973, 468–74; Keesing 1978; 1992, 103–21.
- On Christian syncretic movements and independent churches in Melanesia, see Steinbauer 1979; Trompf 1990; 1991, 212–40; Whitehouse 1995.

7.5. ROAD BELONG CARGO

Since Peter Worsley wrote his pioneering study of millenarian movements in Melanesia, much ethnographic research has been undertaken on specific cargo cults, and, as noted, there is now a considerable literature on religious movements in the region. I want, however, in this section to focus on one specific study, Peter Lawrence's classic ethnographic account of cargo cults in the South Madang district of Papua, New Guinea, *Road Belong Cargo* (1964). It is a vivid historical narrative of the various cult movements that emerged in this region during the colonial period (1900–1950). Undertaking ethnographic studies among the Garia and Ngaing during the 1950s, Lawrence's study not only gives a detailed account of these movements but also is focussed particularly on the career and the movement associated with the rather tragic and enigmatic figure of Yali, the messiah who led and inspired the cargo movement that flourished in the Southern Madang at the end of the Second

World War (1945–1950). Much of the detail regarding Yali's career was given to Lawrence by Yali himself in 1956, when the ethnographer was living in his village.

Since contact began in 1871, the peoples of the Southern Madang have experienced several government administrations, first under German colonial rule and then – after 1914 – for the most part under Australian administration. Plantations were established in the coastal region from the early years of the twentieth century, focussed especially on rubber and copra, and local people tended to be regarded by planters as purely economic assets to be 'exploited with the minimum of outlay and flogged into obedience' (1964, 57). Race relations were therefore tense; there was opposition by the planters to any local initiatives in copra production; and labour strikes, revolts, and anti-white hostilities frequently erupted during the colonial period. The two important Christian missions in the district were the Roman Catholic and Lutheran, and these organizations rivalled and were even more prominent than those of the administration (1964, 51–2). But what was crucial about the colonial impact was that local people developed a strong dependency on western goods – the cargo: steel axes and bush knives, tobacco, cotton goods, flashlights, tinned meat (as well as rifles), not simply as luxuries but as necessities (1964, 59).

The population of Southern Madang numbered around 24,000 and was divided into numerous small ethnic communities, each with its own language. People lived in small villages or hamlets, were primarily subsistence agriculturalists growing taro and yams, with extensive coconut groves in the coastal areas. Each ethnic community comprised a number of descent groups, matrilineal totemic clans among the Ngaing and patrilineal clans among the Garia, and there were extensive trading networks, with the emphasis on reciprocal and equitable exchanges. The keynotes of their social and religious life, according to Lawrence, were materialism and anthropocentrism, and all knowledge, both sacred and empirical, was seen as derived from the deities and spirits. People like the Ngaing and Garia believed that the natural world, its organic life and human beings, were created by the deities [*anut, parambik, tubud*] or by totemic spirits [*sapud*] and that people could control the world and events through ritual, focussed around magic, the deities, or the spirits of the dead [*kabu*]. Importantly, the deities and spirits were seen as just as much a part of the natural order or cosmos as humans, birds, and animals, and they were regarded as a real if not always visible part of the ordinary physical environment. Described as more powerful than humans, the deities, totemic spirits, and the dead were often just as corporeal, taking the form of humans, birds, animals, or insects at will. Using the term 'religion' to connote beliefs about deities, spirits, and totems, Lawrence suggests that these were simply 'superhuman beings' who shared the same world as humans and other animals (1964, 12). But they functioned to explain, through mythology, how the cosmic order came into existence.

The people of the Southern Madang regarded the cosmos as both finite and as almost exclusively a material world. This cosmos consisted of two interdependent realms, one focussed on human relationships (social structure) and their concomitant social values, the other relating to people's interactions with the spirits (deities, totemic spirits, spirits of the dead) focussed around rituals and specific epistemological assumptions. Of particular importance were the complex rituals associated with the men's cult – the boy's initiation, the harvest festival, and the kabu ritual. These tended to involve ceremonial exchanges and were devoted to honouring the dead. Feasts, various dances, often entailing spirit-possession and ritual offerings to the spirits, were intrinsic to these rituals, as well as to the mortuary rites. But Lawrence emphasizes the non-existence of 'spiritual values' or any 'mysticism' in people's ritual practices; these were focussed on material wealth, not simply in terms of their utility but as symbols of social relationships. The emphasis of the latter was on mutual obligations and the attainment of prestige (1964, 29). Thus people of Southern Madang were 'extremely pragmatic' (1964, 31), and the epistemological assumptions underlying their religion, Lawrence concludes, suggested that

> a true relationship existed only when men demonstrated goodwill by reciprocal co-operation and distribution of wealth; and the unswerving conviction that material wealth originated from and was maintained by deities who, with the ancestors, could be manipulated by ritual to man's advantage. (1964, 33)

Thus the pre-contact religion of the Southern Madang people was anthropocentric, pragmatic, and materialistic, little concerned with 'spiritual values', and through ritual and the observance of specific ritual norms (which had little moral significance), humans could maintain a proper relationship with the deities and spirits and thus ensure material benefits (1964, 75).

Throughout the colonial period, Southern Madang evinced a series of cargo cult movements – Lawrence suggests five in number, focussing on specific cargo beliefs. During the initial contact period, a Russian aristocrat, Nikolai Miklouho–Maclay, who visited the Rai coast between 1871 and 1883, was identified by local people as one of their deities [*tibud*] and thus deemed to be a potential provider of material goods. (The notion that early Europeans were often considered gods by people of Melanesia and Polynesia became the subject of a controversial debate between two well-known scholars, Marshall Sahlins [1982, 1995] and Gamanath Obeyesekere [1992]. As all people have multiple perspectives on the world, as Obeyesekere himself suggests [1992, 224], there is some truth in both positions – and the notion of the apotheosis of Europeans may not be simply a product of the European colonial imagination – as Obeyesekere contends. See also Adam Kuper's reflections on this debate and on Sahlin's cultural determinism [1999, 177–200].)

This initial contact with Maclay was, however, fleeting and pragmatic and could hardly be described as a cargo cult (Lawrence 1964, 66).

In the following six decades of colonial rule, several cargo cult movements emerged in Southern Madang, and they had the following general characteristics:

- a belief that European goods (cargo) were not 'man-made' but had a divine source, namely, the cargo deities – whether local deities, God, or Jesus Christ, or the synthetic identity of God with a local deity;
- that the cargo could be obtained through the ancestral spirits by means of a charismatic leader and by the performance of specific rituals, and the observance of certain ritual prohibitions and moral edicts;
- a belief that the cargo would arrive by ship or aeroplane, and preparations were made to receive the cargo, and this had a 'millenarian' tendency;
- that the cargo beliefs and rituals were not fixed but were continually being revised and changed to meet changing circumstances, as well as varying according to specific locations;
- that these movements tended to have a syncretic quality, combining earlier pagan beliefs and rituals with those of Christianity; thus some were 'quasi-Christian' cargo cults;
- though many of the cult members considered themselves Christians, they often expressed hostility towards both the mission churches;
- there was a strong emphasis that either the missionaries were withholding ritual secrets or that Europeans were stealing people's share of the western goods (cargo) that were being sent via the ancestral spirits;
- some of the cults, such as those associated with the prophet Kaum (1942–1944), combined what was essentially a military rebellion with a cargo cult (Lawrence 1964, 63–115).

At the end of the Second World War, another phase of the cargo cult movement developed with the emergence of the 'Yali movement'. During the years 1948–1950, it flourished and was widespread throughout the Southern Madang district, particularly along the Rai coast. Belonging to the Ngaing ethnic community, Yali was born around 1912. His father was a respected community leader, renowned for his warlike process and for his mastery of sacred knowledge. Initiated into the kabu ceremony, Yali left home at a very early age and spent most of his life in close contact with Europeans. Although with little knowledge of his own religious culture, Yali was nevertheless an intelligent and able individual, always respectful and dignified, always neatly and smartly dressed, and with a deep sense of personal loyalty and responsibility. As he had never attended a mission school or been baptised, Yali was illiterate and had little knowledge of English. He always spoke in pidgin English rather than in Ngaing (Lawrence 1964, 117–27). But Lawrence, who knew him well, considered him as essentially a political leader who was a 'born manipulator' (1964, 268).

Yali had a varied career: He worked as an indentured labourer and waiter in a hotel; served as headman [*tultul*] of his own village of Sor and developed extremely cordial relations with Australian administrative officers; and he joined, around

1936, the local police force and loyally served the Australian administration throughout the Second World War at a time when many local people aided and supported the Japanese. He spent six months in Queensland undergoing training in jungle warfare; took part in several campaigns, making a heroic escape from one ambush in which his close friend, a European officer, was killed; and ended his army career with the rank of sergeant-major – the highest rank he could attain as a non-European in the Australian Armed Forces.

Given his personality and abilities and his epic wartime experiences, Yali was highly regarded and respected by the Australian administration when he returned to Madang in June 1945. He soon set about, on his own initiative, organizing a 'rehabilitation scheme' for local people along the Rai coast. Largely a secular affair, Yali advocated that people should cease living in small hamlets in the bush but regroup themselves in large villages with streets and live clean, orderly lives. Pigs were to be kept outside the village, old practices such as polygamy and abortion must be discontinued, and Yali encouraged people to co-operate with the Australian administration and to provide labour for the plantations. He was given a special post as an administrative 'overseer' at £4 per month, and he travelled extensively addressing meetings on behalf of the administration. But Yali was not involved in any cargo cult activity and even urged local people to show a greater interest in Christianity (Lawrence 1964, 142–65).

But then events began to take a different turn, and two developments occurred that tended to coalesce. On the one hand, Yali became increasingly disillusioned and embittered with the Australian administration. Given his undoubted talents and loyal service to the administration, he had expected to be given the rank of a 'patrol officer' in the administration, but this was denied him as he could not write or read English; and on a trip to Port Moresby in 1947, he was treated in a very offhand manner by government officials, and this further frustrated him. Yali was also very much aware that, in 1943, in its attempt to enlist local men in the Australian army, the administration had made a promise or pledge that at the end of the hositilities, in return for loyal support, people would be given houses with galvanized iron roofs, electric lights, motor vehicles, good clothes, and ample food – cargo! But for Yali, none of this materialized – only promises of new schools, hospitals, and new business opportunities. As Yali said to Lawrence, he realized that 'we just wouldn't get anything to give us a better life' (1964, 170).

On the other hand, various cargo cult movements were beginning to emerge in the South Madang district, and rumours were afoot that Yali was the new messiah, or the 'Black King', who would bring cargo to the people. He was seen by many local people as a superhuman being who had discovered the source of cargo and 'would see that the cargo deity ushered in the millennium for which they had worked and waited so long' (1964, 138).

Thus when he returned from Port Moresby in December 1947, Yali took a very different stance. He began campaigning against Christianity, and set about organizing a widespread revival of paganism. He began to associate closely with the prophet Gurek, who had been a Catholic Catechist and whose visionary experiences suggested that people should abandon Christianity and go back to their own religion – in order to receive cargo. The kabu ritual was reinstated and to be performed in full: Small tables were also set up and decorated with flowers, and

offerings of food and tobacco were to be placed on them for both the deities and the spirits of the dead, who were to be invoked to send cargo. (1964, 194)

As Yali was illiterate and 'no theologian', Gurek tended to act as his 'theological secretary' and adviser, but, given his formal status in the administration and his widespread popularity, Yali soon became the undisputed leader of the cargo cult movement. As Lawrence writes, Yali set himself up as a 'virtually independent autocrat' (1964, 204).

He ascribed to himself occult powers and set up his own political organization with 'boss boys' in practically every village of Southern Madang; and in his own area, Yali became the de facto judicial authority. Although at first restricted to an area around Yali's own village of Sor, the cargo cult movement during 1948 spread throughout the whole Rai coast, and the 'pagan revival' flourished. The kabu ceremony was held: Tables were decorated, food offerings made to the deities and spirits of the dead, and invocations made for the sending of cargo.

As cargo activities were illegal during the colonial period, the Australian administration repudiated Yali and denounced this cargo cult, and they were joined in this by the Lutheran Mission and their evangelists who always opposed Yali and the local rituals he had advocated. They depicted Yali as a 'Man of Satan'. By the early months of 1950, Yali himself became disillusioned with the failure of the kabu ceremony to bring the promised cargo, as envisaged by Gurek. But in July 1950 Yali was imprisoned for five years, not for promoting the cargo cult but for illegally depriving people of their liberty and for inciting others to rape. The trial took place in an atmosphere of acute racial tension. This marked the end of cargo cult activity in Southern Madang, at least as a widespread coordinated movement (Lawrence 1964, 215–21; for other studies of cargo cults and millenarian–type movements in Melanesia, see Burridge 1960; Schwartz 1962; Steinbauer 1979; Gesch 1985; Whitehouse 1995).

7.6. THE INTERPRETATION OF MILLENARIAN MOVEMENTS

'Cargo' cults, and millenarian movements more generally, have been subject to a plethora of interpretations – and in this section I review some of this literature, focussing on some key texts that relate to the Melanesian context.

In his study, *The Trumpet Shall Sound* (1957), Peter Worsley noted the similarities between Melanesian 'cargo cults' and the prophetic and millenarian movements described in other parts of the world. These include such movements as the Ghost

Dance religion among the Sioux at the end of the nineteenth century, the Mwana Leza movement in Zambia (described in Chapter 5), the Taiping revolution in China (1850–1865), the millenarian movements that have arisen within the Hindu and Buddhist context, as well as the millenarian movements described in medieval and early modern Europe (1957, 221–4; Mooney 1896; Cohn 1957; Mair 1959; Fuchs 1965; Burridge 1969; La Barre 1972; Wilson 1973).

Many anthropologists have seen such religious movements as constituting a specific type of movement that is associated particularly with social change and cultural dislocation. For example, in a seminal article, Anthony Wallace has described such innovatory cults as 'revitalization movements', which he has defined as a 'deliberate, organized, conscious effort by members of a society to construct a more satisfying culture' (1956, 422), and he indicates that they are recurrent features of human history, occurring at times of acute stress. He considered that both Christianity and Islam (and possibly Buddhism) had originated in revitalization movements. In the process of formation and eventual (or possible) routinization of these cults, Wallace saw the emergence of a prophet as of crucial importance:

> Every religious revitalization movement . . . has been originally conceived in one or several hallucinatory visions by a single individual. A supernatural being appears to the prophet-to-be, explains his own and his society's troubles as being entirely or partly a result of the violation of certain rules, and promises individual and social revitalization if the injunctions are followed and the rituals practiced, but personal and social catastrophe if they are not. (1956, 425)

Such visions are said by Wallace to indicate the dreamer's wish for a satisfying parental figure, to incorporate world-destruction fantasies (the apocalyptic millennial content), as well as expressing feelings of guilt and the need to establish an ideal state of stable and satisfying human relationships. Weber's concept of 'charismatic' leadership is acknowledged as being exemplified by the prophet, the latter's unique relationship with a divine being giving the visionary person moral authority (1965, 46–7).

Worsley, however, is critical of Weber's concept of 'charisma'. Taking a Marxist standpoint, and critical of the dubious division between historical or sociological studies as well as offering a lucid critique of Weberian sociology, Worsley suggests that the notion of charisma is not an explanatory concept but is itself an element in the sociological analysis – datum, something that people in the cults believe in. Moreover, although some cult leaders may be striking individuals and may be involved in healing rites or alleged miracles, he argues that charisma is essentially a social relationship rather than a personal attribute or a mystical quality (cf. Wilson 1973, 499). For often the personality of the prophet is unimportant in the emergence of such cults; what is crucial, Worsley suggests, is the social significance of the leader as symbol, catalyst, and message-bearer. Indeed, the founder of a cult may be treated as a prophet or a messiah – as with André Matswa's relation to the

Congolese messianic cults – without the person himself or herself having made claims to divine inspiration. The popular imagination, as it were, takes over. And as Burridge stresses, there are many different kinds of prophets; ranging from the sickly lad who dreams a dream on which others act but who is then heard of no more; or a half-crazed woman or visionary who is given to trances; to a shrewd man of stature, as Muhammad appears to have been, with real organizing ability (1969, 12). But as Worsley notes, compared with other forms of leadership whose authority or power may rest on patronage, the 'charismatic' leader or prophet is highly dependent on his followers, and an appropriate cult leader emerges only because he or she articulates and consolidates *their* aspirations. He boldly asserts that the personality of the prophet is often unimportant in so-called 'charismatic movements'. Worsley also notes that messianic cults often have a dual leadership, involving both an 'inspired' prophet who is often a recluse, given to visionary experiences, and a 'political organizer', who deals with the more secular affairs of the cult (1957, 271).

In the 'typical' case, however, the dreamer or visionary, having experienced a revelation, begins to preach his or her message in an evangelistic or messianic way. Converts are made by the prophet, and often, in the new prophetic cult, various forms of possession or ecstatic trance are displayed by the cult followers. Besides the advocacy of ritual procedures, there is always a moral component to the prophet's teaching. To what degree there is an affirmation or rejection of the 'traditional' moral code is variable. In the John Frum cargo cult, traditional dancing, drinking, and polygamy were restored, and in many African religious movements there is often, in reaction to the Christian missions, a tendency to emphasize 'traditional' practices. But equally possible, messianic cults may indicate an opposition to tribal religious and moral teachings. But as Worsley suggests in discussing the fact that both ritual obscenity and sexual asceticism may be expressed by such movements, the important point is that the millenarian sect represents a 'rejection' of the present order. 'All prophets', he writes, 'therefore, stress moral renewal; the love of one's cult brethren; new forms of sexual relationship; abandonment of stealing, lying, cheating, theft, devotion to the interests of the community' (1957, 251).

These prophets represent a spiritual and moral renewal, a 'radical break', or, as Burridge puts it, they provide the basis of a new integrity and are thus to be seen as a redemptive process (1969, 171) – though in *defining* religion generally as a set of assumptions about power that imply redemption, Burridge tends to obscure the fact that religion is not only concerned with the 'quality of one's humanity' (and there are echoes here of Turner's *communitas*) but may also function to maintain the status quo. Worsley's reminder, that though religion is 'always potentially innovatory', it is neither intrinsically conservative nor revolutionary, needs to be heeded (1957, xxix)

Millenarian cults therefore vary to the degree to which they stress the old cultural order. There is therefore a clear contrast, which Lucy Mair has explored (1959) in an interesting essay, between the ghost dance religion and the cargo cults. The former movement can justly be described as a 'nativistic' movement in that there was an attempt to 'revive or perpetuate selected aspects of its culture' (Linton 1943). For the ideal world revealed by Wovoka represented a return to the past and a rejection of much of the material culture of the Europeans, which, as Mair writes, has aroused the envy of most tribal peoples. In contrast, a characteristic feature of the cargo cults was an intense interest in material things and a full acceptance of material technology. There was little yearning for the past, and though ancestral spirits were important for the Melanesians, they were the harbingers of a new material well-being that they felt they were being denied. Mair links this difference to the fact that the Melanesian peoples, unlike the Plains Indians, were not 'forcibly detached from their accustomed environment and whole way of life' (1959, 334).

But though there is some variation in the degree to which millennial movements, in their rites, symbols, and morality, represent a rejection of the old order, in an important sense such movements have an essentially syncretic quality. As processes of 'revitalization' or as new religious expressions, they inevitably combine elements of a 'traditional' or 'ethnic' cult, as well as those of the dominant ideology and culture.

There is also some variation in the degree to which the 'millennial' is stressed by such messianic cults. In the taro cult, there was little millennial expectation, whereas in the later cargo cults and in the ghost dance religion – as well as in other millennial sects – there is an anticipation of the millennium in the immediate future, and preparations may be made for this event. Variable too is the degree to which ecstatic rites are expressed, and in terms of Douglas' distinction between 'ritualism' and 'effervescence' (1970, 103–4), millennial cults can by no means be seen as an 'unstructured breaking out' from the dominant ideology. Millennial and ecstatic tendencies do not necessarily coincide. Nonetheless, as many anthropologists have stressed, no sharp line of demarcation can be drawn – or should be drawn – between specifically millennial cults and other related religious movements. In terms of their context, nature, and social function, there are indeed close affinities between millennial-type cults and witch-finding movements, separatist churches, and prophetic cults. Worsley notes the functional similarities of millenarian cults, religious movements led by prophets that were not specifically millenarian (the Sudanese Mahdiya, for example), and separatist sects without prophets but with millennial tendencies.

Worsley suggests that the crucial distinction is not between millenarian and non-millenarian movements but between activist and passivist cults (1957, 236).

Almost all writers on millenarian cults have stressed that such movements have found support and have arisen largely among people who feel themselves oppressed and who are longing for deliverance. The basic condition, writes Worsley, is 'a situation of dissatisfaction with existing social relations and of yearnings for a happier life' (1957, 243). Such conditions are to be found specifically in colonial situations and among discontented and landless peasants in feudal societies (as Cohn observed). La Barre indeed describes such movements as 'crisis cults' (1972, 253). Worsley's study is a sustained attempt to provide an explanation of cargo cults in terms of the radical social changes brought about by colonial rule in New Guinea – the impact of the missions, the introduction of cash crops, and the effect of the migrant labour system, as well as the apparent vagaries of the market economy – from the viewpoint of the Papuans. Although, to my mind, no one has offered any substantial criticisms of Worsley's thesis, many anthropologists have expressed some dissatisfaction with the tenor of the work. Shepperson (1962) has stressed that millennial-type sects often occur as marginal cults among high-status groups – but though perhaps true, this fact does not invalidate Worlsey's argument. Wilson (1973, 499) has noted that there are many cases of societies in which exploitation and relative deprivation are identifiable but in which no millennial tendencies have occurred, but this observation calls for further research, rather than a dismissal of the causal connection that Worsley postulates. And, finally, both Mair (1958) and La Barre (1972, 262) have queried Worsley's *stress* on political and economic 'factors' in his explanation of cargo cults. But as the preceding writers themselves have a tendency to explain such cults in terms of social oppression, Worsley has every right to feel 'unrepentant' about his basic theory, namely, that millennial cults are 'movements of the disinherited' (1957, xiii).

But Worsley argues that such cults must not be seen as an 'irrational flight from reality' (1957, 242); they are rather to be viewed as a rational response and a criticism of a situation that is not only intolerable but inexplicable in terms of the existing cultural ethos. This is a viewpoint that was taken up and developed by Jarvie (1964) in his theoretical study of cargo cults but which has been challenged by other writers. La Barre, in his psychoanalytic interpretation of religious movements, indeed asserts that 'cargo' ideology 'was not rational-economic but irrational-religious' (1972, 267). Worsley, of course, does not deny that millennial cults are essentially religious movements in their ideology, but he also sees these cults as having important political functions. For in the Melanesian context, the cults had an 'integrative role' in welding together previously hostile and separate tribal groups (1957, 228); thus, millenarian cults may be seen as being 'proto-political' movements, representing a phase in the political and economic development of a region. They may, of course, *coexist* with more overtly political forms of protest, but in both colonial and feudal situations, the earliest forms of protest tend to have a religious guise. And Worsley indicates that in the suppression of the cults by the authorities, two developments are possible – either the cult becomes a quietist sect and rarely looks forward to the millennial in the *immediate* future, or the cult develops away from the apocalyptic mission and towards a more secular political organization. In other words, the millennial sect becomes an incipient political organization. He notes, however, that in the Melanesian situation, 'cargo' cults were mostly associated with rural populations and that within the urban context, secular forms of protest tended to predominate. For Worsley then, the cargo cults were the 'first stirrings' of Melanesian nationalism. This thesis, however, has been questioned by other anthropologists.

In his study, *Road Belong Cargo* (1964), Peter Lawrence, like many other social anthropologists, makes a clear distinction between the 'actual situation', relating to practical experiences and actual social relationships between human beings, and religion or 'ideological relations' – specifically with deities and spirits – that imply sacred knowledge and certain epistemological assumptions. But the two aspects of social life among the people of the Southern Madang (Garia, Ngaing) are seen by Lawrence as closely interdependent. Thus religion, specifically beliefs relating to cargo, is not seen as an 'epiphenomenon' nor simply reduced to social relations (social structure).

In his social analysis of cargo cults in Southern Madang, Lawrence acknowledged that these movements could be seen as a rudimentary form of revolutionary 'nationalism' – an attempt to establish a new social order and to achieve independence from colonial rule. But he also emphasized that there was no wholesale cultural disintegration in the region, and that the cargo movement represented a continuity with earlier religious forms and was 'conservative rather than revolutionary' (1964, 223). It was engendered not by too much change but rather, from the local people's point of view, by too little change. His analysis is essentially focussed around three questions or issues.

The first relates to why the people of the Madang district placed so much emphasis and social value on European goods or cargo. The main reason for this – the 'precipitating' causes – Lawrence relates to the social and economic impact of the colonial contact itself, the introduction of the plantation economy along with European commodities. The 'obsession for cargo' thus reflected not only what had come to be seen by local people as necessities but also was an index of people's own 'self-respect'. The lack of cargo became a 'symbol of European oppression' and its appropriation an expression of reciprocal and equitable social relationships on which local people placed so much social value and to which they hoped to aspire vis-à-vis Europeans. The principal motivations of the cargo cult movement therefore expressed a real need for European goods (cargo) and an emphasis on equal and humane treatment – derived from the values of the local culture.

The second question relates to why people felt that material wealth, the cargo, could best be obtained not through secular activity but by means of ritual. The reason for this, Lawrence contends, was due to the 'epistemological' assumptions that were inherent in the earlier religious traditions: These implied that material well-being was achieved through ritual propitiations to the deities and ancestral spirits. Thus the conviction of the people of the Madang district that they could obtain cargo 'almost exclusively by ritual' must be seen as their attempt to control the new situation by the same sorts of ritual techniques that had served them well in the past. Thus Lawrence suggests that the cargo movement was 'strongly conservative' and 'represented the continuation of the essential features of the people's old way of life under new external conditions' (1964, 232).

The third question relates to the effects or consequences of the cargo cult movement, namely, its political significance. Lawrence emphasizes that the cargo movement was in no sense a 'nativistic' movement, simply attempting to revive the past cultural tradition (Linton 1943), for the movement was primarily forward-looking. Thus, Lawrence writes, 'its overall aim was not to turn the clock back to the pre-contact past but to enrich the present and future with European goods' (1964, 256).

The reason people reacted to the European occupation in terms of their old values and epistemological assumptions was largely because they knew of no other alternative. Thus the cargo movements' 'steadfast conservatism' prevented it from becoming a fully fledged revolutionary, proto-nationalist movement. Nevertheless, in its opposition to colonial rule and in bringing together people of many different ethnic communities and developing a 'sense of solidarity', the cargo cult movement did eventually give rise to a form of 'embryonic nationalism' (Lawrence 1964, 257).

In his study, *Big Men and Cargo Cults* (1970), which includes accounts of the Vailala Madness and the cargo cults of the Solomon Islands, Glynn Cochrane affirms that these movements were largely about power, wealth, and status. He eschews concepts such as 'nativistic' and 'revitalization', which are largely descriptive terms with little explanatory power, and questions the validity of many psychological theories. He also agrees with Worsley that concentration on the 'prophet' and his message is a suspect form of analysis. His own account suggests that traditional notions of wealth and political status, which focussed around the 'big men', largely remained unchanged during the colonial period in spite of the harsh impact of European rule. Thus the leaders of the cargo cult movements were, in essence, new 'big men', and they were chosen as leaders by the community specifically because it was felt that they could solve the problems that had been created by the colonial encounter. But in all these movements, Cochrane suggests that the new 'big men' gained their status in conformity with traditional epistemological assumptions regarding the nature of power and wealth (1970, 145–66).

In contrast, G. W. Trompf's reflections on the interpretation of cargo cults in Melanesia is largely a sermon on the limitations of sociological analysis. The use of general sociological categories is likened to the 'incantations of sorcery' (although Trompf himself uses them throughout his own text); psychological explanations are dismissed as 'glib' or 'Eurocentric'; all social-scientific explanations of cargo cults are seen as 'superficial', 'one track', or as reducing religion to the status of 'epiphenomena'; and modern sociology itself is likened to the conjuring up of a 'witches' brew'. He pleads that scholars should recognize the 'intrinsically religious or spiritual nature' of cargo cults (as if in the past anthropologists and sociologists had failed to recognize that these were in fact religious movements) and suggests that then 'an openness to particular historical contexts and to a variety of causal factors and explanations is required before an adequate general theory of cargo cults' can be achieved. Such a strategy has long been advocated by social scientists and runs completely counter to the religious phenomenology he flaunts and adopts in his own critique! (Trompf 1991, 188–211).

Although Worsley had emphasized the limitations of 'ideal type' analysis, which is formal, abstract, and simply creates 'pigeonholes', as well as being tautologous and lacking any explanatory power, it is this kind of analysis that is taken up by Harvey Whitehouse (2000) in a recent study of Melanesian religion. It has long been recognized by anthropologists that there are often two styles of religiosity, and throughout this study we have discussed the varying contrasts between 'world' religions (Buddhism, Christianity) and folk religions (the spirit cults), the great and little traditions in Hinduism (Marriott), clerical and ecstatic styles in Islam (Gellner), and the distinction between central and peripheral cults (Lewis). Whitehouse systematized this contrast and posits two 'modes of religiosity', with concomitant ways of revelation – the disclosure of sacred knowledge – codification, cognition, and social organization. This conceptual schema can be summarized thus:

	Doctrinal	**Imagistic**
Revelation through transmission	Codified body of doctrine routinized worship (language–dialogue)	Sporadic collective rituals multivocal imagery (ecstatic–ritual)
Memory	Semantic (cultural schemas)	Episodic (personal)
Religious outlook	Universal	Particularistic
Cognition	Digital	Analogic
Social organization	Anonymous communities (hierarchy)	Small-scale groups, solidarity (egalitarian)

In his study, Whitehouse relates these two forms of 'religiosity' to four specific case studies – initiation rites among the Baktaman, and three cargo cult movements: the taro cult among the Orokaiva (discussed in this chapter), the Paliau movement of Manus, and the Pomio Kivung of New Britain. In the chapter on 'Indigenous Religions', Whitehouse focusses almost exclusively on boys' initiation rites, for unlike other rituals, such as those relating to marriage, magic, ceremonial exchange, and mortuary rites, initiations have a 'revelatory' emphasis, disclosing through ritual the sacred knowledge concerning the structure of the cosmos and the place of humans within it. Initiation rites are a once-in-a-lifetime experience for the boys, and such experiences are traumatic – Whitehouse describes them as 'rites of terror' that are unforgettable, vivid, and haunting. The solidarity and social cohesion generated among the initiates is functionally related to a 'political landscape' that is composed of small autonomous local groups standing in relationship of hostility or rivalry to each other – such as we find also among the Kwaio and Tsembaga'. Unsurprisingly, such initiations express the Imagistic or Iconic mode of religiosity (Whitehouse 2000, 30–2). The taro cult, likewise, as discussed in Subsection 7.4.1, with its emphasis on spirit-possession and the harvesting of taro, also expressed the imagistic mode of religiosity, for the stress was on fragmented local ritual congregations and the generation and spread of its 'revelations' through the medium of rituals (2000, 66–8). In contrast, Whitehouse argues, both the Paliau movement and the Pomio Kivung were cult movements that exhibited the 'doctrinal' mode of religiosity, for there was an emphasis on hierarchical structures, discipline, and language-based systems (derived from Christianity and the colonial administration), and they provided a 'doctrine–based ideology' – which, again, is hardly surprising, given the definition of the doctrinal mode! (2000, 58–63).

But interestingly, Whitehouse emphasizes that these cargo cult movements were not so much 'proto-nationalist' movements, with respect to the modern state of Papua, New Guinea, but rather had a 'micro-nationalist' or regional significance (2000, 47–8).

In a discussion of various explanations of millenarian movements, Kenelm Burridge suggests that Marxist interpretations, exemplified by Worsley's study, are themselves part of a 'millennial' tradition – though we're never told exactly when Marx claimed to have had a divine inspiration. But although allegedly a part of every ethnographic and socio-historical explanation, the Marxist explanation is unable to explain, according to Burridge, 'the divine intervention demonstrated by the prophet' (1969, 136). But then, only the divinity knows the answer to that!

8

Neopaganism and the New Age Movement

8.1. PROLOGUE

Over the past fifty years in Western Europe and North America, there has been a tremendous upsurge of what has generally been described as 'new religious movements'. Although mainly associated with western societies and with the 'counterculture' of the 1960s, these movements have not been confined to the western world, and their social significance and impact have been both profound and worldwide. Among the best known of these religious movements are the Church of Scientology, the Divine Light Mission, the Unification Church, the Order of the Solar Temple, the Children of God, Subud, the People's Temple, and a movement that we have discussed in Chapter 4 – the Hare Krishna movement. Most of these religious movements started as social organizations that were largely community based, and, as Elizabeth Arweck writes, they 'drew clear boundaries between themselves and the wider society, developed hierarchical structures, and had a distinct set of beliefs and teachings formulated by the leadership and put down in writing' (2002, 265).

These teachings were often syncretic in nature, drawing from various religious traditions. "New" religions are not, of course, entirely a new phenomena, as innovative religious developments have occurred throughout history, but contemporary religious movements have tended to be distinctive in being highly syncretic and in utilizing modern means of communication, including the Internet. Membership of many of these movements has also tended to be rather restrictive – mainly young, well educated, and of a largely middle-class or even affluent background. Although in their beliefs, practices, and activities these new religious movements are extremely diverse, the authority structure of many is often focussed around male charismatic leaders and put an emphasis on authoritative texts. Many of these movements have also had a millennial emphasis, and some, such as the People's Temple, associated with the Reverend Jim Jones, came to an end in tragic circumstances (Hall 2003). Others have been surrounded in controversy and have generated a good deal of resentment and opposition, which has culminated in what has been described as the 'anti-cult movement.' Thus many new religious movements reject being labelled a 'cult'. Estimates regarding the number of new religious movements are varied, but Peter Clarke has estimated that over 400 'new' religious movements have emerged in Britain alone since 1945, and the figure is much higher for North America and post-war Japan. Even so, although the membership of new religious movements may run into millions, it is estimated that less than one per cent of the population of Europe and North America have a long-term commitment to such religious movements (Clarke 1988, 149; Arweck 2002, 274–5).

The literature on new religious movements is now vast, and it is beyond the scope of this present study to engage with this literature. I instead focus in this chapter on two religious movements – Neopaganism and the New Age movement – that are not usually considered under the rubric 'new religious movements'. The reason for this is not entirely clear, but the suggestion is that Neopaganism and the New Age movement indicate a resistance to establishing formal institutional structures, place a strong emphasis on personal religious experience and hence on purely individual authority, and have a this-worldly emphasis, with a corresponding stress on ritual magic, spiritual healing, and self-realization (Arweck 2002; for useful studies of new religious movements, see Beckford 1986; Wilson and Cresswell 1999; Dawson 2003).

The first part of this chapter is focussed on Neopaganism. In Section 8.2, I discuss the notion that this movement is a 'rebirth' or 'revival' of the ancient religion of Western Europe, which is self-consciously acclaimed by many of its devotees. Noting that it is more accurately conceived of as a contemporary manifestation of western esotericism, I outline the basic principles of modern paganism as a worldview. These include the following: radical polytheism, an ecological and feminist emphasis, decentralized politics, the celebration of ritual, a stress on personal experience, and the embrace of esotericism – the notion that divinity is within the human personality.

In Section 8.3, I examine the historical 'roots' of modern paganism and emphasize the important influence of two key figures – Margaret Murray and Gerald Gardner. After a short biographical sketch of Murray, I critically examine her thesis that a 'witch cult' existed in early modern Europe, and that the 'great witch hunt' of the period 1450–1650 was largely an attempt to stamp out a religion that was focussed around women and fertility rites. I then turn to a discussion of Gerald Gardner who, while uncritically accepting Murray's thesis and allegedly discovering an ancient witch cult still existing in England in the 1930s, was nevertheless instrumental in the founding of Neopaganism as a viable movement. I note the importance of Doreen Valiente in shaping the ethos of Neopaganism and conclude the section with a discussion of some of the major cultural trends within Britain that have been important in the 'revival' of Neopaganism as a religious movement.

Neopaganism is a diverse and eclectic movement, and in Section 8.4, I critically discuss the four 'pagan pathways' that constitute the movement, namely, Wicca, Feminist Witchcraft, Druidry, and the Northern tradition. Within the section, I devote some discussion to the notion of a supposedly 'golden age of matriarchy' and the idea of a universal mother goddess, as well as to the link that has often been made between the Northern pagan tradition and national socialism.

In Section 8.5, I turn to the 'Western Mystery tradition', and after discussing the important influences of two early twentieth-century occultists, Aleister Crowley and Dion Fortune, I outline the basic elements of this tradition, otherwise known as western esotericism. These elements include the concept of a 'world soul' and the notion of 'occult' powers that can be harnessed through ritual magic; the doctrine of correspondences; and the importance of gnosis, divine knowledge, the recognition of a 'higher self', and that divinity lies within the human personality.

In the following section – Section 8.6 – I focus on ethnographic studies of contemporary ritual magic, specifically on Tanya Luhrmann's study *Persuasions of the Witch's Craft* and on Richard Sutcliffe's seminal discussion of the various groups, which, influenced by Crowley, follow the 'left-hand path' of magic.

The final part of the chapter is devoted to a discussion of the New Age Movement, and in the final section I discuss some of the key elements and manifestations of New Age spirituality – the importance of ritual magic and channelling, its emphasis on 'self-spirituality' and its equation of the higher self with divinity, as well as its 'countercultural' and millennial aspects. I conclude the section with a review of critiques of the New Age movement and its contrast with Neopaganism.

8.2. THE CONTEMPORARY NEOPAGAN REVIVAL

Over the past thirty years, there has been a self-conscious resurgence or revival of pre-Christian Paganism in both Western Europe and the United States. This new religious movement, which is often described as 'Neopaganism' or 'modern witchcraft', tends to present itself as a revival or as a contemporary manifestation of the 'old religion', the witch cult of Western Europe, as Margaret Murray described it (1931, 19). But what is clearly evident is that Neopaganism is an extremely diverse and eclectic movement – both in its beliefs and ritual practices – and that it is less of a 'nature religion' than the latest manifestation or development of the hermetic tradition, or what has also been described as 'ritual magic' or 'Western esotericism'. Indeed, Susan Greenwood suggests that the notion that Neopaganism or witchcraft is an 'ancient pagan practice' of the common people in a rural setting is largely a romantic 'construction' of people like Gerald Gardner in the middle of the twentieth century (1998, 102). Of interest is that the main advocates of Neopaganism have been anthropologists like Gardner; indeed, two books by anthropologists have been particularly influential in the resurgence of Neopaganism – the 'Wiccan revival' – Margot Adler's *Drawing Down the Moon* and Starhawk's *The Spiral Dance*, the latter book bearing the significant subtitle *A Rebirth of the Ancient Religion of the Great Goddess.* Both books were published in the same year (1979) and both Adler and Starhawk (Miriam Simos) were trained as anthropologists and have a radical Jewish background. This close association of Neopaganism with academia still continues, and many of the leading figures and advocates of 'polytheistic pagan religion' tend to be university teachers, either in anthropology or religious studies departments. Yet although many Neopagans stridently deny that 'Wicca' is a part of the New Age movement (Pearson 1998), nevertheless one has to recognize that there is considerable overlap in the beliefs and rituals of the two movements – Neopaganism and the New Age movement. Both can be seen as divergent expression of western esotericism.

Modern Paganism has been described as a new religion that emerged at the end of the twentieth century, a religion based on 'nature worship' and 'ancient indigenous traditions' – particularly drawing on Celtic and northern (Germanic and Scandinavian) religious traditions. It is estimated that there are around 50,000 Neopagans in Britain – more than twice that number in the United States – and it is considered one of the fastest growing new religious movements (Adler 1979, 455; Hardman and Harvey 1996, ix). Yet it is singularly ignored by many texts on new religious movements, or it is simply seen as a part of the New Age culture (e.g., Wilson and Cresswell 1999; Dawson 2003).

The term 'Pagan', it is thought, is derived from the Latin *pagus*, which essentially means the 'countryside' or a 'rural locality' – in contrast to the city [*civitas*]. A Pagan [*paganus*] thus simply means a country dweller, although this meaning has been challenged by some scholars (Fox 1986, 30–1). 'Pagan' thus tends to have pejorative connotations, particularly as the prophetic religions, such as Christianity, have denigrated and attempted over the centuries to eradicate the pre-Christian religious traditions. These were essentially polytheistic and involved ecstatic rites and ritual magic. The pre-Christian religious culture of Western Europe, whether in respect to the religions of the Celtic or Germanic tribes or that of classical antiquity (Greek or Roman) – collectively known as Paganism – were all, in essence, polytheistic, many different spiritual entities (gods, deities, spirits, fairies) being recognized, and these were often immanent in natural phenomena. Such European Pagan traditions, as Prudence Jones writes, fulfilled their 'age-old function of making human beings feel at home in the world around them' (1998, 85; for useful studies of the Pagan religions of Europe, see Burkert 1985; Fox 1986; Hutton 1991; Jones and Pennick 1995).

Whether or not Neopaganism is simply an 'invented' or 'imagined' tradition, part of a reaction against Christianity and the vicissitudes of capitalist 'modernity', or whether it is a 'survival' or 'revival' of pre-Christian beliefs and rituals has long been the subject of debate. Scholars and adherents within the Neopagan movement, however, tend to stress that it is not some 'New Age fad' but the reaffirmation of a religious tradition that goes back to antiquity; it is thus something of a 'revivalist' movement (Adler 1979, 80–6; Jones 1998).

Modern Paganism has been described as a 'worldview' or theology that is characterized by a certain number of principles or 'basic beliefs'. These include the following:

8.2.1. Radical Polytheism

It espouses a 'radical polytheism' that entails the view that reality is multiply and diverse and that divinity is manifested in, that is, immanent, in all natural phenomena. Although some feminist witches place a fundamental emphasis on the 'great mother goddess', which almost suggests a strident monotheism, most Pagans seem to happily combine and advocate animism, spiritism, pantheism, panentheism, and polytheism (Adler 1979, 4; Carpenter 1996, 49–57). There is a sense in which nature, culture, and life in all its diversity are considered sacred, and the earth itself the 'embodiment' of the 'goddess' or a pantheon of spirits and deities. Neopaganism is thus described as a 'religion of immanence' – contrasting with the doctrinal and transcendental emphasis of Christianity. In essence, then, Neopaganism recognizes a plurality of spiritual beings and views the material world as a theophany, a manifestation of divinity (Adler 1979, x; Jones 1996, 34).

8.2.2. Ecological Perspective

Although virtually equating polytheism and mother-goddess religion with an ecological worldview – which is a secular tradition stemming from Darwin (see Morris 1996) – Neopaganism nevertheless puts a fundamental emphasis on ecology and on the environment. It advocates a sacred ecology that repudiates the Baconian ethic of human domination over nature and the capitalist outlook that views nature simply as a commodity or as a resource to be exploited. An ecological critique of capitalism and mechanistic philosophy goes back, of course, to the nineteenth century, but Neopagans reaffirm this critique and advocate a love for and a 'kinship' with nature. Neopaganism is thus conceived as a religious outlook that is 'nature venerating' (although rituals and prayers are usually addressed to the spirits or the mother goddess, perceived as anthropomorphic beings), and Adler concludes that all the Pagan traditions emphasize a 'reverence for nature' (Adler 1979, 23; Carpenter 1996, 63–4; Harris 1996).

8.2.3. Feminism

There are close affinities between feminism and Neopaganism, for both put an emphasis on the 'feminine', and Pagan theologians like Starhawk indeed define the 'ancient' religion or witchcraft as 'goddess religion'. The goddess in thus not only pantheistically equated with the world or with 'reality' but is seen also as immanent in both humans and the natural world. The world, Starhawk writes, 'is the manifestation of the goddess', and this 'model' of the goddess, who is immanent in nature, 'fosters respect for the sacredness of all living things' (Starhawk 1979, 22–6). Neopaganism is thus seen as a form of 'feminist spirituality' that is opposed to the patriarchal religions such as Islam and Christianity (Adler 1979, 22).

8.2.4. Decentralized Politics

Neopaganism is a very diverse and decentralized religious movement. Adler not only describes Neopagan groups as 'eclectic, individualist and often fiercely autonomous' but the movement as a whole as displaying a 'gentle anarchism, and a remarkable tolerance of diversity' (1979, 3–5). There is therefore little emphasis on 'gurus' and spiritual 'masters', and this is combined with a tendency to repudiate all forms of hierarchy, or what Starhawk refers to, appropriating without acknowledgement of the basic tenets of anarchism, as 'power-over'. This entails a rejection of asceticism, sadomasochistic forms of thought, and all forms of hierarchy and coercive power (Starhawk 1982, 140). It also involves an affirmation of sexuality – although this tends to be spiritualized as 'numinous and sacred' (Starhawk 1979, 27). The Pagan ethic is therefore proclaimed as 'do what thou wilt but harm none', with an emphasis on community rather than on hierarchical organization (Hardman and Harvey 1996, xi).

8.2.5. The Celebration of Ritual

Neopaganism not only has links with the ecology and feminist movements, but it is, according to Adler, also closely interwoven with visionary and artistic traditions. It thus puts an important stress on drama, music, myth-making, and ritual. The important Pagan rituals are the festivals that celebrate the main seasonal days of the year that are associated with the equinoxes and the solstices. These festivals, such as Hallowe'en (Samhaim) (October 31) and Beltane (May 1) were important in the Celtic and Anglo-Saxon religious traditions and were later incorporated into Christianity. Today they are celebrated as Neopagan festivals (Burnett 1991, 149–63; Crowley 1996b, 84–103). Equally important, ceremonial magic is a crucial aspect of modern withcraft. As Starhawk writes, 'Magic, the art of sensing and shaping the subtle, unseen forces that flow through the world . . . is an element common to all traditions of witchcraft' (1979, 27).

Thus, in common with tribal religions generally and unlike many other new religious movements, Neopaganism puts an emphasis on ritual and magical practices rather than on doctrine and belief. As one scholar puts it, 'Pagan religion is magical' (Jones 1996, 39; Lewis 1996, 4).

The emphasis and the value that are placed on ritual magic are two of the distinguishing features of modern witchcraft – as compared with other religious traditions, and indeed, they tend to undermine the familiar distinction between magic and religion. Magical practice among Neopagans is in fact redefined as religious ritual – namely, as communication with an 'other-worldly reality', the domain of gods, goddesses, spirits, fairies, and 'magical powers' (Greenwood 2000, 33–5). As Hutton puts it, 'for Neopagans both religion and magic are a "means" by which humans negotiate with supernatural beings', and they do so by ritual. By these criteria, of course, almost all religions are 'magical'. But Neopagans show little concern with regard to propitiating the Pagan deities, and the concept of sacrifice is usually absent from their ritual practices (Hutton 1999, 394). This focus on ritual magic among Neopagans indicates the important influence of western esotericism (discussed in Subsection 8.2.7) on the movement.

8.2.6. Emphasis on Spiritual Experience

The stress in Neopaganism is not on reason, nor on issues of faith, nor on prophetic revelation but rather on personal religious experience. Such experience relates to a sense that the natural world is alive and the site of 'numinous' or 'occult' powers. As Prudence Jones puts it, for Pagans, 'the divine, transcendent powers seem to be present within nature itself' (1996, 37). Such 'empiricism' she sees as essentially anti-authoritarian, but as it might also entail a loss of human agency, she advocates restricting communion with the 'divine world' to ritual occasions (1996, 38). Her notion that Marxism entails the idea that humans are 'helpless' and lack agency 'before the great tides of class and history' is, of course, a complete distortion of Marxism. But all scholars stress that Neopagans, like advocates of the New Age, put an important emphasis on the 'primacy' of spiritual experience – whether this is a visionary experience of some deity, the numinous experience of a divine 'presence', or the mystical or ecstatic experience of union with the divinity – especially with the goddess (Carpenter 1996, 65–7).

8.2.7. Esotericism

Strongly influenced by western esotericism and Jungian psychology, many scholars emphasize that Wicca or Neopaganism is a 'mystery religion' and akin to 'spiritually oriented psychotherapy'. It is thus centrally focussed on self-knowledge, inner harmony, and self-realization, the achievement of a 'stable core of personality' – the self (Crowley 1996a, 81–3). Following the Occultist Dion Fortune, Starhawk affirms, in New Age fashion, that Neopagan rituals involve a change of consciousness, a state of ecstasy in which there is 'union with the divine' – with the goddess as a real being (1979, 28). In its emphasis on immanence, magic, and self-empowerment, Neopaganism is clearly a variant of the western esoteric tradition.

In his history of modern Pagan witchcraft, Ronald Hutton emphasizes from his own observations that the key features of the movement are essentially esoteric – in aiming to engender and enhance the divinity within each human being and in being a 'mystery' religion, with its initiations and lack of any public rituals (1999, 391–7).

These then are the main tenets of the Neopagan 'revivalist' movement – a radical polytheism with an emphasis on immanence, on ecological perspective, a stress on the feminine and on the mother goddess, decentralized politics, a celebration of ritual magic and drama, and an experiential and esoteric approach to the 'divine'. But what is also very evident with regard to Neopaganism as a religious movement is that it is extremely eclectic and protean, and, like the New Age movement, it contains 'a rich Kaleidoscope of cultural borrowings from all over the globe, fashioned according to the tastes of the person or group working within it' (Hutton 1999, 398–9).

8.3. THE ROOTS OF NEOPAGAN WITCHCRAFT

The history or 'roots' of Neopaganism seem to centre largely around two key figures, Margaret Murray and Gerald Gardner. The revival of Neopaganism has, in fact, served to redeem both these scholars from relative obscurity.

Margaret Murray (1863–1963) was a remarkable woman, an Egyptologist by profession, who taught at University College, London, and whose lively autobiography bears the striking title, *My First Hundred Years* (1963). Doreen Valiente, who knew Murray well in her later years, described her as a tiny woman, 'bright-eyed and alert', who had a mischievous sense of fun (1973, 248). Murray was a pioneer suffragette, conducted archaeological excavations in Egypt, and wrote over eighty books and articles on the ancient Near East. Her most famous book, however, is *The Witch Cult in Western Europe* (1921). This book suggested that witchcraft in early modern Europe represented the continuing existence and relevance of a pre-Christian Pagan religion focussed around fertility rites. Her thesis was not exactly original: The radical French scholar Jules Michelet in his book *La Sorciere* (1862) and the American folklorist and mystic Charles Leland (1899) had many years earlier suggested similar ideas regarding the existence of a 'Medieval Witch Cult' (Hutton 1999, 137–49). But Murray's study had an important impact and influenced many later scholars: It forms the basis of the studies of witchcraft by, for example, Hughes (1952) and Lethbridge (1962).

Basing her researches on documents relating to the early witchcraft trials and unwilling to accept that the witch beliefs and accusations could be dismissed as pure nonsense, Murray argued that there was in fact a 'Witch Cult', a religious cult that was not a heretical form of Christianity but rather a survival of an earlier Pagan religion. The cult involved the worship of the goddess Diana and had the following characteristics. First, the witches met regularly at their 'Sabbath' and formed 'covens' of thirteen, the leader usually being a man. The meeting was essentially a religious gathering, a fertility ritual with feasting and dancing. The women would rub themselves with the witches 'flying' ointment, and as Pennethorne Hughes suggests, the group leader would go into a trance state and be possessed by the deity (1952, 141). Murray thus argues that the rituals of this underground cult were simply Pagan rituals, and that it was the Christian priests and theologians who, in opposition to the cult, came to describe it in negative terms, such as involving a compact with the devil.

Second, the 'devil' worshipped by members of the witch cult was in reality the 'horned god', a spirit of antiquity. The spirit was made manifest through masked dances, the leader of the cult impersonating the spirit. The term *devil*, derived from the same root as the Hindu term *devas*, originally carried more positive connotations. But again, Murray argues that the Christian church, in seeking to stamp out this rival cult, identified the 'horned god' with Satan and with immoral and diabolical practices. In her later study, *The God of the Witches* (1931), Murray identified the 'horned god' with images and notions drawn from many different cultural contexts – the famous 'sorcerer' depicted in Palaeolithic rock art at Trois Freres in the Pyrenees; the Egyptian deity Amon who is usually represented by a ram with curved horns; Cernunnus, the Gallic deity with antlers that were viewed as symbols of potency and fertility; and Herne the hunter, the phantom of Windsor Park, who was associated with witchcraft. All these are interpreted by Murray as manifestations of the Pagan 'horned god' (1931, 23–45). This horned god was seen as the principal deity of the 'old religion' – the Pagan witch cult. Murray also emphasizes the importance of witches or 'wise women' as healers, diviners, and rainmakers, and the fact that they often utilized spirit-familiars – hare, dog, cat, toad – in their divination rituals (1931, 145–6). Interestingly, Murray puts little emphasis on the mother goddess.

There is some evidence to suggest that during the early medieval period, two forms of religion did in fact exist: the dominant cult, Christianity, and a pre-Christian Pagan religion. The Venerable Bede (circa 672–735 C.E.), for instance, described how King Redwald maintained two altars in the same temple, one for Christian worship and the other for sacrifices to the Pagan gods (Hole 1947, 27); and in the same century, the Archbishop of Canterbury made a famous injunction proclaiming that any person wearing an animal mask shall do 'penance for three years because it is devilish' (Hughes 1952, 54). But Murray argued that such Pagan cults were important well into the seventeenth century and constituted a vibrant and rival religion to Christianity and were supported by the bulk of the peasant population.

Murray's thesis, though accepted by writers like Hughes, has come in for a good deal of criticism, some of it rather disparaging. The historian Trevor-Roper (1967) described her ideas as the products of her own 'fancies', while Lucy Mair suggested that Murray simply 'invented' a religion for the purposes of her own argument (1969, 229). In his important study on the popular beliefs of sixteenth- and seventeenth-century England, Keith Thomas, though accepting that there were many 'pagan survivals' – beliefs in magic, divination, astrology, calendrical and fertility rites, folk herbalism – argues that there is little evidence to suggest that the accused witches were either devil-worshippers or members of a Pagan fertility cult (1971, 514–16). Likewise, Norman Cohn, though accepting the reality of 'ritual magic', seriously questions Murray's thesis as well as criticizes her mode of scholarship. The misleading emphasis on 'fertility cults' he puts down to the influence of James Frazer, whose classic study, *The Golden Bough* (1922), was then in vogue (Cohn 1975, 107–9).

Whether or not there existed an organized witch cult in the manner Murray suggested is perhaps open to dispute, but clearly the existence of a pre-Christian Pagan religion cannot be dismissed as simply the product of Murray's own imagination – for the existence of various cults have been noted by later historians.

Cohn admits that the cult of Diana enjoyed a certain popularity in the early medieval period and notes that the church became increasingly more severe in its dealings with women who thought themselves followers of Diana (1975, 212–17). Recent research by historians like Le Roy Ladurie (1974) has also in some ways tended to support Murray's thesis. Carlo Ginzburg describes the role and activities of a group who called themselves the Benandanti, 'the good walkers', who were brought before the Inquisition in Italy in the late sixteenth century. They claimed to be healers who fought against witchcraft, as well as being involved in crop protection. Ginzburg considered the Benandanti's role was a survival from fertility rituals once widespread throughout Europe. But he emphasized that a distinction needs to be made between a coherent and widespread set of beliefs and practices and an organized local cult group. Yet the discovery of an agrarian cult having an ecstatic character in Italy led Ginzburg to look more favourably at Murray's discredited thesis (1984, 1991, 9–10). But the general opinion of scholars is that the people tried for witchcraft in early modern Europe were not members of any surviving Pagan religion (Hutton 1999, 362).

It is beyond the scope of the present study to outline the history and the many interpretations of the great witch-hunt in early modern Europe (1450–1650); in fact, there is now a vast literature on this topic. But it is worth noting that it mainly involved the judicial torture and murder of poor elderly women – it is estimated that there were around 60,000 executions – and about half of these lived within the Holy Roman Empire. Witch-hunts also tended to be local and sporadic (Levack 1987, 21–5). In accounts of European witchcraft, four 'elements' are generally involved: the Pagan beliefs and ritual practices evident among the rural peasants; the recorded experiences of the witches, which were almost certainly the effect of taking hallucinogenic drugs such as henbane and mandrake as 'flying ointment' (Harner, 1973, 125–50; Hansen 1978); the practice of maleficium, witchcraft accusations levelled against neighbours; and finally, there is the diabolical component, the notion articulated by the Christian theologians that the accused women were devil-worshippers and had made a pact with the devil. (For useful studies of the witch-hunt in early modern Europe, see MacFarlane 1970; Russell 1980; Larner 1984; Levack 1987; Ankarloo and Henningsen 1990; Clark 1997; Greenwood 2001; 94–159. For reflections of contemporary scholars and Neopagans on Murray's thesis, see Adler 1979, 47–56; Crowley 1998, 172; Hutton 1991, 302–6; 1999, 194–201.)

Among many historians the general consensus seems to be that Margaret Murray was unscholarly and was generally ignorant about the ancient Paganism of Western

Europe, and that there is little real evidence of any Pagan 'witch cult'. Indeed, Hutton stridently affirms that not a single person tried for witchcraft in Europe during the early modern period 'has been demonstrated to have adhered to a Pagan religion' (1999, 379–380; Levack 1987, 19–20).

However, these findings did not prevent the second figure in the rise of modern Pagan witchcraft, Gerald Gardner (1884–1964), from uncritically accepting Murray's thesis about an ancient 'witchcraft' cult. Indeed, Murray wrote a preface to Gardner's well-known book on *Witchcraft Today* (1954), which many have considered to be the 'foundation text' of modern witchcraft (Russell 1980, 154).

Gardner was an amateur folklorist and anthropologist who spent most of his early life as a rubber planter and customs official in colonial Malaya and Borneo. He took a great interest in the culture of the local people, such as the Malays and Dyaks, and according to Doreen Valiente, made a 'substantial fortune' from his colonial ventures. He was always interested and involved in the occult and spiritualism, and when Gardner returned to England on his retirement in 1936 he made contact with some local occultists near his home in the New Forest area of Hampshire. His neighbours were members of an occult fraternity that called itself the Fellowship of Crotona and claimed to be Rosicrucian. He also made contact with the daughter of the well-known theosophist Annie Besant and with the Ordo Templi Orientis, an occult fraternity led by the famous (or notorious) magician Aleister Crowley. Gardner met Crowley in 1947, shortly before Crowley died, and appears to have greatly admired the occultist. Gardner himself seems to have been an amiable man, generous, lovable, free of malice – someone who radiated charm, friendliness, and understanding. But his scholarship was limited, and Gardner was not the 'oracle of knowledge' that some of his witchcraft devotees considered him to be (Valiente 1973, 151–8; Hutton 1991, 332–3).

What, however, is significant about Gardner, in relation to the history of Neopaganism, is that he claimed to have discovered around 1938 in the New Forest a secret 'witch cult' led by a woman named 'Old Dorothy' – the 'last remains of an old-time witch coven'. Apart from Gardner's own writings, there is little substantive evidence for the existence of such a cult; nevertheless, with the repeal of the Witchcraft Act in 1951, Gardner began to propagate the idea of 'witchcraft' as a religion that was a direct descendent of the ancient rituals and beliefs practiced by the medieval witches. In his book, *Witchcraft Today* (1954), Gardner claimed that there had been witches in all ages and countries, that they worshipped the spirits; that aboriginal 'little people' had once inhabited England prior to the Celts and Saxons, and had later become identified with the 'fairies'; and that early witches met in 'covens', danced in circles in the nude, and worshipped the great mother goddess. Witches he considered to be Wicca, or 'wise people'; they possessed herbal knowledge and occult powers and conducted seasonal rituals in honour of the goddess or female deities. He also suggested that 9 million people died by torture during the premodern witch-hunt (1954, 102) – a figure that later scholarship has found something of an exaggeration. Gardner drew eclectically from many different sources, which is hardly surprising when one considers that he was 'a freemason, a Rosicrucian, a spiritualist, a friend and a probable member of the Ordo Templi Orientis, a member of the governing council of the Folk Lore Society, a fervent admirer of Margaret Murray, and a member of one of the divisions of the Order of Woodcraft Chivalry' (Hutton 1996, 12). Gardner was thus not only one of the founders of Neopaganism but also an advocate of New Age spiritualism. Surprisingly, he is barely mentioned in Starhawk's *The Spiral Dance* (1979).

There has been a great deal of debate and controversy surrounding Gardner: as to whether he was ever initiated into an authentic witchcraft coven that had survived in the New Forest since ancient times, and to what extent the revivalist version of Wicca was his own invention, or that of Crowley, or his colleague Doreen Valiente. One Neopagan priestess wrote to Adler to suggest that fifty per cent of modern Wicca is an invention derived from Gardner, via Crowley; ten per cent borrowed from books like Leland's text *Arcadia, or the Gospel of the Witches* (1899); and the remaining forty per cent from Asian religions and philosophies (Adler 1979, 64). This seems to indicate the eclectic nature of contemporary Neopaganism. Another Neopagan suggests that there is no basis for the claim that Gardnerian witchcraft derives from the ancient Pagan religions of Europe and suggests that it was Doreen Valiente who was mainly responsible, in a number of books, for establishing the basic theology of modern witchcraft – particularly the emphasis on rituals that focussed around the goddess (Adler 1979, 83–4; Valiente 1973, 1989). Indeed, Susan Greenwood has suggested that Doreen Valiente was a key figure in formulating and redefining Gardner's ideas, to create a relatively new form of Paganism, and that she can rightly be described as the 'Mother of Wicca'. A modest, unassuming woman, Valiente, Greenwood writes, 'brought a down-to-earth, yet poetic vision to modern witchcraft practice, as well as a greater emphasis on attaining harmony with nature' (2001, 200).

In his history of modern Pagan witchcraft, Ronald Hutton (1999) not only seriously questions the existence of a 'Pagan cult' in early modern Europe but also doubts the existence of any coven in the New Forest that was actually practising 'ancient' rituals in the years prior to the Second World War. 'Old Dorothy', it appears, was a wealthy woman who lived in Christchurch and was a church-going Anglican and staunch supporter of the local Tory Party (1999, 207–12). But Hutton established beyond doubt that Gardner played a central role in developing and propagating a new religion and can rightly be considered as a 'founder' of modern Paganism (1999, 239). Even in the United States, the influence of Gardner is 'omnipresent' in the Neopagan subculture (Lewis 1996, 2).

In his seminal writings on the roots of modern witchcraft, Ronald Hutton suggests that the link between ancient Pagan religion in Britain and the current revival of Neopaganism was essentially mediated by a number of 'elements', or what he describes as a combination of 'major cultural trends' (1999, 272). These include the following: freemasonry and the western esoteric tradition, involving ceremonial magic (hermeticism), secret initiation, and arcane knowledge, particularly as promoted by Dion Fortune and Aleister Crowley – which we shall discuss later in the chapter (Hutton 1999, 52–83; on freemasonry and western esotericism, see Stevenson 1988; Faivre 1994; Hanegraaff 1996); the interest during the nineteenth century in 'hedge witchcraft' or 'low magic' – the folk traditions relating to herbal medicine, amulets, and charms, and the practices of the 'cunning folk' (Hutton 1999, 84–111); and the general 'love affair' that western intellectuals have for the art, literature, and philosophy of classical antiquity, especially as expressed in the writings of James Frazer, Jane Harrison, and Robert Graves. Influenced by the romantic movement, this led to the emergence in the western literary imagination of the image of the 'great goddess' as a single, universal, ancient deity (Hutton 1999, 32–42; see Harrison 1903; Frazer 1922; Graves 1981); and finally, the interest in folklore studies and the 'modern cult of rural nostalgia' that was expressed, especially towards the end of the nineteenth century – as reflected in the writings of Richard Jefferies, W. H. Hudson, and Harold J. Massingham, and in the development of the woodcraft movement (Hutton 1999, 117–22, 162–70; on this rural nostalgia and the woodcraft movement, see Morris 1970; Williams 1973; Keith 1975). Thus Hutton concludes that Neopaganism was neither the descendant of a continuous 'sectarian' witchcraft or Pagan tradition nor was it simply the invention of one man, Gerald Gardner, but rather it is the 'incarnation' of several deep cultural impulses within British society and culture (1996, 13). Yet although Hutton acknowledges the influence of the Enlightenment in the emergence of modern Paganism and in the articulation of a religion of nature (as opposed to Christian revelation), he suggests that for the philosophers, Cicero and Lucretius were the main inspiration, and they therefore saw the ancients mainly as 'signposts for secularism'. Hutton therefore suggests that Neopaganism is more the heir to German Romanticism, with its nostalgia for a vanished past and its vision of an organic unity and a sacramental nature, than of the Enlightenment (Hutton 1999, 21; see Gay 1967; Eilberg-Schwartz 1989).

It is important to note, of course, that the Pagan revival is not unique to Britain; it has also flourished in other parts of Europe, as well as in North America. In an earlier text, Hutton was, however, adamant that contemporary Paganism has 'virtually nothing in common with that of the past, except in name, which is itself of Christian coinage'. Yet if Wicca is considered a form of ritual magic, then it has, indeed, Hutton suggests, a long and distinguished pedigree, going back to the order of the Golden Dawn, an esoteric group formed at the end of the nineteenth century, and beyond that to the Rosicrucians and the Freemasons (1991, 337). Thus Neopagan witchcraft is seen by Hutton as very much a part of the western esoteric tradition. But Hutton suggests that Neopaganism is neither a sect nor a cult. The former concept implies the separation of a group from an existing religious organization or tradition – which Neopaganism is not, its own self-image implying that it is a 'survival' of an 'ancient' Pagan religion. It is not even a 'new' religious movement by this criterion.

Although the term 'cult' was used positively by both Murray and Gardner to describe Pagan religion, given its current negative connotations, no contemporary Pagans use the term to describe their own religion, and the diversity and complexity of their system of belief makes the term 'cult' inappropriate. Equally, as noted earlier, most Neopagans repudiate any affinities with the New Age movement. Nor can Neopaganism be described as a prophetic or charismatic movement, for Gardner proclaimed no prophetic message and lacked the disposition and qualities to be a charismatic religious leader. Hutton thus concludes that Neopaganism is simply a fully developed independent religion (1999, 409–13).

What is also significant about Neopaganism as a religious movement is that its membership is overwhelmingly white, European, and of either aspirant working-class or lower-middle-class background. They tend not to come from deprived backgrounds and by occupation are either skilled artisans or belong to the professions – teachers, psychologists, civil servants – and seem to share a commitment to self-education (Hutton 1999, 402–5).

8.4. PAGAN PATHWAYS

Modern paganism is a diverse and eclectic movement, even though Neopagans themselves tend to emphasize the fact that they constitute a revival of the beliefs and practices of pre-Christian religions of Europe. As Starhawk described her own brand of witchcraft, it is the rebirth of the 'Ancient Religion' of the great goddess. Thus Neopaganism has generally been described as consisting of several 'major streams' or 'pathways', each associated with particular organizations, cult groupings, and periodicals. Some of these groups draw heavily on western esotericism and modern science, and so there is a good deal of overlap between modern Paganism and that of the New Age movement, while some radical esoteric groups fit uneasily into either of these broad cultural traditions. Leaving aside neo-shamanism, which I discussed at some length in Chapter 1, I discuss briefly in this section four Pagan pathways – Wicca, Feminist Witchcraft, Druidry, and the Northern tradition. Ritual magic will be discussed in the following sections.

8.4.1. Wicca

Most closely identifying with the theories of Margaret Murray and Gerald Gardner, Wicca is the name that its devotees give to the supposedly ancient 'religion of witchcraft'. Also described as the 'craft', its own 'self-image' is that of the 'old religion', specifically the 'reawakening' of the religious ideas, values, and ritual practices of pre-Christian European Paganism. It takes Gerald Gardner to be the 'founding father' of Wicca, though acknowledging the formative influence of Doreen Valiente, who, it is suggested, shifted the emphasis away from 'fertility rites' (which were stressed by Murray) and towards the celebration of the seasons. Calendrical rites, it was felt, would enhance or invoke a sense of 'one's harmony with nature'. Wicca is thus a philosophy of life, according to Valiente, that would bestow peace of mind and spiritual well-being, as well as material satisfaction (1973, 135; V. Crowley 1988, 170–5).

The followers of Wicca continually attempt to counter the negative image of Paganism, fostered by Christian fundamentalists and by a sensational media, and emphasize that they are not 'Satanists', nor do they engage in animal sacrifices; neither are they anti-Christian, and certainly they do not engage in any form of ritual child abuse (V. Crowley 1996b, 10–11).

Wicca, like other Pagans, organize themselves into small autonomous groups, usually called 'covens' or 'circles', and eschew large formal organizations and charismatic leaders. Besides engaging in seasonal rites that embrace a cycle of eight festivals, Wicca is also conceived as a mystery religion that involves a series of initiations, often performed naked (skyclad) and sometimes involving ritual sex or a sacred marriage (V. Crowley 1996a, 86–92). Wicca thus puts an emphasis – as with Gardner – on both the 'great mother goddess' and the 'horned god', and both deities are interpreted in a very erotic fashion. In an important sense, therefore, Wicca combines polytheistic religion, ritual magic, and esoteric mysticism.

Within Wicca there are many different strands, which is inevitable given the fact that it is a decentralized movement, and each coven is to some degree autonomous, not only in organization but also in the beliefs, principles, and rituals that they embrace. A distinction is often made, however, between two strands of Wicca: the Gardnerian tradition that tends to follow the teachings of Gerald Gardner, and the Alexandrian tradition, associated with Alex Sanders (1926–1988), the self-styled 'King of the Witches'. Claiming to have been initiated into witchcraft by his grandmother when he was seven years old, Sanders combined most of the ritual elements of Gardnerian witchcraft – both work 'skyclad' – with the ritual magic of the hermetic (esoteric) tradition, and thus Alexandrian witchcraft is often described as 'high church' Wicca, for it embraces many complex and highly ritualized ceremonies (Adler 1979, 95; Farrar 1971, 1–2; Hutton 1999, 329–32; Greenwood 2001, 202–3).

Putting an emphasis on both the goddess and the horned god, Wicca tends to emphasize a complementary gender opposition as a fundamental working principle. Thus sexual polarity, as Greenwood writes, is the basis of Wicca ritual practices, and this tends to focus on 'heterosexual dynamics' as a means of raising magical 'energy' during the circle rituals (Greenwood 1998, 105–6).

After the initial impact of the writings of Gardner and Valiente, the spread of Wicca was given further impetus during the 1980s through the publication of two key texts – Starhawk's *The Spiral Dance* and Adler's *Drawing Down the Moon*. The latter title referred to a ritual, said to have originated in antiquity, whereby the priestess or devotee becomes possessed by the goddess (Adler 1979, 168). During the 1960s, the Gardnerian tradition of Wicca was taken to the United States largely through the efforts of Raymond Buckland. He had met Gardner in the Isle of Man, where Gardner, towards the end of his life, had established a witchcraft museum. Buckland was to go on to develop his own brand of Wicca, Seax (Saxon) Wicca (Adler 1979, 92–3; Greenwood 2001, 204–5). Many other forms of Wicca subsequently developed in the United States, including the following: Aidan Kelly's New Reformed Orthodox Order of the Golden Dawn, which flourished in the San Francisco area during the 1970s and consisted of many autonomous covens – 'an assemblage of natural anarchists, bootstrap witches and alienated intelligentsia' (Adler 1979, 162–3; Hopman and Bond 1996, 248–54); and the circle sanctuary established by Selena Fox near Madison, Wisconsin, in 1974, which was quite eclectic and aimed to serve, through networking circles, a wide variety of groups and individuals embracing 'Nature Spirituality' (Carpenter 1996, 47; Hopman and Bond 1996, 215–28). In fact, in contrast to Britain, in the United States a wide assortment of Wiccan churches emerged, but as Aidan Kelly noted, 'the vast majority of the witchcraft movement in America is Gardnerian officially or by extension' (Hopman and Bond 1996, 252).

It is worth noting that many of the advocates of Wicca, such as Vivianne Crowley and Selena Fox, are either psychologists or practising psychotherapists and that the writings of Jung have had an important influence on the work of many witches (for useful studies of Wicca, see Farrar and Farrar 1981, 1984; V. Crowley 1989, 1994).

8.4.2. Feminist Witchcraft

Feminist witchcraft is essentially a form of Wicca, often described as Dianic witchcraft, after the Roman moon-goddess Diana. All forms of Wicca venerate the goddess and, unlike Christianity, tend to celebrate the earth, the feminine, and the 'dark' aspects of nature rather than putting an emphasis on spiritual 'light'. Given this stress on the goddess, many pagan groups focus their devotion almost exclusively on this all-embracing deity; an example is the Fellowship of Isis, based at Clonegal Castle in Ireland. Some Dianic covens seem to worship the goddess in more or less monotheistic fashion. A key figure in feminist witchcraft, however, is Starhawk, who is somewhat critical of the overemphasis on heterosexuality in other Wicca groups. She suggests that the 'erotic energy flow' that (supposedly) sustains the universe is not enhanced by the emphasis on a male–female polarity; to stress this polarity, she therefore argues, is to enshrine heterosexual relationships as the 'basic pattern' for all beings (1979, 9). Even so, while acknowledging the need for flexibility and fluidity in sexual relationships and emphasizing that groups like the 'Reclaiming Collective' are much more 'gay positive' than the Gardnerian Wicca tradition, she nevertheless includes men in her vision of witchcraft, and often tends, it seems, to celebrate the joys of monogamy (Hopman and Bond 1996, 305). In fact, unlike other Dianic Wicca groups, Starhawk affirms the relevance of the 'horned god'. This deity seems to be a fanciful projection of her own ideal 'man' – 'free to be wild without being cruel, angry without being violent, sexual without being coercive, spiritual without being unsexed and able to truly love' (1979, 109).

Her theology regarding the goddess, however, is far from straightforward and is complex if not incoherent. It is discussed in an article on the "Reclaiming Collective" by Jone Salomonsen (1998). Written from the perspective of 'theological hermeneutics' and virtually devoid of any sociological insights about either Starhawk or the Collective, the article and Starhawk's own writings give the impression that the goddess – the 'great mother goddess' – is simply a human projection, a construct of the human imagination. Yet the goddess is also, from the perspective of esoteric Neoplatonism, an 'archetypal being'. In addition, the goddess is represented as a spiritual experience of an 'extraordinary divine reality', and as an anthropomorphic being who not only reveals herself in visionary experiences but also is the 'eternal life' that is immanent and embodied in the material world. Starhawk's feminist witchcraft, as interpreted by Salomonsen, is both shamanic and a 'magico-mystical religion within Western esotericism'. Thus feminist Wicca is a new form of mysticism seeking *unio mystica* with the divine goddess, as well as the experience of one's own 'deep self' (Salomonsen 1998, 143–50). This seems hardly different from New Age theology, though Starhawk's own vision of witchcraft combines political activism with both mystical psychotherapy (that Salomonsen describes) and a religious system that is loosely based on Gardnerian Wicca. With respect to the latter, Starhawk's book *The Spiral Dance* (1979) gives a wealth of detail regarding spells, chants, rituals, crystal-gazing, meditations, magical symbols, and 'energy workings' – drawn from the literature or from Starhawk's own fertile imagination. The book has become a bestseller, given its fashionable appeal, poetic, literary style, and the fact that it provides a practical guide to Pagan feminist witchcraft. Starhawk thus seems to reinterpret ritual magic in terms of mystical 'energy' and human psychology and as a set of spiritual techniques for achieving self-discovery and self-empowerment. Largely given to poetry and rhetoric, Starhawk seems, from a philosophical or theological perspective, to make an intellectual virtue out of incoherence, vacuity, and evasion (Hutton 1999, 345–50).

The person, however, who is most closely identified with feminist witchcraft and the 'Dianic tradition' is the feminist witch Zsuzsana Budapest. Originally from Hungary and inspired by the writings of Jane Harrison, Budapest is a strong advocate of the tradition of 'women's mysteries' and Central European shamanism. In 1971, Budapest founded the Susan B. Anthony coven in California, named after the early American suffragette, and later became director of the Women's Spirituality Forum. Budapest placed a crucial emphasis on rituals involving the 'mother goddess' and repudiated the male gods – the sight of the Christian crucifix (a dead man on a dead wooden cross) Budapest said made her feel nauseous. Although she conceives of Neopaganism as 'decentralized', men are excluded from the covens, and Dianic witches are either celibate or lesbian (Budapest 1990; Hopman and Bond 1996, 326–30; Greenwood 2001, 211).

Most advocates of feminist witchcraft in their emphasis on the 'mother goddess', envisaged as either 'great' or 'cosmic', uncritically accept a bipolar conception of European history, put forward by feminist theologians and by archaeologists such as Marija Gimbutas (1974, 1989). In fact, in recent decades there has been a veritable explosion of literature on the 'mother goddess' and goddess spirituality from eco-feminists and feminist theologians, as well as from Neopagans (Eisler 1987; Sjoo and Mor 1987; Spretnak 1991). What these writings offer is a lyrical account of a universal egalitarian matriarchy – an Eden-like 'golden age' of gender equality and harmony with nature – that existed prior to patriarchy, the state and religious cults focussed around a transcendental deity or deities. Essentially a reaffirmation of Jacob Bachofen's (1967) historical speculations, such a theory tends to see an intrinsic relationship between matriliny and mother-goddess religion, both being associated with an Eden-like phase of European history – or at least that of Western Europe and the Mediterranean. Ronald Hutton has indicated that the image of a single universal goddess is largely the product of the western literary imagination – Jane Harrison and Robert Graves being key figures in its construction (1998, 1999, 32–42), and I have elsewhere offered a critique of this currently fashionable account of European prehistory and the questionable conflation of matrilineal kinship with mother-goddess religion (Morris 1998).

8.4.3. Druidry

Druidry, as a spiritual path, has of course a long history and has been a part of the religious and cultural life of Western Europe, particularly of the British Isles, since the end of the eighteenth century. Druids, in the popular image, are associated with the oak tree and Stonehenge, and the archetypal Druid, writes Graham Harvey, is a 'bearded man in a white robe greeting the rising sun at Stonehenge' (1997, 19). The term 'Druid' is said to derive from the Indo-European terms for the oak tree [*drus*] and knowledge [*wid*], and thus Druid essentially means 'one with knowledge of the oak' or 'priest of the oak cult' (Spence 1947, 14–17; Carr-Gomm 1991, x).

As a tradition, Druidry is essentially the religion of the 'Celtic' peoples who are alleged to have migrated into Western Europe around the third century B.C.E. (Piggott 1968, 26–7). Spence simply refers to the Druids as the 'medicine men' of the Celtic peoples – who combined herbalism, divination, and shamanism (1947, 11). Much of the early literature on the Druids is derived from classical writers such as Julius Caesar, but in recent years the well-known Welsh texts *Mabinogion* and the *Book of Taliesen* have come to play a vital role as source material on the Druid tradition.

Druidry, it seems, is continually being 'reborn', and during the eighteenth century a number of scholars – among them John Aubrey, John Toland, and William Stukeley – began to express an interest not only in the classical writings on the Druids, but also on the great stone monuments of Avebury and Stonehenge. Thus an association was made between these megalithic sites and Druidry, and the Druids themselves were portrayed as mystical priests or philosophical sages, worshipping deities in the forest groves or at stone circles. Aubrey, in particular, was not only a pioneer archaeologist but is seen by Carr-Gomm as the 'real founder of the modern Druid movement' (1991, 21–4; Piggott 1968, 133–5).

In the recent decades there has again been a resurgence of Druidry, beginning in 1964 with the formation of the 'Order of Bands, Ovates and Druids', although many other groups of Druids were then in existence – usually holding their ceremonies at Stonehenge or on Primrose Hill. Of interest is that the ritual of the Druids at Stonehenge in 1964 is described by Piggott as 'vaguely mystical' with the singing of etiolated versions of Christian hymns, giving the event the flavour of non-conformist pietism (1968, 182).

There are still many active Druid organizations, not only in Britain but also in France and the United States. The Ancient Order of Druids, founded in 1781 as part of the Romantic movement, is still flourishing with over 3,000 members. It is organized into lodges, and many of these are restricted to men. In contrast, the 'Order of Bands, Ovates and Druids' upholds gender equality, and its current chief, Philip Carr-Gomm, emphasizes that its teachings relate to artistic and environmental issues, as well as to spiritual concerns. There is also a Secular Order of Druids, for many Druids like to portray Druidry as a way of life and a philosophy rather than as a 'religion' (Valiente 1973, 98; Shallcrass 1996, 66).

There is no central Druid theology, but according to Philip Shallcrass, who is Joint Chief of the British Druid Order, contemporary Druidry is no longer specifically 'Celtic' in its rituals but draws eclectically on many other religious traditions, particularly Native American and shamanic traditions, from Asian religions (meditation techniques), and on the Kabbalistic teachings of the Hermetic tradition. What is of interest, however, is the close association between Druidry and the Wicca tradition; many of the founders of the recent Druid Orders, like Shallcrass, had been initiates of Wicca, and there has been a growing emphasis among Druids on goddess spirituality (Shallcrass 1996, 72; Hutton 1999, 372). Shallcrass himself has been a devotee of the goddess since the age of six months, apparently, when from his pram he looked up at the blue sky and saw the goddess (1998, 159). But he does make the suggestion that Druidry implies a belief in a 'great spirit' or a 'spiritual power' that is immanent in the world and that is specifically intense in certain people, places, and things. This 'power' or 'energy', which he describes as 'Awen', seems to be identified not only with the Christian 'holy spirit' but with the 'mother goddess'. Yet, like Starhawk, Shallcrass is quite agnostic and vague as to whether the goddess is looked on as 'a living spiritual entity capable of directly affecting human lives, as a Jungian archetype, as a poetic fancy [or] as an aspect of the individual psyche' (1996, 75–6; 1998, 164). He makes, however, an interesting contrast between Druidry and Wicca, suggesting 'that Druids reverence the sun and perform rites in daylight, whereas witches revere the moon and operate at night. By the same token, Druidry is seen as rational and patriarchal, witchcraft as intuitive and feminist' (1996, 67).

As with Wicca and feminist witchcraft, Druids celebrate the seasons by means of eight festivals and conduct initiation rituals into the various orders. Sacred Groves – described by the Celtic term *Nemeton* – stone circles, such as those at Avebury and Stonehenge, and tree-lore are given particular emphasis in Druidry (Carr-Gomm 1991, 66–114). Unlike in the earlier Celtic religious tradition, contemporary Druids do not practice animal sacrifices, nor do they involve themselves in the kind of spiritualism that entails contacting the ancestral spirits through spirit-mediums. Great play is put on the contrasts among three groups within the Celtic tradition, each with its specific function: the bards (poets and keepers of the sacred traditions), ovates (philosophers or 'seers' – diviners – who are the repository of 'tribal wisdom'), and the Druids – essentially the priests and teachers who in the pre-Christian era were advisors to the kings (Carr-Gomm 1991, 43–64; Harvey 1997, 20–31). As with other Pagan groups, many Druids emphasize that Druidry is a 'nature religion' and essentially an 'animistic faith' (Restall-Orr 1998, 128).

In the United States, many Druid groups have formed over the past few decades, one of the best known being Ar Ndraiocht Fein [Our Own Druidism], formed by Isaac Bonewits around 1983. It was a splinter movement from the Reformed Druids of North America that had begun in 1963 as a protest movement at Carleton College – a protest against a regulation that required all students to attend a certain number of chapel services. Bonewits' vision of Druidry was not, however, entirely Celtic but rather pan-European, and he has often been critical of the Wicca tradition. Margot Adler described him as 'extremely opinionated and often difficult' and as dismissive of the 'myth of Wicca' (1979, 327) – for Bonewits has been very critical of the scholarship of Lewis Spence, Margaret Murray, and Robert Graves and dismisses the 'golden age of matriarchy' as a rather fanciful concept, good to believe in but without any real historical evidence to support it. He is also critical of the small-group orientation of Wicca – the Pagan movement he describes as a 'collection of elite cliques' and adjudges the typical Wiccan group to be unnecessarily small, esoteric, and exclusive. He also questions the theology of Wicca with its exclusive emphasis either on the goddess (monotheism) or on the couplet goddess and horned god (duotheism). In contrast, Bonewits puts an emphasis on pluralism or polytheism, and the unique individuality of many diverse deities. A Neopagan Druidry, as he envisages it, will not only emphasize an attitude of the reverence towards nature but will also embrace contemporary historical scholarship and ecological and biological knowledge with regard to how the environment 'actually functions'. Bonewits thus advocates a form of Pagan Druidry that is open, synthetic, large-group oriented, ecological, and free of fantasies of a past romantic 'Golden Age' (Hopman and Bond 1996, 3–11). Small wonder that Bonewits' relationship with Wicca has been a 'stormy one' (Adler 1979, 67). (For other interesting studies of Druidry and the Celtic religious tradition, see Ross 1967; Nichols 1990; Ellis 1994;

Spence 1996; MacCulloch 1991; Carr-Gomm 2003). The important writings of John and Caitlin Matthews (C. Matthews 1989; J. Matthews 1991; Matthews and Matthews 1994). The 'Celtic Mysteries' have had a significant influence on Neopaganism and in the emergence of the 'second romantic movement', although their limitations as historical accounts have been questioned by some scholars (Hutton 1991, 143). (For personal accounts of Druidry by devotees, see Restall-Orr 1998; Shallcrass 1998.)

8.4.4. The Northern Tradition

Some scholars view the 'Celtic Mysteries' as an intrinsic part of the Northern tradition – and, as has been noted, most Neopagans, whether belonging to Wicca or Druidry, claim Celtic origins for their own religious tradition. Yet a distinction is usually drawn between Wicca and Druidry on the one hand, and what is often described as heathenism, or the North European Pagan tradition. Heathens, or the practitioners of the Northern tradition, attempt to reclaim and follow the ancient beliefs and rituals of Germanic (Teutonic, Anglo-Saxon) and Scandinavian (Nordic) peoples. 'Heathen', of course, has similar connotations to that of 'Pagan', and it evokes a contrast not only with the Judaeo–Christian tradition but also with the western esoteric tradition, or the 'Western Mystery tradition', as some have described it (Hartley 1968).

There are many forms of the Northern tradition, but the main tradition is known as Odinism or Asatru. Odin was one of the principal deities in early Scandinavian (Norse) culture (Wota in Germanic, Woden in Anglo-Saxon cultures), a male deity variously associated with metallurgy, writing (the sacred runes), ritual magic, wisdom, shamanic rituals, as well as with a warrior culture. The term *Asatru* is derived from the Icelandic term that means 'belief in Aesir', or trust in the gods, which is something of a misnomer given the radical polytheistic nature of the Northern tradition. Other Neopagans write of Vanatru – 'trusting in the Vanir', the elemental gods. Some scholars have even made a distinction between Odinism and Asatru on both sociological and theological grounds (Kaplan 1996, 197; Harvey 1996, 53).

Drawing on the early Icelandic, Nordic, and Germanic literature, especially the 'Eddas' and the writings of Snorri Sturluson (1179–1241), the devotees of Odinism and Asatru describe and affirm the rich cosmological system of the Northern tradition. This tradition is essentially polytheistic, and the world is conceived as consisting of several different realms of existence, linked by a cosmic tree [*Yggdrasil*]. Within these realms there are many different kinds of beings (giants, elves, dwarfs), as well as various divinities and nature spirits. The Northern tradition, in fact, has a rich and diverse pantheon of spiritual beings, the term *Aesir* generally referring to the 'gods'. Odin was the father of the gods, the 'Allfather', but there were many other important deities (gods and goddesses) recognized – Thor, Balder, Freya, Frigg, Tyr,

Mani. The term *Vanir*, the 'fertility gods of the earth', also seems to have been a generic name for the deities. Valhalla, in the mythology of the Northern tradition, was a great hall built by Odin where the souls of warriors killed in battle rested, and the Valkyries were Odin's wild maidens who rode out to collect the dead warriors. Of interest, of course, is that many place names in Britain – like Wednesbury – reflect the Northern tradition, as do the names of the days of the week. In many respects, the Nothern tradition reflects the religion of the early chiefdoms of Europe and a warrior culture. Yet although contemporary Odinists draw on this tradition, specifically for ideas with respect to various deities and rituals, one can but agree with Hutton that this contemporary form of paganism has little in common with that of the past – particularly in regard to context and function (Hutton 1991, 337; for useful studies of the Northern tradition as a pre-Christian religious ideology, see Davidson 1964; Dumezil 1973; Branston 1980; Pennick 1989).

Contemporary heathens tend to celebrate a polytheistic worldview, seeing the world as inhabited by numerous deities, each of which is a manifestation of a 'transcendental divinity' (Pennick 1989, 41). As with Wicca and Druidry, there is a celebration also of the seasonal festivals, and an emphasis is put on the sacredness of nature. Also important are three further ritual items: the magical rites focussed around the sacred writings (runes); the importance of talismans and amulets; and the rituals focussed around oracular divination [*seidr*], associated with the goddess Freya and female spirit-mediums [*volva*]. But, generally speaking, Odinism and Asatru are seen as more male-oriented that other Neopagan pathways (Pennick 1989; V. Crowley 1996b, 50).

In Britain there are several groups that express allegiance to the Northern religious tradition – including the Odinic Rite, founded in 1980, which puts a crucial stress on 'faith, folk, and family' and has a strong racial orientation; Odinshof, which is organized into local 'hearths' and whose aim is to 'promote the ancient teachings and philosophy of Odin'; and the Rune Gild-UK, which focuses on the study and mysteries of the runes and stresses more the shamanic rituals [*seidr*] (Harvey 1996, 54–9). The latter group takes its inspiration from the writings of the charismatic figure, Edred Thorsson (1992).

In the United States there are, similarly, many different groups following the Northern (Norse/Germanic) tradition, and in a lucid essay Jeffrey Kaplan (1996) has discussed the complex relationships that exist between and the history of these various groups. These groupings include the following:

1. The Odinist Fellowship that, taking its inspiration from the racist doctrines expressed by Alexander Rud Mills (1930), was founded by Else Christensen in Florida in 1971. It is focussed around the cult of Odin and an explicit racial mysticism.
2. The Asatru Alliance associated with Michael Murray, who was a staunch follower of George Lincoln Rockwell and his American Nazi Party. The

Alliance saw itself as exclusively a religion for people of European descent, and its membership was overwhelmingly white, male, and comparatively young (most adherents were between thirty and forty years of age). It thus competed with the racist movement Christian Identity – though its emphasis was spiritual rather than political.

3. The Ring of Troth was founded by Edred Thorsson in 1987, at the same time as the Asatru Alliance, and was essentially his 'brainchild', although Thorsson had earlier, in 1980, established the Rune Gild. Described as a 'true visionary but a hopeless administrator', Thorsson began the process of both distancing Asatru from its association with racist doctrines and the 'white supremacist constellation', as well as training an embryonic cadre of priests and priestesses and establishing what was essentially an ecclesiastical organization (Kaplan 1996, 194–225; on Nordic racial paganism, see Goodrick-Clarke 2002, 257–78).

Membership of these three groupings was generally small, and it is noteworthy that Odinism and Asatru received no mention in the first edition of Margot Adler's *Drawing Down the Moon* (1979). She was later to conclude that 'Odinism attracts people who are more politically conservative than the majority of neopagans. They are uncomfortable with feminism, anarchism, and diversity in sexuality and lifestyle'. She also notes their stress on martial arts and warrior values (1979, 279).

Much has been written on the occult roots of German National Socialism, and particularly the influence of Guido Von List (1848–1919), who advocated a religion of Wotanism, based on the ancient religion of the Teutons as expressed in the Eddas and the Runes. This was an important aspect of Volkisch ideology, embraced by many National Socialists. Indeed, it was the Nazis who coined the term 'Neopagan'. This ideology was a volatile mixture of deep anti-Semitism, eco-mysticism, authoritarian politics, and an adherence to Germanic Neopaganism (Goodrick-Clarke 1992, 49–55; Biehl and Staudenmaier 1995). A link between the Nazis and Neopaganism cannot therefore be denied. Many contemporary neofascist political groups embrace both eco-mysticism and a Neopagan spiritual worldview. As Kaplan suggests, many Odinist groups in the United States have pronounced neo-Nazi sympathies (1996, 193–5), while Turner notes that some heathens in Britain 'certainly hold Neo-Nazi views' (1996, 62). But there is no intrinsic connection between the Northern tradition, or Neopaganism in general, and fascist politics, any more than there is an intrinsic connection between Christianity and fascism, even though the Christian Identity movement in the United States combines reactionary politics, a white supremacist ideology, and Christian fundamentalism (Barkun 1997). Hitler repudiated many of the Volkisch and Neopagan elements, especially if these conflicted with bourgeois values, and persecuted, along with Jews, Socialists and others, many Neopagans. Unlike Himmler, many leading Nazis, including Hitler, were dedicated Christians. Nonetheless, many Nordic Pagans are appalled and embarrassed by the links with Nazi ideology (Jones and Pennick 1995, 218–9, Harrow 1996, 15–16).

To conclude this section, it is worth noting that many Neopagans do not belong to any group but prefer to 'work' alone. They often describe themselves as 'solitaries' or as a 'hedge witch', and books have been written especially for this kind of Wiccan who belongs to no coven or formal organization (Beth 1990).

8.5. THE WESTERN MYSTERY TRADITION

A clear contrast is often made between 'pagan spirituality', encompassing Wicca, Feminist Witchcraft, Druidry, and the Norse–Germanic tradition, and the contemporary 'Western Mystery tradition'. This latter tradition is often described as 'magical religion', 'Western esotericism', 'occultism', or simply as 'ritual magic'. Its formative influences are not Murray and Gardner and the notion of a 'revival' of an 'ancient' Pagan tradition but rather the occultists Aleister Crowley and Dion Fortune. Ritual magic is thus concretely bound up with the 'occult revival' of the late nineteenth century, which itself has its roots in the earlier hermetic tradition of the Renaissance (subsequently discussed) – the so-called 'Western Mysteries', as some contemporary groups, in fact, describe themselves.

Perhaps the most important influence on the many forms of ritual magic is the notorious occultist of the twentieth century, Aleister Crowley (1875–1947). Brought up as a strict Plymouth Brethren, Crowley came to repudiate Christianity at an early age, and as he put it in his autobiography, he 'simply went over to Satan's side'. In an act of strident blasphemy, he declared himself the Beast 666 of the Book of Revelation, always craving notoriety. He thus described himself as the 'wickedest man alive'. While an undergraduate at Cambridge at the end of the nineteenth century, Crowley became interested in the 'occult revival' then taking place, and in 1898 he became a member of the Hermetic Order of the Golden Dawn. Founded ten years earlier by William Wescott and S. L. MacGregor Mathers, it included the Irish poet W. B. Yeats among its members and established 'temples' in various parts of Britain, though its membership was always small – only around 300 people. The Order was devoted to the propagation and practice of esoteric studies and ritual magic – astrology, theosophy, magic, alchemy, geomancy, kabbalah, tarot, and channelling – particularly of Egyptian deities. It was not in any real sense a 'Pagan' organization. What was crucial about the order was that it did not interpret magic as simply an instrumental activity, like medicine, designed to achieve specific ends, but rather it suggested that the magician or hermeticist could through ritual come into contact and thus control cosmic forces – associated with demons, angels, deities, and various aspects (names) of god (Hutton 1999, 81–2; on the history of the esoteric order of the Golden Dawn, see Howe 1972; Gilbert 1983; Cicero and Cicero 2003, 33–66).

Yet although the Order of the Golden Dawn has been seen as the culmination of the nineteenth-century occult revival, it was soon beset by schisms, and in 1900 Crowley left the Order and came to found his own occult order, the Fraternity of the Silver Star, in 1907.

In his early life, Crowley was essentially a rich playboy and adventurer who travelled widely and was a member of several mountaineering expeditions to the Himalayas, including an attempt to climb Kanchenjunga in 1905. But a year earlier, when in Egypt with his wife Rose, Crowley had a mystical experience that he later considered to be the most important event in his life. For his clairvoyant wife became a medium not only of Crowley's guardian spirit, which he called Aiwass, but of the Egyptian god Horus. He was informed by Horus that a new epoch was dawning, and that he should write down what the deity dictated to him. Thus he wrote – 'received' – *The Book of Law* [*Liber Legis*], a book of mystical nihilism and complex symbolism that is seen as heralding the age of Horus and the establishment of a new religion – the teachings of Thelema. For the remainder of his life, Crowley travelled extensively, settling for several years in Sicily, where he lived in a farmhouse at Cefalu. It was called the Abbey of Thelema. By all accounts, Crowley seems to have been a strange, eccentric, and rather unpleasant character, always seeking publicity – engaging in sadistic behaviour towards others, practicing sexual magic, indulging in all kinds of drugs from mescalin to heroin and opium, conducting blood sacrifices, distrusting and even professing to despise women, and trying to convince everyone that he was the devil incarnate. Crowley was also an Expressionist painter and wrote many books on the occult, as well as novels; yet although he thought himself a genius, he had rather limited talents. But his occult writings nevertheless have had an important impact on many groups embracing in some form the 'Western Mysteries' – ritual magic. (On Crowley's life, see Symonds 1951; Wilson 1971, 457–91; Valiente 1973, 73–6; Suster 1988; Hutton 1999, 171–80).

In an interesting overview of the historical and philosophical aspects of Thelemic Magick, Richard Sutcliffe (1996) outlines some of the basic 'components' or elements of the western esoteric tradition, of which Crowley's Thelemic, or left-hand path of ritual magick, is but a contemporary form. The term *Thelema* is said to derive from the Greek word meaning *will* or *intention* and was appropriated by Crowley from the writings of François Rabelais who had in the sixteenth century written about the Abbey of Thelema. It was a place devoted to the promotion of human virtue. Crowley used the archaic term *magick* to describe his own system of occult practice and saw it as less of a religion than a science – the 'most divine knowledge of natural philosophy'. In fact, he defined magic as 'the art and science of causing change to occur in conformity with the will' and actually described 'magick' as a branch of physics (A. Crowley 1973, 131–7; Hutton 1999, 174).

But before the basic elements of the Western Mystery tradition are outlined, some discussion may be devoted to the second important influence on contemporary ritual magic – and Neopaganism – the occultist Dion Fortune.

A Christian Scientist in her youth – like her mother – and considered one of the leading occultists of her own generation, Dion Fortune was actually the pen name of Violet Firth (1890–1946). Like Crowley, she came from a wealthy background and adopted the family motto *Deo Non Fortuna* [God not luck] as her magical name. Described by Colin Wilson as one of the 'greatest of modern occultists' (1971, 590), Fortune at the early age of twenty-four became a theosophist. However, like Rudolph Steiner, she disapproved of the emphasis that the Theosophical Society placed on Asian religious mysticism and thus came to play a more prominent role in the Christian mystical lodge of the Society. In 1919, she was initiated into the occult fraternity Alpha et Omega, an offshoot of the earlier Hermetic Order of the Golden Dawn, and three years later she founded her own occult group, 'Society of the Inner Light'. This she conceived as a 'Mystery School' working within the western esoteric tradition. Although in many ways a devout Christian, who looked on 'the Master Jesus' as her personal spirit guide and often invoked the sacred name of Jesus in her occult rituals, Fortune tended to be critical of the Christian clergy and saw the Western Mystery tradition as essentially having its origin in Egypt, mediated through the Hermetic tradition – of the Kabbalists and Alchemists (1987, 101). Tending to view religious traditions in social terms, Fortune had a very elitist view of reincarnation, and her political sentiments were decidedly reactionary and conservative. She considered homosexuality as 'unnatural vice' and made a categorical distinction between the right-hand path of magic, which she considered 'god-centred', and the left-hand magical path, which she associated with greed, lust, the desire for power, the taking of drugs, and self-empowerment (1987, 76–85). Although in her magical novels, such as *The Sea Priestess* (1938), Fortune placed an emphasis on the goddess, as well as on the mythical island of Atlantis (reputed to be the home of divine wisdom), she nevertheless, in contrast to Valiente, lacked any real ecological sensibility. As a forerunner of the New Age, Fortune thus placed a crucial emphasis not on the natural world but on divine light and spirituality and suggests that the more a person concentrates on 'spiritual things', the less interest they will have in the 'things of the senses' (1987, 81). She also placed great emphasis on the need for binary oppositions and gender polarity, and wrote that without a relationship with men, women became neurotic, and that if a man associates too closely with a woman, he loses 'his personality' (1987, 164–5). However, through her magical novels and occult writings, particularly her well-known text, *The Mystical Qabalah* (1935), Dion Fortune, like Crowley, came to play an important role in the development of contemporary ritual magic. The Society of Inner Life is still active today, and many other groups describing themselves as adherents of the 'Western Mysteries' have affinities with or are offshoots of the Society. Indirectly, Fortune was also an influence on many Neopagans, given her emphasis on the goddess and ritual magic, even though she herself always remained a rather devout esoteric Christian (Luhrmann 1989, 59; for useful biographies of Dion Fortune, see Richardson 1987; Chapman 1993; Hutton 1999, 180–8; Knight 2000).

The 'Western Mystery' or esoteric tradition that was embraced by both Crowley and Fortune can be characterized by a number of key elements or themes.

The term *occult* means what is hidden (Latin *occultus*) and refers to the notion that there are hidden or concealed forces or powers within nature or the cosmos. This suggests either the existence of an 'unseen realm' or a magical 'other-world', or that there is a 'world soul' (Latin *anima mundi*), as described by Plato, which is the animating principle of the cosmos. But this tends not to imply a 'two-world' theory as with Plato but rather the idea that the 'unseen' world consists of several 'planes' of existence, a complex, multilayered spiritual hierarchy. Thus there is not only a material plane of existence, but more subtler planes – the realms of mind, spirit, and the 'astral kingdom' (Fortune 1987, 129; Luhrmann 1989, 298–9).

Magic was defined by S. L. MacGregor Mathers as an occult science that seeks to 'control the secret forces of nature', and such forces or powers are intrinsically related to the doctrine that suggests that there are real or symbolic correspondences between all parts of the visible or invisible universe. All things are interrelated and linked by a network of 'sympathies', and such linkages are structured and symbolic. Occultism is thus a term that refers to a system of ritual practices – such as kabbalah, alchemy, astrology, geomancy – that are based, in one way or another, on the doctrine of correspondences. Magic, as a concept, implies the knowledge of this 'network of sympathies' and its concrete implementation through ritual practices (Faivre 1987; R. Sutcliffe 1996, 115–6).

The occult powers, however, which are ultimately derived from God, make their influences felt through the 'world soul' by means of celestial beings, identified with the sun, moon, planets, and the more distant stars. As one occult scholar put it, 'By this [world] spirit, therefore, every occult property is conveyed into herbs, stones, metals and animals, through the sun, moon, planets and through stars' (Barrett 1989, 87).

Thus every material object in the world is, in the Western Mystery tradition, believed to be full of occult 'powers', 'virtues', or 'forces', all of which are linked through a symbolic logic and utilized through magical practices. The world soul or spirit is thus the 'divine essence' that permeates all things.

The term *esotericism*, coined by the nineteenth-century French occultist Eliphas Levi (1810–1875), is derived from the Greek term *esoteros*, meaning *inner*. This suggests that divinity is also within the human person, and that divine knowledge [*gnosis*] is derived through a special kind of inner or 'self-knowledge' and thus one is thereby able to obtain enlightenment or individual salvation. This divine knowledge contrasts with both reason (intellectual knowledge) and faith. There is thus the notion of a 'higher self' or the 'spark of the divine spirit' within each human person, and the focus is thus on the 'realm of inner experience' through which an occult initiate is motivated by 'the desire for light on the path of spiritual development that ends in divine union', as Fortune puts it (1987, 23). The Western Mystery tradition therefore embraces a form of mysticism (Luhrmann 1989, 202–4).

Besides its emphasis on magic and on mystical experience [*gnosis*], the esoteric tradition also places a crucial emphasis on the existence and importance of numerous spiritual agencies – spirit guides, angels, deities – that act as essentially intermediaries between the devotee and the godhead, or what Fortune describes as the 'divine spirit' (1987, 128). This implies not only the positing of a 'world of images' [*mundis imaginals*], which is duly conflated with a 'spiritual', 'magical', or 'divine' realm, but also the cultivation of an 'active' or 'esoteric' imagination (Sutcliffe 1996, 116). Contact with the world of spirits, deities, angels, celestial beings, or 'hidden masters' is thus achieved through the development of an 'analogical consciousness' and 'visualization' – the 'seeing' or experiencing of vivid mental images that are interpreted as real spiritual beings (Luhrmann 1989, 207). But as Dion Fortune notes with regard to such contacts with the 'unseen', 'Because a spirit calls itself Victor Hugo does not mean that it *is* Victor Hugo, and even if it were, what is the use of listening to it if it talks nonsense' (1987, 33).

The Western Mystery tradition also makes great use of the doctrine of karma or reincarnation, and the evocation of subconscious memories and 'past lives', acknowledging the influences of 'previous incarnations'. It is thus considered helpful to have knowledge of one's past 'incarnations' (Fortune 1987, 136–50).

No rigid division is made in the Western Mystery tradition among magic, religion, science, or philosophy. Esotericism is considered an 'occult philosophy' and magic, astrology, divination, geomancy, kabbalah, invoking spirit guides, alchemy, and making talismans are all considered to be part of what is described as 'sacred' or 'occult science' (Fortune 1987, 40–3). The nineteenth-century occultist Eliphas Levi thus wrote, 'Magic combines in a single science that which is most certain in philosophy with that which is eternal and infallible in religion' (1957, 29).

It thus reconciles faith and reason, science and belief, authority and liberty, and conceives of the divinity as both transcendent, the source of all being, and immanent in the natural cosmos.

Thus, in very general terms, are the basic elements of the Western Mystery tradition, otherwise known as 'Western esotericism' (on the Western Mystery tradition, see Waite 1961; King 1975; Matthews and Matthews 1994; Faivre 1994, 1998; Ivakhiv 1996; Cicero and Cicero 2003, 1–31).

8.6. CONTEMPORARY RITUAL MAGIC

Tanya Luhrmann's interesting and pioneer ethnographic study, *Persuasions of the Witch's Craft* (1989), is not in fact about Pagan witchcraft but is largely devoted to a study of ritual magic in contemporary Britain. Influenced by Gellner, and following the ultra-rationalist and intellectualist approach of Evans-Pritchard, Luhrmann's study is primarily a work of psychological anthropology. But it offers interesting insights into the belief systems and ritual practices of various occult groups that describe themselves as belonging to the 'Western Mysteries'. Her focus is thus on what she describes as 'modern magic', which is described as a highly eclectic social phenomenon and a mixture of many different ritual activities and ideas – Paganism, astrology, mysticism, the range of alternative therapies, neo-Nordic shamanism, feminist witchcraft, and ritual imagery drawn from Egyptian, Celtic, and Greek sources. Adherents of ritual magic, she suggests, seem to tolerate a 'surprising spiritual diversity' in their ritual practices, which they generally describe by the term 'magic' (1989, 6). Such devotees are seen as situating themselves within the New Age movement, which heralds the advent of the Aquarian age (1989, 32). Most practitioners of ritual magic are white, middle class, and usually well educated, and work as computer analysts, civil servants, therapists, or business executives. Luhrmann has the mistaken impression that with the disappearance of 'primitive societies' and the end of empire, anthropologists are now turning 'inward' towards the study of their own society (1989, 4). In fact, there is a long tradition within anthropology both of 'anthropology at home' and of the study of complex societies like China and India, and at the present time many countries in Africa and Latin America are literally awash with anthropologists (and missionaries)!

The practitioners of ritual magic that Lurhmann studied were largely 'middle-class urbanites' in London. They belonged essentially to two 'types' of organizations – Pagan witchcraft and Western Mysteries. The first type, Pagan witches, met in small groups or covens, under the leadership of a high priestess, and, following the tradition of Gardner, claimed to be practising a pre-Christian nature religion. Seasonal rituals were held, often skyclad, with the priestess 'drawing down the moon' – becoming the goddess incarnate. The goddess, as the 'personification of nature', was of central importance of these witchcraft groups (Luhrmann 1989, 45–57). In addition to the organized covens, there were various ad hoc study groups and networks, focussed around Neopaganism – conceived as a polytheistic nature religion. These included the Green Circle founded by Marian Green in 1982 and the network PAN (Pagans Against Nukes) that, like Starhawk, combine spiritual ecology with radical political activism (Green 1983, 1989; Luhrmann 1989, 82–8).

The Western Mysteries, in contrast to the Neopagans, are organized in occult fraternities, focussed around 'adepts', dress in formal magical robes, and have a much more hierarchical structure. They largely follow the occultist or esoteric tradition associated with Dion Fortune and her Society of the Inner Light, and place an emphasis on secret initiations and rituals focussed around the kabbalah glyph, and on drawing spiritual power from various ethereal beings or spirit guides. Groups within the 'Western Mysteries' spiritual tradition include not only the Society of the Inner Light – which is essentially an esoteric Christian organization – but the 'Servants of Light' and the Western Mysteries group associated with the occultist Gareth Knight, as well as various ad hoc groups of ritual magic like the 'Glittering Sword'. This group combines Egyptian and Nordic ritual elements (1989, 58–81; Knight 1976).

What is important for Luhrmann is that all of these groups, whether Neopagan or occultist, are interested in ritual, and they all talk about magic, viewing magic as both a religion and as a pragmatic activity. She suggests that all magicians accept the basic premise that 'mind affects matter' and that through ritual and the imagination, people can alter the physical world. As she writes, 'It is the mind that works magic. Modern magic holds that thought affects the world directly – even though it is patently obvious that most of the time it does not, without action' (1989, 128).

She is not concerned whether such claims regarding the efficacy of magic are true or not, or whether the spirits or deities invoked actually exist – have ontological status – but rather in understanding why 'apparently irrational beliefs are held by apparently rational people' (1989, 14). The focus of her study is therefore on psychological issues. Two issues have particular salience for Luhrmann, namely, (a) how a practitioner of magic comes to be involved in such practices, and the way in which this entails a shift in perception and cognition; and (b) the intellectual strategies that practitioners employ to come to terms with the 'disjunction' between ritual magic and what they themselves describe as scientific understanding.

With regard to the first issue, relating to the magician's involvement in ritual magic, Luhrmann's discussion ranges over many different topics: the acquisition of a rich body of esoteric and hermetic knowledge by the magician; the development of a capacity to interpret events so that they conform with ritual practices and expectations; learning to engage in such ritual practices as visualization, meditation, ritual nudity, and creating a sacred circle in order to unsettle ordinary consciousness; and, finally, the development of a creative and highly personalized approach to ritual symbolism (Luhrmann 1989, 189–283). What is of interest is that Luhrmann recorded no evidence of the use of drugs to achieve ecstatic states, and noted both that 'analogy' was considered an important source of knowledge and that most modern magicians saw ritual magic itself as a religion (1989, 191).

With regard to the second psychological issue explored by Luhrmann, namely, the way in which magicians justify their magical practices in terms of a culture that tends to see such practices as either irrational or pure fantasy, Luhrmann suggests that magicians employ essentially four strategies. These four 'primary rationalizations', as Luhrmann describes them, are *realism*, the magician's strident claim that magic is on par with science and common sense, that magic works, and that occult forces are indeed part of the physical reality; the *two-worlds* theory, which suggests that magical forces are real, but that they cannot be experienced or known by ordinary scientific understanding; *relativism*, which follows postmodern scholarship in suggesting that people create their own realities, and that magic, science, and common sense are simply alternative and equally valid ways of understanding the world, 'objectivity' being an illusion; and finally, the *metaphysical* approach, which claims that magic is probably invalid, but ritual practices are not really about pragmatic ends but are a religious way of life and a mode of spiritual experience. Luhrmann contends that contemporary theologians essentially follow the same intellectual strategies in attempting to explicate the existence of god (Luhrmann 1989, 307–31).

In her conclusions, Luhrmann suggests that becoming a magician is not a sudden conversion but involves what she calls a process of 'interpretive drift', the gradual and often unacknowledged shift in the way in which someone interprets events and makes sense of particular activities (1989, 340). She also emphasizes that practitioners of ritual magic are generally ordinary, well-educated people and that they can in no sense be considered as belonging to a 'deprived' socio-economic category. But rather their motivations for embracing ritual magic entails a search for a 'powerful emotional and imaginative religious experience' rather than for a religion per se. She also suggests that the contemporary 'occult revival', rather than involving people who are simply alienated from 'scientific-rational society' or being an aspect of the current resurgence of religious enthusiasm, 'has more to do with a commercial success story' and is a 'fad' that 'now appeals to people because it meets some basic need for spiritual, imaginative, emotional play in a remarkably tolerant cultural Milieu' (1989, 370). True – but hardly advancing our sociological understanding of such phenomena.

Luhrmann's study has been seen as a 'prominent milestone' in academic anthropology. But given that it is a pioneering work and takes an intellectualist approach that focusses unduly on the 'efficacy of magic', it has become the subject of much critical debate. It is thus suggested that she ignores the unique 'subjective motivations' of the magical practitioners themselves and assumes that magic is performed to achieve certain ends – rather than the *performance* itself being of the greatest significance; that she ignores the basic principle of magic, which is communication with the 'other world' and thus empowerment; and finally, there is the general feeling that Luhrmann is dismissive of magical practices, seeing them as founded on a 'delusion' (Reid 1996, 145–7; Hutton 1999, 375; Greenwood 2000, 41).

One can debate as to what degree these are valid criticisms of her work, but in adopting a cognitive approach to ritual magic, she hardly explores the sociological dimensions of this social phenomena. And the notion that the contemporary resurgence of occultism is a 'postmodern response to the disenchanted and depersonalised worldview of modernity' (Ivakhiv 1996, 255) is hardly more enlightening. (For a further important ethnographic study of both Wicca and ritual magic, see Greenwood 2000, which focusses specifically on issues of power, identity, and morality.)

In spite of the emphasis on ritual magic, Luhrmann devoted little attention in her study to the kind of groups associated with the 'left-hand path' of magick, who take their inspiration not from Gardner (Pagan witchcraft) nor from Dion Fortune (Christian esotericism) but rather from Aleister Crowley. These are the various, rather anarchistic, ad hoc groups that are organized around 'a sexual, somewhat violent ideology', as Luhrmann describes it (1989, 36). Such groups have been lucidly discussed by Richard Sutcliffe (1996).

Crowley as an occultist was deeply influenced by the Western Mystery tradition and was not only a member of the Hermetic Order of the Golden Dawn (as earlier noted) but also became head of the English section of the Ordo Templi Orientis, which he joined in 1912. This Order first made its appearance in Germany in 1904, an offspring of mystical freemasonry. It was founded by Karl Kellner, a German occultist, and combined an interest in Indian yoga and tantric rituals with the eighteenth-century myth regarding the Knights Templars, and was strongly influenced by the writings of the French occultist Alphonse Constant (1810–1875), who took the pen name Eliphas Levi. This ex-priest wrote a classic text, *The History of Magic* (1957), and is often credited with having initiated the late nineteenth-century 'occult revival' (Wilson 1971, 423–4; see also McIntosh 1972). Gerald Gardner was also a member of the Ordo Templi Orientis. But Crowley was, in addition, strongly influenced by the writing of the philosopher Nietzsche, and thus Crowley's own brand of the Western Mysteries came to have its own unique stamp. In particular, he emphasized a radical individualism, stressing that magick (his term for his own religion of Thelema) was centrally concerned with the expression and realization of one's own 'true will'. He developed the following maxim: 'Do what thou wilt shall be the whole of the law', suggesting that everyone had the right to express or fulfil their own will, which of course was identified with occult or divine powers immanent in the universe. But this did not imply pure egoism, for Crowley also stressed the importance of love in his aphorism: 'Love is the law: love under will'. Like Nietzsche, he was thus propounding a strident individualistic philosophy and an ethic of self-realization that was also summed up in an aphorism: 'every man and every woman a star'. For Crowley, however, firmly situated in the western esoteric tradition, the will was identified with a higher self, which is both unique and divine. As Sutcliffe puts it, 'Magick is less about exerting one's egoism than about transcending the ego in order to align oneself with the harmony of the cosmos' (1996, 124).

This implied, of course, going beyond the dichotomy 'good and evil' (central to Christian theology) and liberating oneself from conventional morality and everyday narrative patterns of authority. The 'antinomian ethos' of Crowley's left-hand path did not entail, however, Sutcliffe suggests, any 'ill-conceived anarchism' – that is, it was devoid of any social content or concern with social justice. It was more to do with overcoming 'one's own inhibitions and limitations' that were bound up in earlier patterns of socialization (1996, 111). Equally important for Crowley was ritual sex and tantric yoga.

There seems to be many ad hoc groups that follow Crowley's Thelemic Magick, which Sutcliffe describes as the 'left-hand path' of ritual magic. These include various developments and offshoots of the Ordo Templi Orientis, the

Kaula-Nath community, which combines western esotericism with Indian tantric yoga, the Temple of Psychick Youth, and the Church of Satan, founded in San Francisco by Anton LaVey (Barton 1990). But some of the most interesting and well known of the recent developments in ritual magic are the various ad hoc groups that self-consciously adopt 'Chaos Magick'. Historically, Chaos Magick seems to have emerged in the late 1970s from the 'Leeds occult scene' and is particularly associated with the 'Illuminates of Thanateros', founded in 1978 by Peter Carroll and Ray Sherwin, both university graduates. The term *thanateros* was derived from what Carroll described as humanity's two greatest obsessions and motivating forces – sex [*eros*] and death [*thanatos*]. 'Illuminates' refers to the aim of the 'order', namely, illumination or the achievement of 'enlightenment' through mind control, ritual magick, and shamanic trance (Carroll 1987, 9–13). Chaos Magick has been described as the 'emergent magical ethos' of postmodernism, and though firmly entrenched in the western esoteric tradition – with its emphasis on ritual magic, kabbalah, symbolic schemas, reincarnation, and divine knowledge [*gnosis*] – it also eclectically incorporates neo-shamanism, quantum physics, and chaos theory. Chaos Magick has thus been described as 'postmodern shamanism', embracing a relativistic epistemology, neo-technophilia (with its fascination towards cyberspace and virtual reality), the fragmentation of subjectivity, and its emphasis on the immediacy of experience (Hine 1993, 65; Sutcliffe 1996, 127).

Chaos magicians are thus self-consciously eclectic, and, according to Phil Hine, Chaos Magick currently embraces the Crowley cult, shamanism, Reichian therapy, eastern thought, voodoo, situationist theory, H. P. Lovecraft, Walt Disney, and 'anything else you might care to add to that list' (1993, 11). But besides chaos theory and Crowley's Thelemic Magick, two other important influences on Chaos Magick are also worth noting. The first is the artwork and writings of the occultist Austin Osman Spare (1886–1956), who was a pupil of Crowley and who emphasized the creation of personal symbols or sigils, which could be utilized in magical rituals, as well as postulating the notion of Kia. This is a fragment of the 'life-force' of the universe, which is also unique to the individual, combining the functions of will and perception. It seems akin to the notion of a 'world soul' or spirit (Carroll 1987, 28–9). The other important influence on chaos magicians are the writings of the American atheist H. P. Lovecraft (1890–1937), which are pure science fiction. Lovecraft's books, mostly written in the 1930s, have as a basic theme the notion that there is a group of alien, extraterrestrial entities called the 'great old ones' who once ruled the earth and wish to make contact with the earth again. Cthulthu is the high priest of the 'great old ones', who are said to be associated with wild places and stone circles, and contact with Cthulthu is said to 'unite the chthomic roots of primeval consciousness to the stellar magicks of the future'. The Cthulthu mythos is therefore said to contain all the key elements of a 'magical belief system' that is embraced by chaos magicians (Hine 1993, 220–2; Greenwood 2001, 244–5).

The social metaphysics of Chaos Magick follows Crowley in embracing a radical individualism and an extreme epistemological and moral relativism. The basic principles of Chaos Magick are expressed in a number of maxims, which include these:

Nothing is true, everything is permitted.
Change is a constant phenomenon.
Oh, let me worship the randomness of things.
Blasphemy shall be our liberation.
I require no justification.
I will believe whatever brings me joy, power and ecstasy.
(Carroll 1987, 154–5)

The emphasis is thus on personal experience and validation and the avoidance of any form of dogmatism. Although adherents of Chaos Magick often suggest that they dispense with the 'need for religion', the invocation or visualization of spiritual entities such as Baphomet, the horned theriomorphic deity, or various Egyptian deities, or the 'great old ones', is a central aspect of their ritual practices. As Phil Hine humorously puts it, they often invoke 'the great god Pan from a bedsit in Basingstoke' (1993, 15). But the central aim of Chaos Magick is to give life a sense of meaning and to achieve gnosis as a form of inner knowledge through the creation of a magical self (Carroll 1987, 179; Hine 1993, 57).

Let me now turn finally to New Age religion.

8.7. NEW AGE SPIRITUALITY

The latest manifestation of western esotericism, New Age has been seen as less of a religion than as a 'do-it-yourself' or a 'postmodern' form of spirituality. A 'cultic milieu', it essentially consists of a blend of eastern mysticism, Neopaganism, western esotericism, and a perchance for psychic and occult phenomena. Initially, it had a pronounced millenarian vision for, as Doreen Valiente put it, 'the present-day revival of interest in witchcraft, magic and the occult generally, is all part of the onset of the Aquarian age' (1978, 13).

Thus in a restricted sense – New Age *sensu stricto*, as Hanegraaff describes it – the New Age movement is seen as a form of millenarianism, although in the New Age context this usually involves a spiritual agency rather than a charismatic personality who is divinely inspired (Hanegraaff 1996, 98–103).

Although an emphasis is often put on New Age as a form of 'spirituality', it undoubtedly expresses a religious metaphysic. God is therefore conceived as a divine being by New Age adherents, less as a personal being, however, than as the 'mind' of the universe, or as a divine 'source' of occult powers, or as an impersonal 'world soul'. As Marilyn Ferguson puts it, 'God is experienced as flow, wholeness, the infinite kaleidoscope of life and death, ultimate course, the ground of being' (1982, 420).

The divinity in New Age theology is thus seen in impersonal terms, as the 'energy' or 'life-force' that keeps the universe alive and whole. Yet equally important in New Age religion are the myriad spiritual beings or 'meta-empirical' entities – planetary deities, angels, spirits, discarnate entities, elementals, or simply subjectively experienced 'presences' – which, along with the Cosmic Christ, act as intermediaries or 'channel' their messages through certain psychic or spirit-mediums. 'Channelling', whether or not this involves spirit-possession or trance states, is thus a key feature of New Age religion. Well-known mediums include Jane Roberts, who was the 'channel' for the spirit-guide Seth; J. Z. Knight, who acts as a spirit-medium for Ramtha, allegedly an ancient warrior from Atlantis; and Helen Schucman, who produced 'A Course in Miracles' (1975), the author of which is thought to have been Jesus Christ himself (Hanegraaff 1996, 37–40).

'Channelling' is obviously akin to spirit-possession and shamanism in other contexts, although automatic writing or painting is an important feature of modern channelling and the books produced by the spirit-guides or 'personalities' like Seth have made their spirit-mediums rich and famous. But what is important about writers and spirit-mediums like Jane Roberts is that religion and psychology tend to be conflated, and thus New Age shows a strong tendency towards a 'psychologizing of religion' along with a 'sacralization of psychology' (Hanegraaff 996, 197).

Much has been written on the notion that New Age implies a 'self-spirituality', and thus that the 'human potential movement' was a key influence in the emergence of New Age as a social phenomenon. This movement focussed around the humanistic and transpersonal psychology of such scholars as Abraham Maslow, Fritz Perls, and later Ken Wilber. The key notion behind this psychology was the attainment of 'peak experiences' or 'personal growth', or the development of 'higher' levels of consciousness. This invariably entailed the idea of people, through various 'mind-expanding techniques', getting in touch with their own 'inner divinity' and achieving 'self-actualization'. Combined with spirit-healing and alternative therapies, New Age psychology has thus come to be associated with a variety of approaches for the promotion of 'holistic health' – acupuncture, chiropractic, iridology, psychic and crystal healing, reflexology, meditation and visualization, auras, enneagrams, numerology, rebirthing, yoga, soul travel, aromatherapy, kinesiology, magnetic therapy, reiki, and much else besides (Hanegraaff 1996, 42–54; Clifford and Johnson 2001, 80–100).

Yet although this would seem to express an extreme eclecticism and indicate an 'extraordinary mish-mash' of ideas and practices, nevertheless many scholars have emphasized that a key and constant feature of New Age religion is the notion of 'self-spirituality' – the assumption that the 'self itself is sacred' and that following the esoteric tradition spirituality or the divine lies 'within the person' (Heelas 1996, 2). As David Spangler expressed it, the true 'real self' is a 'sacred identity' beyond the ego and is a point of transcendence that implies mutuality, love, connectedness, and community (1984, 58–9).

The identification of the real or 'higher self' with divinity, or the idea that divinity is 'within' as a divine spark, or as a refraction of a universal mind or spirit, seems to be a common theme of New Age spirituality. If the person is, in essence, a spiritual being, then it implies that to fully experience the 'self' is also to experience 'god' (or the goddess), and this would seem to have a number of correlates: an 'epistemological individualism' such that truth is simply the outcome of subjective experience; an extreme form of idealism that suggests that we create our own reality, or, as one New Age mystic puts it, 'the physical world is our creation' (Shakti Gawain 1988, 26); and, finally, a rejection of external authority and an emphasis on autonomy, although New Age enthusiasts seem to quite freely accept the authority of enlightened 'masters' and spiritual agencies who 'channel' their messages through well-known spirit-mediums. (On the 'self-spirituality' of New Age advocates, see Hanegraaff 1996, 203–18; Heelas 1996, 18–27; S. Sutcliffe 1998).

Equally significant is that, in spite of their extreme eclectism, many New Age advocates see their form of spirituality as an expression of a 'perennial philosophy'. They therefore stress the 'transcendent unity' of all religions and align themselves with such esoteric scholars as Rene Guenon and Frithjof Schuon (on perennial philosophy, see Huxley 1946; Sharpe 1986, 262–6; Al-Rawandi 1994).

This, of course, does not prevent New Age enthusiasts also from drawing on modern science, especially theoretical physics and systems theory, to validate what is essentially a magical or spiritual worldview. They particularly draw on the writings of Fritjof Capra (1976), who argues that there are significant parallels between quantum physics and oriental mysticism; David Bohm (1980) and his notion of implicate order, and on such system theorists and holistic thinkers as Ilya Prigogine, Gregory Bateson, and James Lovelock (Hanegraaff 1996, 128–40). Many of these scholars repudiate a religious metaphysic; in fact, Bateson suggests that the magical notion of the 'power of mind over matter' is simply 'nonsense' (1987, 59). Hanegraaff emphasizes the fact that New Age religion is an 'organic' or 'holistic' worldview and that historically, western esotericism was a 'counterforce' against both secular philosophy and the mechanistic worldview associated with Galileo and Newton (1996, 388). New Age religion thus attempts to combine science, magic, and religion and expresses a 'cultural critique' against both Cartesian dualism and 'reductionism' – the latter misleadingly equated with 'modern scientific materialism' (1996, 515–6). But, of course, critiques of both Cartesian metaphysics and reductive materialism go back to Marx and, long before Capra, have been expressed by Marxists, evolutionary biologists, naturalists, philosophical pragmatists like Dewey and Mead, and a host of social scientists. It is fallacious to equate secular rationalism and contemporary science with either mechanistic philosophy or reductive materialism. In fact, New Age spirituality is both dualistic – in postulating a transcendental realm or 'other-worldly' reality – and reductive, in that the natural world is seen as having its 'ground' or 'ultimate source' in some divine being or 'transcendent absolute'.

But Hanegraaff also emphasizes that New Age believers tend to have a this-worldly orientation, and this world is seen neither as an illusion (as in Vedanta philosophy), nor as an inherent disaster (as in Gnosticism), nor as something 'irrelevant' to the aim of enlightenment (as in Buddhism) (1996, 114). Hanegraaff thus concludes that New Age religion has five basic tendencies, namely, holism, an evolutionary perspective, 'self-spirituality' – the conflation of psychology and religion, a this-worldly orientation, and the expectations of a New Age – ranging from moderate improvement to 'total bliss' (1996, 365–6). Thus the emphasis on 'inner spirituality' is essentially seen as serving to bring about a 'world of harmony, peace and bliss' (Heelas 1996, 75).

The New Age movement is often seen as arising from the 'counterculture' of the 1960s, with its emphasis on psychedelic drugs and left-wing politics. But over the past two decades, it has proved to be a rather conservative movement, and in his sociological analysis of the New Age culture, Paul Heelas affirms that it has increasingly come to provide a way of 'sanctifying capitalism'. Although Heelas suggests that the New Age often appeals to those who have 'identity problems', given the pressures and uncertainties of 'modernity' – modern capitalism and industrial technology – he also stresses the 'certainties' at the 'heartland' of capitalism, namely, the 'search for prosperity'. Thus he explores the 'turn to prosperity' among New Age adherents and what may well be described as the 'unholy alliance' between the New Age movement and capitalism, with centres like Findhorn running workshops on the 'spirit of business'. Many New Age gurus, in fact, embrace the utopian vision provided by the capitalist system itself. New Age is thus less a 'counterculture' than the means of obtaining wealth and prosperity and has thus come to epitomize some of the central features of modernity (Heelas 1996, 135–52). Through the media of the New Age, spirituality has now become a commodity, and the means of self-transformation is readily available through the market. Thus New Age has often been described as a form of 'spiritual consumerism' (Arweck 2002, 266). The movement has therefore come to be identified by its critics with the 'culture of narcissism' and as providing the ultimate philosophy of the 'me generation' (Lasch 1979; Ritchie 1991, 173).

The feminist artist and writer Monica Sjoo, a strident advocate of goddess religion, is even more critical of the New Age movement, describing it as reactionary and patriarchal, with a 'sinister hidden agenda'. The movement is dominated, she suggests, by people from white, upper-middle-class backgrounds, and in a critical examination of the writing of Blavatsky, Alice Bailey, and the 'right wing' David Spangler, she argues that they are obsessed with transcendence, fire, light, and the

'Aryan race'. Spangler, she writes, advocates a 'cold intellectualism' and a New Age 'elitism' and views multinational corporations as 'ways of securing the planet – strategies for establishing planetary consciousness' (Spangler 1980, 61; Sjoo 1992, 120). She thus insists that many of the covert ideas of the New Age are 'racist, misogymist, reactionary and right-wing, inherited from a mish-mash of both Eastern and Western occult sources', and concludes that New Age thinking is full of 'dishonest, smug, self-righteous and right-wing double think paraded as "spirituality"' (1992, 4–10).

Both Hanegraaff and Heelas tend to view Neopaganism as a constituent part of the New Age movement, given its emphasis on ritual magic, and Hanegraaff indeed writes that 'Neopaganism is a continuation of nineteenth-century occultist ritual magic' (1996, 85). As we noted earlier, many Neopagans repudiate this identification of Wicca and Neopaganism with the New Age movement (Pearson 1998), and in a comparative study of both movements, Michael York (1995) tends to draw out some of the contrasts.

There is a good deal of overlap and common ground between the New Age and Neopagan movements. Both are largely a product of people's disenchantment with the materialism and ethos of contemporary industrial capitalism and with the orthodox religious institutions of the 'West', specifically, theistic Christianity. Both are situated in the western esoteric tradition and draw heavily on its occult theology and ritual magic. And both movements are closely related to the 'human potential movement' and have been influenced by Jungian and transpersonal psychology, so there is a common emphasis on self-transformation and self-realization by means of occult (magical) practices. But there are also key differences in the emphases of each movement, which are summed up succinctly by York with this phrase: 'Where New Age per se pursues a transcendent metaphysical reality, Neopaganism seeks an immanent locus of the deity' (1995, 2). He also notes that whereas New Age thinks of itself as a *new* form of religion or spiritual orientation, Neopaganism thinks of itself more as a 'reawakening' or the 'rebirth' of a *past* ancient tradition. But drawing on the earlier discussions, the different emphases of the two movements may be summarized as follows:

New Age	**Neopagan**
Esotericism	Paganism
Transcendence	Immanence
Spiritual	Ecological
Hierarchy	Egalitarian
Masculine	Feminine
Individualist	Communal
Meditation/channelling	Earth rituals
Millenialism	Revivalism
Panentheism	Polytheism

Several surveys by New Age magazines and organizations have indicated that the majority of occultists have college or university backgrounds and belong to professional occupations – as teachers, engineers, journalists, civil servants, health workers, or computer operators (York 1995, 187–90). This tends to confirm Luhrmann's observations that the majority of adherents of New Age esotericism are white, middle-class, well-educated professionals. Heelas comments favourably that New Age is perhaps 'the secret religion of the educated classes' (1996, 124). (On the New Age movement, see Bloom 1991 for a useful anthology, and Lewis and Melton 1992 for a comparative perspective; other important studies include Campbell 1972; Ritchie 1991; Van Den Broek and Hanegraaff 1998.)

Conclusions

The literature on the anthropology of religion is now so extensive that it might well be described as 'vast'. For over the past three or four decades, books and articles on the anthropology of religion have continued to be published by the hundreds, and even within the past decade several important anthologies have appeared (e.g., Glazier 1997; Klass and Weisgrau 1999; Lambek 2002), this in spite of the fact that the anthropology of religion was said to be in the 'doldrums' and to have been somewhat 'marginalized' within the anthropology curriculum. Given the impossibility of covering even a fraction of this literature within a single text, the present study has focussed specifically on the social anthropology of religion, namely, on those ethnographic studies that have followed the 'dual heritage' of anthropology, as Maurice Bloch described it, combining hermeneutics, the interpretation of religious beliefs and practices, with a sociological approach that situates religion within its socio-historical context. Recent religious-studies scholars have emphasized the need to study religion not only in its 'own terms' as a tradition but also in relation to the 'wider society'. Social anthropologists, of course, have been thus engaged for over half a century.

In my earlier study (1987), I outlined the various theoretical approaches to the study of religious phenomena – intellectualist, psychoanalytic, psychological, interpretive, phenomenological, structuralist, as well as the various sociological approaches to the study of religion that derive from the seminal work of Marx, Weber, and Durkheim. Although in recent years there has been a tendency among so-called postmodernist anthropologists to reduce the study of religion to semiotics, or hermeneutics (or even autobiography!), producing, as Roger Keesing remarked, a kind of 'cultural theology', the 'dual' approach of social anthropology has been the dominant tendency over the past half century or so. The sociological approach has, of course, been embraced also by several very influential recent scholars – Habermas, Bourdieu, Foucault, Giddens, Wallerstein, for example, yet significantly such scholars have tended to treat religion as of somewhat marginal interest.

Eschewing both a thematic approach, one centred around specific conceptual terms – such as ritual, sacrifice, gender, rationality, the body, witchcraft – and the approach that I earlier adopted, which examined religion with reference to broad theoretical perspectives, the present text has, in contrast, taken a regional approach. It has therefore focussed on eight specific ethnographic or substantive areas. Equally important, the study has been focussed around what I consider to be key ethnographic texts – though admittedly, given limitations of space, I have been unable to discuss many other excellent ethnographies. Thus the study has a pronounced ethnographic focus. Such ethnographic studies were viewed not simply as 'case studies' to illustrate some 'theory' but rather as substantive contributions to the study of religion in their own right, and in the text I have critically examined their ethnographic content in relation to some specific context and their theoretical importance within the social anthropological paradigm. Given this ethnographic focus, the whole book is in fact about hermeneutics – descriptive accounts of religious beliefs and practices – but such phenomena are explicated, by the anthropologists I discuss, by situating them within their wider 'social setting'. Those particularly influenced by Marx and Weber – such scholars as Van Binsbergen, Keesing, Worsley, and Obeyesekere – thus deal not only with the phenomenology of religious traditions and ritual practices but also place them in their social context, one that includes the wider political economy, specifically global capitalism.

Throughout the book there are a number of recurrent themes that can usefully be highlighted in these concluding reflections.

The first is that it is evident, as both Lewis and Bourguignon earlier indicated, that spirit rituals, and specifically spirit-possession, is a phenomenon that is not restricted to tribal societies but is found throughout the world. Scholars like De Heusch and Eliade earlier made a clear distinction between shamanism, which involved contact with spirits through an out-of-body experience and the subsequent 'mastery of the spirits' and spirit-possession. The latter entailed the involuntary possession of a person by a spirit-being. But the evidence suggests that within any specific ethnographic context, such phenomena as the visionary trance, the soul flight, spirit-mediumship, and spirit-possession (which normally involves a trance state) coexist and cannot be viewed as self-sustaining forms of religiosity. But what is equally clear is that such spirit rituals, usually involving contact with or possession by some spiritual agent – spirits of the dead, various deities, or in the Christian context, the holy spirit – are found worldwide and are a constituent part of most religious systems. Ecstatic rituals involving spirits are therefore an important part of the lives of many people throughout the world – as we have indicated, in relation, for example, to Buddhists in Tibet and Burma, Muslims in the Sudan (where Zar spirits are significant), Catholics in Haiti and Brazil (particularly among people in African-derived 'cults' such as Vodou and Candomblé), and with regard to the various spirit rituals throughout South Asia and sub-Saharan Africa. Trance states and spirit-possession are equally important in such contemporary movements as neo-shamanism and charismatic Christianity. In many parts of the world, there is a close association between such spirit rituals and people of the lower classes or of low status, especially women.

With regard to such spirit rituals, a number of recurrent themes may be noted. Through possession, and even through the act of worship [*puja*] in the Hindu context, a close identification is made between the spirit or deity and the devotee, and thus the spirit has an immediacy or a presence in the lives of the people. The existence of the spirits is in fact confirmed by the possession. But a distinction is often made between god, or various deities, which have a transcendental quality, and the spirits, which are immanent in the world, and it is only the latter that are involved in ecstatic or possession rites. Equally, a distinction may be made between the village context and a specific 'moral order' and the 'outside' or 'bush', and those spirits associated with the latter domain are often deemed to be amoral, capricious, or even malevolent. Throughout the world, the spirits of people who have died in a violent manner are often deemed to be unsettled and thus malevolent. In fact, spirit rituals often entail the 'settling' of a spirit and thus forming an ongoing relationship with an initially offending spirit. This may be done by the creation of a shrine or by marriage, the spirit henceforth being deemed a 'helping' or 'guardian' spirit. As noted, many anthropologists have described this relationship as akin to that of 'patron–client' relationships among humans.

Second, given the diversity of ritual forms and the existence of ecstatic forms of religiosity, particularly spirit rituals focussed around healing, within the main religious traditions – Islam, Buddhism, Hinduism, Christianity – anthropologists have always been tempted to suggest the presence of two distinct forms of religious expression. During the 1950s, Robert Redfield was conscious of the fact that there was something of a division of labour between humanistic scholars and orientalists in religious-studies departments, who focussed their studies on the literate tradition embodied in sacred texts (as they still do), and the writings of anthropologists, who focussed their ethnographic studies on tribal or village communities, often treating these communities as if they were social isolates. Thus was initiated the distinction between the 'great' and 'little' traditions that was utilized by many early anthropologists studying folk Catholicism and Hinduism. Such a distinction was soon found to be misleading or inadequate. What is of interest is that similar dichotomies have continued to be invoked by anthropologists, as the present study has shown. Thus we have the distinction between scripturalist and ecstatic religious styles within Islam (Gellner); the distinction between shamanic and clerical Buddhism in Tibet (Samuel); the stark dichotomy between spirit rituals and Buddhism in Burma, which is seen as reflecting the Buddhist distinction between this-worldly [*laukika*] and other-worldly [*lokottara*] concerns [Spiro]; the distinction made by David Mandelbaum between two basic functions of religion, namely, the transcendental (concerned with long-term welfare and the ultimate goal of salvation) and the pragmatic (focussed on earthly concerns and personal and local problems), which specifically relates to Hinduism; and finally, with respect to Melanesian religion, the distinction between doctrinal and imagistic (ecstatic–ritualistic) 'modes of religiosity' (Whitehouse). As these distinctions seem to crop up throughout the text, the distinction between the pragmatic and what might be described as the 'salvation' aspects of religion may well be seen as one of the leitmotifs of the present text. But as I have indicated, although such dichotomies may have a certain heuristic validity, they are nonetheless problematic in attempting to describe the richness and diversity of religious traditions and practices. A further point may be made, namely, whether these distinctions, say between the clerical and the ecstatic, correlate with the class structure or with the distribution of power within a society. For Ioan Lewis' distinction between 'peripheral' possession cults and 'central' non-ecstatic religions – Buddhism, Islam, Christianity, and Brahmanic Hinduism – certainly implies such a correlation. Yet although there may be exceptions, the ethnographic data presented within the present text do tend to support the suggestion that there is indeed a close relationship between the class structure and the distribution of power in a society, and its forms of religiosity.

Third, with respect both to tribal religions generally and to the many forms of ecstatic religion, which focus particularly on spirit-healing, many anthropologists have emphasized the pragmatic attitude that surrounds such religious forms. The well-known scholar of African religion, John Mbiti, for example, described African people's relationship with the spirit world as essentially one that was pragmatic and utilitarian rather than spiritual and mystical. Throughout the present study, in fact, many ethnographers were noted who emphasized the pragmatic attitudes of the people they studied towards their religion. For example, Maya Deren, with respect to Vodou religion, suggested that life for the ordinary peasant in Haiti was too urgent and pressing to permit the luxury of idealism or mysticism, and that Vodou was not so much a reason for living as a 'means' of living. Likewise, many scholars discussing religious beliefs and practices in Melanesia (Lawrence, Worsley) have stressed that the prevailing attitudes of Melanesians towards religion was essentially pragmatic and materialistic and that there was little emphasis on 'salvation'. Keesing, in fact, described Kwaio religious cosmology as less a spiritual metaphysics than a 'pragmatic philosophy'. Yet although the spirits have been described as 'immanent' in the world, many anthropologists have also emphasized that the worldview of many people throughout the world implies a dualistic metaphysic, a distinction being made between the empirical world, manifested in everyday life, and what is described as the 'spirit world' or the 'unseen world' of the 'occult', embracing deities, spirits, and other spiritual beings. An example is MacGaffey's description of Kongo religious culture as consisting of two realms – 'this world' [*nza yayi*] and the 'land of the dead' [*nsi a bafwa*]. But whether this implies a dualistic metaphysic is perhaps debatable. What is also of significance – and this has a worldwide relevance – is the close relationship between religious rituals and various symbolic schemas, for the transgressing of certain ritual prohibitions relating to these schemas seems to be intrinsically related to misfortunes. And such misfortunes invariably involve spirits or deities that have to be placated through various rituals, oblations, or sacrifices. Hence, the close relation between spirit rituals and healing and the notion that ecstatic rites are not about salvation but rather about 'survival in this world'.

A fourth recurrent theme relates to the issue of syncretism, for many scholars have emphasized that many religious movements and churches throughout the world have a syncretic quality, combining religious ideas and ritual practices from different cultural contexts. The concept 'syncretism' in fact has become the focus of much debate among anthropologists, scholars such as MacGaffey repudiating the concept entirely, given that it has pejorative connotations, particularly in the hands of some theologians, and the fact that all religious systems are to some degree 'syncretic'. Other scholars, as I have described, have emphasized the cultural 'purity' of certain religious movements – the authenticity of Kimbanguism as a Christian church and of Candomblé as pristine African religion, are examples – and have thus also tended to denigrate or even repudiate the notion of syncretism. Other scholars, however, have reaffirmed the usefulness of the concept of syncretism – involving the intermixing, through convergence, linkage, or juxtaposition of different religious traditions – at least as a descriptive concept referring to what happens concretely when peoples and cultures meet.

The concept of syncretism introduces the final theme, namely, the importance of religion in the contemporary world, especially with regard to the intrusions of global capitalism and the relationship more generally between religion and politics. The relationship between religion and so-called 'modernity' is, of course, diverse and complex and takes many different forms. Religion as a mode of knowledge or an ideology often upholds forms of power and authority, as Marxists, like Foucault, have long emphasized, and throughout the text we have seen illustrations of this – for example, ritual practices sustaining systems of authority in local communities; religious gurus with the Hindu tradition sanctifying a resurgent Hindu nationalism; and evangelical forms of Christianity entailing a cultural logic – utilitarian individualism – that served to facilitate the emergence of capitalism in Southern Africa – as a 'forerunner of colonial rule. In other contexts, however, religion has served as a form of rebellion or 'reaction' against an encroaching global capitalism, and its accompanying state power, particularly the colonial state, or even against the more orthodox religions with their focus on salvation and transcendental concerns. There are many examples of such resistance throughout the text: Zar cults in the Sudan being described as 'counter-hegemonic'; the Rastafari and other African-derived religious movements in the Americas, as well as the Zionist churches in South Africa, serving as 'cultures of resistance' to colonial rule and an expanding global capitalism; and the cargo cults and other religions in Melanesia that have been described as 'movements of the disinherited' and that may take either a millennial form or, as with the Kwaio, reflect a 'siege mentality', people through their religion resisting both the encroachment of global capitalism and an expanding evangelical Christianity. Even the rise of new religious movements, such as

Neopaganism and Hare Krishna, has been interpreted as movements of resistance – part of a reaction against either Christianity or the vicissitudes of capitalist 'modernity'. Whether such religions emphasize a 'revival' or reaffirmation of past religious tradition (as with Neopaganism and Candomblé) or have a millennial emphasis on a coming 'new heaven, new earth' (as with many religious movements like the cargo cults, the Kitawala movement in Zambia, or New Age spirituality) or have an essentially 'reformist' character – as, for example, Protestant Buddhism in Sri Lanka or reformist movements within Islam – depends on the nature and development of a specific religion and its particular socio-historical context. Often these latter movements have a 'fundamentalist' character, combining an emphasis on past religious traditions, affirmed as orthodoxy, with a political project – as in relation to the Iranian revolution and the resurgence of Hindu nationalism. In an era of global capitalism, what is significant with regard to these various religious movements is their syncretic nature, their widespread use of modern communication technology, and their sheer diversity. Such that in many parts of the world anthropologists have described the local situation as one where there is a religious 'marketplace' with a tremendous diversity of different forms of religious expression.

Unlike many religious-studies texts, which focus on religious traditions as 'faiths', this present study has attempted to describe the diversity of religious forms found throughout the world as social institutions. It has thus situated these institutions, whether cultural traditions, churches, or movements, within their specific socio-historical context and has focussed principally not on religious texts but on ethnographic studies, which have concretely described the beliefs and ritual practices of these varied religious forms.

References

Aberle, D. F. 1966. *The Peyote Religion Among the Navaho.* London: Aldin.

Abrahamian, E. 1989. *Radical Islam: The Iranian Mojahedin.* London: Tauris.

———. 1993. *Khomeinism.* London: Tauris.

Abrahams, R. (Ed.). 1994. *Witchcraft in Contemporary Tanzania.* Cambridge, UK: African Studies Centre, Cambridge University.

Abram, D. 1996. *The Spell of the Sensuous.* New York: Random House.

Abun-Nasr, J. H. 1965. *The Tijaniya: A Sufi Order in the Modern World.* Oxford, UK: Oxford University Press.

Adler, M. 1979. *Drawing Down the Moon.* Boston: Beacon Press. (Reprinted 1986.)

Ahmed, A. S. 1976. *Millennium and Charisma Among Pathans.* London: Routledge & Kegan Paul.

———. 1988. *Discovering Islam.* London: Routledge.

Ahmed, A. S. and D. M. Hart (Eds.). 1984. *Islam in Tribal Societies.* London: Routledge & Kegan Paul.

Aiyappan, A. 1965. *Social Revolution in a Kerala Village.* Bombay: Asia Publishers.

Akin, D. 1996. 'Local and Foreign Spirits in Kwaio, Solomon Islands', in J. M. Mageo and A. Howard (Eds.), *Spirits in Culture, History, and Mind*, pp. 147–71. New York: Routledge.

Allen, D. 1978. *Structure and Creativity in Religion.* The Hague, The Netherlands: Mouton.

Allen, M. 1967. *Male Cults and Secret Initiations.* Melbourne, Australia: Melbourne University Press.

Al-Rawandi, I. 1994. 'Esoteric Evangelicals'. *New Humanist* 109(2): 10–12.

Altizer, T. J. 1963. *Mircea Eliade and the Dialectic of the Sacred.* Philadelphia: Westminster.

Ames, M. M. 1964. 'Magical Animism and Buddhism', *Journal of Asian Studies* 23: 21–52.

———. 1968. 'Ritual Prestations and the Structure of the Sinhalese Pantheon', in M. Nash (Ed.), *Theravada Buddhism*, pp. 27–50. New Haven, CT: Yale University Press.

Anderson, A. 1993. *Tumelo – The Faith of African Pentecostals in South Africa.* Pretoria, South Africa: Unisa Press.

Andersson, E. 1958. *Messianic Popular Movements in the Lower Congo.* Uppsala, Sweden: Almquist & Wiksells.

Ankarloo, B. and G. Henningsen (Eds.). 1990. *Early Modern European Witchcraft.* Oxford: Clarendon.

Appiah, K. A. 1992. *In My Father's House.* London: Methuen.

Arberry, A. J. 1950. *Sufism: An Account of the Mystics of Islam.* Washington, DC: Georgetown University Center for Contemporary Arab Studies.

Armstrong, K. 2000. *Buddha.* London: Weldenfeld and Nicolson.

Arweck, E. 2002. 'New Religious Movements', in L. Woodhead (Ed.), *Religions in the Modern World*, pp. 264–87. London: Routledge.

Asad, T. 1986. *The Idea of an Anthropology of Islam.* Washington, DC: Georgetown University Center for Contemporary Arab Studies.

______. 1993. *Genealogies of Religion.* Baltimore: Johns Hopkins University Press.

Atkinson, J. M. 1987. 'The Effectiveness of Shamans in an Indonesian Ritual'. *American Anthropology* 89: 342–55.

______. 1992. 'Shamanisms Today'. *Annual Review of Anthropology* 21: 307–30.

Auslander, M. 1993. 'Open the Wombs! The Symbolic Politics of Modern Ngoni Witchfinding', in J. Comaroff and J. Comaroff (Eds.), *Modernity and Its Malcontents*, pp. 167–92. Chicago: University of Chicago Press.

Babb, L. A. 1986. *Redemptive Encounters.* Berkeley, CA: University of California Press.

Bachofen, J. J. 1967. *Myth, Religion and Mother Right.* Princeton, NJ: Princeton University Press. (Originally published 1861.)

Bainbridge, W. S. 1997. *The Sociology of Religious Movements.* New York: Routledge.

Baldick, J. 2000. *Animal and Shaman.* New York: New York University Press.

Balikci, A. 1963. 'Shamanistic Behaviour Among the Netselik Eskimos'. *South Western Journal of Anthropology* 19: 380–96.

______. 1970. *The Netselik Eskimo.* Prospect Heights, IL: Waveland Press.

Balzer, M. M. 1983. 'Doctors or Deceivers: The Siberian Kanty Shaman and Soviet Medicine', in L. D. Romanucci-Ross et al., *The Anthropology of Medicine*, pp. 54–76. South Hadley, MA: Bergin and Garvey.

______. 1995. 'The Poetry of Shamanism', in G. Harvey (Ed.), *Shamanism: A Reader*, pp. 307–33. London: Routledge.

______. 1996. 'Sacred Genders in Siberia', in S. P. Ramet (Ed.), *Reversals and Gender Cultures*, pp. 164–82. London: Routledge.

______. 1997. (Ed.). *Shamanic Worlds.* Armouk, NY: North Castle.

Banton, M. 1970. 'African Prophets', in J. Middleton (Ed.), *Black Africa*, pp. 222–33. London: Macmillan.

Barkun, M. 1997. *Religion and the Racist Right.* Chapel Hill, NC: University of North Carolina Press.

Barnet, M. 1997. 'The Religious System of Santeria', in M. F. Olmos and L. Paravisini-Gebert (Eds.), *Sacred Possessions*, pp. 79–100. New Brunswick, NJ: Rutgers University Press.

Barrett, D. V. 2001. *The New Believers.* London: Cassell.

Barrett, F. 1989. *The Magus: A Complete System of Occult Philosophy.* Wellingborough: Aquarian Press. (Originally published 1801.)

Barrett, L. 1976. *The Sun and the Drum.* Kingston: Sangsters.

______. 1977. *The Rastafarians.* Kingston: Sangsters.

Barth, F. 1959. *Political Leadership Among the Swat Pathans.* London: Athlone.

______. 1975. *Ritual and Knowledge Among the Baktaman of New Guinea.* New Haven, CT: Yale University Press.

______. 1987. *Cosmologies in the Making.* Cambridge, UK: Cambridge University Press.

Bartholomeusz, T. 1999. 'First Among Equals: Buddhism and the Sri Lankan State', in I. Harris (Ed.), *Buddhism and Politics in Twentieth Century Asia*, pp. 173–93. London: Continuum.

Barton, B. 1990. *The Secret Life of a Satanist.* Los Angeles: Feral House.

Basham, A. L. 1967. *The Wonder That Was India.* Calcutta: Fontana.

Bashiriyeh, H. 1984. *The State and Revolution in Iran 1962–1982.* London: Croom Helm.

Bastide, R. 1951. 'Religion and the Church in Brazil', in T. C. Smith and A. Marchant (Eds.), *Brazil*, pp. 334–35. New York: Dryden.
______. 1971. *African Civilizations in the New World*. London: Hurst.
______. 1978. *African Religions of Brazil*. Baltimore: Johns Hopkins University Press.
Bastien, J. W. 1978. *Mountain of the Condor*. St. Paul, MN: West Publications.
Batchelor, S. 1987. *The Jewel in the Lotus*. London: Wisdom Publishing.
______. 1994. *The Awakening of the West*. Berkeley, CA: Parallax.
Bateson, G. 1972. *Steps to an Ecology of Mind*. St. Albans, UK: Granada.
______. 1980. *Naven*. London: Wildwood House. (Originally published 1936.)
______. 1987. *Angels Fear*. London: Rider.
Baumann, M. 1995. 'Creating a European Path to Nirvana'. *Journal of Contemporary Religion* 10: 55–70.
Beals, A. R. 1962. *Gopalpur: A South Indian Village*. New York: Holt, Rinehart.
Beattie, J. and J. Middleton (Eds.). 1969. *Spirit Mediumship and Society in Africa*. London: Routledge & Kegan Paul.
Bechert, H. 1984. 'To be Burmese is to be Buddhist' and 'Buddhist Revival in East and West', in H. Bechert and R. Gombrich (Eds.), *The World of Buddhism*, pp. 147–58 and 273–85. London: Thames and Hudson.
Beckford, J. A. 1975. *The Trumpet of Prophecy*. New York: Wiley.
______. (Ed.). 1986. *New Religious Movements and Rapid Social Change*. London: Sage.
______. 2003. *Social Theory and Religion*. Cambridge: Cambridge University Press.
Beckwith, M. W. 1929. *Black Roadways*. Chapel Hill, NC: University of North Carolina Press.
Behrend, H. 1999. *Alice Lakwena and the Holy Spirits*. Oxford, UK: Currey.
Behrend, H. and U. Luig (Eds.). 1999. *Spirit Possession: Modernity and Power in Africa*. Oxford, UK: Currey.
Beidelman, T. O. 1997. *The Cool Knife*. Washington, DC: Smithsonian Institution.
Bell, C. 1992. *The Religion of Tibet*. Delhi, India: Motilal Banarsidass. (Originally published 1930.)
Bell, C. 1992. *Ritual Theory, Ritual Practice*. Oxford, UK: Oxford University Press.
Bellah, R. N. 1964. 'Religious Evolution'. *American Sociological Review* 29: 358–74.
Ben-Amos, P. G. 1994. 'The Promise of Greatness: Women and Power in An Edo Spirit Possession Cult', in T. A. Blakely et al. 1994, pp. 119–34.
Benedict, R. 1934. *Patterns of Culture*. London: Routledge & Kegan Paul.
______. 1948. 'Anthropology and the Humanities'. *American Anthropologist* 30: 585–93.
Berglund, A. 1976. *Zulu Thought-Patterns and Symbolism*. London: Hurst.
Berndt, R. M. 1974. *Australian Aboriginal Religion*. Leiden, The Netherlands: Brill.
Besson, J. 2002. *Martha Brae's Two Histories*. Chapel Hill, NC: University of North Carolina Press.
Beteille, A. 1971. *Caste, Class and Power*. Berkeley, CA: University of California Press.
Beth, R. 1990. *Hedge Witch*. London: Aquarian Press.
Beyer, P. 1994. *Religion and Globalization*. London: Sage.
Bhaktivedanta, A. C. 1977. *The Science of Self-Realization*. London: Bhaktivedanta Book Trust.
Bharati, A. 1963. 'Pilgrimage in the Indian Tradition'. *History of Religions* 3: 135–67.
______. 1976. *The Light at the Center*. Santa Barbara, CA: Ross-Erikson.
______. 1985. 'The Self in Hindu Thought and Action', in A. J. Marsella et al. (Eds.), *Culture and Self*, pp. 185–230. London: Tavistock.

Bhardwaj, S. M. 1973. *Hindu Places of Pilgrimage in India.* Berkeley, CA: University of California Press.

Bhatt, C. 2001. *Hindu Nationalism.* Oxford: Berg.

Biehl, J. 1991. *Rethinking Eco-Feminist Politics.* Boston: Southend Press.

Biehl, J. and P. Staudenmaier. 1995. *Ecofascism: Lessons From the German Experience.* Edinburgh: AK Press.

Blakely, T. D., W. E. Van Beek, and D. L. Thomson (Eds.), *Religion in Africa.* London: Currey.

Blavatsky, H. P. 1972. *Isis Unveiled.* Pasadena, CA: Theosophical University Press. (Originally published 1877.)

———. 1982. *The Secret Doctrine.* Los Angeles: The Theosophical Company. (Originally published 1888.)

Bloch, M. E. F. 1983. *Marxism and Anthropology.* Oxford, UK: Clarendon.

———. 1986. *From Blessing to Violence.* Cambridge, UK: Cambridge University Press.

———. 1989. *Ritual, History and Power.* London: Athlone.

———. 1998. *How We Think They Think.* Boulder, CO: Westview.

Bloom, W. (Ed.). 1991. *The New Age: An Anthology of Essential Writings.* London: Rider.

Bockie, S. 1993. *Death and the Invisible Powers.* Bloomington, IN: Indiana University Press.

Boddy, J. 1989. *Wombs and Alien Spirits.* Madison, WI: University of Wisconsin Press.

———. 1994. 'Spirit Possession Revisited: Beyond Instrumentality. *Annual Review of Anthropology* 23: 407–34.

Bohm, D. 1980. *Wholeness and the Implicate Order.* London: Ark.

Bourdieu, P. 1990. *The Logic of Practice.* Cambridge, UK: Polity Press.

Bourdillon, M. 1991. *Religion and Society.* Gweru: Mambo Press.

Bourguignon, E. 1973. (Ed.). *Religion, Altered States of Consciousness and Social Change.* Columbus, OH: Ohio State University Press.

———. 1976. *Possession.* San Francisco: Chandler & Sharp.

———. 1979. *Psychological Anthropology.* New York: Holt, Rinehart & Winston.

Bowie, F. 2000. *The Anthropology of Religion – An Introduction.* Oxford, UK: Blackwell.

Boyer, P. (Ed.). 1993. *Cognitive Aspects of Religious Symbolism.* Cambridge, UK: Cambridge University Press.

———. 2001. *Religion Explained.* London: Heinemann.

Branston, B. 1980. *Gods of the North.* London: Thames & Hudson.

Brazier, D. 2001. *The New Buddhism.* London: Constable.

Bricmont, J. 2001. 'Sociology and Epistemology', in J. Lopez and G. Potter (Eds.), *After Postmodernism.* London: Athlone.

Brohm, J. 1963. 'Buddhism and Animism in a Burmese Village'. *Journal of Asian Studies* 22: 155–67.

Bromley, D. G. and L. Shinn (Eds.). 1989. *Krishna Consciousness in the West.* Lewisberg, PA: Bucknell University Press.

Brown, D. 1979. 'Umbanda and Class-Relations in Brazil', in M. L. Margolis and W. E. Carter (Eds.), *Brazil: Anthropological Perspectives,* pp. 270–304. New York: Columbia University Press.

———. 1986. *Umbanda: Religion and Politics in Urban Brazil.* Ann Arbor, MI: University of Michigan Press.

Brown, K. M. 1987. 'Voodoo', in M. Eliade (Ed.), *The Encyclopaedia of Religion,* Vol. 15, pp. 296–301.

———. 1991. *Mama Lola.* Berkeley, CA: University of California Press. (Reprinted 2001.)

Brown, L. C. 1971. 'The Sudanese Mahdiya', in R. Rotberg (Ed.), *Rebellion in Black Africa*, pp. 3–23. Oxford, UK: Oxford University Press.

Brunton, R. 1980. 'Misconstrued Order in Melanesian Religion'. *Man* 15(1): 112–28.

Buchowski, M. 1997. *The Rational Other.* Poznan, Poland: Wydawnictno Fund Humaniora.

Budapest, Z. 1990. *The Holy Book of Women's Mysteries.* New York: Harper & Row.

Bunge, M. 1996. *Finding Philosophy in Social Science.* New Haven, CT: Yale University Press.

Bunnag, J. 1973. *Buddhist Monk, Buddhist Laymen.* Cambridge, UK: Cambridge University Press.

Burch, E. S. 1999. 'The Caribou Inuit', in R. B. Lee and R. Daly (Eds.), *The Cambridge Encyclopaedia of Hunters and Gatherers*, pp. 56–60. Cambridge, UK: Cambridge University Press.

Burghart, R. 1978. 'Hierarchical Models of the Hindu Social System'. *Journal of the Royal Anthropological Institute* 13(4): 519–36.

______. 1983. 'Renunciation in the Religious Traditions of South Asia'. *Journal of the Royal Anthropological Institute* 18: 635–53.

Burkert, W. *Greek Religion.* Oxford, UK: Blackwell.

Burkert, W., R. Girard, and J. Z. Smith (Eds.). 1987. *Violent Origins.* Stanford, CA: Stanford University Press.

Burkett, R. 1978. *Garveyism as a Religious Movement.* Metuchen, NJ: Scarecrow Press.

Burnett, D. 1991. *Dawning of the Pagan Moon.* Eastbourne, UK: Monarch Publications.

Burofsky, R. (Ed.). 1994. *Assessing Cultural Anthropology.* New York: McGraw-Hill.

Burridge, K. O. L. 1960. *Mambu.* London: Methuen.

______. 1969. *New Heaven, New Earth.* Oxford, UK: Blackwell.

Burt, B. 1994. *Tradition and Christianity: The Colonial Transformation of a Solomon Island Society.* New York: Harwood Academic.

Butt, A. 1966. 'Akawaio Shamanism', in S. Wavell, A. Butt, and N. Epton (Eds.), *Trances.* London: Allen & Unwin.

Callinicos, A. 1997. *Postmodernism: A Critical Diagnosis in Great Ideas Today*, pp. 206-55. Chicago: Encyclopedia Brittanica.

______. 1999. *Social Theory.* Cambridge, UK: Polity Press.

______. 2003. *An Anti-Capitalist Manifesto.* Cambridge, UK: Polity Press.

Campbell, C. 1972. 'The Cult, the Cultic Milieu and Secularization'. *Social Yearbook of Religion in Britain* 5: 119–36.

Campbell, H. 1980. 'Rastafari: Culture of Resistance'. *Race and Class* 22(1): 1–22.

______. 1985. *Rasta and Resistance.* London: Hansib.

Capra, F. 1976. *The Tao of Physics.* London: Fontana.

Carey, S. 1987. 'The Indianization of the Hare Krishna Movement in Britain', in R. Burghart (Ed.), *Hinduism in Britain*, pp. 81–99. London: Tavistock.

Carpenter, D. D. 1996. 'Emergent Nature Spirituality', in J. R. Lewis (Ed.), *Magical Religion and Modern Witchcraft*, pp. 35–72. Albany, NY: State University of New York Press.

Carr-Gomm, P. 1991. *The Elements of the Druid Tradition.* Shaftesbury, UK: Element Books.

______. (Ed.). 2003. *The Rebirth of Druidry.* London: Element Books.

Carrithers, M. 1983a. *The Buddha.* Oxford, UK: Oxford University Press.

______. 1983b. *The Forest Monks of Sri Lanka.* Delhi, India: Oxford University Press.

Carroll, P. J. 1987. *Liber Null and Psychonout.* York Beach, ME: Weiser.

Carneiro, R. L. 1964. 'The Amahuaca and the Spirit World', *Ethnology* 3: 6–11.

Cashmore, E. 1979. *Rastaman.* London: Allen and Unwin.

Castenada, C. 1968. *The Teachings of Don Juan.* Berkeley, CA: University of California Press.
Chapman, J. 1993. *Quest for Dion Fortune.* York Beach, ME: Weiser.
Charlesworth, M. H. Morphy, D. Bell, and K. Maddock (Eds.). 1984. *Religion in Aboriginal Australia: An Anthology.* St. Lucia, West Indies: University of Queensland Press.
Chattopadhyaya, D. 1959. *Lokayata: A Study in Ancient Indian Materialism.* New Delhi: People's Publishing House.
______. 1969. *Indian Atheism.* New Delhi: People's Publishing House.
Chaudhuri, N. C. 1974. *Scholar Extraordinary.* Delhi: Vision Books.
Chennakesavan, S. 1960. *Concept of Mind in Indian Philosophy.* Delhi: Motilal Banarsidass.
Chevannes, B. 1978. 'Revivalism: A Disappearing Religion', *Caribbean Quarterly* 24: 1–17.
______. 1994. *Rastafari: Roots and Ideology.* Syracuse, NY: Syracuse University Press.
______. (Ed.). 1995. *Rastafari and Other African-Caribbean World Views.* London: Macmillan.
Chomé, J. 1959. *La Passion de Simon Kimbangu.* Paris: Presence Africaine.
Churchill, W. 1992. *Fantasies of the Master Race.* Monroe, LA: Common Courage Press.
Cicero, C. and S. T. Cicero. 2003. *The Essential Golden Dawn.* St. Paul, MN: Llewellyn.
Clark, S. 1997. *Thinking With Demons.* Oxford, UK: Oxford University Press.
Clarke, P. 1988. 'Introduction to New Religious Movements', in S. Sutherland and P. Clarke (Eds.), *The Study of Religion, Traditional and New Religion*, pp. 149–53.
Clarke, P. B. 1986. *Black Paradise: The Rastafarian Movement.* Wellingborough, UK: Aquarian Press.
Clifford, R. and P. Johnson. 2001. *Jesus and the Gods of the New Age.* Oxford, UK: Lion.
Clottes, J. and D. Lewis Williams. 1998. *The Shamans of Prehistory.* New York: Abrams.
Cochrane, G. 1970. *Big Men and Cargo Cults.* Oxford, UK: Clarendon.
Cohn, B. S. 1955. 'The Changing Status of a Depressed Caste', in M. Marriott (Ed.), *Village India*, pp. 53–77. Chicago: University of Chicago Press.
Cohn, N. 1957. *The Pursuit of the Millennium.* London: Paladin.
______. 1975. *Europe's Inner Demons.* London: Heinemann.
Collier, A. 1994. *Critical Realism.* London: Verso.
Collins, S. 1982. *Selfless Persons.* Cambridge, UK: Cambridge University Press.
Comaroff, J. 1985. *Body of Power, Spirit of Resistance.* Chicago: University of Chicago Press.
Comaroff, J. and J. L. Comaroff. 1991. *Of Revelation and Revolution: Christianity, Colonialism and Consciousness in South Africa.* Chicago: University of Chicago Press.
______. 1992. *Ethnography and the Historical Imagination.* Boulder, CO: Westview.
Combs-Schilling, M. E. 1989. *Sacred Performances.* New York: Columbia University Press.
Constantinides, P. 1977. 'Ill at Ease and Sick at Heart: Symbolic Behaviour in a Sudanese Healing Cult', in I. M Lewis (Ed.), *Symbols and Sentiments*, pp. 61–84. New York: Academic.
______. 1978. 'Women's Spirit Possession and Urban Adaptation', in P. Caplan & J. Bujra (Eds.), *Women United, Women Divided*, pp. 185–205. London: Tavistock.
______. 1985. 'Women Heal Women: Spirit Possession and Sexual Segregation in a Muslim Society'. *Social Science and Medicine* 21: 685–92.
______. 1991. 'The History of Zar in the Sudan', in I. M. Lewis, A. Al-Safi, and S. Hurreiz (Eds.), *Women's Medicine*, pp. 83–99. Edinburgh: Edinburgh University Press.
Conze, E. 1951. *Buddhism: Its Essence and Development.* Oxford, UK: Cassirer.
Corbridge, S. and J. Harriss. 2000. *Reinventing India.* Cambridge, UK: Polity Press.

Cornell, V. J. 1998. *Realm of the Saint: Power and Authority in Moroccan Sufism.* Austin, TX: University of Texas Press.
Cox, J. L. 1992. *Expressing the Sacred.* Harare, Zimbabwe: University of Zimbabwe Press.
Cranston, S. 1994. *HPB.* New York: Putnam.
Crapanzano, V. 1973. *The Hamadsha.* Berkeley, CA: University of California Press.
Crawford, J. R. 1967. *Witchcraft and Sorcery in Rhodesia.* London: Oxford University Press.
Cronon, E. D. 1962. *Black Moses.* Madison, WI: University of Wisconsin Press.
Crowley, A. 1973. *Magick in Theory and Practice.* London: Routledge.
Crowley, V. 1989. *Wicca: The Old Religion in the New Age.* London: Aquarian Press.
______. 1994. *Phoenix From the Flame.* London: Aquarian Press.
______. 1996a. 'Wicca as Modern Day Mystery Religion', in C. Hardman and G. Harvey (Eds.), *Pagan Pathways*, pp. 81–93. London: Thorsons.
______. 1996b. *Principles of Paganism.* London: Thorsons.
______. 1998. 'Wicca as Nature Religion', in J. Pearson, R. H. Roberts, and G. Samuel (Eds.), *Nature Religion Today*, pp. 170–9. Edinburgh: Edinburgh University Press.
Cunningham, G. 1999. *Religion and Magic.* Edinburgh: Edinburgh University Press.
Czaplicka, M. A. 1914. *Aboriginal Siberia.* Oxford, UK: Oxford University Press.
Da Costa, U. C. 1983. *Umbanda.* São Paulo: Copala.
Daneel, M. L. 1970. *The God of the Matopo Hills.* The Hague: Mouton.
Daner, F. J. 1976. *The American Children of Krsna.* Holt, Rinehart & Winston.
Daniel, E. V. 1984. *Fluid Signs: Being a Person the Tamil Way.* Berkeley, CA: University of California Press.
Danquah, J. B. 1944. *The Akan Doctrine of God.* London: Cass.
Dargyay, E. K. 1978. *The Rise of Esoteric Buddhism in Tibet.* New York: Weiser.
Das, V. 1977. *Structure and Cognition: Aspects of Hindu Caste and Ritual.* Delhi: Oxford University Press.
Davidson, H. R. 1964. *Gods and Myths of Northern Europe.* Harmondsworth, UK: Penguin Books.
Davis, J. 1987. *Libyan Politics.* London: Tauris.
Davis, W. 1986. *The Serpent and the Rainbow.* London: Fontana/Collins.
______. 1988. *Passage of Darkness: The Ethnobiology of the Haitian Zombi.* Chapel Hill, NC: University of North Carolina Press.
Dawson, L. L. (Ed.). 2003. *Cults and New Religious Movements: A Reader.* Oxford: Blackwell.
Dayan, J. 1997. 'Vodoun, or the Voice of the Gods', in M. F. Olmos and L. Paravisini-Gebert (Eds.), *Sacred Possessions.* pp. 13–36. New Brunswick, NJ: Rutgers University Press.
De Camargo, C. 1961. *Kardecismo E. Umbanda.* São Paulo: Pioneira.
De Craemer, W. 1977. *The Jamaa and the Church.* Oxford, UK: Clarendon.
de Heusch, L. 1981. 'Possession and Shamanism', in *Why Marry Her?* Cambridge, UK: Cambridge University Press.
De Marquette, J. 1965. *Introduction to Comparative Mysticism.* Bombay, India: Bharatiya Vidya Bhavan.
De Mille, R. 1976. *Castenada's Journey.* Santa Barbara, CA: Capra Press.
Deren, M. 1953. *The Voodoo Gods.* St. Albans, UK: Granada. Reprinted 1975.
Devereux, G. 1961. 'Shamans as Neurotics', *American Anthropology* 63: 1088–90.
Devisch, R. 1993. *Weaving the Threads of Life.* Chicago: University of Chicago Press.
Dimock Jr., E. C. 1968. 'Doctrine and Practice Among the Vaisnavas of Bengal', in M. Singer (Ed.), *Krishna: Myths, Rites and Attitudes*, pp. 41–63. Chicago: University of Chicago Press.

Dioszegi, V. and M. Hoppal (Eds.). 1978. *Shamanism in Siberia.* Budapest: Akademiai Kiado.
Dirks, N. 1987. *The Hollow Crown.* Cambridge, UK: Cambridge University Press.
Diwakar, R. R. 1980. *Bhagawan Buddha.* Bombay: Bharatiya Vidya Biyavan.
Doore, G. (Ed.). 1988. *Shaman's Path.* Boston: Shambhala.
Douglas, M. 1966. *Purity and Danger.* Harmondsworth, UK: Penguin Books.
———. 1970. *Natural Symbols.* Harmondsworth, UK: Penguin Books.
———. 1975. *Implicit Meanings.* London: Routledge & Kegan Paul.
Dow, J. 1986. *The Shaman's Touch: Otomi Indian Symbolic Healing.* Salt Lake City, UT: University of Utah Press.
Dow, J. W. and A. R. Sandstrom (Eds.). 2001. *Holy Saints and Fiery Preachers.* Westport, CT: Praeger.
Dowman, K. 1988. *The Power Places of Central Tibet.* London: Routledge & Kegan Paul.
Droogers, A. 1980. *The Dangerous Journey.* The Hague: Mouton.
Drury, N. 1989. *The Elements of Shamanism.* Shaftesbury, UK: Element Books.
———. 1991. *The Visionary Human.* Shaftesbury: Element Books.
Dumezil, G. 1973. *Gods of the Ancient Northmen.* Berkeley, CA: University of California Press.
Dumont, L. 1970a. *Homo Hierarchicus.* London: Weidenfeld and Nicholson.
———. 1970b. *Religion, Politics and History in India.* The Hague: Mouton.
———. 1986. *A South Indian Subcaste: Social Organization and Religion of the Pramalai Kallar.* Delhi: Oxford University Press.
Durkheim, E. 1915. *The Elementary Forms of the Religious Life.* London: Allen and Unwin.
Eck, D. 1981. *Darsan: Seeing the Divine Image in India.* Chambersburg, PA: Anima Books.
Eickelman, D. F. 1976. *Moroccan Islam.* Austin, TX: University of Texas Press.
———. 1982. 'The Study of Islam in Local Contexts. *Contributions to Asian Studies* 17: 1–16.
———. 2002. *The Middle East and Central Asia: An Anthropological Approach.* Englewood Cliffs, NJ: Prentice-Hall.
Eilberg-Schwartz, H. 1989. 'Neopaganism and Goddess Worship as Enlightenment Religions'. *Journal of Feminist Studies in Religion* 5 (1): 77–95.
Eisler, R. 1987. *The Chalice and the Blade.* London: HarperCollins.
Eliade, M. 1958. *Yoga: Immortality and Freedom.* London: Arkana.
———. 1964. *Shamanism: Archaic Techniques of Ecstasy.* New York: Princeton University Press.
———. 1975. *Patanjali and Yoga.* New York: Schocken Books.
Elkin, A. P. 1977. *Aboriginal Men of High Degree.* St. Lucia, Queensland: University of Queensland Press.
Ellis, P. B. 1994. *The Druids.* London: Constable.
Emboden, W. 1979. *Narcotic Plants.* London: Studio Vista.
Erricker, C. 1999. 'Phenomenological Approaches', in P. Connolly (Ed.), *Approaches to the Study of Religion*, pp. 73–104. London: Continuum.
Esposito, J. 1988. *Islam: The Straight Path.* Oxford, UK: Oxford University Press.
Evans-Pritchard, E. E. 1937. *Witchcraft, Oracles and Magic Among the Azande.* Oxford, UK: Clarendon.
———. 1949. *The Sanusi of Cyrenaica.* Oxford, UK: Clarendon.
———. 1956. *Nuer Religion.* Oxford, UK: Oxford University Press.
Everden, N. 1985. *The Natural Alien.* Toronto: Toronto University Press.
Evers, H. D. 1972. *Monks, Priests and Peasants.* Leiden, The Netherlands: Brill.

Fabian, J. 1983. *Time and the Other.* New York: Columbia University Press.
______. 1994. 'Jamaa: A Charismatic Movement Revisited', in T. D. Blakely et al. 1994, pp. 257–74.
Faivre, A. 1987. 'What is Occultism?', in L. E. Sullivan (Ed.), *Hidden Truths*, pp. 3–9. London: Macmillan.
______. 1994. *Access to Western Esotericism.* Albany, NY: State University of New York Press.
______. 1998. 'Renaissance Hermeticism and the Concept of Western Esotericism', in R. Van Den Broek and W. J. Hanegraaff (Eds.), *Gnosis and Hermeticism From Antiquity to Modern Times*, pp. 109–23. Albany, NY: State University of New York Press.
Farb, P. 1969. *Man's Rise to Civilization.* London: Secker & Warburg.
Farrar, J. and S. Farrar. 1981. *The Witches' Bible.* London: Hale.
______. 1984. *The Witches' Way.* London: Hale.
Farrar, S. 1971. *What Witches Do.* New York: McCann & Geo Ghegan.
Ferguson, M. 1982. *The Aquarian Conspiracy.* London: Paladin.
Fernandez, J. W. 1978. 'African Religious Movements'. *Annual Review of Anthropology* 7: 198–234.
______. 1982. *Bwitti: An Ethnography of the Religious Imagination in Africa.* Princeton, NJ: Princeton University Press.
Ferretti, M. M. R. 2001. 'The Presence of Non-African Spirits in an Afro-Brazilian Religion', in Greenfield and Droogers, 2001, pp. 99–111.
Fiedler, K. 1996. 'Power at the Receiving End: The Jehovah's Witnesses Experience in One-Party Malawi' in K. R. Ross (Ed.), *God, People and Power in Malawi*, pp. 149–76. Blantyre: Claim.
Fields, K. E. 1985. *Revival and Rebellion in Colonial Central Africa.* Princeton, NJ: Princeton University Press.
Firth, R. 1940. *The Work of the Gods in Tikopia.* London: Percy Lund.
______. 1967. *Tikopia Ritual and Belief.* London: Allen & Unwin.
______. 1996. *Religion: A Humanist Interpretation.* London: Routledge.
Flaherty, G. 1992. *Shamanism and the Eighteenth Century.* Princeton, NJ: Princeton University Press.
Fortes, M. 1959. *Oedipus and Job in West African Religion.* Cambridge, UK: Cambridge University Press.
Fortune, D. 1935. *The Mystical Qabalah.* London: Williams & Norgate.
______. 1938. *The Sea Priestess.* London: Author Publishers.
______. 1987. *Sane Occultism.* London: Aquarian Press. (Originally published 1929.)
Fox, R. L. 1986. *Pagans and Christians.* London: Penguin Books.
Frazer, J. 1922. *The Golden Bough.* London: Macmillan. (Reprinted 1976.)
Freed, R. S. and S. A. Freed. 1964. 'Spirit Possession as Illness in a North Indian Village. *Ethnology* 3: 152–71.
Friedman, J. 1974. 'Marxism, Structuralism and Vulgar Materialism'. *Man* 9: 444–69.
Fry, P. 1976. *Spirits of Protest.* Cambridge, UK: Cambridge University Press.
Fuchs, S. 1965. *Rebellious Prophets.* Bombay: Asia Publishing House.
Fuller, C. J. 1976. *The Nayars Today.* Cambridge, UK: Cambridge University Press.
______. 1984. *Servants of the Goddess.* Cambridge, UK: Cambridge University Press.
______. 1992. *The Camphor Flame.* Princeton, NJ: Princeton University Press.
______. (Ed.). 1996. *Caste Today.* Delhi: Oxford University Press.
Furst, P. T. (Ed.). 1972. *Flesh of the Gods.* New York: Praeger.

Gadgil, M. and R. Guha. 1995. *Ecology and Equity.* London: Penguin Books.
Galeano, E. 1973. *Open Veins of Latin America.* New York: Monthly Review Press.
Garde, R. K. 1975. *Ayurveda for Health and Long Life.* Bombay: Tavaporevala Sons.
Gardner, G. B. 1954. *Witchcraft Today.* New York: Magickal Childe. (Reprinted 1988.)
Gawain, S. 1988. *Living in the Light.* London: Eden Grove.
Gay, P. 1967. *The Enlightenment.* London: Weidenfeld & Nicolson.
Geertz, C. 1968. *Islam Observed.* Chicago: University of Chicago Press.
———. 1975. *The Interpretation of Cultures.* London: Hutchinson.
Gelfand, M. 1967. *The African Witch.* Edinburgh: Livingstone.
Gell, A. 1975. *Metamorphosis of the Cassowaries.* London: Athlone.
Gellner, D. N. 1999. 'Anthropological Approaches', in P. Connolly (Ed.), *Approaches to the Study of Religion*, pp. 10–41. London: Continuum.
Gellner, E. 1969. *Saints of the Atlas.* Chicago: University of Chicago Press.
———. 1972. 'Political and Religious Organisation of the Berbers of the Central High Atlas', in E. Gellner and C. Micaud (Eds.), *Arabs and Berbers*, pp. 25–58. London: Duckworth.
———. 1981. *Muslim Society.* Cambridge, UK: Cambridge University Press.
———. 1984. 'Doctor and Saint', in A. S. Ahmed and D. M. Hart (Eds.), *Islam in Tribal Societies*, pp. 21–38. London: Routledge & Kegan Paul.
———. 1992. *Postmodernism, Reason and Religion.* London: Routledge.
———. 1994. *Conditions of Liberty.* London: Penguin Books.
———. 1995. *Anthropology and Politics.* Oxford, UK: Blackwell.
Gesch, P. 1985. *Initiative and Initiation.* St. Augustin: Anthropos Institute.
Geschiere, P. 1997. *The Modernity of Witchcraft.* Charlottesville, VA: University of Virginia Press.
Gibb, H. A. R. 1969. *Islam: A Historical Survey.* Oxford, UK: Oxford University Press.
Gifford, P. 1991. *The New Crusaders: Christianity and the New Right of South Africa.* London: Pluto.
Gilbert, R. A. 1983. *The Golden Dawn: Twilight of the Magician.* Wellingborough: Aquarian Press.
Gillison, G. 2001. 'Reflections on Pigs for the Ancestors', in E. Messer and M. Lambek (Eds.), *Ecology and the Sacred*, pp. 219–99. Ann Arbor, MI: University of Michigan Press.
Gilsenan, M. 1973. *Saint and Sufi in Modern Eygpt.* Oxford, UK: Clarendon.
———. 1983. *Recognizing Islam.* London: Croom Helm.
Gimbutas, M. 1974. *The Goddesses and Gods of Old Europe.* London: Thames & Hudson.
———. 1989. *The Language of the Goddess.* London: Thames & Hudson.
Ginzburg, C. 1984. *The Night Battles.* London: Routledge & Kegan Paul.
———. 1991. *Ecstasies.* London: Penguin Books.
Glassé, C. 1989. *The Concise Encyclopaedia of Islam.* London: Stacey.
Glazier, S. D. (Ed.). *Anthropology of Religion: A Handbook.* Westport: Praeger.
Glock, C. Y. 1964. 'The Role of Deprivation in the Origin and Evolution of Religion Groups', in R. Lee and M. Marty (Eds.), *Religion and Social Conflict.* New York: Oxford University Press.
Godwin, J. 1994. *The Theosophical Enlightenment.* Albany, NY: State University of New York Press.
Gold, A. G. 1988. *Fruitful Journeys: The Ways of Rajasthani Pilgrims.* Berkeley, CA: University of California Press.
Goldman, I. 1970. *Ancient Polynesian Society.* Chicago: University of Chicago Press.

Gombrich, R. 1971. *Precept and Practice.* Oxford, UK: Clarendon.
______. 1984. 'Introduction: The Buddhist Way', in H. Bechert and R. Gombrich (Eds.), *The World of Buddhism*, pp. 9–14. London: Thames and Hudson.
______. 1988. *Theravada Buddhism.* London: Routledge & Kegan Paul.
Gombrich, R. and G. Obeyesekere. 1988. *Buddhism Transformed.* Princeton, NJ: Princeton University Press.
Goodman, F. D., J. H. Henney & E. Pressel (Eds.). 1974. *Trance, Healing and Hallucinations.* New York: Wiley.
______. 1990. *Where the Spirits Ride the Wind.* Bloomington, IN: Indiana University Press.
Goodrick-Clarke, N. 1992. *The Occult Roots of Nazism.* London: Tauris.
______. 2002. *Black Sun.* New York: New York University Press.
Gordon, J. 1987. *The Golden Guru: The Strange Journey of Bhagwan Shree Rajneesh.* Lexington: Stephen Greene Press.
Gore, C. 2002. 'Religion in Africa', in Woodhead 2002, pp. 204–30.
Graves, R. 1982. *The White Goddess.* London: Faber. (Originally published 1948.)
Green, M. 1983. *Magic for the Aquarian Age.* Wellingborough: Aquarian Press.
______. 1989. *The Elements of Natural Magic.* Shaftesbury, UK: Element Books.
Greenfield, S. M. 1999. 'Hypnosis and Trance Induction in the Surgeries of Brazilian Spiritist, Healer-Mediums', in M. Klass and M. K. Weisgrau (Eds.), *Across the Boundaries of Belief*, pp. 211–26. Boulder, CO: Westview.
______. 2001. 'Population Growth, Industrialization and the Proliferation of Syncretized Religions in Brazil' and 'The Re-Interpretation of Africa: Convergence and Syncretism in Brazilian Candomblé', in Greenfield and Droogers 2001, pp. 55–70, 113–29.
Greenfield, S. M. and A. Droogers (Eds.). 2001. *Reinventing Religion.* Lanham, MD: Rowman and Littlefield.
Greenwood, S. 1998. 'The Nature of the Goddess', in J. Pearson, R. H. Roberts, and G. Samuel (Eds.), *Nature Religion Today*, pp. 101–10. Edinburgh: Edinburgh University Press.
______. 2000. *Magic, Witchcraft and the Otherworld.* Oxford: Berg.
______. 2001. *The Encyclopaedia of Magic and Witchcraft.* London: Lorenz Books.
Guenther, M. 1999. *Tricksters and Trancers.* Bloomington, IN: Indiana University Press.
Guiart, J. 1951. 'John Frum Movement in Tanna'. *Oceania* 12: 165–77.
Gunawardana, R. A. 1979. *Robe and Plough.* Tucson, AZ: University of Arizona Press.
Guthrie, S. 1993. *Faces in the Clouds.* New York: Oxford University Press.
Gyekye, K. 1987. *An Essay in African Philosophical Thought.* Cambridge, UK: Cambridge University Press.
Halifax, J. 1979. *Shamanic Voices.* Harmondsworth, UK: Penguin Books.
Hall, J. R. 2003. 'The Apocalypse at Jonestown', in L. L. Dawson (Ed.), *Cults and New Religious Movements: A Reader*, pp. 186–220. Oxford, UK: Blackwell.
Hall, S. 1985. 'Religious Ideologies and Social Movements in Jamaica', in R. Bocock and K. Thompson (Eds.), *Religion and Ideology*, pp. 269–96. Manchester: Manchester University Press.
Hamilton, M. 2001. *The Sociology of Religion.* London: Routledge.
Hanegraaff, W. 1996. *New Age Religion and Western Culture.* Leiden, The Netherlands: Brill.
______. 1998. 'Reflections of New Age and the Secularization of Nature', in J. Pearson, R. H. Robert, and G. Samuel (Eds.), *Nature Religion Today*, pp. 22–32. Edinburgh: Edinburgh University Press.

———. 2002. 'New Age Religion', in L. Woodhead (Ed.), *Religions in the Modern World*, pp. 249–63. London: Routledge.
Hansen, H. A. 1978. *The Witch's Garden*. York, ME: Weiser.
Happold, F. C. 1963. *Mysticism: A Study and an Anthology*. Harmondsworth, UK: Penguin Books.
Hardman, C. and G. Harvey (Eds.). 1996. *Pagan Pathways*. London: Thorsons.
Harner, M. 1980. *The Way of the Shaman*. New York: Bantam Books.
———. (Ed.). 1973. *Hallucinogens and Shamanism*. Oxford, UK: Oxford University Press.
Harper, E. B. 1957. 'Shamanism in South India'. *South Western Journal of Anthropology* 13: 267–87.
———. 1959. 'A Hindu Village Pantheon'. *S. W. Journal of Anthropology* 15: 227–34.
Harris, A. 1996. 'Sacred Ecology' in C. Hardman and G. Harvey (Eds.), *Pagan Pathways*, pp. 149–56. London: Thorsons.
Harris, I. (Ed.). 1999. *Buddhism and Politics in Twentieth Century Asia*. London, Continuum.
Harris, M. 1964. *Patterns of Race in the Americas*. New York: Walker.
———. 1980. *Cultural Materialism*. New York: Vintage Books.
Harrison, J. 1903. *Prolegomena to the Study of Greek Religion*. Cambridge, UK: Cambridge University Press.
Harrow, J. 1996. 'The Contemporary Neo-Pagan Revival', in J. R. Lewis (Ed.), *Magical Religion and Modern Witchcraft*, pp. 9–24. Albany, NY: State University of New York Press.
Hart, D. M. 1984. 'Segmentary Systems and the Role of the "Four Fifths" in Tribal Morocco', in A. S. Ahmed and D. M. Hart, *Islam in Tribal Societies*, pp. 66–105. London: Routledge & Kegan Paul.
Hartley, C. *Western Mystery Tradition*. London: Aquarian Press.
Harvey, G. 1996. 'Heathenism: A North European Pagan Tradition', in C. Hardman and G. Harvey (Eds.), *Pagan Pathways*, pp. 49–64. London: Thorsons.
———. 1997. *Listening People, Speaking Earth*. London: Hurst.
———. 2003. *Shamanism – A Reader*. London: Routledge.
Hay, P. 2002. *A Companion in Environmental Thought*. Edinburgh: Edinburgh University Press.
Haynes, J. 1996. *Religion and Politics in Africa*. London: Zed Books.
Heelas, P. 1996. *The New Age Movement*. Oxford, UK: Blackwell.
Hefner, R. 2000. *Civil Islam*. Princeton, NJ: Princeton University Press.
Herskovits, M. J. 1937. *Life in a Haitian Valley*. New York: Knopf.
———. 1958a. *The Myth of the Negro Past*. Boston: Beacon.
———. 1958b. *Acculturation: The Study of Culture Contact*. Gloucester, MA: Peter Smith. (Originally published 1938.)
Hess, D. J. 1991. *Spirits and Scientists*. University Park, PA: Pennsylvania State University Press.
———. 1994. *Samba in the Night*. New York: Columbia University Press.
Hinde, R. A. 1999. *Why Gods Persist*. London: Routledge.
Hine, P. 1993. *Prime Chaos*. Tempe, AZ: New Falcon.
Hiriyanna, M. 1949. *The Esssentials of Indian Philosophy*. London: Allen and Unwin.
Hiro, D. 1988. *Islamic Fundamentalism*. London: Collins.
Hitti, P. K. 1971. *Islam: A Way of Life*. Chicago: Regnery.
Hobsbawn, E. J. 1957. 'Methodism and the Threat of Revolution in Britain'. *History Today* 7: 115–24.

Hodges, T. 1976. *Jehovah's Witnesses in Central Africa.* London: Institute of Commonwealth Studies Minority Rights Group Report 29.
Hodgson, M. G. S. 1974. *The Venture of Islam*, 3 vols. Chicago: University of Chicago Press.
Hoffmann, H. 1979. *The Religions of Tibet.* Westport, CT: Greenwood.
Hogbin, I. 1970. *The Island of Menstruating Men.* London: Chandler.
Hole, C. 1947. *Witchcraft in England.* New York: Collier Books.
Holt, P. M. 1958. *The Mahdist State in the Sudan 1881–1898.* Oxford, UK: Clarendon.
Holy, L. 1991. *Religion and Custom in a Muslim Society.* Cambridge, UK: Cambridge University Press.
Hopman, E. V. and L. Bond. 1996. *Being a Pagan.* Rochester, VT: Destiny Books.
Horton, R. 1971. 'African Conversion'. *Africa* 41: 85–108.
______. 1993. *Patterns of Thought in Africa and the West.* Cambridge, UK: Cambridge University Press.
Horton, R. and R. Finnegan (Eds.). 1973. *Modes of Thought.* London: Faber.
Hountondji, P. J. 1983. *African Philosophy: Myth and Reality.* London: Hutchinson.
Howe, E. 1972. *The Magicians of the Golden Dawn.* New York: Weiser.
Hubert, H. and M. Mauss. 1964. *Sacrifice.* Chicago: University of Chicago Press. (Originally published 1899.)
Hughes, P. 1952. *Witchcraft.* Harmondsworth, UK: Penguin Books.
Hultkrantz, A. 1988. 'Shamanism: A Religious Pehnomenon?', in G. Doore (Ed.), *Shaman's Path*, pp. 33–42. Boston: Shambhala.
______. 1989. 'The Place of Shamanism in the History of Religions', in M. Hoppal and O. Von Sadovsky (Eds.), *Shamanism: Past and Present.* Los Angeles: Istor Books.
______. 1997. *Shamanic Healing and Ritual Drama.* New York: Crossroads Publications.
Humphrey, C. 1980. 'Theories of North Asian Shamanism', in E. Gellner (Ed.), *Soviet and Western Anthropology*, pp. 243–54. London: Duckworth.
______. 1996. *Shamans and Elders.* Oxford, UK: Clarendon.
Humphrey, C. and N. Thomas (Eds.). 1994. *Shamanism, History and the State.* Ann Arbor, MI: University of Michigan Press.
Humphreys, C. 1951. *Buddhism.* Harmondsworth, UK: Penguin Books.
______. 1987. (Ed.). *The Wisdom of Buddhism.* New Delhi, India: Promilla.
Hurbon, C. 1986. 'New Religions Movements in the Caribbean', in J. A. Beckford (Ed), *New Religions Movements and Rapid Social Change*, pp. 146–76, London: Sage.
______. 1995. *Voodoo – The Search for the Spirit.* New York: Abrams.
Hurston, Z. N. 1981. *Tell My Horse.* Berkeley, CA: Turtle Island. (Originally published 1938.)
Hutton, R. 1991. *The Pagan Religions of the Ancient British Isles.* Oxford: Blackwell.
______. 1996. 'The Roots of Modern Paganism', in C. Hardman and G. Harvey (Eds.), *Pagan Pathways*, pp. 3–15. London: Thorsons.
______. 1998. 'The Discovery of the Modern Goddess', in J. Pearson, R. H. Roberts, and G. Samuel (Eds.), *Nature Religion Today*, pp. 89–100. Edinburgh: Edinburgh University Press.
______. 1999. *The Triumph of the Moon.* Oxford, UK: Oxford University Press.
______. 2001. *Shamans.* London: Hambledon and London.
Huxley, A. 1946. *The Perennial Philosophy.* London: Fontana.
Huxley, F. 1966. *The Invisibles.* London: Rupert Hart.
Idowu, E. B. 1962. *Olodumare: God in Yoruba Belief.* London: Longman.
______. 1973. *African Traditional Religion.* Mary Knoll, NY: Orbis Books.

Iteanu, A. 1995. 'Rituals and Ancestors', in D. Coppet and A. Iteanu (Eds.), *Cosmos and Society in Oceania*, pp. 135–63. Oxford: Berg.
Ivakhiv, A. 1996. 'The Resurgence of Magical Religion', in J. R. Lewis (Ed.), *Magical Religion and Modern Witchcraft*, pp. 237–65. Albany, NY: State University of New York Press.
Jackson, M. 1989. *Paths Towards a Clearing*. Bloomington, IN: Indiana University Press.
Jakobsen, M. 1999. *Shamanism*. New York: Berghahn.
James, C. L. R. 1938. *The Black Jacobins*. London: Allison and Busby.
Janzen, J. M. 1992. *Ngoma*. Berkeley, CA: University of California Press.
———. 1994. 'Drums of Affliction', in Blakely et al. 1994, pp. 161–81.
Jarvie, I. C. 1964. *The Revolution in Anthropology*. London: Routledge & Kegan Paul.
Jaspers, K. 1953. *The Origin and Goal of History*. London, New Haven: Yale University Press (Original 1949) pp. 1–6.
Jensen, J. S. and L. H. Martin (Eds.). 1997. *Rationality and the Study of Religion*. London: Routledge.
Jensen, T. and M. Rothstein (Eds.). 2000. *Secular Theories of Religion*. Copenhagen: Tusculanum Press.
Johnson, C. 2003. *Claude Levi-Strauss*. Cambridge, UK: Cambridge University Press.
Johnson, G. 1976 'The Hare Krishna in San Francisco', in G. Glock and R. N. Bellah (Eds.), *The New Religious Consciousness*, pp. 31–51. Berkeley, CA: University of California Press.
Johnson, P. C. 1995. 'Shamanism From Ecuador to Chicago'. *Religion* 25: 163–78.
Jonas, H. 1958. *The Gnostic Gospels*. Harmondsworth, UK: Penguin Books.
Jones, P. 1996. 'Pagan Theologies', in C. Hardman and G. Harvey (Eds.), *Pagan Pathways*, pp. 32–46. London: Thorsons.
———. 1998. 'The European Native Tradition', in J. Pearson, R. H. Roberts, and G. Samuel (Eds.), *Nature Religion Today*, pp. 77–88. Edinburgh: Edinburgh University Press.
Jones, P. and N. Pennick. 1995. *A History of Pagan Europe*. London: Routledge.
Joshi, V. 1982. *The Awakened One: The Life and Work of Bhagwan Shree Rajneesh*. San Francisco: Harper & Row.
Judah, S. 1974. *Hare Krishna and the Counter Culture*. New York: Wiley.
Juillerat, B. (Ed.). 1992. *Shooting the Sun: Ritual and Meaning in West Sepik*. Washington, DC: Smithsonian Institution.
Jules-Rosette, B. 1975. *African Apostles: Ritual and Conversion in the Church of John Maranke*. Ithaca, NY: Cornell University Press.
Kahn, J. S. and J. R. Llobera. 1981. *The Anthropology of Pre-Capitalist Societies*. London: Macmillan.
Kakar, S. 1981. *The Inner World*. Delhi: Oxford University Press.
———. 1982. *Shamans, Mystics and Doctors*. Delhi: Oxford University Press.
Kalilombe, P. A. 1980. 'An Outline of Chewa Traditional Religion'. *African Theological Journal* 9(2): 39–51.
Kalweit, H. 1992. *Shamans, Healers and Medicine Men*. Boston: Shambhala.
Kapferer, B. 1983. *A Celebration of Demons*. Bloomington, IN: Indiana University Press.
———. 1988. *Legends of People, Myths of State*. Washington, DC: Smithsonian Institution Press.
Kaplan, J. 1996. 'The Reconstruction of the Asatru and Odinist Traditions', in J. R. Lewis (Ed.), *Magical Religion and Modern Witchcraft*, pp. 193–236. Albany, NY: State University of New York Press.
Kaplan, M. 1995. *Neither Cargo Nor Cult*. Durham, NC: Duke University Press.

Katz, R. 1976. 'Education for Transcendence: Kia Healing With the Kalahari !Kung', in R. Lee and I. De Vore (Eds.), *Kalahari Hunter–Gatherers*. Cambridge, MA: Harvard University Press.

______. 1982. *Boiling Energy*. Cambridge, MA: Harvard University Press.

Katz, S. T. (Ed.). 1983. *Mysticism and Religious Traditions*. Oxford, UK: Oxford University Press.

Keddie, N. R. (Ed.). 1972. *Scholars, Saints and Sufis*. Berkeley, CA: University of California Press.

______. 1981. *Iran: The Roots of Revolution*. New Haven, CT: Yale University Press.

Keer, D. 1988. *Veer Savarkar*. London: Sangam Books.

Keesing, R. M. 1978. 'Politico-Religious Movements and Anti-Colonialism on Malaita'. *Oceania* 48: 241–61; 49: 46–73.

______. 1982. *Kwaio Religion*. New York: Columbia University Press.

______. 1992. *Custom and Confrontation: The Kwaio Struggle for Cultural Autonomy*. Chicago: University of Chicago Press.

Keith, W. J. 1975. *The Rural Tradition*. Toronto: University of Toronto Press.

Kenyon, S. M. 1995. 'Zar as Modernisation in Contemporary Sudan. *Anthropology Quarterly* 68(2): 107–20.

Keown, D. 1996. *Buddhism*. Oxford, UK: Oxford University Press.

King, F. 1975. *Magic: The Western Tradition*. London: Thames & Hudson.

Kitzinger, S. 1969. 'Protest and Mysticism: The Rastafari Cult of Jamaica'. *Journal for Scientific Study of Religion* 8: 240–64.

Klass, M. and M. Weisgrau (Eds.). 1999. *Across the Boundaries of Belief*. Boulder, CO: Westview.

Kleinman, A. 1979. 'Why Do Indigenous Healers Successfully Heal?' *Social Science and Medicine* 13: 7–26.

Knight, G. 1976. *The Practice of Ritual Magic*. Wellingborough: Aquarian Press.

______. 2000. *Dion Fortune and the Inner Light*. Loughborough, UK: Thoth Publishers.

Kolenda, P. 1978. *Caste in Contemporary India*. Prospect Heights, IL: Waveland Press.

Kopytoff, I. 1971. 'Ancestors as Elders in Africa'. *Africa* 41: 129–42.

______. (Ed.). 1987. *The African Frontier*. Bloomington, IN: Indiana University Press.

Kramer, F. 1993. *The Red Fez*. London: Verso.

Krige, J. D. 1947. 'The Social Function of Witchcraft'. *Theoria* 1: 8–21.

Kuper, A. 1982. *Wives for Cattle*. London: Routledge & Kegan Paul.

______. 1988. *The Invention of Primitive Society*. London: Routledge.

______. 1999. *Culture: An Anthropologist's Account*. Cambridge, MA: Harvard University Press.

Kurtz, P. 1983. *In Defense of Secular Humanism*. Amherst, MA: Prometheus Books.

Kuznar, L. A. 1997. *Reclaiming a Scientific Anthropology*. London: Sage.

Kvaerne, P. 1984. 'Tibet: The Rise and Fall of a Monastic Tradition', in H. Bechert and R. Gombrich (Eds.), *The World of Buddhism*, pp. 253–70.

La Barre, W. 1972. *The Ghost Dance: Origins of Religion*. London: Allen and Unwin.

______. 1975. 'Anthropological Perspectives on Hallucinations and Hallucinogens', in R. K. Siegel and L. J. West (Eds.), *Hallucinations*. New York: Wiley.

La Fontaine, J. S. 1985. *Initiation*. Harmondsworth, UK: Penguin Books.

Laguerre, M. 1987. *Afro-Caribbean Folk Medicine*. South Hadley, MA: Bergin and Garvey.

______. 1989. *Voodoo and Politics in Haiti*. London: Macmillan.

Laing, R. D. 1967. *The Politics of Experience.* Harmondsworth, UK: Penguin Books.
Lambek, M. 1981. *Human Spirits: A Cultural Account of Trance in Mayotte.* Cambridge, UK: Cambridge University Press.
———. 2002. (Ed.). *A Reader in the Anthropology of Religion.* Oxford, UK: Blackwell.
Lame Deer, J. and R. Erdoes. 1972. *Lame Deer: Seeker of Visions.* New York: Simon and Schuster.
Lanternari, V. 1963. *The Religions of the Oppressed.* New York: Knopf.
———. 1988. 'Melanesian Religions', in S. Sutherland and P. Clarke (Eds.), *The Study of Religion: Traditional and New Religions,* pp. 85–95.
Larner, C. 1984. *Witchcraft and Religion.* Oxford, UK: Blackwell.
Larose, S. 1977. 'The Meanings of Africa in Haitian Vodu', in I. M. Lewis (Ed.), *Symbols and Sentiments,* pp. 85–116. London: Academic.
Lasch, C. 1979. *The Culture of Narcissism.* New York: Norton.
Lawrence, P. 1964. *Road Belong Cargo.* Manchester, UK: Manchester University Press.
Lawrence, P. and M. J. Meggitt (Eds.). 1965. *Gods, Ghosts and Men in Melanesia.* Melbourne, Australia: Oxford University Press.
Leach, E. 1954. *Political Systems of Highland Burma.* London: Bell.
Leacock, S. and R. Leacock. 1975. *Spirits of the Deep.* Garden City, NY: Doubleday.
Lee, R. B. 1968. 'The Sociology of !Kung Bushman Dance Performances', in R. Prince (Ed.), *Trance and Possession States,* pp. 35–52. Montreal: R. M. Bucke Memorial Society.
Legesse, A. 1994. 'Prophetism, Democharisma and Social Change', in T. D. Blakely et al. (Eds.), *Religion in Africa,* pp. 315–41. London: Currey.
Lehman, F. K. 1971. 'Doctrine, Practice and Belief in Theravada Buddhism'. *Journal of Asian Studies* 31: 372–80.
Leland, C. G. 1899. *Arcadia, of the Gospel of the Witches.* London: David Nutt.
Le Roy Ladurie, E. 1974. *The Peasants of Languedoc.* Urbana, IL: University of Illinois Press.
Lessnoff, M. 2002. *Ernest Gellner and Modernity.* Cardiff, Wales: University of Wales Press.
Lethbridge, T. C. 1962. *Witches: Investigating an Ancient Religion.* London: Routledge & Kegan Paul.
Lett, J. 1997. 'Science, Religion and Anthropology', in S. D. Glazier (Ed.), *Anthropology of Religion: A Handbook,* pp. 103–20. Westport, CT: Praeger.
Levack, B. P. 1987. *The Witch-Hunt in Early Modern Europe.* London: Longman.
Levi, E. 1957. *The History of Magic.* York Beach, ME: Weiser.
Levi-Strauss, C. 1963. *Structural Anthropology.* Harmondsworth, UK: Penguin Books.
———. 1966. *The Savage Mind.* London: Weidenfeld and Nicolson.
Lewis, I. M. 1955. 'Sufism in Somaliland: A Study in Tribal Islam'. *African Studies* 17: 581–602.
———. 1963. 'Dualism in Somali Notions of Power', *Journal of the Royal Anthropological Institute* 93: 109–16.
———. 1969. 'Spirit Possession in Northern Somaliland', in J. Beattie and J. Middleton (Eds.), *Spirit Mediumship and Society in Africa,* pp. 188–219. London: Routledge & Kegan Paul.
———. 1971. *Ecstatic Religion.* Harmondsworth, UK: Penguin Books.
———. 1986. *Religion in Context.* Cambridge, UK: Cambridge University Press.
———. 1991. 'Introduction', in I. M. Lewis, A. Al-Safi, and S. Hurreiz (Eds.), *Women's Medicine,* pp. 1–16. Edinburgh: Edinburgh University Press.
———. 1999. *Arguments With Ethnography.* London: Athlone.
Lewis, J. R. (Ed.). 1996. *Magical Religion and Modern Witchcraft.* Albany, NY: State University of New York Press.

Lewis, J. R. and J. G. Melton (Eds.). 1992. *Perspectives on the New Age.* Albany, New York: State University of New York Press.

Lewis, R. 1987. *Marcus Garvey: Anti-Colonial Champion.* London: Karia.

Lewis, T. T. 1997. 'Buddhist Communities', in S. D. Glazier (Ed.), *Anthropology of Religion*, pp. 319–68. Westport, CT: Praeger.

Lewis, W. P. 1993. *Soul Rebels: The Rastafari.* Prospect Heights, IL: Waveland Press.

Lewis-Williams, D. 1983. *New Approaches to South African Rock Art.* Cape Town, South Africa: South African Archaeological Society.

Lewis-Williams, D. and T. A. Dowson. 1988. 'The Signs of All Times: Entopic Phenomena in Upper Paleolithic Art. *Current Anthropology* 29: 201–45.

Linden, I. 1979. 'Chisumphi Theology in the Religion of Central Malawi', in J. M. Schoffeleers (Ed.), *Guardians of the Land*, pp. 187–207. Gwelo, Zimbabwe: Mambo Press.

Ling, T. 1968. *A History of Religion East and West.* London: Macmillan.

Lings, M. 1983. *Muhammad, His Life Based on the Earliest Sources.* Cambridge, UK: Islamic Texts Society.

Linton, R. 1943. 'Nativistic Movements'. *American Anthropologist* 45: 230–40.

Long, N. 1968. *Social Change and the Individual.* Manchester, UK: Manchester University Press.

Lopez, D. 2002. *Modern Buddhism.* London: Penguin Books.

Ludwig, A. M. 1968. 'Altered States of Consciousness', in R. Prince (Ed.), *Trance and Possession States.* Montreal: R. M. Bucke Memorial Society.

Luhrmann, T. M. 1989. *Persuasions of the Witch's Craft.* London: Macmillan.

Luling, V. 1991. 'Some Possession Cults in Southern Somalia', in I. M. Lewis, A. Al-Safi, and S. Hurreiz (Eds.), *Women's Medicine*, pp. 167–77. Edinburgh: Edinburgh University Press.

Luna, L. E. 1986. *Vegetalismo.* Stockholm: Almqvist & Wiksell.

MacCulloch, J. A. 1991. *The Religion of the Ancient Celts.* London: Constable. (Originally published 1911.)

MacFarlane, A. 1970. *Witchcraft in Tudor and Stuart England.* London: Routledge & Kegan Paul.

Mackie, L. 1987. *The Great Marcus Garvey.* London: Hansib.

MacGaffey, W. 1983. *Modern Kongo Prophets.* Bloomington, IN: Indiana University Press.

______. 1986. *Religion and Society in Central Africa.* Chicago: University of Chicago Press.

______. 1994. 'Kimbanguism and the Question of Syncretism in Zaire', in Blakely 1994, pp. 241–56.

MacLaine, S. 1983. *Out on a Limb.* Toronto: Bantam Books.

Macy, J. 1991. *Mutual Causality in Buddhism and General Systems Theory.* Albany, NY: State University of New York Press.

Madan, T. N. 1997. *Modern Myths, Locked Minds.* Delhi: Oxford University Press.

Mageo, J. M. and A. Howard (Eds.). 1996. *Spirits in Culture, History and Mind.* New York: Routledge.

Mahadevan, T. M. 1977. *Ramana Maharshi: The Sage of Arunacala.* London: Allen and Unwin.

Mahmood, C. K. 1997. 'Hinduism in Context', in S. D. Glazier (Ed.), *Anthropology of Religion*, pp. 305–18. Westport, CT: Praeger.

Mair, L. 1958. 'The Pursuit of the Millennium in Melanesia'. *British Journal of Sociology* 9: 175–82.

______. 1959. 'Independent Religious Movements in Three Continents'. *Comparative Studies in Society and History* 1: 113–36.

———. 1967. 'Independent Religious Movements in Three Continents', in J. Middleton (Ed.), *Gods and Rituals*, pp. 307–36. New York: American Museum of Natural History.
———. 1969. *Witchcraft*. London: Weidenfeld and Nicolson.
Malinowski, B. 1922. *Argonauts of the Western Pacific*. London: Routledge & Kegan Paul.
———. 1974. *Magic, Science and Religion and Other Essays*. London: Souvenir Press. (Originally published 1925.)
Mandelbaum, D. 1966. 'Transcendental and Pragmatic Aspects of Religion'. *American Anthropologist* 68: 1174–91.
Mann, M. 1986. *The Sources of Social Power*. Cambridge, UK: Cambridge University Press.
Mann, W. E. 1991. *The Quest for Total Bliss*. Toronto: Canadian Scholars Press.
Marcus, G. E. 1995. 'The Redesign of Ethnography After the Critique of Its Rhetoric', in R. Goodman and W. Fisher (Eds.), *Rethinking Knowledge*. Albany, NY: State University of New York Press.
Marriott, M. 1955. 'Little Communities in an Indigenous Civilization', in M. Marriott (Ed.), *Village India*, pp. 171–222. Chicago: University of Chicago Press.
Marriott, M. (Ed.). 1955. *Village India*. Chicago: University of Chicago Press.
Martin, B. G. 1976. *Muslim Brotherhoods in Nineteenth Century Africa*. Cambridge, UK: Cambridge University Press.
Martin, D. 2002. *Pentecostalism: The World Their Parish*. Oxford, UK: Blackwell.
Martin, M. L. 1975. *Kimbangu*. Oxford, UK: Blackwell.
Marwick, M. 1950. 'Another Modern Anti-Witchcraft Movement in East-Central Africa'. *Africa* 20: 100–12.
———. (Ed.). 1970. *Witchcraft and Sorcery: Selected Readings*. Harmondsworth, UK: Penguin Books.
Ma Satya Bharti. 1980. *Drunk on the Divine*. New York: Grove.
Matthews, B. 1999. 'The Legacy of Tradition and Authority: Buddhism and the Nation in Myanmar', in I. Harris (Ed.), *Buddhism and Politics in Twentieth Century Asia*, pp. 26–53. London: Continuum.
Matthews, C. 1989. *The Elements of the Celtic Tradition*. Shaftesbury, UK: Element.
Matthews, C. and J. Matthews. 1994. *The Western Way*. London: Penguin Books.
Matthews, J. 1991. *Taliesin: Shamanism and Bardic Mysteries in Britain and Ireland*. London: Aquarian Press.
Mauss, M. 1979. *Seasonal Variations of the Eskimo*. Trans. J. J. Fox. London: Cohen & West. (Originally published 1906.)
Mawdudi, A. A. 1980. *Towards Understanding Islam*. London: UK Islamic Mission.
Mazrui, A. A. 1986. *The Africans: A Triple Heritage*. London: BBC Publications.
Mbiti, J. S. 1969. *African Religions and Philosophy*. London: Heinemann.
———. 1970. *Concepts of God in Africa*. London: Society for Propogation of Christian Knowledge.
McCauley, R. N. and E. T. Lawson. 2002. *Bringing Ritual to Mind*. Cambridge, UK: Cambridge University Press.
McIntosh, C. 1972. *Eliphas Levi and the French Occult Revival*. London: Rider.
McKean, L. 1996. *Divine Enterprise*. Chicago: University of Chicago Press.
Mead, M. 1954. *Growing Up in New Guinea*. Harmondsworth, UK: Penguin Books. (Originally published 1930.)
———. 1956. *New Lives for Old*. New York: Mentor Books.
———. 1963. *Coming of Age in Samoa*. Harmondsworth, UK: Penguin Books. (Originally published 1928.)

Meebelo, H. S. 1971. *Reaction to Colonialism.* Manchester, UK: Manchester University Press.

Menon, Y. K. 1976. *The Mind of Adi Shankara.* Bombay: Jaico.

Merkur, D. 1985. *Becoming Half-Hidden: Shamanism and Initiation Among the Inuit.* Stockholm: Almqvist & Wiksell.

Mernissi, F. 1993. *Islam and Democracy.* London: Virago.

Messer, E. and M. Lambek (Eds.). 2001. *Ecology and the Sacred.* Ann Arbor, MI: University of Michigan Press.

Messing, S. D. 1958. 'Group Therapy and Social Status in the Zar Cult of Ethiopia'. *American Anthropology* 60: 1120–6.

Metraux, A. 1959. *Voodoo.* London: Sphere Books. (Reprinted 1974.)

Meyer, B. 1999. *Translating the Devil.* Edinburgh: Edinburgh University Press.

Michelet, J. 1862. *La Sorciere.* Paris.

Middleton, J. 1960. *Lugbara Religion.* London: Oxford University Press.

———. 1969. 'Spirit Possession Among the Lugbara', in Beattie and Middleton 1969, pp. 220–31.

Middleton, J. and E. H. Winter (Eds.). 1963. *Witchcraft and Sorcery in East Africa.* London: Routledge & Kegan Paul.

Milingo, E. 1984. *The World in Between.* London: Hurst.

Mills, A. R. 1930. *The Odinist Revision.* Melbourne, Australia: Author.

Mills, C. W. 1959 *The Sociological Imagination.* London: Oxford University Press.

Minor, R. N. 1981. 'Sarvepalli Radhakrishnan and "Hinduism"', in R. D. Baird (Ed.), *Religion in Modern India,* pp. 305–38. New Delhi: Manohar.

Mintz, S. W. and R. Price. 1976. *The Birth of African–American Culture.* Boston: Beacon Press.

Mitchell, J. C. 1956. *The Yao Village.* Manchester, UK: Manchester University Press.

Moerman, D. E. 1979. 'Anthropology of Symbolic Healing', *Current Anthropology* 20: 59–66.

Moffat, M. 1979. *An Untouchable Community in South India.* Princeton: Princeton University Press.

Mooney, J. 1896. *The Ghost Dance Religion and the Sioux Outbreak of 1890.* Chicago: University of Chicago Press. (Reprinted 1965.)

Moore, H. L. and T. Sanders (Eds.). 2001. *Magical Interpretations, Material Realities.* London: Routledge.

Morinis, E. A. 1984. *Pilgrimage in the Hindu Tradition.* Delhi: Oxford University Press.

Morris, B. 1970. 'Ernest Thompson Seton and the Origins of the Woodcraft Movement'. *Journal of Contemporary History* 5: 183–94.

———. 1975. 'Jesus the Shaman'. *New Humanist* 91: 149–50.

———. 1976. 'Whither the Savage Mind?' *Man* 11: 542–57.

———. 1979. 'The Hare Krishna Cult'. *New Humanist* 95: 73–5.

———. 1981. 'Hill Gods and Ecstatic Cults'. *Man in India* 61: 203–36.

———. 1987. *Anthropological Studies of Religion.* Cambridge, UK: Cambridge University Press.

———. 1990. 'Indian Materialism'. *The Secularist* (Pune) 123: 63–72.

———. 1991. *Western Conceptions of the Individual.* Oxford, UK: Berg.

———. 1994. *Anthropology of the Self.* London: Pluto Press.

———. 1996. *Ecology and Anarchism.* Malvern Wells, UK: Images.

———. 1997. 'In Defence of Realism and Truth', *Critique of Anthropology* 17: 313–40.

———. 1998. 'Matriliny and Mother Goddess Religion'. *Journal of Contemporary Religion* 13(1): 91–102.

———. 1998. *The Power of Animals.* Oxford, UK: Berg.
———. 2000. *Animals and Ancestors.* Oxford, UK: Berg.
Morrish, I. 1982. *Obeah, Christ and Rastaman.* Cambridge, UK: J. Clarke.
Motta, R. 2001. 'Ethnicity, Purity, The Market and Syncretism in Afro-Brazilian Cults', in Greenfield and Droogers 2001, pp. 71–85.
Mottahedeh, R. P. 1985. *The Mantle of the Prophet.* New York: Simon & Schuster.
Mudimbe, V. Y. 1988. *The Invention of Africa.* Bloomington, IN: Indiana University Press.
Munson Jr., H. 1988. *Islam and Revolution in the Middle East.* New Haven, CT: Yale University Press.
———. 1993a. *Religion and Power in Morocco.* New Haven, CT: Yale University Press.
———. 1993b. 'Rethinking Gellner's Segmentary Analysis of Morocco's Ait 'Atta', *Man* 28: 267–80.
Murphy, J. M. 1964. 'Psychotherapeutic Aspects of Shamanism on St. Lawrence Island, Alaska', in A. Kiev (Ed.), *Magic, Faith and Healing,* pp. 53–83. New York: Free Press.
Murray, M. 1921. *The Witch Cult in Western Europe.* Oxford, UK: Clarendon.
———. 1931. *The God of the Witches.* London: Oxford University Press. (Reprinted 1970.)
———. 1963. *My First Hundred Years.* London: Kimber.
Murti, T. R. V. 1955. *The Central Philosophy of Buddhism.* London: Unwin.
Myers, J. E. 1985. 'Rajneeshpuram: The Boom and Bust of a Buddhafield', in A. C. Lehmann and J. E. Myers (Eds.), *Magic, Witchcraft and Religion,* pp. 366–75. Mountain View, USA: Mayfield.
Nadel, S. F. 1954. *Nupe Religion.* London: Routledge & Kegan Paul.
Naipaul, V. S. 1962. *The Middle Passage.* London: Andre Deutsch.
Nash, M. 1965. *The Golden Road to Modernity.* Chicago: University of Chicago Press.
Nasr, S. H. 1981. *Islamic Life and Thought.* Albany, NY: State University of New York Press.
Needham, R. (Ed.). 1973. *Right and Left: Essays in Dual Symbolic Classification.* Chicago: University of Chicago Press.
Nettleford, R. M. 1970. *Mirror, Mirror: Identity, Race and Protest in Jamaica.* Kingston: Collins and Sangster.
Ngubane, H. 1977. *Body and Mind in Zulu Medicine.* London: Academic.
Nichols, R. 1990. *The Book of Druidry.* London: Aquarian Press.
Nicholson, R. A. 1914. *The Mystics of Islam.* London: Routledge & Kegan Paul.
Nicholson, S. (Ed.). 1987. *Shamanism: An Expanded View of Reality.* Wheaton, IL: Theosophical Publishing House.
Nirvedananda, S. 1944. *Hinduism at a Glance.* Calcutta: Ramakrishna Mission.
Noel, D. C. 1997. *The Soul of Shamanism.* New York: Continuum.
Noll, R. 1983. 'Shamanism and Schizophrenia', *American Ethnology* 10: 443–59.
———. 1994. *The Jung Cult.* Princeton, NJ: Princeton University Press.
———. 1997. *The Aryan Christ.* London: Macmillan.
Obeyesekere, G. 1981. *Medusa's Hair.* Chicago: University of Chicago Press.
———. 1992. *The Apotheosis of Captain Cook.* Princeton, NJ: Princeton University Press.
O'Connor, M. I. 1997. 'The Pilgrimage to Magdelena', in S. D. Glazier (Ed.), *Anthropology of Religion: A Handbook,* pp. 369–89. Westport, CT: Praeger.
Omari, M. S. 1994. 'Candomblé: A Socio-Political Examination of African Religion and Art in Brazil', in T. D. Blakely et al. (Eds.), *Religion in Africa,* pp. 135–59. London: Currey.
Organ, T. W. 1970. *The Hindu Quest for the Perfection of Man.* Athens, OH: Ohio University Press.

Ott, M. 2000. *African Theology in Images.* Blantyre: Claim.
Ottenberg, S. 1989. *Boyhood Rituals in an African Society.* Seattle, WA: University of Washington Press.
Otto, T. 1992. 'The Paliau Movement in Manus and the Objectification of Tradition'. *History and Anthropology* 5: 427–54.
Owens, J. 1976. Dread: *The Rastafarians of Jamaica.* London: Heinemann.
Owusu, M. 1997. 'The Ethnography of Africa: The Usefulness of the Useless', in R. Grinker and C. B. Steiner (Eds.), *Perspectives on Africa,* pp. 704–23. Oxford, UK: Blackwell.
Pagels, E. 1982. *The Gnostic Gospels.* Harmondsworth, UK: Penguin Books.
Pals, D. L. 1996. *Seven Theories of Religion.* Oxford, UK: Oxford University Press.
Parry, J. P. 1970. 'The Koli Dilemma'. *Contributions to Indian Sociology* 4: 84–104.
______. 1979. *Caste and Kinship in Kangra.* London: Routledge and Kegan Paul.
______. 1985. 'The Brahmanical Tradition and the Technology of the Intellectual', in J. Overing (Ed.), *Reason and Morality.* London: Tavistock.
Parsonson, G. S. 1975. *The John Frum Movement in Tanna.* Dunedin, New Zealand: University of Otago Press.
Patai, R. 1952. 'The Middle East as a Cultural Area', *Middle East Journal* 6(1): 1–21.
Pattee, R. 1988. 'Ecstasy and Sacrifice', in G. Doore (Ed.), *Shaman's Path,* pp. 17–31. Boston: Shambhala.
Patterson, O. 1967. *The Sociology of Slavery.* London: McGibbon and Kee.
Paul, R. A. 1982. *The Tibetan Symbolic World.* Chicago: University of Chicago Press.
Peacock, J. 1978. *Muslim Puritans.* Berkeley, CA: University of California Press.
Pearson, J. 1998. 'Assumed Affinities: Wicca and the New Age', in J. Pearson, R. H. Roberts, and G. Samuel (Eds.), *Nature Religion Today.* Edinburgh: Edinburgh University Press.
Pearson, J. L. 2002. *Shamanism and the Ancient Mind.* Lanham, MD: Altamira.
Pearson, J., R. H. Roberts, and G. Samuel (Eds.). 1998. *Nature Religion Today.* Edinburgh: Edinburgh University Press.
Peel, J. D. Y. 1968. *Aladura.* Oxford, UK: Oxford University Press.
Pennick, N. 1989. *Practical Magic in the Northern Tradition.* Loughborough, UK: Thoth Press.
Peters, L. 1981. *Ecstasy and Healing in Nepal.* Malibu, CA: Undena.
Pfeiffer, J. E. 1982. *The Creative Explosion.* New York: Harper & Row.
Piggott, S. 1968. *The Druids.* London: Thames & Hudson.
Poewe, K. O. 1981. *Matrilineal Ideology.* London: Academic.
Poole, F. J. P. 1982. 'The Ritual Forging of Identity: Aspects of Person and Self in Bimin-Kuskusmin Male Initiation', in G. H. Herdt (Ed.), *Rituals of Manhood,* pp. 99–154. Berkeley, CA: University of California Press.
Prabhavananda, S. 1953. *The Yoga Aphorisms of Patanjali.* Mylapore, India: Sri Ramakrishna Math.
Pressel, E. 1974. 'Umbanda, Trance and Possession in São Paulo, Brazil', in I. I. Zaretsky (Ed.), *Trance, Healing and Hallucinations.* New York: Wiley.
Preston, J. J. 1980. *Cult of the Goddess.* New Delhi: Vikas.
Pye, M. 1979. *The Buddha.* London: Duckworth.
Quigley, D. 1993. *The Interpretation of Caste.* Oxford, UK: Clarendon.
Rabinow, P. 1975. *Symbolic Domination.* Chicago: University of Chicago Press.
Radhakrishnan, S. 1927. *The Hindu View of Life.* London: Allen and Unwin.
______. 1932. *An Idealist View of Life.* London: Allen and Unwin.
______. 1933. *Indian Philosophy.* Vol. I. London: Allen and Unwin.

Radice, W. (Ed.). 1998. *Swami Vivekananda and the Modernization of Hinduism.* New Delhi: Oxford University Press.

Ragatz, L. J. 1963. *The Fall of the Planter Class in the British Caribbean 1763–1833*. New York: Octagon Books.

Raheja, G. 1988. *The Poison in the Gift.* Chicago: University of Chicago Press.

Rahman, F. 1967. *Islam.* Chicago: University of Chicago Press.

Rahula, W. 1959. *What the Buddha Taught.* London: Fraser.

———. 1974. *The Heritage of the Bhikkhu.* New York: Grove.

———. 1978. *Zen and the Taming of the Bull.* London: Fraser.

Ramachandra Rao, S. K. 1985. *The Temple Rituals and Festivals.* Bangalore, India: IBH Prakashana.

Ranger, T. 1975. 'The Mwana Lesa Movement of 1925', in T. O. Ranger and J. Weller (Eds.), *Themes in the Christian History of Central Africa*, pp. 45–75. London: Heinemann.

———. 1986. 'Religious Movements and Politics in Sub-Saharan Africa'. *African Studies Review* 29(2): 1–69.

———. 1991. 'Religion and Witchcraft in Everyday Life in Contemporary Zimbabwe', in P. Kaarsholm (Ed.), *Cultural Struggle and Development in Southern Africa*, pp. 149–65. London: Currey.

Rappaport, R. A. 1968. *Pigs for the Ancestors.* New Haven, CT: Yale University Press.

———. 1979. *Ecology, Meaning and Religion.* Berkeley, CA: North Atlantic Books.

———. 1999. *Ritual and Religion in the Making of Humanity.* Cambridge, UK: Cambridge University Press.

Rasmussen, K. 1927. *Across Arctic America.* New York: Putnam.

———. 1929. *The Intellectual Culture of the Iglulik Eskimos.* Copenhagen: Glydendalske.

Rasmussen, S. J. 1995. *Spirit Possession and Personhood Among the Kel Ewey Taureg.* Cambridge, UK: Cambridge University Press.

Ray, B. C. 1976. *African Religions.* Englewood Cliffs, NJ: Prentice-Hall.

Reay, M. 1960. 'Mushroom Madness in the New Guinea Highlands'. *Oceania* 31: 3–27.

Redfield, R. 1956. *Peasant Society and Culture.* Chicago: University of Chicago Press.

Reichel-Dolmatoff, G. 1975. *The Shaman and the Jaguar.* Philadelphia: Temple University Press.

———. 1997. *Rainforest Shamans.* Dartington, UK: Themis Books.

Reid, S. 1996. 'Magic as Metaphor in Neo-Pagan Witchcraft', in J. R. Lewis (Ed.), *Magical Religion and Modern Witchcraft*, pp. 141–67. Albany, NY: State University of New York Press.

Restall-Orr, E. 1998. *Spirits of the Sacred Grove.* London: Thorsons.

Rexroth, K. 1975. *Communalism.* London: Owen.

Reyna, S. P. 2002. *Connections.* London: Routledge.

Rhys Davids, C. A. F. 1912. *Buddhism.* London: Home University Library.

Richards, A. I. 1935. 'A Modern Movement of Witch Finders'. *Africa* 8: 448–61.

———. 1939. *Land, Labour and Diet in Northern Rhodesia.* Oxford, UK: Oxford University Press.

———. 1956. *Chisungu.* London: Tavistock.

Richardson, A. 1987. *The Life and Magic of Dion Fortune.* Wellingborough: Aquarian Press.

Riches, D. 1994. 'Shamanism: The Key to Religion', *Man* 29: 381–405.

Ripinsky-Naxon, M. 1993. *The Nature of Shamanism.* Albany, NY: State University of New York Press.

Ritchie, J. 1991. *The Secret World of Cults.* London: Angus & Robertson.
Roberts, A. 1970. 'The Lumpa Church of Alice Lenshina', in R. I. Rotberg and A. Mazrui (Eds.), *Protest and Power in Black Africa*, pp. 513–68. New York: Oxford University Press.
Rodinson, M. 1971. *Mohammed.* Harmondsworth, UK: Penguin Books.
______. 1987. *Europe and the Mystique of Islam.* Seattle, WA: University of Washington Press.
Rodman, S. and C. Cleaver. 1992; *Spirits of the Night.* Dallas, TX: Spring Publications.
Rodney, W. 1972. *How Europe Underdeveloped Africa.* London: Bogle L'Ouverture.
Romanucci-Ross, L., Moerman, D., and Tancred, L. R. (Eds). 1983. *The Anthropology of Medicine.* S. Handley, Mass.: Bergen & Garvey.
Rose, H. and Rose, S. (Eds.). 2000. *Alas, Poor Darwin.* London: Cape.
Rosenbaum, S. (Ed.). 2003. *Pragmatism and Religion.* Urbana, IL: University of Illinois Press.
Ross, A. 1967. *Pagan Celtic Britain.* London: Routledge & Kegan Paul.
Rotberg, R. I. 1961. 'The Lenshina Movement in Northern Rhodesia'. *Rhodes-Livingstone Journal* 29: 63–78.
______. 1965. *The Rise of Nationalism in Central Africa.* Cambridge, MA: Harvard University Press.
Rowe, M. 1980. 'The Women in Rastafari'. *Caribbean Quarterly* 26(4): 13–21.
Rowlands, M. and J. P. Warmer. 1988. 'Sorcery, Power and the Modern State in Cameroon'. *Man 23: 118–32.*
Roy, M. N. 1940. *Materialism.* Delhi: Ajanta.
Russell, J. B. 1980. *A History of Witchcraft.* London: Thames & Hudson.
Ruhela, S. P. and D. Robinson (Eds.). 1985. *Sai Baba and His Message.* New Delhi: Arnold-Heinemann.
Saddhatissa, H. 1976. *The Life of Buddha.* London: Unwin.
Sahlins, M. 1976. *Culture and Practical Reason.* Chicago: University of Chicago Press.
______. 1982. 'The Apotheosis of Captain Cook', in M. Izard and P. Smith (Eds.), *Between Belief and Transgression.* Chicago: University of Chicago Press.
______. 1995. *How "Natives" Think.* Chicago: University of Chicago Press.
Said, E. 1978. *Orientalism.* London: Routledge & Kegan Paul.
Saladin D'Anglure, B. 1996. 'Shamanism', in A. Barnard and J. Spencer (Eds.), *Encyclopaedia of Social and Cultural Anthropology*, pp. 504–7. London: Routledge.
Salehi, M. M. 1988. *Insurgency Through Culture and Religion: The Islamic Revolution in Iran.* New York: Praeger.
Saler, B. 1993. *Conceptualizing Religion.* Leiden, The Netherlands: Brill.
Sallnow, M. J. 1987. *Pilgrims of the Andes.* Washington, DC: Smithsonian Institution.
Salomonsen, J. 1998. 'Feminist Witchcraft and Holy Hermeneutics', in J. Pearson, R. H. Roberts, and G. Samuel (Eds.), *Nature Religion Today.* Edinburgh: Edinburgh University Press.
Samuel, G. 1990. *Mind, Body and Culture.* Cambridge, UK: Cambridge University Press.
______. 1993. *Civilized Shamans.* Washington, DC: Smithsonian Institute.
Sanders, A. *A Deed Without a Name.* Oxford, UK: Berg.
Sangharakshita. 1986. *Alternative Traditions.* Glasgow: Windhorse.
______. 1987. *Crossing the Stream.* Glasgow: Windhorse.
______. 1990. *A Guide to the Buddhist Path.* Glasgow: Windhorse.
______. 1992. *Buddhism and the West.* Glasgow: Windhorse.
______. 1996a. *Tibetan Buddhism.* Birmingham, UK: Windhorse.
______. 1996b. *Buddhism for Today – and Tomorrow.* Birmingham, UK: Windhorse.

Sardesai, S. G. and D. Bose. *Marxism and the Bhagavant Geeta.* New Delhi: People's Publishing House.
Savishinsky, N. J. 1999. 'Transnational Popular Culture and the Global Spread of Jamaican Rastafarian Movement', in M. Klass and M. Weisgrau (Eds.), *Across the Boundaries of Belief,* pp. 347–66. Boulder, CO: Westview.
Schapera, I. 1971. *Married Life in an African Tribe.* Harmondsworth, UK: Penguin Books.
Schieffelin, E. L. 1976. *The Sorrow of the Lonely and the Burning of the Dancers.* New York: St. Martin's.
Schoffeleers, J. M. (Ed.). 1979. *Guardians of the Land.* Gwero: Mambo Press.
———. 1994. 'Christ in African Folk Theology', in Blakely et al. 1994, pp. 73–88.
Schucman, H. 1975. *A Course in Miracles.* London: Arkana.
Schuler, M. 1979. 'Myalism and the African Religious Tradition in Jamaica', in M. E. Crahan and F. Knight (Eds.), *Africa and the Caribbean,* pp. 65–79. Baltimore: Johns Hopkins University Press.
Schultes, R. E. and A. Hofman. 1979. *Plants of the Gods.* London: Hutchinson.
Schwartz, R. D. 1999. 'Renewal and Resistance: Tibetan Buddhism in the Modern Era', in I. Harris (Ed.), *Buddhism and Politics in Twentieth Century Asia,* pp. 229–53. London: Continuum.
Schwartz, T. 1962. 'The Paliau Movement in the Admirality Islands 1946–1954'. *Anthropology, Papers. American Museum of Natural History* 49: 210–421.
Seabrook, W. 1929. *The Magic Island.* New York: Harcourt Brace.
Searle, J. 1999. *Mind, Language and Society.* London: Weidenfeld and Nicolson.
Sen, K. M. 1961. *Hinduism.* Harmondsworth, UK: Penguin Books.
Sergei, K. 1991. 'Shamanism and Christianity', *Ethnohistory* 38: 363–87.
Shallcrass, P. 1996. 'Druid Today', in C. Hardman and G. Harvey (Eds.), *Pagan Pathways,* pp. 65–8. London: Thorsons.
———. 1998. 'A Priest of the Goddess', in J. Pearson, R. H. Roberts, and G. Samuel (Eds.), *Nature Religion Today,* pp. 157–69. Edinburgh: Edinburgh University Press.
Sharma, U. 1973. 'Theodicy and the Doctrine of Karma'. *Man* 8: 347–63.
———. 1999. *Caste.* Buckingham: Open University Press.
Sharpe, E. 1986. *Comparative Religion: A History.* La Salle, Canada: Open Court.
Shepperson, G. 1962. 'Nyasaland and the Millennium', in J. Middleton (Ed.), *Black Africa,* pp. 234–47. London: Macmillan.
Shirokogoroff, S. M. 1935. *The Psychomental Complex of the Tungus.* London: Kegan Paul.
Shorter, A. 1988. *Toward a Theology of Inculturation.* London: Chapmen.
———. 1996. *Christianity and the African Imagination.* Nairobi: Paulines Publications.
Shweder, R. A. 1984. 'Anthropology's Romantic Rebellion Against the Enlightenment', in R. A. Shweder and R. A. Levine (Eds.), *Culture Theory,* pp. 27–66. Cambridge, UK: Cambridge University Press.
Siegel, P. N. 1986. *The Meek and the Militant.* London: Zed Books.
Siikala, A.-L. 1978. *The Rite Technique of the Siberian Shaman.* Helsinki: F. F. Communications No. 20.
Siikala, A-L. and M. Hoppal. 1998. *Studies on Shamanism.* Helsinki: Finnish Anthropological Society.
Silverman, J. 1967. 'Shamans and Acute Schizophrenia', *American Anthropology* 69: 21–31.
Simpson, G. E. 1956. 'Jamaican Revivalist Cults'. *Social and Economic Studies* 5: 321–442.
———. 1962. 'The Shango Cult in Nigeria and Trinidad'. *American Anthropologist* 64: 1204–19.

Singer, M. 1968. 'The Radha-Krishna Bhajanas of Madras City', in M. Singer (Ed.), *Krishna: Myths, Rites and Attitudes*, pp. 90–138. Chicago: University of Chicago Press.
———. 1972. *When a Great Tradition Modernizes.* Chicago: University of Chicago Press.
Singh, K. *Gurus, Godmen and Good People.* New Delhi: Orient Longman.
Siskind, J. 1975. *To Hunt in the Morning.* Oxford, UK: Oxford University Press.
Sjoo, M. 1992. *New Age and Armageddon.* London: Women's Press.
Sjoo, M. and B. Moor. 1987. *The Great Cosmic Mother.* New York: Harper & Row.
Sjøslev, I. 2001. 'Possession and Syncretism: Spirits as Mediators in Modernity', in Greenfield and Droogers 2001, pp. 131–44.
Smart, N. 1996. *Dimensions of the Sacred.* London: Harper Collins.
Smith, D. E. 1965. *Religion and Politics in Burma.* Princeton, NJ: Princeton University Press.
Smith, M. G., R. Augier, and R. M. Nettleford. 1960. 'Report on the Rastafari Movement in Kingston, Jamaica', in *Social and Economic Studies.* Kingston: University of the West Indies.
Smith, W. C. 1957. *Islam in Modern History.* New York: Mentor Books.
Snelling, J. 1987. *The Buddhist Handbook.* London: Century.
Southwold, M. 1978. 'Buddhism and the Definition of Religion', *Man* 13: 363–79.
———. 1982. 'True Buddhism and Village Buddhism in Sri Lanka', in J. Davis (Ed.), *Religious Organization and Religious Experience*, pp. 137–51. London: Academic.
———. 1983. *Buddhism in Life.* Manchester, UK: Manchester University Press.
Spangler, D. 1980. *Explorations: Emerging Aspects of the New Culture.* Findhorn, UK: Findhorn Press.
———. 1984. *The Rebirth of the Sacred.* London: Gateway Books.
Spence, L. 1947. *The History and Origins of Druidism.* Van Nuys, CA: Newcastle. (Reprinted 1995.)
———. 1996. *The Magical Arts of Celtic Britain.* Van Nuys, CA: Newcastle. (Originally published 1945.)
Spencer, J. (Ed.). 1990. *Sri Lanka: History and the Roots of Conflict.* London: Routledge.
Spencer, P. 1965. *The Samburu.* Berkeley: University of California Press.
Spiro, M. E. 1967. *Burmese Supernaturalism.* New York: Prentice-Hall.
———. 1970. *Buddhism and Society.* New York: Harper & Row.
———. 1987. *Culture and Human Nature.* Chicago: University of Chicago Press.
Spretnak, C. 1991. *States of Grace.* San Francisco: Harper.
Srinivas, M. N. 1952. *Religion and Society Among the Coorgs of South India.* London: J. K. Publishers.
———. 1962. *Caste in Modern India and Other Essays.* London: J. K. Publishers.
Starhawk. 1979. *The Spiral Dance.* New York: HarperCollins. (Originally published 1989.)
———. 1982. *Dreaming the Dark.* London: Unwin Hyman.
Starrett, G. 1997. 'The Anthropology of Islam', in S. D. Glazier (Ed.), *Anthropology of Religion*, pp. 279–303. Westport, CT: Praeger.
Stein, J. 1986. *The World of Marcus Garvey.* Baton Rouge, LA: Louisiana State University Press.
Steinbauer, F. 1979. *Melanesian Cargo Cults.* London: Prior.
Stevenson, D. 1988. *The Origins of Freemasonry.* Cambridge, UK: Cambridge University Press.
Storr, A. 1996. *Feet of Clay: A Study of Gurus.* London: HarperCollins.
Sundkler, B. G. 1948. *Bantu Prophets in South Africa.* Oxford, UK: Oxford University Press.
Suster, G. 1988. *The Legacy of the Beast.* London: Allen.

Sutcliffe, R. 1996. 'Left Hand Path Ritual Magic', in C. Hardman and G. Harvey (Eds.), *Pagan Pathways*, pp. 109–37. London: Thorsons.
Sutcliffe, S. 1998. 'Between Apocalypse and Self-Realization', in J. Pearson, R. H. Roberts, and G. Samuel (Eds.), *Nature Religion Today*, pp. 33–44. Edinburgh: Edinburgh University Press.
Suzuki, D. T. 1957. *Mysticism: Christian and Buddhist.* London: Allen and Unwin.
Swain, T. and G. W. Trompf. 1995. *The Religions of Oceania.* London: Routledge.
Symonds, J. 1951. *The Great Beast.* London: Rider.
Tambiah, S. J. 1970. *Buddhism and Spirit Cults in North-East Thailand.* Cambridge, UK: Cambridge University Press.
______. 1976. *World Conqueror and World Renouncer.* Cambridge, UK: Cambridge University Press.
______. 1990. *Magic, Science and Religion, and the Scope of Rationality.* Cambridge, UK: Cambridge University Press.
______. 1992. *Buddhism Betrayed?* Chicago: University of Chicago Press.
Taussig, M. 1980. *The Devil and Commodity Fetish in South America.* Chapel Hill, NC: University of North Carolina Press.
______. 1987. *Shamanism, Colonialism and the Wild Man.* Chicago: University of Chicago Press.
Taylor, D. 1987. 'Charismatic Authority in the Sathya Sai Baba Movement', in R. Burghart (Ed.), *Hinduism in Britain*, pp. 119–133. London: Tavistock.
Taylor, J. V. and D. A. Lehmann. 1961. *Christians of the Copperbelt.* London: Society for Christian Missions Press.
Temple, R. C. 1906. *The Thirty Seven Nats.* London: Griggs.
Ter Haar, G. 1992. *Spirit of Africa.* London: Hurst.
Terwiel, B. J. 1975. *Monks and Magic.* Scandinavian Institute of Asian Studies, Monograph 24. London: Curzon.
Thomas, K. 1971. *Religion and the Decline of Magic.* London: Weidenfeld & Nicolson.
Thompson, D. 1996. *The End of Time.* Hanover, NH: University Press of New England.
Thompson, E. P. 1963. *The Making of the English Working Class.* London: Gallancz.
Thompson, J. and P. Heelas. 1986. *The Way of the Heart.* Wellingborough: Aquarian Press.
Thorsson, E. 1992. *The Book of Troth.* St. Paul, MN: Llewellyn.
Townsend, J. B. 1988. 'Neo-Shamanism and the Modern Mystical Movement', in G. Doore (Ed.), *Shaman's Path*, pp. 73–83. Boston: Shambhala.
______. 1997. Shamanism in S. D. Glazier (Ed.), *Anthropology of Religion*, pp. 429–69. Westport, CT: Praeger.
Toynbee, A. 1976. *Mankind and Mother Earth.* London: Paladin.
Trevor-Roper, H. 1967. *The European Witch-Craze in the 16th and 17th Centuries.* New York: Harper.
Trompf, G. W. (Ed.). 1990. *Cargo Cults and Millenarian Movements.* Berlin: Mouton.
______. 1991. *Melanesian Religion.* Cambridge, UK: Cambridge University Press.
Tucci, G. 1980. *The Religions of Tibet.* London: Routledge & Kegan Paul.
Turner, E. 1992. 'The Reality of Spirits'. *Revision* 15 (1): 28–32.
Turner, H. W. 1979. *Religious Innovation in Africa.* Boston: Hall.
Turner, V. W. 1957. *Schism and Continuity in an African Society.* Manchester, UK: University of Manchester Press.
______. 1967. *The Forest of Symbols.* Ithaca, NY: Cornell University Press.
______. 1968. *The Drums of Affliction.* Oxford, UK: Oxford University Press.

______. 1969. *The Ritual Process.* Harmondsworth, UK: Penguin Books.
______. 1974. *Dramas, Fields and Metaphors.* Ithaca, NY: Cornell University Press.
Tyler, S. 1986. 'Postmodern Ethnography', in J. Clifford and G. Marcus (Eds.), *Writing Culture*, pp. 122–140. Berkeley, CA: University of California Press.
Tylor, E. 1871. *Primitive Culture.* London: Murray.
Valiente, D. 1973. *An ABC of Witchcraft Past and Present.* London: Hale.
______. 1978. *Witchcraft for Tomorrow.* London: Hale.
______. 1989. *The Rebirth of Witchcraft.* Custer, WA: Phoenix.
Van Binsbergen, W. M. 1981. *Religious Change in Zambia.* London: Kegan Paul.
Van Den Broek, R. and W. J. Hanegraaf (Eds.). 1998. *Gnosis and Hermeticism from Antiquity to Modern Times.* Albany, NY: State University of New York Press.
Van Der Veer, P. 1988. *Gods on Earth.* London: Athlone.
______. 1994. *Religious Nationalisms.* Berkeley, CA: University of California Press.
Van Gennep, A. 1960. *The Rites of Passage.* London: Routledge & Kegan Paul. (Originally published 1908.)
Van Wetering, I. 2001. 'Polyvocality and Constructions of Syncretism', in Greenfield and Droogers 2001, pp. 183–200.
Vaswani, T. L. 1960. *The Face of Buddha.* Poona, India: Gita.
Vitebsky, P. 1995a. *The Shaman.* London: Macmillan.
______. 1995b. 'From Cosmology to Environmentalism', in R. Fardon (Ed.), *Counterworks*, pp. 182–203. London: Routledge.
Waddell, L. A. 1972. *Tibetan Buddhism.* New York: Dover. (Originally published 1894.)
Wadley, S. 1985. *Shakti.* New Delhi: Munshiram Manoharlal.
Waite, A. E. 1961. *The Book of Ceremonial Magic.* New York: University Books.
Wallace, A. 1956. 'ReVitalization Movements'. *American Anthropologist* 58: 264–81.
______. 1979. 'ReVitalization Movements'. in W. A. Lessa and E. Z. Vogt (Eds.), *Reader in Comparative Religion*, pp. 421–9. New York: Harper & Row.
Walsh, R. N. 1990. *The Spirit of Shamanism.* Los Angeles: Tarcher.
Walvin, J. 1992. *Black Ivory.* London: Fontana.
Washington, P. 1993. *Madam Blavatsky's Baboon.* London: Secker and Warburg.
Wasson, R. G. 1972. 'The Divine Mushroom of Immortality', in P. T. Furst (Ed.), *Flesh of the Gods*, pp. 185–213. London: Allen and Unwin.
Waterbury, J. 1970. *The Commander of the Faithful.* London: Weidenfeld & Nicholson.
Watt, W. M. 1961. *Muhammad: Prophet and Statesman.* Oxford, UK: Clarendon.
Weber, M. 1947. *The Theory of Social and Economic Organization.* New York: Free Press.
______. 1958. *The Religion of India.* Glencoe, IL: Free Press.
______. 1965. *The Sociology of Religion.* London: Methuen.
Weil, A. 1986. *The Natural Mind.* Boston: Houghton Mifflin.
Werbner, R. P. 1977. *Regional Cults.* London: Academic.
Wexler, A. 1997. 'The Artistry of a Haitian Vodou Flagmaker', in M. F. Olmos and L. Paravisini-Gebert (Eds.), *Sacred Possessions*, pp. 59–78. New Brunswick, NJ: Rutgers University Press.
White, C. S. J. 1972. 'The Sai Baba Movement: Approaches to the Study of Indian Saints'. *Journal of Asian Studies* 31: 863–78.
Whitehead, H. 1921. *The Village Gods of South India.* Calcutta: Associated Press.
Whitehouse, H. 1995. *Inside the Cult.* Oxford, UK: Oxford University Press.
______. 2000. *Arguments and Icons.* Oxford, UK: Oxford University Press.
Wiebe, D. 1981. *Religion and Truth.* The Hague, The Netherlands, Mouton.

Wilbert, J. 1972. 'Tobacco and Shamanistic Ecstasy Among the Warao of Venezuela', in P. Furst (Ed.), *Flesh of the Gods*, pp. 55–83. New York: Praeger.
Willems, E. 1969. 'Religious Pluralism and Class Structure: Brazil and Chile', in R. Robertson (Ed.), *Sociology of Religion*, pp. 195–217. Harmondsworth, UK: Penguin Books.
Williams, E. 1964. *Capitalism and Slavery.* London: Andre Deutsch. (Originally published 1944.)
Williams, F. E. 1923. 'The Vailala Madness and the Destruction of Native Ceremonies in the Gulf Division'. Port Moresby; Papua New Guinea: *Papuan Anthropology Report* No. 4.
______. 1928. *Orokaiva Magic.* London: Oxford University Press.
______. 1976. *'The Vailala Madness' and Other Essays* (E. Schwimmer, Ed.). Brisbane, Australia: University of Queensland Press.
Williams, G. M. 'Swami Vivekananda: Archetypal Hero or Doubting Saint', in R. D. Baird (Ed.), *Religion in Modern India*, pp. 197–226. New Delhi: Manohar.
Williams, R. 1973. *The Country and the City.* London: Chatto and Windus.
Williams, R. 1980. *Problems in Materialism and Culture.* London: Verso.
Williams, R. B. 1984. *A New Face of Hinduism: The Swaminarayan Religion.* Cambridge, UK: Cambridge University Press.
Willis, R. (Ed.). 1975. *The Interpretation of Symbolism.* London: Malaby.
Willis, R. G. 1968. 'Kamcape: An Anti-Sorcery Movement in Southwest Tanzania'. *Africa* 38: 1–15.
Willoughby, W. C. 1928. *The Soul of the Bantu.* New York: Doubleday.
Wilson, B. R. 1973. *Magic and the Millennium.* St. Albans, UK: Paladin.
Wilson, B. and J. Cresswell (Eds.). 1999. *New Religious Movements.* London: Routledge.
Wilson, C. 1971. *The Occult.* St. Albans, UK: Granada.
______. 1985. *Rudolf Steiner: The Man and His Vision.* Wellingborough: Aquarian Press.
Wilson, M. 1936. *Reaction to Conquest.* London: Oxford University Press.
______. 1971. *Religion and the Transformation of Society.* Cambridge, UK: Cambridge University Press.
Winkelman, M. 1997. 'Altered States of Consciousness and Religious Behavior', in S. D. Glazier (Ed.), *Anthropology of Religion*, pp. 393–428. Westport, CT: Praeger.
Wolf, E. R. 1982. *Europe and the People Without History.* Berkeley, CA: University of California Press.
Wood, E. 1959. *Yoga.* Harmondsworth, UK: Penguin Books.
Woodhead, L. (Ed.). 2002. *Religions in the Modern World.* London: Routledge.
Woodward, M. 1989. *Islam in Java.* Tucson, AZ: University of Arizona Press.
Worsley, P. 1957. *The Trumpet Shall Sound.* New York: Schocken Books. (Reprinted 1968.)
Yalman, N. 1964. 'The Structure of Sinhalese Healing Rituals', in E. Harper (Ed.), *Religion in South Asia*, pp. 115–50. Seattle, WA: University of Washington Press.
Yinger, J. M. 1970. *The Scientific Study of Religion.* London: Macmillan.
York, M. 1995. *The Emerging Network.* Lanham, MD: Rowman & Littlefield.
Zaehner, R. C. 1957. *Mysticism: Sacred and Profane.* Oxford, UK: Oxford University Press.
______. 1962. *Hinduism.* Oxford, UK: Oxford University Press.
Zartman, I. W. (Ed.). 1987. *The Political Economy of Morocco.* New York: Praeger.
Zips, W. 2001. 'Ragga Cowboys', in Greenfield and Droogers 2001, pp. 163–81.
Zubaiba, S. 1993. *Islam: The People and the State.* London: Tauris.
Zuesse, E. M. 1979. *Ritual Cosmos.* Athens, OH: Ohio University Press.

Index